REFERENCE

THE REFORM OF UNITED KINGDOM COMPANY LAW

Cavendish
Publishing
Limited

London • Sydney • Portland, Oregon

THE REFORM OF
UNITED KINGDOM
COMPANY LAW

Edited by
Dr John de Lacy
Senior Lecturer in Law,
University of Manchester

Cavendish
Publishing
Limited

London • Sydney • Portland, Oregon

First published in Great Britain 2002 by
Cavendish Publishing Limited, The Glass House,
Wharton Street, London WC1X 9PX, United Kingdom
Telephone: + 44 (0)20 7278 8000   Facsimile: + 44 (0)20 7278 8080
Email: info@cavendishpublishing.com
Website: www.cavendishpublishing.com

Published in the United States by Cavendish Publishing
c/o International Specialized Book Services,
5804 NE Hassalo Street, Portland,
Oregon 97213-3644, USA

Published in Australia by Cavendish Publishing (Australia) Pty Ltd
3/303 Barrenjoey Road, Newport, NSW 2106, Australia

© Cavendish Publishing Limited 2002
Reprinted 2002

British Library Cataloguing in Publication Data
Data available

Library of Congress Cataloguing in Publication Data
Data available

ISBN 1-85941-693-4

3 5 7 9 10 8 6 4 2

Printed and bound in Great Britain

CONTRIBUTORS

John Birds, LLM, FRSA, is Professor of Commercial Law at Sheffield University.

David Booton, BSC, LLM, is Lecturer in Law at Manchester University.

Diana Faber is a Circuit Judge and was formerly a Law Commissioner with responsibility for company and commercial law reform.

Stephen Griffin, LLB, MPhil, is Reader in Law at Wolverhampton University.

Andrew Griffiths, BA, solicitor, is Senior Lecturer in Law at Manchester University.

John de Lacy, LLB, PhD, DPhil, is Senior Lecturer in Law at Manchester University.

Andrew Lidbetter, MA, BCL, is a solicitor and Commercial Litigation Partner at Herbert Smith in London.

Lisa Linklater, MA, is a barrister in private practice at Chancery House Chambers in Leeds.

Mike Lower, LLB, MPhil, solicitor, is Lecturer in Law at Manchester University.

John Lowry, LLB, LLM, is Reader in Law at Queen Mary and Westfield College, University of London.

Gerard McCormack, BCL, LLM, PhD, barrister, is Professor of Law at Manchester University.

Jonathan Marsh, BA, LLM, is a solicitor and Head of Legal and Compliance at Sempra Metals Ltd.

David Milman, LLB, PhD, FRSA, is CMS Cameron McKenna Professor of Corporate and Insolvency Law at Manchester University.

Peter Muchlinski, LLB, LLM, barrister, is Professor of Law and International Business at Kent Law School, University of Kent at Canterbury.

Sir David Neuberger is a Justice of the High Court (Chancery Division) and was formerly a QC practising in the Chancery Division.

Jonathan Rickford, CBE, MA, BCL, solicitor, was Project Director for the Company Law Review, formerly Chief Legal Advisor for British Telecommunications plc and Head of Company Law with the DTI (1979–82).

John Parkinson, BA, solicitor, is Professor of Law at Bristol University. He served as a member of the Company Law Review Steering Group.

Chris Riley, LLB, solicitor, is Reader in Law at Durham University.

Celia Wells, LLB, LLM, is Professor of Law at the Cardiff Law School, University of Wales.

CONTENTS

PART 1

THE COMPANY LAW REVIEW

PART 2

CONTEMPORARY COMPANY ISSUES

PART 3

CORPORATE GOVERNANCE AND ACCOUNTABILITY

PART 4

CORPORATE SECURITY AND INSOLVENCY

PART 5

FINANCIAL SERVICES AND MARKETS

Contents

TABLE OF CASES

TABLE OF STATUTES

International legislation

Australia

Canada

TABLE OF STATUTORY INSTRUMENTS

INTRODUCTION

Modern company law effectively began with the enactment of the Companies Act 1862,[1] famously described as the 'magna carta' of company law.[2] Prior to this Act and, indeed, to the turn of the 20th century, two main themes dominated the subject of company law. These were, firstly, should the corporate form be freely available, and secondly, if so, should it be accompanied with limited liability for those incorporating or joining the new company? Via a process of trial and error, by the end of the Victorian era both of these themes had been embraced by UK law.[3] As we enter the 21st century it is now taken for granted that the limited liability corporation is the pre-eminent form of business association throughout the developed world. The corporation has become the centre of, or even the driving force behind, the modern global economy.[4] This is not to say, however, that the growth of the corporation and, in particular, the large multi-national corporation has been an altogether good thing. One only has to refer to the collapse of the US company Enron to realise that unsustained corporate growth can have disadvantages.[5] The growth of corporate power has also threatened the power and role of nation states who some have accused of abandoning their role as the protector of the national interest in search of corporate investment.[6] Whatever the merits of the arguments of those who do not embrace the development of the modern corporation as we now recognise it, it has to be said that the present corporation is a fact of life and it is difficult to see any immediate candidate to replace it as the main collective vehicle for economic exchange throughout the developed world.

That being so, it falls upon us to address issues of regulation and how the form and power of the corporation can be, or rather should be, shaped. In April 2000 the Centre For Law and Business held a conference at Manchester University School of Law entitled 'Company Law for the New Millennium'.[7] A number of distinguished persons involved in the company law area attended and spoke at the conference, which proved to be a great success. The conference was designed to highlight, and provide a forum for discussion of, some of the more important topics which were, at that time, being reviewed by the Company Law Steering Group as part of the DTI sponsored Company Law

---

1   For a general treatment of companies as they existed before this time see PL Davies *Gower's Principles of Modern Company Law* (London, Sweet & Maxwell, 6th edn, 1997) at Chapters 2 and 3.

2   See FB Palmer *Company Law* (London, Stevens, 1st edn, 1898) at p 1; see now *Palmer's Company Law* (London, Sweet & Maxwell, 25th edn, 1992) Vol 1 at para 1.110.

3   Culminating in the leading case of *Salomon v Salomon & Co Ltd* [1897] AC 22. See now Companies Act 1985, s 1.

4   'The private corporation is the most remarkable institutional innovation of the past two centuries. Today's economy would be unimaginable without its dynamism and flexibility.' Martin Wolf 'A manager's real responsibility' *Financial Times* 30 January 2002.

5   Enron was the seventh biggest company in the USA – valued in excess of $70 billion – and filed for bankruptcy in December 2001 following the exposure of accounting and profit irregularities suggesting a wholesale fraudulent operation by senior management figures. The case has wide implications for all large companies and led Patricia Hewitt, the Trade and Industry Secretary, to announce, in February 2002, that two separate reviews would be held in the UK examining the roles of non-executive directors and the adequacy of existing arrangements for financial reporting and auditing; see DTI Press Notice Nos 128 and 234 of 2002. In March 2002 the Enron scandal led President Bush to announce new corporate governance proposals based upon a 10 point action plan; see 'Bush blueprint for US corporate governance attacked as too weak' and 'Bush blueprint on investor protection said to lack bite' *Financial Times* 8 March 2002.

6   See, for example, G Monbiot *Captive State: The Corporate Takeover of Britain* (London, Macmillan, 2000).

7   The Conference was generously sponsored by Halliwell Landau solicitors.

Review. Given the success of the conference and the importance of the material discussed, it was felt that a wider audience would benefit from access to this material. Therefore, it was decided to publish the fruits of this conference and to take the opportunity to expand the coverage of materials. This book contains the expanded versions of most of the conference papers along with a number of new essays. Taken together they provide a comprehensive discussion of many of the more important issues that face our system of company law as it currently stands at the crossroads of reform. It should not be thought, however, that company law is confined to issues arising out of the reform of the Companies Act 1985. Although the latter is naturally the most prominent example, the subject of company law reform should be taken in a broad sense. With that in mind, the book also includes contributions on insolvency law[8] and financial services.[9]

We still await the final fate of the labours of those behind the Company Law Review,[10] although it is expected that a new Companies Bill will be available for comment later this year (2002) and that a Companies Act will follow in 2003. In the meantime the essays presented here offer a glimpse of some of the more pressing problems which the legislature will need to address. Publication and time constraints have meant that this collection cannot possibly cover every area that might interest the student of company law. Pressing commitments meant that some leading commentators were unable to meet the publication schedule and had to withdraw from this project. That aside, the final collection offers the reader the opinions of many leading commentators and it is to be hoped that this will help to shape the continuing reform debate. Any imperfections that might remain in the reform proposals post the Company Law Review can hopefully be corrected before a new Companies Act emerges. If that is achieved then the UK will at last have a system of company law that is fit for a developed economy in the 21st century.[11]

It is believed that the essays in this collection are up-to-date as of October 2001. However, later additions have been made where circumstances permitted.[12]

John de Lacy
School of Law, University of Manchester
April 2002

---

8   See the essay by Milman at p 415 below.
9   See the essays by Marsh and Linklater at pp 439 and 459 below.
10 See generally *Modern Company Law for a Competitive Economy: Final Report* in 2 volumes (London, DTI, July 2001).
11 We cannot continue with the present system contained in the Companies Act 1985 which bears an uncanny resemblance to its forebear the Companies Act 1862; for a chronological history of UK companies legislation see Appendix 3 at the end of this book.
12 At the time of going to press the Enterprise Bill 2002 was published by the government. This Bill, if later enacted (as seems probable), will make significant changes to our current system of insolvency law. In particular it will replace the current law on administration and also strengthen the position of unsecured creditors by, for example, abolishing Crown preference and also limiting the ambit of floating charges in certain circumstances. It was not possible to incorporate these developments in this book but readers should consult the Enterprise Bill 2002 Part 10 for further details.

PART 1

THE COMPANY LAW REVIEW

CHAPTER 1

A HISTORY OF THE COMPANY LAW REVIEW*

Jonathan Rickford[1]

1 PURPOSE AND APPROACH

This essay offers an historical account of the progress of the three-year project set in hand in March 1998 to review the whole of British 'core'[2] company law, and to make proposals for its reform. It is said that, when asked to assess the French Revolution, Mao Tse Tung replied that it was too soon to say. Even greater diffidence needs to be shown in such an historical essay written within weeks of the Review's conclusion, particularly by an author deeply involved in its processes. Accordingly, I shall focus on events and immediate assessment of the direct effects of decisions made. More fundamental judgment of the value of the Review will surely need to be based largely on the quality and performance of any legislation which results. But a factual account and explanation seem likely to be of value while events are still reasonably fresh, as a record and for those considering similar projects.

The essay considers, in chronological order, first, the state of company law in early 1998 (unchanged in substance at the time of writing) and the case for reform. I shall then move on to describe the establishment of the Review and the events of the first few weeks as preliminary issues were resolved. It will then be convenient to track the subsequent structure of the Review, which broadly fell into four stages: the first, Strategic, phase when key principles, strategic thrusts and working methods and the various options for these were identified, analysed, tested and consulted upon; the second, Development, phase, when the results of this work were developed and applied, to produce reasonably firm high-level policy proposals; the third, Completion, phase when reasonably firm conclusions were reached on these matters and co-ordinated to a level where the developed policy outcomes could be proposed as parts of an internally coherent and balanced system. The final phase then took account of consultation on these proposals to produce a complete and firm *Final Report*, with, it was hoped, sufficient detail in all areas to provide confidence that the recommendations as a whole were sound, coherent and viable.

---

* © Jonathan Rickford 2002.

1   The author served as Project Director of the Company Law Review. Factual assertions and judgments offered without reference to sources represent the personal recollections and judgments of the author.

2   Issues of definition of the boundaries of a pervasive area of law such as the law of associations are of course problematic, indeed insoluble. However, broadly speaking, by 'core' company law was meant what is generally regarded as such – ie, the law relating to the formation, operation, control and dissolution of private law incorporated associations (the DTI had separately commissioned a review of the law of partnership law by the Law Commissions), including non-statutory rules of corporate governance, but excluding insolvency and financial services regulation, except to the extent that there were 'knock-ons' between these fields and company law in that sense. The law on co-operatives (industrial and provident societies) and charities was also excluded, but it was recognised that where either form of association took the form of a registered company, they would need to be considered.

Each of these four phases culminated in a major consultation document, entitled, respectively (under the common heading *Modern Company Law for a Competitive Economy* – itself the title of the document with which the department launched the Review),[3] *The Strategic Framework, Developing the Framework, Completing the Structure* and, of course, *The Final Report*.[4] The very widespread and active consultation which followed each document formed part of the basis for the next phase; but the work in hand necessarily continued vigorously while these consultations took place and in each phase more original work was also added to the ongoing process. It is convenient to structure this account around this fourfold framework, once we have examined the background and preliminaries. It will emerge that much of the core of the Review, particularly the process of reaching firm recommendations on company governance (rules about directors, shareholders/members and transparency and information provision) progressed in accordance with the fourfold structure; but it will also emerge that the nature of the subject and the time constraints made it essential simultaneously to progress a number of different topics respectively at different levels of principle and detail. This was necessary to ensure that the various levels of policy mapping and analysis, detail completion and refinement, from high-level policy to more carefully worked out proposals and in some cases fully detailed legislative drafting, were all fully exposed to consultation. Those subjects which were interdependent, related and conditional on outcomes elsewhere also had to be dealt with in an appropriate time frame.

Constraints of time and subject matter also sometimes led to the stages being combined in consultation – for example, the proposals on the institutional structure of regulation emerged at the end of the third phase, without prior publication of significant initial analysis or examination of options (though these were, of course, addressed in the working groups and steering group before the publication).

This all led to subjects being consulted on at particular levels of development at different stages, to the interstitial generation of six further consultation documents on particular subjects at various points, and in the latter stages to two further urgent and informal consultation letters with restricted circulation, to clear up relatively minor matters.[5] The result was that while some topics were fully developed in draft clauses in *The Final Report*, others, such as the proposed structure for regulatory institutions, had, even by then, reached only the status of firm high-level recommendations. A few, notably company charges and their registration, were still at the initial proposal stage.

From the perspective of the management of the process, this parallel, iterative, and staggered method of proceeding represented the only solution to the problems of the subject matter. It proved, surprisingly, relatively free of fundamental problems in itself.

---

3   *Modern Company Law for a Competitive Economy* (London, DTI, March 1998), hereafter *The Launch Document*.

4   Respectively: *Modern Company Law for a Competitive Economy: The Strategic Framework* (London, DTI, February 1999), hereafter *The Strategic Framework*; *Modern Company Law for a Competitive Economy: Developing the Framework* (London, DTI, March 2000), hereafter *Developing the Framework*; *Modern Company Law for a Competitive Economy: Completing the Structure* (London, DTI, November 2000), hereafter *Completing the Structure*; and *Modern Company Law for a Competitive Economy: Final Report* (London, DTI, July 2001), hereafter *The Final Report*.

5   These were on re-registration of companies with different status, eg, limited as unlimited, and on the unanimous consent rule. Both letters were published on the Review website; see www.dti.gov.uk/cld/review.htm.

The major issues were of course those of the merits of substantive policy choices; but the process, and the sequence and interrelationship of those choices within it, are inevitably the main theme of this historical account. Methodology also developed as the Review progressed. It will, however, be convenient to give complete accounts of the main methodological topics, the operation of working groups, the consultative committee and the public consultations, when they first arise.

Finally, it is proposed, after this account of the process by reference to its four stages, to offer a few very broad conclusions and observations on what appear at this juncture to have been its successes and failures.

2 BACKGROUND – THE CASE FOR REFORM

By May 1997, when the new Labour Government came to power, it was quite widely (but not universally) recognised that the state of British company law was no longer acceptable. It had, over its 150-year history since Gladstone's Act in 1844,[6] which first made provision for the formation of incorporated joint stock companies by registration with publicity, and the critical addition of limited liability in 1855,[7] been reviewed at approximately 20-year intervals by royal commissions, culminating in the Jenkins Committee of 1962.[8] These took evidence on the current problems and made recommendations, typically incorporated into an amending Act, which was subsequently consolidated. This usually led to numerous technical amendments and additions to meet current needs or abuses, but no coherent re-examination of the whole. Very rarely was the basic structure adjusted, or anything, however obscure or outmoded, removed.[9]

The Jenkins Committee proposals themselves were never fully implemented. After 1972 the legislative programme was dominated by the need to implement European Community harmonising directives with primary legislation for this purpose in 1972,[10] 1980,[11] 1981[12] and 1989.[13] Each of these Acts grafted Community law provisions onto the

---

6 See Joint Stock Companies Act 1844.
7 See Limited Liability Act 1855. The two Acts and some interstitial legislation were consolidated in 1856. Significant remnants of the Victorian language remain – see below. There was a very active period of legislation on the law of associations in the closing years of the century; see generally PL Davies *Gower's Principles of Modern Company Law* (London, Sweet & Maxwell, 6th edn, 1997) at pp 46–48.
8 See: *The Loreburn Report* (1906) Cd 3052; *The Wrenbury Report* (1918) Cd 9138; *The Greene Report* (1926) Cmd 2657; *The Cohen Report* (1945) Cmd 6659; and *The Jenkins Report* (1962) Cmnd 1749.
9 For example, the law on private companies was developed in the period 1906–08 as a modification of the basic 1862 Companies Act model, which was designed for large, widely held, capital intensive railway and canal companies. Yet the private company rapidly overtook the public company in numbers and legal significance and would, quite early in the last century, have justified a reframing of the Act to correspond to their needs.
10 See European Communities Act 1972, implementing the First Directive on the Harmonisation of Company Law D68/151 (1968) OJ 41, dealing with publicity and capacity.
11 See Companies Act 1980, implementing the Second Directive D77/91 (1977) OJ L 26/1, dealing again with publicity and capital maintenance.
12 See Companies Act 1981, implementing the Fourth Directive D 78/660 (1978) OJ L 222/11 on individual company accounts.
13 See Companies Act 1989, implementing the Seventh Directive D83/349 (1983) OJ L 193/1 on group accounts, and the Eighth Directive D84/253 (1984) OJ L 126/30 on audit.

existing code, sometimes with great difficulty in achieving a fit (the first Directive provisions on corporate authority and *vires*, for example, are still the subject of uncertainty and criticism, after 30 years and two attempts at primary legislation).[14] This was combined with sometimes hasty, and often complex, attempts to add domestic law provisions, often late in the legislative process, to deal with the current corporate scandals. The addition of insider dealing provisions to the 1980 Companies Act provisions on conflicted director transactions and the 'warehousing' of shares to the 1981 Companies Act, and provisions on auditor regulation, charges and the private company elective regime to the 1989 Companies Act, are all good examples of the latter trend.

Both these kinds of change, Community and domestic, were often made without considering the implications for other statutory provisions – for example, to what extent did the additional Second Directive provisions on subscriptions require reconsideration of the existing provisions on commissions and discounts? The additions in 1989 to the existing code on the appointment and removal of auditors created a complex minefield of provisions.[15] In some cases the approach to implementing Community obligations led to incorporation into primary legislation of complex, detailed and technical provisions fit neither for Parliament nor the statute book.[16] In others, the domestic law proposals proved so hasty and ill-considered that they were incapable of implementation. The most notorious examples were, perhaps, the 1989 Companies Act replacements of Part XII on registration of charges and s 159A on terms of redemption for redeemable shares. Other provisions, such as the elective regime and written resolution provisions in the 1989 Act, while effective in themselves, paid little attention to their uncertain secondary effects. More minor Community law provisions were added by statutory instrument. Predictably, this paid even less attention to the need to ensure coherent modification of the code and was further bedevilled by the dogmatic adoption of a minimalist approach to implementation of Community obligations.[17]

---

14 See European Communities Act 1972, s 9(1), and now ss 35–35B of the Companies Act 1985 (hereafter the Act), inserted by the Companies Act 1989. See too Charities Act 1993, s 98. Note, for example, that the revised s 35(1) and (2) of the 1985 Act, after a valiant attempt to repeal the *ultra vires* doctrine, then makes provision for the effect of a transaction which would, before that repeal, have been *ultra vires*, thus retaining the old law for some purposes; and see s 711A, abolishing constructive notice for most purposes and arguably part of the same picture, enacted at the same time, but defective and never commenced.

15 For similar criticism of other parts of the 1989 Act see the Law Society paper cited at n 24, below.

16 For example: how to lay out a balance sheet; see Companies Act 1985 Schedule 4, Part 1, s B; how to determine the purchase price or production cost of an asset; see Companies Act 1985 Schedule 4, paras 26–28.

17 Admittedly, there are limits on what is achievable under s 2 of the European Communities Act 1972; but excessive caution (or increasing Euroscepticism) seems evident. Thus, implementation of the Eleventh Directive on company branches resulted in two codes for regulation of overseas companies operating in Britain, one for those with 'places of business', and another, with different provisions, for those with 'branches' (a distinction which was obscure in itself). The result was 21 sections and 4 Schedules (see Companies Act 1985 Part XXIII and Schedules 21A–21D) of bewildering complexity to deal with an essentially minor and simple technical problem. The Directive on one man companies (D89/667 (1989) OJ L 395/40; SI 1992/1699) was implemented by adding to s 1 of the Act, which begins by providing that any two or more persons associated together for a lawful purpose may by subscribing to a memorandum of association form a company, a subs (3A), to the effect that, notwithstanding this, one person may by subscribing to a memorandum of association do likewise! It was not explained with whom this person was associating. The section is itself based on the method of company formation by deed of settlement which preceded 1844. The total effect on anyone unwise enough to attempt to understand how to form a company by beginning to read the Act can be imagined.

While criticism tended to focus on these more recent legislative attempts at reform, the basic structure of the Companies Act itself showed signs of strain. Victorian language and concepts had become enshrouded in mystery in some cases;[18] the episodic reforms propounded by the various royal commissions were usually sound in themselves, but this was by no means always the case; some showed an absence of principled thought which ultimately turned the legislation, and, in one notorious case Community Law as well, septic; others were attractive but proved unworkable – a defect which might have been remedied by more comprehensive consultation.[19] Already by 1979, Professor Gower[20] had reached the conclusion that our company law was 'in greater disarray than at any time this century, both in content and in form, and likely to remain so', a view which grew stronger with the adoption of the subsequent legislation.[21]

In short, by 1997 our company legislation was in many parts an incoherent, overdetailed and inaccessible jumble of provisions, many of them outmoded, deriving from the vicissitudes of our economic history since the Victorian age. Moreover, much of our company law was to be found in voluminous and contentious (and therefore costly) case law, in many cases with an even longer history and even less pertinent provenance.[22] While the law still worked surprisingly well in terms of legal certainty, the case for a radical review was widely recognised as overwhelming, not least because with each new legislative and judicial overlay the problem of achieving a coherent and accessible body of law was becoming technically and politically more difficult. Other countries had, by now, judged the British model of company law unacceptable. Once adopted by most Commonwealth countries, it had been abandoned successively by Canada, Australia, South Africa and New Zealand, and a similar departure was under consideration in Hong Kong.

The prospects for addressing these problems also looked unpromising and a tone of despair was beginning to appear in the views of commentators. The DTI was far from inactive. A series of proposals had been put forward during the 1990s by DTI officials and ministers for consultation on such subjects as the need for a simpler law for small and

---

18 Consider: the structure of Part I of the Companies Act 1985, including the survivals of the deed of settlement company; the language of s 14; or the meaning of ss 97–100.

19 For example, the Greene Committee's proposal to outlaw 'financial assistance'; see *The Greene Report*, above n 8, at paras 30 and 31 (now embodied in Companies Act 1985, s 151). This was later adopted in Article 23 of the Second Directive at the suggestion of the UK and applied, in differing forms, to all European public companies. The absence of a principled policy objective for this proposal led to 70 years of increasing expense, unfairness and uncertainty, to be ended, one hopes, by the Review (see *Completing the Structure*, above n 4, at paras 7.12–7.15 and earlier documents there referred to) for private companies, but destined to continue for public companies, until the Directive is amended. Other examples are the indeterminate s 310, another *Greene Report* recommendation, and the unfocused palm-tree justice 'unfair prejudice' provision of s 459, recommended by *The Jenkins Report*, above n 8, to thwart the attempts by judges to impose some certainty on 'oppression' – hopefully now remedied by *O'Neill v Phillips* [1999] 1 WLR 1092. On the scope of 'unfair prejudice' see the Lowry essay below at p 229.

20 See LCB Gower *Principles of Modern Company Law* (London, Stevens, 4th edn, 1979) at p 56.

21 The 1985 consolidation itself, like previous consolidations, could make no attempt to deal with issues of content. Its improvements as to form were almost immediately partly unpicked by the Insolvency and Financial Services Acts of 1986 and by the other subsequent primary and secondary legislation referred to above.

22 Consider, for example, *Regal (Hastings) Ltd v Gulliver* [1967] 2 AC 134n (HL) and its derivation from *Keech v Sandford* (1726) Sel Cas Ch 61.

private companies, simplification of the law on conflicted directors, clarification and relaxation of the notoriously obscure and unpredictable provisions on financial assistance by a company in connection with the acquisition of its own shares and simplification of the provisions of Part VI of the Act on transparency for interests in share capital.[23] While there was strong and clear recognition by the professions and representative bodies of the need for many of these reforms and the damaging effect that neglect would have on business and employment, ministers had found neither the time nor the inclination to make progress and all the indications were that this would continue. Companies legislation was notoriously difficult and time consuming, as the legislative attempts of the 1980s had shown, and there was perceived to be little or no political credit to be gained.

In 1991, in a hard-hitting paper,[24] the Law Society, supported by the General Council of the Bar, had pointed out the importance of company law and the lack of attention given to it by recent governments. They noted the dysfunctional, reactive approach of amending legislation over the history of the various Companies Acts and stressed the absence of coherent review, the inadequacies of consultation on recent primary legislation and the cautious approach to vires in amending secondary legislation. The paper proposed the establishment of a Company Law Commission, modelled on Commonwealth precedents, and consisting of 'civil servants, practitioners[25] and academic lawyers' with a continuing obligation to keep the law under review and to propose a series of reforms, of 'moderate scope and reasonable time span'. However, it was not clear how the problem of securing ministerial backing was to be solved, nor how the Commission, using this limited approach, could deal effectively and quickly with all these problems.

3 THE REVIEW – PRELIMINARY STAGES

While there was nothing in the manifesto of the new Labour Government to suggest that reform of commercial law would be a priority, there was much about the need to modernise our institutions. This was vigorously applied in constitutional reforms, devolution, the House of Lords and human rights law in the early months. Establishing a competitive climate for business was also a key priority. So there was, no doubt, a receptive climate in which to make the case for addressing the company law issue.

3.1 Preliminary stages – the launch

Whatever the precise sequence of events within Government – and one may suspect that there were doubts about the political expediency of the ambitious and novel proposal which emerged – by March 1998 Margaret Beckett, the Secretary of State for Trade and

---

23 This by no means exhausts the list of proposals considered by officials; some of the others are referred to below.
24 See Law Society Standing Committee on Company Law *The Reform of Company Law*, Law Society Legal Practice Directorate, No 255, July 1991 (London, Law Society, 1991).
25 It is not clear whether it was intended that these were to be practising lawyers or to include business people and economists with an understanding of the wealth creation process.

Industry, was able to announce a three-year fundamental and comprehensive review, with a view to legislation in the following Parliament.[26]

In *The Launch Document*[27] Mrs Beckett described the task as to create 'a modern law for a modern world' instead of the present 'complex ... outdated, patchwork'. The new law should be clearly expressed for the non-specialist. The review process was to be independent, open and tightly managed, and conducted by an independent, widely based, non-political steering group which would include an independent review project director and be chaired by the DTI's Director of Company Law and Investigations.[28] International and comparative aspects were to be taken full account of. The Review should address the 'overformality of language', 'excessive detail', 'overregulation', and 'complexity of structure' of the present law. An example of this was said to be the financial assistance provisions, costing 'more than £20 million per year' in professional fees alone.[29] Other issues thought fit for re-examination included the relationship between the law and the various 'best practice' codes, notably that on corporate governance.[30] On the latter, there was speculation that the code might be made legislative, but Mrs Beckett supported 'best practice ... provided best practice is seen to be working' (widely interpreted as a threat). However, *The Launch Document* did envisage new legislation as possible in some areas, such as directors' remuneration, fiduciary duties[31] and more effective shareholder participation. Secondary legislation was also advocated to achieve greater flexibility in the context of a review of the structure of regulation generally.[32]

The Steering Group's terms of reference were lengthy, but amounted, in their own summary, to the creation of 'a framework of company law which promoted the competitiveness of British companies, struck the proper balance between the interests of

---

26 The public launch took place at a conference on 4 March 1998 convened by Pensions and Incomes Research Consultants Ltd. There were speeches by Mrs Beckett and John Monks of the TUC, who strongly advocated a stakeholder view of corporate governance, referring to a speech by the Prime Minister some months before, when leader of the opposition, to the same effect; see www.pirc.co.uk.

27 See *The Launch Document*, above n 3.

28 See *The Launch Document*, above n 3, at chapter 7.

29 See *The Launch Document*, above n 3, at Foreword, chapter 1 and paras 3.2 and 3.3. For the author's view of the real problem with these provisions see n 17 above. Most experts appear to believe that £20 million is a substantial underestimate of their cost. The Review's conclusion from comparative work was that they probably had little, if any, benefit.

30 At the time of the launch, the Stock Exchange had begun the task of incorporating into a 'Combined Code' the latest report on this by Sir Ronald Hampel which had been published in January 1998; see: *Committee on Corporate Governance: Final Report* (London, Gee, 1997); *The Hampel Report*. During the course of the Review the Combined Code was published and 'annexed' to the Stock Exchange listing rules, responsibility for which was in turn transferred to the UK Listing Authority within the Financial Services Authority; for rationale see FSA, Paper 37, *Transfer of the UK Listing Authority* (London, FSA, 1999).

31 The DTI and the Lord Chancellor's Department had referred the law on directors' conflicted transactions (Part X of the Act) and on fiduciary duties to the Law Commissions for England and Wales and Scotland in 1997. Codification was a possibility, though the first consultative paper on the subject was not enthusiastic; but see Law Commission Report No 261, *Company Directors: Regulating Conflicts of Interest and Formulating a Statement of Duties* (1999) Cm 4436 (London, TSO, 1999) at Part 4, for their final position.

32 See *The Launch Document*, above n 3, at paras 3.8 and 5.8.

those concerned with companies, in the context of straightforward, cost-effective and fair regulation, and promoted consistency, predictability and transparency in the law'.[33]

3.2   Preliminary stages – appointment of the Steering Group

The Launch Document had stressed the need for a highly qualified but broadly based group with the necessary authority and credibility to control the Review. Its members were appointed by the Secretary of State, on the basis of advice from officials, and from members themselves once appointed, over a period from December 1997 to April 1998. Its independence was emphasised by the participation of a High Court judge with a high reputation as a company lawyer.[34] The other lawyers in the group included a distinguished member of the company bar, a Scottish solicitor with extensive commercial and public experience, a leading academic expert on company law and a corporate lawyer with broad government and company strategy experience.[35] Nevertheless, lawyers were in a minority. The business perspective was very strong; it was represented by: the chairman/chief executive officer of one major public company and a managing director of another, the experienced CEO of a number of small businesses (with extensive experience of public policy in the small business sector), a practising economist, an academic economist and business strategy expert, and a business analyst and commentator from the press and broadcasting.[36] This group, which represented a wide range of opinions as well as experience, was chaired by a senior DTI official.[37] At later stages of the Review a practising accountant, a further professor of company law and a leading economist, accountant and regulator joined the group.[38]

3.3   Preliminary stages – reactions to the launch

The response to the announcement of the Review and the composition of the group was overwhelmingly favourable. In around 160 responses many of the themes and criticisms mentioned above were raised. The TUC and a number of non-governmental organisations advocated adoption of a 'stakeholder' view of corporate governance; many others adopted the contrary view. Only one response opposed the project, asserting it was merely make-work for DTI officials. But privately some commentators expressed doubt whether the case for radical reform had been made out, or declined co-operation on the

---

33   A description at the end of the day; see *The Final Report*, above n 4, at para 1.3; see also Annex A to that report for the original full terms of reference.

34   The Rt Hon Lady Justice Mary Arden DBE, then Chairman of the Law Commission, and later appointed to the Court of Appeal in 2000.

35   Respectively, Richard Sykes QC, Robert Bertram, Professor John Parkinson (Bristol University) and Jonathan Rickford CBE, the project director.

36   Respectively, Sir Stuart Hampson (John Lewis Partnership), Bryan Sanderson CBE (BP Chemicals), Colin Perry (Chairman LTE Scientific and CBI Small Business Council), Rosemary Radcliffe CBE (Chief Economist, PricewaterhouseCoopers), Professor John Kay (of the London Business School and, at that time, Director of the Said Business School, Oxford), and John Plender (*The Financial Times*). The project director's most recent experience had also been in business strategy (British Telecommunications plc).

37   Richard Rogers, Director, Company Law and Investigations.

38   Martin Scicluna (Deloitte and Touche), Professor Paul Davies (London School of Economics) and Sir Bryan Carsberg (then Director General, International Accounting Standards Commission).

ground that the project could not succeed within the political and practical constraints and proposed timescales.

4 THE FIRST PHASE OF THE REVIEW – STRATEGIC

The Steering Group first met in June 1998. As a first priority a basic philosophy and plan were required. This in turn implied an agreed view on core purposes, philosophy and guiding principles, a clear substantive analysis ('mapping') of the key areas of the legislation and common law to be considered and of the interdependencies between them, and a prioritisation of these areas. The outcome of these deliberations would need to be consulted on, and was indeed in due course reflected in *The Strategic Framework*. The group decided to address these 'overarching', or high-level and general issues of principle immediately. However, it was agreed that, given the shortage of time, it would also immediately be essential to consider in working groups the analysis and approach to those of the high-level issues which were amenable to consideration in that way. Some substantive issues of law at a more basic level should also be subjected to working group treatment at once. These were selected partly on the basis that they were urgent and fundamental to further work, which would be dependent on their resolution. But such topics were also chosen because they were complex and therefore likely to require long-term consideration, or because they represented 'low-hanging fruit' (in the marketing jargon), that is, the case for reform was well recognised and thinking well advanced, so that 'early wins' could be achieved. Some of these topics showed all these characteristics.

4.1   Strategic phase – 'overarching' issues of principle

The high-level issues were of three kinds. First, there were the 'philosophical' issues, such as what was the purpose of company law and what was to be the touchstone or test for the success of the review recommendations. Related to this, but different, was the question what were companies for, and how should the character of the law reflect that? The second kind of high-level issues were ones of substance which the law needed to address which were at such a high level of generality that they were likely to be no less pervasive. Here the problem of the needs of the small company, the character and style of the regulation to be adopted, and the mismatch between the philosophy on which the legislation was founded and the real modern needs of incorporated businesses, lay at the root of discussions. On this latter point it was recognised that at the technical level the law had failed to exploit the potential of modern technology and also that, at a more fundamental level, it had failed, in both its substantive and its transparency rules, to reflect sound perceptions of the real sources of value and performance in the modern economy. The third set of high-level issues related to process, and discussion began on these at once. These included: How was the Review to be conducted? What were the rules on openness and confidentiality to be? What should be the role of the Consultative Committee, proposed as a wider sounding board in *The Launch Document*?[39] How could

---

39   See *The Launch Document*, above n 3, at chapter 7. In chapter 8 there had been put forward a timetable, which, it was quickly recognised, failed to take full account of the iterative character of the task – see above.

the group ensure that the output would be 'viable', in the sense that it would be acceptable to an incoming administration in the next Parliament? This, given the scale of any legislative implementation, clearly required a very broad and positive consensus in support of the outcome – how could this best be achieved while preserving the integrity of the Review? How could the proposals to be put forward be made immune to the problems which had led to the establishment of the Review, which, it was evident, was not an exercise which could be repeated at regular intervals? There seemed to be a relationship between the structure of the Review and the structure of the legislation to be proposed – both would require continuous development and improvement. The comparative and international dimension was plainly also pervasive. In this context and across the field there were important empirical and factual issues requiring research and investigation, for which a method and definition of needs had to be developed. The reactive approach which merely took the existing law as a given and decided how to change it was to be abjured. The unachievable, but formative, ideal was to start from a zero base of factual need.

It was clear that at least an initial analysis and identification of options for consultation was required on all these matters in an initial 'strategic' phase. However, on some matters a working hypothesis was immediately needed as a basis for progress.

4.2   Strategic stage – the first seven working group topics

It was essential to allocate work to working groups and to get them up and running, if possible before the summer break. While discussion proceeded on many of the high-level issues within the Steering Group, it was decided to allocate the issue of the purpose of a company (so-called 'scope'), which plainly raised the stakeholder issue but would pervade the approach to all rules on company operation and control (hereafter 'governance'), to a working group.

The small company problem raised technical, factual and comparative issues which had stubbornly resisted solution for many years. This again seemed to require the breadth and focus of immediate working group attention. Information technology issues were all-pervasive but technical and seemed to require early consideration on a similar basis. Two fundamental areas, where the law was antique and/or complex, where some defects were readily identifiable and major progress could probably be readily made, but which were likely to require more than one phase of consultation, were company formation and capital maintenance. Finally, in two other areas it was clear that the problems would be deep-seated and would require consideration from a number of perspectives as the Review proceeded; these were comparative law and international issues and issues about the structure of regulation and legislation. On the former, it was decided that research projects were to be set up to publish reports which could be drawn on by all participants, but that the international competitiveness of the present regime and the approach to international jurisdictional issues were best considered, in the time available, through a working group of international practitioners. The structure of regulation was clearly an issue which would permeate the whole Review and deserved immediate high-level discussion within the Steering Group, but an initial appreciation of the detail and a 'mapping' analysis was required. The latter task seemed fit for an expert working group.

Accordingly, seven topics were allocated between three working groups, each to be led by a chairman drawn from the Steering Group: the first addressed scope and the needs of small and closely held companies; the second, company formation, capital maintenance and the structure of the legislation ('boundaries'); and the third, international issues and information and communications technologies.[40]

4.3 An aside on the steering and working group method

While the working group process was refined as the Review progressed, it remained constant in its essentials. All groups were led by a chairman from the Steering Group. The latter met monthly, with very few gaps, throughout the Review period, including a number of intensive overnight 'awaydays' at which the broad structure and direction of the Review and a number of key documents were discussed. At every Steering Group meeting minutes of the current working group discussions and an oral report on their progress and direction was presented by the chairman of each active group, or by the project director.[41]

The membership of the working groups was decided on by the Steering Group on the basis of advice from the DTI, the project director, other Steering Group members and, of course, critically, the agreement of the chairman of the group in question, making use of all their contacts. The objective was to ensure that all relevant perspectives and sources of technical expertise were represented on each group. The members were chosen for their personal authority and expertise, but also for their access to networks and organisations which would be able to provide wider expertise, experience and resources as well as a sounding board for ideas. However, the members were invited to participate in a personal and not a representative capacity. In consequence, while ideas and proposals generated within these groups were not to be kept confidential, their sources and attribution were. The intention, which was broadly achieved, was that working groups should hammer out authoritative analysis and proposals which were tested in the course of their development within the groups from all relevant perspectives and which represented a viable and practical consensus of expert but non-partisan participation. Thus, some of the discipline of consultation, wide argument, persuasion and consensus building could be achieved early, at the stage of idea generation. In the most successful cases this led to unanimity and commitment on the part of the expert authorities involved. However, in some cases it became clear to a particular participant that the thinking within the group was moving away from his or her personal views. In only one case did such a participant feel unable to continue as a member. But in all other cases

---

40 These working groups were chaired by Professor John Parkinson, Richard Sykes QC and Jonathan Rickford, respectively. For full membership of all these groups see *The Strategic Framework*, above n 4, at Annex A.

41 The project director attended almost every working group and sub-group meeting, but in the later stages of the Review he was supported by a senior manager from the DTI, Kate Harre, who became in substance deputy project director and shared the burden of these reports and managed the growing team of officials. The ground rules for the operation of the Steering Group were broadly similar to those for working groups – as to which see below. In particular, the attribution of views of members and thus the papers provided were as such confidential, though the issues and arguments discussed were not.

participants continued to contribute constructively and conscientiously, and to test and improve the ideas which finally emerged.

Working groups typically met monthly, but they often spawned sub-groups on particular topics (for example, directors' fiduciary duties; the operating and financial review; company charges). At some points meetings were taking place at the rate of three or four per week. Initial papers for groups were typically provided by their chairman, by the project director, or by a DTI official.[42] Subsequently individual members would often offer papers or presentations. At critical or difficult points the project director, who was a member of all groups and co-ordinated them in co-operation with their chairmen, would table a paper.[43] On some issues working groups failed to establish a consensus, and on a few the Steering Group declined to accept their view, in every case, so far as I can recall, as a result of further consultation and new perspectives. Generally the technical and consensus-establishing work of the groups was very successful. On every issue the work produced was of very high quality, which is attributable to the outstanding quality of the participants and their unstinting generosity in time, constructive thought and expertise. In all there were over 200 members and expert participants in such groups, excluding DTI officials, who also provided very valuable input, analysis and support. The secretarial burdens were enormous and were superbly managed, in many cases by officials who continued to do their 'day jobs'.[44]

4.4   The first phase – the strategic framework emerges

The Steering Group drew all this work together in its first consultation document, *The Strategic Framework*, published in February 1999. This account can give only the most cursory of summaries of the progress of the thinking embodied in such documents, sufficient to explain the progress of the story.

In chapter 2 of the document the Group set out its conclusions on the issues bearing on the overall approach. Consistently with *The Launch Document* and the terms of reference, it adopted as its generally overriding objective the need for the law to promote and facilitate efficient wealth generation (in the broadest sense) for all, best achieved through freely operating markets in a climate of transparency and accountability. Minimal complexity, and maximum accessibility, for the law were advocated and a 'think small first' principle propounded at the outset.[45] Key underlying factors identified as requiring attention included changing patterns of ownership and the importance of institutional investors, changing perceptions of the sources of value ('modern asset mix'), new technology, regulatory techniques and globalisation. The document had been extensively discussed in the Consultative Committee (see below). The minutes of those discussions together with the document itself and a body of empirical material on

---

42 Each group was under the tutelage of a departmental official, who ensured secretarial servicing, chased or provided materials, and supervised record keeping.

43 Providing, for example, a draft on fiduciary duties, an approach to the operating and financial review and a 'default private company' approach to the small company problem.

44 The initial staff commitment to the Review consisted of the Project Director (in theory part-time) and a full-time Review Secretary (Edwin James); but by the close of the Review there were about 15 full-time equivalent staff, including a full-time senior manager from the DTI and a parliamentary draftsman.

45 See *The Strategic Framework*, above n 4, at p v and paras 2.24 and 2.25.

international, European and European Community developments[46] and an extensive review of related literature on all aspects of the review, were published on a special part of the DTI website, which provided a valuable source of information on all aspects of the Review.[47]

The output of the working groups, together with the Steering Group's views on the relevant topics, was set out in chapter 5 of the document. On 'scope' the objective was to describe the present law (in terms capable of being understood by all those with a concern for the proper orientation of companies' operations), to explain the economic and political arguments and to identify the main policy options for addressing the issue in legal rules. It was explained that the current law on the operation and control of companies by directors and members/shareholders, provides that at present companies are ultimately controlled by, and to be run by directors for the benefit of, shareholders. Two main lines of approach to the 'scope' issue were then identified. These were the 'shareholder value' and 'pluralism' approaches. The former approach essentially reflected the shareholder orientation of the present law; the latter approach would permit, or require, directors to serve the interests of others whose welfare depended on, and whose risks were bound up with, those of the company. A version of shareholder value which recognised that true advantage to shareholders could not be achieved without proper recognition of the need for the management of the company to take proper account of a wider body of interests, over a broad, strategic range in time and substance, was designated 'enlightened shareholder value'. A third approach, that directors should serve the interests of their company 'as an entity in its own right' was tentatively dismissed, as not resolving the issue of which individual interests should be preferred in a case of conflict, and adding little of substance in the absence of such conflict.[48]

The enlightened shareholder value view was recognised as a broadly[49] correct statement of the law, but as not widely recognised as such in practice. The pluralist view was perceived to be preferable in theory, as recognising the wider impacts of company behaviours and their consequences for all those at risk, but as raising major practical problems, if applied to directors' duties, in terms of the dangers of diluting the focus of directors, extending the range of their discretion, and failing to provide a secure basis for the justiciable enforceability of the resulting duties to the wider community.[50] The inconsistency between shareholder control and a pluralist view of directors' duties was also identified; it was suggested that pluralist duties might require structural change, perhaps through two-tier boards and a wider source of board authority. The Steering Group recognised that there was little support for such radical change and came very close to rejecting pluralist solutions and suggesting that enlightened shareholder value,

---

46 See too *The Strategic Framework*, above n 4, at chapters 3 and 4.

47 See www.dti.gov.uk/cld/review.htm.

48 See *The Strategic Framework*, above n 4, at para 5.1.15.

49 But with some doubts about the effect of s 309 of the Act (interests of employees); see *The Strategic Framework*, above n 4, at para 5.1.17 onwards.

50 See *The Strategic Framework*, above n 4, at paras 5.1.17–5.1.113, but note the recognition that s 309 of the Act was ambiguous and could carry either an enlightened shareholder value or a pluralist interpretation.

combined with greater disclosure, might better meet the needs identified.[51] It was hoped that, by this exposure of the scope issues, the stage had been set for a public debate on the practical options for addressing stakeholder interests in company law.

On small and closely held companies, two possible approaches were examined – a 'free-standing' approach, providing such companies with separate tailor-made legislation,[52] or an 'integrated' approach, retaining them within the current framework, but restructuring it to meet their needs on a 'think small first' basis. The latter was favoured, perhaps combined with greater relaxations in the law for all private companies, or some kinds of them, and the implications for more detailed reform were opened up for consultation. The possibility of erecting barriers to exclude small firms from incorporation and limited liability was rejected.[53]

On company formation,[54] proposals were made for abolition of the memorandum and articles in favour of registration through a simple form and a single integrated constitutional document, for abolition of authorised share capital as a superfluous concept and for simplification of company capacity and authority rules by total abolition of the external effect of objects clauses (*ultra vires*), as well as clarification of the rules on the external authority of boards and abolition of the constructive notice doctrine.

After a general question for consultation about the real significance of share capital as a source of security to creditors and others, similarly straightforward, but rather radical, proposals were made on capital maintenance. These included the removal of the mandatory court approval for capital reductions and the abolition of nominal, in favour of no par value, shares for all companies, if an appropriate amendment to the European Second Directive could be achieved, but if not, for private companies. The Second Directive also inhibited major reform of financial assistance for public companies. The document recognised the weakness of the policy basis for the prohibition and flirted with the idea of a very substantial curtailment of the law for private companies, but was 'inclined to think this may be too radical' and proposed a system of solvency certification and general meeting authorisation.[55] This matter was destined to be revisited by the second phase. The working group considered the issues from the small companies' perspective, and with the benefit of the answers to the question about the real value of capital maintenance, a more radical line was adopted (see below).

On the structure of regulation and 'boundaries', the document raised key issues of principle and set out a 'map' of the existing institutions and their jurisdictions,[56] which proved invaluable in later stages of the Review and in consultation.

On international issues, the relative attractiveness of the British regime, its certainty and flexibility, were recognised in the working group of international practitioners, but they compiled a significant list of 'irritants' which inhibited establishment here, by

---

51 See *The Strategic Framework*, above n 4, at para 5.1.32, and see in particular paras 5.1.44–5.1.47 – 'The Relevance of Transparency and Public Accountability'.

52 Comparative models were set out and analysed in Annex E to *The Strategic Framework*, above n 4.

53 See *The Strategic Framework*, above n 4, at chapter 5.2, but see the discussion of sanctions policy and directors' duties towards creditors in the third phase, below.

54 See *The Strategic Framework*, above n 4, at chapter 5.3.

55 See *The Strategic Framework*, above n 4, at paras 5.4.23 and 5.4.24.

56 See *The Strategic Framework*, above n 4, at chapter 5.5 and Annex F.

companies with a choice of possible host countries;[57] all of these matters were considered at later stages, and are discussed below. The opportunity was also taken to consider the basic 'incorporation' choice of law doctrine, which determines to which companies British company law is generally applied by reference to their registration here, and thus enables those who operate companies here to adopt foreign law governance systems. The possibility of taking a power by secondary legislation to apply parts of our code to companies founded under foreign law but based here, as is done in California, and more crudely in Germany, was raised. However, the idea was conclusively rejected after consultation. On Part XXIII of the Act (overseas companies with establishments in Britain), a radical simplification of the law was proposed, aligning the regime on a single approach, that adopted by Community law for regulation of overseas companies' branches.[58]

Finally, on information technology, a 'technology neutral' approach to the legislation was suggested, based on a recognition of the need to regulate for the potential beneficial effects of technology and its possible abuses, and a broad secondary legislative power to amend the law to address the issues was proposed. It was suggested that at this stage it was too early to compel the use of new technologies as opposed to enabling it, but that this might change, particularly in relation to compelling companies and the registrar of companies to offer a choice.[59] Particular areas where it was proposed that electronic methods should be possible were: company formation and registration; company communication with shareholders on proxy forms and by distribution of accounts; and the holding of meetings using new technologies. It was also proposed that the rules on company publication of corporate information on business documents should be extended to their electronic equivalents.[60] The broad approach of these proposals was adopted in the Electronic Communications Act 2000 and the first three specific proposals were embodied in the first order under that Act.[61]

It was clear that, although no work had been done on company reporting in the first phase, except certain aspects in relation to scope and small companies, transparency was bound to be a key component of the final settlement and would need to be addressed fully in the next phase. Accordingly, the Steering Group decided to include in the document a description of what it believed to be the key issues, with a call for comment, to assist in the planning of the coming work. After some liaison with the Institute of Chartered Accountants and some rather lively discussion in the Consultative Committee, the key issues were thought to include: the relationship between law, standards and 'best practice'; international accounting standards; small company issues, including audit; qualitative reporting and the directors' report; auditor independence and auditor liability; and the impact of technology, in particular on timing and publication of information.[62]

---

57 See *The Strategic Framework*, above n 4, at para 5.6.4.
58 See *The Strategic Framework*, above n 4, at paras 5.6.23–5.6.29.
59 In fact in *The Final Report* mandatory use of the internet for some quoted company reporting was firmly recommended; see *The Final Report*, above n 4, at para 8.80 onwards.
60 See *Developing the Framework*, above n 4, at chapter 5.7.
61 See Companies Act 1985 (Electronic Communications) Order 2000, SI 2000/3373, which came into force on 22 December 2000. See too the related Institute of Chartered Secretaries and Administrators *Guide to Best Practice* (London, ICSA, 2000), referred to by the Order.
62 See *The Strategic Framework*, above n 4, at chapter 6.

The rest of *The Strategic Framework* document examined the legislative form to be adopted for the group's proposals and the possible structure of the legislation as a vehicle for further development (related to the structure of regulation and boundaries issues), on which the Steering Group adopted firm and radical views, and set out the plans for the next phase.[63]

4.5 An aside on the roles of consultation documents and the Consultative Committee

The need for a consultative committee had been identified in *The Launch Document* and the Steering Group also recognised that there was a need for a very broadly based consultative body to act as a sounding board and discussion forum for its proposals in advance of their publication. Unlike the working groups, to be effective this body would need to be representative of all the interested constituencies, business, the professions, the trade unions, investors large and small, government departments, regulatory bodies and non-government organisations, though some additional members were invited to participate on the basis of their personal expertise.[64] Its members would need to be equipped to commit those bodies, at least on a preliminary basis, as to the likely outcomes of consultation. However, it was clearly understood that final commitments could only be given after full consideration and consultation at the end of the relevant consultation periods. On the other hand, it was hoped (and indeed it turned out) that as the Review progressed a broad and committed consensus would emerge within this representative body. Such a very broadly based body was accordingly established mainly on the basis of nominations by the key organisations. It met approximately every three months, though only when there were sufficient matters to discuss, a total of 10 times over the three-year course of the Review.

All major consultative documents were presented to this committee in draft in advance of publication, though timing constraints sometimes made full consultation on every detail difficult. It proved a very valuable forum for candid exchange of views, consensus building and early warning of likely difficulties.

Documents, except *The Final Report*, were all framed around policy questions, except where the issues referred to had already been consulted on at least once and firm conclusions reached. The questions would be worded in an open form except where the Steering Group was strongly inclined to adopt a view, in which case questions would be slanted – 'Do you agree that ...?'. This was intended to enable answers to be focused, to encourage more vigorous and argued dissent where there was a clear provisional Steering Group view, and to facilitate systematic analysis of the issues raised, but the practice was widely misunderstood in the early stages. The normal period allowed for responses was three months, but for *Developing the Framework*, apart from the urgent small company aspects which had already been covered to some extent in *The Strategic Framework*, four-

---

63 See *The Strategic Framework*, above n 4, at chapters 8 and 9, respectively. Chapter 7 of *The Strategic Framework* was a progress report on the work of the Law Commissions on directors' duties and Part X of the Companies Act 1985 (directors' conflicted transactions), as to which see below.

64 For a full list of the 52 members see *The Final Report*, above n 4, at Annex E. Steering Group members were also members *ex officio* and the chairman and project director attended all meetings.

and-a-half months were allowed. These lengthy periods of consultation were essential, but they presented formidable logistical problems within the three-year timeframe. Allowing for the notice requirements of the Consultative Committee and of the Steering Group itself, which needed to approve final drafts after the Consultative Committee had opined, at the beginning of each consultation document process, and for the completion of the analysis of responses, which were often late, at the end of it, there was a minimum period of four-and-half to six months for the completion of each major consultation stage. These timing constraints created major problems for management of a Review which required three such consultations and six minor ones in the two years after the reaching of initial strategic conclusions. It was clear that work would have to continue on the relevant issues as the consultations progressed. Happily, our public readily recognised this.

Each major document provoked between 100 and 200 responses, occasionally more, many of which were complex, lengthy and closely reasoned.[65] These had to be read, assimilated and evaluated and the outcome incorporated into the work of the next phase. A method was developed of analysing the results by issue (the structure of the questions in the originating consultation document was vitally important in securing valuable input, enabling such analysis and shaping ongoing policy formation) and providing a digest of all responses by reference to these issues for use by the project director, working groups and others proposing policy conclusions for later phases. These digests were published on the website, except where a response requested confidentiality. The sequence of consultation and timing of successive phases (including processing of responses) was accelerated as experience was gained. However, the targets for the final phase proved too ambitious. The consultation period for *Completing the Structure* ended at the end of February 2001 and the target for *The Final Report* was April. Many responses were late and lengthy. Some respondents took the opportunity, perfectly properly, to reopen positions on a whole range of interrelated issues covered by the Review. In the event the interval for analysis and decisions proved to be too short. Fortunately, the Government was content that, in the period running up to the general election in May the final stage should be delayed, thereby enabling the Steering Group to report in June 2001. The moral for others embarking on such an exercise is to allow for a longer period for the final phase than would, at first sight, appear necessary, and certainly not to rely on further improvements in performance at that stage.

The approach to responses was to consider the weight and experience of any body offering empirical judgements and to consider the force of the reasoning offered. 'Yes/no' answers were of course taken account of according to the credibility of their source, and the breadth and direction of any consensus noted. However, reasoned and substantiated assertions carried most weight and the process of reaching conclusions was certainly not one of counting heads. In spite of the importance of achieving consensus, on no occasion was the Steering Group influenced by the numbers of responses to adopt a view which it did not accept on the merits. But only on rare occasions did the view adopted differ from

---

65 All except the very few which demanded confidentiality were made available publicly by respondents, or the DTI, or both. *The Final Report*, above n 4, attracted well over 400 responses, but almost half of these were on one issue – the retention of the requirement for private companies to appoint a company secretary.

that of the overwhelming majority, on the grounds that the arguments were compelling[66] and almost all the Steering Group proposals did finally achieve an overwhelming majority endorsement.

5 THE SECOND PHASE – DEVELOPING THE STRATEGY

After publication of *The Strategic Framework* in February 1999, work began immediately on the next phase in accordance with the programme announced. This phase was, as has been noted, destined to conclude with the *Developing the Framework* document in March 2000.

Five working groups were established to carry forward the work on the topics of: small companies and wider questions about the range of legal structures available to business ('vehicles'); 'scope' issues and the role of directors; the role of shareholders and technical issues on shares; accounting and reporting; and registration of information.[67] Sub-groups emerged on the subjects of: not for profit companies; the model constitution for private companies; the structure and drafting of directors' fiduciary duties; Part X of the Act; qualitative reporting and the operating and financial review; company names; and company dissolution and restoration to the register. At a relatively late stage preliminary work also began in a sub-group on the registration of charges.

The target was to publish reasonably firm conclusions, in the form of a balanced package of proposals to include all the key policy issues relating to company governance, by early spring 2000. This would leave time for one further major consultation document, taking account of the reception for these proposals and covering the outstanding second- and third-order issues, of which the structure of regulation and sanctions policy seemed likely to be the most important. This last major consultation document was to be published before the final period allowed for completion of the Review, with a *Final Report* due in spring 2001.

Intensive work by the working groups over the summer and early autumn of 1999 (taking account of the responses to *The Strategic Framework* received in June and July) led to reports to the Steering Group in the late autumn. This allowed for intensive drafting and final decisions on the *Developing the Framework* document (which ran to 460 pages) to be made over December 1999 and into January/February 2000.

It is now appropriate to consider the achievements in this second phase, some of which proved to be wrong turnings, in more detail.

---

66 Leading examples were decisions to abandon a fiduciary duty of honesty and to codify the unanimous consent rule.

67 These groups were led, respectively, by Professor Paul Davies, Professor John Parkinson, Martin Scicluna and Robert Bertram.

5.1 Second phase – working groups[68] and Steering Group conclusions

The key proposals which emerged on small companies[69] were provisional. Nevertheless, there was firm adoption of the 'integrated' rather than the 'free-standing' approach, based on the simplification of the law for all private companies in a range of areas, including: a firm recommendation in favour of the abolition of financial assistance rules for all private companies; simplification of capital issues and of capital maintenance rules; and much greater flexibility in the rules for member decision making in writing.[70] Consideration of the practical implications of the 'think small first' approach led to a decision that the existing 'elective'[71] option for private companies, to opt out of the general meeting regime and a number of related provisions (some of which were to be abolished altogether), should become the norm. It would be for companies which sought the more elaborate regime to 'opt in'. General proposals were also put forward for simplifying the model constitution for private companies[72] and for the provision of an arbitration scheme for the resolution of shareholder disputes.

More surprisingly perhaps, the Steering Group was persuaded by the working group recommendations not to relax the rules for private companies on conflicted directors' transactions in Part X of the Act, but rather to tighten them up. There had been pressure in this direction from small business representatives themselves; it was recognised that companies are customers for the good governance of their corporate trading partners.

While this 'integrated' and 'think small first' philosophy had been strongly (but with some heavyweight opposition) endorsed in consultation, there remained a substantial body of opinion, in the working group and elsewhere, that there was a case for trying to develop a special structure within the Act for companies whose shareholders and directors were the same individuals, so that agency problems did not (allegedly) arise. This proved highly controversial, with those opposed pointing out the difficulties which would arise in such a structure when such identity of members and directors ceased to be the case. In the end the consultation document put forward two possible models of such an owner-managed structure for consultation, but pointed out the difficulties they raised and invited solutions.[73] A new separate corporate vehicle for charities was proposed[74] and issues raised about whether its use should be restricted to charities, or extend to other voluntary organisations, and should be mandatory or voluntary.

---

68 For the plan for second phase working groups as at February 1999 (end of the first phase) see *The Strategic Framework*, above n 4, at Annex I. This plan included, in addition to the four groups described below, two further working groups on the progress of detailed issues from the first phase (capital, formation, etc) and a group to address a series of further issues. In the event this plan proved unduly ambitious – the first of these was dealt with by the project director and the team working with the relevant chairmen's approval – see the description of the intermediate consultations below; the other issues were partly postponed until the third phase and partly subsumed in other groups' work during the second.

69 See generally *Developing the Framework*, above n 4, at chapter 7.

70 A further, more controversial, proposal was for abolition of the requirement for private companies to have a company secretary. See *Developing the Framework*, above n 4, at para 7.34.

71 See Companies Act 1985, s 379A.

72 See *Developing the Framework*, above n 4, at para 7.70 onwards and the scheme for modifying Table A which would result, in Annex D.

73 See *Developing the Framework*, above n 4, at para 7.95 onwards.

74 See *Developing the Framework*, above n 4, at chapter 9 on alternative 'vehicles', and at para 9.14 onwards, reflecting very helpful input from the Charity Commission.

The key proposals which emerged on the role of directors and 'scope', after lively discussion and some considerable differences of view in the working group,[75] included a codification of fiduciary duties with an 'inclusive' duty of loyalty setting out the purpose for which the company was to be run. It was decided that companies should be run on enlightened shareholder value lines, centred on an obligation to 'promote the success of the company for the benefit of its members as a whole' with a duty to take account of wider relationships and impacts and corporate reputation, where and to the extent that this was necessary to achieve that overriding objective.[76] This was to be combined with a new qualitative reporting obligation, developed in the transparency working group, for public and large private companies in the form of a statutory operating and financial review. In both cases where wider interests were relevant they were to be taken account of, as were the longer-term and dynamic effects of company policy and strategy.[77]

The Law Commission for England and Wales and for Scotland had, by this time, reported in favour of codifying directors' fiduciary duties at a high level of generality, to allow for flexibility and judicial development.[78] The key influence on the Commissions had been the results of two empirical surveys of company directors which had shown a remarkable degree of ignorance on the part of many directors of their general legal obligations and a desire for authoritative clarification of the position. The main objections[79] to such codification had come from legal bodies who regarded it as impractical, in terms of reconciling certainty and flexibility. Because this was essentially an empirical question, a 'trial draft' of flexible 'high-level principles', prepared by the project director and refined in the working group (but broadly,[80] following an earlier non-legislative guidance draft prepared by the Law Commissions, which had been well received in their consultation) was published in the document. It was proposed that the existing provision, in s 309 of the Act, on the position of employees in relation to fiduciary duties would be subsumed within the new loyalty duty. The case for including a duty towards creditors was raised, but rejected in favour of guidance.[81] A proposal by the Commissions that the statement of duties should be included in the notification of appointment to be acknowledged, signed and registered by directors was accepted.[82]

---

75 The allegedly 'polarised' analysis in *The Strategic Framework*, above n 4 (enlightened shareholder vs pluralism) had been strongly criticised by advocates of strong stakeholder views; but no convincing alternative analysis was offered. See further on directors' duties the essay by Birds, below at p 149.

76 The problems with a pluralist approach to directors' duties and their enforceability were thought to be overwhelming. On enforceability, the TUC had proposed that duties to the wider Community might be enforceable through the courts at the suit of the Secretary of State.

77 See *Developing the Framework*, above n 4, at para 3.12 onwards; and at para 5.74 onwards.

78 They reported in September 1999, see above n 31. Their recommendations on Part X were largely accepted by the Steering Group, but with some significant modifications; see *Developing the Framework*, above n 4, at para 3.86 onwards and at Annex C.

79 Maintained particularly by the Law Society for England and Wales, the General Council of the Bar and the Scottish Faculty of Advocates.

80 There were a number of important differences, notably a completely new loyalty and related obedience and proper purpose duty, a reframed duty of independence and a radically reformed set of duties on conflicts of interest. There were also important drafting changes on care and skill.

81 See *Developing the Framework*, above n 4, at paras 3.72–3.73.

82 See *Developing the Framework*, above n 4, at para 3.18.

Amongst numerous other important issues[83] on the role of directors was the question whether the rules of best practice incorporated in the combined code on corporate governance[84] could be incorporated into mandatory rules. It was argued that this would ensure the monitoring and balancing role and independence of non-executive directors. But this also raised important and very controversial issues of principle about the structure of corporate governance regulation and tricky definitional issues.[85]

The third working group operating at this stage was concerned with the position of shareholders and here there were a number of major concerns. The first was the need to ensure that companies catered effectively for the interests of 'real' shareholders (that is, those with control rights, and corresponding risks), represented on the share register by nominees and custodians, in some cases through intermediate funds managers. As the importance of the shareholder in the general scheme of corporate governance gained prominence, so information issues and the protection of his governance powers came to the fore. After careful analysis, some minor amendments to the Companies Act were proposed to facilitate this.[86]

The role of the company general meeting and its justification emerged as important issues, as it was recognised that for quoted companies real power lay with institutional investors outside the general meeting, while for small companies such meetings could be expected to become a very exceptional event. On the other hand, the importance of members in the emerging scheme cut the other way, and there was widespread concern that public company general meetings were mere charades, with the real decision making taking place elsewhere. These concerns, which had been expressed vigorously in responses to *The Launch Document* and *The Strategic Framework*, prompted the issue of an intermediate consultation document in October 1999,[87] raising the possibility of allowing public as well as private companies to dispense with their AGMs. Few respondents were prepared to countenance this, though many recognised the weaknesses of the institution. There were almost no practical suggestions for substantive improvement. The *Developing the Framework* document, issued five months later, raised the issue of whether the rules on annual general meetings, their agendas and information provision in connection with them, should be tightened up, but rejected the proposal that public companies, like private ones, should at this stage be free to dispense with such meetings altogether. However, it was suggested that the Secretary of State should have power to introduce such a reform if and when modern technology allowed this through the provision of acceptable substitutes.[88] Transparency and technology issues were recognised as highly

---

83 Including: the definition of directors, shadow and alternate directors; relief, exemption and indemnity from liability; attribution rules; qualifications and training; and the wider disciplinary effect of the market for corporate control and the capital market. See *Developing the Framework*, above n 4 ,at chapter 3. The important issue of whether the codified duties should be exhaustive of their field or should allow for judicial development of new fiduciary duties was also raised, with a provisional preference for exhaustiveness; see *Developing the Framework*, above n 4, at paras 3.82–3.83 and question 3.17.

84 Stock Exchange (now UK Listing Authority) rule 12.43A, London Stock Exchange, July 1998.

85 See *Developing the Framework*, above n 4, at para 3.112 onwards.

86 See *Developing the Framework*, above n 4, at paras 4.7–4.18.

87 *Modern Company Law for a Competitive Economy – Company General Meetings and Shareholder Communication* (London, DTI, October 1999).

88 See *Developing the Framework*, above n 4, at para 4.25 onwards.

relevant.[89] The powers of company members unanimously to govern their affairs without formalities were also considered and the unanimous consent rule endorsed, but it was proposed at this point in the Review that it should not be codified,[90] a position which was reversed later (see below).

Having considered such collective institutions for company members' decision making, the focus of discussion then moved to individual, personal or minority rights of members. General principles on the approach to this were propounded and the discussion then moved on to consider individual rights of members under the constitution, 'oppression', or 'unfair prejudice', remedies, derivative actions, and the general law on the limits of the powers of the majority by general meeting action to control the company's affairs.[91] A statutory statement of personal rights of shareholders was proposed, departing from the contractual model, and based on an illustrative list and a residual general principle for their identification. This idea was destined to be abandoned in the light of consultation. Earlier recommendations of the Law Commission for England and Wales[92] on derivative actions and unfair prejudice were adopted with substantial modifications, including a statutory derivative action abandoning the fraud on the majority doctrine. Work was begun in this phase, but not completed, on the remaining general principles of law limiting the powers of the majority.[93] The Steering Group contented itself with describing the issues and inviting responses on them. A number of more technical issues on shares and shareholders were also raised, some of them of considerable significance.[94]

The work on accounting and reporting led to a series of proposals to reform radically the reporting cycle, its structure and timing, the boundary between law and standards, the extent of qualitative as opposed to financial reporting, and the role and liabilities of auditors. On the structure of reporting, proposals were made to render the core document for listed companies the preliminary announcement of results, which should be made mandatory by statute and should be made available to all shareholders as a matter of right within 70 days of the year end. It was envisaged that this might replace the summary financial statement option (though a firm proposal to this effect was watered down as a result of criticism in the Consultative Committee) or that that option might become an alternative to the new 'statutory prelims'.[95] The full annual report would become a document which was available on demand, but not automatically distributed to shareholders, within 90 days of the year end. Here, once again these initial proposals on the structure of the reporting cycle were destined to be radically changed in the next phase in the light of consultation.

---

89 See *Developing the Framework*, above n 4, at paras 4.25–4.45. It was proposed, however, that wholly owned subsidiaries should be free to dispense with AGMs – modified in the *Final Report* to dispensation by unanimous resolution.

90 See *Developing the Framework*, above n 4, at paras 4.21–4.23.

91 See *Developing the Framework*, above n 4, at paras 4.65–4.144.

92 See Law Commission Report No 246 *Shareholder Remedies* (1997) Cm 3769 (London, TSO, 1997). This project had begun in February 1995; see too Law Commission Consultative Paper No 142 *Shareholder Remedies* (London, TSO, 1996).

93 See: *Greenhalgh v Arderne Cinemas Ltd* [1951] Ch 286 (CA); and *Gambotto v WCP Ltd* [1995] ALR 417 (High Court of Australia).

94 See *Developing the Framework*, above n 4, at paras 4.145–4.181.

95 See *Developing the Framework*, above n 4, at paras 5.22–5.25; and 5.33–5.35.

On the law and standards, it was proposed that the whole of the law on the form and content of company accounts, apart from the list of reporting documents and their basic purpose, should be made a matter of standards. However, given the fact that much of this area was Community law, the standards should become legally enforceable. This raised important issues about sanctions for breach of such rules. By way of possible solution three options were floated: first, full legal enforceability of all standards, with criminal and civil penalties; second, for such enforceability only to be available for the standards implementing European directives; and a third option, for such legal enforceability to apply only to the statutory rules and for enforceability of all standards only to be effected through the specific enforcement mechanism of the Financial Reporting Review Panel and discretionary judicial director disqualification.[96]

On qualitative reporting, it was proposed that the current Accounting Standards Board guidance on the annual operating and financial review (OFR) should be made mandatory, at least for listed and perhaps for all public and very large private companies.[97] The concept was that a report should be given by the board which gave their honest appreciation of the factors which needed to be considered to assess the performance and prospects of their company. The content should in all cases include a 'fair review' of performance and an explanation of the overall orientation, purposes and strategies for the company operated by the board. These 'mandatory' items were to be supplemented by coverage of all other factors the directors judged relevant to users of the report (which was to be published) for assessing performance and prospects. An illustrative list of matters to be considered, which included the factors covered in the similar list in the draft loyalty duty, was included in the report.[98] This report was largely envisaged as replacing the directors' report, but the need for a residual public interest reporting power in the hands of the Secretary of State was also recognised.[99] It was also envisaged that the OFR should be reviewed by the auditors[100] for consistency with financial statements, the accuracy of its factual basis, compliance with applicable standards and consistency with the auditor's other information, and that the auditor's report would state whether the OFR had been 'properly prepared'.[101] General questions were also raised about the possible use of communications technology in reporting.[102]

On audit, a balanced package of reform of the law on auditors' duties and liabilities was proposed. This was to include a wider role for auditors in verifying accounting statements and the OFR and a tightly limited[103] extension of the range of the auditors'

---

96 See *Developing the Framework*, above n 4, at para 5.64.
97 See *Developing the Framework*, above n 4, at paras 5.79 and 5.100. Difficult issues on application to groups of companies were raised in para 5.101.
98 See *Developing the Framework*, above n 4, at paras 5.88–5.92. A confidentiality exemption was envisaged in para 5.87.
99 See *Developing the Framework*, above n 4, at paras 5.102–5.105.
100 And/or perhaps other experts, see *Developing the Framework*, above n 4, at para 5.143 onwards, an idea abandoned as unnecessary in the next phase of the Review.
101 See *Developing the Framework*, above n 4, at paras 5.98 and 5.99.
102 Including verification of internet publications; see *Developing the Framework*, above n 4, paras 5.114–5.128.
103 Doubts were expressed about the method and feasibility of such a limitation, however, see *Developing the Framework*, above n 4, at paras 5.146–5.155.

duty of care beyond the common law *Caparo* rule.[104] This would allow auditors to limit their liability by agreement with the company,[105] but subject to safeguards, and also extend the duties of company directors and employees to assist the auditors in the conduct of the audit. For the audit of small companies[106] it was proposed to extend the exemption from audit to all small companies (within the Fourth Directive definition), but to require a lighter version of audit verification (known as 'independent professional review') for larger small companies.[107] The facility for small companies to file 'exempt' accounts and the exemptions for 'medium-sized' companies should, it was suggested, be abolished as providing inadequate information,[108] but a significantly shorter, simpler and more informative model for small company accounts was advanced.[109] A substantial acceleration of the reporting timetable was also proposed, shortening the interval for the preparation of private company annual accounts from 10 to seven months, with a shortening to five months in due course.[110]

The work on company registration and information provision and dissolution and restoration was voluminous,[111] but largely uncontroversial. However proposals for less extensive disclosure of shareholders' particulars in private companies and to allow directors to register their home addresses in confidential files at the companies registry, in exchange for the provision of published 'service' addresses, provoked considerable interest. The work on company charges registration was reached late in this phase and proved technically very difficult and as a result it was decided to deal with this topic in a special working group in the third phase.

The Review research and information programme was by now in full swing and was drawn on in support of many of these provisional conclusions and analytical approaches. An account of it was given in chapter 12 of *Developing the Framework*. Effective research and empirical studies require careful definition by reference to the issues to be addressed and frequently require lengthy periods for data capture and analysis. This meant that it was not possible to commission work until the Review was well under way and that the window within which such work could be usefully completed was tight.[112] Further empirical work was done, particularly on corporate governance and the practicalities of the OFR, but by the close of this second phase in spring 2000, the opportunity to begin new major work was already restricted. This led one to reflect that a focused continuing

---

104 See *Caparo Industries plc v Dickman* [1990] 2 AC 605.

105 Repealing Companies Act 1985, s 310 for auditors.

106 See *Developing the Framework*, above n 4, at chapter 8.

107 The value of such a review became the subject of an Institute of Chartered Accountants for England and Wales (ICAEW) research study. The Steering Group finally took the view that whether the idea should be adopted should be determined by the results of this study; see *The Final Report*, above n 4, at para 4.49.

108 This significant tightening of the rules for small companies was supported by small and medium sized business experts in the working group and it proved in wider consultation.

109 See *Developing the Framework*, above n 4, at paras 8.36 onwards and Annex E. This required minor amendments to the Fourth Directive but was thought valuable even if these were not achievable.

110 See *Developing the Framework*, above n 4, at para 8.40. In *The Final Report*, above n 4, the five-month proposal was abandoned in favour of a general power to amend the accounting requirements by statutory instrument, already contained in Companies Act 1985, s 257.

111 Reflected in chapter 10 of *Developing the Framework*, above n 4.

112 European Community public contracts tendering rules also imposed formal constraints on the commissioning of work, which proved demanding of time and staff.

programme independent of the Review timetable, commissioned by a well informed and responsible body, was desirable.

5.2   Second phase – intermediate consultation – progressing the detail

The responses to *The Strategic Framework* were received by late June, and were processed and assessed during July and August 1999. On the detailed issues of company formation, capital maintenance and overseas companies these were sufficiently positive to make it feasible to progress the development of the policy to the level of detailed policy statements sufficient to found lawyers' drafting instructions. It was clearly also highly desirable to make progress in this way. Companies legislation is an object lesson in the devil lying in the detail and policies needed to be tested to this level, at least in technical areas. It was agreed that the Review should provide a detailed and 'bankable' body of legislative input and that its audience should have the opportunity to see the detail and, if possible, the legislative style proposed for the final product, over as wide an area as was feasible in the time available. The objective should never be lost sight of and the Review would be useless unless it was structured in a way which led to legislation. Moreover, the general objective of accessibility could be little more than an aspiration if the policies being developed at this stage could not be illustrated, in at least some areas, by actual draft legislation.

Accordingly, it was decided to publish detailed policy proposals on these three areas. These proposals would be made available at the same time as the *Company General Meetings* document, so that the audience should suffer the minimum of separate consultation approaches.[113] Consultation on these intermediate documents (October 1999) was to be completed by 7 January 2000, allowing just enough time to include conclusions based on the outcomes in *Developing the Framework* in March. In fact, while the output from consultation on *Company General Meetings* contributed substantially to the working group proposals on shareholders, the output on formation and overseas companies proved so supportive that it was possible to begin immediately to prepare for the drafting of instructions to parliamentary counsel.[114] On capital maintenance, however, a number of thorny technical issues had arisen on which it was decided that a very small expert working party would be required in the third phase (see below).

6 THE THIRD PHASE – COMPLETING THE PICTURE

By the end of the second phase (March 2000) the Steering Group had put out for consultation a series of provisional, but fairly firm, proposals on the key policy issues relating to company governance, namely scope; directors; shareholders; and

---

113 But the October consultation was divided into three documents: (i) Formation and Capital Maintenance; (ii) on Overseas Companies; and (iii) General Meetings.

114 This work was done by two small working parties chaired by the project director, which referred their conclusions to Richard Sykes QC, who approved the interim consultation documents before their endorsement by the Steering Group. The detailed work on formation and capital maintenance was, however, largely done, within very tight deadlines, by John Healey, a retired DTI official who had been the secretary to the Hampel Committee on Corporate Governance, and by departmental lawyers.

transparency; and the special issues in relation to all of these which arose for small and private companies. The published thinking had also advanced to a more detailed level on a number of more technical issues, namely: formation; capital; registration of information; and overseas companies. So long as the thinking on all these matters proved reasonably robust in the light of consultation, the time was ripe to move on to fill in the overarching issues. The latter issues were contingent on the soundness of this approach, notably the structure of regulation and legislation – a subject which had been encountered in numerous different contexts[115] during the second phase work – and sanctions policy (which had been ventilated at the level of high-level principle in *The Strategic Framework*, but which was plainly contingent on work elsewhere). Third phase working groups were accordingly established on these topics.[116] There were also more detailed areas to be filled in. Small 'working parties'[117] seemed appropriate on capital maintenance and company charges[118] and the remaining issues on minority rights,[119] but fully fledged working groups were needed to address issues relating to groups of companies, issues on company reconstructions, takeovers and migration between jurisdictions, and transitional regime issues.[120]

The intention was to progress the working group and working party issues at least to the level of high-level policy conclusions for consultation, in a document to be called *Completing the Structure* (a title signalling that conclusions were becoming firm), due out by November 2000. This should leave a tight, but just sufficient, interval for consultation once more, and to deal with any resulting difficulties or surprises, in time for a *Final Report* in April 2001. This was planned to provide a complete picture of a system of policies which would already have achieved substantial consensus. It was thought essential that the way should by then have been prepared, through thorough and sustained argument and consensus building, to ensure that this *Final Report* was not significantly controversial.

6.1 Third phase – indications of Government views

Midway through this third phase, at a conference in June 2000,[121] a significant indication was given of likely Government views on some key aspects of corporate governance in a speech by Stephen Byers, the then new Secretary of State for Trade. He stressed the value he attached to maintaining the Review's independence. However, the key points which emerged from this speech were an indication of support for something close to the

---

115 Particularly in work on the board, shareholders, general meetings and disclosure.
116 Led by Sir Bryan Carsberg on Institutions, and Dame Mary Arden on Sanctions.
117 See *Developing the Framework*, above n 4, at para 12.8 for the full list of working parties planned to be operating at this stage. Such 'working parties' were intended to have a smaller membership and lighter structure more easily and speedily serviced by the team.
118 These were led by Jonathan Rickford.
119 Led by Richard Sykes QC.
120 These were chaired by Rosemary Radcliffe, Richard Sykes and Jonathan Rickford.
121 A joint seminar called by the Institute for Public Policy Research and the TUC on 7 June 2000. The other speakers were: Brendan Barber of the TUC, who spoke forcibly in favour of stakeholder views and employee involvement; Will Hutton of the Industrial Society, who criticised the deal making culture of British management, which militated against value creation through organic growth; and John Cridland of the CBI, who expressed support for the proposed codification of directors' duties.

enlightened shareholder, or 'inclusive', view of directors' duties within a climate of broader accountability, and a general preference for 'best practice' approaches in matters within the corporate governance code. There was also an encouraging indication that matters of company governance would be a high priority for the Labour Government in the next Parliament. This speech probably did not influence Steering Group members' views, which had already been provisionally expressed publicly, but the speech was widely noted and affected the overall climate within which the Review proceeded to develop its proposals, generating confidence in the Government's commitment to the Review and to subsequent implementation.

6.2 Third phase – emerging consensus on governance issues

The plan for now achieving firm conclusions on governance proved feasible – but not without difficulty. On the critical scope issues there was overwhelming support in the responses to *Developing the Framework*, as they emerged in early August 2000, for the proposed codification of directors' duties and for the OFR. While there was persistent opposition to the former in principle from two respondents,[122] much of the reasoned objection was based on technical issues which were believed to be soluble in drafting. On the OFR there was significant demand[123] for more extensive obligations, but argument from only a few that the regime should remain one of best practice rather than be made mandatory. This argument was based in part on the feared burdensomeness and inflexibility of mandatory provisions and the dangers of such rules inducing defensive, perfunctory and 'boiler-plate' compliance.[124] In its 'Conclusions' on scope as published at the end of the third phase in *Completing the Structure* in November 2000, the Steering Group rejected both these views, but responded to the concerns of those who wanted a tighter requirement by proposing stronger audit of the process of preparation of the OFR. It also set in hand the commissioning of an empirical study of the preparation of OFRs in accordance with the proposed obligations, to be conducted by the Industrial Society, to explore, so far as possible, the validity of the practical concerns of the opponents of a mandatory rule.[125] However, a number of further issues had arisen from the consultation concerning conflicted transactions and the effect of insolvency in relation to directors' duties, and standards in relation to the OFR, and views were invited on these.[126]

On other matters relating to directors, the most important feedback from consultation was a strong aversion to revision, or statutory underpinning, of the Combined Code. It was only in its second year of operation and the case was strong for retaining the Combined Code's flexibility in rules for company governance through mandatory disclosure on a 'comply or explain' basis. The Steering Group accepted this view after discussions in autumn 2000, but believed that the Code should be kept under review under the supervision of the proposed new Standards Committee and be subject to enforcement by the new Monitoring and Enforcement Committee (for these bodies, see

---

122 The Law Society for England and Wales and the Faculty of Advocates.
123 Mainly from the TUC, many NGOs and some accountants.
124 Mainly the CBI and some accountants.
125 For the outcomes see below and *The Final Report*, above n 4, at paras 8.30 onwards.
126 See *Completing the Structure*, above n 4, at questions 3.1–3.8.

below). However, it was also proposed that this standards body should have power to require disclosure in general meeting notices of information sufficient to enable the members appointing directors to be satisfied that code requirements on independent directors were being met.[127] The responses to the other proposals, including those on conflicted director transactions (see Part X of the Act) were broadly favourable,[128] but the proposal to reduce the maximum term of employment of a director to three years on first appointment and one year thereafter (subject to general meeting authorisation of longer terms) was strongly opposed in some quarters. The Steering Group nevertheless maintained it and proposed a further corresponding limitation of covenanted payments on loss of office.[129]

On shareholders, the responses were again generally supportive.[130] Voluntary, but not mandatory provisions for companies to recognise 'real' shareholders were favoured; but there was significant, though not majority, support for codification of the unanimous consent rule. There was also general support for the proposals on annual general meetings, including the extended rights to have shareholder resolutions circulated at company expense where effectively supported and received in time (the revised proposals on annual accounts publication would enable such resolutions to be properly informed – see below), but not for a statutory minimum agenda for the AGM. The Steering Group abandoned this in favour of best practice guidance.

Further original thinking in the working group on minority rights (influenced in part by the responses) did, however, lead to some revision of the recommendations in this area. In particular, the Steering Group concluded that personal rights of shareholders should be presumed to arise under the constitution unless expressly excluded, thereby abandoning the illustrative list definition approach that had been proposed in the second phase. The Steering Group were also of the opinion that the recent judicial limiting of the unfair prejudice remedy[131] should be retained. They thought that the only other constraints on the exercise of majority power in general meetings should be that it should be exercised *bona fide* in the interest of the company where an alteration of the constitution or class rights were in issue and that the wrongdoers and those subject to their influence should be disqualified from voting where a wrong to the company was being authorised, condoned or ratified.[132]

Greater difficulties were encountered with the second phase proposals on accounting and reporting and these difficulties led to their being radically revised. The proposal to make the 'statutory prelims' the core document for all shareholders, which had been based on a desire to ensure speed and equality of information for all shareholders, was shown by respondents not to be feasible. There was also very strong support for the retention of summary financial statements and for these together with the full annual report, in spite of its wider scope, to remain the 'core document'. The key argument was that 'prelims' were now a lengthy, detailed and highly technical document designed to

---

127 See *Completing the Structure*, above n 4, at para 4.47.
128 See *Completing the Structure*, above n 4, at chapter 4.
129 See *Completing the Structure*, above n 4, at paras 4.19 and 4.20.
130 See generally *Completing the Structure*, above n 4, at chapter 5.
131 Ie, contained in Companies Act 1985, s 459; see *O'Neill v Phillips* [1999] 1 WLR 1092.
132 See *Completing the Structure*, above n 4, at para 5.59 onwards.

meet the needs of expert investors. They could not sensibly and usefully be modified also to meet the needs of the general body of shareholders, which were better met by the full annual report, or the summary of it which summary financial statements would provide. It was also pointed out that the new OFR would be an important source of information for shareholders, though not a time-critical one, and that this or a summary of it should be part of the core document. Bodies representing individual shareholders also proposed that if the full annual report could be published electronically it should be possible to adjust the timetable so that shareholders could requisition resolutions at the annual general meeting on the basis of the relatively up-to-date information which such reports contained – an idea which proved very attractive to the Steering Group. The proposed 90-day deadline for publication of accounts was also criticised by some as too tight, but the major accounting and industry bodies thought it feasible (it is the SEC requirement).[133] The Steering Group concluded in favour of a requirement that where prelims were published they should be published on an accessible website, so as to achieve equality of information for all those interested, at least where they were 'wired'. The full annual report should also be published in this way within the 90-day period, but distributed in hard copy within the 120 days to be allowed for the notice of the annual general meeting. There should also be a minimum 15-day interval between publication and notice, to permit informed requisitioning of resolutions. The AGM and filing of accounts should be within 150 days of the year end.[134] All this should apply at least to listed companies and perhaps to all quoted companies, though here interesting issues arose about the relationship with the jurisdiction of the UK Listing Authority and the London Stock Exchange; but unquoted public companies should be subject merely to the 120/150-day limits.[135]

Devolution of the whole of the law on the form and content of financial accounts and standards for the OFR was practically unanimously supported in the responses and the Steering Group agreed without difficulty to adopt this, with a sanction based on an extended jurisdiction for the proposed Monitoring and Enforcement Committee (as to which, see below). This clearly had major implications for the structure of the institutions being dealt with in the new third phase working group.

On auditors, further work[136] on attribution and extension of the auditors' duties had led to a recognition that these represented intractable problems of the common law of agency and tortious (or delictual) liability. The suggested extension of the auditors' duty of care and the suggestion that companies should be liable vicariously, and by way of contribution and contributory fault, for the negligence and fraud of directors in the preparation of accounts, had wide and indeterminate implications for directors' and companies' liability more generally. New questions were raised in *Completing the Structure* on these aspects, on the possible limits for such a duty, and possible protections against its abusive exploitation. It was suggested that there should be civil liability for directors and employees who breached the proposed new duties to assist the auditors and such

---

133 After more research opinions changed on this – see below.
134 See *Completing the Structure*, above n 4, at paras 6.16–6.31.
135 See *Completing the Structure*, above n 4, at paras 6.32–6.40.
136 Including an opinion commissioned from Ian Glick QC, published on the Review website, on attribution rules and the implications of the earlier proposals.

breaches should be imputed to their companies.[137] On auditor independence, the Steering Group examined the recently introduced regime for the regulation of accountants and concluded that change would be premature, but that it should be kept under review and a reserve power to legislate if necessary retained.[138]

The second phase proposals for small and private companies received a much easier reception. It should, however, be remembered that this subject had received a more thorough airing in the first phase. The Steering Group decided firmly to adopt its proposals for simplifying the law for private companies, including making the elective regime the normal or 'default' regime and simplifying the law on company decision making and on capital.[139] New detailed issues were raised on: sole directors; on the practical implications of shortening the timetable for accounts; on the proposed independent professional review to replace audit for larger 'small' companies; and on the distinction between public and private companies (that is, the prohibition on the latter from offering securities to the public and its relationship with prospectus law).[140]

6.3　Third phase – output from working parties – initial drafting

The small working party on capital maintenance[141] dealt with a number of technical, but very stubborn, problems in this field leading to the publication of a consultation document in June 2000 which sought responses by August. This allowed time for a final position to be adopted on this subject by the Steering Group upon publication of the *Completing the Structure* at the end of the third phase in November 2000.[142]

By July 2000 it was clear that thinking was sufficiently advanced on formation, capital maintenance and directors' duties for it to be possible to contemplate draft clauses for the final document. An arrangement was agreed between the DTI and a member of the office of Parliamentary Counsel and instructions were prepared on formation and capital maintenance between July and the close of the Review. The Steering Group was clear that

---

137 See *Completing the Structure*, above n 4, at para 6.98 for a convenient summary of this.

138 See *Completing the Structure*, above n 4, at para 6.71.

139 See generally *Completing the Structure*, above n 4, at chapter 2. Further research was first done with the help of the American Bar Association on the effects of the abolition of financial assistance prohibitions for private companies. The 'owner-managed' concept was abandoned due to the fact that no responses proposed practical solutions to the difficulties it posed. The separate corporate vehicle for charities was also adopted and subsequently the Scottish executive also declared its intention to adopt this model for Scottish charities; see: *Completing the Structure*, above n 4, at paras 9.2–9.7; and *The Final Report*, above n 4, at para 4.63 onwards.

140 This had been raised in *Developing the Framework*, above n 4, at para 4.160 with a suggestion that company law and prospectus law should be aligned. However, the Steering Group had by now concluded, contrary to the views of most respondents, that this looked inappropriate on the ground that the purposes of the two regimes differed. Instead a power to amend, align and clarify so far as possible was proposed, together with a new criminal offence for private companies of assisting any application for a quotation on a prescribed exchange; see paras 2.77–2.82. It may be asked whether the basic distinction between public and private companies was questioned. It was; but the group took the view that the distinction between companies with the economic power to call on the public capital markets and those without was inherently sound as a basis for determining the proportionality of governance regulation; it was also a fundamental component of Community law.

141 For membership and sources of outside evidence see the document *Modern Company Law for a Competitive Economy – Capital Maintenance: Other Issues* (London, DTI, June 2000), at Annex A; hereafter *Capital Maintenance*.

142 See *Completing the Structure*, above n 4, at chapter 7.

draft clauses on directors' duties were also required; but drafting instructions on these could not be completed until resolution of outstanding issues after the end of the third phase.

The process of drafting what was, in many ways, to be a new style of Bill proved challenging and time consuming; it also absorbed very substantial resources. The project team, which began to be regarded as the core of a future Bill Team, grew within the DTI, and the team and its management was perhaps distracted from other possible Review work. On the other hand, this was the only way of proving the viability of the project to the public, and perhaps within Government. It also provided an opportunity to assess the resources which would be needed later for a full legislative implementation project.

The other main area of working party activity[143] during this third phase concerned company charges. A consultation document on this vexed area[144] finally emerged in October 2000.[145] This took its basic policy line, in favour of detailed improvements but no fundamental reform to the system, from a relatively recent consultation by the DTI.[146] However, this document stimulated a very wide range of differences of view on almost every major issue raised, and unexpectedly strong support for fundamental change to the system in the direction of 'notice filing' – that is, constitutive rather than confirmatory registration.[147] This was the only consultation in the course of the Review which failed to produce a viable basis for consensus in the responses. The Steering Group decided to call together a further working group with additional participants to reconsider the issues and provide input in the final phase of the work in early 2001 (as to which, see below). However, it was recognised that there was no longer time to provide Government with final recommendations which would be securely founded on a widely achieved public consensus on this issue.

6.4 Third phase – new work from working groups

As has been already noted, the two main overarching areas where the structure needed to be completed were the institutional structure of regulation and a general policy (including its detailed application) on sanctions. There was now time for only one consultation on these critical issues before final recommendations were needed on the whole system.

After intensive work in the working group on the institutional structure, a new Companies Commission was proposed to keep company law under review. The new Companies Commission would also advise ministers on legislation and be consulted by

---

143 Minority rights work was covered above. Work on unregistered companies and company reregistration was completed within the team, largely by John Healey. The former appeared in *Completing the Structure*, above n 4, at chapter 9, the latter in a separate informal consultation letter and in chapter 11 of *The Final Report*, above n 4.

144 It raises issues of personal property and land law and the law of trusts and must reconcile competing systems of registration of property rights. For a more detailed treatment of this subject in general see the de Lacy essay below at p 333.

145 See *Modern Company Law for a Competitive Economy – Registration of Company Charges* (London, DTI, October 2000); hereafter *Registration of Company Charges*.

146 See *Registration of Company Charges*, above n 145, at paras 1.9–1.14.

147 See further the de Lacy essay below at p 380.

them on secondary legislative proposals. The consultation was to be a mandatory requirement, with an obligation on ministers to explain their position on the relevant issue. This Commission was to have three 'subsidiaries'. These subsidiaries were first, a new Standards Committee, responsible for accounting and reporting standards and for a wide range of rule making in disclosure and other technical areas.[148] Secondly, there was to be a separate Private Companies Committee, responsible for advising the other bodies on the implications for small and private companies of any proposals and with a right to be consulted by them. Thirdly, there was to be a Monitoring and Enforcement Committee replacing the Financial Reporting Review Panel, to monitor compliance and enforce the reporting requirements, including a power to issue binding enforcement orders. Finally there was also to be an independent specialised Reporting Tribunal, to which appeals from action by the Monitoring and Enforcement Committee could be referred for expert adjudication, rather than to the High Court.[149] As we shall see below, these ideas were significantly modified in the final phase.

On sanctions, there was again intensive work from a widely based and highly experienced working group; the key proposals were for: the retention of the great range of regulatory offences, which though numerous were shown in working group discussion to be a very efficient means of securing compliance; creation of a series of more serious 'second-tier' offences, with more severe penalties where technical offences were committed with dishonest intent; and extension of the law on fraudulent trading. A proposed list was developed of general principles to be applied to the detailed provisions as they were revised in detail, and proposals were made for reforming the outdated law on 'officers in default', improving the system of civil sanctions for public law purposes (disqualification and enforcement orders), for disclosure of offences committed in relation to companies ('naming and shaming'), for codifying the private civil remedies against defaulting directors, and for tightening up the legal provisions which applied to 'phoenix' companies (companies trading on the assets and goodwill of other companies which have failed, in such a way as to disguise that failure).

The other two third phase working groups were concerned with the remaining more technical areas which still required examination: the law of groups of companies and the law on reconstructions, takeovers and jurisdictional migration. On groups, radical reform on enterprise liability lines was not favoured, but a limited proposal allowing wholly owned subsidiaries exemption from individual accounting and reporting requirements in exchange for a parent company guarantee was developed; this proved to be quite complex.[150] On reconstructions the possibility of aligning Companies and Insolvency Acts' provisions[151] was raised, together with a limited proposal for 'statutory' mergers within wholly owned groups without court approval or creditors' meetings. Part XIIIA of the Act, on takeovers, was examined and 32 general and more detailed questions on

---

148 Eg, conduct of general meetings, corporate governance, rules on public offers by private companies and rules on the allocation of responsibility between the board and the general meeting, such as the 'Super Class 1' listing rule on major acquisitions and disposals.

149 See *Completing the Structure*, above n 4, at chapter 12. It was suggested that appeals from the tribunal should only lie on matters of law, not including the meaning of 'true and fair', nor of standards.

150 See *Completing the Structure*, above n 4, at chapter 10.

151 See: Companies Act 1985, s 425; and Insolvency Act 1986, s 110. See generally *Completing the Structure*, above n 4, at chapter 11.

possible reforms were raised. Finally, a detailed proposal for jurisdictional migration was floated, based in part on the provisions of the Community Statute for a European Company.

7 THE FINAL PHASE

Plans were now in place for the final phase bringing together all the recommendations on the whole of core company law. These plans would need to take account of comments received on *Completing the Structure*, particularly those on the new material which had originated from third phase working groups. They would also need to identify and resolve any difficulties which had come to light with previous proposals, and, if possible, deal with the major outstanding issue of company charges.

7.1 The new material

The most important and contentious of the new proposals which had originated in the third phase working groups were those about the institutional structure. Some concern was expressed in responses that these represented a prescription for over regulation, through an excessively elaborate bureaucratic structure. At the more detailed level, objections of principle were raised to the conferring of a devolved jurisdiction on a body such as the proposed Standards Committee for major issues of public policy. These were thought to include the 'Super Class 1' listing rule on merger authorisations, and rules involving criminal penalties, such as the 'offer to the public' criterion, which fixed the boundary between public and private companies. More contentiously, it was also suggested that any rules which applied by reference to whether a company was quoted should be a matter for financial services regulation and not for company law. This implied that the developed regime for quoted company reporting and the Combined Code corporate governance reporting rules should, if at all, be a matter for the Financial Services Authority and not, like other accounting and reporting rules, for the proposed standards body.

The Steering Group proposals had been quite widely misunderstood. In their essence they represented no more than a development of the existing Financial Reporting Council, Accounting Standards Board and Financial Reporting and Review Panel structure, and took into account the review proposals on qualitative reporting,[152] with the addition of a body to secure the interests of smaller companies and a specialised adjudication system. However, the Group was persuaded that the standards body's role should be limited primarily to reporting and to the arguably related subjects of provision of information and use of technology in connection with the general meetings.[153] It sought to emphasise the continuity of the proposals with the existing highly regarded structure of the FRC, ASB and FRRP by rechristening the main bodies the Company Law

---

152 There was a significant interrelationship, and even overlap, between financial reporting, the OFR and Combined Code reporting.

153 But that the Secretary of State should have power to devolve additional competences; see *The Final Report*, above n 4, at paras 5.47–5.70.

and Reporting Commission, the Standards Board and Reporting Review Panel. The Reporting Tribunal and the mandatory enforcement order proposals were abandoned, the former mainly on the ground that it might, by reducing the standing of the adjudicator, tempt companies more readily to challenge RRP rulings, and the latter as unnecessary.

It was also recommended that the Standards Board should have power to issue guidance on any matter within its jurisdiction, including all aspects of the OFR, and that the CLRC should have similar powers for the rest of company law. The Steering Group continued to favour these bodies as a more efficient source of law in these fields, more expert, flexible and fleet of foot, but recognised that, for these advantages to accrue, the relationship between the bodies and Government, their statutory authorisation, composition and funding would be very important matters in principle and practice. So in *The Final Report* a set of statutory objectives was proposed, recognising that there had not been time for consultation on these, and a clear preference for strong business and professional involvement and funding on the present lines was expressed; but the peculiar interest of Government and Parliament in these questions was recognised.[154]

On the other major new area of general principle exposed in this phase, sanctions policy, there was much less argument. All the main proposals from *Completing the Structure* were adopted with some refinements, notably a more detailed set of recommendations on 'officers in default' and 'phoenix' companies.[155]

The conclusions in the light of responses on the more detailed working group work in the third phase[156] were: that the proposal for an accounting exemption for wholly owned subsidiaries guaranteed by their parent was in insufficient demand to justify the complexities and losses in transparency which would result; that there was similarly no case for major alignment of the reconstruction provisions, though detailed improvements were required; and that there was a case for a number of detailed reforms to the takeover provisions in Part XIIIA.[157] The schemes for statutory mergers within wholly owned groups and for jurisdictional migration were also endorsed.[158]

7.2   Incidental issues on governance

As we have noted, by the end of the third phase the Steering Group's position on the main aspects of company governance – scope, directors, shareholders and transparency and the small company aspects of these – were quite well settled and had achieved a wide measure of support. However, a number of important incidental issues had arisen which required final resolution. These were dealt with in *The Final Report* in the context of a general description of the overall recommendations.

The first such area was the detail of the provisions on directors' duties. A draft clause and schedule to the bill on these had been prepared and were published in *The Final Report* with a set of explanatory notes.[159]

---

154 See *The Final Report*, above n 4, at paras 5.81–5.101.
155 See *The Final Report*, above n 4, at chapter 15.
156 See *The Final Report*, above n 4, at paras 8.23–8.28, and at chapters 13 and 14.
157 Some 30 in all; see *The Final Report*, above n 4, at paras 13.19–13.65.
158 See *The Final Report*, above n 4, at chapters 13 and 14.
159 See *The Final Report*, above n 4, at Annex C.

A number of issues had arisen in drafting, or as a result of consultation and further thinking within the Review. First, it was decided to reopen the decision not to include in the codified statement any reference to the special duties of directors towards creditors in circumstances of likely insolvency. It was agreed that s 214 of the Insolvency Act 1986 should be incorporated in the statement without substantial amendment; this provides an overriding duty towards creditors enforceable in an insolvent winding up once all reasonable hope of saving the business has been lost. But agreement could not be reached on whether the common law rule[160] providing protection at a point when insolvency is likely should also be incorporated. The merits of this rule proved highly contentious. The issue had only fully emerged once a decision in favour of codification was taken. It was finally decided to publish a draft codification of this rule to enable further consultation to take place after the end of the Review. It was clear that the arguments on this were very evenly balanced, with legal, theoretical, economic and commercial perspectives in contention.[161]

A further area of difficulty on directors' duties concerned the authorisation on behalf of companies of directors' exploitation of their property, information and opportunities. The draft hitherto proposed had followed the familiar *Regal (Hastings)*[162] principle, requiring general meeting authorisation, or, more dubiously, authorisation by (or perhaps under?) the constitution of the company.[163] A significant body of responses had suggested that this was impractical, unfair and economically damaging in the modern age and had advocated authorisation by an independent board. The Steering Group had already proposed in *Completing the Structure* that, for private companies only, such board authorisation might be allowed if in turn authorised by the constitution, and that the model constitution should include such a provision.[164] Now it went further and recommended that this should be lawful unless prohibited by the constitution (thus enabling existing companies), so long as the authorisation was specific to the particular case, independent and disclosed after the event in the report and accounts; but it also proposed that the only constitutional permission to be allowed by public companies should be such authorisation.[165] These were significant new proposals, but in an area which had been well traversed by consultation.

On qualitative reporting, the main changes were for the addition of an item ('dynamics') to the list of matters to be covered by the directors in their OFR in all cases – this resulted from the Industrial Society study, referred to above, which had been generally very positive on the practical issues, but which stressed the case for this change and for guidance on the OFR. Some refinements of the criteria for audit review were also adopted.[166]

---

160 See *West Mercia Safety Wear Ltd v Dodd* [1988] BCLC 250 (CA).
161 The essence of the argument was that from the legal and economic point of view as the probability of insolvency increases and businesses are run more at the risk of creditors so their interests deserve greater protection as against those of shareholders. The commercial and practical argument is that such a rule will 'chill' enterprise; see *The Final Report*, above n 4, at paras 3.12–3.20.
162 See *Regal (Hastings) Ltd v Gulliver* [1967] 2 AC 134n.
163 See the trial draft in *The Final Report*, above n 4, at para 3.40, 3b.
164 See *The Final Report*, above n 4, at paras 3.26–3.27.
165 See *The Final Report*, above n 4, at para 3.21 onwards.
166 See *The Final Report*, above n 4, at paras 3.33–3.45.

On shareholders, the main new area of work during this final phase concerned the position of institutional shareholders and the effectiveness and integrity of vote registration on behalf of beneficial investors. The main concerns were about the diligence, effectiveness and propriety of the exercise of voting powers held by such investors in a fiduciary or quasi-fiduciary capacity, particularly in conflict of interest situations. Responses to questions raised on this area in *Completing the Structure* had indicated a major body of concern. A special Discussion Group was established on this,[167] which held two meetings in the early weeks of 2001. The Group found important evidence of significant problems and considered a range of remedies, including a new criminal offence of corrupting the exercise by fiduciary investors of their shareholder powers. However, the Group concluded that this would not be justified and recommended transparency in the relationships between fiduciary investors and investee companies. They also recommended mandatory audit of the voting process on resolutions called on shareholder requisition and where such audit was demanded by an appropriately qualified minority of shareholders. Mandatory disclosure by fiduciary investors to their clients of the way in which they had exercised their powers was also proposed. The Steering Group considered whether to recommend general publication of this information, but finally recommended a reserve power for the Secretary of State to require this.[168] This was new material, but it followed naturally from the questions asked in *Completing the Structure*[169] about the role of institutional investors in company governance and the growing recognition of the importance of this within the emerging shareholder-orientated system for monitoring and disciplining company management.

On small and private company issues, the main innovations at this stage were a proposal to codify the unanimous consent rule and a consultation draft of the model constitution for private companies.[170] The former of these constituted a reversal of the Group's own initial position and a rejection of the majority support which it had raised, on the ground that the rule was of particular importance in small and private companies, where accessibility of the law was at a premium, and that the rule was far from clear in its case law form. The proposed codification involved a generous conferring of unlimited power for the membership to decide unanimously without formalities on any course of action which it was lawful for the company to take.[171]

On minority remedies, the main recommendations from the earlier stage were confirmed. However, after consideration, one member had reservations about the view expressed in *Completing the Structure* that, beyond alterations of the constitution and class rights and resolutions ratifying or authorising wrongs on the company, there should be no restriction on the powers of the majority, other than the unfair prejudice remedy.[172] An alternative solution was not proposed, but would presumably involve some unspecified power on the part of the courts to strike down majority resolutions, or perhaps reversal of

---

167 Led by John Plender.
168 See *The Final Report*, above n 4, at paras 3.52–3.55 and at chapter 6, para 6.22 onwards.
169 See *The Final Report*, above n 4, at paras 4.49–4.62.
170 See *The Final Report*, above n 4, at Volume II, chapter 17.
171 See *The Final Report*, above n 4, at para 2.14.
172 See *The Final Report*, above n 4, at paras 7.52–7.62.

the limitations on the unfair prejudice remedy set by the House of Lords in *O'Neill v Phillips*.[173]

On transparency more generally, consultation on the reporting cycle had shown that the targets for reporting and the holding of general meetings were unduly tight and rigid for practical purposes. The targets for publication of annual reports were relaxed from 90 to 120 days for public companies and to seven months for private companies, and greater flexibility was allowed in the timing of general meetings, which were regarded as less time-critical.[174]

7.3   Final phase – unfinished business?

It has been noted that the work on company charges was in some disarray following the inconclusive consultation from October to December 2000. In *The Final Report*, as a result of the work in the expanded working party during the fourth stage, an alternative, new scheme was proposed for 'notice filing'. This proposal also gave an indication of how the detailed improvements proposed could be incorporated into either this or a more traditional, *'ex post'*, filing scheme. However, the Steering Group recognised that the notice filing version represented a preferred course through a series of contentious interrelated issues on which there had been no final consultation and also that the proposal to adopt notice filing arguably had wider implications for property law. There were also important Scottish private law complications (a devolved matter) which would need to be addressed. It therefore recommended that the matter should be referred to the Law Commissions – a recommendation which is currently under active consideration.

It has also been noted that the Steering Group's consideration of the agency and tort (delict) law problems surrounding the attribution of liability of directors to their company, and of the duty of care of directors, auditors and others in relation to company accounts, raised far reaching issues of general law. The Steering Group now finally concluded that a viable basis for extending *Caparo*[175] liability and the correlative liabilities of directors and companies had not been achieved. Accordingly, they recommended that the matter should be one for judicial case-by-case development, in the context of the retention of the other recommendations on the position of auditors. It proposed that the liability of those failing in their obligations to assist auditors, and vicarious liability of their companies, should be owed to auditors, in apparent response to concern about the range of this liability. The Steering Group concluded that the broader questions on attribution of acts and wrongs to companies were matters of general law which did not require resolution in order to achieve a satisfactory outcome on auditor liability (that is, a fair allocation of loss between auditors, defaulting directors and employees and their company). It was felt that this could be achieved by an effective system of civil liability for breach of the proposed more extensive obligations of directors and employees to assist in the audit. Further examination of the wider issues was effectively left to one side, on the basis that 'there might well be merit' in such examination.[176]

---

173 [1999] 1 WLR 1092. See further the Lowry essay below at p 229.
174 See *The Final Report*, above n 4, at para 8.96 onwards.
175 See *Caparo Industries plc v Dickman* [1990] 2 AC 605.
176 See *The Final Report*, above n 4, at para 8.142.

A further area where the Review failed to reach conclusions of any kind concerned directors' remuneration. Mrs Beckett had mentioned this area as possibly meriting legislation at the time the Company Law Review was launched. It has been noted above that recommendations were made on terms of employment and compensation for loss of office. However, on remuneration the Review remained silent. The reason was that the DTI began its own consultation on this topic in July 1999 and reached conclusions in a press release in March 2001, as *The Final Report* was being completed. The matter was thus being treated as one of immediate government policy for the majority of the period of the Review and by the time the Government reached its conclusions it was not possible – nor perhaps politic – for the Review to consider them. Any Review recommendations would have required further consultation and consideration of evidence, and perhaps empirical research. So *The Final Report* contented itself with an account of the facts, recognition of the relevance of the issue to the integrity of shareholder control[177] and some minor refinements of the earlier proposals on terms of employment and compensation for loss of office.[178]

7.4 Final phase – *The Final Report* – an appraisal

This account of the final phase inevitably focuses on the main[179] changes and developments in the orientation of the Review which arose at this point, rather than the overall impact of the final document. It should, however, be recorded that in this document the Steering Group went back to first principles and set out to justify by reference to those principles the whole interconnected system of recommendations made. The principles adopted strongly resembled the original ones set out in *The Strategic Framework*, published two years before, but there was less emphasis on decriminalisation, and more on codification. There was a description of the Review working method and a complete but inevitably high-level description of the totality of the recommendations. Finally, there was a chapter consisting of a complete set of draft clauses on company formation, a significant part of the capital maintenance regime, key parts of the private company regime, principles governing directors' duties and overseas companies. The overall objective was clearly to give a complete picture of the Review, its processes, conclusions and the proposed outcomes.

8 AFTERMATH AND REFLECTIONS

The reception given to *The Final Report* in the press and by interested bodies on its publication in July 2001 was practically unanimously supportive.[180] The new Secretary of

---

177 See *The Final Report*, above n 4, at para 6.23.

178 See *The Final Report*, above n 4, at paras 6.10–6.14.

179 Inevitably not all. For example, there had been substantial work on company information and disclosure in trading documents, etc, with an informal consultative document issued in February 2001 for comment by 12 April 2001. The outcomes of this and a number of other significant recommendations on company information and registration were included in chapter 11 of *The Final Report*, above n 4.

180 The CBI, IOD, National Association of Pension Funds (NAPF), Law Society and TUC, amongst others, issued press releases welcoming the report and encouraging the Government to legislate.

State for Trade, Patricia Hewitt, while naturally reserving her position on detailed issues, declared her intention to consult on draft legislation. It can thus be fairly safely asserted that the Review succeeded in achieving the objectives set for it. Practically speaking, substantially the whole of 'core' company law had been covered. The Steering Group had failed to reach agreed recommendations on only two relatively minor aspects (the full extent of directors' duties towards creditors and restrictions on majority powers). In one major, but technical area, registration of company charges, it had made provisional proposals, but recognised that the wider implications of the subject deserved broader review by the Law Commissions. There was good reason to hope that this could be completed in time for incorporation in the legislative outcome.

Perhaps the greatest success had been the devising of a method for covering such a wide area of law comprehensively in a way which achieved consensus. Consultation on companies legislation is not new. However, previous exercises had been more limited and taken relatively much longer.[181] The novelty in the approach adopted was that it was participative, that is to say, those with in-depth practical knowledge of the implications of policy proposals were engaged with legal and public policy experts in the process of developing review proposals in the Steering Group, working groups and the Consultative Committee. That Committee enabled representative bodies to scrutinise legislative proposals which already had a degree of legitimacy as a result of working and Steering Group work. The process as a whole led to the progressive consolidation of support for the conclusive recommendations for reform. The result was not only wide endorsement of the proposals but also recognition of their positive value and thus widespread active support. 'Coregulation' – a process which involves a partnership between government and market participants – is increasingly recognised, including by the European Commission, as a beneficial means of achieving better regulation in complex commercial areas, as for example, in the Lamfalussy recommendations on financial services regulation.[182] The process developed by the Review might, perhaps, be described as 'colegislation'. At a very early stage in the Review, in a conversation with a very senior member of the Office of Parliamentary Counsel (a body which generously supported the Review throughout), the latter referred to a widely held view that the main components of our commercial law had become so complex and vast in scale that effective legislative reform was no longer feasible – Government lacked the resources, capacity and will to embark upon such projects. It may, perhaps, be that the approach adopted in the Review offers an answer to this concern.

The question remains, was this consensus bought at too high a price? A major criticism was expressed towards the end, by some leading members of the academic community in particular,[183] that the outcome was insufficiently radical and offered insufficient change to justify the efforts invested. This criticism has not so far been taken up by the many users of the law, business and professional, who have commented on the

---

181 For example, the Law Commission review of shareholder remedies took over three years (including further inconclusive consultation by the DTI) to cover a very limited area.

182 See: *Financial Times*, 20 July 2001, 'Law must reach out to disgruntled voters'; and *European Governance: A White Paper*, Commission of the European Communities, 25 July 2001, COM (2001) 428.

183 At a seminar helpfully called at the invitation of Sir Roy Goode QC in Oxford in early 2001. This seminar contributed to a more radical view being adopted on company charges; for an analysis of the work of the Steering Group on charges see the de Lacy essay below at p 380.

final outcome. On the contrary, many constituencies, not least that representing small businesses, have expressed the strong belief that the proposals are a prescription for fundamental change.

There can be no doubt that errors and flaws in our proposals will emerge over time. The recommendation for a flexible, responsive and effective ongoing institutional structure is, of course, designed to provide, amongst other things, a dynamic mechanism for retrieving such errors. To ensure that this works we rely, as ever, on the sympathetic and responsive efforts of Government, and Parliament.

CHAPTER 2

INCLUSIVE COMPANY LAW

John Parkinson[1]

1 INTRODUCTION

The Company Law Review was set up in 1998 by Margaret Beckett, the then Secretary of State for Trade and Industry, to devise a framework of company law which 'facilitates enterprise and promotes transparency and fair dealing'.[2] Its terms of reference invited it, among other things, to identify a set of provisions that would support the creation of wealth, while at the same time protecting the interests of those involved with the company, including shareholders, creditors, and employees.[3] The most fundamental task that faced the Review in meeting this challenge was to determine the objective or objectives in accordance with which companies should be run, and correspondingly the range and priority of interests that company law should seek to further. In the words of the consultation documents issued by the Review, the aim was to establish the proper 'scope' of company law.

The Review's conclusion is that the current obligation of company directors to give precedence to the interests of shareholders should be retained, but that that obligation should be understood in a way that reflects a principle of 'inclusivity'. The inclusivity principle recognises the dependence of the successful operation of the company, and hence benefit for shareholders, on the quality of its relationships with the other economic participants in the business and the way in which it manages its broader social and environmental impacts. The priority afforded to shareholders in this scheme reflects not so much a belief that their interests are inherently more deserving of protection than those of other groups, as acceptance of the traditional economic analysis[4] that argues that the greatest contribution to 'wealth and welfare for all' is likely to be made by companies with a primary shareholder focus.[5] Shareholder interests should not be the directors' only concern, however, and in order to give effect to the inclusive approach the Review recommends the adoption of a statutory statement of directors' duties in an inclusive form and a complementary regime of wider reporting through a mandatory Operating and Financial Review ('OFR'). The aim of the latter is to increase transparency in relation to the non-financial aspects of a company's operations, among other things facilitating an

---

1   John Parkinson was a member of the Company Law Review Steering Group and chaired the working groups that considered the 'scope' issue and directors' duties. He writes here in a personal capacity.
2   See *Modern Company Law for a Competitive Economy* (London, DTI, 1998), Foreword, at p i; hereafter *Company Law for a Competitive Economy*.
3   See *Company Law for a Competitive Economy*, at chapter 5.
4   For a recent statement of this position, see Henry Hansmann and Reinier Kraakman 'The End of History for Corporate Law', Yale Law School Law and Economics Working Paper No 235 (2000).
5   See Company Law Review Steering Group *Modern Company Law for a Competitive Economy: Developing the Framework* (London, DTI, 2000) at chapter 2; hereafter *Developing the Framework*.

assessment by users of how well the company is managing its relationships and impacts, thereby improving accountability and in turn, performance, in each area. This essay will first examine the background to the Review's conclusions on the 'scope' issue, and then look in more detail at the proposals relating to the inclusive duty and the OFR.

2 THE BACKGROUND

The first consultation document issued by the Review set out two alternative models around which a new Companies Act might be constructed, which it labelled the 'enlightened shareholder value' and 'pluralist' models.[6] The key difference between them lies in what should happen on those occasions when there is a clash of interests between the shareholders and other affected groups. The former model, which is the precursor of the inclusive approach, dictates that the shareholders' interests should prevail. The pluralist model, on the other hand, holds that the directors should balance the relevant interests, without giving automatic priority to those of shareholders, with a view to maximising the welfare of the parties in aggregate. After reflecting on the issues in the light of the responses to consultation, the Review decided not to take further the pluralist approach, but instead to give effect to the concept of inclusivity. To that end the follow-up consultation document set out a trial draft of the inclusive duty and proposals concerning the OFR.[7] With some modifications of detail, these arrangements have been carried forward into the Review's final recommendations.[8] Why company law should adopt an inclusive approach, as opposed to one that focuses narrowly on shareholder interests, will now be considered, before examining the Review's reasons for preferring inclusivity to pluralism.

2.1   The case for inclusivity

Two factors underpin the case for inclusivity. The first is a belief in the importance to the efficient creation of wealth of co-operative relationships between a company and its employees, suppliers, and customers. The second is a recognition of a company's need to take account of its ethical, social and environmental performance if it is to be a success in the long term. Dealing with the former issue first, the aim of the Review was to establish a legal framework which was conducive to the formation and maintenance of co-operative relationships where they were likely to be wealth creating.

As regards employment relationships, these will usually be more productive where there is a measure of trust and goodwill on each side. Optimal levels of employee effort, skill, and inventiveness cannot simply be contracted for, nor is a company likely to achieve the best possible performance from its employees through reliance on the exercise

---

6   See Company Law Review Steering Group *Modern Company Law for a Competitive Economy: The Strategic Framework* (London, DTI, 1999) at chapter 5; hereafter *The Strategic Framework*.

7   See *Developing the Framework*, above n 5, at chapter 2; and at paras 3.9–3.58; 5.74–5.105.

8   See Company Law Review Steering Group *Modern Company Law for a Competitive Economy: Completing the Structure* (London, DTI, 2000) at chapter 3; hereafter *Completing the Structure*; and *Modern Company Law for a Competitive Economy: Final Report* (London, DTI, 2001) at paras 3.5–3.11 and Annex C; 3.28–3.48 and 8.29–8.71; hereafter *The Final Report*.

of hierarchical authority. Rather, an important additional factor is that employees possess a degree of commitment to the goals of the organisation. Such commitment is unlikely in the absence of a well-founded expectation that they will share in the company's success over time.[9] This will tend of necessity to be an 'expectation' rather than a right, because just as it is not feasible for the company to contract for exemplary conduct on the part of the workforce, so also it is not practicable to protect contractually the understanding that the employees will obtain commensurate rewards; problems of measuring employee inputs are generally too great and future contingencies affecting the employment relationship too difficult to anticipate and provide for.[10] Employment relationships are, therefore, to varying degrees contractually incomplete and so depend for their success on the parties' ability to trust each other – to perform to a high standard, and to fulfil implicit obligations about continuity of employment and rewards, respectively.

That companies should enjoy such relationships with their employees is particularly important in the modern economy, in which technological advances and the demand for customisation make the knowledge and problem-solving abilities of the workforce key determinants of a company's ability to compete.[11] These changes in the nature of the economy also mean that companies are increasingly dependent on the acquisition and use by employees of firm-specific knowledge and skills (that is, knowledge and skills which add to their productivity within the employment but which are of little value outside it). These include 'knowledge of operating procedures in the firm, of local information sources, of locally specialised language usage, and of customer, supplier, coworker and machine idiosyncrasies; special skills in tasks peculiar to the firm, and membership in the social networks within the firm and between the firm and its suppliers and customers'.[12] For employees to have appropriate incentives to make the necessary investments in firm-specific human capital, they need some assurance that they will see a return on it by sharing in the resulting productivity gains. If employees anticipate that the company will attempt opportunistically to bargain down their returns *ex post*, or prematurely foreclose their ability to earn these returns by terminating their employment, they will be deterred *ex ante* from acquiring relevant knowledge and skills at a socially efficient level.[13]

Co-operative relationships and firm-specific investment are also important in the supply chain, especially in a world in which all but 'core' functions are increasingly

---

9   And a wider sense of the legitimacy of managerial authority; see further Jackson 'Comparative Corporate Governance: Sociological Perspectives' in John Parkinson, Andrew Gamble and Gavin Kelly (eds) *The Political Economy of the Company* (Oxford, Hart, 2001) at p 279.

10 See further Blair 'Firm-Specific Human Capital and Theories of the Firm' in Margaret M Blair and Mark J Roe (eds) *Employees and Corporate Governance* (Washington, 1999) at p 58. While explicit incentive pay schemes can go some way towards aligning employee with shareholder interests, they have limitations; see, generally, Paul Milgrom and John Roberts *Economics, Organization and Management* (Englewood Cliffs, Prentice-Hall International, 1992) at chapter 12.

11 See, for example, Peter F Drucker *Post-Capitalist Society* (Oxford, OUP, 1993), at pp 19–47; Rajan and Zingales 'The Governance of the New Enterprise' in Xavier Vives (ed) *Corporate Governance: Theoretical and Empirical Perspectives* (Cambridge, CUP, 2000) at p 201.

12 See Milgrom and Roberts *Economics, Organization and Management*, above n 10, at p 345.

13 See Margaret M Blair *Ownership and Control: Rethinking Corporate Governance for the Twenty-First Century* (Washington, The Brookings Institution, 1995), especially at chapter 7.

contracted out.[14] A relationship in which customer and supplier 'internalise' each other's interests, as opposed to dealing at arm's length or in an adversarial way, will often be mutually advantageous where transactions are complex and the relationship ongoing. In a co-operative relationship the parties may be willing, for example, to adjust quantities at short notice, avoiding protracted and expensive renegotiations, or to share information about opportunities for cost reduction or product innovations.[15] A precondition for such extra-contractual co-operation, however, is a secure expectation that the other party will reciprocate and that the relationship will be long-lasting, so that co-operativeness benefits both parties over time. Similar issues arise as regards relationship-specific investment. Investment by a supplier in capital equipment or systems specialised to the needs of a particular customer will often be a potential source of productive efficiency, but such investments are unlikely to be made unless the supplier is confident that it will earn an appropriate return. In particular, the supplier must have some assurance that the relationship will be enduring and that the other party will not attempt to exploit its position of strength (created by the lock-in effect of the investment)[16] to alter unfairly the terms of trade in its own favour.

Two major reports during the last five years have attributed, in part, the poor performance of many British companies (relative to their overseas competitors) to a failure to cultivate long-term, co-operative relationships with employees and relationships in the supply chain of the kind that have just been described. Other factors they identify include underinvestment in physical capital and research and development.[17] A common theme is an unhealthy preoccupation with short-term financial returns. Companies with a short-term focus will find it difficult to sustain co-operative relationships because they will be reluctant to bear the costs that may be associated with them. For example, co-operativeness may require that the company retain employees in a temporary downturn or expend resources to meet the urgent needs of a customer without the immediate possibility of reimbursement. Overall, these costs will often be justified because of the gains that are likely to flow to the company from the relationship over time, but it is evident that if the benefits from co-operation are to be realised the company must be prepared to work within an appropriate time frame. The aim of the inclusive approach is accordingly to encourage companies to adopt the

---

14 See: John Kay *Foundations of Corporate Success: How Business Strategies Add Value* (Oxford, OUP, 1993) at chapters 3–5; Kester 'Governance, Contracting, and Investment Horizons: A Look at Japan and Germany' in Donald H Chew (ed) *Studies in International Corporate Finance and Governance Systems* (New York, OUP, 1997) at p 227.

15 Chrysler has estimated that following the adoption of a co-operative approach to its supplier relationships, it made cost savings of over US $500 million in one year as a result of ideas suggested by suppliers; see D Pyke 'Strategies for Global Sourcing' in *Financial Times Supplement* 'Creating the Global Organisation' 20 February 1998, cited in Claudia Gonella, Alison Pilling and Simon Zadek *Making Values Count: Contemporary Experience in Social and Ethical Accounting, Auditing, and Reporting* ACCA Research Report No 57 (London, ACCA, 1998).

16 See Oliver Williamson *The Economic Institutions of Capitalism: Firms, Markets, Relational Contracting* (New York, Free Press, 1985) at chapter 12.

17 See RSA Inquiry *Tomorrow's Company: The Role of Business in a Changing World* (London, RSA, 1995) and Commission on Public Policy and British Business *Promoting Prosperity: A Business Agenda for Britain* (London, Vintage, 1997) at chapters 1 and 4. Recent figures indicate that research and development (R&D) intensity (R&D as a percentage of sales) is below international levels in most sectors; see 2000 R&D Scoreboard available at www.innovation.gov.uk. The position is similar in relation to capital investment; see 2000 Capex Scoreboard at www.innovation.gov.uk.

necessary longer-term perspective, and within it to recognise the importance of co-operative relationships in building competitive strength.

It should be mentioned that for many routine supplies of goods and services there will be no need for a long-term relationship or one other than at arm's length; inclusivity does not require a company's management to be 'inclusive' where there is no economic case for it. More generally, there are sectors of the economy in which committed relationships are of particular value, while in others a prime consideration is the flexibility to terminate relationships quickly as the company's circumstances change. In the former category are sophisticated manufacturing industries that depend on a highly skilled workforce, access to the technological expertise of suppliers, and close collaboration in the supply chain. In certain high-tech and start-up sectors and others undergoing fundamental change, on the other hand, there is a premium on rapid entry and exit and long-term commitments here may be counter-productive.[18]

The second factor lying behind the Review's support for the inclusive approach is the importance of the connection between ethical, social and environmental responsibility and commercial success. Often responsible behaviour makes a direct contribution to profits by reducing costs; this is the case with many environmental measures aimed at recycling waste and reducing energy consumption.[19] Alternatively for some companies, such as the Body Shop and the Co-operative Bank, developing a reputation for high standards of ethical, social and environmental responsibility has given them a distinctive presence in their markets and increased market share.

More generally, companies which are seen to behave irresponsibly are liable to suffer market penalties. Consumers may decide to buy elsewhere, sometimes as a result of an organised boycott.[20] Companies with poor reputations tend to find it difficult to recruit and retain high-quality employees.[21] Increasingly investors are scrutinising company policies on wider social responsibilities, associated management systems, making investment and sometimes voting decisions, as well as applying informal pressure to managements. In many cases this scrutiny is for conventional financial reasons, since investments in companies which are deficient in these areas may carry unacceptable risk. Such companies may face future difficulties in their consumer markets, significant legal liabilities (for example, for clean-up costs), and major expenditures in adapting to toughened regulatory regimes, all of which may reduce shareholder returns. But there is also a growing number of individual investors and investment institutions (such as ethical funds and public-sector pension funds) that have an explicit commitment to responsible investment principles. These investors are able to draw on the advisory services of specialist agencies that monitor companies from a responsibility perspective,

---

18 See Wendy Carlin and Colin Mayer 'How Do Financial Systems Affect Economic Performance?' in Vives *Corporate Governance*, above n 11, at p 137; Richard Whitley *Divergent Capitalisms: The Social Structuring and Change of Business Systems* (Oxford, OUP, 1999) at chapter 1.

19 See John Braithwaite and Peter Drahos *Global Business Regulation* (Cambridge, CUP, 2000) at pp 267–69.

20 Well-known campaigns include those against Nestlé (promotion of infant formula milk in developing countries), Shell (disposal of Brent Spar oil facility in the North Sea), and Nike (employment conditions in overseas production facilities).

21 Survey evidence indicates that a good corporate reputation is regarded as more important than starting salary, fringe benefits, or sports and social facilities by potential employees: see Just Pensions *Socially Responsible Investment and International Development* (London, 2001) at p 5.

exercising their voting rights and other governance efforts accordingly.[22] Further impetus is likely to be given to these developments by the new statutory requirement for pension fund trustees to state their policy, if any, on responsible investment.[23]

To sum up, inclusivity recognises that there is a substantial commonality of interests between shareholders and the other participants in the business; the commercial success that benefits the former is often linked to the development of constructive, long-term relationships with the latter, which generally serve their interests too. It also recognises that long-term profitability may depend on the pursuit of ethically, socially and environmentally responsible policies.[24] The aim of inclusive company law is to encourage businesses to take maximum advantage of these overlaps.

2.2   The pluralist alternative

To acknowledge that shareholder and other interests overlap is not the same thing as saying that they necessarily coincide, that is, that there can be no conflict between them, so long as an appropriately lengthy timescale is adopted.[25] This proposition is manifestly false. For example, there will be occasions when it will be clear to management that serving the interests of the shareholders, even when their interests are viewed as long-term ones, requires discontinuing an activity and making part of the workforce redundant. This will be detrimental to those laid off, their dependants and often the local community more generally. In addition, it will not necessarily, in all cases, be an economically efficient response. Where employees have made investments in firm-specific knowledge and skills the economic surplus generated by the project is likely to be divided between the shareholders and the employees; their bargaining relationship is such that pay will no longer be determined by the external market for labour. In these circumstances, a decision to reduce (or not to expand) the scale of an activity that is based exclusively on furthering the interests of the shareholders will not necessarily maximise

---

22 Eg, the PIRC Corporate Responsibility Service and the Ethical Investment Research and Information Service.

23 They must state their policy in their statement of investment principles on 'the extent (if at all) to which social, environmental or ethical considerations are taken into account in the selection, retention and realisation of investments' and 'their policy (if any) in relation to the exercise of the rights (including voting rights) attaching to investments'; see Pensions Act 1995, s 11A, added by the Occupational Pension Schemes (Investment, and Assignment, Forfeiture, Bankruptcy etc) Amendment Regulations 1999, SI 1999/1849. For an early review of the impact of this requirement, see Eugenie Mathieu *Response of UK Pension Funds to the SRI Disclosure Regulation* (London, UK Social Investment Forum, 2000).

24 There is a substantial research literature on the connection between various forms of responsible behaviour and financial performance. A survey undertaken for the Company Law Review suggests that, on balance, the evidence supports the hypothesis of a positive relationship, but notes the considerable methodological problems that such research faces: see *Literature Survey on Factual, Empirical and Legal Issues* undertaken by the ESRC Centre for Business Research, University of Cambridge at chapter 1. This is available at www.dti.gov.uk/cld/review.htm.

25 Cf Phillip Goldenberg 'Shareholders v Stakeholders: The Bogus Argument' (1998) 19 *Company Lawyer* 34. For a fuller treatment than provided in this chapter of the differences between inclusive and pluralist approaches, see John Parkinson 'Corporate Governance: The Company Law Review and Questions of "Scope"' (2000) Vol 8 No 1 *Hume Papers on Public Policy, Corporate Governance and the Reform of Company Law* at p 29.

wealth overall.[26] The same may be true in relation to supply-chain relationships. More generally, where it is known that priority will automatically be given to shareholder interests, employees and others may be deterred from making firm-specific investments at a socially efficient level. The pluralist position, therefore, questions the efficiency argument on which the case for affording primacy to shareholder interests in all cases rests, by challenging the view that it is the shareholders alone who are the recipients of the firm's residual income and exposed to its residual risk. A related perspective questions the ability of companies to sustain the trust on which long-term relationships depend when management is obliged to favour shareholder interests in all cases of conflict.[27]

Nor is it true that maximising long-term profits and acting in an ethically, socially or environmentally responsible way are always consistent. The latter forms of behaviour may increase costs or require profitable opportunities to be foregone resulting in a net loss to the company. Further, although a company's reputation is important to its long-term commercial success, it does not follow that all forms of socially undesirable behaviour will result in reputational damage, especially damage that inflicts costs on the company that exceed the gains arising from the questionable acts. It will not always be the case that a sufficient number of a company's customers, for example, will be concerned, or concerned enough, say, about its dubious labour practices in a developing country[28] or the impact of its operations on local wildlife, for there to be a significant adverse effect on revenues. Companies which do not sell directly into consumer markets may be less exposed to market pressures to behave responsibly. Also crucial to the existence or otherwise of a 'market penalty' for antisocial behaviour is that there be adequate information in the public domain about corporate performance in relation to ethical, social and environmental issues. While specific instances of abuse by large, big-name enterprises may be well known, there is little public consciousness of the day-to-day social and environmental impacts of the bulk of companies and particularly their performance relative to each other. So it is possible for companies to behave inclusively, but still in ways that cause unacceptable damage to others or are otherwise offensive to notions of responsible business behaviour.

The pluralist analysis draws attention, then, to these potential conflicts of interest between the shareholders on the one hand and the other economic participants in the company and third parties and society as a whole on the other. For reasons just noted, these conflicts may not always be best resolved by giving automatic precedence to the interests of shareholders. The pluralist prescription is accordingly that the directors should balance the relevant interests with a view to obtaining the best attainable outcome overall. This may, for example, involve the company respecting its implicit, but legally unenforceable obligations to non-shareholder participants in the business even when

---

26 More specifically, if the total returns to all the investments in the firm are positive, the firm should continue with an activity, even though the returns to the shareholders alone are not sufficient to justify continuance. See Blair *Ownership and Control*, above n 13, and Gavin Kelly and John Parkinson 'The Conceptual Foundations of the Company: A Pluralist Approach' [1998] *Company Financial And Insolvency Law Review* 174.

27 See John Kay and Aubrey Silberston, 'Corporate Governance' (August 1995) *National Institute Economic Review* 84 at p 90.

28 For a vivid account of such practices, see Naomi Klein *No Logo* (London, Flamingo, 2000) at chapter 9.

there are no obvious benefits to shareholders, or voluntarily taking steps to internalise the costs that its activities might otherwise impose on third parties or society at large.

2.3 The preference for inclusiveness

Although the Review expresses some support for the pluralist analysis and the objectives that lie behind it, it ultimately rejects the adoption of pluralist directors' duties, a key objection it makes to them being the problems that arise from the practical difficulties of enforcement.[29] A pluralist duty, that is, one requiring the directors to balance the relevant set of interests, would be feasible only as a subjective duty. It would not be realistic, or probably desirable, to expect a court to sit in judgment, as an objective duty would require, on whether the directors had struck what it considered to be an appropriate balance. Whether the company should close down one of its operations with consequent job losses, or retrain otherwise redundant employees, or whether it should sacrifice profits in order to reduce environmental damage are not issues that lend themselves to legal analysis. However, a subjective duty – one in which the directors were required to strike what in their judgment was a suitable balance – would in practice amount to no more than a discretion, even though it might be couched in mandatory language. One problem with such a discretion is that directors might attach disproportionate weight to a particular set of interests. Rather than leading to an outcome superior overall to one to be expected from compliance with an inclusive duty, the outcome might actually, therefore, be worse. After all, complex issues of ethics or social policy may be at stake with which business managers are not necessarily well equipped to deal. An alternative possibility is that directors might exploit the reduced accountability that a broadened discretion would entail to act in their own interests at the expense of others involved in the company.[30] What is perhaps the most likely outcome, however, is that altering directors' duties would not change company conduct in any noticeable way. Given the lack of enforceability, and in view of the other incentives and pressures that directors face to act in the interests of shareholders, it seems implausible that the introduction of a pluralist duty would result in a significant re-orientation of behaviour.

The reality is that the adoption of pluralist duties makes little sense in the absence of more thorough-going reform aimed at altering companies' decision making structures and the location of ultimate control. Such duties would be likely to have little effect, for example, where control, in the sense of the ability to appoint and remove the directors, remains exclusively with the shareholders. There were very few suggestions in responses to consultation, however, that shareholders' control rights should be altered, and the position of the Review is that shareholder control, exercised through voting and the capital market, is a crucial part of the system of accountability on which corporate efficiency depends. While reform of the board to permit wider representation, certainly of

---

29 See *Completing the Structure*, above n 8, at para 3.5. For other factors that the Steering Group regarded as telling against the adoption of the pluralist position, see *Developing the Framework*, above n 5, at paras 3.20–3.26.

30 It is possible to exaggerate the significance of this point. The current duty to act in the interests of the shareholders is a subjective one: the courts do not review business decisions. Only egregious failure to pursue a commercial objective is likely to ground liability. It would not be impossible, though perhaps more difficult, to establish that a similar failure constitutes a breach of a pluralist duty.

employees, is a workable possibility, as continental European, especially German, experience shows,[31] very little support was voiced for it during the Review, including from organised labour. Nor would mandatory employee board representation be likely to be attractive to Government.

It is worth noting in passing that board representation is not the only mechanism for ensuring that more extensive consideration is given to the interests of employees in making decisions that affect them. A less radical alternative (not necessarily requiring the adoption of a pluralist duty) is the appointment of works councils. In so far as these might be framed as consultative, rather than decision making bodies, works councils would not be part of the company's constitutional structure[32] and hence do not fall within the scope of a review of company law. Now that agreement has been reached on the proposal for a European directive on informing and consulting employees, however, consultative structures will in due course be created via that route.[33] As regards other interests and concerns, it is now not uncommon for companies to consult a range of bodies, for example, neighbourhood groups or NGOs, in respect of such issues as the likely impact of a corporate decision on the local community or the environment. While such consultation is highly desirable and would often be an appropriate way of responding to the inclusive duty, an obligation to consult about the company's impacts generally would be of doubtful practicability.

Returning to the inclusive duty itself, while increased litigation is not anticipated or intended as a result of its adoption, the duty, unlike a pluralist duty, is capable of enforcement, including where failure to pay proper regard to relationships and impacts is in issue (as discussed further below). For this reason one might expect an inclusive duty to have more significant behavioural effects. A more important role in promoting behaviour in line with the inclusive duty is, however, attributed to increased transparency, effected by the proposed OFR.

In principle, an obligation to report more widely than on financial performance, including on such matters as the management of the company's relationships and environmental and social impacts, may have a number of beneficial consequences. First, the process of collecting information and analysing it for the purposes of presentation may lead to improved performance in the areas that are the subject of disclosure. The

---

31 For recent reviews see E Gerum and H Wagner 'Economics of Labor Co-Determination in View of Corporate Governance' in KJ Hopt *et al* (eds) *Comparative Corporate Governance: The State of the Art and Emerging Research* (Oxford, OUP, 1998) at p 341; Ronald Dore *Stock Market Capitalism: Welfare Capitalism: Japan and Germany versus the Anglo-Saxons* (Oxford, OUP, 2000) at chapter 9.

32 Even where works councils enjoy some co-determination rights, as in Germany, they tend to be regarded as a matter of labour law rather than company law. For a brief survey see Mark Hall *Works Councils for the UK? Lessons from the German System* Warwick Papers in Industrial Relations (Warwick, 1993).

33 See *Proposal for a Council Directive Establishing a General Framework for Informing and Consulting Employees in the European Community: Latest Developments*, available at www2.dti.gov.uk/er/consultation/proposal.htm. For a recent call for the introduction of mandatory domestic works councils see Patrick Burns *The Silent Stakeholders: Reforming Workplace Consultation Law* (London, The Industrial Society, 2000). See also Robert Taylor 'Worker Rights and Responsibilities in the Modern Company' in Parkinson, Gamble and Kelly *The Political Economy of the Company*, above n 9, at p 101. Companies with over 1,000 employees in total and at least 150 employees in two member states are already required to establish a European Works Council if requested by the designated number of employees as a result of the European Works Council Directive, implemented by the Transnational Information and Consultation of Employees Regulations 1999, SI 1999/3323.

requirement to disclose may act as a stimulus to better internal information flow and monitoring, helping in the identification of problems or opportunities that were previously undiscovered or ignored. Secondly, disclosure facilitates monitoring by shareholders and other interested parties of how well the company is managing its relationships and impacts. The resulting increase in accountability and the prospect or fact of external pressure is likely to bring about improvements in performance. This pressure may come from shareholders concerned about the adverse effect of poor management of relationships and impacts on financial performance, and also from shareholders with a more direct interest in ethical, social and environmental responsibility issues. It may come in addition from other groups such as consumers or NGOs alerted by more extensive and reliable information to a company's shortcomings in these areas. Thirdly, with fuller information available to the capital market a company's securities are likely to be more accurately priced. If share prices more faithfully reflect the value to the company of stable, long-term relationships with employees or suppliers or of a positive reputation for corporate responsibility, then short-termist pressures from the capital market that are liable to undermine such relationships or militate against responsible behaviour should be lessened. More positively, the company should be more fully rewarded by the market for its success in these respects.

To conclude, although the inclusive duty requires directors to take account of relationships and impacts only to the extent that this is necessary to further the interests of the shareholders, it should be borne in mind that the environment in which directors make decisions and the degree of importance that must be attached to relationships and impacts in pursuit of the company's goals are not static. In particular, as general awareness of corporate responsibility issues increases and civil society pressure on companies to improve their records grows, the more managements will be obliged to heed social responsibility considerations in order to serve the interests of their shareholders. The proposals for wider disclosure are likely themselves to alter the balance of this dynamic relationship, by increasing the quantum, reliability and comparability of information and thus the effectiveness of civil society controls. To that extent the inclusive and pluralist approaches are not entirely discrete, and the former may go some way to achieving the objectives of the latter.

3 THE PROPOSALS

The remainder of this chapter will now look in more detail at the content of the proposed inclusive duty and at what the projected OFR will entail.

3.1   The inclusive duty

The Review proposes that directors' duties under the general law should be set out in statute, at a high level of generality, capturing the essential principles, but not in the form of detailed behavioural rules. This proposal follows the earlier recommendation of the Law Commission.[34]

As far as the current law is concerned, the content of directors' duties must be extracted from a complex body of case law. While the directors' core duty is expressed as a duty to act in the interests of the company (and is undoubtedly owed to the company),[35] it is generally accepted that the duty is to further the interests of the shareholders.[36] It is often suggested that it is the interests of present and also future shareholders that count for this purpose.[37] Although a forward-looking element is of great importance, this particular formulation is problematic since it is difficult to understand why directors should be required to serve the interests of those who as yet have no connection with the company. Recent developments have also indicated that when a company is insolvent or insolvency is threatened, the directors must have regard to the interests of creditors, since it is their interests rather than those of shareholders that will be affected by conduct that depletes the company's assets.[38] The main significance of this appears to be that breaches that damage creditors are unratifiable. To the position at common law s 309 of the Companies Act 1985 must also be added. This provides that 'the matters to which the directors of the company are to have regard in the performance of their functions include the interests of the company's employees in general, as well as the interests of the members'. The meaning of this section is unclear. While there was undoubtedly no intention to create a pluralist duty, entitling the directors to give precedence to employee interests over those of shareholders where they consider it appropriate,[39] this is a possible interpretation of the section. It is one that has some judicial support,[40] though it seems unlikely, given the ambiguity of the wording, that a court would conclude, in a case that turned on the point, that such a radical change had been made to the common law duty. The provision is defective, on the other hand, as an inclusive duty, in that it fails to make explicit that the obligation to have regard to employee interests is an integral part of the directors' duty to promote the success of the company and potentially enforceable as such.

In proposing a statutory statement of directors' duties, an important objective is to remedy the inaccessibility of the current law and its lack of clarity. These features are in themselves obviously undesirable, but there is also some evidence that they have contributed to a potentially damaging misunderstanding of what the law actually

---

34 See Law Commission *Company Directors: Regulating Conflicts of Interests and Formulating a Statement of Duties* (1999) Cm 4436 (London, TSO, 1999). The Company Law Review differs from that of the Law Commission in recommending a full rather than a partial codification: see *Developing the Framework*, above n 5, at paras 3.16 and 3.82 and *Completing the Structure*, above n 8, at para 3.31.

35 See, eg, *Re Smith & Fawcett Ltd* [1942] Ch 304 at p 306.

36 See: *Greenhalgh v Arderne Cinemas Ltd* [1951] Ch 286 at p 291; *Parke v Daily News Ltd* [1962] Ch 927 at p 963.

37 This proposition appears to have originated in the report of the inspector appointed by the Board of Trade to investigate the Savoy Hotel affair: see Board of Trade *The Savoy Hotel Ltd and the Berkeley Hotel Company Ltd: Investigation under Section 165(b) of the Companies Act 1948: The Report of E Milner Holland QC* (London, HMSO, 1954).

38 See: *West Mercia Safetywear Ltd v Dodd* [1988] BCLC 250; and note Keay 'The Director's Duty to Take into Account the Interests of Company Creditors: When is it Triggered?' (2001) 25 *Melbourne University Law Review* 315.

39 See *The Strategic Framework*, above n 6, at para 5.1.21.

40 See *Fulham Football Club Ltd v Cabra Estates plc* [1994] 1 BCLC 363.

demands. A significant number of directors appear to believe that they are required to give precedence to the immediate interests of shareholders by maximising current profits, even though this may prejudice longer-term returns.[41] They may as a result be reluctant to make investments that are necessary to secure the company's prospects into the future. While misconceptions about directors' duties are unlikely to be a major causative factor in the adoption of short-termist approaches of this kind, it is important that the law should not reinforce short-termist attitudes but rather make clear that the directors' obligation is to take a balanced view consistent with maximising overall economic performance. Similarly, the intention is to make explicit the duty of directors to take responsibility for the company's relationships and broader impacts and for protecting its reputation. These obligations are already implicit in the common law duty, but by increasing their visibility the aim is to alter the climate in which company decisions are made. So although the Review's proposals do not to change the law in this area (other than as may be necessary in the interests of making the law more certain), it is the intention that they should change behaviour.

Turning to the statutory statement itself, the trial draft prepared earlier in the Review[42] has now been superseded by a draft clause by Parliamentary Counsel.[43] The content of the statement will be considered here only in so far as it relates to the inclusivity issue.[44] The core obligation is to promote the success of the company for the benefit of the shareholders.[45] This makes plain that as in the current law, the interests of shareholders override those of other groups.[46] How to promote success and what constitutes it are matters for directors' good faith judgment, but in the case of an ordinary commercial company, the objective will no doubt be understood in terms of enhancement of shareholder wealth.[47] The formulation addresses the important timescale issue by providing that directors should take account of both the short- and the long-term consequences of their acts. It then goes on to stipulate that the circumstances to which the directors must have regard in fulfilling the duty include the company's need to foster its business relationships with employees, suppliers and customers, the impact of its operations on communities affected and the environment, and its need to maintain a reputation for high standards of business conduct. The phrase 'the success of the company' emphasises that it is the shareholders' interests as members of an association, rather than as individuals, that are in issue. It also ties all the elements together. While the ultimate objective is to benefit the shareholders, this is achieved by building a successful business, which in turn depends on the adoption of an appropriate timescale and paying proper attention to relationships, impacts and reputation.

---

41 See Institute of Directors *Good Boardroom Practice* (London, IOD, 1999).
42 See *Developing the Framework*, above n 5, at para 3.40.
43 See *The Final Report*, above n 8, at Annex C, which also includes an explanatory note.
44 For the proposals on directors' duties more generally see the Birds essay below at p 149.
45 Subject to compliance with the company's constitution and the duty to act for a proper purpose.
46 Assuming continuing solvency. The Review was undecided about the merits of going beyond the current Insolvency Act 1986, s 214 and including a statutory provision aimed at reflecting common law developments as regards obligations in relation to creditors where insolvency is a less certain prospect; see *The Final Report*, above n 8, at paras 3.12–3.20.
47 Where the intention is otherwise, eg, where the company exists, or exists in part, for philanthropic purposes, as indicated in its constitution, the duty will be interpreted accordingly.

Consistent with the duty's inclusive rather than pluralist character, damage to non-shareholder interests will not in itself be indicative of breach. For there to be a breach of duty, damage or potential damage to the company would need to be shown. Similarly, the duty is not enforceable by non-shareholders, but as now, by the company, or in default by a shareholder if the requirements for standing to bring a derivative action are satisfied.[48] The duty also distinguishes between the obligation to identify relevant factors, which must be performed with appropriate care, skill and diligence, and decisions about how to act, which are matters for good faith judgment. It does not follow from all this, however, that the obligation to have regard to wider interests is for practical purposes unenforceable. For example, a company might make a decision that causes serious environmental damage without giving proper prior consideration to its environmental effects. If the decision results in loss to the company (it may incur environmental liabilities or lose sales following injury to its reputation) and it could be shown that the failure to take account of the environmental implications of the decision was negligent, then in principle liability could ensue.

3.2 The operating and financial review

The proposals for a mandatory OFR respond to the criticisms of the current company reporting regime that it is excessively backward-looking, is narrowly financial in scope, and pays too little attention to the intangible assets, such as human capital and reputation, which are a major component of the total value of modern companies. Given these deficiencies, present disclosure requirements fail to make directors give a full account of their stewardship of the business and to satisfy the information needs of the wide range of users of company reports. In order to increase transparency and improve the associated disciplines, it is intended, therefore, that sizeable public companies and the relatively small number of very large private companies should produce an OFR,[49] the purpose of which is to 'provide a discussion and analysis of the performance of the business and the main trends and factors underlying the results and financial position and likely to affect performance in the future, so as to enable users to assess the strategies adopted by the business and the potential for successfully achieving them'.[50] This requirement would make mandatory, and expand, the current Accounting Standards Board statement of best practice in this area with which many listed companies currently comply on a voluntary basis.

---

48 For the proposed new rules concerning the OFR see: *Developing the Framework*, above n 5, at paras 4.112–4.139; *Completing the Structure*, above n 8, at paras 5.82–5.90; *The Final Report*, above n 8, at paras 7.46–7.51.

49 *The Final Report*, above n 8, at para 3.44, indicates that the exact thresholds need further research, but provisionally recommends that public companies should be required to prepare an OFR when they satisfy at least two out of the three criteria of turnover in excess of £50 million, balance sheet total in excess of £25 million, and number of employees in excess of 500. For private companies the corresponding thresholds are £500 million, £250 million and 5,000. It is also suggested that as the OFR becomes established these thresholds should be reduced so that the requirement applies to all companies of significant size; see *The Final Report*, above n 8, at para 3.45.

50 See *Developing the Framework*, above n 5, at para 5.79. On the OFR generally, see: *Developing the Framework*, above n 5, at paras 5.74–5.103; *Completing the Structure*, above n 8, at chapter 3; *The Final Report*, above n 8, at paras 3.28–3.48 and 8.29–8.71.

Of the subject headings that make up the proposed OFR, coverage in respect of three of them is expressed to be mandatory in all cases, since they will be important to an understanding of the business of all the companies to which the OFR requirements apply. These are 'the company's business and business objectives, strategy and principal drivers of performance', a 'fair review of the development of the company's business', and the 'dynamics of the business – that is, known events, trends, uncertainties and other factors which may substantially affect future performance, including investment programmes'. The other headings, many of which are relevant to the inclusive approach, need not be covered in all cases, but must be included where the directors consider that they are material in terms of the fulfilment of the purpose of the OFR as indicated above. That is, they are important to an understanding of the performance of the business, factors likely to affect it in future, and management's strategy for dealing with these factors. The categories in question include an account of the company's key relationships (for example, with employees, suppliers and customers), environmental policies and performance, and policies and performance on community, social, ethical and reputational issues. Whether to report under these heads is, therefore, a matter for directors' good faith judgment. Further, the report is to be written from the perspective of the directors as managers of the business. So the focus of a report on environmental policies and performance, for instance, would be on the challenges environmental management presents to the company as an operating business and its response to those challenges. While there is likely to be a wide measure of overlap, such a report would not necessarily have the same coverage as a report the purpose of which was to make a full assessment of the company's environmental impacts.

Where an item is reported on, the report will be required to comply with reporting standards to be laid down by the standards body that will form part of the proposed Company Law and Reporting Commission.[51] Such standards are likely to require, for example, information on trends in performance over time. Compliance with them should also significantly improve consistency of reporting between companies, facilitating comparison, and reduce the scope for the provision of one-sided information that presents the company's performance in a misleadingly favourable light.[52] In recognition of the specialised skills involved in setting standards, it is intended that the standards body should be required by statute to include members with expertise in reporting in relation to each of the types of relationship and impact that are identified in the inclusive duty.

As well as laying down reporting standards, the new reporting regime will require a limited auditor review of the content of the OFR.[53] This will involve, first, a review of the propriety of the directors' process in preparing it. In order to perform this function the auditors will need to examine how the directors satisfied themselves that the decision

---

51 On the Company Law and Reporting Commission see *Completing the Structure*, above n 8, at chapter 12 and *The Final Report*, above n 8, at paras 3.56–3.66 and at chapter 5.

52 These are problems with current voluntary reporting. As regards environmental performance, see P Kirkman and C Hope *Environmental Disclosure in UK Company Annual Reports* (Cambridge, CUP, 1992) and, more generally, Deborah Doane *Corporate Spin: The Troubled Teenage Years of Social Reporting* (London, New Economics Foundation, 2000). See also PIRC *Reporting on Employment Issues: A Survey of the FTSE 100* (London, PIRC, 2000); *Environmental Reporting 2000: The PIRC Survey of the FTSE All-Share Index* (London, PIRC, 2000).

53 See *The Final Report*, above n 8, at paras 8.58–8.63.

whether or not to include material in the OFR was made on the basis of adequate and supportable information, and that there were proper grounds for statements made, whether factual or judgmental. Secondly, the auditors will need to review statements in the OFR for consistency with their knowledge obtained from the audit of the accounts and with the accounts themselves, and other knowledge obtained during the course of their review of the OFR, and finally for compliance with applicable reporting standards.

In that companies are not in all cases required to report under all the heads that it is proposed the OFR should cover and reporting is to be from the point of view of the company as an operating concern, these recommendations might be regarded by some as not going far enough to satisfy the information needs of the full range of users of company reports. As to the first of these issues, the proposal just mentioned that the process by which the directors determine materiality and thus whether an issue should be covered in the OFR should be subject to auditor review, is a response to criticisms raised in consultation on the original proposals. So while the decision about inclusion is one for the good faith judgment of the directors, if a proper decision making process has not been conducted it will be possible to require the company to produce a revised OFR.[54]

As regards the second point and more generally, an attempt has been made to strike a balance between maximum transparency on the one hand and excessive reporting burden and rigidity on the other. A particular concern has been that an overly prescriptive regime might actually reduce transparency by encouraging boiler-plate or perfunctory reporting. A number of companies have experimented with reporting on a range of non-financial issues and there are several initiatives under way aimed at developing guidelines for reporting on social, ethical and environmental performance. It is clear, however, that the field of wider reporting is still in an early stage of development.[55] The creation of a dynamic and responsive standard-setting regime should ensure that company reporting requirements keep pace with evolving best practice. The resulting standards, together with the statutory underpinning of the OFR, should in due course bring about a significant increase in transparency while at the same time leading to improvements in the reliability and comparability of material disclosed.

4 CONCLUSIONS

The intention of the proposals in this area is to encourage companies to take an appropriately long-term perspective, to develop productive relationships with employees and in the supply chain and to take seriously their ethical, social and environmental responsibilities. There are, it must be accepted, limits to what directors' duties and

---

54   It is proposed that within the Company Law and Reporting Commission structure there should be a Monitoring and Enforcement Committee, which would be entitled to apply to a specialist tribunal for a declaration that a company's accounts do not comply with the requirements of the Act, and an order requiring directors to prepare revised accounts. These arrangements would replace the current functions of the Financial Reporting Review Panel. See *Completing the Structure*, above n 8, at paras 12.44–12.48; *The Final Report*, above n 8, at paras 5.76–5.80.

55   For a review see: Gonella *et al Making Values Count*, above n 15; Doane *Corporate Spin*, above n 52. See also the work of the Global Reporting Initiative available at www.globalreporting.org; the New Economics Foundation at www.neweconomics.org; and Accountability at www.accountability.org.uk.

reporting requirements can achieve. The broad features of the corporate economy within which these mechanisms must function also exert a powerful influence on management behaviour. The UK listed sector is characterised by wide dispersal of shareholdings, with many shareholders feeling little loyalty to the companies in which they invest, and an active market in control. It is arguable that the resulting environment is unsupportive of, and even antagonistic towards long-term commitments and the adoption of policies that build long-term value but impose short-term costs.[56] Another cause for concern is management pay schemes that create incentives to maximise relatively near-term results at what may be the expense of longer-term performance. As to the first of these, increasing concentration of holdings and trends towards a more 'relational' style of investing give some cause for optimism.[57] Similarly, as the governance role of non-executive directors becomes more firmly entrenched, there may be less need for reliance on hostile takeovers as a source of management discipline.[58] How to establish procedures for determining directors' rewards that circumvent the inherent conflicts of interest, on the other hand, has so far proved an intractable problem.[59] In the years to come there will no doubt be continuing developments in each of these areas. In the meantime the clarification of directors' duties and increased transparency have an important role to play by altering the climate of decision making, reducing share mispricing and concomitant adverse short-term pressures, and sharpening accountability, both to shareholders and the wider community.

---

56 In essence, the arguments are that the threat of takeover encourages managements to maximise share price, which may be at the expense of longer-term performance; changes in control are likely to disrupt relationships; and gains from takeover may result in part from breach of implicit undertakings to participants, particularly employees. In its consideration of these issues, the Company Law Review thought the evidence inconclusive, but has recommended that a revised OFR should be issued by offeror and offeree at the time of a takeover offer, and that the possibility of lowering the size thresholds for shareholder consent in offeror companies be kept under review. Otherwise, however, it was accepted that the takeover market was a useful discipline, and that in general company law should not inhibit its operation; see: *Developing the Framework*, above n 5, at paras 3.162–3.168; *Completing the Structure*, above n 8, at paras 4.49–4.62; *The Final Report*, above n 8, at para 6.19.

57 See John Plender 'Short-Termism and the Limits of Company Law' *Financial Times* 15 June 2000. On the other hand, the Review expresses concern over conflicts of interest affecting investing institutions and other problems that inhibit the exercise of shareholder governance responsibilities, and makes some recommendations for ameliorating them; see *The Final Report*, above n 8, at paras 6.22–6.40.

58 The Company Law Review was not satisfied that non-executive directors were operating effectively as monitors of management in all cases. While it considered it premature to recommend strengthening the Combined Code, it proposes that the Code become the responsibility of the Company Law and Reporting Commission and be kept under active review; see: *Developing the Framework*, above n 5, at paras 3.112–3.153; *Completing the Structure*, above n 8, at paras 4.44–4.47; *The Final Report*, above n 8, at paras 5.42–5.46. Following the collapse of the US company Enron, the OTI has now announced a further review of the role of non-executive directors; see DTI Press Notice number 128 of 2002 (27 February 2002).

59 The Company Law Review makes some proposals relating to directors' pay; see: *Completing the Structure*, above n 8, at paras 4.19–4.20 (duration of service contracts) and para 6.16 (facilitating shareholder resolutions); *The Final Report*, above n 8, at paras 6.10–6.14 and 8.96–8.101, respectively. Otherwise, the Government has consulted on ways of increasing shareholder involvement in pay issues, and has subsequently announced proposals for revised disclosure requirements aimed at improving the linkage between pay and performance and strengthening the position of shareholders; see: *Directors' Remuneration: A Consultative Document* (London, DTI, 1999); and *Directors' Remuneration: A Consultative Document* URN 01/1400 (London, DTI, 2001).

CHAPTER 3

COMPANY LAW REFORM: THE ROLE OF THE COURTS

David Neuberger

1 INTRODUCTION

The recently published *Final Report* of the Company Law Review Steering Group[1] serves to focus our attention on the future reform of UK Company Law. It has long been recognised that our current system is, in many ways, outmoded. Given the sterling work of the Company Law Review it is to be expected and hoped that their efforts will eventually be translated into legislation in the form of a new Companies Act. Company law is one of the most vibrant and practical subjects that one could encounter. Although some may think of the subject as largely academic, perhaps witnessed by the fact that our law is highly complex and largely the preserve of experts, it still remains a subject with enormous practical significance. There are currently 1.3 million companies on the register at Companies House, ranging from the smallest one-man operation to the largest plc.[2] At the Bar, I did not specialise in company law, but I came across points in that field quite often, as anyone with any sort of commercial practice, even someone specialising in real property law (as I did), would expect to do. On becoming a judge, I must confess to having been somewhat nervous to find myself from time to time being responsible for the Companies List, and indeed dealing with points of difficulty in relation to company law generally. As I have become more familiar with company law, I can understand its attraction to those who are interested in substantive points of legal theory or procedure, and the commercial and practical aspects of this vitally important subject. In this essay I will offer a broad survey of some of the more topical matters which have come before the courts in recent years and note, in particular, the role and influence of the courts on the topic of company law reform.

2 THE ROLE OF THE COURTS IN CORPORATE AFFAIRS

Over the past few years one can detect a certain tension between various forces pulling in different directions as to the extent to which the court should involved itself with company matters. On the one hand, both the legislature and the executive seem to consider it desirable that the courts' policing of the way in which companies are run should be increased; on the other hand, the courts themselves appear to think it right to leave those who own or run companies to get on with it.[3]

---

1 See *Modern Company Law for a Competitive Economy: Final Report* (London, DTI, 2001), hereafter *The Final Report*.

2 See *Companies in 1999–2000* (London, TSO, 2000) at p 24 Table A1.

3 The general principle that the courts should not readily involve themselves in the management of companies is well established; see: *Carlen v Drury* (1812) 1 V & B 154 at p 158 *per* Lord Eldon LC; *Shuttleworth v Cox Bros & Co* [1927] 2 KB 9 at p 23 *per* Scrutton LJ.

I should like to refer to two recent examples, of a rather different nature, where the court has taken the view that interference was not, in principle, desirable. The first is the decision of the House of Lords in *O'Neill v Phillips*.[4] This was a case in which it was alleged that the company's affairs were being conducted in a manner unfairly prejudicial to the interests of the minority shareholders.[5] Lord Hoffmann said that, while s 459 of the Companies Act 1985 involved the choice of 'fairness as the criterion by which the court must decide whether it has jurisdiction to grant relief',[6] this did not mean that 'the court can do whatever the individual judge happens to think is fair'.[7] Accordingly, s 459 could only be invoked where the minority could either show that there had been some breach of the terms on which it had been agreed that the company's affairs should be conducted, or where equitable considerations would render it unfair for those running the company to rely upon their strict legal powers. However, even on that latter basis, the minority would have to establish some sort of equitable wrong, such as the breach of a promise by the majority, in circumstances where the promise might not be legally enforceable as a matter of contract, but would be enforceable in equity.

In reaching this decision, and reversing the Court of Appeal,[8] it seems to me that the House of Lords was emphasising (or perhaps re-emphasising) that s 459 could not be invoked simply because some might say that, in some vague sense, the minority was being unfairly treated. In order to establish unfairness, it is necessary to identify something which the law would recognise, that is a legal or equitable wrong, against the minority. Thus, the courts should not get involved save where there are normal common law (that is, contractual) or equitable grounds for doing so. The court is not there to administer palm tree justice.[9]

It is interesting to note that, consistent with the modern approach of the court, as embodied, perhaps, in the new Civil Procedure Rules 1998 (CPR),[10] the House of Lords was anxious to encourage agreement between shareholders who had fallen out. Lord Hoffmann (with whom the other members of the House of Lords agreed)[11] said that 'parties ought to be encouraged, where at all possible, to avoid the expense of money and spirit inevitably involved in such litigation by making an offer to purchase at an early stage'.[12]

In a somewhat different context, there is the decision in *Re T & D Industries plc*[13] where an administrator had been appointed pursuant to Part I of the Insolvency Act 1986. He had received an attractive offer to purchase almost all the assets of the company on a 'going concern' basis, and he needed to reach a quick decision as to whether to accept it or not. Indeed, the pressure of time was such that there was no question of his being able to defer deciding whether or not to accept the offer until after the meeting of creditors to

---

4   [1999] 1 WLR 1092. See also section 5 below.
5   Ie, it was a petition made pursuant to Companies Act 1985, s 459(1).
6   See [1999] 1 WLR 1092 at p 1098D.
7   See [1999] 1 WLR 1092 at p 1098D.
8   The decision of the Court of Appeal in this case can be found at [1997] 2 BCLC 739.
9   Cf *Re Cade & Son Ltd* [1992] BCLC 213 at p 227 *per* Warner J.
10 See SI 1998/3132.
11 Lord Jauncey, Lord Clyde, Lord Hutton and Lord Hobhouse.
12 See [1999] 1 WLR 1092 at p 1106H.
13 [2000] BCC 956.

be called in accordance with provisions of the Act.[14] The question for consideration was whether, in view of his inability to get the formal consent of the creditors, or even to enable the creditors carefully to consider the proposal, the administrator could validly accept the offer without the need for him to obtain the sanction of the court. There had been earlier decisions which suggested that, in such circumstances, the administrator needed the leave of the court before he could validly proceed to sell assets of the company, if he did not have the formal consent of the creditors.[15]

I concluded, differing from a number of earlier decisions (including one of my own), that the administrator could validly proceed with the sale without the need to come to court for approval. So far as the question of a pure construction of the Insolvency Act 1986 was concerned, I did not find it easy, although it seemed to me that, on balance, the way in which the 1986 Act was worded pointed to that conclusion. However, it seemed to me that the result was right for practical reasons. The decision whether or not to sell assets of a company, and if so when and on what terms, is a commercial decision, which an insolvency practitioner should be well able to judge, and which should rarely involve the court. By contrast, particularly given that the application to the court for permission to effect the sale will be made *ex parte* (that is, without opposition), I thought that the court's consent would in practice be of little value. Faced with, at least normally, cogent reasons from the administrator as to why it was urgent and sensible that he should sell on the proposed terms, the court would have little alternative in most circumstances but to sanction the proposed sale. Accordingly, it seemed to me that concluding that the administrator needed leave would merely represent extra cost and delay in the administrator having to make an application, which the court would almost always be bound to grant.

3 THE COURTS AND ADMINISTRATION ORDERS

In contrast to this relatively *laissez-faire* attitude on the part of the court, the legislature and the executive seem to be adopting a more 'proactive' attitude. In terms of volume of work, the two most notable changes have been the law of administration and the disqualification of directors, both now enshrined in statutes passed in 1986.[16] It could be said that the introduction of administration has not increased the court's role, because it is merely an alternative to liquidation. Given that compulsory liquidation would be the fate of most companies if the administration route was not available, there is obvious force in that point. However, the increase in the court's involvement arises from the very fact that administration orders are sought from the court almost exclusively in circumstances where, if the administration route were not available, there would be no question but that the company would be wound up. In other words, administration is unlikely to be sought in circumstances where the company could have had any realistic prospect of challenging

---

14 On which see Insolvency Act 1986, s 24.
15 The cases are reviewed in the judgment at [2000] BCC 956 at pp 962–65.
16 See Insolvency Act 1986, Part II ss 8–27 (on administration) and on which see generally the Milman essay below at p 419 onwards; Company Directors Disqualification Act 1986 (as amended) (on the directors' disqualification regime), and on which see generally the Griffin essay below at p 203 onwards.

a winding-up petition. A petition for an administration order takes up more time, effort and cost than an unopposed winding-up petition. Even though administration orders are not normally opposed, the court has to consider the evidence said to justify the administration order in a little detail. I might add that the continuation of an administration petition is not infrequently opposed, although it is also uncommon.

At least from the judge's point of view, the trouble with the fact that an administration petition is hardly ever opposed is that, in the great majority of cases, he feels that he has little alternative but to make the administration order as sought. Sometimes, however, the evidence available will suggest either that an administration order is inappropriate or unnecessary, or that there are simply gaps in the information provided which need to be filled before the court can conclude that an administration order is appropriate. Although an accountant normally has to prepare a report in accordance with Rule 2.2 of the Insolvency Rules,[17] his report will normally suffer from three disadvantages. The first is the very fact that he will have produced his report in a great hurry. The second is that he will normally be unfamiliar with the company or its affairs until he was instructed to prepare his report. Thirdly, he will often be the accountant who is being put forward as the proposed administrator. In these circumstances, the information which the court is given by an apparent 'independent' expert has been provided by someone who is really dependant on what he has been told by the directors (who are very frequently also the shareholders), and not only do they have an interest in an administration order being made, but so does he.

Regrettably, but perhaps inevitably, there also appear to be occasions where there is something of a 'cosy' arrangement between the proposed administrator and the directors, either from the time that the administrator is first instructed or from some later date. This relationship can lead to actions and decisions by the administrator which are to the prejudice of the company's general creditors. How often this happens is a matter of speculation, but it is obviously to be hoped that it is infrequent.[18]

I am not sure what the answer to these problems should be. One solution is that it should be an independent accountant who investigates the company and then prepares the Rule 2.2 Report. This independent accountant would then be prevented from becoming the administrator after the administration order was granted by the court. Such an idea is attractive in theory. However, bearing in mind the urgency with which administration orders normally have to be sought, and the fact that, almost by definition, there is a limited amount of money at stake,[19] it seems to me that such an idea would be impractical in many cases. In theory, considerable control over the work of the administrator should be exercised by creditors committees,[20] but I am not convinced that that always happens.

It is, I think, desirable that, when a petition for administration is presented, the court should be told how much the costs of the proposed administration are expected to be. I think it is also appropriate that, when the administration order is later discharged or varied, the court should be told the actual costs of the administration at that time and also

---

17 See Insolvency Rules 1986, SI 1986/1925.
18 See further the Milman essay below at p 431.
19 Most companies will either be insolvent or on the verge of insolvency.
20 See generally Insolvency Rules 1986, at chapter 4.

the originally estimated costs at the time of the original application for the order. The court should also be shown how the results of the administration compare with what was estimated at the time the court was invited to make the administration order. I believe that a requirement that the court has this information at the time it makes the administration order, and the knowledge that it will have this information at the time that it is invited to discharge or vary the administration order would, at least help concentrate minds. Of course, it is possible that a *bona fide* estimate of costs or values will turn out to be wrong, but I think that the court should know how successful or otherwise its administration orders are, and, in an appropriate case, that the court should know why things have gone wrong or estimates have turned out to be wrong, in cases where that has occurred.

The administration order procedure, established by the Insolvency Act 1986, is still relatively new. Many of the concepts introduced have still to be fully defined and implemented. This process of acclimatisation has, on occasion, led to conflicting decisions as the courts have struggled to map the contours of the new legislation and, in particular, its interrelationship with other areas of law. The moratoria provisions contained in ss 10 and 11 of the Insolvency Act 1986 are a good example of this. Section 11 is designed to prevent creditors of a company, which suffers from financial difficulties, from enforcing their security interests and other proprietary rights against the company during the duration of an administration order.[21] Obviously if individual creditors were allowed to proceed against the company then the administration order, which is founded on more collectivist principles (and a rejection of the normal self-help principle which tends to underpin English law via the freedom of contract notion), would be largely frustrated.

Problems have arisen in this context with regard to the ambit of the term 'security' which is used in the Act. For example under s 11(3)(c) during the duration of an administration order 'no other steps may be taken to enforce any security over the company's property' without the consent of the administrator or the leave of the court.[22] It is a natural reaction for any creditor of a financially distressed company to seek to enforce their rights before other creditors and then get out while they can. This section is designed to prevent secured creditors from doing just this. However, the provision can only operate if the creditor is seeking to enforce a 'security' interest against the company. The concept of security interests has troubled English law for a long time and is a separate subject in need of reform.[23] Whilst the traditional forms of security interest namely, the mortgage, charge, pledge and lien[24] present no problems in this context, it is the more modern contract-based techniques which avoid the traditional conveyance of proprietary rights from debtor to creditor that cause the problems. Although the latter can loosely be described as security in that they perform a security function, at law these devices cannot be classified as security interests. This is the reason why devices such as retention of title and hire purchase had to be treated specifically by the administration legislation to ensure

---

21 Section 10 of the Act applies in a similar manner when a petition for an administration order has been made to the court but before the order has been made.
22 See also Insolvency Act 1986, s 10(1)(b) to like effect.
23 See further the essay by de Lacy below at p 333.
24 See Insolvency Act 1986, s 248(b)(i) for a definition of 'security'. In this context it is submitted that the only other type of 'or other security' is the pledge.

that they were also caught by the moratoria provisions.[25] This recognition did not, however, extend to all forms of interest that might be classified as operating by way of security. The problem arose in the case of *Exchange Travel Agency Ltd v Triton Property Trust plc*[26] whether the landlord's right of re-entry to premises for non-payment of rent could be classified as a security interest for the purposes of the administration order regime. Harman J held that it could, taking a broad interpretation of the new legislation and looking to its underlying purpose (that is, the prevention of individuals enforcing security rights against the company outside the collectivist regime the administration order was designed to impose). This point was subsequently followed in other first instance cases.[27]

Despite the commendable result in these cases they were, nevertheless, in danger of placing policy considerations above those of legal analysis. Although it was correct that the right of re-entry had been described as a security for a long time,[28] the use of the term 'security' was merely one of convenience rather than as a term of legal art. This was made clear from the Court of Appeal decision in *Ezekiel v Orakpo*.[29] The latter case was not cited to the court in the *Exchange Travel Agency* case,[30] which serves to demonstrate the dangers associated with interpreting new legislation: there is always a risk of adopting an overenthusiastic approach to policy to the detriment of the wider issues of established legal principle. As Sir Nicholas Browne-Wilkinson VC once warned:

> On the other hand, however desirable it may be to construe the [Insolvency] Act in a way calculated to carry out the parliamentary purpose, it is not legitimate to distort the meaning of the words Parliament has chosen to use in order to achieve that result. Only if the words used by Parliament are fairly capable of bearing more than one meaning is it legitimate to adopt the meaning for which it gives effect to, rather than frustrates, the statutory purpose.[31]

With this warning in mind Lightman J and I were each able to view the issue in, perhaps, clearer perspective when it came before us respectively in the cases of *Razzaq v Pala*[32] and *Re Lomax Leisure Ltd*.[33] We both concluded that the earlier approach of the courts to the question of 'security' had been wrong and the right of an unpaid landlord to re-enter premises could not be classified in law as the enforcement of a security interest. I reached this decision with regret since it was clear that the underlying purpose of the legislation was designed to prevent such things happening. Nevertheless, in such cases it is for the legislature to intervene if they have got it wrong in the first place. The courts cannot correct defective draftsmanship if it would amount to a subversion of legal principle.

---

25 See Insolvency Act 1986, ss 10(1)(b), 11(3)(c) and 11(4) covering a 'hire purchase agreement'.

26 [1991] BCC 341.

27 See *Re Olympia & York Canary Wharf Ltd* [1993] BCC 154 at p 158C *per* Millett J; *Doorbar v Alltime Securities Ltd (No 2)* [1995] BCC 728 at p 734E *per* Knox J; *March Estates plc v Gunmark plc* [1996] 2 BCLC 1 at pp 7C–8A *per* Lightman J.

28 See, eg, *Wadman v Calcraft* (1804) 10 Ves Jun 67 at p 68 *per* Sir William Grant MR.

29 [1977] QB 260 at pp 267H–268A *per* Shaw LJ.

30 [1991] BCC 341.

31 See *Bristol Airport plc v Powdrill* [1990] Ch 744 at p 759A–B.

32 [1998] BCC 66.

33 [2000] BCC 352. Note also *Re Park Air Services plc* [2000] 2 AC 172 at p 186B–D *per* Lord Millett.

Parliament has indeed now intervened to rectify the position and the right of re-entry is now caught by the administration order regime.[34]

4 THE COURTS AND THE COMPANY DIRECTORS DISQUALIFICATION ACT 1986

The specialist company law report publications *Butterworths Company Law Cases*[35] and *British Company Cases*[36] are littered with decisions under the Company Directors Disqualification Act 1986, which represents another big change in company-related litigation. One can well understand the policy behind the Company Directors Disqualification Legislation: there should be some sanction against those who unfairly take advantage of creditors, whether government departments, trade creditors or the public generally, by sheltering dishonestly or ineptly behind the protection of limited liability.[37] Furthermore, the penalty imposed on people who act in such a manner appears commensurate with their wrongdoing, namely disqualification from being able to act as a director, or in any senior management capacity of a company.[38] The Act is fairly well drafted and has not led to many problems of principle. From the point of view of the courts, however, the devil, as usual, is in the detail.

An application to disqualify a director can involve a hearing for days, even weeks, exceptionally even months, particularly when the grounds upon which it is said that the respondent is unfit are numerous, or where the allegations span a long period.[39] This undesirable feature of the disqualification procedure was identified in the Court of Appeal in *Re Westmid Packing Services Ltd*,[40] where Lord Woolf MR referred to the 'overelaboration in the preparation and hearing of these cases and a technical approach as to what evidence is and is not admissible',[41] and suggested that the parties should be limited to 'sufficient evidence to enable the court to adopt a broad brush approach'.[42]

My experience suggests that this is entirely desirable, but I think it will be very difficult to achieve without running the real risk of an injustice. Whether a respondent is disqualified, and for how long he is disqualified, are matters of great importance to him or her, as it is, indeed, to the public. Although the Disqualification Act is not criminal in its effect (and indeed it would lead to procedural difficulties in terms of human rights if it were otherwise),[43] its consequences can be said to be fairly penal, and justifiably penal, in relation to a person who is disqualified. Accordingly, it seems to me questionable whether

---

34 See Insolvency Act 2000, s 9, which amends the Insolvency Act 1986 to bring this about.
35 Published by Butterworths and has been reporting company law matters since 1983.
36 Now published by Sweet & Maxwell (formerly by CCH) and has been reporting company law matters since 1983.
37 See generally *Salomon v Salomon & Co* [1897] AC 22.
38 See Company Directors Disqualification Act 1986, s 1. The maximum period that a director can be disqualified for is 15 years.
39 Cf *EDC v UK* [1998] BCC 370; *R v Secretary of State for Trade and Industry ex p Eastaway* [2001] BCC 265.
40 [1998] 2 BCLC 646.
41 See [1998] 2 BCLC 646 at p 658f.
42 See [1998] 2 BCLC 646 at p 658f.
43 See generally *Official Receiver v Stern* [2000] 1 WLR 2230.

anything other than a fairly detailed investigation of the charges can be just so far as any respondent is concerned. Furthermore, if the investigation is too superficial, it will be difficult for the court to arrive at a decision whether to disqualify or not, in cases which are close calls, and, even in cases where it is fairly clear that a disqualification order should be made, a fairly detailed appreciation of the facts will normally be necessary before the court can fairly determine the appropriate period of disqualification.

Clearly, the 'Carecraft Procedure'[44] whereby the Secretary of State and a respondent can agree the basic facts (which almost inevitably involve a degree of give and take) with the view to the court deciding whether to disqualify (which is normally conceded by the respondent) and if so for how long, at a fairly short hearing is a good example of the flexibility shown by the court when dealing with novel situations. In *Re Carecraft*[45] the court demonstrated that it would not be hide-bound when called upon to interpret the scope of the Directors Disqualification Act 1986 such that no full trial would be required when the evidence supported, and the parties agreed, that a case should be dealt with on a summary basis. The resulting Carecraft Procedure has, therefore, provided a welcome procedural alternative in many cases thereby saving much time and money.[46] The latter has been achieved whilst still protecting the public interest which is, of course, the overriding purpose of the disqualification regime.

Nevertheless, expediency and cost-saving are not, and should not become, the sole determinants involved in the exercise of judicial policy making. For example, in the case of *Re Blackspur Group plc*[47] it was urged upon the court that a director should be allowed to offer an undertaking to the Secretary of State in lien of director disqualification proceedings being taken against him. Factors in favour of such an approach included the saving of massive costs[48] estimated to flow from a formal trial of the disqualification case; the saving of much time and also the fact that the undertaking on offer was more restrictive than any order the court could have made upon finding that the director was unfit to be involved in the management of a company. The Court of Appeal, however, concluded that primacy must be given to the statutory scheme, and that the proposed course of action amounted almost to giving the director a power of veto over the procedures established under the 1986 Act. Of particular concern was the fact that the statutory scheme was predicated on the assumption that persons subject to disqualification orders were 'unfit' to be concerned in the direction or management of companies.[49] In the present case the director was not prepared to make an admission of unfitness such that the case could have been disposed of under the Carecraft Procedure. This position served to underline the stigma effect of the disqualification regime and its primary purpose, namely to expose and then prevent unfit persons being concerned in the direction and management of companies. The director was trying to avoid the stigma

---

44 See *Re Carecraft Construction Co Ltd* [1994] 1 WLR 172.
45 [1994] 1 WLR 172.
46 In *Re Blackspur Group plc* [1998] 1 WLR 422 at p 429A, Lord Woolf MR described it as a 'commendable cost-saving procedure'.
47 [1998] 1 WLR 422.
48 The director in this case stated that he believed his own costs would be in the region of £900,000; see [1998] 1 WLR 422 at p 428A.
49 See generally Company Directors Disqualification Act 1986, ss 6(1)(a), 8(2).

of a finding of unfitness and simply go straight to the 'punishment'. To use a criminal law analogy one cannot be sentenced for an offence before one has been convicted.[50]

The conceptual similarities between disqualification and criminal proceedings are quite apparent. The court is not only deciding whether a respondent has done anything wrong, but what is the appropriate period, albeit that it is a period of disqualification rather than one of imprisonment. In *Re Westmid*,[51] as in earlier decisions, the Court of Appeal has been anxious to emphasise that the decision whether to disqualify, and the period of disqualification are very much for the judge or registrar hearing the case, and an appellate court should be slow to interfere.

5 THE COURTS AND SECTION 459 PETITIONS

The desire to reduce the issues, the complexities, and the length of the hearing is to be found not only in the context of disqualification cases. Perhaps not surprisingly, the Court of Appeal has expressed not dissimilar views in connection with petitions made pursuant to s 459 of the Companies Act 1985. In *North Holdings Limited v Southern Tropics Ltd*[52] Aldous LJ referred to the CPR as 'a new way of conducting litigation' and to the duty 'of the courts to manage cases actively' leading to 'a new approach by the registrar to proceedings such as this one'.[53] He suggested that s 459 petitions would, as a result, be 'quick and cheap'.[54]

Again, one can have no doubt but that this represents a highly desirable procedural target to aim for, but I am bound to say that in many cases it will be difficult to achieve. The observations seem to support the view that the court should, if possible, cut down the matters which need to be determined on a s 459 petition. That was a course proposed to me in *Re Rotadata Ltd*,[55] and, while it was obviously attractive for the reasons given by Aldous LJ,[56] it seemed to me that I could not properly adopt it. The applicant's case was that a series of actions by the respondents, when taken together, constituted a breach of the applicant's rights such that a purchase order ought to be made in respect of his shares against the respondent. In order to assess the seriousness of the allegations, and the reliability of the evidence called on behalf of the parties, I concluded that it would be very dangerous to remove some of the matters complained of from the dispute. Nonetheless, it did seem to me right to point out that certain issues were so marginal and so potentially expensive to deal with, not in terms of court time but in terms of having witnesses called from abroad, that I very much doubted that, even if a party would otherwise have been entitled to its costs, any order for costs would be made in its favour in relation to those

---

50 On a positive note, the legislature has recently recognised that there should be scope for directors to give an undertaking in lien of proceedings in certain cases if the Secretary of State thinks it appropriate; see Insolvency Act 2000, s 6, introducing a new s 6(1)A to the Company Directors Disqualification Act 1986.

51 [1998] 2 BCLC 646.

52 [1999] 2 BCLC 625.

53 See [1999] 2 BCLC 625 at p 638e–g.

54 See [1999] 2 BCLC 625 at p 638e–g.

55 [2000] 1 BCLC 122.

56 See above nn 53 and 54 and the main text thereat.

items. Certainly, the spirit and terms of the CPR give the court, when exercising its companies jurisdiction, just as much as when exercising any other jurisdiction, flexible powers, and that should certainly not be overlooked.

The most important judicial development in this area is the decision of the House of Lords in *O'Neill v Phillips*.[57] Prior to this decision there was a danger that things were getting out of hand with regard to the number of s 459 petitions being presented and the grounds upon which such petitions were being sustained. There can be no doubt that such cases were a drain on the time of the courts and often involved the courts being called upon to sort out the mess created by personal disputes in small, often family run, companies. Clearly the courts are often unsuitable forums for such disputes which are dressed up in company law language in order to maintain a s 459 petition with the courts often being called upon to act almost as surrogate marriage guidance counsellors. Many disputes which, to an outsider, would seem rather trivial and unimportant were a cause for substantive concern. For example, the Law Commission noted one case where the hearing lasted 43 days leading to costs of £320,000 to establish the value of shares at £24,600 which had originally cost £40,000![58] It is to be hoped that the decision in *O'Neill* will help eradicate the belief that s 459 is a universal panacea for all the ills that might befall a shareholder and that an allegation of 'unfair prejudice' will result in summary justice being awarded to the aggrieved shareholder. Lord Hoffmann has rightly identified the ideal as being that a lawyer should be able to advise his client with confidence in advance whether the s 459 petition will be successful.[59] The conditions to be satisfied before s 459 can be invoked, namely that a shareholder can demonstrate a breach of the terms on which he became a member or that some equitable interest of the member has been infringed,[60] should aid the determination of the strength of an individual case. Interestingly, the Company Law Steering Group has recommended that the *O'Neill v Phillips* approach to s 459 be maintained.[61] This was despite the fact that the majority of respondents to earlier consultations thought that *O'Neill* was unduly restricting access to s 459 and that this might lead to cases of injustice. However, although noting such concerns the Steering Group felt that 'the interests of certainty and the containment of the scope of s 459 actions'[62] dictated that the *O'Neill* criteria[63] should remain as a gateway to s 459 actions.

The Law Commission had tried to face up to the problems of s 459 petitions prior to the decision in *O'Neill v Phillips*.[64] It proposed a number of ways of dealing with the long, exhausting and expensive petitions to which s 459 frequently led and to which reference has already been made. The Law Commission suggested[65] that one way in which the

---

57 [1999] 1 WLR 1092. See further the Lowry essay below at p 229.
58 See Law Commission Report No 246 *Shareholder Remedies* (1997) Cm 3769 (London, TSO, 1997) at p 3 n 14.
59 See *O'Neill v Phillips* [1999] 1 WLR 1092 at p 1099G.
60 See [1999] 1 WLR 1092 at pp 1098H–1099A *per* Lord Hoffmann.
61 See *The Final Report*, above n 1, at para 7.41.
62 See *The Final Report*, above n 1, at para 7.41.
63 See above n 60 and the main text thereat for these criteria.
64 [1999] 1 WLR 1092.
65 See *Shareholder Remedies*, above n 58, at para 2.4.

problem could be alleviated was pursuant to the CPR,[66] very much along the lines suggested by Aldous LJ[67] as I have discussed. I have already expressed some scepticism about this, although I enthusiastically support it in so far as it is consentient with justice, and in particular a fair trial. The Law Commission also suggested that a minority could require to be bought out by the majority, but not to ask for any other relief, where the unfairness alleged was exclusion of the minority from the management of the company.[68] This would go further than suggested by Lord Hoffmann in the *O'Neill* case,[69] because it would permit an application to be brought for relief even where the applicant could not establish any breach of contract or breach of any other sort of promise by the majority. It would have the benefit of being justifiable without the applicant having to establish any fault on the part of the respondent. The proposed remedy would be limited to small companies. This would plainly render the role of the court rather easier, because it would have, ultimately, to decide only one issue on an application, namely whether the minority had in fact been excluded from the management of the company. So long as other grounds still existed, I wonder whether this aspect of the proposal would actually make any difference. I suspect that in many cases it would simply be thrown in by the minority as an additional ground for granting them the relief sought pursuant to s 459. However, given the recent conclusions of the Steering Group[70] it must be doubtful whether the Law Commission's approach will be adopted.

The Law Commission did not limit themselves to discussing the ambit and problems of s 459. In order to prevent disputes arising before the courts they called for Table A[71] to be amended in order to provide simple solutions in the event of future membership conflicts arising.[72] The main solution in this context was the provision for an exit article[73] to be introduced allowing an aggrieved shareholder, in defined circumstances, to demand that his shares be purchased from him.[74] Given that the majority of s 459 petitions involve claims for, or solutions by way of, a buyout of the minority shareholder this is perhaps a sensible measure that should help in many situations. However, this is not a measure that the Company Law Steering Group have adopted in their *Final Report*.[75]

Although the courts are given a wide discretion[76] as to the remedy[77] available to an aggrieved shareholder who succeeds in his petition under s 459, in practice such an order will almost invariably be that the majority buy out the aggrieved minority. In short, s 459 actions tend to involve the ability to terminate a company membership by an individual. This leads me to turn to the situation where a member seeks redress which does not

---

66 Above n 10.
67 See above nn 52–54 and the main text thereat.
68 See *Shareholder Remedies*, above n 58, at para 3.30.
69 [1999] 1 WLR 1092. See also *Re Guidezone Ltd* [2000] 2 BCLC 321.
70 On which see above n 62 and the main text thereat.
71 See Companies Act 1985, s 8 and SI 1985/805.
72 See generally *Shareholder Remedies*, above n 58, at chapter 5.
73 See *Shareholder Remedies*, above n 58, at paras 5.32 and 5.49.
74 See *Shareholder Remedies*, above n 58, at pp 133–36 for the details of this new article.
75 See n 1 above, Volume II at chapter 17.
76 See Companies Act 1985, s 461(1): the court may make such order 'as it thinks fit' for giving relief under s 459.
77 See also Companies Act 1985, s 460(2), which provides some examples of the types of remedy available.

involve him seeking to terminate membership or the claim that the affairs of the company have been conducted in an 'unfairly prejudicial'[78] manner.

6 THE COURTS AND MINORITY SHAREHOLDER PROTECTION

At the heart of any company is its membership.[79] Excluding the one-man company, most companies will inevitably suffer from internal disagreements between members over policies and decisions taken on behalf of the company. In the majority of situations the democratic principle of majority voting will determine which viewpoint prevails in the event of a dispute. Company law has already differentiated here between issues requiring an ordinary resolution which requires a simple majority of those voting (51%) and those requiring a special (or extraordinary)[80] resolution which requires a special majority of 75% of those voting on the relevant issue.[81] However, there will always be occasions when the minority, unable to control the respective vote, is not content to accept the majority position. In these circumstances the question arises as to the proper circumstances in which that minority should be able to challenge the position of the majority, reflected as the decision of the company, in the courts. The courts naturally do not want to get involved in internal company decisions which are often acrimonious and can reflect political viewpoints, and normally result from a breakdown in personal relationships.[82] Given that the nature of any corporate endeavour involves the taking of business risks in the hope of achieving profits, it is only right that the court should be wary of involving itself in such type of disputes. On the other hand, the courts must be alive to the possibility that the majority controlling a company might be abusing their position to inflict damage on the company and/or the minority members of the company usually in the furtherance of their own agenda. In such a case, the court should be prepared to become involved and, in an appropriate case, overturn a decision purportedly taken in the name of the company. A difficult problem has always remained, however. In what circumstances should the courts get involved or, in other words, in what circumstances should a minority shareholder be allowed to challenge a decision in the courts?

Since the foundation of our company law system in Victorian times, this question has troubled the courts. In the famous case of *Foss v Harbottle*[83] the courts attempted to establish some ground rules in this area. Here the proper plaintiff rule was firmly established: the court acknowledged, that in general, it was for the company itself to sort out internal problems and the court should not allow shareholders to act behind the back of the company and challenge or seek to enforce the rights and obligations which were, in

---

78 See Companies Act 1985, s 459(1).
79 For the position of the Company Law Steering Group on this area see *The Final Report*, above n 1, at chapter 7.
80 See *The Final Report*, above n 1, at para 7.14, where the Company Law Steering Group recommends the abolition of extraordinary resolutions.
81 See generally Companies Act 1985, s 378.
82 See also at n 3 above.
83 (1843) 2 Hare 461. See also *Edwards v Halliwell* [1950] 2 All ER 1064 (CA).

reality, vested in the company. Given the fact that a company possesses a distinct personality it is right in principle that this should be the starting point. Apart from this doctrinal justification there is also the practical argument that it would simply be unworkable for every aggrieved shareholder to be able to petition the courts for redress.[84] Nevertheless, rigid adherence to this rule would virtually exclude minority shareholders from having an avenue of redress. It comes as no surprise, therefore, to learn that the courts have always sought the prevention of injustice or the oppression of minorities by majorities when considering the proper application of the rule in *Foss*. Therefore, the courts have sought to create exceptions to the rule in *Foss* whereby, in certain circumstances, a minority shareholder will be allowed to bring an action either to right a wrong against himself or to enforce a right of action vested in the company which the majority has deemed should not be exercised. It has to be said however, that the courts have not always been clear in determining precisely which acts will allow a shareholder access to the courts.

Nonetheless, it can be said that the courts have been all too aware that they must prevent a majority from using their position to commit a fraud on the minority. In this situation a minority will be able to bring an action.[85] Nevertheless, if a majority of the 'minority' class of shareholders do not wish to see an action brought in the company name, and they are genuinely independent of the 'majority' of shareholders who control the corporate decisions, then an individual member of that 'minority' will be prevented from taking action.[86] The courts have also appreciated the economics of attempting to bring an action to right a wrong in this situation. Therefore, in *Wallersteiner v Moir (No 2)*[87] the Court of Appeal recognised that a minority shareholder should have a right to his costs in bringing the matter before the court via an indemnity from his company so long as the shareholder had acted in a 'reasonable and prudent' manner in bringing the action.[88] Conversely, the courts must also be alive to the possibility that allowing a derivative action to proceed might amount to 'killing the company with kindness'[89] due to the costs associated with the action. A relatively minor dispute could be dwarfed by the costs of establishing the 'misconduct' such that the financial viability of the company was imperilled.[90] These are factors which the minority shareholders would have to consider in deciding whether or not to proceed with a derivative action.

---

84 See also: *Gary v Lewis* (1873) 8 Ch App 1035 at p 1051 *per* James LJ; *MacDougall v Gardiner* (1875) 1 Ch D 13 at p 25 *per* Mellish LJ.

85 See *Burland v Earle* [1902] AC 83. See also *Konameneni v Rolls-Royce Industrial Power (India) Ltd* [2002] 1 All ER 979.

86 See *Smith v Croft (No 2)* [1988] Ch 114.

87 [1975] QB 373.

88 See *Wallersteiner v Moir (No 2)* [1975] QB 373 at p 392B *per* Lord Denning MR. Note also Prentice 'Wallersteiner v Moir: The Demise of the Rule in *Foss v Harbottle*?' [1976] *The Conveyancer* 51.

89 See *Prudential Assurance Co Ltd v Newman Industries Ltd (No 2)* [1982] Ch 204 at p 221E (CA).

90 In the *Prudential Assurance* case the Court of Appeal described the costs of bringing the case as being 'horrendous'; see [1982] Ch 204 at p 220H.

Quite apart from this aspect, difficulties remain with defining the precise circumstances[91] in which an action will be allowed to proceed. There can be no doubt that the courts will allow an action where illegal conduct[92] or *ultra vires* transactions[93] are involved. Beyond this a minority shareholder will have to demonstrate that a personal interest is involved such that he has a direct right of action rather than enforcing a right derived from the company. The proper boundaries of shareholders' 'personal interests' are difficult to define and represent a topical subject.

The case of *Johnson v Gore Wood & Co* served to highlight the problematic state of the law in this regard. Here, the Court of Appeal[94] had to do its best to reconcile earlier, while fairly recent, decisions of the Court of Appeal[95] stemming from the decision in the *Prudential Assurance* case.[96] The Court of Appeal freely acknowledged the difficult nature of this area[97] and, perhaps, unsurprisingly the problem went to the House of Lords to resolve.[98] At issue was whether in a situation where a company suffers loss caused by a breach of duty owed both to the company and to a shareholder the shareholder can recover for the loss independent of the company. In other words can the shareholder recover in his own right or is he bound by the proper plaintiff rule thereby restricting the right to bring an action to the company alone? The issue had become complicated because although the earlier authority had suggested that a strict approach should be taken thereby preventing a shareholder from bringing an action in this situation,[99] more recent authority suggested that if the justice of the situation favoured the shareholder then he might be allowed to bring an action (distinguishing the authorities which might

---

91   The courts have not been alone in trying to identify the correct principles in this area and the subject remains controversial, see further: Wedderburn 'Shareholders' Rights and the Rule in *Foss v Harbottle*' [1957] CLJ 194 and [1958] CLJ 93; Bastin 'The Enforcement of a Member's Rights' [1977] *Journal of Business Law* 17; Smith 'Minority Shareholders and Corporate Irregularities' (1978) 41 MLR 147; Baxter 'The Role of the Judge in Enforcing Shareholder Rights' [1983] CLJ 96; Drury 'The Relative Nature of a Shareholder's Right to Enforce the Company Contract' [1986] CLJ 219. However, many of the problems identified by the academic commentators will be resolved if the Company Law Steering Group's proposals are implemented; see *The Final Report*, above n 1, at para 7.34 where it is recommended that every shareholder be given *standi* to enforce obligations provided for by the corporate constitution (ie, the articles and memorandum of association), unless the breach in question was 'trivial or the remedy fruitless'. Regard should also be had to the issue of whether the claimant has 'clean hands', see further Payne 'Clean Hands in Derivative Actions' [2002] CLJ 76.

92   See *Hope v International Financial Society* (1876) 4 Ch D 327.

93   See: *Simpson v Westminster Palace Hotel Co* (1860) 8 HL Cas 712; *Clinch v Financial Corp* (1868) LR 5 Eq 450, affirmed at LR 4 Ch App 117. However, at common law a majority of the disinterested and independent minority shareholders may prevent action being taken by one of their class in this situation; *Smith v Croft (No 2)* [1988] Ch 114. In limited circumstances, a shareholder now has a statutory right to prevent *ultra vires* activities by the company; see Companies Act 1985, ss 35(2), 35A(4).

94   [1999] BCC 474.

95   On which see: *Heron International Ltd v Lord Grade* [1983] BCLC 244; *Howard Ltd v Woodman Matthews & Co* [1983] BCLC 117; *Fisher (GB) Ltd v Multi Construction Ltd* [1995] BCC 310; *Christensen v Scott* [1996] 1 NZLR 271; *Barings plc v Coopers & Lybrand* [1997] BCC 498; *Gerber Garment Technology Inc v Lectra Systems Ltd* [1997] RPC 443; *Stein v Blake* [1998] 1 All ER 724; *Watson v Dutton Forshaw Motor Group Ltd* [1998] EWCA 1270; available at www.baillii.org.

96   [1982] Ch 204.

97   See [1999] BCC 474 at pp 487G and 497C.

98   On which see [2001] 2 WLR 72.

99   See *Prudential Assurance Co Ltd v Newman Industries Ltd (No 2)* [1982] Ch 204.

suggest the contrary).[100] In the latter situation it would be up to the court to examine the merits of each case in order to resolve the issue of whether a shareholder could bring an action.[101] The former, strict, approach would reduce this issue to a relatively simple mechanical question and answer affair[102] without the need for any court determination in most cases.[103]

The House of Lords resolved this matter by taking a relatively strict approach and following the weight of historical precedence,[104] thereby reinforcing the legitimacy of the proper plaintiff rule. As Lord Millett explained:

> If the shareholder is allowed to recover in respect of such loss, then either there will be double recovery at the expense of the defendant, or the shareholder will recover at the expense of the company and its creditors and other shareholders. Neither course can be permitted. This is a matter of principle; there is no discretion involved. Justice to the defendant requires the exclusion of one claim or the other; protection of the interests of the company's creditors requires that it is the company which is allowed to recover to the exclusion of the shareholder.[105]

On this basis it is for the company to pursue wrongdoers and if it fails to do so to the satisfaction of its shareholders then the shareholders' complaint is against the company and/or its officials[106] responsible for the omission or defect in pursuing the cause of action.[107] In the latter situation the loss is caused to the shareholder by the company's failure to take action and not by the third party/defendant directly.

The stricter approach of the House of Lords in the *Johnson* case[108] has effectively overruled many decisions which might otherwise have led to the abandonment of the proper plaintiff rule. As a result of this approach the law is now at least tolerably clear.[109] The Company Law Steering Group recently endorsed this approach.[110]

---

100 See: *Fisher (GB) Ltd v Multi-Construction Ltd* [1995] 1 BCLC 260 at p 266h *per* Glidewell LJ; *Barings plc v Coopers & Lybrand* [1997] 1 BCLC 427 at p 435 *per* Leggatt LJ; *Christensen v Scott* [1996] 1 NZLR 273 at pp 280–81 *per* Thomas J.

101 See *Johnson v Gore Wood & Co* [2001] 2 WLR 72 at p 114E–G *per* Lord Hutton.

102 Ie, is the loss claimed by the shareholder merely reflective of that suffered by the company? If 'yes' then the shareholder cannot bring an action and it will be for the company to proceed with the matter. In *Day v Cook* [2002] 1 BCLC 1 at p 3g, Arden LJ referred to this as the 'no reflective loss principle'. Note also *Walker v Stones* [2001] QB 902.

103 In the event of any doubt (at least at the strike out stage), the benefit should be given to the shareholder; *Johnson v Gore Wood & Co* [2001] 2 WLR 72 at p 95E *per* Lord Bingham.

104 Ie, following *Prudential Assurance Co Ltd v Newman Industries Ltd (No 2)* [1982] Ch 204 and rejecting the authorities cited at n 100 above, insofar as they questioned the decision in *Prudential*.

105 See *Johnson v Gore Wood & Co* [2001] 2 WLR 72 at p 121E–F; and note also at pp 125F–26C.

106 In many situations it will be the relevant insolvency official controlling the companies affairs (eg, liquidator, receiver, administrative receiver, etc) who will decide not to take action on behalf of the company, usually because he considers it uneconomic or speculative.

107 See *Johnson v Gore Wood & Co* [2001] 2 WLR 72 at p 125E *per* Lord Millett; cf *Giles v Rhind* [2001] 2 BCLC 582.

108 [2001] 2 WLR 72.

109 However, a note of caution might need to be added if the Court of Appeal allow the appeal in *Giles v Rhind* [2001] 2 BCLC 582. In *Giles*, at pp 595f–96b, Blackburne J reluctantly followed *Johnson v Gore Wood* in holding that a shareholder cannot maintain a personal claim against a third party in a reflective loss situation even if the company cannot pursue the matter such that there can never be any double recovery for that loss. It is probable that we have not heard the last on this topic and the House of Lords may well be called upon to review the scope of their decision in *Johnson v Gore Wood & Co* [2001] 2 WCR 72 in the near future. Note also my decision in *Humberclyde Finance Group Ltd v Hicks* (unreported) 14 November 2001 (available on Westlaw 2001 WL1346978).

110 See *The Final Report*, above n 1, at para 7.51.

The Law Commission looked at this area in 1997.[111] They considered that the circumstances in which a minority shareholder could bring a derivative action had become 'complicated and unwieldy'.[112] They endorsed the basic rationale behind the rule in *Foss v Harbottle*[113] in that it was only in 'exceptional circumstances' that a shareholder should be allowed to proceed with a derivative action.[114] In order to simplify matters the Law Commission proposed a new statutory-based derivative action which would replace the old common law on the subject.[115]

Under this new statutory scheme a member of a company would be entitled to maintain a derivative action to enforce any cause of action vested in the company if it arose as a result of an actual or proposed act or omission involving the negligence or breach of duty by a director of the company, or as a result of a director having put himself in a position where his personal interests conflicted with his duties to the company.[116] The management of any derivative action under this proposed scheme would be vested in the court which would be under a duty to fix a case management conference, once the action had commenced.[117] At that case management conference, the minority shareholder claimant would be required to seek the permission of the court to continue the derivative action.[118] From the point of view of such a member, particularly an unreasonable member, it could be said that the views of the Law Commission involve taking away with one hand what had been given with the other. The Law Commission recognised that a derivative action should only proceed in exceptional circumstances and that such proceedings should not be brought without good cause.[119] As the Law Commission accepted, this proposal would involve the replacement of what may be said to be an existing strict rule[120] with a new rule depending upon the exercise of judicial discretion on a case-by-case basis.

The Law Commission's proposals would involve a degree of uncertainty, and, as the Commission recognised, proceedings could only be brought in the name of the company by a member in an appropriate case. As the Law Commission accepted, this would involve a judge exercising (at the case management conference) what amounted to a discretion to decide whether any particular derivative litigation should be permitted to proceed. The Law Commission recommended that the court should exercise its discretion taking into account 'all the relevant circumstances without limit' in an individual case.[121] However, in order to guide the court in the exercise of its wide discretion the Law Commission also provided a set of non-exclusive relevant matters to take into account.[122]

---

111 See generally *Shareholder Remedies*, above n 58, at Part 6.
112 See generally *Shareholder Remedies*, above n 58, at para 6.4.
113 (1843) 2 Hare 461.
114 See generally *Shareholder Remedies*, above n 58, at para 6.4.
115 See generally *Shareholder Remedies*, above n 58, at para 6.55. However, the Law Commission noted that this new scheme would not prevent a member sustaining a personal action which would continue to be a common law matter; at para 6.57.
116 See generally *Shareholder Remedies*, above n 58, at para 6.49 and p 116 Clause 458A.
117 See generally *Shareholder Remedies*, above n 58, at para 6.69.
118 See generally *Shareholder Remedies*, above n 58, at para 6.69.
119 See above n 114 and the main text thereat.
120 Ie, the rule in *Foss v Harbottle* (1843) 2 Hare 461.
121 See generally *Shareholder Remedies*, above n 58, at para 6.73.
122 See generally *Shareholder Remedies*, above n 58, at paras 6.74–6.93 and p 131 Draft Rule 50.10.

This is throwing quite a burden on the court, particularly as the competing factors raised by each side are unlikely, at least on all occasions, to be satisfactorily met. In other words, what would be involved would be a balancing exercise, and there is an obvious danger that the law will develop in a somewhat haphazard, inconsistent and hence undesirable manner.[123] Nonetheless, there is no doubt that there have been quite a few cases where the absence of the members' right to bring a derivative action has wrought an injustice, and to that extent the Law Commission's proposal must be welcomed. On the other hand, the proposals, if implemented, will involve the court in a new sort of involvement in the affairs of companies, but it is to be hoped that this would not turn out to be a particularly dangerous development.[124] The Company Law Steering Group have recently endorsed these proposals.[125]

7 THE COURTS AND PUBLIC PROTECTION

The apparent tension between the courts' preference for letting those managing and owning companies get on with it, and the apparent preference of the legislature and executive for a degree of interference can, to a substantial extent at any rate, be explained by the difference between disputes within the ambit of the company and protection of members of the public. That, perhaps, is well illustrated by the fact that the courts have been prepared to adopt a fairly wide construction of legislation, and a generous approach to public policy, when considering petitions brought by the Secretary of State for Trade and Industry to wind up companies running trading schemes where members of the public are encouraged to participate in what ultimately amounts to a pyramid scheme, even though it may have been dressed up as something else. The leading case is *Re Senator Hanseatische Verwaltungsgesellschaft mbH*.[126] That case has been followed by a number of subsequent cases, many of which are unreported, and one of the most recent is *Re Delfin International (SA) Ltd*.[127] Like the Secretary of State, the court has taken the view that it is right and proper to protect the public from these sort of schemes, as a matter of public policy, giving a very generous meaning to the definition of trading schemes in Part XI of the Fair Trading Act 1973. There is, undoubtedly, room for the view that it is a matter for members of the public whether or not they should take part in such schemes, and it is unjustifiably protective for the court to interfere with schemes provided that the prospectuses and other promotional material are honest.

The Court can go too far in seeking to apply policy to the construction of statutes, and, indeed, the Court of Appeal held me guilty of that particular offence in *Re Mineral Resources Ltd*,[128] when they decided *Re Celtic Extraction Ltd*.[129] The facts were

---

123 Ie, there is a danger of the courts starting to administer 'palm tree justice'; see above n 9 and the main text thereat.

124 As Paul Davies states in *Gower's Principles of Modern Company Law* (London, Sweet & Maxwell, 6th edn, 1997) at p 678: '... the modern Chancery judges have a good record of developing the discretion conferred upon them by the statutory unfair prejudice remedy.'

125 See *The Final Report*, above n 1, at para 7.46.

126 [1997] 1 WLR 515.

127 [2000] 1 BCLC 71.

128 [1999] 2 BCLC 516.

129 [1999] 2 BCLC 555.

comparatively simple. A company held a Waste Management Licence, which effectively entitled the company to dump certain types of waste in a large hole in the ground. However, as is now invariable, the licence was subject to certain obligations in relation to looking after the site not only while the waste was being dumped, but for a substantial time thereafter. When the hole was virtually full, the company got into financial difficulties, and went into liquidation. The question was whether the Waste Management Licence was 'onerous property' which the liquidator could disclaim.[130] I held that the licence was 'property'[131] (at least I got that right) but that, in light of the provisions of the Environmental Protection Legislation,[132] it could not be disclaimed by the liquidator.[133] This meant that the remaining money in the company had to be devoted to looking after the site rather than for paying out to creditors.

The Court of Appeal held that this was wrong, and that the liquidator was entitled to disclaim.[134] I must confess to having been heavily influenced by policy considerations. It was not merely that I thought it was desirable from the public interest point of view that the company's remaining money was used to keep the site as safe as possible in accordance with the terms of the Waste Management Licence, albeit that this was at the expense of the company's creditors. It was also the fact that, if a liquidator could disclaim a Waste Management Licence, then it would be open to a rich and substantial company to go into voluntary liquidation, have the liquidator disclaim the licence, and, at least as I saw it, he could do so without any penalty. That is because, although a disclaimer normally results in the company having to pay compensation to the person who suffers as a result of the disclaimer,[135] it appeared to me very difficult to see how anyone could claim compensation under that provision when a Waste Management Licence is disclaimed.[136] The Court of Appeal took the view that the terms of the legislation did not prevent the liquidator from disclaiming the licence.

8 CONCLUSIONS

Since the foundation of our modern system of company law about 150 years ago, the courts have played a central role in the development and application of the law. This is a role the courts continue to perform to this day. When the work of the Company Law Steering Group is finally implemented in a new legislation the courts will be expected to continue in this tradition. We have come to expect a great deal from the courts in this field, and I hope that the courts have generally lived up to this high public expectation. Although the courts have on occasion jumped the gun in interpreting certain statutory provisions, their endeavours have usually served only to pre-empt intervention by Parliament on the relevant matter. By a process of trial and error, I think that we have usually arrived at the correct solution. This is not, however, a call for complacency.

---

130 See Insolvency Act 1986, s 178.
131 See generally Insolvency Act 1986, s 436.
132 See generally Environmental Protection Act 1990, Part 2.
133 See [1999] 2 BCLC 516.
134 See [1999] 2 BCLC 555.
135 See Insolvency Act 1986, s 178(6).
136 See generally [1999] 2 BCLC 516 at pp 530–32.

Although the courts will continue to play a central role in the development of company law, they cannot be expected to bear the sole burden. In this respect the proposal for a new Company Law and Reporting Commission (CLRC) and also a new Standards Board to advise and review the law is to be welcomed.[137]

---

137 See generally *The Final Report*, above n 1, at pp 98–130.

PART 2

CONTEMPORARY COMPANY ISSUES

CHAPTER 4

LEGAL STRUCTURES FOR SMALL BUSINESSES

Diana Faber

1 INTRODUCTION

This essay presents a chronological account of the various law reform projects that have affected small businesses in recent years. The essay focuses on small businesses for two main reasons. The first is that they are of vital importance to the UK economy and the second reason, which is linked to the first, is the extent to which recent law reform projects have focused on them. The Small Business Service of the DTI defines as 'small' a business with 50 or fewer employees. Over 99% of businesses in the UK are small and they account for 44% of non-government employment and 37% of turnover.[1] In the purely corporate sphere 29.5% of companies fall within that definition of small.[2] The Small Business Service of the DTI has said, 'Most of the moderate growth in the business population between 1995 and 2000 has been in the number of 'micro' businesses employing fewer than 10 people and in the number of one-person companies'.[3] This essay shows that, during the last 40 years, consideration of the problems encountered by small businesses has led to repeated mention of eight important issues. Not all of these issues are relevant to all small businesses in that some are run by sophisticated entrepreneurs who are not troubled by ignorance of the law, or ineptitude in running a business. The recurring issues are:

(a) restriction of access to limited liability;

(b) creation of a new form of limited liability corporate body;

(c) burden of companies legislation relating to disclosure;

(d) difficulties in sourcing finance;

(e) ignorance as to the effect of company law;

(f) general difficulties in running businesses;

(g) simplification and restructuring of companies legislation; and

(h) reform of partnership law.

Most of these issues have been, or are, the subject of detailed consideration and debate. The historical review has led the author to conclude, however, that there should be further debate and research, not as to limiting access to limited liability, but as to whether or not governments and trade bodies should be encouraging the use by small business of limited liability structures. They may well not be economically efficient, particularly for

---

1   See 'Small and Medium-Sized Enterprise (SME) Statistics for the UK, 2000' (DTI Small Business Service press release, 21 June 2001), available at www.sbs.gov.uk.
2   Statistics on the Small Business Service website at www.sbs.gov.uk/statistics.
3   See n 1 above.

the smallest companies and for their small business creditors. There should also be greater dissemination of information as to the consequences of incorporating with limited liability and as to the consequences of doing business with such structures. The outcome of further research and debate may suggest that it would be better for small businesses if governments and others were to promote the use by small businesses of ordinary partnerships rather than limited liability structures.

2 DEFINITIONS

In 1994 the Department of Trade and Industry published a consultative document seeking views on the Law Commission's feasibility study on reform of the law applicable to private companies.[4] In their study the Law Commission pointed out the lack of consensus as to the definition of a small company.[5] They set out nine different definitions which came variously from the European Observatory for Small and Medium Size Enterprises, clearing banks, the Bank of England, VAT legislation, corporation tax legislation, the Fourth Company Law Directive, the Companies Act definition and the 1971 *Bolton Report*.[6] The definition contained in the Companies Act 1985 relates to a company as being a small company if it is a company which satisfies at least two of the following:[7] turnover not exceeding £2.8 million, balance sheet not exceeding £1.4 million and number of employees not exceeding 50. The definition in *The Bolton Report*[8] covered businesses with less than 200 employees. Rather than opt for one of these definitions, or yet another, the Company Law Review Steering Group has sensibly said:

> A company may be regarded as small either because of its economic significance or because of the small number of its shareholders. In the latter case all the shareholders are often also involved in management and such companies are frequently described as 'closely-held' or 'close' companies. Most companies are small on both counts and the Steering Group is concerned with both aspects of small.[9]

3 HISTORICAL REVIEW

The first major review of small company business occurred in 1962 when the Board of Trade set up the Jenkins Committee to review the workings of the Companies Act 1948

---

4   See *The Law Applicable to Private Companies* (London, DTI, November 1994) Document URN 94 529; a consultative document seeking views on the Law Commission's feasibility study on reform of private companies.

5   See *The Law Applicable to Private Companies*, above n 4, at p 7.

6   See generally: *The Law Applicable to Private Companies*, above n 4, at Appendix A; Income and Corporation Taxes Act 1988, s 13 (as amended); Companies Act 1985, s 247; Report of the Committee of Inquiry on Small Firms *Small Firms* (1971) Cmnd 4811 (London, HMSO, 1971); hereafter *The Bolton Report*.

7   See Companies Act 1985, s 247.

8   See above n 6.

9   See Company Law Review Steering Group, consultation document *Modern Company Law for a Competitive Economy: The Strategic Framework* (London, DTI, February 1999); hereafter *The Strategic Framework*, at paras 2.19, 5.2, 5.2.2.

and other companies legislation.[10] The subsequent *Jenkins Report* recorded that the Board of Trade had referred to '[t]he irresponsible multiplication of companies' and to the dangers of abuse to which incorporation by small undercapitalised businesses could give rise.[11] The Committee considered that there was a need to check unnecessary incorporation while making it easier for businesses that would genuinely benefit from incorporation.[12] It gave brief consideration to the issue of whether a new form of corporate body described as a corporate partnership should be created and concluded that it would be undesirable to create another corporate legal vehicle.[13] In considering the issue of disclosure of financial information it recommended the abolition of the distinction between exempt and non-exempt private companies. Exempt private companies were those under the Companies Act 1948 that were not required to file accounts or to have them audited.[14] The Committee considered that the administrative disadvantages of the disclosure requirements should be accepted because disclosure was right 'in principle and necessary to protect those who trade with and extend credit to limited companies'.[15] As a result of *The Jenkins Report*, the Companies Act 1967 abolished exempt private companies.[16]

The next development was in 1969 when the Board of Trade commissioned a Committee of Enquiry known as The Bolton Committee to carry out the first official comprehensive study and report on small firms.[17] The subsequent *Bolton Report* was to serve as a basis for recommendations for future policy. *The Bolton Report* presented an economic analysis of the characteristics, functions and performance of small firms. It identified problems that were specific to small businesses and these were notably in the areas of finance, taxation, general relations with government, management skills, sources of advice, the disclosure provisions of the Companies Act 1967 and form-filling.[18] As a result of one of its recommendations the Small Firms Division of the DTI was established.[19] The division is currently known as 'the Small Business Service'. In 1973, the Government issued a White Paper reviewing the Companies Act 1967 and re-examined some of the unimplemented recommendations of *The Jenkins Report* of 11 years earlier.[20]

---

10 See Board of Trade *Report of the Company Law Committee* (1962) Cmnd 1749 (London, HMSO, 1962); hereafter *The Jenkins Report*.
11 At the request of the Committee, the Board of Trade collected statistics which showed that 20% of companies registered in 1954 had, by mid-1961, gone into liquidation, been struck off the register or become seriously in default in filing returns; see *The Jenkins Report*, above n 10, at para 20.
12 See *The Jenkins Report*, above n 10, at para 20.
13 See *The Jenkins Report*, above n 10, at para 72.
14 See Companies Act 1948, s 129 and Schedule VII, 127.
15 See *The Jenkins Report*, above n 10, at para 61. The Report adhered to this view despite its recognition, at para 60, that accounts are filed some months after the period to which they relate. It considered that, while the accounts may be an unreliable guide as to the present position of the company, over a period of years they are a good indication of the profitability and stability, or otherwise, of the company.
16 See Companies Act 1967, s 2.
17 See *The Bolton Report*, above n 6.
18 See *The Bolton Report*, above n 6, at chapters 12 (finance), 13 (taxation), 9 (relations with government), 10 (management skills and sources of advice), 17 (disclosure) and 15 (form-filling).
19 See the *The Bolton Report*, above n 6, at para 19.10.
20 See White Paper, *Company Law Reform* (1973) Cmnd 5391 (London, HMSO, 1973).

The White Paper stated that the public interest did not require the same amount of disclosure (involving the same amount of administration by the company and the DTI) from smaller companies as from larger companies. It said that there was a case for grading disclosure requirements in accordance with the size and status of the individual company.[21] The government considered that the statutory definitions of public and private companies should be modified to reflect more accurately different responsibilities and requirements of the two corporate forms and suggested that a minimum paid-up capital requirement should be imposed for public companies.[22] The Government considered the adoption of an additional corporate form for small firms but did not commit itself at that time. Instead, it required further evidence in relation to the desirability of a new corporate structure. The Government said that the machinery provided by the Partnership Act 1890, the Limited Partnerships Act 1907 and unlimited company provisions was sufficient or could be made so by amendment.[23] Therefore, no legislation resulted from this White Paper.

In 1981 a DTI Consultative Document specifically addressed the issue of a new form of incorporation and sought comments as to its desirability and characteristics.[24] It annexed a proposal advanced by Professor Gower for a separate, simplified regime for incorporated firms with limited liability. Professor Gower also advocated giving corporate personality to partnerships that would retain unlimited liability status.[25] He suggested that the only way to encourage traders (as opposed to professional practitioners) to use that structure would be to introduce a minimum capital requirement for limited liability private companies in order to encourage use of the unlimited structure.[26] A practical response to Professor Gower's papers came in the Law Society's memorandum by its Standing Committee.[27] This memorandum served to highlight the difficulties of persuading small incorporated companies to change to a new regime. Although, the Law Society Standing Committee was in favour of enabling partnerships to become separate legal entities with unlimited liability status, they argued that, in practice, most small firms would want limited liability.[28] The Standing Committee also pointed out that Professor Gower's suggested new limited liability regime permitted all members to participate in management and this was not considered to appeal to the large numbers of existing incorporated small firms with members who did not wish to participate in this way.[29] In any event, the Standing Committee considered that the numerous different forms of business organisations that existed should not be increased unless there was evidence of a clear demand for change.[30] Its preferred approach was to structure certain

---

21 See *Company Law Reform*, above n 20, at paras 30 and 31.
22 See *Company Law Reform*, above n 20, at para 32.
23 See *Company Law Reform*, above n 20, at para 34.
24 See Department of Trade and Industry *A New Form of Incorporation for Small Firms* (1981) Cmnd 8171 (London, HMSO, 1981).
25 See *A New Form of Incorporation for Small Firms*, above n 24, at para 11.
26 See *A New Form of Incorporation for Small Firms*, above n 24, at para 11.
27 See Law Society, Memorandum by the Society's Standing Committee on Company Law *A New Form of Incorporation for Small Firms* (1981) No 79 (London, The Law Society, 1981).
28 See *A New Form Of Incorporation For Small Firms*, above n 27, at para 3.
29 See *A New Form Of Incorporation For Small Firms*, above n 27, at p 7.
30 See *A New Form Of Incorporation For Small Firms*, above n 27, at para 1.

requirements of the Companies Act, such as the accounting rules, by reference to the size, rather than the classification of the company.[31] No action was taken in relation to the 1981 Consultative Document. In 1994 the author of this essay enquired of the DTI as to the reasons for this and she was told that there had been no overwhelming support for any of the changes proposed. It was not possible, however, to obtain copies of other responses to the DTI's consultation document other than that of the Law Society.

In 1981 the new Companies Act did not create a new form of incorporation for small firms. However, the legislation, now consolidated in Part VII of the Companies Act 1985, did enact a more lenient regime for small and medium-sized companies in relation to the filing of accounts. The Companies Act 1989 brought further deregulation to private companies. Written resolutions were allowed in certain circumstances in place of notices and meetings. An elective regime was introduced under which shareholders could, by unanimous resolution, resolve not to hold AGMs and to dispense with requirements to lay accounts and to appoint auditors at such meetings. It should be noted that a number of these reforms reflected European Directives, for example as to the filing, preparation and auditing of accounts.[32] When, in 1992, Regulations were brought into force which permitted the creation of single member private limited liability companies these too reflected the provision of a European Directive.[33]

In the 1990s, a number of business organisations and academics conducted empirical research and published papers that examined the problems of small businesses and considered possible options for reform. These included the Manchester Business School,[34] Freedman and Godwin,[35] Professor Sealy,[36] Hicks, Drury and Smallcombe[37] and The Institute of Advanced Legal Studies.[38]

The next Government project started in November 1992 when the DTI announced a review of a wide range of specific company law topics. One of the areas chosen for review at that time was the law related to private companies and the DTI set up a working group to examine the needs of small private companies. The group identified as the type of company which might benefit most from simplification of company law as the private company in which there was no division of ownership and control and which had a small number of owners. It denominated those companies as 'proprietary' and, by the end of 1993, it had identified three options for reform in this area. The first option was a new form of incorporation as, effectively, an incorporated partnership, possibly modelled on

---

31 See *A New Form Of Incorporation For Small Firms,* above n 27, at para 3.

32 See: First Company Law Directive, 68/151/EEC (OJ Sp Ed 1968, at p 41); Fourth Company Law Directive, 78/660/EEC (OJ L222, 14.8.1978, at p 11).

33 See: Twelfth Company Law Directive, 89/667/EEC (OJ L395, 30.12.1989, at p 40) and Companies Act 1985, s 1(3A).

34 See Forum of Private Business *A Report into Business Legal Structures* (1991), research by Manchester Business School.

35 See Freedman and Godwin 'Incorporating the Micro Business: Perceptions and Misperceptions' in Hughes and Storey (eds) *Finance and the Small Firm* (London, Routledge, 1995). See also Freedman 'Small Businesses and the Corporate Form: Burden or Privilege?' (1994) 57 MLR 555.

36 See Sealy 'Small Company Legislation' (1993) *Law Society Gazette,* 8 December, at p 16.

37 See Hicks, Drury and Smallcombe, *Alternative Company Structures for Small Businesses,* Association of Chartered Certified Accountants (1995) Research Report 42 (London, ACCA, 1995).

38 See 'The Quest for an Ideal Legal Form for Small Businesses' in Rider and Andenas (eds) *Developments in European Company Law Volume 2* (London, Kluwer Law International, 1997).

the South African Close Corporations Act 1984. The second option was to disapply all the sections of the Companies Act 1985 that were unnecessary for proprietary companies and to draw together the remaining sections in a separate part of the Act or in separate legislation. The provisions governing a company's internal relations would be replaced by more flexible ones. The third option was to extend the elective regime by using the regulation-making power contained in s 117 of the Companies Act 1989.

At the beginning of 1994, when the author joined the Law Commission, the DTI asked the Commission (in consultation with the Scottish Law Commission) to continue the work on private companies building on the working group's proposals. However, the Law Commission had a number of anxieties. Their first concern was that they did not think it correct that the DTI had sought to limit their considerations to the options set out in the working group's paper. South Africa was not the only country that had introduced legislation designed to assist small businesses and they wanted to look at the structure of the legislation in other jurisdictions. The working group had concentrated on proprietary companies but, at that time, there were no published statistics evidencing that there were a significant number of such companies in this country. The Law Commission wanted to know whether a reform of company law concentrating on proprietary companies would assist a significant number of small businesses in this country. The DTI needed a result within three or four months and the Law Commission formed the view that all that could be done within that time was to determine the extent to which a reform of company law would be useful to small businesses and, if reform would be useful, what direction it should take. The Law Commission therefore carried out a feasibility study that the DTI later published in a Consultation Document.[39]

The Law Commission identified certain desirable features which should underpin any future reform of the structures available for small businesses. The first was simplicity and brevity in legislation and, in particular, the removal of legislative provisions which did not apply to such businesses. The second desirable feature was flexibility in order to meet the varying needs of small businesses, including those with sleeping owners or those where shares were inherited. Part of the issue of flexibility was whether there should be a limit on the availability of the business vehicle by reference to the number of shareholders. A third feature was that it should be inexpensive, in other words there was a suggestion that the statute should itself provide a variety of standard form packages of rights and obligations from which people could select the most appropriate vehicle for their business. A fourth, and probably the most important feature, was the need for an incremental approach to company law. By this was meant that future conversion to a larger form of corporation or expansion should not involve taking on a completely new legal structure with different rights and obligations. Instead, the requirements necessary for the larger form of corporation should be added to those of the existing structure allowing members to build on the knowledge and experience which they have already acquired.

The Law Commission also considered whether people would want an entirely new legal structure in which to conduct their business. An examination of the research available at that date suggested there would be an equivocal response. The Law

---

39   See n 4 above.

Commission also discussed whether a new structure would solve the problems of small businesses. They considered the available literature and research and held discussions with more than 70 people, some of whom represented organisations and others who gave individual views. Their investigations produced a fairly obvious result, which was that the main problems encountered by small businesses related to the financial and administrative burdens. The financial problems were compounded by a lack of financial management and marketing skills in those running the business. The Law Commission noted that, by facilitating access to limited liability, the financial problems felt by the general business community might be increased if small undercapitalised firms were encouraged to incorporate. This was because their creditors might well be other small businesses whose inability to collect debts (for example, if the company became insolvent) would be exacerbated by an increase in the number of such companies. These points reflected the evidence which had been presented to the Jenkins Committee in 1962. The Law Commission also pointed out that incorporation could cause problems not only for creditors but also for the owners of small businesses themselves. Empirical research showed that many people believed that incorporation with limited liability would provide status and credibility for their businesses; they also wanted the protection of limited liability. The research also found that they may have been using such structures in response to pressure from banks or other third parties to do so.[40] However, the research also revealed incorporators' disappointment with the reality of the limited liability company because it was undermined, in practice, by the demands of the banks and other major trade creditors for personal guarantees from the businesses' owners or from their family members and because the use of that form led to external burdens such as auditing and filing accounts.

There was also an external obstacle to the Law Commission pursuing the creation of a new legal structure at that time. That was the DTI's own review, which was considering a number of topics relevant to such an exercise. The Law Commission's work could not have ignored the outcome of the Government review so the timing was wrong for work on the creation of a new legal structure or the simplification of the existing regime. It had to wait in any event until the outcome of the DTI work.[41]

The Law Commission's feasibility study did suggest that a number of areas of company law could be usefully reformed to advance the interests of small businesses. These included a requirement for clarification as to the law relating to directors' duties and the simplification of the shareholder remedies regime.[42] The study also revealed calls for the reform of partnership law. It was suggested that a reform of partnership law could assist as many, if not more, small businesses as would a reform of company law. In this

---

40   See Freedman and Godwin, above n 35.

41   At about the same time as the Law Commission was working in this area in 1994, the European Commission launched a new integrated programme directed at improving conditions for small and medium-sized enterprises. It published a communication in relation to improving the tax environment for smaller companies and a recommendation on late payments. It consulted on proposals to provide a favourable tax environment and simple procedures to facilitate business transfers (for example, on death or retirement) and to encourage growth; see European Commission *Programme for Improving Conditions for Small and Medium-Sized Enterprises*: COM(94)207 Final and COM(94)206 Final.

42   The Law Commissions later carried out projects on both those topics; See: *Shareholder Remedies* Report No 246 (1997) Cm 3769 (London, TSO, 1997); *Company Directors: Regulating Conflicts of Interests and Formulating a Statement of Duties* Report No 261 (1999) Cm 4436 (London, TSO, 1999).

regard the impact of partnerships on the UK economy is often underestimated. There are almost as many partnerships in the UK as there are trading companies. For example, in 2000 there were 670,905 partnerships and 825,445 trading companies (private and public).[43] When the DTI published the feasibility study they sought views on its content. Of the 42 respondents to the DTI consultation, 29 supported the idea of partnership law reform and five considered that a new incorporated limited liability structure would assist small business.

The next development occurred in February 1997 when the DTI published a Consultation Document inviting comments on proposals for the introduction of a Limited Liability Partnership (LLP) vehicle in the UK. In May of that year the Government announced its intention of consulting on draft legislation to introduce the LLP and in 1998 the draft Bill was published.[44] The introduction to the Consultation Document on the Bill recorded that a number of professions proposed that they should be able to trade with limited liability while retaining the organisational flexibility of a partnership. It was pressure from the large firms of accountants that resulted in this Government initiative. They were concerned about the unlimited liability of partners for very large legal claims, particularly for professional negligence. In large partnerships one partner may have no opportunity to assist another in avoiding such claims. Partners may not know each other and one partner may have no knowledge of another's specialism. By the time the consultation on the Bill had begun, the new Company Law Review had been announced, as had the Law Commission's review of partnership law.[45] According to the DTI, taken together, these studies would represent a comprehensive examination of the range of forms of legal association available to business in Great Britain. However, the introduction went on:

> As any resulting legislation could not be introduced for some considerable time, the Government is now planning to proceed with legislation on the specific question of limited liability partnership in response to a widespread demand to bring legal entities available in Great Britain up-to-date with good international practice in this respect.

The introduction of a new legal structure should, logically, have been postponed until after the fundamental review. Nevertheless, this was not done and the Limited Liability Partnerships Act 2000 came into effect on 1 April 2001. An LLP is a legal entity separate from its members and it has unlimited capacity.[46] The terms on which the members agree to run the LLP between them are confidential and, for the purposes of the Tax Acts, the trade or profession carried on by the LLP will be treated as carried on in partnership by the members, not by the LLP.[47] For these purposes its property will be treated as that of the members. In many other respects, however, the LLP will, effectively, be a company. The new Act provides for regulations to apply provisions of the Companies and Insolvency Acts, in particular on financial disclosure, fraudulent trading and winding up

---

43 See n 2 above for the source of these figures.
44 Department of Trade and Industry *Limited Liability Partnerships, A Consultation Document* URN 98/874; and *Limited Liability Partnerships, Draft Regulations: A Consultation Document* URN 99/1025.
45 See Law Commission *Partnership Law* Consultation Paper No 159 (London, TSO, 2000) which makes a number of provisional recommendations.
46 See Limited Liability Partnerships Act 2000, s 1(2) and (3).
47 See Income and Corporation Taxes Act 1988, s 118ZA (as amended).

and to LLPs and the Limited Liability Partnerships Regulations 2001 came into effect on 6 April giving effect to those.[48] The option of using an LLP is not confined to the regulated professions, as was initially proposed. Paragraphs 7 and 8 of the Regulations contain provisions governing the running of the LLP and relations between members that will apply in the absence of any agreement to the contrary. The latter provisions will be helpful in the event of a small business taking up the form without proper advice as to the type of provisions that they should make.

Apart from the question of limited liability there is another reason why the LLP might be attractive to large or small sophisticated professional partnerships. It is that an incorporated limited liability entity is easier to sell off to larger businesses than a general partnership governed by the Partnership Act 1890. The new LLP will make it much easier for law firms to sell themselves to accountancy practices or to large insurance companies. The former are looking for lawyers with tax and other financial expertise and the latter may want litigation firms.

4 CURRENT WORK

The latest law reform project to affect small businesses is the DTI Company Law Review which commenced in March 1998. The first publication in relation to this Review referred to the availability of different legal structures for small businesses.[49] One of the objectives of the Review was stated to be '[t]o consider whether company law, partnership law, and other legislation which establishes a legal form of business activity together provide an adequate choice of legal vehicle for business at all levels'. It also said, 'The Government believes that those responsible for managing a business enterprise should be given the maximum freedom to select the business vehicle which is most appropriate for their business. Companies are one option ... partnerships are another'.

The Company Law Review Steering Group recognised the economic importance of small companies and, in February 1999, stated that at the start of 1997 small companies accounted for 45% of non-government employment and 40% of turnover.[50] The Steering Group also noted the problems faced by small companies as revealed from responses to their earlier 1998 publication.[51] The first problem was that the legislation was not accessible to those managing and advising small companies because many of the provisions of the Companies Act 1985 did not apply to small private companies and the structure of that Act (which tends to be based on large public companies with detailed adaptations for other companies) is such as to render it opaque and inaccessible for small business users. The determination of which parts of the Companies Act apply to a small company requires a thorough knowledge of the whole Act, the exemptions and

---

48 See generally: Limited Liability Partnerships Act 2000, ss 14 and 15; SI 2001/1090 at paras 4 and 5; and note also para 6 applying certain provisions of the Financial Services and Markets Act 2000 to LLPs.

49 See *Modern Company Law for a Competitive Economy* (London, DTI, March 1998) at chapter 5, paras 5.2 and 5.7.

50 See *Modern Company Law for a Competitive Economy: The Strategic Framework* at paras 2.19, 5.2 and 5.2.2; hereafter *The Strategic Framework*.

51 See n 49 above.

adaptations available and in what circumstances they are available. Another major concern was that the Act contains many provisions that were irrelevant to the requirements of small companies. Thirdly, there was a concern as to the regulation in the Act being too burdensome and failing to serve the purposes of creditor protection for which it was originally designed. The Review document *The Strategic Framework* recognised that for some small businesses the Companies Act form, however improved, might be unduly burdensome as compared to the partnership approach and that an improved partnership form might be particularly beneficial in that context.

The Strategic Framework also noted that there was another important issue which merited further attention relating to the potential for abuse of the limited liability company and the subsequent risk of insolvency and non-payment of debts to which easy access to limited liability status might give rise.[52] However, the Steering Group was not aware of any evidence suggesting that the ease of incorporation (which is cheaper and quicker in the UK than almost anywhere in Europe) had led to unusually high levels of corporate failure or abuse by the standards of international comparison. The Steering Group stated that it had set in hand enquiries on this matter and, in particular, relating to the 'phoenix company' phenomenon (that is, registration of substantially the same company after an insolvent winding up or dissolution) and that it would be addressed in the next phase of their work. The next reference to the phoenix company problem came in November 2000 in the document *Completing the Structure*.[53] This was not linked in any way with the the Steering Group's earlier discussion as to limiting access to limited liability in their March 2000 document, *Developing the Framework*, in which the Steering Group reflected on the responses to this issue as raised in the February 1999 document *The Strategic Framework*.[54] In *Developing the Framework*[55] the Steering Group recorded that a significant majority of respondents said that restricting access to limited liability was undesirable. A number of respondents thought that limited liability status acted as a spur to entrepreneurship and innovation but some cautioned that there was a regulatory 'price' to balance the benefit of limited liability, namely the imposition of enforceable duties and responsibilities on the owners and directors of the company. Very few respondents argued that there should be restricted access to limited liability and the arguments in favour of it fell into two main categories. The first category was that too easy incorporation as a limited liability company meant that people chose the form without fully appreciating the requirements and duties which accompanied it. Secondly, as limited liability restricted the ability of creditors to pursue debts their interests should be adequately protected. In responding to the two arguments in favour of restricting access to limited liability, the Steering Group stated that the first of those concerns could best be tackled through education and information, for example, in a statutory statement of directors' duties and confirmation by directors on appointment that they have read and understood the statement. As for restricting access to limited liability, the most frequently

---

52 See *The Strategic Framework*, above n 50, at para 5.2.12.

53 See *Modern Company Law for a Competitive Economy: Completing the Structure* (London, DTI, November 2000) at para 13.102, hereafter *Completing the Structure*.

54 See *Modern Company Law for a Competitive Economy: Developing the Framework* (London, DTI, March 2000) at pp 305–07, hereafter *Developing the Framework*.

55 See n 54 above.

suggested means of achieving this aim was the minimum capital threshold for incorporation. The Steering Group doubted whether it would provide any meaningful protection for creditors because capital provided on incorporation could be dissipated in trading or by directors' remuneration. They also considered it to be disproportionate and overregulatory. In addressing the second argument in favour of restricting access to limited liability, the Steering Group stated that creditors should have access to information which they needed in order to assess a company's financial status and should be able to rely on controls which operated after incorporation and which could be targeted on those cases where things were likely to go wrong. The Steering Group recommended that small companies which fell below the audit threshold should, nevertheless, be subject to some kind of professional review of their business accounts. They said that this would not require all the evidence necessary for an audit but might give users some confidence in the company's figures while imposing fewer costs on the client.

In May 2000 a review group consisting of officials from the Treasury, the DTI and the Insolvency Service, together with some outside experts, published *A Review of Company Rescue and Business Reconstruction*.[56] In consultation the group had identified 'the apparent reluctance on the part of directors (particularly of small companies) to recognise or respond to the onset of financial difficulties'. Responses to consultation referred to directors' ignorance as to their obligations and called for basic education of directors to include the acquisition of some financial skills.[57] The Review recorded that:

> The lack of a statutory audit requirement for most companies with turnovers below £350,000 (now to be extended to £1 million and possibly in the future to companies with turnovers up to £4.8 million) was felt by many to send the wrong signal to many directors of small businesses. For many small, owner-managed companies the audit was felt to provide an almost unique opportunity for someone outside the company to take a detached view of its activities and prospects and to offer an early warning of problems on the horizon.

In contrast with the Company Law Reform Steering Group, the group conducting the Review of Company Rescues did link the issue of repeat insolvency with the issue of limiting access to limited liability. They said:

> To the extent that a limited liability company is an effective and convenient legal vehicle for the undertaking of enterprises large and small, any restriction on individuals' ability to avail themselves of the facility would clearly be a restriction on enterprise. Where, however, an individual was involved as a director in a second or subsequent failure, there could be an argument for requiring that individual to demonstrate that he or she did in fact possess the basic financial and/or management skills required to discharge the obligations of the position.[58]

Recognising that to be a matter of company law, however, they left it to the Company Law Review to further consider these matters. However, it is important to note the reluctance of the Company Rescue Review Group to subject all company directors to

---

56   See *A Review of Company Rescue and Business Reconstruction* (London, DTI, 2000).
57   Above n 56, at paras 102–03.
58   Above n 56, at para 113.

mandatory qualification requirements because, as they put it, 'only a small minority of companies ... become insolvent in any year, a requirement on all company directors [to be subject to qualification requirements] driven by insolvency considerations would appear to be an example of the dog being wagged by its tail'.[59]

The Company Law Reform Steering Group's consideration of the phoenix company phenomenon in *Completing the Structure* in November 2000 focused on the deliberate abuse of limited liability and contrasted it with the failure of businesses for reasons outside the control of directors such as bad debts or the loss of a major customer.[60] The Group stated that, 'The nature of entrepreneurial risk means that not every business succeeds. It is not our intention to deter honest risk takers from setting up in business again where no misconduct has occurred'. They did not, however, consider repeat failure due to a lack of the necessary managerial or financial skills on the part of the directors of such companies. In the *The Final Report* issued by the Company Law Steering Group, where further consideration was given to phoenix companies, once again the focus was on the deliberate abuse of limited liability.[61] At one point in *The Final Report*, however, there was another approach to protection of creditors. It was to be found in the chapter dealing with directors' duties.[62] Here, the Steering Group recommended that a new highlevel statutory statement of directors' duties should be introduced which was to be located in a schedule to a newly reformed Companies Act.[63] On formation each company director would be required to provide the registrar of companies with a statement confirming that he had read the new statutory statement of directors' duties.[64] The Steering Group also noted in *The Final Report* that there has been criticism that the responsibility of company management not to abuse limited liability had not been given sufficient attention. Responding to this criticism the Steering Group recommended that there should be incorporated into the statutory statement of directors' duties principles requiring directors to have regard to the interests of creditors.[65] In the author's view, however, when considering small businesses it would be better if the directors were informed of the consequences of not paying attention to the interests of creditors. Instead of, or in addition to, dealing with the issue as a legal duty, the information shown to directors should set out the risks of personal liability should the company become insolvent.[66] This would encourage directors to act properly from the outset and, where in doubt, to seek advice.

Turning now to the recommendations in *The Final Report* as to accounts and auditing. The Steering Group proposed that the small companies accounting regime should apply to companies that met any two of the following criteria:

(a) turnover of no more than £4.8 million;

---

59 Above n 56, at para 113.

60 See *Completing the Structure*, above n 53, at paras 13.102–13.110.

61 See *Modern Company Law for a Competitive Economy: The Final Report* in 2 Volumes (London, DTI, 2001) at paras 15.55–15.77, hereafter *The Final Report*.

62 See *The Final Report*, above n 61, at paras 3.12–3.20.

63 See *The Final Report*, above n 61, Vol II, at p 376 clause 17; and p 412 Schedule 2.

64 See *The Final Report*, above n 61, Vol II, at p 369 clause 5(1)(j).

65 See *The Final Report*, above n 61, at para 3.13.

66 See Insolvency Act 1986, s 214.

(b) balance sheet total of no more than £2.4 million; and

(c) number of employees of no more than 50.[67]

Such companies would no longer be able to file 'abbreviated accounts' and the form and content would, in future, be set entirely by standards and not in part by statute. Accounts would have to be filed within seven months from the financial year-end. The Government has already raised the company audit threshold to £1 million turnover[68] and the Steering Group noted that the Government had also announced its intention to exempt all small companies from the audit requirement once the Steering Group had finished its work on the independent professional review (IPR). The Steering Group contemplated that the IPR would be used only for companies with turnovers of more than £1million.[69] If that were the case then 84% of companies would be exempt from any independent financial review.[70]

Turning now to the proposals for substantive company law reform for small businesses. The Steering Group's document *Completing the Structure*[71] distinguished between two broad approaches to the reform of company law for small businesses. The first was to create a separate free-standing vehicle for small companies and the second was an integrated approach perhaps based on New Zealand legislation.[72] Earlier research had shown that more than 70% of UK companies had one or two shareholders and 90% have fewer than five.[73] It was not possible to ascertain the number of companies where there was a complete identity of directors and shareholders although a small-scale survey of company auditors indicated that a significant proportion of companies fell into this category.[74] There is still no statistically significant evidence on this issue although it is six years since the Law Commission pointed to its absence. The Steering Group examined whether there was any benefit in creating a specific set of provisions designed for owner-managed companies and concluded that the benefit to owner-managed companies of such a set of provisions would be very small compared to significant disadvantages. The document *Completing the Structure* reflected the outcome of consultation on three models for owner-managed companies. It recorded that there was very little enthusiasm for any of them.[75] The majority view was that the proposals addressed to the needs of private companies would meet the needs of small companies while avoiding transitional problems for companies that wish to grow. The Steering Group remained of the view that a separate form of incorporation for small companies would be unwise because the company that outgrew the criteria for being small would need to re-incorporate or to go

---

67   See *The Final Report*, above n 61, at para 2.32.
68   See the Companies Act 1985 (Audit Exemption) (Amendment) Regulations 2000, SI 2000/1430.
69   See *The Final Report*, above n 61, at para 2.33.
70   See *Statutory Audit Requirement for Smaller Companies, A Consultative Document* (London, DTI, October 1999) document URN No 99/1115 which states that of 750,000 active companies, 520,000 had turnovers of up to £350,000 and 110,000 had turnovers of between £350,000 and £1 million.
71   See n 53 above.
72   See the New Zealand Companies Act 1993.
73   See *Developing the Framework*, above n 54, at paras 6.8–6.9.
74   See *Developing the Framework*, above n 54, at para 6.9.
75   See *Completing the Structure*, above n 53, at para 2.35.

through some form of conversion process.[76] That would constitute a barrier to growth and act as a trap for the unwary in that a company might find that, inadvertently, it had ceased to satisfy the criteria for being considered small and yet had failed to take the steps necessary for conversion.[77]

The final recommendations of the Steering Group contain significant reforms insofar as they affect small companies.[78] For example, the common law rule that if a decision of the company's members is unanimous, then there is no need to comply with any formalities, will be given statutory effect.[79] The package of reforms for small companies includes: reducing the period of notice for shareholder meetings; relaxing the requirement for unanimity to pass written resolutions; introducing a simpler capital maintenance regime; removing requirements for shareholder authorisation for directors to allot shares; abolishing the requirement for a company secretary; a modified Part 10 relating to directors' conflicts of interests; provisions to encourage the use of arbitration rather than litigation in shareholder disputes; the production of a separate and updated model constitution (that is, a revised Table A) for private companies focusing on the needs of very small and/or closely held companies; and the automatic inclusion of all the provisions currently within the elective regime. It follows that, unless on registration, or later, members opted to include them, there would be no requirement to hold AGMs, nor to lay accounts or to appoint auditors annually in such meetings. This package of proposals for private companies affects all aspects of a company's operations and in substance it amounts to comprehensive simplification of the law.

One of the recurring themes of the Company Law Review was the difficulties posed by the structure of the current companies legislation with regard to accessibility and difficulty of understanding for small businesses and their advisers. These problems are addressed in Chapter 2 of *The Final Report* and in Volume II of that Report which includes 84 draft clauses of a new proposed Companies Bill in an attempt to clarify these matters.[80] The Steering Group's aim in producing *The Final Report* was that the new legislation should be structured in such a way that the provisions that apply to small companies are easily identifiable. It was not possible for the Steering Group to draft an entire Companies Bill and so *The Final Report* is more modest in its approach, setting out some of the more crucial aspects which should underpin a new Companies Act. It states that provisions applying to private companies should not be tailpieces to those for public companies. It states that in some areas separation of provisions for public and private companies would be artificial and so would lead to more complex legislation; in those areas the Steering Group considers that law must be as simple as possible for all types of company. It states the desirability of the core provisions of the legislation being based on the needs of private companies. The Steering Group has not adopted the New Zealand approach of a basic Companies Act which governs all private companies leaving the provisions which apply only to those companies which sell shares publicly and/or list to be dealt with in other additional legislation and/or standards and/or codes. The author regrets that the Steering Group did not follow the New Zealand approach. This is

---

76 See *The Final Report*, above n 61, at para 2.7.
77 See *The Final Report*, above n 61, at para 2.7.
78 See generally *The Final Report*, above n 61, at Chapter 2.
79 See *The Final Report*, above n 61, at para 2.14.
80 See *The Final Report*, above n 61, Volume 1 at paras 2.34–2.37; and Volume II at pp 362–415.

especially the case given that 99% of UK companies are private. That approach would keep irrelevant provisions out of the legislation to which private companies and their advisers refer. In this respect the draft clauses proposed by the Steering Group do not augur well for the simplicity or accessibility of any new legislation.[81] Clauses 13–15 and 29–46 contained in *The Final Report* apply only to public companies. Although the headings of these clauses indicate clearly that they only apply to public companies, they should, nevertheless, be physically separated from the provisions applicable to private companies. The author does not accept that an overlap of some provisions is a good reason to leave those applicable solely to public companies in the middle of provisions applicable to private companies. The effect of this approach is to burden private companies with unnecessary complexity in reading the proposed legislation. It is hoped that these provisions will be separated in any final version which is enacted.

The Steering Group also recommended mechanisms be put in place for keeping the operation of company law and governance under review.[82] A standing commission or committee on company law established for that purpose is vital to the future maintenance of quality and utility of any new legislation. The Steering Group further suggested that a separate committee be established to deal with the needs of private companies by way of providing advice to the main committee and to the bodies responsible for standard setting.[83] It would not have any power itself to issue rules or guidance or take enforcement action. Provided that the main committee does indeed take its views into account then a lack of such powers would not be fatal to its effectiveness. It should, as a minimum, however, be entitled to funds to enable it to publish its own annual report.

In September 2000 the Law Commission published a consultation paper on the reform of ordinary partnership law.[84] They found the major problems in partnership law to be threefold.[85] The first major problem was the lack of separate legal personality for the partnership which led to practical difficulties in relation to property ownership and to continuity of rights and obligations. The second problem concerned the current law which often led to unnecessary dissolution of partnerships. The third major problem related to the rules on winding up the affairs of dissolved partnerships which led to protracted and expensive proceedings. The Law Commission made a number of provisional proposals for radical law reform in this area to tackle these problems. First, they suggested that legal personality be granted to partnerships thereby allowing a continuity in business despite changes in the membership of the partnership. Second, they provisionally proposed that whether or not partnerships had legal personality, partnerships should not necessarily be dissolved on a change in membership. The Law Commission also made suggestions as to how continuity could be achieved in particular circumstances such as death or departure of one partner. Detailed proposals were also made for dealing with winding up dissolved partnerships. A wide range of other topics were also considered in the Consultation Paper.

---

81 See generally *The Final Report*, above n 61, Volume II at pp 362–415.
82 See generally *The Final Report*, above n 61, at Chapter 5.
83 See *The Final Report*, above n 61, at para 5.75.
84 See Law Commission *Partnership Law* Consultation Paper No 159 (London, TSO, 2000).
85 See *Partnership Law*, above n 84, at paras 3.1–3.5.

5 FUTURE WORK

The eight issues outlined at the start of this essay have all been subjected to extensive debate and research and much of this work is ongoing. Nevertheless, a major theme or issue has been neglected in the UK. This relates to the question of whether or not the use of limited liability structures by small businesses should be positively encouraged. The Company Law Steering Group has taken the view that law reform should facilitate the use of limited liability vehicles by small businesses. The author of this essay supports law reform that clarifies the law so as to enable those governed by it to ascertain its effect. Those small businesses which are run to produce an income for a small number of people who work in them but which do not produce large profits should not be forced to employ specialists to advise them on their rights and obligations. The law applicable to such businesses should be accessible to and comprehensible by non-specialist lawyers and to lay advisers to small businesses. The author does not suggest that limited liability should *not* be available to small businesses. She supports the view of the Government that those responsible for managing a business enterprise should be given maximum freedom to select the business vehicle most appropriate for their business. This does not, however, obviate the need for research and debate as to whether Government should be encouraging small businesses to take up limited liability. As the above chronological review shows, the problems arising from small business using the corporate form are not restricted to dealing with legislative complexity and administrative burdens. Both small companies and those dealing with them encounter other difficulties. There is a need for further research and then principled debate based on such research. Professor Freedman has set the process going in a recent article.[86] Supporters of the use of limited liability rely heavily on its purported efficiency based on economic analysis. This analysis can be challenged, particularly in relation to closely held companies. Freedman, for example, mounts a most convincing challenge and the following account is drawn entirely from that article which should be read in its entirety.

In economic analysis, the test for efficiency in a legal structure is threefold:

(a) it should allocate risk to those most capable of bearing it;

(b) it should create optimal levels of risk taking, that is, ventures with net positive value to society but not others should be undertaken; and

(c) it should reduce transaction and monitoring costs.

It is said that limited liability meets these tests for the following reasons. It decreases the need to monitor agents in that the less risk a shareholder has the less it is worth monitoring the company directors. There is less need to monitor other shareholders as their wealth is irrelevant. Limited liability promotes the free transfer of shares; they trade at one price regardless of the identity of the seller or purchaser thus limiting the amount of investigation and negotiation needed on the part of the buyer. Trading facilitates the control of the managers of the company through the market price of the shares. Investors in a limited liability company reduce their risk through diversification but in an unlimited liability regime diversification increases risk since the investor could lose all his wealth on the failure of one firm. Diversification by investors in turn enables the managers to enter

---

86   See Freedman 'Limited Liability: Large Company Theory and Small Firms' (2000) 63 MLR 317.

into risky ventures without risking the entire wealth of their investors. This increases the capital available for potentially risky projects.

Freedman goes on to set out the arguments that undermine these points. There is a challenge to the statement that a limited liability company allocates risk to those most capable of bearing it. Rather it shifts the risk of failure onto creditors from shareholders. This is said to be more efficient than a system in which shareholders bear all the risks for a number of reasons. Creditors such as banks often have specialist knowledge and skills and so are better than shareholders at monitoring managers. They can protect themselves by charging interest and taking security. Such measures, of course, *increase* transaction costs. The description of this shift of risk as 'efficient' does not take account of the risks run by small creditors, who may well be other small businesses and who do not have the bargaining power of banks to protect themselves nor of the risks of involuntary creditors such as tort victims. The desirability of diversification has been challenged on the basis that if there is a concentration of holding, the owner will have a greater incentive to monitor the managers without others 'free-riding' on his efforts.

Turning to small closely held businesses, Freedman points out that it is in respect of these entities that the efficiency theory is most clearly challengeable. So far as savings of monitoring costs are concerned, owners and managers may be an identical group or even a single person so in the absence of the separation of ownership and control this benefit of limited liability falls away. Additionally, because the number of shareholders is small, they can monitor each other. Shares in such companies are not usually freely marketable and so the control through market forces is missing. As for diversification, the owners of an owner-managed firm, even if they incorporate with limited liability, may still have to commit all their assets because of a demand for personal guarantees by large creditors. But probably the most important argument against limited liability in the closely held business sphere is that efficient risk bearing may not be achieved. Owner-managers, it is said, have a stronger incentive to attempt to invest insufficient capital to support the ventures they undertake than do those who are diversified shareholders and non-shareholding managers. Freedman and Godwin's research[87] showed that in a small private company it is often the case that the direct investment of the shareholder is very small or even negligible. In that event, risk is not shared at all but just shifted to others. Major lenders will often contract round the limited liability enjoyed by those owning/directing the company such as by taking security or by other means and this, in itself, produces transaction costs which it is said that limited liability removes. Trade creditors with less bargaining power and involuntary creditors cannot shift the risk back.

---

87 See n 35 above.

6 CONCLUSIONS

In the UK there is a need for more research and principled debate of the issues raised in Freedman's article.[88] Empirical studies should compare the costs of setting up and of running limited liability businesses against those of unlimited liability businesses. They should also compare the costs to third parties of doing business with the different types of business structure. There should also be an investigation into the capitalisation of small companies and the effect of the failure of small limited liability businesses on other small businesses. Insolvency practitioners should assist such work by disgorging papers on the insolvency of small firms so that statistics could be obtained on the following issues: whether after government creditors, other small businesses suffer more than large businesses from such failures and whether small businesses suffer more from the failure of limited liability companies than from the failure of unlimited liability firms. Socio-legal research could investigate whether the proprietors of small limited liability businesses are less concerned about accretion of debt than partners and sole traders.

In an ideal world such research and debate would have been conducted before the LLP legislation was introduced and before the most recent consideration of company law reform for small businesses. Now that all that work has been completed, however, it would be unattractive to delay further legislation for the additional research and debate to take place. It could be organised and reviewed by the proposed new standing bodies on company law and taken into account in their future recommendations. Such research and debate would enable government and non-governmental bodies alike to make informed decisions as to whether to encourage the use of limited liability structures by small businesses or whether it would be better for the proprietors and their creditors if they were encouraged to use unlimited liability structures.

---

88 See n 86 above.

CHAPTER 5

AN ASSESSMENT OF SECTIONS 35-35B AND 322A OF THE COMPANIES ACT 1985 AND THE PROTECTION OF THIRD PARTIES DEALING WITH COMPANIES

Andrew Griffiths

1 INTRODUCTION

This essay will examine the current state of the law governing the validity and effectiveness of contracts made or authorised by the board of directors (the directors) of a company.[1] A company cannot, of course, 'make' a contract for itself since it does not physically exist. Its existence is a legal fiction and 'its' actions can only be those actions of its directors or other agents purporting to act on its behalf which, in the circumstances, the law attributes to the company.[2] In the United Kingdom's unitary board system of corporate governance,[3] the directors are the principal agent of the company in charge of the management of its affairs and, therefore, the principal repository of the power to make contracts attributable to the company. They are supposed to exercise their powers of management in the best interests of their company, which usually means maximising the overall financial return to the company's shareholders, or 'shareholder value', although the directors do have some discretion to balance the interests of shareholders against those of other 'stakeholders' in the company such as its employees and creditors.[4]

The powers of management vested in the directors of a company are derived from its constitution, which has effect as a contract among the company's shareholders.[5] These powers, including the power to make contracts attributable to the company, can therefore be altered by a resolution sufficient to amend the relevant provision in the constitution.[6] The directors may exercise their powers in their own right or delegate them to subordinate agents, so far as the constitution permits them to do this.[7] When the directors

---

1   In this chapter, the expression 'the directors' will be used to refer to the board of directors of a company, as it is in the Companies Act 1985. The expression will be used in the plural, although in practice a company may have only one director.

2   *Meridian Global Funds Management Asia Ltd v Securities Commission* [1995] 2 AC 500 at p 506 (PC).

3   This expression is used to differentiate this system from dual systems, such as in Germany, where powers to manage the affairs of a company are split between two separate boards, one being responsible for supervising the affairs of the other. It was used in this way in the *Report of the Committee on the Financial Aspects of Corporate Governance* (London, Gee, 1992), hereafter *The Cadbury Report*; and the *Final Report of the Committee on Corporate Governance* (London, Gee, 1998), hereafter *The Hampel Report*.

4   See generally the DTI's Company Law Review referred to in n 10 below. See in particular the proposed restatement of the general principles by which directors are bound in *The Final Report*, below n 10, at Annex C, Schedule 2.

5   Companies Act 1985, s 14.

6   This will usually require a special resolution, but it is possible to entrench provisions and make their removal or amendment more difficult; see n 22 below and the related text.

7   There is usually a general power to delegate the powers of the directors, as in Regulation 72 of Table A; see Companies (Tables A–F) Regulations 1985, SI/1985/805 (Table A). However, certain powers of the directors may not be delegable in this way, at least not unless there is an express provision in the company's constitution permitting delegation. This applies to the directors' power to award remuneration to directors: see *Guinness v Saunders* [1990] 2 AC 663.

exercise the powers vested in them by the constitution, they can be viewed as the company itself, although they do not constitute an 'organ' of the company in the sense used in certain other jurisdictions such as Germany.[8] In particular, the directors' powers are not prescribed by law or set at a minimum level, although law does impose some limits in this respect.[9] The powers of the directors of a particular company depend on the particular terms of its constitution. The DTI's Company Law Review (the Company Law Review) has not recommended any change in this respect.[10] The Company Law Review has, however, recommended certain changes to the form of companies' constitutions and certain other changes that may have an impact on the making of contracts attributable to a company and these recommendations will be considered later in this essay.

This essay will focus on the power of the directors to make contracts attributable to a company and the role of a company's constitution in setting limits on that power. It will examine the legal nature of these limits and the legal consequences of exceeding them. It will consider, in particular, the effect of exceeding the directors' power on the validity of the resulting contract and on the ability of the other party to the contract (the 'third party') to be able to enforce the contract against the company. This essay will review the current state of the law, which was reformed by the Companies Act 1989, and consider what further impact the proposals in the Company Law Review may have on this law. It will not, however, consider the additional legal issues raised when the directors delegate authority to make contracts for their company to a subordinate agent of some kind, such as a managing director or a committee of directors, or when a subordinate agent of this kind has purported to make a contract on behalf of a company. The validity of a contract made in the name of a company by a subordinate agent is still governed by the common law of agency, although the power of the directors of a company to authorise others to act on its behalf has a pivotal role in this respect and that power will be addressed in this essay.

2 THE CONSTITUTION OF A COMPANY AND THE POWER OF ITS BOARD

The constitution of a company establishes a governance structure for the management of its affairs. It must divide the necessary powers between the two bodies available in the unitary board system, that is the directors and the company's shareholders in general

---

8   See *El Ajou v Dollar Land Holdings* [1994] 2 All ER 685.

9   See, for example, Part X of the Companies Act 1985.

10 The DTI's Company Law Review Steering Group was set up in March 1998 and published its final report in June 2001: *Modern Company Law for a Competitive Economy: Final Report* (London, DTI, 2001), hereafter *The Final Report*. It raised issues and made provisional recommendations in three wide ranging interim reports: *Modern Company Law for a Competitive Economy: The Strategic Framework* (London, DTI, February 1999), hereafter *The Strategic Framework*; *Modern Company Law for a Competitive Economy: Developing the Framework* (London, DTI, March 2000), hereafter *Developing the Framework*; and *Modern Company Law for a Competitive Economy: Completing the Structure* (London, DTI, November 2000), hereafter *Completing the Structure*. It also published some more focused reports, including one on *Company Formation and Capital Maintenance* (London, DTI, October 1999), hereafter *Company Formation*.

meeting,[11] and may impose restrictions on the scope of these powers or their manner of exercise.[12] In practice, there will be little point in reserving significant powers of management to the shareholders. In small private companies, they are likely to be identical with the directors or at least to overlap with them extensively.[13] In larger companies, and especially in listed public companies, the shareholders are likely to be too large in number to be able to function as an alternative decision making body, unlike, for example, a supervisory board. It is, therefore, usual for extensive powers of management to be vested in a company's directors, but for limits to be set so that certain transactions have to be referred to the shareholders for their approval, giving them a power of veto. Such an approach avoids the need for shareholders to engage in active decision-making and in larger companies the shareholders are likely in any event to have to rely on the directors' guidance to form a view.[14] Limits of this kind may in fact be required by legislation or other regulation.[15]

A company's articles of association usually contain a general vesting of powers of management in its directors in the form of Regulation 70 of Table A and this includes the power to make contracts attributable to the company and to engage in other transactions in the name of the company that may be necessary to conduct its business. Insofar as these powers are not expressly vested in the directors, they vest by default in the shareholders.[16] However, both parts of a company's constitution may affect the scope of the directors' power to make contracts. The objects clause in the Memorandum of Association specifies the goals of the company and thus of its management. It therefore defines the purposes for which the directors may use their powers, including any powers expressly listed in the objects clause,[17] although the typical objects clause will give them a very wide scope in practice.[18] Both the Memorandum and the Articles of a company may impose further limits and restrictions on the extent of these powers beyond those stemming from the objects clause. These limits may take different forms. Certain powers vested in the directors may be expressly qualified, such as the limit on the directors' power to borrow money that was included in older versions of Table A, for example that

---

11   The shareholders in this context may also be referred to as 'the company' or the 'company in general meeting'.

12   It is possible for the constitution to vest powers in a third body by, for example, giving them a power of veto over the decisions of the directors on certain matters; see *Quin & Axtens v Salmon* [1909] AC 442.

13   In such companies, individual shareholders may face the potential problem of being removed from the board of directors and excluded from the company's management. However, simply reserving powers of management to the shareholders would not of itself mitigate this danger, since the shareholders also operate by majority voting. There would need to be more elaborate devices based on entrenched rights such as those referred to in n 22 below.

14   On this, and the directors' distinct fiduciary duty to the shareholders to express an honest opinion, see, for example: *John Crowther v Carpets International* [1990] BCLC 460; and *Rackham v Peek Foods* [1990] BCLC 895.

15   See, for example: Part X of the Companies Act 1985; and the Listing Rules for the London Stock Exchange.

16   The Company Law Review acknowledged this in its survey of the current provisions of Table A; see *Developing the Framework*, above n 10, at Annex D.

17   *Rolled Steel v British Steel* [1986] 1 Ch 246.

18   See, for example, the objects clauses at issue in: *Cotman v Brougham* [1918] AC 514; *Bell Houses v City Wall Properties* [1966] 2 QB 656; *Re New Finance & Mortgage Co* [1975] Ch 420.

annexed to the Companies Act 1948. Some limits, however, may be much harder to discover or to recognise as such. A limit on the directors' powers may, for example, be drafted in the form of rights attached to certain classes of share and these rights may only arise in certain eventualities.[19] Limits drafted in this form may not only be hard to discover, but when they are discovered their meaning may be hard to discern.

There may, therefore, be uncertainty and ambiguity as the precise scope of the directors' powers. Any limit on the directors' powers can only be overridden by obtaining a resolution from the company's shareholders or a class of shareholders sufficient to override the provision setting the limit in question, but this may be time consuming and costly in practice, especially in the case of a public company. Limits on the directors' power to make contracts can, therefore, be graded according to the kind of resolution by which they can be overridden. A simple limit on a power vested in the board means that a complementary power to override the limit vests in the shareholders, who can exercise it by an ordinary resolution.[20] A limit may, however, be more firmly entrenched in the constitution so that it can only be overridden by a resolution sufficient to alter the terms of the constitution itself or by a resolution of a particular class of shareholders.[21] This normally requires at least a special resolution of the shareholders, but it is possible to entrench terms of the constitution so that they cannot even be amended by special resolution, for example by putting them in the Memorandum.[22]

The Company Law Review has recommended that the structure of companies' constitutions be overhauled and that a single document should replace the Memorandum and Articles of Association. It has, however, also recommended that it should still be possible to entrench provisions in the constitution.[23] It has not recommended any revision of the legal role of the constitution as the source of the directors' powers and thus as the source of the limits and restrictions on their power to make contracts for the company. The existing legal consequences that flow from the directors exceeding the limits of their power will therefore continue to apply. Directors have a fiduciary role in relation to their company and have duties analogous to trustees when dealing with the company's assets and property.[24] In particular, the company's constitution governs their powers like a trust deed. The directors therefore owe their company a duty to comply

---

19 See, for example, *Re Torvale Group* [1999] 2 BCLC 605. See also 'QMH restores £2 billion' *The Times* 9 March 1994, which describes a situation in which the directors of a company discovered that they had incurred very substantial debts on its behalf in violation of its constitution.

20 See *Grant v UK Switchback Railway* (1880) 40 Ch D 135.

21 See: *Boschoek v Fuke* [1906] 1 Ch 148; *Quin & Axtens v Salmon* [1909] AC 442; *Re Torvale Group* [1999] 2 BCLC 605.

22 Other such 'entrenching' devices include attaching rights to particular shares, thereby making them class rights: *Cumbrian Newspapers v Cumberland & Westmorland Herald* [1987] Ch 1; giving certain shares enhanced voting rights in certain circumstances: *Bushell v Faith* [1970] AC 1099; and using extrinsic contracts such as a shareholders' agreement to restrict the shareholders' use of their voting rights; *Russell v Northern Bank* [1992] 1 WLR 588.

23 It has recommended that the new form of constitution include an equivalent regulation to Table A's Regulation 70 conferring all the powers of the company on the board, subject to the Companies Act and the terms of the constitution: 'It is suggested that a provision along these lines should be retained, since where the articles do not confer a company's powers on its directors then the power of management vests in the company in general meeting.' See *Developing the Framework*, above n 10, at Annex D.

24 See: *Belmont Finance Corporation v Williams Furniture* [1979] Ch 250; *Bairstow v Queen's Moat Houses* [2001] 2 BCLC 531.

with the terms of its constitution, including the limits on their powers, and face personal liability to their company if they fail to do.[25] The Company Law Review has not proposed the removal or any mitigation of this personal liability and has included an express reference to the duty of directors to act in accordance with their company's constitution in the proposed restatement of the general principles by which directors are bound.[26]

The crucial issue for third parties dealing with a company has been the effect of the directors exceeding their powers on the validity of the resulting contract and their own ability to enforce the contract against the company. The common law principles were a source of great confusion and difficulty, but have been subject to major statutory reform. The impact of this reform on third parties will, therefore, be analysed in the next section of this essay.

3 THE POTENTIAL SETS OF LEGAL CONSEQUENCES OF EXCEEDING THE DIRECTORS' POWERS

If the directors of a company exceed their powers under its constitution when making or authorising the making of a contract, up to three distinct areas of company law may govern the legal consequences. At common law, each of these areas could affect the validity of the contract, and thus the ability of a third party to enforce it, in quite different ways. Statutory reform has mitigated the consequences for third parties stemming from two of these areas, but this mitigation is subject to differing conditions of availability. It is therefore important to address each of these areas in isolation. Case law has not always done this. In particular, the term *'ultra vires'* has often been used indiscriminately to cover a number of distinct legal issues, adding to the confusion and complexity of the law.[27]

The first relevant area of company law is that governing a company's own intrinsic legal ability to make a contract. The power of a company's directors to act on behalf of a company cannot, by definition, exceed the company's own legal ability. There are two principal limits to note in this context. First, statute or some other rule of law may prohibit the company from entering into certain transactions. Natural persons are also, of course, limited in this way and it is in essence an aspect of the general issue of 'illegal contracts'. However, company law prevents companies from making certain kinds of contract that would not be a problem for natural persons. In particular, companies are subject to detailed regulation concerning the raising and maintenance of share capital and this includes the prohibition of the payment of dividends and the repayment of capital to shareholders except in accordance with a strict formal procedure and subject to

---

25 The Companies Act 1989, which mitigated the impact of the directors exceeding their powers on third parties, reiterated this duty and the consequential personal liability in its revision of the Companies Act 1985; see Companies Act 1985, ss 35(3) and 35A(5).

26 'A director of a company must act in accordance with (a) the company's constitution, and (b) decisions taken under the constitution (or by the company, or any class of members, under any enactment or rule of law as to means of taking company or class decisions), and must exercise his powers for their proper purpose', *The Final Report*, above n 10, at Annex C, Schedule 2.

27 See, for example, the Court of Appeal's analysis of *Re David Payne & Co* [1904] 2 Ch 608, *Charterbridge Corporation v Lloyds Bank* [1970] Ch 62, and *Introductions v National Provincial Bank* [1970] Ch 199 in the case of *Rolled Steel v British Steel* [1986] 1 Ch 246.

compliance with strict conditions.[28] Such prohibited contracts are void for illegality and cannot be enforced by the third party.[29] The courts have indicated that, when considering whether a particular transaction is in fact one prohibited by statute, they will look at its substance rather than the form in which it is presented.[30] Thus, when considering a payment to a shareholder of a company that is presented as a legitimate transaction, the courts will consider whether the apparent transaction is genuine or whether in reality it is an illegal dividend or an illegal repayment of capital.

A company's intrinsic ability to make contracts is also limited by the objects clause in its Memorandum,[31] although the practical impact of this limitation has been blunted, first by the general practice of drafting objects clauses in the widest possible terms,[32] and secondly by statutory mitigation. This limit stems from the so-called 'ultra vires doctrine' expounded by the House of Lords in the 19th century in Ashbury Railway Carriage v Riche,[33] which holds that a company only exists for the pursuit of the objects set out in its Memorandum of Association and therefore lacks the contractual capacity to act beyond the limit defined by those objects. In the absence of statutory mitigation, the impact of contractual incapacity on the validity of a contract would be the same as when the company does not legally exist.[34] The contract would be a legal nullity, unenforceable by either party.[35] The statutory mitigation, which will be examined below, has not given a company unlimited contractual capacity, but in practice does appear to have removed contractual incapacity as a significant danger facing third parties. However, a company's objects clause still operates as an overall limit on the powers of a company's directors. The effective removal of contractual incapacity as a legal problem affecting third parties does not, therefore, of itself remove the significance of a company's objects clause for third parties. If a contract is authorised by the directors alone, without the sanction of a

---

28 See generally E Ferran *Company Law & Corporate Finance* (Oxford, OUP, 1999) at pp 355–429.

29 See: *Heald v O'Connor* [1971] 1 WLR 497; *Aveling Barford v Perion* [1989] BCLC 626; *Bairstow v Queen's Moat Houses* [2001] 2 BCLC 531.

30 *Re Halt Garage* [1982] 3 All ER 1016; *Aveling Barford* [1989] BCLC 626. The decision in *Aveling Barford* has been criticised for creating uncertainty about the validity of intra-group transfers of assets which are based on their book value rather than market value; see Mair *'Ultra Vires* and *Aveling Barford'* [1991] *International Company & Commercial Law Review* at p 37. However, the Company Law Review has proposed amending the definition of 'distribution' in the Companies Act 1985, s 263 to reduce this uncertainty: *Completing the Structure*, above n 10, at paras 7.20–7.23; *The Final Report*, above n 10, at para 10.6.

31 See *Ashbury Railway Carriage Co v Riche* (1875) LR 7 HL 653.

32 A practice noted with some consternation by the House of Lords in *Cotman v Brougham* [1918] AC 514. Objects clauses can be given even greater scope by the use of 'sweeper' clauses, which give the directors power to extend the range of the company's activities at their discretion; see, for example, *Bell Houses v City Wall Properties* [1966] 2 QB 656. Note also the very wide definition given to the expression 'to carry on business as a general commercial company' by the Companies Act 1985, s 3A (inserted by the Companies Act 1989), although this does not seem to have led to any reduction in the size of the typical objects clause in practice. The Company Law Review has proposed that s 3A not be retained; see *Company Formation*, above n 10, at para 2.17.

33 (1875) LR 7 HL 653.

34 The House of Lords in *Ashbury* expressly rejected the view that contracts beyond the scope of the objects clause were in effect prohibited by statute and therefore void for illegality. Instead, companies were viewed as having an inherently limited legal existence.

35 There are no cases in which a third party attempted to rely on a company's contractual incapacity to resist enforcement of a contract, although this was acknowledged as a theoretical possibility in the *Bell Houses* case [1966] 2 QB 656.

special resolution of the shareholders,[36] the third party would still have to overcome the distinct legal problem presented by the directors' lack of power to bind the company and that would depend on a different piece of statutory mitigation.

The directors' own lack of power to bind the company is the second area of company law that must be considered. This has also been referred to by the term *'ultra vires'*, although the Court of Appeal in *Rolled Steel v British Steel Corporation* indicated that, to avoid confusion, the term should be used only to refer to a lack of contractual capacity on the part of the company.[37] Lack of power by the directors is an aspect of the general law of agency. The directors act as an agent of their company when exercising their powers and therefore can only bind the company if they have actual or apparent authority to do so.[38] The actual authority of the directors of a company reflects their powers derived from the constitution. It is therefore limited by the terms of the constitution, including the objects clause of the Memorandum. The objects clause may well limit the actual authority of the directors much more narrowly than the contractual capacity of the company itself, in particular where the objects clause lists powers to enter into various kinds of transaction as independent objects of the company. In *Rolled Steel v British Steel*,[39] the Court of Appeal held that the actual authority of the directors to exercise any power derived from the objects clause, whether express or implied, is limited by reference to the purposes of the company as set out in that clause.[40] In other words, when determining the scope of the directors' actual authority as opposed to the company's contractual capacity, sub-clauses setting out mere powers must be construed by reference to those sub-clauses that specify the proper business objectives of the company.

If the directors make a contract for their company that is beyond the scope of their actual authority to bind it, the contract is potentially void and unenforceable by the third party. However, the contract's voidness in this context is conceptually very different from the legal nullity that results from a company's non-existence or its lack of contractual capacity.[41] The third party can enforce the contract if, despite their lack of actual authority, the directors have apparent (or ostensible) authority to make it and the third party does not have actual or constructive notice of the directors' lack of actual authority. The apparent authority of the directors of a company may be much wider that their actual

---

36 This is what is required to amend the objects clause and should therefore be sufficient to override its restrictive effect; see Companies Act 1985, s 35(3).

37 [1986] 2 Ch 246.

38 See generally Markesinis and Munday *An Outline of the Law of Agency* (London, Butterworths, 4th edn, 1998).

39 [1986] 1 Ch 246.

40 [1986] 1 Ch 246 at p 295. See also *Re David Payne* [1904] 2 Ch 608.

41 At common law, a contract made with a company that proves not to exist at the time of contracting is null and void, enforceable by neither party. Such a contract can only have validity if the parties intended that the agent acting on behalf of the non-existent company should be party to the contract, in which case it would have effect as one made with the agent personally. Section 36C of the Companies Act 1985 (originally s 9(2) of the European Communities Act 1972) now provides that all pre-incorporation contracts, that is, contracts made in the name of a company that has not been formed, should take effect as contracts made with the agent personally, unless this result is expressly excluded by the parties; *Phonogram v Lane* [1982] 1 QB 938. However, this provision does not apply to post-dissolution contracts, where the company has been formed but has since been struck off the register, and such a contract may still therefore be a legal nullity under the common law rules; *Cotronic v Dezonie* [1991] BCLC 721. See generally Griffiths 'Agents without Principals' (1993) 13 LS 241.

authority and may reflect the full scope of a company's contractual capacity in relation to those sub-clauses setting out powers as if they were objects.[42] At common law, though, third parties were deemed to have notice of the contents of the company's public file maintained by the Registrar of Companies at Companies House, including those terms of its constitution defining the limits of the directors' powers. At common law therefore, third parties were unable to rely on the directors' apparent authority if their lack of actual authority would have been revealed by an inspection of the constitution. As will be seen below, however, the prejudicial effect of deemed knowledge of a company's constitution has been substantially mitigated by statute, although on different terms from the mitigation of contractual incapacity. A second difference from legal nullity is that the company can validate a contract made by the directors without actual authority by ratifying it, provided that the contract is one that the company is legally able to make. If the contract is ratified, it has the same legal effect as if it had been made with the necessary actual authority. For a company to ratify a contract, there must be a resolution of its shareholders sufficient to override the relevant limit in the constitution on the directors' powers.

A contract made without actual authority therefore has potential validity, which a legal nullity does not enjoy. However, if the third party cannot rely on the directors' apparent authority and if the company does not ratify the contract, then the contract has no legal effect and the third party cannot enforce it. The contract can give the third party no rights against the company. In other words, the company is under no obligation to perform the contract and may recover any consideration that has already passed to the third party.[43] This lack of validity is also conceptually distinct from the provisional validity or 'voidability' that may ensue in other circumstances.[44] A voidable contract has to be rescinded by the company and is valid and effective until rescission. Further, rescission of a voidable contract may be barred, for example if there has been unreasonable delay or the company cannot make restitution of any benefits received by it under the contract.[45] A contract made without actual or apparent authority and which has not been ratified does not have to be rescinded. It simply fails to bind the company. There is a lack of precise terminology to describe the status of such a 'contract', as Nourse LJ recognised in the *Jyske Bank* case:

> Where an agent is known by the other party to a purported contract to have no authority to bind his principal, no contract comes into existence. The agent does not purport to contract on his own behalf and the knowledge of the other party unclothes him of ostensible

42 *Rolled Steel v British Steel* [1986] 1 Ch 246.
43 See: *Rolled Steel v British Steel* [1986] 1 Ch 246; *Guinness v Saunders* [1990] 2 AC 663; *Jyske Bank v Spjeldnaes* (1999) WL 819062.
44 For example, that arising under the Companies Act 1985, ss 322 and 322A. This is also the legal consequence of a contract made in breach of the self-dealing rule: see Lord Goff's judgment in *Guinness v Saunders* [1990] 2 AC 663 and the Court of Appeal's judgments in *Hely-Hutchinson v Brayhead* [1968] 1 QB 549.
45 See: *Guinness v Saunders* [1990] 2 AC 663; *Runciman v Runciman* [1992] BCLC 1084. It has been argued that having these differing sets of consequences is not satisfactory and that establishing a modified version of statutory voidability as the standard set of consequences would be better for third parties in general; see Nolan 'Enacting Civil Remedies in Company Law' (November 2000), available at www.dti.gov.uk/cld/review.htm.

authority to contract on behalf of the principal. Whether or not such a transaction is accurately described as a void contract, it is plainly not voidable. If no contract comes into existence, there is nothing to avoid or rescind, nor can any property pass under it.[46]

At common law therefore, a third party with actual or constructive notice of the directors' lack of authority would have been in the same position as one faced with the company's lack of contractual capacity.

The third relevant area of company law when the directors exceed the limits of their powers derives from the law of equity and reflects the fact that directors have a fiduciary status analogous to that of trustees. Directors owe their company a duty not to exceed the limits of their powers. They also owe it a fiduciary duty not to abuse their powers. They must exercise their powers in good faith in the best interests of the company and not for any collateral or improper purpose.[47] In practice, the limit set on the directors' powers by this duty may extensively coincide with the formal limits set by the constitution,[48] but it triggers a different set of legal consequences reflecting its equitable foundation. If the directors' of a company breach their duties by exceeding or abusing their powers under the constitution, they are personally liable to the company.[49] Third parties may be liable as well, but their liability depends on whether they have actual or constructive knowledge of the directors' breach of duty.[50] Thus, if a third party with such knowledge receives property or other assets from the company, the beneficial ownership of these assets remains with the company and the third party is liable to the company as a constructive trustee.[51] The basis of the third party's liability in this context has been termed 'knowing receipt' or 'recipient liability'.[52]

The next few sections of this essay will examine in more detail the legal consequences for third parties resulting from the general areas of company law described above and the impact of the statutory reform on these consequences. They will also consider how the recommendations of the Company Law Review might affect the relevant law.

---

46 (1999) WL 819062. See also the emphasis on the lack of legal effect of such a contract in *Guinness v Saunders* [1990] 2 AC 663.

47 See: *Re Smith & Fawcett* [1942] Ch 304; *Howard Smith v Ampol* [1974] AC 821. The Company Law Review has proposed that this duty be restated in the following terms: 'A director of a company must in any given case (a) act in the way he decides, in good faith, would be most likely to promote the success of the company for the benefit of its members as a whole ... and (b) in deciding what would be most likely to promote that success, take account in good faith of all the material factors that it is practicable for him to identify,' going on to give an extended definition of these 'material factors'; see *The Final Report*, above n 10, at Annex C, Schedule 2.

48 This was the case in *Rolled Steel v British Steel* [1986] Ch 246 and *Jyske Bank*, above n 43.

49 See: *Re Sharpe* [1892] 1 Ch 154; *Selangor United Rubber Estates v Craddock* [1968] 1 WLR 1555. This liability is strict, but individual directors may be relieved under the Companies Act 1985, s 727.

50 The difference between the terms 'notice' and 'knowledge' in this context will be examined in more detail below. For a general review of judicial attempts to define these terms in detail and distinguish them, see G Moffat *Trusts Law: Texts and Materials* (London, Butterworths, 1999) at pp 553–61.

51 See: *Rolled Steel v British Steel* [1986] 1 Ch 246; *El Ajou v Dollar Land Holdings* [1994] 2 All ER 685; *Jyske Bank v Spjeldnaes* (1999) WL 819062.

52 This is one of the two kinds of accessory liability identified by Lord Selborne in his judgment in *Barnes v Addy* (1874) 9 Ch App 244. See generally *Trusts Law: Texts and Materials*, above n 50, at pp 553–61 and Lord Nicholls 'Knowing Receipt: The Need for a New Landmark' in Cornish, Nolan, O'Sullivan and Virgo (eds) *Restitution: Past, Present and Future* (Oxford, Hart, 1998).

4 EXCEEDING THE COMPANY'S LEGAL CAPACITY

The law regulating a company's capacity is now governed by s 35(1) of the Companies Act 1985 ('s 35'), which was inserted in its current form by the Companies Act 1989:[53]

> The validity of an act done by a company shall not be called into question on the ground of lack of capacity by reason of anything in the company's memorandum.

This reform followed a report commissioned by the DTI (*The Prentice Report*).[54] However, whereas *The Prentice Report* recommended that companies be given the contractual capacity of a natural person, the actual reform held back from going so far and instead sought to counter the impact of contractual incapacity on the validity of the resulting contract and its enforceability by either party.[55] The wording of the section is not completely free from ambiguity and could be interpreted in a way that would negate its obvious intention, for example by holding that an act done by the directors in breach of their duties or of the company's constitution cannot be regarded as 'an act done' by the company.[56] To remove any remaining doubt that the old *ultra vires* doctrine has been abolished and that contractual incapacity is no longer a significant problem for third parties, the Company Law Review has recommended that companies should expressly be given unlimited contractual capacity and that the Companies Act should be amended to include a provision to that effect.[57]

Another potential problem with the current version of s 35 is that the word 'company' may apply only to those companies registered under the Companies Act itself, thus excluding companies incorporated in Northern Ireland, the Isle of Man and the Channel Islands, as well as foreign companies. Section 735(1) of the Companies Act 1985 provides that the word 'company' should be interpreted in this restrictive way 'unless the contrary intention appears' and there is nothing in s 35 that expressly indicates a contrary intention. The Court of Appeal, in an unreported decision on the predecessor of s 35,[58] indicated that 'company' should be interpreted in accordance with s 735(1). Harman J also took this view in *Rover International v Cannon Film Sales*[59] in relation to s 36C of the Companies Act 1985, which gives pre-incorporation contracts effect as contracts made with the agent purporting to act for the non-existent company. In that context, the

---

53 The revised section was inserted by the Companies Act 1989, s 108 and took effect on 4 February 1991.

54 Prentice *Reform of the Ultra Vires Rule: A Consultative Document* (London, DTI, 1986), hereafter *The Prentice Report*. *The Prentice Report* followed an earlier reform of the law by s 9(1) of the European Communities Act 1972, later consolidated as the original version of the Companies Act 1985, s 35. This reform was required to implement the EC's First Directive on the harmonisation of company law (EEC/68/151), which required much greater 'security of transaction' for third parties dealing with companies and provided that limits on the powers of the company's organs should not be relied on against third parties, even if these limits had been disclosed.

55 See the Companies Act 1985, s 35(1).

56 '[D]irectors like any other agents can only bind the company by acts done in accordance with the formal requirements of their agency ... Acts done otherwise than in accordance with these formal requirements will not be the acts of the company'; *per* Browne-Wilkinson LJ in *Rolled Steel v British Steel* [1986] 1 Ch 246 at p 304. See generally E Ferran *Company Law and Corporate Finance* (Oxford, OUP, 1999) at pp 89–97.

57 See *The Final Report*, above n 10, at para 9.10.

58 *Janred Properties v Ente Nazionale Italiane per Il Turismo* (14 July 1983), concerning the European Communities Act 1972, s 9(1).

59 [1987] 1 WLR 1597.

distinction introduced by the restrictive interpretation seems particularly bizarre since s 36C applies to contracts made by non-existent companies, which have not yet been incorporated and may never be incorporated.[60] The specific decision in *Rover International* was reversed by the Foreign Companies (Execution of Documents) Regulations 1994,[61] but these do not apply to s 35.

There are two further limitations on the scope of s 35. First, its effect is restricted in relation to companies which are charities.[62] Whilst the Company Law Review has not recommended any change in this respect, it has not indicated that its proposal that companies should have unlimited contractual capacity should not extend to such companies.[63] Secondly, it only applies to the limitation of a company's contractual capacity by the terms of its objects clause. It does not, therefore, apply to any other restrictions on the intrinsic ability of a company to be a party to a contract and in particular it does not mitigate the impact of statutory prohibitions. Thus, if a contract is found to involve the payment of an illegal dividend or an illegal repayment of capital, a third party cannot use s 35 to overcome the legal consequences of that illegality.[64] Again, there is a need for caution with the terminology used in this area since judges have sometimes referred to contracts that are void for illegality as being *ultra vires* the company.[65]

5 EXCEEDING THE POWERS OF THE BOARD

Section 35 has substantially removed contractual incapacity as a problem facing third parties, but that does not mean that the terms of a company's objects clause are no longer relevant. The powers of the directors are still circumscribed by their company's objects clause and this can only be overridden by a special resolution of the shareholders.[66] Section 35 by itself is therefore only sufficient to ensure the validity of a contract that is not only made or authorised by the directors, but is also ratified by a special resolution. Otherwise, a third party may still have to overcome the distinct legal problem presented by the directors' lack of actual authority to bind the company. This potential problem is now governed by s 35A(1) of the Companies Act 1985 ('s 35A'), which was also inserted by the Companies Act 1989:[67]

> In favour of a person dealing with a company in good faith, the power of the directors to bind the company, or authorise others to do so, shall be deemed to be free of any limitation under the company's constitution.

---

60 See generally on this point Griffiths 'Agents without Principals' (1993) 13 LS 241 at pp 250–52.
61 See SI 1995/1729.
62 See the Companies Act 1985, s 35(4).
63 It has, however, proposed that a specific corporate vehicle be introduced for charities; see *The Final Report*, above n 10, at paras 4.63–4.67.
64 See *Aveling Barford v Perion* [1989] BCLC 626, but see n 30 above on this decision.
65 See, for example: *Aveling Barford v Perion* [1989] BCLC 626; *Bairstow v Queen's Moat Houses* [2000] 1 BCLC 549 and [2001] 2 BCLC 531 (CA).
66 See the Companies Act 1985, s 4.
67 See the Companies Act 1989, s 108.

Section 35A(3) provides that the relevant limitations on the directors' power should include those deriving from resolutions of or agreements between the company's shareholders or a class of shareholders. Unlike s 35, s 35A does not purport to negate the legal problem, but it reduces its impact substantially. Thus, any lack of actual authority on the part of a company's directors due to the terms of its constitution remains a problem for those third parties who are not 'dealing with the company in good faith'. Further, a third party who is also a director of the company, or of its holding company, or a person connected to or a company associated with such a director, is subject to the provisions of s 322A of the Companies Act 1985 ('s 322A'), which qualifies the impact of s 35A. Section 322A will be examined in a later section of this essay. The Company Law Review has proposed that s 35A be retained in its current form.[68] The doubts about the meaning of the term 'company' noted in relation to s 35 also apply here.[69]

Assuming that a third party is not caught by s 322A, s 35A eliminates the potential problem of the directors' lack of actual authority provided that the third party is dealing with the company in good faith. Section 35A(2)(a) provides that 'a person deals with' a company if he is a party to any transaction or other act to which the company is a party', which extends the protection to voluntary and non-commercial transactions as well as contracts in the usual sense. The meaning of 'good faith' is therefore of crucial importance to third parties dealing with companies. Sections 35A provides some elaboration of this term, as does s 35B. Section 35A(2)(b) provides that 'a person shall not be regarded as acting in bad faith by reason only of his knowing that an act is beyond the powers of the directors under the company's constitution'. Section 35A(2)(c) provides that 'a person shall be presumed to have acted in good faith unless the contrary is proved'.[70] Section 35B provides that a third party 'to a transaction with a company is not bound to enquire as to whether it is permitted by the company's Memorandum or as to any limitation on the powers of the board of directors to bind the company or authorise others to do so'. The Company Law Review has proposed that these three refinements should all be retained in their current form.[71]

6 THE EFFECT OF UNAUTHORISED CONTRACTS AT COMMON LAW

It is useful to analyse the elaborations set out in ss 35A and 35B by reference to the common law position, which they were designed to improve. As noted already, a contract made by the directors acting in excess of their powers under the constitution had no legal effect at common law and could not be enforced by the third party unless the directors had apparent authority to make the contract in question or it had been properly ratified by the company. The apparent authority of the directors of a company was governed by two common law doctrines of company law, namely the 'indoor management rule' (also

---

68 See *Company Formation*, above n 10, at paras 2.37–2.40.
69 This protection is also qualified in relation to companies which are charities; see the Companies Act 1985, s 35A(6).
70 See the Companies Act 1985, s 35A(2)(b) and (c).
71 See *Company Formation*, above n 10, at paras 2.37 and 2.40.

known as the 'rule in *Turquand'*) and the doctrine usually referred to by the term 'constructive notice'.

At common law, the presumption that the directors of a company would have unlimited authority to act on its behalf was cut down by the fact that third parties were deemed to know the contents and meaning of the company's public documents and were therefore fixed with knowledge of the terms of its constitution, including the limits on the powers vested in the directors.[72] In any event, the powers of the directors could not exceed the actual contractual capacity of the company. Third parties could not therefore rely on the directors having apparent authority if their lack of actual authority could have been discerned by inspecting the company's public documents.[73] Beyond this, however, third parties dealing with a company in good faith were entitled to assume that acts within its constitution and powers had been properly and duly performed and were not therefore bound to check up on acts of internal management.[74] They did not, for example, have to inquire whether those acting as directors had been properly appointed or that procedural formalities had been properly complied with where due compliance would not itself be a matter of public record.

There is, however, a need for caution with the term 'constructive notice' in this context since it and the related expression 'constructive knowledge' both have wider significance.[75] For this reason, the company law doctrine that third parties are deemed to know the contents of a company's public file will be referred to as 'deemed notice'.[76] The terms 'constructive notice' and 'constructive knowledge' are used to refer to the fact that parties should be taken to know not only what they actually do know, but also what in the circumstances they ought to know. This ensures that the law does not give an unfair advantage to the careless, the reckless and those who deliberately close their minds to the obvious. Thus, constructive notice has been described as 'fault of a lesser degree', which 'embraces everything that a recipient acting with reasonable prudence would have discovered and everything that an agent acting for the recipient in the transaction discovered or should reasonably have discovered'.[77] This does, of course, beg the question of what it is reasonable to expect a third party to infer from the particular circumstances of a transaction and to find out about those acting on behalf of the other party.

---

72 See: *Mahony v East Holyford Mining* (1875) LR 7 HL 869; *Rolled Steel v British Steel* [1986] 1 Ch 246.

73 For example, if the terms of the contract itself violate a limit imposed on the directors or if the contract falls into a category which the constitution expressly requires to be approved by the company's shareholders.

74 The rule derives from *Royal British Bank v Turquand* (1856) 6 E & B 327. This statement of the rule was approved by the House of Lords in *Morris v Kanssen* [1946] AC 459 at p 474 and applied by the Court of Appeal in *Rolled Steel v British Steel* [1986] 1 Ch 246 at p 283.

75 The so-called 'doctrine of constructive notice' in fact originated in the context of conveyancing and it has been argued that it should not be extended to other contexts. The real issue here is the level of knowledge that should in the circumstances be attributed or imputed to a third party and some judges have suggested that the issue should be addressed in those terms: see, for example, the remarks of Vinelott J in *Eagle Trust v SBC Securities* [1993] 1 WLR 484, cited with approval by Knox J in *Cowan de Groot v Eagle Trust* [1992] 4 All ER 700 at p 759d–j.

76 It was referred to as 'deemed notice' in the Companies Act 1989, which abolished it, although this provision was never implemented; see the Companies Act 1989, s 142. The Company Law Review has also used this term in recommending its abolition; see *Company Formation*, above n 10, at para 2.42.

77 *Per* Lord Nicholls in his chapter in *Restitution: Past, Present and Future*, above n 52, at p 235.

The idea of a third party's constructive knowledge has featured in both company law's indoor management rule and in agency law's concept of apparent authority, but it has been given a different emphasis in each case. In the context of the indoor management rule, it is reflected in the principle that third parties cannot rely on the rule if the circumstances are such as to 'put them on inquiry' about the propriety of the transaction. A third party is put on such an inquiry if the transaction is unusual or suspicious, such as where the transaction would appear to be detrimental to the company and especially if any of those acting on behalf of the company are known to have a conflicting personal interest that would give them an incentive to act against its interests.[78] However, where a third party is making an arm's length commercial transaction with a company and giving consideration, as opposed to receiving a gift, the idea of the third parties being put on inquiry must take account of their right to pursue their own commercial interests and they should not, for example, be expected without more to inquire into the reasons lying behind an apparent bargain that is being offered to them.[79] In the context of apparent authority, however, the impact of a third party's constructive knowledge is reflected in the scope of the representation of authority or 'holding out' on which the apparent authority of any agent must be based. Thus, in *Freeman & Lockyer v Buckhurst Properties*,[80] the leading case on the application of the concept of apparent authority to agents acting for companies, Diplock LJ explained a series of previous decisions on the basis that where an agent's apparent authority is based on appointment to an office it does not cover transactions that are unusual for such an agent or which are surrounded by suspicious circumstances, especially if the suspicions of the third party have already been aroused.[81] The third party's constructive knowledge has the same legal effect of exposing them to the consequences of the agent's lack of actual authority, but the route there is different. This difference may, however, have some bearing on how far s 35A has modified the position of third parties at common law when they are dealing with the directors of a company.

At common law, contracts made or authorised by the directors in excess of their powers presented two major problems for third parties. First, it was generally accepted as unrealistic to expect third parties to know and understand the constitution of every company with which they dealt and therefore to know the precise limits set by the constitution on the powers of its directors.[82] Such a presumption went far beyond the kind of prudent and reasonable conduct envisaged by constructive notice in its broader sense. In practice, therefore, the company law doctrine of deemed notice simply exposed third parties to an unpredictable danger that contracts made with companies would prove to be invalid and unenforceable. It also violated the principle of 'security of transaction' enshrined in the EC's First Directive.[83] Secondly, there was a specific problem

---

78   See: *Underwood v Bank of Liverpool* [1924] 1 KB 254; *Rolled Steel v British Steel* [1986] 1 Ch 246; *Northside Developments v Registrar-General* (1990) 170 CLR 146.

79   See the comments of Knox J in *Cowan de Groot v Eagle Trust* [1992] 4 All ER 700 at pp 760–61.

80   [1964] 2 QB 480.

81   See [1964] 2 QB 480 at pp 506–09 discussing: *Biggerstaff v Rowatt's Wharf* [1896] 2 Ch 93; *Houghton v Nothard, Lowe & Wills* [1927] 1 KB 246; *Kreditbank Cassel v Schenkers* [1927] 1 KB 826; *British Thomson-Houston v Federated European Bank* [1932] 2 KB 176; *Rama Corporation v Proved Tin & General Investments* [1952] 2 QB 147.

82   See generally *The Prentice Report*, above n 54.

83   See EEC/68/151.

for third parties that were in fact companies themselves. An agent acting for such a third party in a transaction with another company might be quite unaware of information already acquired about that company by another agent of the third party. This problem of 'institutional knowledge' had to be taken into account when redrawing the boundaries of the knowledge that would be attributed to third parties in general.

7 THE CIRCUMSTANCES IN WHICH THIRD PARTIES CANNOT RELY ON SECTION 35A

The main effect of s 35A is to negate the impact of the doctrine of deemed notice and replace it with a presumption that the directors of a company have unlimited power to make contracts on its behalf. It does not, however, confer unlimited actual authority on the directors of a company, nor does it entitle third parties to rely on their unlimited apparent authority in all circumstances. The third party must be 'dealing with a company in good faith' which begs the question of when would a third party not be so dealing with a company and thus be unable to rely on the directors' unlimited apparent authority. Section 35A places the burden of proving the third party's lack of good faith on the company or whoever else is challenging a third party's ability to rely on the validity of the contract.[84] It also provides that the fact that a third party knows that an act is beyond the powers of the directors does not of itself mean that he is acting in bad faith.[85]

The wording of s 35A implies that bad faith entails something more than knowledge of the directors' lack of authority to bind the company, even where the third party's knowledge is actual rather than constructive. This would go further than *The Prentice Report* recommended. *The Prentice Report* proposed that a third party with actual knowledge of the directors' lack of authority should only be able to enforce a transaction against the company if the company, that is the shareholders, expressly ratified it.[86] Further, *The Prentice Report* proposed that this should also apply where the third party had certain kinds of constructive knowledge, arguing that actual knowledge should extend to a situation where a third party 'wilfully shuts his eyes' or 'wilfully and recklessly fails to make such inquiries as an honest and reasonable man would make'.[87] It concluded on this point:[88]

> The concept of actual knowledge in all likelihood embraces this type of knowledge. A third party should be able to trust appearances, but not appearances known to be false. Also, there will at least be a tincture of a want of probity where a third party proceeds with a contract despite a director's or a board's lack of authority.

The wording used in s 35A must therefore be scrutinised with care to see whether it does in fact go further than this. The reference to 'want of probity' is significant. Directors are

---

84 See the Companies Act 1985, s 35A(2)(c).
85 See the Companies Act 1985, s 35A(2)(b).
86 See *The Prentice Report*, above n 54, at p 32.
87 *The Prentice Report* drew this formulation of constructive notice from *Belmont Finance Corporation v Williams Furniture* [1979] Ch 250 at 267. It also cited Harpum 'The Stranger as Constructive Trustee' (1986) 102 LQR 114 at pp 122–23.
88 See *The Prentice Report*, above n 54, at p 32.

in a position analogous to trustees and are in fact treated as if they were trustees when engaging in transactions involving the transfer of property or assets belonging to the company.[89] Exceeding powers and abusing powers both amount to a breach of trust. If a third party knows that the directors do not have the power to transfer money or other assets of the company through the particular transaction proposed, it is hard to see how that third party can claim to be acting in good faith when accepting the transfer from the directors. The same reasoning should apply where the third party has been put on inquiry because the transaction is unusual or suspicious and thereby has constructive knowledge of the directors' lack of authority.

It is here that the difference in emphasis between the indoor management rule and the concept of apparent authority may have significance. If the unusualness of the transaction or the presence of suspicious circumstances simply removes the transaction from the ambit of the directors' apparent authority at common law, then this effect is negated by the overriding presumption made by s 35A. The third party is protected by s 35A despite these factors. If, however, these factors impose a responsibility on third parties to make further inquiry and it is that which prevents them from being able to rely on the directors' apparent authority, it is arguable that their effect is not negated by s 35A. Instead these factors are relevant to determining whether or not a third party is dealing with the company in good faith. The latter conclusion would be more consistent with the fiduciary nature of the directors' power to make contracts. The impact of the law of agency on the directors' exercise of their powers of management in fact overlaps extensively with the impact of the law of equity and in particular the directors' potential liability for knowing receipt. Thus, in *Rolled Steel v British Steel*,[90] the Court of Appeal held that if a third party received property or assets from a company as a result of a transaction that involves an excess or abuse of its directors' powers and has actual or constructive notice of that excess or abuse, then the third party is liable as a constructive trustee and the company can recover its property accordingly. The Court of Appeal has subsequently endorsed this view in *Jyske Bank v Spjeldnaes*.[91]

The key point to note is that exceeding powers is of itself a breach of the directors' fiduciary duties and s 35A provides that it does not 'affect any liability incurred by the directors, or any other person, by reason of the directors' exceeding their powers'.[92] This essay will, therefore, digress at this point and examine a third party's potential liability for knowing receipt in more detail and then return to consider what guidance this may provide on the meaning of s 35A.

---

89 See *Belmont Finance v Williams Furniture* [1979] Ch 250.
90 [1986] 1 Ch 246 at pp 297–98 and pp 303–04.
91 (1999) WL 819062. This case concerned a company which was the wholly owned Gibraltar subsidiary of a Danish bank. Section 35A was not raised as a defence and it is arguable that it would not apply to such a company. In any event, there was evidence of fraudulent abuse of power as well as the excess of power.
92 See the Companies Act 1985, s 35A(5).

8 ABUSING THE POWERS OF THE DIRECTORS

Third parties face liability for knowing receipt if the directors or any other agent of the company act in breach of their fiduciary duty to exercise their powers in good faith in the best interests of the company. This is still governed by the relevant law of equity. This liability renders the third party a constructive trustee of any property or other assets of the company received by them from the directors or agent in question and this obviously negates the effectiveness of the transaction from the third party's perspective.

In *El Ajou v Dollar Land Holdings*, Hoffmann LJ held that to establish a constructive trust on the basis of knowing receipt, it was necessary to show: (a) a disposal of assets in breach of fiduciary duty; (b) receipt of assets which are traceable as representing those assets; and (c) knowledge on the part of the recipient that the assets are traceable to a breach of fiduciary duty.[93] For third parties dealing with companies, the breach of fiduciary duty may include the directors purporting to exercise powers that have not been vested in them by the constitution, although this form of liability has been associated with fraud or breach by the directors of their duty to exercise their powers in good faith in the best interests of the company.[94] Abuse of power may overlap extensively with excess of power. The component of this liability that has proved most difficult is the third party's knowledge of the breach of fiduciary duty.[95] This includes constructive knowledge as well as actual knowledge, but there is uncertainty as to the standard of fault or carelessness that should be used to gauge a recipient's constructive knowledge.

In *Baden Delvaux and Lecuit v Société Générale*,[96] Peter Gibson J referred to five different mental states that are relevant in this respect: (a) actual knowledge; (b) wilfully shutting one's eyes to the obvious; (c) wilfully and recklessly failing to make such inquiries as an honest and reasonable man would make; (d) knowledge of circumstances which would indicate the facts to an honest and reasonable man; and (e) knowledge of circumstances which would put an honest and reasonable man on inquiry.[97] Where a third party is dealing with an agent acting for a company and is a purchaser of the relevant assets rather than a volunteer, it is clear that the third party's knowledge extends to include that covered in categories (a)–(c), but doubt has been expressed about categories (d) and (e). Thus, in *Cowan de Groot Properties v Eagle Trust*,[98] Knox J recognised the need to weigh the presence of suspicious circumstances against the right of a third party to a commercial transaction to obtain the best possible terms and the particular difficulties that might otherwise arise where the third party is itself a company acting through directors or other agents, who themselves have a fiduciary duty to act in its best interests:

> The duty of directors of a purchasing company is to buy as cheaply as they can in the light of the mode and terms of the proposed sale and it would in my judgment be a slippery

---

93 [1994] 2 All ER 685 at p 700g. This formulation was endorsed by the Court of Appeal in *Brown v Bennett* [1999] 1 BCLC 649.
94 See: *International Sales & Agencies v Marcus* [1982] 3 All ER 551; *Rolled Steel v British Steel* [1986] 1 Ch 246; *Jyske Bank v Spjeldnaes* (1999) WL 819062.
95 See generally Lord Nicholls's chapter in *Restitution: Past, Present and Future*, above n 52.
96 [1993] 1 WLR 509.
97 See generally the discussion of these levels of knowledge in relation to subsequent case law in *Trusts Law: Texts and Materials*, above n 50, at pp 556–61.
98 [1992] 4 All ER 700 at pp 754–61.

slope upon which to embark to impose upon directors of a company a positive duty to make inquiries into the reasons for an offer being made to their company at what appears to be a bargain price. The line should in my judgment be drawn at the point where the figure in question, regard being had not only to the open market value but also to the terms and mode of sale, is indicative of dishonesty on the part of the directors of a vendor company.[99]

He went on:

In my judgment it may well be that the underlying broad principle which runs through the authorities regarding commercial transactions is that the court will impute knowledge, on the basis of what a reasonable person would have learned, to a person who is guilty of commercially unacceptable conduct in the particular context involved.[100]

Lord Nicholls approved this reference to 'commercially unacceptable conduct' in his judgment for the Privy Council in *Royal Brunei Airlines v Philip Tan Kok Ming*,[101] a case concerning 'knowing assistance', the other form of accessory liability.[102] As Knox J recognised in *Cowan de Groot*, the standard of knowledge necessary to render a party liable for knowing assistance had been more clearly set (compared to that necessary for knowing receipt) at a level which excluded *Baden* categories (d) and (e). In *Royal Brunei Airlines*, Lord Nicholls reviewed the relevant case law on knowing assistance and held that the touchstone of liability is 'dishonesty'. He said that this is an objective standard meaning simply 'not acting as an honest person would in the circumstances'. He elaborated on the meaning of dishonesty by saying that 'for the most part it is to be equated with conscious impropriety', but acknowledged that it is something that must depend on the particular circumstances of each case:

In most situations there is little difficulty in identifying how an honest person would behave ... *Unless there is a very good and compelling reason*, an honest person does not participate in a transaction if he knows it involves a misapplication of trust assets to the detriment of the beneficiaries.[103]

He held that the reference to 'commercially unacceptable conduct' by Knox J in *Cowan de Groot* captured the necessary flavour of this objective standard in a commercial setting.[104] He said that the court would look at all the circumstances known to the third party and 'the reason why he acted as he did' before deciding whether or not the third party had been dishonest.[105] In relation to knowing receipt, there is a case for setting the standard at the same level to take account of the concerns raised by Knox J in *Cowan de Groot* and in

---

99 [1992] 4 All ER 700 at p 761b–61c.

100 [1992] 4 All ER 700 at p 761h.

101 [1995] 2 AC 378. See also *Twinsectra Ltd v Yardley* [2002] 2 All ER 377 (HL).

102 This is a fault-based liability, analogous to that for procuring a breach of contract, where the defendant is not actually the recipient of the relevant property or assets. See Lord Nicholls [1995] 2 AC 378 at pp 386–87: '... if, for his own purposes, a third party deliberately interferes with that [trust] relationship by assisting the trustee in depriving the beneficiary of the property held for him by the trustee, the beneficiary should be able to look for recompense to the third party as well as the trustee. Affording the beneficiary a remedy against the third party serves the dual purpose of making good the beneficiary's loss should the trustee lack financial means and imposing a liability which will discourage others from behaving in a similar fashion.'

103 [1995] 2 AC 378 at 389 (emphasis added).

104 See above n 100 and the main text threat for the approach of Knox J. And see now *BCCI (Overseas) Ltd v Akindele* [2001] Ch 437.

105 See [1995] 2 AC 378 at pp 390–91.

other cases reviewed by him. Also, a flexible standard expressed in such terms is likely to prove more useful in a commercial setting than the elaboration of different mental states set out in the *Baden Delvaux* case.

However, where a third party receives property or other assets from a company for no consideration or where the transaction is clearly motivated by factors other than the best interest of the company, then there is a case for holding that the third party must proceed with caution and make further inquiry that the transaction does not involve a breach of duty by those acting for the company. In other words, the knowledge of a third party who is a volunteer should extend to include *Baden* categories (d) and (e).[106] However, the question remains of how far a third party's liability for knowing receipt has been affected by s 35A where the relevant breach of fiduciary duty involves an excess of their powers by the directors of the company.

9 WHEN IS A THIRD PARTY NOT DEALING WITH A COMPANY IN GOOD FAITH FOR THE PURPOSES OF SECTION 35A?

The key question that has been left open so far is whether a third party's knowledge that the directors of a company are exceeding their powers under its constitution when making a contract, or authorising someone else to do so on behalf of the company, is sufficient to negate that third party's good faith and thus the protection afforded by s 35A. If so, the further question arises of what further knowledge should be imputed to the third party by way of 'constructive knowledge' for the purpose of this exercise. If not, the question remains of what would be required to negate the third party's good faith. The transaction would have to involve some breach of fiduciary duty on the part of the directors apart from the excess of their powers. In other words, the third party would be liable for knowing receipt in any event on the basis discussed above. In particular, except for third parties who are volunteers, their liability should depend on whether or not they are guilty of 'commercially unacceptable conduct' in accordance with the judgments of Knox J in *Cowan de Groot* and Lord Nicholls in *Royal Brunei Airlines*. Another possibility, however, is that the concept of 'commercially unacceptable conduct' could be used as a standard for determining the required lack of good faith.[107] This would mean that knowledge of the directors' excess of powers could negate the third party's good faith, but that other factors should also be taken into account such as whether the third party had a good and commercially acceptable reason for not insisting on the proper formalities being observed. At this stage, the policy factors underlying s 35A must be examined in more detail.

There is a good case for arguing that the good faith proviso in s 35A should be interpreted in a way that gives full effect to the goal of 'security of transaction' enshrined in the First Directive, which s 35A was, among other things, designed to implement.[108] On this basis, third parties should be entitled to act on the assumption that the directors

---

106 See *International Sales & Agencies v Marcus* [1982] 3 All ER 551.

107 Lord Nicholls's treatment of dishonesty in *Royal Brunei Airlines* has also been used as a basis for discerning the meaning of the term 'bad faith' in the context of the Trade Marks Act 1994: see *CA Sheimer's TM Application* [2000] RPC 484 at pp 506–11. Note also *Twinsectra Ltd v Yardley* [2002] 2 All ER 377.

108 See EEC/68/151.

of a company have unlimited power to bind the company even if they are aware of the limits set on that power by the constitution of a particular company. This would give full effect to the idea that third parties need have no concern with the terms of the constitution, which would then be an internal matter for the directors and the company's shareholders. This would move the relevant British law much closer to that in jurisdictions in which the directors are treated as a genuine organ of the company, whose powers are prescribed by law.[109] Third parties would be able to enforce any transaction made or authorised by a company's directors, and would not face any liability for knowing receipt in relation to such a transaction, unless they know that the directors are abusing their powers as well as exceeding the limits on those powers, as was found in the *International Sales & Agencies, Rolled Steel* and *Jyske Bank* cases. The argument that lack of good faith should entail more than knowledge of the directors' excess of power would also remove an anomaly whereby a careful and diligent third party would be at a disadvantage in situations where the time needed to overcome the directors' lack of authority in accordance with the constitution is costly for the third party.

There are also good arguments in favour of equating lack of good faith with knowledge of the directors' lack of authority, provided that this knowledge is limited by reference to 'commercially unacceptable conduct'. The duty of a company's directors to observe the limits set by its constitution is clear and third parties should respect those limits once they are aware of them. On this basis, the role of ss 35A and 35B is to make it clear that third parties have no duty to inquire into these limits and should not, without more, suffer a penalty for failing to make such an inquiry. The knowledge attributable to a third party in the form of constructive knowledge should be set on this basis. Further, the sections may also be designed to exclude, without more, knowledge without understanding, where a third party has received notice of the relevant terms of a company's constitution, but cannot be shown to have appreciated their restrictive effect on the directors' powers. In particular, the sections should limit the extent to which the knowledge of a corporate third party can be equated with the cumulative knowledge of all of its agents and that 'institutional knowledge' should be limited to that acquired by agents engaged on the transaction in question.

A median possibility is the one canvassed above, that a third party's lack of good faith should be determined on the basis of a standard such as 'commercially unacceptable conduct' and that knowledge of the directors' lack of authority should be a relevant, but not conclusive, factor. Thus, it is possible to envisage a scenario where a third party has actual knowledge of the directors' lack of power to make a contract and yet arguably would not be engaging in commercially unacceptable conduct by proceeding with the transaction. For example, the directors of a public company may be about to conclude a transaction with a third party when they discover that its terms are beyond their powers, due to some obscure and perhaps not immediately discernible provision in the constitution. Overcoming this restriction means obtaining the approval of the shareholders in general meeting. Nevertheless, these directors may honestly believe that the transaction is in the best interests of the company and that it would be damaging to the company to wait for the shareholders' approval to be obtained. The directors may

---

109 As is the case, for example, in the German system of corporate governance: see the comments of Hoffmann LJ in *El Ajou v Dollar Holdings* [1994] 2 All ER 685 at p 705.

therefore decide to take the risk of proceeding with the transaction and of obtaining the shareholders' approval afterwards. However, they may decide to inform the third party of the problem. The third party may have good commercial reasons for wanting a completed agreement and not merely one that is conditional on the shareholders' approval subsequently being obtained. The contract may thus be concluded by the company's directors who purport to bind the company. However, before the shareholders' approval is obtained, some major and unexpected change of circumstances may then occur, which completely undermines the commercial value of the transaction to the company and perhaps even renders it highly damaging.[110] A third party who had remained ignorant about the directors' lack of power would be protected by s 35A. The question is whether the third party's actual knowledge of the directors' breach of the constitution should in such circumstances undermine this protection. To put it another way, if the directors of the company are prepared to take the risk of proceeding with the transaction, is that enough to ensure that the third party is protected by s 35A?

If the good faith of the third party in the above example were to be determined by using the standard of commercially unacceptable conduct, it is likely that s 35A would still apply. It is arguable that that is the result that would be in accordance with the goal of 'security of transaction'. In this respect, it is worth noting that the liability of the company directors for their breach of duty in such a scenario could be mitigated at the discretion of the court under s 727 of the Companies Act 1985 if it were to appear to the court that the directors had acted honestly and reasonably and in the circumstances ought fairly to be excused. It would be more difficult to justify this conclusion if the third party had superior knowledge or business judgment in relation to the transaction in question and was more aware than the company's directors of the likely change in circumstances and thus of the fact that the transaction could prove damaging to the company. In that context, the limit on the directors' powers could be seen as providing crucial protection to the company's shareholders, which the third party should not be able to ignore once aware of it. Even so, if the third party was not aware of any breach of fiduciary duty by the directors apart from exceeding their powers, it is still hard to find such a third party guilty of unacceptable commercial conduct. However, in the overall assessment of a third party's conduct, knowledge of the directors' excess of power should at least increase the onus on the third party to ensure that the company's directors are not acting fraudulently or otherwise infringing their duty to act in good faith in their company's best interests.

10 SECTION 322A: CONTRACTS INVOLVING 'INSIDERS'

This section applies to transactions made or authorised by the directors of a company in excess of their powers where the third party is one of a specified list of persons,[111] which broadly includes directors of the company and those with close connections to a director.

---

110 *Rackham v Peek Foods* [1990] BCLC 895 provides a good example of how a sudden change of circumstances can suddenly transform the commercial value of a contract to a company in this way. In that case, however, the contract had been made conditional on the shareholders' approval being obtained and, although the directors had given an undertaking to recommend its approval, it was held that this was overridden by the directors' fiduciary duty to the shareholders to express an honest opinion on the merits of the transaction at the time at which approval was being sought.

111 See the Companies Act 1985, ss 322A(1) and 346 respectively, for the specification and definition of these persons.

Section 322A(2) overrides s 35A for such third parties and renders the transaction voidable at the instance of the company. This means that, unlike voidness or lack of legal effect at common law, the transaction has provisional validity and the company must take action to rescind it.[112] Section 322A(5) lists four sets of circumstances in which the transaction ceases to be voidable, including the impossibility of restitution, the indemnification of the company for any loss or damage, the acquisition of rights by another party 'bona fide for value and without actual notice of the directors' exceeding their powers' and the ratification of the transaction in the appropriate way. Section 322A(3) provides that, whether or not the transaction is avoided, the third party, along with any director authorising the transaction, is liable to account to the company for any gain made from the transaction and to indemnify it against any resulting loss or damage. However, s 322A(6) provides that the third party will not be personally liable in this way 'if he shows that at the time the transaction was entered into he did not know that the directors were exceeding their powers', unless he is a director of the company.

The Prentice Report had recognised the case for expecting directors and other officers of a company to know the limits on the powers of its directors and therefore giving them much less generous protection than that extended to third parties in general. It therefore proposed that a third party in this category should still be treated as having constructive knowledge of the limits on the power of the company's directors where such knowledge 'may reasonably be expected of a person carrying out the functions of that director or officer in relation to that company'.[113] That would have left transactions with such third parties to suffer the common law consequences of the directors' lack of authority. The proposal reflected the common law view that such insiders owe a duty to their company to look after its affairs and to ensure that its transactions are regular and orderly and that no protection should be extended to them which might encourage their ignorance and condone their dereliction from this duty.[114] Thus, at common law, the indoor management rule and the concept of apparent authority were not applied to directors in the same way as to outsiders.

Neuberger J considered the policy considerations underlying s 322A in his judgment in Re Torvale Group.[115] He viewed it as providing a safeguard against conflict of interest rather than as a penalty for unacceptable ignorance, saying:

> [It] seems to me that the purpose of section 322A is to protect a company in circumstances where its directors exceed their powers in connection with transactions entered into by the company with one or more of their number (or their associates) to the disadvantage of the company and to the advantage of one or more of the directors (or associates). It is true that the effect of the section is wider than that, and it may well have been intended to ensure

---

112 See, however, Nolan 'Enacting Civil Remedies in Company Law', above n 45, who recommends that voidability along the lines prescribed in ss 322 and 322A should be the standard legal effect of a contract made in breach of duty. The Company Law Review, whilst acknowledging that this would 'provide an elegant solution to what is an extremely complex problem', has recommended that this 'difficult area' be given further consideration by the DTI; see The Final Report, above n 10, at paras 15.28–15.30.

113 See The Prentice Report, above n 54, at p 33.

114 See Morris v Kanssen [1946] AC 459 at pp 475–76.

115 [1999] 2 BCLC 605.

that directors are penalised if they fail to behave with particular propriety in connection with transactions between the company and themselves. However, I do not think that detracts from the main mischief at which the section is directed.[116]

Third parties subject to s 322A include not only directors of the company itself, but also directors of the company's holding company, if any,[117] persons connected to a director of the company or of its holding company and associated companies of such a director. The latter terms feature elsewhere in Part X of the Companies Act 1985 and are defined by s 346. They include spouses and business partners of directors and companies in which a director, alone or together with persons connected to him, holds at least one-fifth of the equity share capital or of the voting shares.

There has been some doubt as to the precise relationship between s 35A and s 322A. Section 322A(4) states that the provisions of the section should not be construed as 'excluding the operation of any other enactment or rule of law by virtue of which the transaction may be called in question or any liability to the company may arise'. This implies that it should not apply if s 35A would not prevent the transaction from being void at common law and thus should only apply if the third party has been dealing with the company in good faith. Further, if the third party were also liable as a constructive trustee to the company for knowing receipt, this would also prevail over s 322A. However, ss 35A and 322A have sometimes been presented as a simple dichotomy based on whether or not the third party is within any of the categories designated for s 322A. If that were the case, then all third parties within the ambit of s 322A would be subject to s 322A regardless of whether or not they had been dealing with the company in good faith. In other words, where such a third party had been dealing with the company in bad faith, the resulting transaction would enjoy provisional validity under s 322A rather than the mere potential validity that would have ensued at common law. Given that the difference between voidability and lack of legal effect is a significant one,[118] this would not be a defensible position since contracts made with insiders lacking good faith would be treated more favourably than contracts made with outsiders lacking good faith. It would contradict the policy rationale for s 322A envisaged by Neuberger J,[119] as well as the common law's attitude towards insiders. However, the wording of s 322A(4) does seem clear enough on this point to resist that conclusion.

Assuming therefore that an insider third party must be within s 35A for a transaction to be voidable under s 322A rather than void at common law, the question arises whether any special considerations should be taken into account for determining whether such a third party is dealing with the company in good faith. It is arguable that account should be taken of the common law concern that directors should not be given any incentive to remain ignorant about the terms of their company's constitution or to be slack in ensuring

---

116 [1999] 2 BCLC 605 at p 622.
117 See the Companies Act 1985, s 736(1).
118 The difference between the concepts was regarded as crucial in *Guinness v Saunders* [1990] 2 AC 663 and *Jyske Bank v Spjeldnaes* (1999) WL 819062.
119 See *Re Torvale Group* [1999] 2 BCLC 605.

that its affairs are conducted properly. However, in *Re Torvale Group*,[120] the only reported case so far on s 322A, the case proceeded on the basis that the section would apply to a debenture made with the chairman and major shareholder of the company without considering as a preliminary issue whether he would in fact be entitled to rely on s 35A.[121]

Re Torvale Group also concerned two further debentures granted by the company to the trustees of a retirement benefits scheme, including one who was also a director of the company.[122] In relation to these, the trustees invited the court to exercise its discretion under s 322A(7). This applies to transactions involving more than one third party and provides:

> [Where] a transaction is voidable by virtue of [s 322A] and valid by virtue of [s 35A] in favour of [a third party not within s 322A], the court may, on the application of that person or of the company, make such order affirming, severing or setting aside the transaction, on such terms, as appear to the court to be just.

Neuberger J held that s 322A(7) did apply and that, in the circumstances, he would declare the debentures valid. In reaching this conclusion, he took account of various factors which suggested that there was nothing improper about the transaction and that the failure to obtain the approval of the relevant class of shareholders had been a genuine oversight. These factors included the reasonable terms of the loan secured by the debenture and the moderate rate of interest, the fact that the relevant director had received no personal benefit from the transaction and the fact that there was no suggestion that any of the trustees had lacked good faith. However, even with the approach adopted by Neuberger J in *Re Torvale Group*, it is arguable that s 322A(7) undermines the goal of 'security of transaction' underlying s 35A by rendering uncertain the validity of multiparty transactions within its ambit and giving the court a wide and vague discretion.

It is perhaps not surprising that the future of s 322A has been under review. Both the Law Commission and the Company Law Review have reviewed it. The Law Commission in their report on directors' duties did not find any major deficiencies and recommended that it be retained as it stands.[123] However, the Company Law Review considered the suggestion that that the elaborate detail of s 322A is unnecessary and that this section is confusing to the extent that it adds an additional layer of regulation to the principles which would otherwise apply. The Company Law Review has, therefore, proposed that third parties within s 322A simply be denied the protection of s 35A.[124]

---

120 [1999] 2 BCLC 605.

121 The point was in fact left open pending further evidence of whether the breach of the relevant limitation in the constitution had in fact been ratified by the unanimous consent of the relevant shareholders in accordance with the principle in *Re Duomatic* [1969] 2 Ch 365.

122 Again, the question of whether the debentures were in fact valid and binding under the *Duomatic* principle, above n 121, was left open.

123 See *Company Directors: Regulating Conflicts of Interest and Formulating a Statement of Duties* (1999) Cm 4436 (London, TSO, 1999), Law Commission Report No 261, at para 10.38.

124 See *Company Formation*, above n 10, at para 2.41.

11 CONCLUSIONS

This essay has shown that there are still several areas of uncertainty in the law governing the ability of third parties to enforce contracts made, or authorised, by the directors of a company in excess of their powers under the company's constitution. Whilst the Companies Act 1989 effectively abolished the old doctrine of *ultra vires*, in practice giving most companies unlimited contractual capacity, some semantic doubts about s 35 remain. There is greater doubt about the impact of s 35A, in particular as to the meaning of 'good faith' and how the knowledge of third parties about a breach of the constitution should affect their ability to rely on s 35A. A third party's exposure to liability for knowing receipt is also unclear, which reflects a general uncertainty about the precise degree of knowledge required to give rise to this form of liability. Finally, the relationship between s 35A and s 322A in respect of contracts involving directors and other 'insiders' would benefit from clarification and the future of s 322A has in fact been called into question. The treatment of multiparty transactions by s 322A(7) in fact formalises a degree of uncertainty about the validity of certain transactions, which does not accord with the general goal of 'security of transaction'.

The recommendations of the Company Law Review will remove some of these areas of doubt, in particular their proposal that companies should be expressly stated as having unlimited contractual capacity. It would, however, be useful if there were an express statement as to whether or not ss 35 and 35A apply to companies in general or just those incorporated under the Companies Act. Other issues such as the future of s 322A may be considered if the DTI engages in a further review of the remedies available to a company when its directors act in breach of their duties.[125] It would be useful if such a review were to address the nature of the good faith requirement in s 35A and consider what further guidance might be given on the significance of a third party's knowledge in this respect. Otherwise, the necessary direction in this area will have to come from any pertinent case law. A landmark case on knowing receipt of the kind looked for by Lord Nicholls might have wider value in relation to the enforceability of contracts by third parties.[126] The concept of 'commercially unacceptable conduct' introduced by Knox J in *Cowan de Groot*[127] and elaborated by Lord Nicholls in *Royal Brunei Airlines*[128] would provide a useful platform on which such case law development might build.

---

125 See above n 112.
126 See generally Lord Nicholls 'Knowing Receipt: The Need for a New Landmark' in Cornish, Nolan, O'Sullivan and Virgo (eds) *Restitution: Past, Present and Future*, above n 52. And see now *BCCI (Overseas) Ltd v Akindele* [2001] Ch 437.
127 [1992] 4 All ER 700 at p 761.
128 [1995] 2 AC 378 at pp 386–91.

CHAPTER 6

REFORM AND DEVELOPMENT OF THE LAW PROTECTING INTERESTS IN TRADING NAMES

David Booton

1 INTRODUCTION

The Company Law Review Steering Group have not proposed an extensive revision of the existing statutory system regulating the adoption of company names. In its *Final Report*, the Steering Group expressed the view that, for the most part, the existing system of controls works well.[1] Of course, the statutory system of controls is but a small part of the law regulating the adoption and use of names by companies. Indeed this essay is concerned mainly with the common law and, in particular, the proper role, and future development, of the tort of passing off as it applies to protecting interests in trading names. The law of passing off has, over the past five years or so, been undergoing somewhat of a transformation and this essay charts and explains a shift in the interests that are recognised and protected by the tort. The existing statutory system of controls on the adoption of company names and the proposed revisions to this system are thus considered against the background of the development of the common law.

With this in mind, the remainder of the essay is divided into four sections. The first of these presents a brief overview of the law of passing off as it applies to names, and introduces, at a general level, the debate surrounding the interests that are properly protected by the tort. This section charts a shift in thinking which challenges the traditional view that the law of passing off is based upon the notion that a name or mark owes its value to the goodwill and reputation of the business to which the name or mark is attached in favour of the proposition that, in certain circumstances, there can be a property interest in a reputation inherent in the trading name itself.[2] Related to this proposition has been an increasing recognition by the courts that the dilution or erosion of a claimant's reputation as a result of the appropriation of his name can be a relevant head of damage in passing off actions.[3] It is argued that this shift, in part, demonstrates an attempt by the courts to modernise the role of passing off and, in particular, is an acknowledgment that under modern conditions of trade, businesses are often built up around their name such that a name can form part of a trader's goodwill. But, of equal, if not greater, significance has been the pressure from businesses to widen the application of the tort of passing off so as to provide a remedy against injury resulting from certain forms of perceived unfair competition. This argument is further developed in the two sections that follow which demonstrate how the law of passing off has been developed so

---

1   Company Law Review Steering Group, *Modern Company Law for a Competitive Economy: Final Report* (London, DTI, 2001), at pp 240–41, hereafter *The Final Report*.

2   See, in particular, *Harrods Ltd v Harrodian School* [1996] RPC 697 at p 719, considered below at n 15 and the accompanying text.

3   See: *Lego System A/S v Lego M Lemelstrich* [1983] FSR 155; *Taittinger SA v Allbev Ltd* [1993] FSR 641; and *Harrods v Harrodian School* [1996] RPC 697, considered below at nn 16–26 and the accompanying text.

as to remedy 'unfair' business practices arising in respect of the registration of company names and of Internet domain names. As to the former, it is shown that the current statutory system has at least allowed, if not encouraged, the registration of non-trading shelf companies with names that are similar, or identical, to those of existing corporations. The courts have responded by applying the law of passing off so as to restrain this activity,[4] notwithstanding that the juridical basis for doing so has, until recently, been far from certain. It is against this background that the Company Law Review Steering Group has proposed to reform the law so as to give individuals a statutory right to apply for a direction that a company be required to change its name if the name was chosen with the principal intention of seeking monies from the applicant, or in order to restrain the applicant from seeking to use that name.[5] It is argued that both the common law and the Steering Group's recommendations are moving English law away from the notion that a name owes its value to the goodwill and reputation of the business to which it is attached and towards a legal doctrine based on the maxim that a name worth appropriating is *prima facie* worth protecting. Most recently, this doctrine has been applied to the registration and use of Internet domain names. Disputes over the registration of domain names have presented courts with an opportunity to further develop the common law and, in particular, to clarify the juridical basis of the law of passing off as it applies to the practice of registering names that are the same as those of existing corporations.[6] At the same time, courts have sought to introduce limits on the application of passing off to this area.[7]

Conclusions about the developments outlined in the earlier sections are drawn together in the final section where it is argued that, in respect of the interests recognised and protected in trading names, whether these are company names or Internet domain names, the law of passing off has evolved beyond its traditional role and operates to fulfil a much wider function in regulating certain unfair business practices and, to this extent, compensates for the UK's lack of a general law of unfair competition. Unlike the UK, the majority of continental European countries recognise a right of the honest trader to restrain his competitors from causing him injury by unfair conduct which is not consistent with 'honest usages' of the trade.[8] In extending the tort of passing off to fulfil a similar role, the risk is that the tort will become a vehicle for market dominance particularly by those enterprises with advertising power. It is argued that what is now needed is a coherent doctrine of unfair competition at the policy level.

---

4   See: *Glaxo plc v Glaxowellcome Ltd* [1996] FSR 388; and *Direct Line Group Ltd v Direct Line Estate Agency Ltd* [1997] FSR 374, considered below at nn 46–48 and the accompanying text.

5   See *The Final Report*, above n 1, at p 240; and see below at n 49 and the accompanying text.

6   See, in particular: *British Telecommunications plc v One in a Million Ltd* [1998] FSR 265; and [1999] FSR 1 (CA), considered below at nn 63–80 and the accompanying text.

7   See, for example, *French Connection Ltd v Sutton* [2000] ETMR 341, considered below at nn 85–86 and the accompanying text.

8   See: Kirkbride 'The Need for Unfair Competition Law' (1998) 9 *International Company and Commercial Law Review* 343 at p 343; and Robertson and Horton 'Does the United Kingdom or the European Community Need an Unfair Competition Law' [1995] *European Intellectual Property Review* 568 at p 574.

2 THE INTERESTS PROTECTED AGAINST PASSING OFF[9]

In its classic form, the essential elements of passing off are: first, that there is goodwill or reputation attached to the goods or services which the claimant supplies by association with the identifying name under which the goods or services are offered. Secondly, the claimant must show that there is a misrepresentation by the defendant leading or likely to lead the public to believe that goods or services offered by him are the goods or services of the claimant. Finally, the claimant must show that he suffers or, in a *quia timet* action, that he is likely to suffer damage by reason of the erroneous belief engendered by the defendant's misrepresentation.[10]

Where an action is based on the use of trading names alone, to the exclusion of get-up and other factors, a court will have regard to two issues: first, at the time of the defendant's act complained of did the claimant enjoy exclusive reputation in the name used by the defendant; and secondly, if not, is the name used by the defendant deceptively similar to the name in which the claimant does have reputation and goodwill in the sense that the defendant's use of its own name would be likely, if not restrained, to lead people to deal with the defendant on the faith of the claimant's reputation?[11]

The law of passing off has traditionally been based upon the idea that a name or mark owes its value to the goodwill and reputation of the business concerned and it follows that a claimant must establish a goodwill or reputation *attached to the goods or services which he supplies*, by association with the identifying name. Goodwill in this context means 'the benefit and advantage of the good name, reputation and connection of a business ... the attractive force which brings in custom'.[12] Under the traditional view, the law of passing off creates no rights in a name as such and it is not enough for a claimant to demonstrate that his name has a reputation in itself or is well known. So, for example, in refusing to grant an injunction requested by the owners of the Harrods department store against the owners of the 'Harrodian' School, Millet LJ commented:

> Passing off is a wrongful invasion of a right of property vested in the claimant, but the property which is protected by an action for passing off is not the claimant's proprietary right in the name or get up which the defendant has misappropriated but the goodwill and reputation of his business which is likely to be harmed by the defendant's misrepresentation.[13]

In short, as traditionally understood, passing off recognises a property right in the 'customer connection' that emanates from the reputation of the claimant's products or

---

9   For more comprehensive reviews of the action of passing off see: Carty 'Passing Off' in A Dugdale *et al* *Clerk & Lindsell on Torts* (London, Sweet & Maxwell, 18th edn, 2000); D Kitchen *et al Kerly's Law of Trade Marks and Trade Names* (London, Sweet & Maxwell, 13th edn, 2000); and C Wadlow *The Law of Passing Off* (London, Sweet & Maxwell, 2nd edn, 1994).

10   See, in particular: *Reckitt & Colman Products Ltd v Borden Inc* [1990] RPC 341 at p 406; and note also *Consorzio del Prosciuto di Parma v Marks & Spencer plc* [1991] RPC 351 at pp 368–70, where Nourse LJ expresses a clear preference for this 'classic trinity' over the more complex, five-element approach suggested by Lord Diplock in *Erven Warnink BV v Townend & Sons (Hull) Ltd* [1980] RPC 31 at p 93.

11   See: *The British Diabetic Association v The Diabetic Society and Others* [1996] FSR 1 at p 14 *per* Walker J, following Goff LJ in *Bulmer Ltd v Bollinger SA* [1978] RPC 79 at p 117.

12   See *IRC v Muller* [1901] AC 217 at pp 223–24 *per* Lord MacNaghten.

13   See *Harrods Ltd v Harrodian School* [1996] RPC 697 at p 711.

services and protects the goodwill between and trader and his customers which his name sustains.[14] However, during the 1990s, there emerged a new school of thought in respect of the interests that are recognised and protected by the tort. In the *Harrods* case, Sir Michael Kerr, in a dissenting judgment, expressed the view that a distinctive name can, in some cases, form part of a claimant's goodwill and, in itself, constitute a property interest[15] thereby bringing the concept of goodwill closer to that of mere reputation. Admittedly, the views expressed by a single judge in a dissenting judgment, albeit in the Court of Appeal, are hardly evidence of a significant shift in judicial opinion. However, that Sir Michael Kerr was not isolated in his view of the interests protected by passing off has been demonstrated, not in similar overt declarations, but rather in an expansion of the heads of damage recognised in passing off actions.

The concept of goodwill, in defining the interests protected thereby also determines the type of damage recognised as sufficient to bring an action. In the classic form of passing off, where a defendant represents his goods or services as those of the claimant, there is an obvious risk of damage to the claimant's business by substitution. However, it well established that diversion of trade is not the only relevant head of damage and courts have in recent years been inclined to accept that loss of distinctiveness can cause damage to a reputation ultimately leading to a loss of trade. In *Harrods*, Sir Michael Kerr identified two particular aspects to loss of distinctiveness:

> First, a debasement or dilution of the plaintiff's reputation, as the result of the action of the defendant, is a relevant head of damage. Secondly, if the act which constitutes the passing off has the effect of raising in people's minds the mistaken belief of a connection between the defendant and the plaintiff, but which is in fact non-existent, then the court will have regard to the fact that the plaintiff has, to that extent, lost control of his reputation, and that he has therefore suffered damage to his goodwill by a potentially injurious association with the defendant against which the court will protect him by injunction.[16]

That passing off protects against the dilution of a claimant's reputation was accepted by all of the judges in the Court of Appeal in *Taittinger SA v Allbev Ltd*[17] where the producers of Champagne attacked the defendant's use of the word 'champagne' to describe a sparkling elderflower cordial drink. Here, Mann LJ argued that the word 'champagne' had an exclusiveness which would be impaired by a 'gradual debasement, dilution or erosion' of what was distinctive about it if it were used in relation to a product that was not Champagne,[18] whilst Sir Thomas Bingham MR noted that the defendants' use of the word would debase and cheapen the reputation built up by the Champagne houses over the years.[19]

However the consensus in *Taittinger* was not repeated in the later *Harrods* case.[20] Millet LJ, whilst noting the decision and reasoning in *Taittinger*, expressed the concern

---

14 See: Carty 'Passing Off and the Concept of Goodwill' [1995] *Journal of Business Law* 139 at p 139; and W Cornish *Intellectual Property: Patents, Copyright, Trade Marks and Allied Rights* (London, Sweet & Maxwell, 4th edn, 1999) at pp 619–20.

15 *Harrods Ltd v Harrodian School* [1996] RPC 697 at p 719.

16 See [1996] RPC 697 at p 724, *per* Sir Michael Kerr; and note also the judgment of Millet LJ at pp 715–16.

17 [1993] FSR 641.

18 [1993] FSR 641 at p 674 and see also the judgment of Gibson LJ at p 670.

19 See [1993] FSR 641 at p 678.

20 [1996] RPC 697.

that unless care was taken, the recognition of erosion of distinctiveness could mark an unacceptable extension of the tort of passing off. He drew attention to the link between recognising dilution as a relevant head of damage and the interests protected against passing off and noted a paradox:

> To date the law has not sought to protect the value of the brand name as such, but the value of the goodwill it generates; and it insists on proof of confusion to justify its intervention. But the erosion of the distinctiveness of a brand name which occurs by reason of its degeneration into common use as a generic term is not necessarily dependent on confusion at all ... I have an intellectual difficulty in accepting the concept that the law insists upon the presence of both confusion and damage and yet recognises as sufficient a head of damage which does not depend on confusion.[21]

Given that Sir Michael Kerr, in his dissenting judgment, expressed the view that a distinctive name can, in some cases, form part of a claimant's goodwill, it is unsurprising that he disagreed with Millet LJ on the issue of dilution and asserted that this was a relevant head of damage, the authority for this assertion was to be found in all of the judgments in *Taittinger*.[22]

If the division of opinion on the question of dilution as a head of damage is evidence of a more fundamental disagreement as to the interests protected against passing off, it is all the more surprising that Millet LJ and Sir Michael Kerr agreed that the other aspect of loss of distinctiveness – loss of control – was a valid head of damage. Millet LJ noted that where parties were not in competition with each other, the claimant's reputation and goodwill may nevertheless be damaged without any corresponding gain to the defendant. He cited in support of this proposition *Lego System A/S v Lego M Lemelstrich*,[23] where the claimants, who were the manufacturers of the well-known toy construction kits, successfully restrained the defendants' use of the name 'Lego' on plastic garden irrigation equipment. Millet LJ gave the example of a customer who, dissatisfied with the defendant's garden equipment, might as a consequence be dissuaded from buying the claimant's toys believing them to be made by the defendants and pointed out that the danger in such a case was that, without restraining the defendant's use of the name, the claimant would lose control over his own reputation.[24] This particular aspect of the judgment in *Harrods* has been subject to much criticism. Certain commentators have noted that whilst there may be good reason, on the facts of a given case, to anticipate that loss of control over a name will lead to a real risk of harm to goodwill,[25] acceptance by the courts of damage arising from a bare loss of control, without evidence of actual or likely harm to a claimant's goodwill, would amount to a significant extension of the tort.[26]

As has already been noted, the law of passing off is based upon the principle that a trader's name owes its value to the goodwill and reputation of the trader's business.

---

21 See [1996] RPC 697 at p 716.
22 See [1996] RPC 697 at pp 724–25.
23 [1983] FSR 155.
24 See *Harrods v Harrodian School* [1996] RPC 697 at p 715.
25 For example, where the level of confusion is high or where there is a common pool of customers or where the plaintiff is peculiarly vulnerable to an injurious association.
26 See: Carty 'Passing Off at the Crossroads' [1996] *European Intellectual Property Review* 629; and Murray 'A Distinct Lack of Goodwill' [1997] *European Intellectual Property Review* 345.

However, it is undoubtedly true that under modern conditions of trade, there is a tendency for businesses to be built up around a name, such that the reputation of the business is inherent in its name. The divergence of opinion regarding the law of passing off reflects on the one hand a recognition that the law must adapt so as to take account of modern trading circumstances and practices, whilst on the other, a recognition of the need to maintain clearly defined boundaries of protection founded on established principles. It is probably true to say that, in the past, businesses have tended to undervalue if not completely ignore their intangible assets. More recently, it has become recognised that there is considerable value in all forms of intellectual property including a business's trading name.[27] This increased awareness has in turn led to businesses adopting a more aggressive attitude towards protecting the reputation inherent in their name from appropriation or damage. In circumstances where there has been a blatant appropriation of a trader's name, and in the absence of any developed law of unfair competition on which to found a judgment in a claimant's favour, there has been an understandable tendency for courts to press the law of passing off into service even if this results in a widening of its application and a deviation from the established principles underlying the tort. In this role, passing off can be seen as compensating for the lack of a roving concept of unfair competition under UK law.

3 INTERESTS IN NAMES AND THE REGISTRATION OF COMPANIES

To understand how and why the common law has been pressed into service in order to remedy abuses of the system of registration of companies' names, it is first necessary to give a brief overview of the relevant current statutory provisions. There is little by way of statutory control over the choice of a new company's name and, subject to a few restrictions, the incorporators of a company are free to choose any name they wish for it.[28] What few restrictions there are in the Companies Act 1985 have three principal objects: first, to protect persons who have, or wish to have, dealings with a company from being misled into believing that its status or business is other than its name suggests; secondly, to ensure that persons who deal with a company can readily discover essential information about the company; and thirdly, and most fundamentally, the Act, by way of a system of registration, provides for a means by which companies may be identified. The process of incorporation creates a person with full legal capacity and any person, natural or corporate, must have a name as a means of identification. Thus the Memorandum of Association of every company must state the name of that company,[29] and under s 714 of

---

27 So, for example, whilst the rights to continued use of a name following the break up of a business or joint venture may not have been expressly dealt with in any termination agreement, the current perceived importance of the right to trade under a name has led parties to engage in lengthy and complex legal proceedings: see: *Scandecor Development AB v Scandecor Marketing AB* [1999] FSR 26 (ownership of goodwill as between foreign publisher and United Kingdom distributor once part of same multinational group); and *Dawnay Day & Co Ltd v Cantor Fitzgerald International* [2000] RPC 669 (CA) (concerning the right of a company to continue to use a particular name after the termination of a joint venture agreement).

28 For a recent review of the legal obligations concerning a company's name after the initial choice of name has been resolved, see: Hannigan 'Companies and the Law' (2001) 46 *The Register* 3; and R Smerdon and G Morse *Palmer's Company Law Manual* (London, Sweet & Maxwell, 2000) at pp 2,075–98.

29 Companies Act 1985, s 2(1).

the Act, the registrars of companies for England and Wales, and for Scotland, are required to keep an index of the names of companies and certain other bodies such as registered limited partnerships and societies.

In respect of names as means of identification, the key provisions are contained in ss 26 and 28 of the Act. Section 26 includes a prohibition on the registration of any company under a name which is the same as one already appearing in the registrar's index.[30] This prohibition acknowledges that if a name is to identify the person to whom it belongs then it must be unique to that person. Under s 26, priority in a particular name is given to the first in time on the index, and it follows that once a name is entered, then no other company can adopt the same name. In determining whether a name is the same as another within the meaning of s 26, the definite article, where it is the first word of a name, is disregarded. Also disregarded, being no more than indications of status, are the words and expressions: 'company'; 'company limited'; 'limited'; 'unlimited'; 'public limited company'; and 'investment company with variable capital'; as are abbreviations of these words and expressions and their Welsh equivalents. The type and case of letters, accents, spaces between letters and punctuation marks are also ignored for the purpose of determining whether two names are the same. The Act gives little attention to the use of symbols in company names, specifying only that 'and' and '&' are to be taken as the same.[31]

The provisions of s 28 allow the Secretary of State to direct a company, within 12 months of its registration, to change its name where it has been registered by a name which is 'the same as' or is 'too like' a name appearing in the registrar's index.[32] Section 28 thus complements s 26 in two ways. First, it allows rectification of erroneous registrations that may occur because of the registrar's failure to appreciate that two names are the same or because an existing company was omitted from the index. However, s 28's more important role is in the power of the Secretary of State to direct a company to change its name where that name is 'too like' that of an existing company. In practice, s 28 provides a means whereby, for a limited period, existing companies can oppose the registration of companies under names that are 'too like' their own. However, the effectiveness of s 28 is this regard is significantly limited.

First, the Secretary of State can only direct a company to change its name where it has been registered by a name which is the same as or too like a name already appearing in the registrar's index and it follows that any challenge to the registration of a particular

---

30 Companies Act 1985, s 26(1)(c).

31 One manifestation of the desire to exploit the new electronic trading environment has been a relatively widespread wish by incorporators to use, as part of proposed company names, certain symbols, prefixes and suffixes, such as: '@'; 'www.'; and '.com', which are all familiar elements of electronic nomenclature. In light of this trend, Companies House has recently reviewed its policy and in particular the way it applies s 26. Its response has been cautious. Whilst expressly stating that it intends to keep its options open, Companies House has indicated that it will not generally view names containing symbols as the same as their equivalents without them (except possibly for @ and 'at'). Company names incorporating symbols are thus acceptable on incorporation or change of name and will be allowed whether or not the symbols used have an obvious spelled out word equivalent used in another name on the register. Since the current policy treats symbols differently from punctuation, Companies House is intending to produce a list identifying the commonly occurring symbols and distinguishing them from punctuation. See Companies House 'Policy on Company Names' (2000) 44 *The Register* 6.

32 In practice, the Secretary of State's powers under s 28 are exercised by Companies House.

name must be based on the fact that there is an existing entry in the index. This is of particular significance for businesses incorporated overseas which have no subsidiary incorporated in the UK.[33]

Secondly, although the Act does not lay down any criteria by which the s 28 'too like' test is to be applied, Companies House has indicated that the sole evidence that will be admitted must be to do with the names alone. The test involves primarily a visual comparison, however account may also be taken of phonetic similarities between names.[34] In general, a name will only be considered 'too like' another if the differences between the two are confined to single letters, especially plurals, or the use of short, meaning-starved words such as 'UK' or 'GB' or '.com'.[35] Companies House will not consider the existing or intended nature of business activities of the two companies concerned, nor their geographical field of activity. Nor does Companies House accept evidence of confusion over trading activity based on the trading style of the company. Section 28 is thus not concerned in any way with protecting the consumers of a company's products or services from confusion as to the source of those products or services. The provisions do not provide rights in a registered name that are analogous to those in a registered trade mark. Nor are the provisions a statutory form of the action of passing off in the sense of protecting any goodwill associated with a trader's name. Indeed, whether or not a registered company is dormant is of no significance in the determination of whether two names are 'too like' each other within the meaning of s 28. Rather s 28 is concerned simply with ensuring that the registrar's index provides an accurate, and not manifestly misleading, means of identifying companies.

The final limitation on the effectiveness of s 28 arises because Companies House does not set the grounds for a direction under this section so widely as to prevent companies in a corporate group taking up similar names.[36] Bearing in mind that the ownership of a company has no bearing on whether a name is considered 'too like' another on the register, this policy significantly restricts a broad interpretation being given to s 28 which is applied consistently and irrespective of whether the names under consideration belong

---

33 Such companies may be further disadvantaged in so far as goodwill must exist in the jurisdiction in order to sue in passing off, and under the orthodox view, such goodwill must be the product of actual trading by a claimant within the jurisdiction. However, there have been conflicting decisions in this regard, and some courts are seemingly prepared to accept that an international reputation is sufficient to establish goodwill. For a review and comment on the circumstances in which international and foreign companies can be said to have goodwill in the UK, see Carty, above n 14.

34 See Companies House, above n 31.

35 Although the revised policy allows a name incorporating symbols onto the register under s 26, there may nevertheless be an objection and direction under s 28. Companies House has indicated that a company name distinguished from another only by the use of '@' will almost certainly be considered 'too like' another with '@' replaced by 'at', 'a' or nothing. Furthermore, the use of other symbols as the sole differentiation from a company name already on the register, especially when applied in a meaning-starved way, will similarly, generally, result in 'too like' names; see Companies House, above n 31.

36 See Companies House, above n 31. On how that law of passing off has been applied in the cases of group companies if the corporate or the contractual connection is severed and there are no express post-termination contractual provisions designed specifically to regulate the future use of the corporate name, see: *Habib Bank Ltd v Habib Bank AG Zurich* [1981] 1 WLR 1265; *Fyffes plc v Chiquita Brands International Inc* [1993] FSR 83; *Scandecor Development AB v Scandecor Marketing AB* [1999] FSR 26; and *Dawnay Day & Co Ltd v Cantor Fitzgerald International* [2000] RPC 669.

to companies which are related through ownership and are part of the same group.[37] Again, this reflects the fact that s 28 is not concerned with protecting the consumers of companies' products or services from confusion nor with the protection of trading goodwill.

The conclusions drawn by the Company Law Review Steering Group in its *Final Report* were that, for the most part, the existing system of controls on the adoption of company names works well. The Steering Group accordingly recommended little by way of reform. The Steering Group has proposed that there continue to be restrictions on the choice of a name for a company on formation and clause 69 of the draft Bill essentially follows s 26 of the current Act. However, whereas s 26 applies to a name under which a company may not be registered, clause 69 applies to a name under which it may not be formed.[38] The Steering Group have not yet drafted a clause following s 28 of the Act but have signalled the need to do so and have proposed that the law be reformed to introduce a time limit of 12 months from a company name's registration for others to object to it being the same as or too like a name already on the register and that the time limit for the Secretary of State to make a direction be extended from 12 months of the name's registration to 15 months.[39]

To understand the most significant reform recommended by the Steering Group in respect of company names, it is necessary to take account of a relatively common practice which takes advantage of the fact that priority in a particular name is given to the first in time on registrar's index. This practice involves attempting to anticipate the activities of existing corporations by incorporating new companies with names very similar to or even identical to those of existing corporations and thereby removing from those available, names which existing corporations may have chosen, either in expanding into some new activity or into the UK market. The motives for this behaviour are, of course, financial: once registered, the individual concerned then offers to sell the newly registered company, or its name, to the existing corporation.[40]

As has already been noted, although s 28 provides a means by which existing companies can challenge the incorporation of companies under names that are 'too like' their own, the effectiveness of s 28 is limited.[41] In principle, a company could be directed

---

37 In practice it is unlikely that a company will seek a direction under s 28 in respect of another company in the same group and, since s 28 does not seem to be applied unless there is an objection, it is more than possible that a name may be admitted onto the index that would otherwise be opposed as 'too like' an existing name if the companies concerned were not related. It follows that that index itself is a poor guide as to how the s 28 'too like' test is applied. Accordingly, it is no defence to a direction under s 28 to point out that the register contains pairs of names which are similarly 'too like' the names in issue but which have not been subject to a direction. Companies House is currently giving consideration to publishing a list of directions and refusals to help incorporators understand how s 28 is applied; see Companies House, above n 31.

38 See *The Final Report*, above n 1, at pp 240–41; the explanatory notes, at p 464; and clause 69 of the draft Bill, at pp 402–03. If a name is not permitted under clause 69, then under clause 8, the registrar should not issue a certificate with the effect that the company will not be formed under clause 9.

39 See *The Final Report*, above n 1, at pp 240–41 and the explanatory notes, at pp 465–66.

40 Usually for a sum large enough to generate a profit, but small enough so that it was cheaper for the existing corporation to pay rather than to take legal action to secure the name, see: Karet 'The Name Game' [1996] *European Intellectual Property Review* 47, at p 47; and Watts and Walsh 'Company Names' [1996] *European Intellectual Property Review* 336, at p 336.

41 In addition to the substantive limitations outlined above, it should be noted that, in operation, the statutory procedures are cumbersome and speedier relief may be available by way of an interlocutory application to the court in a passing off action for a mandatory injunction requiring a change of name; see: R Smerdon and G Morse, above n 28, at para 2.423.

to change its name under s 32, which gives the Secretary of State the power to direct a company to change its name if he is of the opinion that the name by which it is registered gives so misleading an indication of the nature of its activities as to be likely to cause harm to the public. However, in practice this provision has been applied to names which are misleading in suggesting some official standard of service rather than in suggesting a connection with an existing business.[42]

In the absence of an effective statutory mechanism for preventing abuses of the system of registration, claimants have attempted to press the tort of passing off into service to provide a remedy. Given that the different objects of the statutory provisions and the common law, it is unsurprising that courts have indicated that they will apply the law of passing off without regard to any concurrent statutory powers of the Secretary of State.[43] However, there are difficulties in relying on the action, as classically understood, to regulate abuses of the system of registration of company names. For example, in *Ben & Jerry's Homemade Inc v Ben & Jerry's Ice Cream Ltd*,[44] the claimant, a US-based ice-cream manufacturer, was prevented from incorporating a UK subsidiary under the name 'Ben & Jerry's' by the prior incorporation of the defendant company, Ben & Jerry's Ice Cream Ltd, a company which had no connection with the claimants. Ferris J accepted that the claimants had goodwill in the name of 'Ben & Jerry's' in the UK; however, he noted that there was no evidence that the defendant company had ever traded nor that it had any immediate intention to do so. The claimant's case was based solely on the existence of the defendant company bearing the name 'Ben & Jerry's' and Ferris J was not convinced that this amounted to passing off.

There are two particular problems facing a claimant in such circumstances. First, to succeed in an action for passing off, the claimant must show that the defendant has made some misrepresentation. If the defendant company has not traded and there is no evidence that it intends to trade, then this begs the question: where is the actual or threatened misrepresentation by the defendant? Secondly, a claimant must show that the defendant's threatened and intended actions would cause injury by appropriating a material part of his business.[45] It is questionable whether a claimant can show such damage to his goodwill in circumstances where the defendant has not traded, nor has any intention to trade.

The decision in *Ben & Jerry's* can thus be seen as consistent with established principles of passing off. However, the decision in *Glaxo plc v Glaxowellcome Ltd*[46] showed signs that courts were prepared to accept claims that manifest abuses of the system of registration of companies' names amounted to passing off, notwithstanding the difficulties of establishing misrepresentation and damage. The claimants in the *Glaxowellcome* case were

---

42 See, for example, *Re Association of Certified Public Accountants of Great Britain* [1997] BCC 736. For a consideration of the possible role of s 32 in regulating the abuse of the system of registration, see Watts and Walsh, above n 40, at pp 336–38.

43 See *The British Diabetic Association v The Diabetic Society and Others* [1996] FSR 1.

44 Unreported, Chancery Division, 19 January 1995, Ferris J (transcript by Marten Walsh Cherer is available on LEXIS).

45 Note, in particular, *Hendriks v Montagu* (1881) 17 Ch D 638, especially the judgment of Brett LJ, at pp 647–49 and see also *Ewing (Trading as the Buttercup Dairy Company) v Buttercup Margarine Company Ltd* (1917) 34 RPC 232; *Tussaud v Tussaud* (1890) 44 Ch D 678; and *Fletcher Challenge Ltd v Fletcher Challenge Pty Ltd* [1982] FSR 1 at p 13 *per* Powell J.

46 [1996] FSR 388.

both major pharmaceutical companies, who announced publicly in January 1995 that their businesses were to merge and that the resulting company would be renamed 'Glaxo-Wellcome plc'. The day following the announcement, the defendant, a company registration agent, filed an application to register a company under the name of 'Glaxowellcome Limited'. On discovering the Glaxowellcome registration, the claimants offered to buy the registered company for what was at the time the defendant's standard price of £1,000. This offer was rejected, the defendant demanding instead the sum of £100,000. The claimants made an interlocutory application for a mandatory order that the defendant should change the name of the newly registered company to one which did not include the words 'Glaxo' or 'Wellcome' or any other confusingly similar words. Lightman J, having noted that both Glaxo plc and Wellcome plc had worldwide reputations and goodwill in their respective names, found that the defendants had been engaged in a dishonest scheme to appropriate the goodwill of the claimants and to extort from them a substantial sum as the price for not damaging the goodwill in the names 'Glaxo' and 'Wellcome'. In granting the injunctive relief sought, Lightman J commented that:

> The court will not countenance any such pre-emptive strike of registering companies with names where others have the goodwill in those names, and the registering party then demanding a price for changing the names. It is an abuse of the system of registration of companies' names. The right to choose the name with which a company is registered is not given for that purpose.[47]

Lightman J found support for this in a series of (unspecified) cases where, in actions for passing off, the courts had granted relief requiring the registered name of a company to be changed, irrespective of whether the registered company has traded or not.[48] In its *Final Report*, the Company Law Review Steering Group has recommended that principle developed in *Glaxowellcome* be put on a statutory basis and has recommended that any new Act makes provision for a person to apply to the court for a direction that a company be required to change its name if: (a) the name was chosen with the principal intention of seeking monies from the applicant; or (b) if the name was chosen in order to bring proceedings to restrain the applicant from seeking to use or using that name. In either case, the applicant will need to show that the name is one in which the applicant (whether or not incorporated) has an established reputation or goodwill.[49] Although this recommendation will do little to change the substantive law, it signals an awareness on the part of the Steering Group of the problem of new companies being incorporated with names that are similar or identical to those of existing corporations. Furthermore, putting the law on a statutory footing may well increase awareness of the law amongst those who would otherwise seek to exploit the system of registration of company names and this move may go some way to reduce this activity. However, given that the recommendation is that a person be given the right to apply to the court for a direction, it is unlikely that there will be a significant reduction in the cost or speed of obtaining relief. Given the

---

47 See [1996] FSR 388 at p 391. Laddie J expressed similar sentiments in *Direct Line Group Ltd v Direct Line Estate Agency Ltd* [1997] FSR 374 at p 376.

48 As no cases were referred to in the judgment, one cannot be sure as to which cases formed the basis for Lightman J's decision, however, for some suggestions see Murray, above n 26.

49 See *The Final Report*, above n 1, at p 240.

current powers exercisable by the Secretary of State, for example, under ss 28 and 32 of the Act, it is not clear why a person should not have a right to apply in the first instance to the Secretary of State for a direction, with the right of appeal to the court. This would potentially reduce costs and furthermore, in instances where there have been manifest abuses of the system where the Secretary of State finds in favour of the applicant, it would transfer the burden of initiating a court action onto the company appealing against the direction to change its name.

No doubt, a prime motivation of the Steering Group in suggesting this reform was to put the law on a more certain foundation. Although the *Glaxowellcome* case indicated in the clearest possible terms that courts were not prepared to countenance abuses of the system of registration of companies' names, the basis of the decision was unclear. It has been noted that although the application to the court complained of passing off, the court's decision seemed based on the perception that the defendants had acted in some way fraudulently.[50] Certainly the question why a defendant chooses a particular name is always highly relevant in passing off actions and if a claimant can show that a defendant had the intent to mislead members of the public, courts will readily infer that deception has indeed resulted or is likely to result.[51] However, it is well settled that proof of intentional deception is not a necessary ingredient of conventional passing off[52] and it would follow that the juridical basis of the decision in *Glaxowellcome* cannot have been the defendant's dishonesty.[53] If this was the basis of the decision, then it would suggest the existence of a peculiar species of passing off founded on the dishonest appropriation of goodwill rather than on the conventional elements of a misrepresentation resulting in damage to the claimant's goodwill.

The decision in *Glaxowellcome* and the Steering Group's recommendations would seem to be founded on the principle that if a name is worth appropriating then it is worth protecting and can be seen as compensating for the UK's lack of a general law of unfair competition. However, it is unlikely that the Steering Group's recommendations, if implemented, will put a brake on the extension the tort of passing off as it applies to the adoption and use of names. In more recent times, the legal issues surrounding the registration and use of company names have been largely eclipsed by developments in respect of the registration and use of Internet domain names.

4 INTERESTS IN INTERNET DOMAIN NAMES

Put simply, the Internet is a global network of computers connected together in such a way as to allow the exchange of information between the machines in the network. From its establishment in the 1970s until the early 1990s, this network was a tool used principally by universities, the military and research organisations. The advent of the World Wide Web in 1994 radically changed the character of the Internet. The previously

---

50 Karet above n 40, at p 48.
51 See, for example, *Office Cleaning Services Ltd v Westminster Window and General Cleaners Ltd* (1946) 63 RPC 39 at p 42.
52 See, for example, *Harrods v Harrodian School* [1996] RPC 697 at p 706 *per* Millet LJ and at p 720 *per* Sir Michael Kerr.
53 [1996] RPC 697 at p 720.

complex, cumbersome and relatively unreliable mechanisms for the exchange of information were replaced by a single 'user-friendly' system that greatly facilitated access to the Internet. Coincidental with this technical development, a number of commercial organisations began to recognise the potential of this new means of mass communication giving rise to the notion of electronic commerce (more commonly referred to as 'e-commerce'). E-commerce embraces a wide range of commercial activities conducted by using, exclusively or partially, electronic communications and digital information-processing technology. By far the great majority of companies engaged in e-commerce conduct some of their business electronically and some in more conventional ways. At its simplest, e-commerce may involve no more than the promotion of an existing business by providing information about the products and services offered to users of the Internet; the actual business, the buying and the selling, is done 'conventionally'. Used in this way, the Internet is used as no more than a promotional tool. At the other end of the spectrum, businesses may be dealing in electronic products and services, such as music, computer software, and electronic design, in which case promotion, sales and distribution may all take place within the electronic environment. Although the recent crash in high-technology stocks would seem to suggest that the business community is becoming more sceptical about the claims made for its commercial potential, there is no doubt that the last decade has seen a widespread desire on the part of businesses of all kinds to take advantage of the commercial opportunities offered by the Internet.

It is in the registration and use of so-called Internet 'domain names' where the law of passing off has been pressed into service. As has already been mentioned, the Internet is a global network of computers. For information to be exchanged, each machine needs an identifying address so that it can be located by other machines connected to the network. In this respect, the Internet is not unlike the telephone network, where, in order to communicate with someone else connected to the network, you must first know their telephone number. In the same way, every organisation or individual connected to the Internet is uniquely identified by a numerical address. However, to make the system more 'user-friendly' such numerical addresses are frequently mapped onto more memorable names. These so-called domain names are structured according to a hierarchy. Top Level Domains (TLDs) are divided into classes based on rules that have evolved over time. The great majority of TLDs are designated to individual countries, however there are a limited number of generic TLDs which do not have a geographic or country designation, by far the best known of which is '.com'.

Since 1998, overall technical management of the Internet's domain name system has been coordinated by the Internet Corporation for Assigned Names and Numbers (ICANN). Based in the US, ICANN is a non-profit-making corporation formed by a broad coalition of members of the Internet community.[54] Under the ICANN coordination policy, country-code TLDs are delegated to managers in the country concerned. Within the United Kingdom, domain name registrations are processed and maintained by Nominet UK, a not-for-profit limited company, which has responsibility for the '.uk' TLD.[55] That

---

54 Information about ICANN is published electronically at www.icann.org; see also Chandrani 'ICANN – Now Others Can' (2000) 11 *Entertainment Law Review* 39.

55 There are a number of second level domains (SLDs) within the '.uk' TLD, the most popular of which are: '.co.uk', for commercial enterprises and which is the largest SLD in the UK; '.org.uk', for non-commercial organisations; and '.plc.uk' and '.ltd.uk', which are for companies.

part of Nominet's register which contains information on who has registered a particular domain name is publicly accessible by way of a so-called 'Whois' search.[56]

Because domain names identify specific locations on the Internet, it is technically impossible for exactly the same name to be allocated to different persons. Nominet processes domain name registrations on a first-come, first-served basis[57] and thus, like the register of company names, priority in any particular name is given to the first person onto the register. However, Nominet does not operate any policy which mirrors the powers exercisable by Companies House under s 28 of the Companies Act 1985. This is significant since a domain name will function technically as a unique identifier even if the differences between it and an existing domain name are very slight. For example, a single character difference between two domain names will be technically sufficient for them to operate as the unique identifiers of two quite different locations on the Internet.

In the same way that certain individuals have taken advantage of the system of registration of company names, so too has the system for registering domain names been exploited. One common way of doing so mirrors the practice of registering company names and takes advantage of the fact that priority in a domain name is given to the first to apply. Aided by the fact that many corporations have been slow to appreciate the commercial opportunities offered by the Internet, so-called cyber-squatters have registered the names of existing corporations as domain names, thereby removing from those available precisely those domain names that the corporations themselves would wish to use. Furthermore, cyber-squatters have been able to take advantage of the fact that the domain name system allows a name to be registered even where this differs from an existing name in a small degree and may thus be confusingly similar to one already in use. For example, if a company registers the domain name 'Greenbottle.com', this does not preclude the subsequent registration by another person of the names 'GreenbottleUK.com' or 'Greenbottle.co.uk'. Thus, even if a company registers a domain name comprising its company name, there will remain a large number of variations on its name that potentially can also be registered as domain names by other persons. In addition to cyber-squatters, another class of individual, better described as cyber-pirates, has taken advantage of this and has deliberately used the names of well-known corporations to draw Internet users to unrelated websites. For example, consumers searching the Internet for information regarding, a well-known brand of toys, such as Nintendo, may be diverted to pornographic or hate websites.[58]

As far as the regulation of cyber-squatting and cyber-piracy is concerned, it is important to appreciate that Nominet is not a governing or regulatory body and expressly refuses to accept any responsibility for the use of any domain name on the UK register and in particular for any conflict with any rights in the name in other contexts.[59] Nominet does offer a dispute resolution system but has no power to impose a solution to any

---

56 Accessible from the Nominet website at www.nic.uk.

57 See para 7.1 of Nominet's standard terms and conditions of registration, published electronically at www.nic.uk.

58 For a brief account of this practice see Louise Kehoe 'Leading Brands on the Run' *The Financial Times* 11 October 2000.

59 See paragraph 7.4 of Nominet's standard terms and conditions. Furthermore, under para 7.9 of the same terms, applicants must indemnify Nominet against any claim that the registration of a domain name or its use infringes the legal rights of any third party.

dispute and cannot transfer a domain name to a third party without either the express consent of the registrant or an order of the court.[60] Nominet does, however, have the option of exercising some contractual power in that persons seeking to register a domain name must warrant that neither the registration of the domain name nor the manner in which the domain name is used infringes the legal rights of any third party.[61] However, Nominet itself will not make judgments as to whether the registration or use of a domain name does infringe the rights of a third party.[62]

The absence of any effective regulation of the domain name system in the UK, together with the perception that the Internet is an important commercial environment, has had the inevitable consequence that commercial enterprises have sought a legal means to restrict the activities of cyber-squatters. The obvious parallels with the system of registration of companies' names and the success of the claimants in *Glaxowellcome* suggested a remedy in the action of passing off. In *British Telecommunications plc v One in a Million Ltd*,[63] the defendant was a dealer in Internet domain names who had registered a large number of domain names which comprised or included the names and trade marks of a number of well-known enterprises. The claimants, who included Marks & Spencer plc, J Sainsbury plc, British Telecommunications plc and Virgin Enterprises Ltd, alleged that the registration by One in a Million of these domain names amounted to passing off and to the threat to pass off.[64] None of the domain names registered by One in a Million were in active use as Internet addresses and the defendants claimed that they had registered the domain names with a view to making a profit either by selling them to the owners of the business goodwill associated with the names or to other persons who might have a legitimate reason for using them. Relying in large part on the decision in *Glaxowellcome*, the court at first instance ordered both negative injunctions, restraining the defendants from passing off, and mandatory injunctions, requiring the defendants to assign the disputed domain names to the claimants.[65]

The sole judgment delivered in the Court of Appeal was that of Aldous LJ, with Swinton Thomas LJ and Stuart-Smith LJ indicating only their unqualified agreement with Aldous LJ's findings and reasoning. Aldous LJ noted that the action of passing off was of ancient origin and had developed over time and that the basis of the action should not be confined so as to prevent the common law evolving to meet changes in methods of trade

---

60 However, under para 7.3 of its standard terms and conditions, Nominet may cancel the registration or suspend the delegation of a domain name in exceptional circumstances, such as where to maintain the registration would put Nominet in conflict with statutory obligations or the terms of a Court Order.

61 See para 7.8 of Nominet's standard terms and conditions of registration.

62 It is to be remembered that Nominet's powers and responsibilities are confined to SLDs within the '.uk' country-code TLD. Other national registries may operate different policies in respect of their own country-code TLDs. In the case of generic TLDs, such as '.com', registrants must agree to submit to ICANN Uniform Dispute Resolution Policy. For a recent review of the ICANN Dispute Resolution Policy see Jones 'A Child's First Steps: The First Six Months of Operation – The ICANN Dispute Resolution Procedure for Bad Faith Registration of Domain Names' [2001] *European Intellectual Property Review* 66.

63 [1998] FSR 265; and [1999] FSR 1 (CA).

64 The domain names in issue included: 'marksandspencer.co.uk' and 'marksandspencer.com'; 'sainsburys.com', 'sainsbury.com' and 'j-sainsbury.com'; 'bt.org', 'britishtelecom.co.uk', 'britishtelecom.net' and 'britishtelecom.com'; and 'virgin.org'.

65 [1998] FSR 265.

and communication as it had in the past.[66] There are two ways in which this statement can be understood. At a superficial level, it can be taken as no more than statement that the law needs to adapt and evolve so as to take account of the peculiarities of any new technical development in trade such as the Internet and e-commerce. However, it can equally be read as endorsing the view that the law must adapt so as to take account of modern trading conditions including the tendency for businesses to be built up around a name and the notion that the goodwill of a business may be inherent in the name itself. As discussed above, this issue has in the past divided opinion within the Court of Appeal; a division which has been manifested in particular in disagreements as to whether dilution is a relevant head of damage in passing off actions. As shall be seen, even if Aldous LJ did not intend his statement to be understood in this way, his judgment in *One in a Million* makes clear that he subscribes to the modernising tendency.

Following an extensive review of decided cases where the defendant had either produced goods which would or could be used by another to pass off or had equipped himself with means of identification similar to that of the claimant, Aldous LJ concluded that:

> ... a court will intervene by way of injunction in passing off cases in three types of case. First, where there is passing off established or it is threatened. Secondly, where the defendant is a joint tortfeasor with another in passing off either actual or threatened. Thirdly, where the defendant has equipped himself with or intends to equip another with an instrument of fraud. This third type is probably mere *quia timet* action.[67]

On the facts, Aldous LJ found that there was clear evidence of the systematic registration by One in a Million of well-known trade names as 'blocking registrations'. He noted that the purpose of such blocking registrations was to extract money from the owners of the goodwill in the name chosen. The ability to do so was mainly dependent upon the threat that One in a Million would exploit the goodwill by either trading under the name or equipping another with the name so he could do so.[68] The activities of the defendants amounted to passing off and, furthermore, the domain names registered by the defendants were instruments of fraud.

As to passing off, Aldous LJ took the view that the registration of a distinctive name such as 'marksandspencer' made a false representation to persons who consulted the register that the registrant was connected or associated with the name registered. Damage, or the likelihood of damage, would result from the registration by the erosion of the exclusive goodwill in the distinctive name.[69]

Aldous LJ thus addressed the question left unanswered by the decisions in *Ben & Jerry's*[70] and *Glaxowellcome*[71] as to the misrepresentation in circumstances where the defendant company does not trade. Aldous LJ argued that the misrepresentation lies in the publicly accessible information held on Nominet's register of domain names. There is

---

66 See [1999] FSR 1 at pp 11–12.
67 See [1999] FSR 1 at p 18.
68 Given that all of the claimants were well known companies, Aldous LJ seems to have taken the view that the threat of the use of their names by cyber-pirates was a very real one.
69 See [1999] FSR 1 at pp 22–23.
70 Unreported, Chancery Division, 19 January 1995, Ferris J.
71 [1996] FSR 388.

some force in this argument. It has long been established that a trader might be injured in his business if there is a misrepresentation that the defendants are connected or 'in some way mixed up' with the claimants.[72] Some assumed commercial or even a philanthropic connection between the claimant and defendant is sufficient to amount to a misrepresentation.[73] If a member of the public consults Nominet's register of domain names, the first two pieces of information displayed are the domain name itself followed by the name of the person for whom the name is registered[74] and this would certainly seem sufficient to suggest to the public that there is a connection between the parties concerned. It might similarly be argued that the existence of a name on the index of company names could be construed as a form of connection misrepresentation between the company registered and an existing company with the same or similar name.[75] This would be so irrespective of whether the registered company traded or not.

As to damage, Aldous LJ simply pointed to the erosion of the exclusive goodwill in the distinctive name that would result from the registration. His recognition of dilution as a head of damage was unequivocal and there was no attempt to engage in the debate triggered by the earlier decisions of the Court of Appeal in *Taittinger*[76] and *Harrods*.[77] It will be recalled that none of the domain names in issue in *One in a Million* were in actual use and interestingly, Aldous LJ suggested that it was the registration which risked the erosion of the goodwill in a name. Yet the appearance of a name on a register presents no more of a risk of erosion than does the appearance of the word 'champagne' in an English dictionary. Both are available to be used, but without use it is hard to see how there can be an erosion of any goodwill in the name. Given that the act complained of was the mere registration of the domain names, a stronger argument, both on the facts and on the basis of supporting authority, would have been to recognise the damage resulting from the claimants' loss of control of their reputation by the defendant's act of registering the domain names. Why Aldous LJ chose to focus on erosion is thus something of a mystery unless it is to indicate his support for the recognition of this head of damage.

In addition to finding passing off established, Aldous LJ also found that the domain names registered by One in a Million were instruments of fraud. As noted above, the decision in *Glaxowellcome* pointed to the existence of a peculiar species of passing off founded on the dishonest appropriation of goodwill rather than on the conventional elements of a misrepresentation resulting in damage to the claimant's goodwill. In *One in a Million*, Aldous LJ confirmed the existence of this species of passing off and in so doing signalled the willingness to provide a remedy against manifestly unfair business practices. On the face of it, the parallels between the registration of company names on the one hand, and Internet domain names on the other are obvious. Both are largely deregulated systems in which priority in a name is determined according to who is first

---

72   See *Ewing (Trading as the Buttercup Dairy Company) v Buttercup Margarine Company Ltd* (1917) 34 RPC 232 at p 237 *per* Lord Cozens-Hardy MR.

73   See *Harrods v Harrodian School* [1996] RPC 697 at p 721 *per* Sir Michael Kerr.

74   The register also contains information concerning who registered the name (usually an Internet service provider), the date when the name was registered and the servers on which the domain is maintained.

75   An argument put forward in relation to the *Glaxowellcome* case by Karet, above n 40, at p 48.

76   [1993] FSR 641.

77   [1996] RPC 697.

to register. However, there are also significant differences. Companies are creatures of statute and there is a strong argument that courts are under an obligation to police the registration of companies so as to protect against manifest abuses of the system. In finding for the claimants, Lightman J in the *Glaxowellcome* case noted that the right to choose the name with which a company is registered is not given for the purpose of allowing the appropriation of goodwill in the name. However, the Internet is not a creation of the law, nor are domain names given for any purpose other than for identifying a location on the Internet. Furthermore, whereas companies exist to trade, the Internet is not exclusively, nor even primarily, a commercial environment. The law of passing off is a branch of commercial law in so far as it exists to protect traders. Its extension into the area of the registration of companies' names is understandable but the registration of domain names, whilst potentially impacting on the activities of traders, is not, in itself, a commercial activity.

As to the circumstances when a name amounts to an instrument of fraud, Aldous LJ drew a distinction between names the use of which would inherently lead to passing off and those where this was not necessarily so:

> Whether any name is an instrument of fraud will depend upon all the circumstances. A name which will, by reason of its similarity to the name of another, inherently lead to passing off is such an instrument. If it would not inherently lead to passing off, it does not follow that it is not an instrument of fraud. The court should consider the similarity of the names, the intention of the defendant, the type of trade and all the surrounding circumstances. If it be the intention of the defendant to appropriate the goodwill of another or enable others to do so, I can see no reason why the court should not infer that it will happen, even if there is a possibility that such an appropriation would not take place. If, taking all the circumstances into account, the court should conclude that the name was produced to enable passing off, is adapted to be used for passing off and, if used, is likely to be fraudulently used, an injunction will be appropriate.[78]

The unqualified recognition by Aldous LJ that dilution is a valid head of damage would suggest that he subscribes to the view that a distinctive name can, in some cases, form part of a claimant's goodwill and, in itself, constitute a property interest. It is unsurprising therefore that he suggests that there are names, the use of which by another person, would inherently lead to passing off.[79] Such a proposition would be unsustainable under the more orthodox view that passing off does not protect the claimant's proprietary right in his name as such, but rather the goodwill and reputation of his business which is likely to be harmed by the defendant's misrepresentation. Even if a name would not inherently lead to passing off, it may nevertheless be an instrument of fraud. Aldous LJ indicated that whether this is so would depend on all the circumstances, but particularly relevant was the similarity of the claimant's and defendant's names and the intention of the defendant in registering the name. These two factors are related in that, the closer the similarity between the parties' names, the harder it will be for a defendant to convince a court that his motive in registering the name was not to extract money from the owners of

---

78 See [1999] FSR 1 at p 18.
79 On the facts, Aldous LJ concluded that the domain names that included the name 'Marks & Spencer' were such instruments of fraud since any realistic use of them as domain names would inherently result in passing off.

the goodwill in the name chosen. Of course mere similarity may signal no more than coincidence. In *One in a Million*, there was no question that the names in issue were distinctive of the claimants' businesses. However, if a name is not so distinctive, for example because it is apt simply to describe the character or quality of the services or goods offered, then passing off will be harder to establish. Thus a claimant who provided a fax to e-mail service under the name 'efax' was unable to obtain an injunction to prevent the defendant from offering a similar service from his website at efax.co.uk.[80] The court took the view that any confusion resulting from the fact that both the claimants and the defendant were offering similar services under similar names was attributable to the descriptive nature of that name, rather than any misrepresentation by the defendant to the effect that he was carrying on the claimant's business. One the other hand, the court in *Britannia Building Society v Prangley*,[81] found incredible the defendant's explanation that the registration of 'BritanniaBuildingSociety.com' was intended to advertise his business of supplying British building workers to Iran.[82] Furthermore, registering a domain name that is not necessarily distinctive of the claimant's business and then setting up a website under that name which has a similar look and style to the claimant's own website may well amount to passing off.[83]

Occasionally it may be that a name, whilst distinctive of the claimant's business in one market, is not so distinctive when used on the Internet. So for example, in *French Connection Limited v Sutton*,[84] Rattee J found that the term 'FCUK', although used by the claimants, French Connection Ltd, as part of an extensive advertising campaign, was well known to Internet users as an alternative to the expletive 'FUCK'.[85] Thus the domain name 'FCUK.com' would not necessarily be understood as a reference to the claimants.[86] Furthermore, although the defendant had at one point offered to sell the domain name to the claimants, he had nevertheless registered the domain name 'FCUK.com', not with a view to extracting money for sale of the name, but for use as his own business's Internet address and it followed that it was not an instrument of fraud.

It is important to appreciate that as far as determining whether a name is an instrument of fraud, what is determinative is evidence that the defendant intends to appropriate the goodwill of another. Even if it can be established that there is at least a possibility that a name may be legitimately used, the court will nevertheless infer that

---

80   *eFax.com Inc v Oglesby* (2000) *The Times* 16 March 2000 (transcript available on Westlaw (2000 WL191200)).

81   Unreported, Chancery Division, 12 June 2000, Rattee J.

82   Cf *MBNA America Bank NA v Freeman* [2001] EBLR 13, and see Sandhu (2000) 11 *Entertainment Law Review* N99.

83   *Easyjet Airline Co Ltd v Dainty*, unreported, Chancery Division, 19 February 2001, Mr B Livesey QC (transcript available on Westlaw (2001 WL272885)). For an interesting consideration of how the registration of domain names comprising generic words potentially impacts on the balance between public and private interests, see Wilkof 'Trade Marks and the Public Domain: Generic Marks and Generic Domain Names' [2000] *European Intellectual Property Review* 571.

84   [2000] ETMR 341.

85   The claimants claimed that the term 'FCUK' used in their advertising campaign was an acronym standing for 'French Connection UK'.

86   However, note that even a purely descriptive name may, by a course of dealing over many years, become so associated with a particular trader that it acquires a secondary meaning such that it may properly be said to be descriptive of that trader's goods and of his goods alone, see: *Reckitt & Coleman Products Ltd v Borden Inc* [1990] RPC 341 at p 412 *per* Lord Oliver; and *County Sound plc v Ocean Sound Ltd* [1991] FSR 367 at pp 373–76 *per* Nourse LJ.

there will be an appropriation of goodwill once the intention of the defendant has been established.

5 CONCLUSIONS

There is no doubt that the last five years has seen a significant extension of the tort of passing off. In an article written in 1995, after the Court of Appeal's decision in *Taittinger*, but before the decisions in *Harrods*, *Glaxowellcome* and *One in a Million*, Robertson and Horton noted that whilst English law protects traders against certain forms of unfair competition, the focus of the law is on the prevention of customer confusion[87] and that it has eschewed a continental European approach to unfair competition based on determinations of what is fair and ethical practice in the marketplace.[88] However, in more recent times, courts have been inclined to recognise a property right in the distinctive character or advertising value of a name as such, particularly in accepting claims for the dilution or erosion of the distinctiveness of a name as a relevant head of damage in passing off actions. In this respect, it can be argued that the law of the UK has developed beyond an action founded on customer confusion. It is interesting to note, for example, that the World Intellectual Property Organisation's (WIPO) Model Provisions on Protection Against Unfair Competition[89] distinguish between acts which cause or are likely to cause confusion with respect to another's enterprise[90] and those acts which damage or are likely to damage the goodwill or reputation of another's enterprise by the dilution of the reputation attached to a trade name.[91] Furthermore, to date, no one has sought to address the paradox noted by Millet LJ in *Harrods*, that whilst action of passing off demands the presence of both confusion and damage, dilution of reputation does not depend on confusion.

The development of the doctrine of instruments of fraud has also significantly extended the tort and, to some extent, points to an erosion of the traditional reticence of UK courts to make determinations of what is fair and ethical commercial practice. The basis of the doctrine is the intention of a defendant to appropriate the goodwill of another. Misrepresentation, customer confusion and damage form no part of the basis for a finding that a defendant has equipped himself with an instrument of fraud. It is interesting to note the similarity of the approach adopted by UK courts to that under the ICANN Uniform Domain Name Dispute Resolution Policy. Under this policy, what amounts to an abusive registration of a domain name is judged according to three criteria: first, that the domain name registered is identical or confusingly similar to a mark in which the complainant has rights; secondly, that the domain name registrant has no rights or legitimate interests in respect of the domain name in question; and thirdly, that the

---

87 See Robertson and Horton, above n 8, at pp 569–70.
88 Robertson and Horton, above n 8, at p 568 and note also the similar observations made by Carty, above n 14, at p 151.
89 On the World Intellectual Property Organisation (WIPO) Model Provisions on Protection against Unfair Competition see Gielen 'WIPO and Unfair Competition' [1997] *European Intellectual Property Review* 78.
90 See WIPO Model Provisions on Protection against Unfair Competition, Art 2.
91 See WIPO Model Provisions on Protection against Unfair Competition, Art 3.

domain name has been registered in 'bad faith'.[92] As to what amounts to a registration made in 'bad faith', para 4(b) of the ICANN Policy sets out the following examples of circumstances that will be considered as evidence of the bad faith registration and use of a domain name:

(a) circumstances indicating that the domain name was registered or acquired primarily for the purpose of selling, renting, or otherwise transferring the domain name registration to the complainant who is the owner of the trademark or service mark or to a competitor of that complainant, for valuable consideration in excess of the domain name registrant's out-of-pocket costs directly related to the domain name; or

(b) the domain name was registered in order to prevent the owner of the trademark or service mark from reflecting the mark in a corresponding domain name, provided that the domain name registrant has engaged in a pattern of such conduct; or

(c) the domain name was registered primarily for the purpose of disrupting the business of a competitor; or

(d) by using the domain name, the domain name registrant intentionally attempted to attract for financial gain, Internet users to the registrant's website or other on-line location, by creating a likelihood of confusion with the complainant's mark as to the source, sponsorship, affiliation, or endorsement of the registrant's website or location or of a product or service on the registrant's website or location.

The fact that the Internet is a true global medium highlights the fact that the absence of a law of unfair competition in the UK puts it out of line with the majority of other Member States of the European Union. As has already been noted, the majority of continental European countries recognise a right of the honest trader to restrain his competitors from causing him injury by unfair conduct which is not consistent with 'honest usages' of the trade.[93] Furthermore, the WIPO Model Provisions on Protection against Unfair Competition and the terms of the ICANN Uniform Domain Name Dispute Resolution Policy evidence the emergence of international norms concerned with the regulation of unfair business practices with which the law of the UK is arguably inconsistent. What is now needed in the UK is the development of a coherent doctrine of unfair competition at the policy level. To date, the law has developed on an ad hoc basis in response to specific instances of manifestly unfair practices relating to the registration of company names and domain names. Whilst the response of the courts to these practices is understandable, what is now needed is a review taking into account the rationale of passing off and whether, in its expanded form, it can fulfil the role of a law of unfair competition whilst striking an appropriate balance between the interests of traders, their competitors and of course customers. What needs to be asked is whether the scope of protection is justifiable once these interests have been taken into account. Without such a consideration, the risk is that the tort will become a vehicle for market dominance, particularly by those enterprises with advertising power.[94]

---

92 See ICANN Uniform Domain Name Dispute Resolution Policy, para 4(a).
93 See above n 8 and accompanying text.
94 See Carty, above n 26, at p 632.

PART 3

CORPORATE GOVERNANCE
AND ACCOUNTABILITY

CHAPTER 7

THE REFORM OF DIRECTORS' DUTIES

John Birds

1 INTRODUCTION

Although the legislation governing companies has never clearly spelt out the role of the directors of companies, leaving this strictly to the constitution of each company, there is no doubt that, as the Cadbury Committee explained, in reality 'boards of directors are responsible for the governance of their companies'.[1] In smaller companies this will probably include the actual management of companies as well, while in larger companies it is more likely to comprise setting strategy and supervising management, and reporting on their stewardship to the shareholders in general meeting. Given this key role of directors, what their duties are is clearly a central issue for company law. Currently, though, these duties are to be found in a mass of rather unwieldy case law reinforced by some provisions in the companies' legislation,[2] supplemented by regulations in companies' articles of association, where appropriate the *City Code on Takeovers and Mergers* and, in the case of listed companies, in the *Listing Rules* and the *Combined Code*.[3]

There has been much consideration of, and comment on, these duties over the years.[4] This includes the Law Commission's 1999 Report, *Company Directors: Regulating Conflicts of Interest and Formulating a Statement of Duties*,[5] and, more recently, has culminated in recommendations from the Steering Group of the Company Law Review that should form the basis of the major reforming legislation promised within the current Parliament. There seems little doubt that the Law Commission's review was necessary, given the complexity and overlap already mentioned and the lack of clarity in some of the current statutory provisions. Their remit was, however, a limited one. Once the Government had instigated the fundamental review of company law, it was inevitable that there would be a further detailed and more fundamental examination of directors' duties. The March 2000 consultation document issued by the Steering Group (*Modern Company Law for a Competitive Economy: Developing the Framework*)[6] devoted considerable attention to this issue. This was followed by further thoughts in the consultation document of November 2000 (*Modern Company Law for a Competitive Economy: Completing the Structure*)[7] and their

---

1 Report on the Financial Aspects of Corporate Governance (London, Gee, 1992), at para 2.5.
2 One consequence is considerable overlap; see the comment in *Gore-Browne on Companies* (Bristol, Jordans, 44th edn, 1986 as updated) at s 27.3, final paragraph.
3 For a review of corporate governance generally, see Birds, Boyle, Ferran and Villiers, *Boyle & Birds' Company Law* (Bristol, Jordans, 4th edn, 2000), at chapter 11.
4 They are perhaps the subject of the greatest amount of academic literature on company law, and are often the subject of DTI Inspectors' reports.
5 Law Commission Report No 261 *Company Directors: Regulating Conflicts of Interests and Formulating a Statement of Duties* (1999) Cm 4436 (London, TSO, 1999).
6 Hereafter, *Developing the Framework* (London, DTI, 2000).
7 Hereafter, *Competing the Structure* (London, DTI, 2000).

conclusions in *Modern Company Law for a Competitive Economy: Final Report* in July 2001.[8] It is the intention of this chapter to review the reforms that seem likely to emanate from the work done by the Law Commission and the Steering Group.[9] This contribution concentrates upon the duties as such, with some brief reference to the consequences of breach, and a passing glance at the question of minority shareholders' remedies for breach of directors' duties.

The work of the Law Commission, as it was developed by the Steering Group, has usefully considered and identified general questions of policy that affect directors' duties and other related areas of company law. In particular there has been identification of the guiding principles which should govern this area of the law. The latter were referred to by the Law Commission as the 'headline principles' and were: (a) accessibility of the law, (b) certainty, (c) graduated regulation of conflicts of interests and (d) efficient disclosure.[10] These principles were heavily influenced by the economic analysis and empirical work done as part of the Law Commission's project on directors' duties.[11] The Steering Group has endorsed this philosophy, one of its core policies being 'an inclusive, open and flexible scheme of company governance', of which one of the main components is:

> ... an accessible codified statement of the general duties which directors owe to their companies as managers and monitors, embodying a modern, inclusive view of the range of decision making and objective standards of professional and skill, tailored to the role of the individual director.[12]

As far as company law more generally is concerned, there is greater clarity regarding the needs of different types of company. The Steering Group enthusiastically espoused the 'think small first' philosophy, which became another core objective. However, it does not seem likely that this particular objective will have much impact on directors' duties as such. Despite the move to real simplification of the law governing private companies,[13] the Steering Group has not recommended that there should be any real differences between the basic law on the duties of the directors of public and large companies and that applicable to the directors of private companies (with the exception of some minor qualifications as regards detailed rules relating to conflicts of interest). Of course, case law application of the duties can develop appropriate differences,[14] but serious questions can

---

8 Hereafter, *The Final Report* (London, DTI, 2001).

9 For detailed consideration of the Law Commission's work, see in particular: (1999) 20(6) *Company Lawyer* (June 1999); [1999] *The Company Financial and Insolvency Law Review*, Part 2 (Autumn 1999). For a valuable comment on the Steering Group's proposals in *Developing the Framework*, above n 6, see Worthington 'Reforming Directors' Duties' (2001) 64 MLR 439. Recent detailed treatment of the duties of directors includes Butcher *Directors' Duties: A New Millennium, a New Approach?* (London, Kluwer, 1999) and Andennas and Sugarman (eds) *Developments in European Company Law, Volume 3, Directors' Conflicts of Interest: Legal, Socio-Legal and Economic Analysis* (London, Kluwer, 2001).

10 See Law Commission Report, above n 5, at Part 3.

11 See Law Commission Report, above n 5, at Appendix B.

12 See *The Final Report*, above n 8, at para 1.56.

13 See Part II of *Developing the Framework*, above n 6, which was confirmed in chapter 2 of *Completing the Structure*, above n 7, and chapters 2 and 4 of the *The Final Report*, above n 8.

14 For example, regarding the application of the duty to act with proper care and skill, as is briefly discussed later at p 167.

be raised about the appropriateness of some proposed duties to smaller companies.[15] More will be said about this below.

In the course of this official lengthy review of directors' duties, consideration has also been given to what, if anything, should be the proper role of non-statutory regulation. Both the Law Commission and the Steering Group came out firmly in favour of the view that the basic duties and principles governing company directors must be covered by traditional legal rules.[16] Of course, this does not deny the importance of self-regulatory rules in amplifying traditional duties. General statements of directors' duties are either very general or framed in terms of prohibitions rather than affirmative statements. General statements, for example, that directors must act in good faith and exercise their powers for a proper purpose and must exercise appropriate care and skill do not actually say what directors should do in the context of taking a particular decision. In the case of a listed company, assistance in determining the scope of these general duties can be found in, for example, the provisions of the *Combined Code* and the *City Code on Takeovers and Mergers*. Indeed, it has been cogently argued that many of the principles that govern the conduct of company directors, especially those that stem from the prohibition on conflicts of duty and interest, as explained below, are not really 'duties' at all.[17] This view argues that the duty of directors is to manage and/or to supervise management, and report as appropriate. The legal and regulatory rules that determine the propriety of their conduct are perhaps better described in general as 'principles', and it is noteworthy that the draft codifying legislation in the Steering Group's *Final Report*,[18] which is discussed below, has partially adopted this language. The title of the draft section and schedule is 'General principles by which directors are bound', although some may be relieved to read that it is still proposed that directors are under a duty to observe these principles and that the word 'must' appears regularly!

After a brief description of the current law, this essay will examine the likely shape of the law for the future under the following headings:

- the codification of directors' duties;
- core duties – the scope of company law;
- good faith and proper purposes;
- independence of judgment and fairness;
- the core equitable principles regulating conflicts of duty and interest and detailed fiduciary duties supplementing those;

---

15 See also Berg 'The Company Law Review: Legislating Directors' Duties' [2000] *Journal of Business Law* 472.

16 Compare the views of some distinguished lawyers such as Lord Hoffmann that there is a role for 'self-regulation' in this area, particularly in his very clear and stimulating discussion of these issues at a public lecture at the University of Manchester's Centre for Law and Business on 13 November 1998. Lord Hoffmann laid particular stress on the third tier of rules overlaying both the general common law and the detailed statutory rules, particularly the self-regulatory rules operating for listed companies under the *Listing Rules* and the *Combined Code*. A version of this lecture is published as chapter 1 in Andennas and Sugarman, above n 9.

17 See especially, for a recent review, Sealy 'Directors' Duties Revisited' (2001) 21 *Company Lawyer* 79. This is supported by some case law, especially *Movitex Ltd v Bulfield* [1988] BCLC 104, but is not accepted by all; see the further brief discussion at p 170, below.

18 Above n 8, at Annex C.

- duties of care and skill;
- the ratification and the enforcement of directors' duties;
- the consequences of a breach of duty.

2 AN OUTLINE OF DIRECTORS' DUTIES

Traditionally, directors' duties are divided into two categories. The first comprises those duties and principles that apply because directors are regarded as standing in a fiduciary relationship with their companies, that is in a broad sense a relationship that requires the display of particular good faith and loyalty by the director/fiduciary to their company/principal. The duties here are derived from equitable principles initially imposed on trustees of property and subsequently applied to persons such as agents and partners. Because directors manage the property of others for the benefit of the latter, it was natural for the law to bring them within the category of those in a fiduciary relationship. This was originally effected entirely by case law, the companies' legislation by itself for many years giving no indication of it. The second category of duties is the duty of care and skill, in other words concerned with the standards by which a director will be liable for acting negligently and liable to compensate the company accordingly.

Different writers classify the fiduciary duties of directors in different ways,[19] but for present purposes there are, it is thought, five main subdivisions. The first is the primary duty to act in good faith in the interests of the company. This is primarily a subjective duty, in the sense that it is for the director to decide, in good faith, what is in the interests of the company,[20] but there is an objective element also, in that the interests of the company means the long-term interests of the members of the company, usually of course the shareholders, and to give primacy to any other interests will be a breach of duty, regardless of the directors' honest belief.[21] The qualifications to this are twofold. The first is the statutory duty to have regard to the interests of the company's employees,[22] but this is clearly subordinate, where it matters, to the interests of the members, and in practice is unenforceable.[23] The second is that the interests of creditors are paramount when a company is insolvent or approaching insolvency.[24] The duty to act in good faith probably comprises a duty to exercise an independent judgment,[25] although this could be separately identified.

---

19 For detailed accounts, see: *Gore-Browne on Companies*, above n 2, at chapter 27; Davies *Gower's Principles of Modern Company Law* (London, Sweet & Maxwell, 6th edn 1997) at chapters 21–23; Farrar and Hannigan *Farrar's Company Law* (London, Butterworths, 4th edn 1998), at chapters 25 and 26.

20 See *Re Smith and Fawcett Ltd* [1942] Ch 304.

21 See: *Hutton v West Cork Railway* (1883) 23 Ch D 654; *Parke v Daily News Ltd* [1962] Ch 929.

22 See Companies Act 1985, s 309.

23 Because it is owed to the company alone. See further *Gore-Browne on Companies*, above n 2, at para 27.4.1. Note, however, the reasonably positive reference to it in the judgment of the Court of Appeal in *Fulham Football Club Ltd v Cabra Estates plc* [1992] BCC 863 at p 876.

24 See the discussion at p 163, below.

25 See *Fulham Football Club Ltd v Cabra Estates plc* [1992] BCC 863.

The second duty requires the directors to exercise the powers vested in them for their proper purpose. This has a substantial objective element according to the case law,[26] in that the proper purpose is determined as a matter of construction of the power, express or implied, in the company's articles of association, although where the exercise of a power can be said to have more than one purpose, one proper and one improper, weight will be given to the honest opinion of the directors as to why they exercised the power.[27]

Thirdly, directors are regarded as being trustees of the property of the company that is under their control and liable for any misappropriation or misapplication thereof.[28] Although it would probably be rare that directors misapplying company property would be acting in good faith, liability is clearly not dependent on a lack of good faith.

Fourthly, directors must not place themselves in a position where there is, or may be, a conflict between their duty to the company and their own interest.[29] Although the boundaries of this principle are regularly the subject of debate, it is traditionally a strict principle, which is supplemented by many of the detailed provisions affecting directors in Part X of the Companies Act 1985. The general equitable principle states that any conflict can be resolved by proper disclosure to and approval by the company in general meeting or, in some cases if the articles allow, the board of directors, but in the absence of that, any transaction involving a conflicted director is voidable[30] and the director liable for any profit they have made.[31] The statutory rules, among other things, ensure that disclosure of interests is made to the board of directors,[32] but in respect of substantial property transactions[33] make general meeting sanction mandatory[34] and prohibit entirely most loans by companies to their directors.[35] They also extend the prohibitions to persons connected with directors,[36] so that they are not easily evaded.

The fifth principle was historically derived from the fourth, but probably stands in its own right. It renders a director accountable for any secret profit they have made through holding the office of director.[37] Again, the presence or absence of good faith is irrelevant,

---

26 See: *Hogg v Cramphorn Ltd* [1967] Ch 254; *Bamford v Bamford* [1970] Ch 212; *Howard Smith Ltd v Ampol Petroleum Ltd* [1974] AC 821; and *Lee Panavision Ltd v Lee Lighting Ltd* [1992] BCLC 22.

27 See Lord Wilberforce in *Howard Smith Ltd v Ampol Petroleum Ltd* [1974] AC 821 at p 837. The proper purposes doctrine was the basis of the much publicised decision in *Equitable Life Assurance Society v Hyman* [2000] 2 WLR 798 (CA) and [2000] 3 WLR 529 (HL) and is clearly, as pointed out by Lord Woolf MR at [2000] 2 WLR 798 at p 806, a doctrine of public law as well as private law.

28 See: *Cook v Deeks* [1916] AC 554; *Selangor United Rubber Estates Ltd v Craddock (No 3)* [1968] 1 WLR 1555 at pp 1,575–76 and *Wallersteiner v Moir (No 1)* [1974] 1 WLR 991. *Gore-Browne on Companies*, above n 2, at para 27.6, has long treated this as a separate head of directors' duties, although most other company texts subsume its consideration within the secret profits rules.

29 See: *Aberdeen Railway Co v Blaikie* (1854) 1 Macq 461; *Guinness plc v Saunders* [1990] 2 AC 663.

30 See *Hely-Hutchinson v Brayhead Ltd* [1968] 1 QB 549.

31 See *Imperial Mercantile Credit Association v Coleman* (1873) LR 6 HL 189.

32 See Companies Act 1985, s 317.

33 Broadly speaking, a deal involving property worth more than £10,000 or 10% of the company's asset value, subject in the latter case to a minimum of £1,000.

34 See Companies Act 1985, ss 320–22.

35 See Companies Act 1985, ss 330–42.

36 Defined in s 346 to include spouses, minor children, business partners and associated companies, the latter broadly being companies in which a director has a 20% or more stake.

37 *Regal (Hastings) Ltd v Gulliver* [1967] 2 AC 134n.

as is whether there was a conflict of duty and interest in the strict sense, but the prohibition is only on secret profits, so that proper disclosure and approval will relieve a director from any possibility of liability.[38] Again there is some statutory amplification of the general principle, principally in connection with payments made for loss of office.[39]

The duty of care and skill was traditionally regarded as low, because directors were not bound to devote their time to the company and were judged by the level of skill that they possessed, that is on a subjective basis.[40] The common law probably now requires an objectively reasonable level of care and skill, and this is certainly the case where a company is insolvent or on the verge of insolvency.[41] Statute here would impose liability on an objectively negligent director[42] and the same standard is used in order to decide whether or not a director should be disqualified for unfitness.[43]

As indicated earlier, the principles sketched out above are derived from a large volume of case law and statutory material. There is also much overlap. There can be no doubt that the careful director, or board of directors, will regularly need their lawyers 'at their side' lest they fall foul of one or more of the principles. The law can hardly be said to be easily accessible to those affected by it. It is also not always clear. While few would quarrel with the proposition that directors should be subject to strict duties and responsibilities, because they manage other people's property and are responsible for actions that affect employees, creditors and indeed the whole community, it needs to be certain that their duties achieve a fair and, perhaps, efficient balance, so that proper entrepreneurship is not unduly stifled. There also needs to be proper consideration of the question whether the same principles should apply to the range of company directors, from the sole director of a one-person private company at one extreme to the board of the large or very large listed company, often part of a multinational group, at the other. A proper and detailed review of directors' duties seems an entirely appropriate exercise to have been undertaken, and as we have seen, this has been done in effect by a two-stage process, first by the Law Commission and secondly by the Company Law Review. It is to the likely result of these deliberations that the remainder of this chapter is devoted.

3 CODIFICATION OF DIRECTORS' DUTIES

Despite objections[44] that have mainly come, it seems, from lawyers, both practising and academic, it looks certain that the next Companies Act will codify all the principal

---

38 Some would argue that the no conflict and no profit principles are not properly *duties* of directors. See p 151 above and briefly further below at p 170.

39 See Companies Act 1985, ss 312–16.

40 See: *Re City Equitable Fire Insurance Co* [1925] Ch 407; *Dorchester Finance Co v Stebbing* [1989] BCLC 498.

41 See: *Norman v Theodore Goddard* [1991] BCLC 1028; *Re D'Jan of London Ltd* [1993] BCC 646; *Re Simmon Box (Diamonds) Ltd* [2000] BCC 275; *Re Westlowe Storage and Distribution Ltd* [2000] BCC 851; and, in Australia, *Daniels v Anderson* (1995) 16 ACSR 607. It could be argued that it is cases on disqualification for unfitness (see Company Directors Disqualification Act 1986, s 6) that are primarily setting the modern standard; see especially the cases cited in n 43, below.

42 See Insolvency Act 1986, s 214.

43 See: *Re Landhurst Leasing plc* [1999] 1 BCLC 286; *Re Barings plc (No 5)* [1999] 1 BCLC 433 at pp 486–89 *per* Jonathan Parker J, affirmed at [2000] 1 BCLC 523.

44 These are referred to in *Completing the Structure*, above n 7, at para 3.6.

fiduciary and other duties of directors.[45] A majority of the respondents to the consultations undertaken by both the Law Commission and the Steering Group supported this, principally on the basis that it would make the law more accessible, and, as we have seen, accessibility of the law was a major component of the Steering Group's thinking.

The Steering Group, though, took a different view from that of the Law Commission on the nature of this codification. The Law Commission proposed a non-exhaustive code that would set out the basic principles but leave room for the common law to develop in the light of, but not necessarily limited by, those principles.[46] Their proposed code was to be primarily educational, with the statutory statement occupying a prominent place on the statutory forms a director must sign on taking up office. Despite the fact that a clear majority of respondents to the Law Commission consultation supported this sort of partial codification, the Steering Group on the other hand favoured an exhaustive code. They stated:

> We have not been able to think of any new principles, nor areas where it is desirable to leave scope for the judges to develop completely new ones. There would also be an objection of principle to the judges inventing wholly new bases of liability for company directors, with retrospective effect, rather than new obligations being imposed prospectively and after democratic debate by Parliament. We are therefore inclined to favour the proposed restatement being treated as exhaustive. Our view at this stage is that the restatement should set out all the general duties which apply to directors in the exercise of their functions as such. The only other duties which apply to them will be those which are imposed by other provisions of the legislation.[47]

To that end, in *Developing the Framework*, the Steering Group put forward a trial statutory code. Because it was intended to be exhaustive, it was more detailed than that recommended by the Law Commission. Further suggestions were made in *Completing the Structure* and in *The Final Report*; the code is one of the matters that is the subject of draft legislation appended to *The Final Report*. The proposed code is still more of a high-level statement than an attempt completely to codify existing case law and is, therefore, less open to objection on the ground that it might stultify development of the law.[48] Although it is stated to replace the present law,[49] there would clearly still be scope for some development where necessary within its terms, as well as the possibility, or indeed likelihood, of using existing case law to explain its meaning.[50]

Despite this, it seems possible that many lawyers will continue to oppose codification in any form, perhaps because previous experience of codifying statutes in English law,

---

45 It is most unlikely, though, that the term 'fiduciary' will be used; see further below at p 158.

46 See the Law Commission Report No 261, above n 5, at Part 4.

47 See *Developing the Framework*, above n 6, at para 3.82.

48 This was arguably a problem with earlier suggestions for codification, particularly that recommended by the Jenkins Committee and included in the abortive Companies Bill 1978; see Birds 'Making Directors Do Their Duties' (1980) 1 *Company Lawyer* 67.

49 See the concluding phrase of draft sub-s (1), set out below at p 158.

50 See *Completing The Framework*, above n 7, at para 3.12. It is hardly likely that chancery practitioners will not continue to cite the traditional authorities on which such a code is based.

chiefly those commercial codes drafted by Chalmers, is not always happy.[51] Whether or not they will be right to do so depends, it is thought, on the nature of the codification. If it is capable of broad interpretation and development, perhaps rather like a traditional civilian code, then it should be unproblematic. What seems vital is that it does not turn out to be the sort of code about whose intricacies lawyers will be able to spend large amounts of time[52] arguing. Evidence of this can be seen from some of the responses to the draft in *Developing The Structure*, which are addressed in *Completing the Structure*, and some of which are referred to below. The ultimate version must take account of this. It is also suggested that the proposed code can still be criticised for not reproducing, even at a 'high level', all the main features of the current law. Detailed points of this sort are made below, where the provisions of the proposed code, as they appear in *The Final Report*, are reproduced and commented on. The form adopted is a short proposed section (set out below), which incorporates a detailed Schedule, the latter including explanatory notes. The Steering Group believes that this facilitates flexibility and accessibility.[53]

A further general point concerns the way in which the duties are to be expressed. It is well known that, in general, directors owe their duties to the company and not, in particular, to members directly.[54] This forms the basis of the 'proper plaintiff' principle regarding the enforceability of duties.[55] There may, though, be some instances where duties are owed directly to members.[56] The first draft produced in *Developing the Framework* did not encapsulate this basic point, but as the Steering Group pointed out at the time,[57] it is a central feature of company law and should be retained. They believed that the case for embodying this principle in legislation was not as strong as the case for embodying the general duties, but subsequently they accepted that it should be explicitly referred to in the code.[58] This seems right. It will not preclude the development and application of duties owed directly to members where that is appropriate, as the proposed code allows for the continued applicability of requirements imposed by any other rule of law.[59]

---

51 For a recent example concerning Marine Insurance Act 1906, s 17 see *Manifest Shipping Co Ltd v Uni-Polaris Shipping Co Ltd* [2001] 2 WLR 170 (HL), but many others could be cited from the case law on that Act and, eg, on the Sale of Goods Act 1979.

52 And earning large sums from their clients!

53 See *The Final Report*, above n 8, at Annex C, para 3.

54 See *Percival v Wright* [1902] 2 Ch 421, recently confirmed as the general principle in *Peskin v Anderson* [2000] 1 BCLC 1, affirmed by the Court of Appeal [2000] All ER (D) 2278; see also Moore 'Fiduciary Duties Owed to Shareholders: The Court of Appeal Applies the Brakes' [2001] *Lloyd's Maritime and Commercial Law Quarterly* 456.

55 Under the rule in *Foss v Harbottle* (1843) 2 Hare 461. On the nature of this rule see the Neuberger essay above at p 70.

56 Classically, if directors act as agents for them in a particular transaction; see *Allen v Hyatt* (1914) 30 TLR 444; or supply information regarding a takeover; see *Gething v Kilner* [1972] 1 WLR 337; but other duties such as the proper purposes duty and the duty to act fairly have also been expressed as owed to members; see: *Re A Company* [1987] BCLC 82; *John Crowther Group plc v Carpets International plc* [1990] BCLC 460 at p 464.

57 See *Developing the Framework*, above n 6, at para 3.79.

58 See *Completing the Structure*, above n 7, at para 3.12.

59 See the proposed sub-ss (2) and (3) set out below.

3.1 Director or directors

An important question regarding the proposed codification is whether duties are to be expressed as owed by 'a director' or by directors collectively. The drafts proposed by both the Law Commission and the Steering Group, including that in *The Final Report*, express the various duties as owed by an individual director. This is clearly a correct approach as regards some of the traditional heads of duties, namely those relating to the no conflict and no profit principles and the duty of care and skill. However, it has been convincingly argued[60] that, as far as the basic duties of good faith and proper purpose are concerned, this approach ignores the collective responsibility of a board of directors. Further, it seems to assume, incorrectly, that a single director has management powers, which is unlikely in the case of companies of any size. It also ignores the supervisory role of the board of directors.[61] It is thought that the code would benefit from redrafting in this respect.

It has also been argued[62] that the draft code ignores completely the position of executive directors and is wholly unclear as to the relationship between it and the duties under a service contract.[63] This criticism is perhaps somewhat harsh. It is true that the Law Commission and the Steering Group have paid little attention to the contractual duties of an executive director, but it can be made clear in the final version that they are distinct from the codified duties owed by a director as an office holder, as indeed the draft contained in *The Final Report* seems to do.[64]

3.2 The proposed introductory section

We have already noted that the codification proposed by the Steering Group is by way of a general section and a detailed Schedule. It is appropriate to set out the draft section at this stage:[65]

General principles by which directors are bound

(1) Schedule 2 sets out:

   (a) the general principles applying to a director of a company in the performance of his functions as director, and

   (b) the general principles

      (i) applying to a director of a company in relation to his entering into transactions with the company, and

---

60 See Berg, above n 15.

61 Emphasised in *Re Barings plc (No 5)* [1999] 1 BCLC 433, affirmed [2000] 1 BCLC 523, one of the sequels to the collapse of the city bank in question. As to the importance of this decision in the context of directors' duties in general, see the cases cited at n 41, above.

62 See Berg, above n 15.

63 Many non-executive directors in public companies now also have a written contract, whether a contract of service or a contract for services.

64 Though whether it does so clearly enough is another matter; see the further comments below. The legislation will also have to make clear the extent to which a contract can exclude or modify the general law duties. The draftsman has not yet addressed this question.

65 See *The Final Report*, above n 8, at Vol 2, p 376.

(ii) applying to a director or former director in relation to the use of property, information and opportunities of the company and to benefits from third parties,

and has effect in place of the corresponding equitable and common law rules.

(2) A director of a company owes a duty to the company to comply with that Schedule, and a former director owes a duty to the company to comply with paras 6 and 7.

(3) Nothing in that Schedule authorises the contravention by a director (or former director) of any prohibition or requirement imposed on him by or under any other enactment or rule of law.

The majority of draft sub-s (1) is designed to incorporate the detail of the Schedule, but the concluding phrase merits some emphasis. In saying that the Schedule has effect 'in place of the corresponding equitable and common law rules', it seeks to give effect to the views of the Steering Group, noted above, that the statutory code should be exhaustive. This will be so, however, only as regards *corresponding* equitable and common law rules. It is, therefore, crucial that the Schedule covers all aspects of directors' duties in equity and at common law. As will appear from the discussion below, this is in most respects the result of the current draft, but it will be argued that there are some omissions of which account must be taken.

Draft sub-s (3) preserves liability arising on a duty by virtue of some other principle of law, that is something other than their basic duties to the company. This could arise because in particular circumstances directors owe a duty directly to shareholders,[66] or indeed to third parties,[67] although it is clear from sub-s (1) that these are not covered by the codification. Similarly liability could arise under specific statutory provisions outside the purview of company law. The sub-section must also cover contractual liability, including that arising by virtue of a director's service contract. This draft sub-section is fairly comprehensible to a lawyer, but would hardly appear so to a non-lawyer. Given that one of the primary purposes of codifying is to make the law more accessible to directors themselves, it is thought that it is a serious omission not to give a clearer indication of what other duties may be owed.

3.3   Fiduciary

Although, as we have seen, most of the duties of directors are traditionally described as fiduciary duties, there is no intention to use this term in the codification. The explanation seems to be that the term cannot properly describe the duties of care and skill and that, as a particularly legal term of art, it should have no place in a code that is, at least partly, educational. With respect this seems somewhat short-sighted. There can be little doubt that judges will continue to use the term whatever the statute says, and, in any event, a further statutory provision could be used to explain the term in a broad and educative way. It is thought that such a description and explanation would add some force to the code.

---

66 See n 56, above.

67 Although in the ordinary way a director is unlikely to owe a tortious duty to outsiders: *Williams v Natural Life Health Foods Ltd* [1998] 1 WLR 830.

4 CORE DUTIES – THE SCOPE OF COMPANY LAW

The Company Law Review Steering Group first addressed in detail the issue of the core duties of directors, namely the duty to act in good faith in the interests of the company and to exercise their powers for the proper purpose, in their Consultation Paper of February 1999 – *Modern Company Law for a Competitive Economy: The Strategic Framework*.[68] There was further and more detailed discussion in Developing the Framework. The central issue here is what are the 'interests of the company' – what the Steering Group refers to as the 'scope' of company law.[69]

It still seems to be the case that our current law on directors' duties is widely understood as not allowing directors to take proper account of interests other than those of members as a whole on a long-term basis.[70] There is, perhaps, in practice an emphasis on the short term rather than the long term, and a feeling that there is no sound basis for considering the interests of other than members.[71] A convincing case can be made for arguing that this view is based on a misunderstanding of the current law; after all, it was famously stated judicially over a century ago that 'The law does not say that there are to be no cakes and ale, *but that there are to be no cakes and ale except such as are for the benefit of the company*'.[72] However, it is thought that the case has been made, in accordance with the principles of clarity and accessibility, for the law to be clearly phrased in a formula that is appropriate for modern times.

The question still remains, however, as to what is an appropriate formula. *The Strategic Framework* devoted much space[73] to weighing the merits of what the Steering Group called a 'stakeholder model'[74] as against a 'pluralist approach'[75] to the scope of company law and hence of the core duty of directors. It is not the intention of this chapter to review the merits of the different approaches, which is of course a matter of broader policy than a purely legal question and which has been addressed by many writers in recent years.[76] What seems clear, as a result of the consultation since February 1999, is that very little support was expressed for a fully pluralist approach, at least as enshrined in core directors' duties, and that in any event there would be real difficulties in

---

68 London, DTI, 1999; hereafter *The Strategic Framework*.

69 See chapter 5.1 of *The Strategic Framework*.

70 And of creditors if insolvency is threatened; as to the interests of creditors, see further below.

71 Apart from the rather uncertain effect of Companies Act 1985, s 309 regarding the interests of employees.

72 See *Hutton v West Cork Railway* (1883) 23 Ch D 634 at p 672 *per* Bowen LJ (emphasis added).

73 Above n 68 at chapter 5.1.

74 A model that would give primacy to members' long-term interests but would expressly allow directors to take account of other interests. See further the Parkinson essay, above at p 43.

75 An approach that would allow directors to take all relevant interests into account and give primacy to none.

76 See: Parkinson *Corporate Power and Responsibility* (Oxford, OUP, 1993); Royal Society of Arts *Tomorrow's Company: The Role of Business in a Changing World* (London, RSA, 1995); Ireland 'Corporate governance, shareholding and the company: towards a less degenerate capitalism' (1996) 23 *Journal of Law and Society* 287; Grantham 'The doctrinal basis of the right of company shareholders' [1998] CLJ 554; Ireland 'Company law and the myth of shareholder ownership' (1999) 62 MLR 32; Kelly and Parkinson 'The conceptual foundations of the law: a pluralist approach' [1998] *Company, Financial and Insolvency Law Review* 174; Goldenberg 'Shareholders v stakeholders: the bogus argument' (1998) 19 *Company Lawyer* 34; Roach 'The paradox of the traditional justifications for exclusive shareholder governance protection: expanding the pluralist approach' (2001) 22 *Company Lawyer* 9.

legislating effectively for that in the sense of producing a meaningful enforceable duty.[77] Indeed, it is clear that s 309 of the Companies Act 1985[78] is destined for the 'scrap heap', being regarded as 'neither desirable nor politically sustainable'.[79]

The overall model that has ultimately been proposed by the Steering Group is a modified stakeholder approach, but perhaps with less emphasis on directors' duties as such than on increased disclosure obligations. In this context, the proposal for a mandatory Operating and Financial Review to be prepared and published by public and large private companies may be more important. This builds on what is currently required for listed companies by the Accounting Standards Board's guidance and best practice.[80]

5 GOOD FAITH AND PROPER PURPOSES

There are a number of different facets of these core directors' duties. The Law Commission draft statement[81] on them was little more than regurgitation of the basic principles as described earlier, with separate paragraphs requiring independence and fairness. Because the Steering Group's approach has been very different, both in terms of the nature of the codification and the importance of directors' duties to their project as a whole, their recommendation is much more substantial. It has gone through three stages.

The first was a draft principle in *Developing the Framework*.[82] On consultation this was felt to be insufficiently clear, especially in terms of the relative importance of the various 'sub-duties' within the draft. Such comments were acknowledged in *Completing the Structure*,[83] and a further draft appears as paras 1 and 2 of the proposed Schedule to which reference has already been made. These paragraphs are as follows.[84]

Obeying the constitution and other lawful decisions

1   A director of a company must act in accordance with -

(a) the company's constitution, and

(b) decisions taken under the constitution (or by the company, or any class of members, under any enactment or rule of law as to means of taking company or class decisions),

and must exercise his powers for their proper purpose.

---

77 See *Completing the Structure*, above n 7, at para 3.5. As many other countries adopt a 'pluralist' approach in their law, this is a little difficult to accept.

78 See above at p 152.

79 See *Completing the Structure*, above n 7, at para 3.22. This seems a little hard on this provision, which was inserted after all by a Conservative Government, originally in the Companies Act 1980! Although its effect remains uncertain, it may perhaps have had some educational value and, as we have seen, it was cited uncritically in the Court of Appeal; see *Fulham Football Club Ltd v Cabra Estates plc* [1992] BCC 863 at p 976.

80 See: *Developing the Framework*, above n 6, at paras 5.83–5.92; *Completing the Structure*, above n 7, at paras 3.32–3.42; and *The Final Report*, above n 8, at paras 3.33–3.45 and 8.29–8.67 for the Steering Group's proposal in this respect.

81 See Law Commission Report No 261, above n 5, at Appendix A.

82 Above n 6 at para 3.40.

83 Above n 7 at paras 3.13–3.19.

84 See *The Final Report*, above n 8, at Vol 2, pp 412–13.

Promotion of company's objectives

2   A director of a company must in any given case -

(a) act in the way he decides, in good faith, would be most likely to promote the success of the company for the benefit of its members as a whole (excluding anything which would breach his duty under para 1 or 5); and

(b) in deciding what would be most likely to promote that success, take account in good faith of all the material factors that it is practicable in the circumstances for him to identify.

Notes

(1) In this paragraph, 'the material factors' means -

(a) the likely consequences (short and long term) of the actions open to the director, so far as a person of care and skill would consider them relevant; and

(b) all such other factors as a person of care and skill would consider relevant, including such of the matters in Note (2) as he would consider so.

(2) Those matters are -

(a) the company's need to foster its business relationships, including those with its employees and suppliers and the customers for its products or services;

(b) its need to have regard to the impact of its operations on the communities affected and on the environment;

(c) its need to maintain a reputation for high standards of business conduct;

(d) its need to achieve outcomes that are fair as between its members.

(3) In Note (1) a 'person of care and skill' means a person exercising the care, skill and diligence required by paragraph 4.

(4) A director's decision as to what constitutes the success of the company for the benefit of its members as a whole must accord with the constitution and any decisions as mentioned in paragraph 1.

It must again be commented that the way in which these core principles are set out does not seem particularly clear to a non-lawyer. Paragraphs 1 and 2 might be acceptable in this respect on the whole, but they have to be read in conjunction with the notes, and that does not look like something that the average company director might easily be able to comprehend.

The Steering Group believed that its proposal in *Developing the Framework*, the substance of which is still reflected in the above draft,[85] would 'have a major influence in changing behaviours and the climate of decision making'.[86] In reality it is difficult to see it as being very much more than an attempt to enact what the present law requires anyway, but perhaps with some changes of emphasis and other qualifications. First, as we have noted earlier, the current law generally and properly expresses these basic duties as being

---

85   The only notable omission from the final draft as opposed to the earlier one is any reference to directors being required to act honestly. This fell into disfavour because it was felt to lead to uncertainty and to be superfluous, as the law requires that directors, like everyone else, act honestly; see *Completing the Structure*, above n 7, at para 3.13.

86   *Developing the Framework*, above n 6, at para 3.58.

the duties of the directors as a whole.[87] Some will rightly continue to find it odd that the duty is expressed in the singular alone. This looks particularly odd as respects the proper purposes doctrine, given that the powers to which that refers will, in the vast majority of cases, be powers such as the power to allot shares and deal with the company's property that are vested in the board as a whole.

There are a number of other potential problems. Paragraph 1 seems largely self-evident, although there is perhaps a change of emphasis from the present law, in that the proper purposes duty is elevated above the duty to act in good faith. Paragraph 2 retains the essentially subjective nature of the duty to act in good faith, but requires the taking account of 'all the material factors that it is practicable in the circumstances for [a director] to identify'. In identifying the interests of the company with the interests of its members, the current law is understood as referring to the long-term interests of the members as a whole. This does not appear in para 2(a), but is incorporated in the definition of the 'material factors' in note (1)(a). This does not appear to have the same emphasis as under the current law. Then come the other 'matters' spelt out in note (2). What is their relationship with the primary duty to act in good faith?

The Steering Group clearly envisages that directors would be under an obligation to consider these matters, because there is a duty to do so (para 2(b)), albeit only to the extent that it is practicable in all the circumstances to identify them. To the extent that the current law may be sometimes misunderstood, the proposed statement may be an improvement. Except as regards the interests of employees, this looks at first sight like a change in the law – a move towards the 'inclusiveness' favoured by the Steering Group. The ability to take account of interests other than those of the members as a whole would be replaced by some sort of obligation to do so. But it is absolutely clear that the long-term interests of members would remain the overriding test of what is in the interests of the company, and that only the duty to exercise powers for the proper purpose would remain as an objective limit on what is otherwise essentially a subjective test of loyalty.[88] The 'obligation' in para 2 is not a very strong obligation; it is merely to 'take account' of the material factors, which is arguably less strong wording than the words 'to have regard' that appeared in the earlier version put forward by the Steering Group.[89] It seems difficult to believe that, faced with this wording, a court would strike down a board decision[90] that was taken in good faith, and with proper care and skill, in the long-term

---

87 See Berg, above n 15, at pp 480–81, where he points out that the duty to act *bona fide* in the interests of the company was classically formulated (in *Re Smith and Fawcett Ltd* [1942] Ch 304) in terms of a power of the board, and the duty to exercise powers for a proper purpose is also normally directed to the board's powers. However, it is thought that in principle these duties can apply to directors acting individually; compare Berg's discussion of Nolan's interpretation of the observations of Hoffmann LJ in *Bishopgate Investment Management Ltd v Maxwell (No 2)* [1994] 1 All ER 261 at p 265 (see Nolan's essay in Rider (ed) *The Realm of Company Law* (Bristol, Jordans, 1998) at pp 10–11). That particular decision, striking down the transfer of shares owned by the company as an improper gift, is perhaps more properly regarded as a case of misapplication of company property; see further below.

88 It is thought that the case law would still be relevant for determining the boundaries of the proper purposes duty as classically in *Howard Smith Ltd v Ampol Petroleum Ltd* [1974] AC 821.

89 In *Developing the Framework*, above n 6. To 'have regard' is the wording that appears in the current s 309, which has led most commentators to express the view that this section imposes a largely meaningless duty. See n 23, above.

90 Presumably a breach of this principle would lead to any transaction being voidable except as against a third party acting in good faith, as is the effect of the current law. This is not currently spelt out, though, and in any event it is not at all clear who would have standing to challenge a decision of the directors; see the later comments on consequences and remedies.

interests of members, and with no hint of improper purpose, even if it could be shown that the directors failed to have regard to the interests of employees or suppliers or customers, etc. It has been suggested that the practical result of enacting this principle would be for board minutes to record expressly that directors had regard to the matters listed in note (2),[91] but it seems difficult to see that happening where there is no evidence that s 309, which has been on the statute book for 20 years, has had that sort of effect.[92] It is submitted that any concerns of this sort are unfounded.[93]

Attention should be drawn to note (2)(d), requiring that the company should achieve outcomes that are fair as between its members. In the earlier draft,[94] this sort of fairness was set out in a separate principle. It may well be better placed here, in the context of the core duty of directors. The principle is established in the case law[95] and seems unobjectionable.

In practice there would seem to be few difficulties in assessing the propriety of directors' conduct by reference to the basic principles of good faith and proper purposes as codified, and, therefore, that no real change to the law would result.[96] Whether or not this would be the right result is, as indicated, a question of policy and outside the scope of this particular discussion.

5.1 The interests of creditors

It seems clear under the current law that, when a company is insolvent or on the verge of insolvency, it is the interests of creditors rather than members that are predominant.[97] This was not reflected at all in the Steering Group's principle 1 as originally drafted, except in so far as the general duty to take account of the company's business relationships already incorporates it. Their view was that this should be left to the insolvency legislation, especially the wrongful trading provision,[98] rather than included in the general code. They did consider, though, that there might be a case for a 'health warning' to this effect on form 288.[99] In general this seemed a sensible view, as in practice the cases where this duty was developed seem to have been superseded by the more specific and perhaps more appropriate provisions in the Insolvency Act.[100] However,

---

91 See: Berg, above n 15, at p 485; and see *Completing the Structure*, above n 7, at para 3.24.

92 This is the view of the Steering Group; see *Completing the Structure*, above n 7, at para 3.24.

93 Query whether or not it would be a problem anyway for a well-run board of directors to record their decisions in this way.

94 Both the Law Commission's recommended statement and the Steering Group's proposal in *Developing the Framework*, above n 6.

95 See: *Mutual Life Insurance Co of New York v Rank Organisation Ltd* [1985] BCLC 11; *Re BSB Holdings Ltd (No 2)* [1996] 1 BCLC 155.

96 Except that employees would lose their current 'special status'.

97 See generally *West Mercia Safetyware Ltd v Dodd* [1988] BCLC 250. Equally clearly, this duty is not enforceable by creditors directly. For further discussion see Keay 'The Director's Duty to Take into Account the Interests of Company Creditors: When is it Triggered?' (2001) 25 *Melbourne University Law Review* 135.

98 See Insolvency Act 1986, s 214.

99 The form that is currently submitted to the Registrar on the appointment of directors and which they have to sign.

100 Although concerns have been expressed about the enforceability of these provisions; see, eg, Berg, above n 15, at pp 475–76.

recognising the force of some comments made, in *Completing the Structure* the Steering Group suggested that there should be a general provision making it clear that the duties operate subject to the supervening obligations to have regard to the interests of creditors where there is no reasonable prospect of avoiding insolvent liquidation.[101]

In *The Final Report*, the Steering Group remains of this view, and para 9 in the draft Schedule in effect incorporates the wording of s 214 of the Insolvency Act 1986, the wrongful trading provision. However, it would seem that this is in effect no more than publicising the duty, since it would be enforceable only in the event of liquidation. The Steering Group was divided as to whether or not the statutory code should incorporate a principle that would apply at a time when it is probable that the company would be unable to pay its debts as they fall due, and not simply when there is no reasonable prospect of avoiding insolvent liquidation, and recommend that the Department of Trade and Industry should consult on this.[102] To this end, a possible draft is contained in para 8 of the draft Schedule, which reads as follows:[103]

Special duty where company more likely than not to be unable to meet debts

At a time when a director of a company knows, or would know but for a failure of his to exercise due care and skill, that it is more likely than not that the company will at some point be unable to pay its debts as they fall due:

(a) the duty under paragraph 2 does not apply to him; and

(b) he must, in the exercise of his powers, take such steps (excluding anything which would breach his duty under paragraph 1 or 5) as he believes will achieve a reasonable balance between

   (i) reducing the risk that the company will be unable to pay its debts, as they fall due; and

   (ii) promoting the success of the company for the benefit of its members as a whole.

Notes

(1) What is a reasonable balance between those things at any time must be decided in good faith by the director, but he must give more or less weight to the need to reduce the risk according as the risk is more or less severe.

(2) In deciding in any case what would be most likely to promote the success of the company for the benefit of its members as a whole, the director must take account in good faith of all the material factors that it is practicable in the circumstances for him to identify.

(3) The Notes to paragraph 2 apply also for the purposes of this paragraph.

(4) In this paragraph, 'due care and skill' means the care, skill and diligence required by paragraph 4.

The argument in favour of the principle as set out in this draft is essentially that it seems a sound principle to require directors to put creditors first when they know or ought to

---

101 See *Completing the Structure*, above n 7, at para 3.12.

102 See *The Final Report*, above n 8, at para 3.20. This whole issue is discussed in some detail in that Report at paras 3.12–3.20.

103 See *The Final Report*, above n 8, Vol 2 at pp 414–15.

recognise that there is a substantial probability of an insolvent liquidation; this is what the current law probably requires anyway. The argument against the principle is essentially that it could lead to excessive caution and cause directors not to risk trading out of insolvency.

This appears to be one of the very few points on which the Steering Group was unable to reach an agreed view, and it will no doubt lead to much discussion in the run up to the next Companies Act. There is a matter of wider principle here. The bulk of *The Final Report* is very much in favour of allowing people to trade with the benefit of incorporation and limited liability; the Steering Group throughout the review process has paid little attention to those who argue that the ease of incorporation sometimes produces undesirable consequences in terms of undercapitalised companies that go to the wall prejudicing creditors, employees and customers. It is thought that imposing a duty on directors to consider the interests of creditors is the very least that should be done to redress the balance a little.

5.2   Group companies

British company law has not hitherto developed much by way of principle in the context of corporate groups, including as regards the duties of directors of companies within a group. Such jurisprudence as there is seems to suggest that the duty to the company of which one is a director is paramount,[104] although that does not preclude taking due account of the wider interests of the group.[105] This seems right as a starting point and it is thought that it is implicit in the proposed codification. The Steering Group considered groups in *Completing the Structure*.[106] In the course of making what some may regard as rather limited proposals for group liabilities, which would impose liability on the group as a whole if this was chosen in return for exemption from the filing of separate accounts and reports,[107] they considered that the principles of the proposed code worked well in relation to the duties of directors of an 'elective subsidiary', which would be a subsidiary whose holding company had elected to assume its liabilities.[108]

However, even the modest proposal for group liabilities has not survived the last period of consultation, and nothing at all is recommended in respect of groups of companies.[109] Regardless of this, it might have been thought that, as one of the principal motives for codification is educational, it would be sensible for the code to have some sort of express statement to inform directors of group companies appropriately. The complete lack of any such thing is unfortunate.

---

104 See *Scottish CWS Ltd v Meyer* [1959] AC 324.
105 Problems only really arise in this context when there are minority interests in group companies or on insolvency. See further the Lower essay below at p 271.
106 Above n 7, at chapter 10.
107 Further consideration is beyond the scope of this chapter.
108 See *Completing the Structure*, above n 7, at para 10.38.
109 See *The Final Report*, above n 8, at paras 8.23–8.28.

6 DELEGATION AND INDEPENDENCE OF JUDGMENT

Paragraph 3 of the proposed Schedule provides for two other principles that in essence flow from the core duties of directors. They are expressed as follows:[110]

Delegation and independence of judgment

A director of a company must not, except where authorised to do so by the company's constitution or any decisions as mentioned in paragraph 1:

(a) delegate any of his powers; or

(b) fail to exercise his independent judgment in relation to any exercise of his powers.

Note

Where a director has, in accordance with this Schedule, entered into an agreement which restricts his power to exercise independent judgment later, this paragraph does not prevent him from acting as the agreement requires where (in his independent judgment, and according to the other provisions of this Schedule) he should do so.

The principle of non-delegation in the absence of authority is long established,[111] and the draft concerning independence of judgment seems to reflect the position reached in the case law.[112] Thus, this paragraph seems unobjectionable so far as it goes. As has been pointed out,[113] however, it does not seek explicitly to reflect the case law regarding nominee directors,[114] which insists that they owe their primary duty to the company and not to their nominator.[115] Even if this is implicit in the formulation, it is not clear why the basic fiduciary position of such directors should not be spelt in a statutory codification that is primarily intended to be educational.

7 CONFLICTS OF DUTY AND INTEREST

This is an area where the current law can be especially described as a mass of somewhat unwieldy principles (derived originally from the law of trusts), supplemented by the detailed statutory rules contained in Part X of the Companies Act 1985. The bulk of the Law Commission's Report was concerned with Part X and, as we shall see, the Steering Group adopts the vast majority of their thinking on this. Different views have been

---

110 See *The Final Report*, above n 8, at Vol 2, p 413.

111 See: *Boschoek Proprietary Co v Fuke* [1906] 1 Ch 148; *Nelson v James Nelson & Sons* [1914] 2 KB 770.

112 See *Fulham Football Club Ltd v Cabra Estates plc* [1992] BCC 863.

113 See Berg, above n 15, at pp 485–86, citing the Law Commission Consultation Paper No 153. See *Company Directors: Regulating Conflicts of Interest and Formulating a Statement of Duties* (London, TSO, 1998), at paras 11.11–11.12.

114 See: *Scottish CWS v Meyer* [1959] AC 324; *Selangor United Rubber Estates Ltd v Craddock (No 3)* [1968] 1 WLR 1555; *Kuwait Asia Bank EC v National Mutual Life Nominees Ltd* [1991] 1 AC 187.

115 See: *Scottish CWS v Meyer* [1959] AC 324; *Selangor United Rubber Estates Ltd v Craddock (No 3)* [1968] 1 WLR 1555; *Lonrho Ltd v Shell Petroleum Ltd* [1980] 1 WLR 627; *Kuwait Asia Bank EC v National Mutual Life Nominees Ltd* [1991] 1 AC 187.

propounded[116] as to the appropriateness today of having strict rules governing conflicts of interest and the making of unauthorised profits, which owe their origins to the rules devised by the Court of Chancery in respect of trustees. However, it seems fair to say that, by and large, the modern case law reveals a strict adherence to those rules.[117] It is appropriate to consider first the general principles and then the current thinking on Part X.

7.1   General principles

In *Developing the Framework*, the Steering Group proposed a general principle (principle 3) along the following lines:[118]

Conflict of interest

A director must not:

a   authorise, procure or permit the company to enter into any transaction in which he has an interest unless the interest has been disclosed to the relevant directors to the extent required under the Act; nor

b   use any property, information or opportunity of the company for his own or anyone else's benefit, nor obtain a benefit in any other way in connection with the exercise of his powers, unless he is allowed to make such use or obtain such benefit by the company's constitution, or the use or benefit has been disclosed to the company in general meeting and the company has consented to it.

This statement of principle was very much based on the Law Commission's suggested statutory statement, but was clearly inadequate as a real codification rather than an educational tool, particularly because it failed to give expression to the full range of traditional fiduciary duties flowing from the no conflict and no profit rules. Further thoughts were propounded in *Completing the Structure*[119] and *The Final Report* proposes a much fuller set of principles, drafted as paras 5, 6 and 7 in the proposed Schedule.[120]

Transactions involving conflict of interest

5   A director of a company must not:

(a)   in the performance of his functions as director, authorise, procure or permit the company to enter into a transaction, or

(b)   enter into a transaction with the company,

---

116 See, for example: Jones 'Unjust Enrichment and the Fiduciary's Duty of Loyalty' (1968) 84 LQR 472, Prentice '*Regal Hastings v Gulliver* – The Canadian Experience' (1967) 30 MLR 450; Prentice 'Directors' Fiduciary Duties – The Corporate Opportunity Doctrine' (1972) 50 *Canadian Bar Review* 623; Beck 'Corporate Opportunity Revisited' in J Ziegel (ed) *Studies in Canadian Company Law* (Toronto, Butterworths, 1973) Vol 2 at p 224; Lowry and Edmunds 'Corporate Opportunity Revisited' (1998) 61 MLR 515.

117 See especially *Guinness plc v Saunders* [1990] 2 AC 663. The decision of the House of Lords regarding a director's accountability for unauthorised remuneration was primarily based on an irreconcilable conflict of interest and duty expressed in the traditional language. There are many other examples, both ancient and modern, involving directors and other fiduciaries.

118 See *Developing the Framework*, above n 6, at p 30.

119 See *Completing the Structure*, above n 7, at paras 3.26 and 3.27.

120 See especially the discussion in *The Final Report*, above n 8, at paras 3.21–3.27; and for the Schedule see Volume 2 at pp 413–14.

if he has an interest in the transaction which he is required by this Act to disclose to any persons and has not disclosed the interest to them to the extent so required.

Personal use of the company's property, information or opportunity

6   A director or former director of a company must not use for his own or anyone else's benefit any property or information of the company, or any opportunity of the company which he became aware of in the performance of his functions as director, unless:

(a) the use has been proposed to the company and the company has consented to it by ordinary resolution; or

(b) the company is a private company, the use has been proposed to and authorised by the board, and nothing in the constitution invalidates that authorisation; or

(c) the company is a public company, its constitution includes provision enabling the board to authorise such use if proposed, and the use has been proposed to and authorised by the board in accordance with the constitution.

Notes

(1) In this paragraph 'the board' means the board of directors acting without the participation of any interested director.

(2) This paragraph does not apply to a use to which the director has a right under a contract or other transaction that he has entered into with the company, or that he has in the performance of his functions authorised, procured or permitted the company to enter into.

Benefits from third parties

7   A director or former director of a company must not accept any benefit which is conferred because of the powers he has as director or by way of reward for any exercise of his powers as such, unless the benefit is conferred by the company or:

(a) acceptance of the benefit has been proposed to the company and the company has consented to it by ordinary resolution; or

(b) the benefit is necessarily incidental to the proper performance of any of his functions as director.

As the Steering Group pointed out,[121] para 5 here states the law as it applies in effect rather than the strict equitable principle which would regard a transaction in which a director has an interest as invoking the conflict principle whether or not he was involved in authorising, procuring or permitting, or entering into, that transaction. Standard form articles of association, as in article 85 of the 1985 Table A, allow a director to have an interest provided it is disclosed, and it would seem eminently sensible to redraft the general law along those lines.[122] Paragraph 5 will be read along with whatever replaces s 317 of the Companies Act 1985, which is briefly discussed below.

---

121 See *Developing the Framework*, above n 6, at para 3.62, discussing the earlier draft, but the same point applies to the latest proposal in para 5.

122 Note the view of the Steering Group and the draftsman of the proposed Schedule that 'permit' includes 'fail to prevent', where a director has or may have the means of preventing; see *The Final Report*, above n 8, at p 353 n 321.

Paragraphs 6 and 7 seek to codify, with some modifications, the strict equitable principles governing the misuse of company property and the obtaining of secret profits.[123] Although they were clearly aware of the arguments[124] that have been propounded against the harshness of the secret profits rule, particularly as it applies to situations where the company itself could not obtain the benefit,[125] in *Developing the Framework*, the Steering Group favoured retaining a strict rule. Subsequently, however, in *Completing the Structure*, they accepted that there was a case for some exemption from the strict rule.[126] Ultimately this is effected in para 6 by allowing disinterested directors to sanction the making of a profit,[127] although it should be noted that there are important differences between private and public companies. In effect for private companies there is a presumption in favour of independent director sanction, that is if there is nothing in the company's constitution to disallow it. In the case of public companies, the constitution must expressly so provide. Another issue that was raised for consultation, reflecting the criticisms of the harshness of the secret profits rule, was whether or not opportunities that the company is incapable of exploiting should be excluded from the principle. Acknowledging that there are real problems in allowing directors themselves to decide what the company can or cannot take up itself,[128] the Steering Group favours retaining the strict principle, although it should be noted that in respect of corporate opportunities, a director must 'become aware of [them] in the performance of his duties as director'. It will not matter, though, in what capacity a director actually exploits such an opportunity. The principle is reinforced by para 7 spelling out that directors must not accept benefits from third parties unless they are appropriately sanctioned or necessarily incidental to the proper performance of any of their functions.

There is still, though, a problem with both paras 6 and 7 if they are intended to be broadly a genuine codification of the law as it currently is, subject to permitting a broader method of sanctioning directors' making of profits. The extent to which directors are trustees of company property, and how far the concept of property extends, are issues that have been much discussed. There are many authorities that directors are treated as trustees to this extent,[129] and the vitality of the principle is well illustrated by recent decisions involving directors' liability for wrongfully declared dividends.[130] Of course, holding directors liable as trustees can overlap with the conflict rule or the no profit rule, but the question is important both because it can determine the proper remedy available to the company (that is whether or not a proprietary or personal remedy is available), and because it seems clear that, under the current law, a misappropriation of property is not

---

123 They are much better drafted that the previous principle, especially in the clear identification of corporate opportunities as distinct from the misuse of property or information of the company.

124 See especially Jones, above n 116.

125 See *Regal (Hastings) Ltd v Gulliver* [1967] 2 AC 134n.

126 See *Completing the Structure*, above n 7, at paras 3.26 and 3.27.

127 See sub-paras (b) and (c), read with note (1).

128 See *The Final Report*, above n 8, at para 3.22. Many others have expressed this view, which is in particular a comment on the well known decision of the Supreme Court of Canada in *Peso Silver Mines Ltd v Cropper* (1966) 58 DLR (2d) 1; see: Prentice (1967) and (1972), above n 116; and Beck, above n 116.

129 See especially those cited at n 28, above.

130 See: *Bairstow v Queens Moat Houses plc* [2001] 2 BCLC 531; *Allied Carpets Group plc v Nethercott* [2001] BCC 81.

capable of being ratified by the company in general meeting in the ordinary way. Problems about ratification or ratifiability may to a large extent disappear under proposals that are examined below, but as it seems unlikely that the detail of proprietary remedies will be codified,[131] other issues arising out of the distinction would remain for development in the case law. In so far as para 6 seeks to codify the existing principles on misappropriations or misapplications of property, it is clearly wrong to state that disclosure to and the consent of the general meeting will enable a director to escape liability.[132] If fundamental changes are to be made to the law governing directors' accountabilities, it is suggested that this should have been spelt out much more fully than has been done either by the Steering Group or by the Law Commission. As neither body is actually purporting to propose fundamental changes, but rather a general codification of existing law, then it is all the more curious.

There is still, perhaps, a more fundamental problem with all these proposed paragraphs. They do not actually encapsulate the basic conflict rule at all.[133] Paragraph 5 is merely an application of it, while paras 6 and 7 are concerned with either or both the arguably separate no profit rule and the rule about misappropriations of property. The same can be said of the Law Commission's draft Statement of Duties,[134] which had a separate para 5 regarding the secret profits rule from para 7, the latter referring to conflicts arising out of transaction involving the company similarly to para 5 of the proposed Schedule. The basic conflict rule prohibits fiduciaries such as directors from putting themselves in a position where their duty and interest may conflict, as has been confirmed in many recent cases.[135] It reinforces the duty of fidelity owed by a fiduciary.[136] It is suggested that the proposed Schedule is seriously defective in not reproducing this basic duty before going on to spell out some of its particular consequences. It is thought that at the very least it should set out the principle that directors are fiduciaries,[137] and as such subject to the long-standing equitable rules.[138]

7.2   Part X of the Companies Act 1985

Despite the general law that paras 5, 6 and 7 of the proposed Schedule seek to codify, it is probably the current provisions in Part X that attract most attention in practice. As is well

---

131 The question of remedies is touched on briefly below.

132 *Cook v Deeks* [1916] 1 AC 554.

133 See also Berg, above n 15, at pp 486–89.

134 See above, n 5, at Appendix A.

135 See generally *Gore-Browne on Companies*, above n 2, at para 27.7 and, among other recent authorities: *Bristol and West Building Society v Mothew* [1998] Ch 1 and *Attorney-General v Blake* [2001] 1 AC 268 at p 280G–H *per* Lord Nicholls.

136 As to whether or not the no conflict and no profits rules are properly duties or disabilities, see the references above at n 17. See also Berg's discussion, above n 15, of the difficulties arising from *Movitex Ltd v Bulfield* [1988] BCLC 104, a decision that was accepted by the Law Commission (see Consultation Paper No 153, above n 113, at para 11.50), but which perhaps conflicts with other authority (especially *Bristol and West Building Society v Mothew* [1998] Ch 1) and which was really concerned with the proper scope of Companies Act 1985, s 310. See also Berg's criticism, above n 15, of the conventional reliance on *London and Mashonaland Exploration Co Ltd v New Mashonaland Exploration Co Ltd* [1891] WN 165 for the proposition that a director can compete with his company.

137 As also argued earlier.

138 Of course, this does not preclude proper modification of the duties duly agreed in the company's constitution, as in Table A, Article 85 and paragraphs 5, 6 and 7 of the proposed Schedule.

known, they consist of a collection of rules introduced at various times to deal with specific abuses of the conflict and secret profit principles, often to ensure that disclosure obligations are reinforced and, in respect of 'large' transactions, reinstating the original equitable principle of disclosure to and approval by the company in general meeting.[139] Both the Law Commission and Steering Group consider that most of the provisions should be retained, but there is likely to be detailed amendment and clarification, and we are promised a coherent set of remedies for breach in place of the differing consequences that now follow breaches of the different provisions. It is also clear that the provisions will continue to apply to all types of company, although there may be minor modifications for private companies, for example extending the written resolution procedure to the appropriate provisions in Part X.[140] As indicated earlier, the fact that some of these rules are in effect duplicated for listed companies under requirements of the *Listing Rules* and the *Combined Code* is not regarded as problematic or as supporting arguments for their removal from the statute.

Both the Law Commission and the Steering Group are content that the provision regarding tax-free payments to directors (s 311), the provisions making directors' service contracts open to inspection (s 318(5)) and exempting from approval contracts for employment overseas (s 318(11)), and the prohibition on directors dealing in share options (s 323) may safely be repealed.[141] However, the substance of the provisions on payments in connection with loss of office (ss 312–16), on declarations of interest (s 317), on service contracts (ss 318 and 319), on substantial property transactions (ss 320–22), on transactions beyond directors' powers (s 322A) and with sole members/directors (s 322B), and on loans and credit transactions (ss 330–42) would remain. The Steering Group invited views on their and the Law Commission's proposals for reform,[142] and in *Completing the Structure*,[143] indicated their likely final views. *The Final Report* adopts these proposals with just a few additional points. The following account briefly highlights what seem to be the most important likely changes.[144]

- Payments for loss of office – both bodies think that these should expressly not apply to covenanted payments,[145] and that they should extend to payments to directors of the company's holding company. The Steering Group also think that they should be extended to payments made to connected persons and, probably, to all types of takeover offers.[146]

---

139 See *Aberdeen Railway Co v Blaikie* (1854) 1 Macq 461.

140 See *Developing the Framework*, above n 6, at paras 7.37–7.44. With respect, it seems doubtful whether it is really necessary to apply all these provisions, as opposed to the basic fiduciary principles, to directors of very small companies, but it would appear that consultees are generally happy that they should remain so applicable.

141 As to the last item, see *The Final Report*, above n 8, at para 6.15 where the Steering Group confirms its view that the prohibition, involving an issue of market manipulation, should be a matter for the Financial Services Authority and the Treasury. On the subject of market abuse see the Linklater essay at p 459 below.

142 See the questions listed in *Developing the Framework*, above n 6, at para 3.89.

143 See *Completing the Structure*, above n 7, at paras 4.8–4.21.

144 The detail is conveniently set out in *Developing the Framework*, above n 6, at Annex C.

145 This is fairly clearly the law anyway; see *Taupo Totara Timber Co v Rowe* [1978] AC 537.

146 See *Completing the Structure*, above n 7, at paras 4.9 and 4.10.

- Declarations of interest – s 317 would have civil consequences, which will clarify the still uncertain question of the relationship between that provision and the general law as modified by standard articles of association.[147] Whether or not the criminal penalty should be retained was considered by the Steering Group as part of their general consideration as to the appropriateness of criminal sanctions under the companies' legislation,[148] and the view is that some form of criminal penalty should remain.[149] It is thought that the duty of disclosure should be limited to material interests of which the director is aware, although the Steering Group favours a rather broader definition of materiality than the Law Commission, with the burden on the director to prove that the board could not reasonably have felt constrained in its decision if it had been aware of the interest.[150] But there should be no duty to disclose what the board is already fully aware of, and no duty where a company has a sole director. In the latter instance, it was suggested in *Completing the Structure*[151] that this might be replaced by a duty to disclose to the general meeting, but the Steering Group's final recommendation is that the obligation should simply be disapplied here.[152] The Steering Group did not support the Law Commission proposal for a register of directors' interests.[153]

- Directors' service contracts – in *Completing the Structure*, it was proposed that the initial period allowed for a service contract without shareholder approval would be reduced to three years, with steps being taken to prohibit abuse of what is now s 319 by the use of rolling contracts and only yearly extensions permitted. Steps should also be taken to limit the damages payable on loss of office to one year's remuneration.[154] These proposals clearly caused some controversy, but the Steering Group has broadly maintained its view,[155] the only concession being that a longer contractual period could be authorised by special resolution.

- Substantial property transactions – a company should be able to enter into a transaction within s 320 contingently on shareholder approval. Transactions with administrators should be exempt and transactions with administrative receivers would be permitted subject to court approval.[156] As already indicated, suggestions that have been made that listed companies might be exempt from s 320 (because of the Listing Rules' requirements) and that transactions approved by independent directors, or put to shareholders without dissent being received or testified to be

---

147 See, eg, the different views expressed in *Guinness Plc v Saunders* [1990] 2 AC 663.

148 This is addressed in detail in *Completing the Structure*, above n 7, at chapter 13; and see *The Final Report*, above n 8, at chapter 15.

149 See *Completing the Structure*, above n 7, at para 13.37, where the possibility is raised of heavier sanctions for a dishonest failure to disclose than a mere failure to disclose.

150 This could be satisfied by proof that the director had in due time notified his fellow directors in writing; see *The Final Report*, above n 8, at para 6.8.

151 See *Completing the Structure*, above n 7, at paras 2.24–2.26.

152 See *The Final Report*, above n 8, at paras 4.8 and 4.9.

153 The Steering Group's original views on s 317 in *Developing the Framework*, above n 6, have been confirmed in *Completing the Structure*, above n 7, at paras 4.11–4.16.

154 See *Completing the Structure*, above n 7, at paras 4.19 and 4.20, and see para 4.17 and 4.18 regarding the proposal that members have a right to a copy of a director's service contract on payment of a fee to cover expenses. See also *The Final Report*, above n 8, at paras 4.19 and 4.20. Paragraph 6.11 also proposes that non-executive directors' terms of engagement be subject to similar disclosure.

155 See *The Final Report*, above n 8, at paras 6.12–6.14.

156 In effect partly reversing and partly qualifying the decision in *Demite Ltd v Protec Health Ltd* [1998] BCC 638.

reasonable by an expert should be exempted, are not favoured by either the Law Commissions or the Steering Group.

- Loans and credit transactions – the Steering Group agrees with the Law Commission that ss 330 to 342 need simplification and that the restrictions on quasi loans and credit transactions should apply to all companies and not simply to public companies and their associates. However, they seem to be taking a stricter line on the question of the exemptions, indicating that they should be reduced to a minimum, 'We subscribe to the view that in principle directors should obtain credit in the market and not from their companies'.[157] There should, though, be a general exception for transactions approved in general meeting.[158]

- Connected persons – both bodies favour the extension of the concept of connected person to cover cohabitants and adult children, parents and siblings of directors.

8 DUTIES OF CARE AND SKILL

Few, if any, would now argue that the traditional view requiring directors to display only a subjective standard of skill and very little diligence is maintainable in a modern system of company law, at least as regards the directors of larger companies. Indeed, it seems fairly clear that the common law, reflecting the introduction of the standard imposed for the purposes of the wrongful trading provision in the Insolvency Act 1986,[159] has now developed in any event.[160] The Law Commission were clear that this higher standard should be clearly enacted and the Steering Group agrees. Paragraph 4 of the proposed Schedule provides:[161]

Care, skill and diligence

A director must exercise the care, skill and diligence which would be exercised by a reasonably diligent person with both:

(a) the knowledge, skill and experience which may reasonably be expected of a director in his position; and

(b) and any additional knowledge, skill and experience which he has.

Quite properly, it is thought, an argument that companies should be able to relax this standard in their articles was rejected on the ground that the community as a whole suffers if companies are run without reasonable competence.[162] A question that has been

---

157 See *Developing the Framework*, above n 6, at para 29 of Annex C.
158 See *Completing the Structure*, above n 7, at para 4.21; confirmed in *The Final Report*, above n 8, at para 6.15.
159 Section 214.
160 See the authorities cited at n 130 above, and see further below.
161 See *The Final Report*, above n 8, at Vol 2, p 413.
162 Berg, above n 15, is critical of this proposal as it applies to small companies, arguing that it would rule out the limited liability company for much of the population as directors of such companies cannot possibly be expected to display an objective standard of skill. It is thought, though, that this is too harsh a view. The words 'in his position' are critical here and should allow for an appropriate degree of flexibility. In any event, the issue in small companies is only likely to arise on insolvency, where an objective standard has to be applied under the Insolvency Act 1986. Surely this is also a proper 'consumer protection' measure to guard against the consequences of undercapitalisation; see n 41, above.

much discussed in other common law jurisdictions, following its case law development in the United States, is whether or not a 'business judgment' rule should be introduced. Such a rule would apply so that directors are not penalised for honestly taking risks that, in hindsight, might be viewed as negligence.[163] The Steering Group feels that the principle allows development of such a rule, traces of which can arguably already be found in our case law,[164] and in any event, as will be seen, propose retention and modification of the general provision allowing directors to be relieved from liability. They are, therefore, firmly against the introduction of a business judgment rule as such in statutory form.[165]

They also see no need for express sanction for directors to be able to delegate and rely on others where appropriate; done reasonably, this is clearly permissible under the general principle. However, it may be wondered whether the educational purposes behind this principle are sufficiently served if it does not give a fuller indication of the developing case law in this area. While the cases under the general law[166] may be viewed as no more than illustrative of the appropriate standard of care and skill, recent case law concerning the disqualification of directors for unfitness contains most useful guidance on directors' duties to acquire and maintain sufficient knowledge and understanding of the company's business and to supervise those to whom functions have been delegated.[167] There is no obvious reason why such principles should not be included in the proposed code, perhaps in the form of notes of guidance.

9 RATIFICATION AND ENFORCEMENT

As is well known, directors' duties are owed primarily to the company and it is, *prima facie*, for the company to take action in respect of alleged breaches. This is, of course, one aspect of the rule in *Foss v Harbottle*.[168] The Law Commission considered this rule in its report on *Shareholder Remedies*,[169] and made a number of important recommendations, including putting the derivative action into statutory form governed by clear principles rather than 150 years of still rather uncertain case law. It still seems fair to say that the essence of the judge made principles would be preserved. In general the Law Commission's recommendations have received official support,[170] echoed by the Steering Group in *Developing the Framework*.[171] However, in certain respects thinking has been

---

163 For an overview, see Pasban, Campbell and Birds 'The protection of corporate directors in England and the US' (1998) 27 *Anglo-American Law Review* 461.

164 See especially the *dictum* in *Howard Smith Ltd v Ampol Petroleum Ltd* [1974] AC 821 at p 835, cited in *Developing the Framework*, above n 6, at para 3.70.

165 It is arguable that para 2 of the proposed Schedule in effect allows for the equivalent of a business judgment rule.

166 Referred to in n 164 above.

167 See especially *Re Barings plc (No 5)* [1999] 1 BCLC 433 at pp 487–89.

168 (1843) 2 Hare 451.

169 Law Commission Report No 246 *Shareholder Remedies* (1997) Cm 3769 (London, TSO, 1997).

170 See Department of Trade and Industry, *Shareholder Remedies, a Consultative Document*, URN 98/994 (London, DTI, 1998). Academic comments have been more critical; see especially Sugarman 'Reconceptualising company law: reflections on the Law Commissions consultation paper on shareholder remedies' (1997) 18 *Company Lawyer* 226 and 274.

171 See *Developing the Framework*, above n 6, at chapter 4.

developed and this development continued in *Completing the Structure*. Although it is not the intention of this chapter to review in detail the question of shareholder remedies for breach of directors' duties, some brief comments are thought to be appropriate.[172]

Probably the key to when a minority shareholder is currently allowed to bring an action (including a personal action) in respect of a wrong done to the company or within the company is whether or not the wrong is capable of being ratified by a majority of shareholders.[173] This is because the underlying principle that sensibly governs the business of any association, including a company, is majority rule. Under the Law Commission's proposals, ratifiability would cease to be wholly determinative of whether or not a derivative action could be brought. Indeed it could not be, as the Law Commission (supported by the Steering Group) wants the action to be available in respect of negligence, which is traditionally regarded as ratifiable.[174] However, it would still be an important factor in the court's decision as to whether or not the action could proceed. Actual ratification, though, would be a bar to a derivative action. Even outside the context of minority shareholders' remedies, the question of ratification has to be considered in a general review of directors' duties.

The Steering Group is clearly of the view that breaches of duty should be capable of ratification where the company itself could lawfully have done the act complained of, and confirmed in *Completing the Structure*[175] that this should be included in legislation. They also think that ratification should not be permitted in cases of threatened insolvency,[176] and suggest that it should not be effective if the effect is to reduce the assets available to creditors. Ratification is linked, of course, to the points made earlier about duties being owed to the company. In *Developing the Framework* (in the context of their discussions of the Law Commission's recommendations),[177] they make the point that ratification should be allowed only by a resolution of disinterested members.[178] What was not, perhaps, immediately apparent was whether this would be effected solely in the context of changes in respect of derivative actions, or whether it would apply more generally. However, in *Completing the Structure*, they clarified the position so that this would apply in both contexts.[179] Present case law would seem to suggest that any breach of duty that involves a misappropriation of company property or a director benefiting at the expense of the company is not capable of ratification except by the unanimous consent of the shareholders.[180] This is not just important in the context of minority shareholders' derivative actions. It could be relevant in a petition under s 459 of the Companies Act or if the liquidator of a failed company wanted to pursue its former directors. The likely

---

172 This writer was somewhat disturbed by the Steering Group's comment (see *Completing the Structure*, above n 7, at para 5.60) that '... Minority rights and remedies are principally of concern to private companies'.

173 See the classic articles by Wedderburn, 'Shareholders' remedies and the rule in *Foss v Harbottle*' [1957] CLJ 194 and [1958] CLJ 93. Note also Neuberger's essay above at p 70.

174 See *Pavlides v Jensen* [1956] Ch 565.

175 See *Completing the Structure*, above n 7, at para 3.30.

176 As suggested by the case law; see, eg, *Rolled Steel Products Ltd v British Steel Corporation* [1986] Ch 246 at pp 296–97, although this was really in the context of ratification by the unanimous assent of members rather than simply by majority.

177 See generally *Developing the Framework*, above n 6, at para 4.134 ff.

178 Thus overruling *North-West Transportation Co v Beatty* (1887) 12 App Cas 589.

179 See *Completing the Structure*, above n 7, at para 5.84.

180 See: *Burland v Earle* [1902] AC 83; *Cook v Deeks* [1916] 1 AC 554.

outcome is that there should be no limit, except in cases of insolvency and assuming the lawfulness of the act, on what can be ratified if this is only effective when a disinterested majority so decides.[181]

10 CONSEQUENCES OF BREACH OF DUTY

There are a number of consequential issues with regard to directors' duties that have been considered during the Review and merit some brief consideration here.

10.1 Exclusion clauses

The Steering Group is clear, and this seems right in general,[182] that the effect of s 310 of the Companies Act 1985, which prohibits exclusions and limitations of liability in the articles and elsewhere, should be retained, although actual implementation may be rather different, with clear provision being made in respect of each duty as to its excludability.[183] It seems likely that the no conflict and no profit rules, however they are ultimately codified, will be capable of modification by the company's constitution,[184] but presumably the core duty of good faith and the duty of care and skill will not be capable of being modified in any way. An important question that does not yet appear to have been addressed concerns the proper purposes duty. At present this would seem to be excludable,[185] and in principle it seems unobjectionable that the company's constitution defines the purposes for which directors may exercise their powers, but it is not clear how this stands with its importance in the hierarchy suggested by the Steering Group.[186]

At least the notorious obscurity of the current provision[187] should be rectified. There is no doubt that companies will be allowed to continue to effect liability insurance for directors.[188]

10.2 Relief from liability

As the Steering Group pointed out,[189] s 727 of the Companies Act 1985, which allows the court to grant relief from liability to a director who has acted honestly and reasonably and

---

181 Note that in the discussions in the *The Final Report*, above n 8, at chapter 7, on shareholder voting generally, it is revealed (at para 7.62) that one member of the Steering Group thought that only a resolution expressly so stating should be regarded as effective to ratify or condone a wrong. The Steering Group recommends further consultation by the DTI on this and related matters.

182 But see Berg, above n 15, at p 477.

183 See: *Developing the Framework*, above n 6, at para 3.74; and *Completing the Structure*, above n 7, at para 3.74.

184 As is permissible now under the articles of association; see *Movitex Ltd v Bulfield* [1988] BCLC 104.

185 See Birds 'The permissible scope of articles excluding the duties of company directors' (1976) 39 MLR 400. For Australian authority to this effect see *JD Hames v MJH Pty Ltd* (1992) 7 ACSR 8.

186 In the light of the decisions in *Equitable Life Assurance Society v Hyman* [2000] 2 WLR 798 and [2000] 3 WLR 529 (HL) the courts might be keen though to look very carefully at such limits.

187 See *Movitex Ltd v Bulfield* [1988] BCLC 104.

188 As is permitted now by Companies Act 1985, s 310(2) (as amended by the Companies Act 1989). See further *The Final Report*, above n 8, at paras 6.2–6.4.

189 See *Developing the Framework*, above n 6, at para 3.76.

ought fairly to be excused, is little used, but of value. There are indeed notable cases in respect of which it seems very surprising that the section was not at least argued.[190] The recommendation that the reasonableness requirement should be omitted,[191] which is inevitable given the stricter negligence test, seems unobjectionable given the wide discretion that would still be available to the court.

10.3 Remedies for and consequences of a breach of duty

There is a wide range of possible remedies for a breach of directors' duties.[192] Action taken by directors, including but not limited to entering into a transaction, may be voidable at the instance of the company against a third party with knowledge of the breach.[193] In an appropriate case directors may be restrained by injunction from a proposed course of action.[194] They may be liable in damages, which could be either common law damages or equitable compensation.[195] They may be accountable for a profit made irrespective of loss to the company.[196] In some situations they may be regarded as constructive trustees of property or money,[197] which in appropriate circumstances may invoke proprietary restitutionary remedies.[198] The boundaries of some of these remedies are still developing and the statutory provisions in Part X invoke some of them in perhaps inconsistent ways.[199]

As far as Part X remedies are concerned, in *Completing the Structure*, the Steering Group shared the view of the Law Commission that there should be a single code of remedies for breach. With regard to the broader remedies, their view was that it would be impossible and undesirable to seek to codify them in detail, pointing out that no other jurisdiction had attempted to do so.[200] However, they did propose a statutory statement

---

190 See, for example, *Regal (Hastings) Ltd v Gulliver* [1967] 2 AC 134n.

191 See: *Completing the Structure*, above n 7, at para 3.29; *The Final Report*, above n 8, at para 6.4.

192 In addition to the traditional remedies outlined here, directors who breach their duties may be sacked without compensation; see *Boston Deep Sea Fishing and Ice Co v Ansell* (1888) 39 Ch D 339. For recent cases confirming directors' liability for the amount of any dividends unlawfully paid, see: *Bairstow v Queens Moat Houses plc* [2001] 2 BCLC 531; *Allied Carpets Group plc v Nethercott* [2001] BCC 81.

193 See, for example, *Rolled Steel Products Ltd v British Steel Corporation* [1986] Ch 246.

194 This will classically be to restrain a breach of the core duties to act *bona fide* in the interests of the company and not to exercise powers for an improper purpose; see, for example, *Hogg v Cramphorn Ltd* [1967] Ch 254. Note also Companies Act 1985, ss 35(2) and 35A(4).

195 See, for example, *Warman International Ltd v Dwyer* (1995) 182 CLR 544 and *Daniels v Anderson* (1995) 16 ACSR 607.

196 See, for example, *Regal (Hastings) Ltd v Gulliver* [1967] 2 AC 134n.

197 See, for example, *Selangor United Rubber Estates Ltd v Craddock (No 3)* [1968] 1 WLR 1555.

198 As the Steering Group says in *Completing the Structure*, above n 7, at para 13.74, this goes well beyond questions solely of company law.

199 For example, Companies Act 1985, s 312 provides that a payment for loss of office as a director not approved in general meeting must be repaid. However, s 313, in contrast, says such a payment made in connection with the transfer of the undertaking or property of the company is unlawful, while s 320 provides that unapproved substantial property transactions are merely voidable.

200 The Steering Group relied heavily on the paper produced for them by Richard Nolan, available at www.dti.gov.uk/cld/review.htm. See also: Nolan 'Enacting civil remedies in company law' (2001) 1 *Journal of Corporate Law Studies* 245; Nolan 'Directors' self-interested dealings: liabilities and remedies' [1999] *Company Financial and Insolvency Law Review* 235.

of the principal remedies, leaving the detail to the case law. On balance, this seemed unobjectionable.[201] In *The Final Report*, though, it is commented that this is a difficult area, which will require considerable further thought.[202] Whether or not the DTI will be inclined to proceed down this route remains to be seen.

11 CONCLUSIONS

It would seem that the move to a code of directors' duties is now unstoppable. The Government is hardly likely to reject what is such a key proposal from the Steering Group. It is also clear that the draft contained in *The Final Report* represents a valiant attempt to capture the essence of the vast majority of the case law, and it is clearly an improvement on the earlier version.[203] But as it is meant to be both exhaustive and accessible, it must be tested against both those criteria.

It is not, with respect, exhaustive. In particular, it does not capture the essence of the fiduciary relationship, whether or not that description is actually used, as expressed in the no conflict rule. It does not explicitly refer to the duties of nominee directors and directors of group companies. It does not reflect the fact that in terms of the core duties of directors, the duties are those that affect the board as a whole and not just individual directors. It does not capture the full force of the current principle that directors must not misappropriate or misapply company property.

One must also question whether the draft Schedule[204] is in fact sufficiently accessible in the sense of being an educational tool for company directors. As is well known, the 'company director' covers a wide range of persons with many different backgrounds and educational experiences, from the single director of a small company, who has incorporated his business for tax or other reasons, to the chief executive of the largest public company. Even the latter, if he or she has no legal or, perhaps, other professional qualifications, may struggle to interpret some aspects of the proposed code without a lawyer at his side.[205] This will surely be the case, in the majority of situations, where the director is a jobbing builder or plumber or a small shopkeeper who will also be subject to the code and expected to read and appreciate it. It is suggested that at the very least the wording of the code needs to be further looked at, and perhaps that use has to be made of clearer notes of guidance.

---

201 Note, however, that Berg, above n 15, at pp 478–79 makes a plea for clarification of the consequences on transactions with a third party of a breach of duty.

202 See *The Final Report*, above n 8, at para 15.30.

203 It would not be fair to judge it against the Law Commission proposal, above n 5, as that was not of course intended as exhaustive.

204 See *The Final Report*, above n 8, at Vol 2, pp 412–15.

205 Recent survey evidence of company directors shows an alarming degree of ignorance in reasonably large companies (average annual turnover £167m) of fundamental directors' duties/obligations; see 'Directors show poor knowledge of legal liabilities' *Financial Times* 1 November 2001. Litigation against failing directors is now on the increase; see the cases cited above at n 192 and note also: 'Equitable targets high flyers to pacify its policyholders'; 'Equitable targets ex-directors' *Financial Times* 30 November 2001; and 'Equitable sues 15 ex-board members for 3bn loss' *Financial Times* 25 April 2002.

CHAPTER 8

THE JURIDIFICATION OF CORPORATE GOVERNANCE

Chris Riley[1]

1 INTRODUCTION

What role should the state play in specifying the governance system of large, public companies? Ought it to regulate, say, for the composition of companies' boards and, if so, what form should such regulation take? One recent influential view holds that these matters should not be subject to mandatory legal rules but should be left instead to 'private ordering' – meaning the bargains struck by shareholders, their appointed managers and, where appropriate, other stakeholders.[2] Such a view resists the 'juridification' of corporate governance,[3] and offers some support instead to the current arrangement in the UK where heavy reliance has been placed on the soft regulation provided by the 'Combined Code'.[4]

The debate about the proper boundary between regulation and private ordering is of considerable legal and political interest, and has featured prominently in the UK government's company law Review, *Modern Company Law for a Competitive Economy*.[5] Superficially, it appears as if the Company Law Steering Group which leads that review ('the Steering Group')[6] was sympathetic to critics of juridification. So, at an early stage, the Steering Group expressed an inclination in favour of increased reliance upon non-legal (and especially non-criminal) regulation generally,[7] and subsequently declared itself

---

1   I am grateful, for comments, to Ian Dawson, Adrian Walters, Lisa Whitehouse and participants at the 2001 annual meeting of the company law section of the SPTL. The usual disclaimer applies.

2   There is a massive literature defending private ordering in corporate law; BR Cheffins *Company Law: Theory, Structure and Operation* (Oxford, Clarendon, 1997) (especially at Parts I and II) provides a good introduction.

3   Garner defines juridification (see BA Garner *A Dictionary of Modern Legal Usage* (Oxford, OUP, 2nd edn, 1995) at p 487) as a translation 'of the German word *Verrechtlichung*, which denotes the process of transforming social relations into legal relations – and social conflicts into legal conflicts – primarily through legislation and judicial decisions'. For further discussion around the meaning of this term, see n 11 below and the main text thereat.

4   See the Committee on Corporate Governance *The Combined Code* (London, Gee, 1998) and the discussion below at section 3; hereafter referred to as the Combined Code.

5   That Review has produced four overarching consultation documents, namely: *Modern Company Law for a Competitive Economy: The Strategic Framework* (London, DTI, 1999), hereafter *Strategic Framework*; *Modern Company Law for a Competitive Economy: Developing the Framework* (London, DTI, 2000), hereafter *Developing the Framework*; *Modern Company Law for a Competitive Economy: Completing the Structure* (London, DTI, 2000), hereafter *Completing the Structure*; and *Modern Company Law for a Competitive Economy: Final Report* (London, DTI, 2001), hereafter *The Final Report*.

6   On the composition of the 'Company Law Review Steering Group', and its relationship to the other organs of the review, see B Pettet *Company Law* (Harlow, Pearson Education, 2001) at p 87.

7   See *Strategic Framework*, above n 5, at para 5.5.5: '... we would expect the general trend to be away from prescriptive rules set out in the statute and enforced by criminal sanctions.'

unconvinced of the case for 'intervention through law' in those matters currently dealt with by the Combined Code.[8]

But this appearance is, as we shall see, misleading. As much as it denies the case for 'intervention through law', the Steering Group also proposes a number of reforms – both to the process for updating the Combined Code and to the disclosure obligations which underpin it – that would considerably increase the role of the State in setting the governance rules here.[9] Moreover, there is good reason to think that the increasingly objectivised duty of care and skill for directors[10] will also 'spill over' into the terrain now occupied by the Combined Code, entailing legal consequences for breaches of its norms. In these various ways, a strong tide seems to be flowing towards the juridification of corporate governance.

The foregoing descriptive claims are set out, and defended, in sections 2–4 of this essay. Thereafter, section 5 takes a normative turn. It argues not only that these moves towards juridification ought to be welcomed, but that they should be pushed still further. In particular, it argues, first, for a more detailed specification of the role of a director, secondly for the strengthening (in the sense of making more detailed and rule-like) the provisions of the Combined Code and, thirdly, for making some of the Combined Code's norms enforceable *ex ante* by injunction. In arguing for such changes, the chapter casts some doubt on the level of compliance achieved under the current, voluntary regime instituted by the Combined Code, and also seeks to qualify the argument for 'flexibility' that is so emphasised by critics of juridification.

The essay thus both welcomes and urges an intensification of current moves towards the juridification of corporate governance. Nevertheless, these proposals fall well short of the statutory design of a single governance straitjacket to be imposed by State regulators on every listed company. They do entail an increased role for the State, and for legal norms and judicial oversight, in constructing and enforcing the UK system of corporate governance. But, importantly, such moves might continue to operate with substantial industry involvement in setting the rules of the game, with norms expressed with some generality, and with shareholders continuing to bear the brunt of the enforcement burden. In these ways, then, the proposals here avoid the worst excesses of juridification which have sometimes given that term such a pejorative connotation.[11]

---

8   *Completing the Structure*, above n 5, at para 4.47. See also *The Final Report*, above n 5, at para 3.49.
9   See below at section 4 of this essay.
10 See below n 82 and the main text thereat.
11 See, for example, Teubner 'Juridification – Concepts, Aspects, Limits, Solutions' in G Teubner (ed) *Juridification of Social Spheres* (Berlin, Walter de Gruyter, 1987). Teubner notes that juridification is about not just an increase in the *quantity* of legal norms ('the flood of law') but also the spread of a particular type of law – 'materialized law' – that employs detailed and 'particularized' (rather than abstract and generalised) norms, that is accompanied by a purposive interpretative style and is associated with the regulatory objectives of the welfare state.

2 CORPORATE GOVERNANCE: THE STRUCTURE AND ROLE OF THE BOARD

As Parkinson observes, corporate governance is often used, in a catch-all way, 'to refer to anything to do with the running of companies'.[12] A narrower definition focuses upon 'the system by which companies are directed and controlled',[13] although even when so restricted the term still encompasses a large range of different mechanisms of control. However, for the purpose of this chapter, the focus will be upon one element within the governance system, namely the board of directors.[14]

Boards of directors lie at the centre of corporate organisations, and the rules that govern their operation are fundamental to the operation of the corporate governance system as a whole. Yet it is in this area of corporate life that UK law has, historically, deferred so heavily to private ordering. Corporate regulation has been based upon a model of the company as a private organisation and has, accordingly, had remarkably little to say, of a mandatory nature, about either the structure or the proper role of boards or their individual members. What is said has usually been put forward as default rules, subject to contractual exclusion or variation by the parties.[15]

To see this, we need to turn to consider the rules that govern the most significant features of the board. In so doing, it is useful to differentiate between two elements thereof. The first is the *structure* of the board, meaning such matters as its size and composition, the existence of board sub-committees, and the like. The second element is one of *role* – meaning the activities required of the board as a whole or of its individual members. I shall return shortly to how these two elements (and the rules governing them) are interconnected. First, just what does the law have to say about them?

Begin with structure. Although UK company law does specify the minimum number of directors a company must have,[16] it does not prescribe by whom such directors should be appointed. It does not follow the German system of insisting on employee-directors,[17] but nor, equally, does it say that directors have to be appointed by shareholders, rather

---

12 See Parkinson 'Company Law and Stakeholder Governance' in G Kelly, D Kelly and A Gamble (eds) *Stakeholder Capitalism* (Basingstoke, Macmillan, 1997). See also PL Davies *Gower's Principles of Modern Company Law* (London, Sweet & Maxwell, 6th edn, 1997) at p 66, noting how corporate governance has become a 'convenient rubric' under which to discuss a wide array of issues relating to the regulation of companies.

13 See the Committee on the Financial Aspects of Corporate Governance *Report and Code of Best Practice* (London, Gee, 1992) at para 2.5; hereafter *The Cadbury Report*.

14 I shall, therefore, say little about changes designed to increase the level of activism by shareholders (and especially institutional shareholders). On that, see Stapledon 'Institutional Investors: What are their Responsibilities as Shareholders?' in J Parkinson, A Gamble and G Kelly (eds) *The Political Economy of the Company* (Oxford, Hart, 2000); P Myners *Institutional Investment in the UK: A Review* (London, HM Treasury, 2001), especially paras 5.73–5.94.

15 Most notably through the relevant regulations within Table A: Companies (Tables A–F) Regulations 1985, SI 1985/805; see especially Regulations 64–98.

16 One director for private, and two directors for public, companies; see Companies Act 1985, s 282. There is no maximum limit to the number of directors a company may have.

17 On the German system, see Hopt 'The German Two-Tier Board: Experience, Theories, Reforms', Theisen 'Empirical Evidence and Economic Comments on Board Structure in Germany' and Semler 'The Practice of the German *Aufsichtsrat*', all in KJ Hopt, H Kanda, M Roe, E Wymeersch and S Prigge (eds) *Comparative Corporate Governance: The State of the Art and Emerging Research* (Oxford, OUP, 1998).

than by any other group of stakeholders within the company.[18] Similarly, it neither precludes, nor requires, a two-tier or a unitary structure, or the use of board sub-committees, nor does it specify any particular mix or balance between, say, executive and non-executive directors ('NEDs'). Likewise, it does not say whether the same person might occupy the position of both Chief Executive and Chairman, nor does it specify any particular *attributes* directors must have (such as being professionally qualified or 'independent').[19]

In fact it would be difficult for these matters of structure to be juridified without the law also doing more to specify *the role* of the board, or of its individual members. What is the point of requiring companies to have two different types of director unless the law also says how the types are to differ (in terms of their role within the company)? Yet on this issue of role, company law has again been largely silent. Take, for example, the role of the board as a whole. The broad managerial power enjoyed by boards is only a default provision found in Table A.[20] Companies could, if they so wished, adopt a very different constitutional role for their board. Moreover, even insofar as they do not, company law still says little about precisely what functions the board should then be seen as having in virtue of that role.[21]

Turn next to the role of *individual* directors. It might appear that company law has indeed already juridified directorial roles through its imposition of mandatory legal duties. But this appearance too is deceptive. Directors are of course subject to a duty of care and skill.[22] This *could* have been developed in such a way as to define the role to be played by individual directors. The law might, for example, have developed a substantive 'job description' for any person appointed a director, specifying the various activities required of someone occupying that position. Or, more ambitiously still, it might have proffered a number of such job descriptions, linked to the different types of director – whether, say, executive or non-executive – that a company might appoint. But, historically at least, company law failed to do that. Rather, in the UK that duty was traditionally seen as an undemanding one, offering few substantive obligations.[23]

We might conclude this section by elaborating the relationship between these elements of *structure* and *role*. We have seen how prescribing board structure makes little sense unless the roles associated with that structure are also defined. Relatedly, enforcing structural norms (ensuring, say, that companies appoint a given number of non-executives) seems ineffective *unless* the roles accompanying those positions are also

---

18 Article 78 of Table A, above n 15, does provide that shareholders may appoint additional directors by ordinary resolution, but this provision is, of course, subject to contrary agreement.

19 Historically, the failure to insist on a professional qualification could be related to the absence of any recognised qualification for directors. But see now the Institute of Directors' (IOD) development of the status of 'Chartered Director'. To be admitted as such, directors must, *inter alia*, pass the IOD's 'Examination in Company Direction'. See further at www.iod.co.uk.

20 See Table A, above n 15, at Regulation 70.

21 Contrast, for example, the detail in the American Law Institute's *Principles of Corporate Governance: Analysis and Recommendations* (St Paul, Minnesota, ALI, 1994) at para 3.02 (Functions and Powers of the Board of Directors).

22 See *Re City Equitable Fire Insurance Co Ltd* [1925] Ch 407.

23 See *Re City Equitable Fire Insurance Co Ltd* [1925] Ch 407. For more recent developments, see section 4.3 below. Some academics have also reinterpreted the older case law as rather less forgiving of directors; see, for example, Hicks 'Directors' Liability for Management Errors' (1994) 110 LQR 390.

enforced. It should also be noted that one might achieve the juridification of a company's structure *indirectly*, through the enforcement of the director's role within the company. In particular, if the director's duty of care and skill required directors to deliberate on, and to adopt, the 'best' board structure for their company, then the law might juridify that without necessarily prescribing, in advance, a single structure for all companies. Directors would, by law, be legally accountable for the structure their companies have adopted. Of course, for the reasons set out above, the historically relaxed nature of the duty of care and skill failed to hold directors to account in this way. An important question for us is whether the strengthening of this duty will change this state of affairs.[24]

3 THE COMBINED CODE

The Combined Code represents the latest gloss on UK company law's long-standing preference for private ordering.[25] The detail of the Combined Code has been well documented elsewhere,[26] and an *aide memoire* will suffice for here. Published in June 1998 by the Committee on Corporate Governance (the 'Hampel Committee'),[27] it consolidated[28] the earlier codes of practice issued by the Hampel Committee itself,[29] and its two predecessors, the Cadbury Committee[30] and the Greenbury Study Group.[31] Applicable to listed companies, it is centrally[32] concerned with developing a board structure, and a set of directorial roles, that will enable the board more effectively to 'lead and control' the company.[33] To achieve this, it recommends that '[t]he board should include a balance of executive and NEDs (including independent NEDs) such that no individual or small group of individuals can dominate the board's decision taking.'[34]

---

24 See section 4.3 below.

25 For a useful summary of developments in other OECD member States up to 2000, see OECD, 'Corporate Governance in OECD Member Countries: Recent Developments and Trends' (undated) available online at www.oecd.org/daf/corporate-affairs/governance/trends.pdf.

26 For a good overview of the content of and background to the Combined Code, see Pettet, above n 6, at chapter 11.

27 The Committee was chaired by Sir Ronald Hampel.

28 Besides consolidating the earlier codes, the Combined Code includes a few changes agreed with the London Stock Exchange; see the Combined Code at p 2, para 2.

29 The Committee on Corporate Governance *Report of the Committee on Corporate Governance* (London, Gee, 1998); hereafter *The Hampel Report*.

30 *The Cadbury Report*, above n 13.

31 The Study Group on Directors' Remuneration *Directors' Remuneration* (London, Gee, 1995); hereafter *The Greenbury Report*. The Greenbury Study Group was chaired by Sir Richard Greenbury.

32 Elsewhere, the Code aims to foster a more constructive dialogue with shareholders, and urges institutional shareholders 'to make considered use of their votes' and 'to enter into a dialogue with companies based on the mutual understanding of objectives' (see Part 2, section 1, provisions E.1–E.3).

33 There has been an ongoing debate about the proper role of NEDs and, in particular, the extent to which their monitoring role should be combined with a collegial contribution towards developing corporate strategy; see Mezzamel and Watson 'Wearing Two Hats: The Conflicting Control and Management Roles of Non-Executive Directors' in K Keasey, S Thompson and M Wright (eds) *Corporate Governance: Economic, Management, and Financial Issues* (Oxford, OUP, 1997).

34 See Combined Code at Part 1, section 1, principle A.3.

More specifically, the Combined Code provides that '[n]on-executives should comprise not less than one-third of the board'[35] and recommends that '[t]he majority of non-executive directors should be independent of management and free from any business or other relationship which could materially interfere with the exercise of their independent judgement.'[36] It also recommends the creation of three board sub-committees to deal with particularly contentious areas of corporate life – namely the nomination of directors,[37] their remuneration,[38] and the audit process.[39]

3.1   The Combined Code as anti-juridification

The Code, like its predecessors, represented a difficult balancing act. On the one hand, there was a perceived need to strengthen corporate governance in response to a variety of claimed governance abuses.[40] On the other hand, it was also born under a government committed to *reducing* the regulatory burdens on business and extending the discipline of market forces.[41] That commitment was already evident in the UK's long-standing resistance to the EC's draft Fifth Company Law Directive, with its provisions on board structure and employee participation.[42] Thus, corporate governance had to be strengthened, but not juridified.

Two features of the Combined Code evidence this anti-juridification philosophy. First, it was the product of a non-governmental committee, composed primarily of industrialists, financiers and City professionals. In this sense, it was a self-regulatory process, with those subject to, or benefiting from, the regulatory framework responsible for its construction. Secondly, the Code is voluntary in that it creates no formal sanctions for non-observance of its provisions. Listed companies are required to *disclose* the extent of their compliance with the Combined Code (and to explain any departures therefrom)[43] but it is left to shareholder voice or the pressure of the capital markets[44] to challenge a company's failure to comply fully with the provisions of the Code.[45] Moreover although,

---

35 See Combined Code at Part 2, section 1, provision A.3.1.

36 See Combined Code at Part 2, section 1, provision A.3.2.

37 See Combined Code at Part 2, section 1, provision A.5.1. It is recommended that nomination committees comprise a majority of NEDs.

38 See Combined Code at Part 2, section 1, provision B.2.1. It is recommended that remuneration committees comprise exclusively independent NEDs.

39 See Combined Code at Part 2, section 1, provision D.3.1. It is recommended that audit committees comprise 'at least three directors, all non-executive ... the majority of whom should be independent ...'

40 See Preface, *The Cadbury Report*, above n 13.

41 For an introduction to the relationship between company law and the 'deregulation debate' see: S Wheeler *A Reader on the Law of the Business Enterprise* (Oxford, Clarendon, 1994) Introduction; Riley 'Public Companies' in D Milman (ed) *Regulating Enterprise* (Oxford, Hart, 1999).

42 On the history of that Directive's various manifestations, see J Du Plessis and J Dine 'The Fate of the Draft Fifth Directive on Company Law: Accommodation Instead of Harmonisation' [1997] *Journal of Business Law* 23.

43 On the nature of the disclosure obligations, see below at n 72 and the main text thereat.

44 For a fuller account of these pressures, written following publication of *The Cadbury Report*, above n 13, see Riley 'Controlling Corporate Management: UK and US Initiatives' (1994) 14 LS 244 at pp 255–62.

45 Note that institutional shareholders are subject to no disclosure requirements in regard to their obligations under the Combined Code.

as Parkinson notes,[46] the Code creates a 'presumption' in favour of compliance, that presumption is a relatively weak one. This is seen, obviously, in the absence of legal sanctions attending non-compliance. However, it is also evident in the Code's heavy reliance on vague and abstract principles[47] (rather than more concrete, prescriptive rules),[48] and in the Code's emphasis that 'those concerned with the evaluation of governance should do so with common sense and with due regard to companies' individual circumstances.'[49] This attempt to limit reliance on prescriptive rules reflects Hampel's own warning against a 'tick box' mentality, in which rules are imposed, and compliance demanded, without adequate regard for 'the diversity of circumstances and experience amongst companies'.[50]

4 THE TURNING OF THE JURIDIFICATION TIDE

Hampel's attempt to strengthen without juridifying corporate governance was always a difficult balance to strike. The New Labour Government, elected in 1997, was less ideologically committed to the deregulatory agenda than its predecessor administrations, and more open to the case for legal intervention.[51] In 1998 it launched a major review of company law under the rubric *Modern Company Law for a Competitive Economy*.[52] The guiding aim of the review was to produce a modernised company law likely to promote 'competitiveness' and, thereby, 'national prosperity'.[53] Whilst much of the rhetoric of the review and its consultation documents remains, as might be expected, *laissez faire* and critical of excessive regulation,[54] still there was a greater readiness to acknowledge both the limits of market forces and the need for legal regulation.[55]

This stance is seen in the first consultation document of the DTI's Review, which declared: 'The Government does not intend to replace the use of best practice by legal rules, provided best practice is seen to be working. There may, however, be a need for

---

46 See Parkinson 'Evolution and Policy in Company Law: The Non-Executive Director' in J Parkinson, A Gamble and G Kelly (eds), above n 14, at p 236, citing Rickford 'Do Good Governance Recommendations Change the Rules for the Board of Directors?' (unpublished paper, 13 March 2000).

47 The Combined Code is divided into two parts. Part 1 contains the general 'Principles of Good Governance', expressed as vague, open-ended standards. Part 2 contains a set of more specific, rule-like provisions, which are collectively labelled 'The Code of Best Practice'.

48 A good example of this reliance on vague principles can be seen in the Combined Code's provisions on the independence of non-executive directors: see Part 2, section 1, provision A.3.2, which provides that '[t]he majority of non-executive directors should be independent of management and free from any business or other relationship which could materially interfere with the exercise of their independent judgment'. It does not, however, specify what 'business or other relationships' could materially interfere with the exercise of an independent judgment.

49 See Combined Code at Preamble, para 6.

50 See *The Hampel Report*, above n 29, at para 1.13.

51 For a longer history of the Labour Party's views on corporate regulation, see Clift, Gamble and Harris 'The Labour Party and the Company' in J Parkinson, A Gamble and G Kelly (eds), above n 14.

52 For a useful overview of the review, see Pettet, above n 6, at chapter 4.

53 See DTI, *Modern Company Law for a Competitive Economy* (London, DTI, March 1998) at para 1.2. See also Armour 'Share Capital and Creditor Protection: Efficient Rules for a Modern Company Law' (2000) 63 MLR 355 at pp 356–58.

54 See, for example, *The Final Report*, above n 5, Foreword at paras 2 and 5–10.

55 See *The Final Report*, above n 5, at para 1.11.

legislation in certain areas which are not covered by the new Code, or where experience shows that some legal underpinning is needed.'[56] As the remainder of this section will demonstrate, the move towards formal legal regulation is evident also in a number of proposals that will, taken together, juridify significant parts of the governance landscape now occupied by the Combined Code. As Jonathan Rickford, Project Director of the Company Law Review, has put it, '[t]he origin of the Code may lie with the markets and practitioners; it is beginning perhaps to become government territory'.[57]

4.1   Reviewing and updating the Combined Code

The first area in which the movement towards juridification can be seen concerns the role of the State in updating and thus determining the future content of the Combined Code. The Combined Code was an exercise in self-regulation, in the sense that it was produced by the business community itself. However, the Steering Group recommended that a significant reassignment of responsibility be made here. As part of the institutional structure for the ongoing development and enforcement of company law, the Steering Group suggested the creation of a 'Company Law and Reporting Commission', 'responsible for the overall operation of the regulatory structure'.[58] Beneath this there would operate a Standards Board,[59] which would be charged with keeping the Code under review.[60]

For the State to take overall control of the process for developing and updating a governance code in this way acknowledges that the scope and content of such a code is a matter of public, and not merely private, concern.[61] This does not, of course, necessarily mean that the State must ensure that the interests of all members of the public, or all corporate 'stakeholders', are taken into account by corporate managers.[62] The latter is one possible model for a governance code, but it does not follow just from the fact that the State is interested in setting the ground rules by which companies must operate. The State might well decide that the public interest is best served by a set of governance rules that promote 'efficiency', and that rules requiring managers to promote the interests of their shareholders best achieve that.[63] However, the important point would remain that such a

---

56   DTI, above n 53, at para 3.7.

57   See J Rickford 'Do Good Governance Recommendations Change the Rules for the Board of Directors?' (unpublished paper, 13 March 2000, copy on file with author) at p 37, footnote omitted.

58   See *Completing the Structure*, above n 5, at para 12.59. The name proposed in *Completing the Structure* (Companies Commission) has been changed to give a more 'accurate reflection of the overarching role we envisage for this body'; see *The Final Report*, above n 5, at para 5.21 and, for a more detailed list of the Company Law and Reporting Commission's functions, see *The Final Report*, above n 5, at para 5.22.

59   See *The Final Report*, above n 5, at para 5.38 (noting the change of name from that of 'Standards Committee' as originally used in *Completing the Structure*, above n 5).

60   See *The Final Report*, above n 5, at para 5.43. This ownership of the review process seems to include making changes to the content of the Combined Code, but not making 'substantive rules' (meaning, it seems, legal rules) on those matters now covered by the Code; see *The Final Report*, above n 5, at para 5.60.

61   One of the best recent discussions of the public interest in the regulation of corporations remains JE Parkinson *Corporate Power and Responsibility* (Oxford, Clarendon, 1993).

62   The literature on stakeholding has become too voluminous to cite in full. For a useful collection of recent essays on the subject, see Parkinson, Gamble and Kelly (eds), above n 14.

63   Indeed, that seems to be the position taken by the Steering Group itself; see above n 53 and the main text thereat.

decision would be taken by a committee appointed by the State, and ultimately accountable through Parliament, enjoying a democratic legitimacy which the Hampel Committee and its predecessors lacked.[64] Furthermore, even if the State takes efficiency as the proper goal, it continues to have an interest in seeing that the rules are indeed efficient. One compelling criticism of Hampel, for example, was that it relied too heavily upon 'casual empiricism', based on its members' own personal experiences, in comparison, say, to the much more extensive and rigorous research which is informing the Government's own Company Law Review.[65]

Will this increased State involvement in the process for updating the Combined Code undermine the claimed advantages of self-regulation? One such advantage is greater sensitivity to the business practices being regulated. Insiders will know better, and sooner, what practices need to be controlled, and how. Their regulation will therefore likely be more effective, better tailored to the differing circumstances and problems of different firms within the regulated industry, and thus more responsive to changes in that environment.[66] Centralised, governmental regulation, by contrast, is seen as a bludgeoning, lumbering creature. It knows too little, and too late, about the industry practices it is seeking to control, it regulates all alike, and is slow to respond to developments within the industry.

But the sensitivity argument seems to apply poorly here, for at least three reasons. First (and a point to which we will return below), the Combined Code itself makes little effort to develop different menus of rules tailored to different types of company. Instead, it achieves 'sensitivity' only indirectly, in the ways mentioned earlier: by using highly generalised principles that can be tailored, *ex post*, to the different situations of different companies, and by permitting a company to opt out of rules which do not 'fit'. The drafters of the Combined Code, then, do not attempt to 'fine tune' their rules to the differing circumstances of different companies, but instead pass that responsibility to those charged with *applying and enforcing* the Code's provisions.

Secondly, the need for a heightened *responsiveness* to changes in business practices also looks doubtful. We are not concerned here with detailed technical regulation of a particular sector of industry where new practices or new scientific knowledge may warrant immediate changes in the regulatory regime. The Code is a pan-industrial regime, written at a level of generality where new thinking is likely to emerge slowly, and hardly require immediate change. Indeed, the process by which the predecessors to the Combined Code were updated was hardly one of great alacrity.[67]

Finally, the sort of Standards Board being proposed can retain a great deal of industry input, even whilst adding a layer of democratic accountability. The Steering Group's

---

64　See *Strategic Framework*, above n 5, at para 5.5.3: 'Regulation by, and enforcement under, statute has the merit of democratic legitimacy in the making of the rules and, in the company law field, the widest consultation beforehand ... Ministers are accountable publicly for the effective operation of the rules.'

65　Relatedly, the Hampel Committee's consultation process looks modest compared to that surrounding the Steering Group's work.

66　See I Ayres and J Braithwaite *Responsive Regulation: Transcending the Deregulation Debate* (New York, OUP, 1992), especially at pp 110–12; Deakin and Cook 'Regulation and the Boundaries of the Law' (August 1999) at chapter 9 of the *Literature Survey on Factual, Empirical and Legal Issues*, carried out by the ERSC centre for Business Research, University of Cambridge for the Steering Group, available online at www.dti.gov.uk/cld/review.htm.

67　See *The Final Report*, above n 5, at para 5.43: 'We would not envisage frequent changes to the Code ...'

stated principle that the board's members should have 'the necessary vision and calibre to ensure that its views and recommendations carried due weight'[68] seems at least to represent an acknowledgment of the issues here. To that end, it constitutes a subtle kind of juridification, which rejects pure self-regulation whilst retaining some of its advantages.

4.2   State-enforced disclosure

The second way in which we are seeing a move towards the juridification of corporate governance concerns the State's role in the *disclosure* of prescribed information that underpins the Code. At a theoretical level, the relationship between disclosure, market forces and regulation is complex.[69] It is widely acknowledged that extensive disclosure is necessary for capital markets to 'work' effectively (meaning, here, for such markets to impose strong disciplinary constraints on the behaviour of corporate managers). Some such disclosure might be achieved itself through market forces – with investors sanctioning companies that fail to reveal reliable information about their activities, or sanctioning securities markets that fail to require such disclosure.[70] However, mandatory rules can also play an important part in establishing the basic framework of institutions necessary for effective disclosure regimes.[71]

As noted above, listed companies are required to say how they apply the general principles of the Combined Code (an 'Appliance Statement') and whether they comply with the provisions of Part 2 of the Code and, to the extent they do not, why not (a 'Compliance Statement').[72] Enforcement of these obligations lies with the Financial Services Authority, as the UK Listing Authority.[73] Already within the current regime, then, we see the intrusion of the State into the disclosure that underpins the Code's enforcement. Moreover, it seems likely that these disclosure obligations will be subject to further, and more intense, State involvement, with the Steering Group suggesting that 'the Combined Code on Corporate Governance, including the *Turnbull* requirements on

---

68 See *Completing the Structure*, above n 5, at para 12.63.
69 See Black 'The Core Institutions that Support Strong Securities Markets' (2000) 55 *The Business Lawyer* 1565, especially p 1571 onwards.
70 For a positive assessment of the effectiveness of market forces and regulatory competition in securing high disclosure standards, see Romano 'Empowering Investors: A Market Approach to Securities Regulation' (1998) 107 *Yale LJ* 2359.
71 See La Porta, Lopez-de-Silanes and Schleifer 'Law and Finance' (1998) 106 *Journal of Political Economy* 1113; Bebchuck and Roe 'A Theory of Path Dependence in Corporate Ownership and Governance' (1999) 52 *Stanford Law Review* 127.
72 See Listing Rules at chapter 12. According to PIRC *Corporate Governance 2000: PIRC's Annual Review of Corporate Governance Trends and Structures in the FTSE All Share Index* (London, PIRC, 2000) all the companies covered by the PIRC Review made an Appliance Statement. It also seems that all the companies made Compliance Statements, although only 91.7% were, on PIRC's criteria, deemed 'satisfactory' (PIRC is the acronym of Pensions & Investment Research Consultants Ltd).
73 Under the Official Listing of Securities (Change of Competent Authority) Regulations 2000, SI 2000/968, the FSA became, with effect from 1 May 2000, the 'competent authority' under the Financial Services Act 1986 with responsibility for, *inter alia*, enforcing the continuing obligations of issuers of securities.

disclosure of risk, should be made a matter for delegated mandatory disclosure standards'.[74]

These reforms can be seen as part of a broader package of proposals by the Steering Group for enhanced disclosure. These include the Operating and Financial Review ('OFR') which companies will be required to publish,[75] the audit process that will support the OFR,[76] and additional disclosure requirements relating to the training and experience of potential directors.[77] Furthermore, outside of the Company Law Review, the DTI has announced its intention of introducing further rules 'to introduce new disclosure requirements on boardroom pay to improve linkage between pay and performance' and to require an annual shareholder vote on the directors' remuneration report.[78]

4.3   Juridifying substance

As important as disclosure rules may be in improving corporate governance, they represent a 'half-way house' towards full juridification. For whilst they require companies to be open about the nature or operation of their governance systems, they still do not prescribe the actual content of that system. However, there have also been some, albeit more limited, moves towards this 'substantive' juridification of corporate governance.

Examples of such include proposed rules on AGMs[79] and restrictions on the length of a director's service contract.[80] However, the most significant development here concerns the duty of care and skill. We noted earlier how, historically, the leniency of that duty contributed towards the non-juridification of corporate governance.[81] For the law to insist on companies having, say, non-executive directors would have achieved little so long as the law also lacked any mechanism for defining and enforcing the distinctive role of such a director. Moreover, a duty that imposed so few substantive obligations on directors was unlikely to lead to an indirect juridification of corporate governance structures. Directors would be unlikely to be held to be in breach of their duty of care just because they had failed to introduce an appropriate board structure.

---

74 See *Completing the Structure*, above n 5, at para 3.35; and now *The Final Report*, above n 5, at paras 5.44–5.47. The board's responsibility in relation to internal risk management was dealt with in principle D.2 and provisions D.2.1–D.2.2, of the Combined Code. It was then set out in greater detail in the 'Turnbull Guidance' (Internal Control Working Party *Internal Control: Guidance for Directors on the Combined Code* (London, ICAEW, 1999). For an overview of that guidance, and its implications for company directors, see Blackburn 'Managing Risk and Achieving Turnbull Compliance' (1999) *Accountants' Digest* Issue 417.

75 See *The Final Report*, above n 5, at chapter 8.

76 See *Completing the Structure*, above n 5, at chapter 6; and *The Final Report*, above n 5, at para 3.43.

77 See *The Final Report*, above n 5, at para 5.49.

78 See: *Directors' Remuneration: A Consultative Document* (London, DTI, 1999); and *Directors' Remuneration: A Consultative Document* (London, DTI, 2001).

79 But note here how, from a fairly wide range of issues that were mooted for possible reform in *Developing the Framework*, above n 5 (at paras 4.24–4.64), a much more limited set of proposals, with greater reliance on non-statutory norms, has now emerged in *The Final Report*, above n 5, at chapter 7.

80 See *The Final Report*, above n 5, at para 6.12.

81 See above n 21 and the main text thereat.

The leniency of the duty of care and skill has, however, been challenged over recent years, and from two sources.[82] First, it seems that recent case law has moved towards a more objective interpretation of the duty.[83] In particular, Lord Hoffmann has stated that the objective standard of liability found in s 214 of the Insolvency Act 1986 also represents the duty of care of a director at common law.[84] Secondly, the Law Commission has proposed the adoption of a statutory statement of the director's duty of care and skill, which statement would expressly incorporate an objective standard of liability.[85] This proposal has in turn been taken up by the Steering Group.[86]

UK company law's adoption of an objective duty of care and skill has the potential for a significant contribution towards the juridification of corporate governance, in two ways. First, in interpreting and applying an objective duty of care and skill, the law might come to articulate a much fuller account of the different roles to be fulfilled by different directors (such as executives and non-executives, the company Chairman, and so on). Secondly, in articulating these roles the law might also begin, indirectly, to spell out the governance structures that directors, in order to fulfil their duty of care and skill, must adopt for their companies.

Whether these two potential contributions towards the juridification of corporate governance are realised depends, of course, upon just how the role of the director (or of different directors) is developed. Currently, we have no statutory statement of that role, and there is resistance to the introduction of such.[87] Rather, it is to be left to the courts to articulate this role, and there are obvious dangers that they will be cautious in so doing, resulting in a very modest account of what is expected of a director (including the governance structure they are expected to adopt). Against this, however, the courts might be encouraged to offer a more expansive account of the director's role as a result of the Combined Code's own norms. The courts could, in other words, reason that the Code provides an account of what is expected of company directors – both in terms of their role within the company, and in terms of the sort of governance structure they ought to ensure their company enjoys.

Is it likely that courts will proceed in this way? This is a question which existing company law doctrine does not really help us to answer, given the novelty of the application of an objective standard in this area. However, arguments can be advanced in favour of the courts so doing. A code of practice can give some indication of current

---

82 See generally BS Butcher *Directors' Duties: A New Millennium, A New Approach?* (The Hague, Kluwer Law International, 2000).

83 For an early move in this direction, see *Dorchester Finance Co Ltd v Stebbing* [1989] BCLC 498.

84 See *Norman v Theodore Goddard (A Firm)* [1991] BCLC 1028; *Re D'Jan of London Ltd* [1994] 1 BCLC 561. This view was subsequently applied in *Bairstow v Queens Moat Houses plc* [2000] 1 BCLC 549 at p 559d–g.

85 See Law Commission Report No 261, *Company Directors: Regulating Conflicts of Interests and Formulating a Statement of Duties* (1999) Cm 3769 (London, TSO, 1999) at Part 5. More technically, the Law Commission and the Steering Group have advocated a 'mixed' objective/subjective duty. This would judge a director's behaviour against both the knowledge and experience that may reasonably be expected of a person in the same position as the director and any actual knowledge and experience the director has.

86 See *Developing the Framework*, above n 5, at para 3.40 and paras 3.66–3.71; *The Final Report*, above n 5, at paras 3.4 and 3.10 and Annex C (at para 4) containing a draft statutory statement of the duty of care and skill.

87 See below at n 104 and the main text thereat.

standards of behaviour and practice within the community. Or a code might provide evidence of the 'best' (meaning something like 'the most efficient') means of organising a company's governance structure (whether or not existing practice is reflected in the code). Furthermore, whilst these arguments in favour of reliance on codes are not uncontroversial,[88] we also know that courts dealing with negligence claims in other areas of professional life do seem to place an emphasis (albeit a critical one) on common standards of practice.[89]

The foregoing offers reasons why a court might give some weight to the Combined Code in applying the director's duty of care and skill. However, for two reasons this process is likely to be a modest one. For one thing, the Code, as now drafted, falls well short of providing a detailed blueprint. It is best seen as a starting point in determining the role of directors, with a good deal of further argument and analysis needed in applying its general principles to real-world situations. For another, the Code's emphasis that its provisions do not necessarily apply to all companies prevents easy reliance upon the Code in any particular case.[90] There might, at best, be a *presumption* that the Code should be followed by companies, with directors then bearing the onus of showing why their non-compliance was acceptable.

The argument that juridification of corporate governance is under way here might also be thought to be strengthened by reference to at least two other areas of company law doctrine, namely the regime for disqualifying directors under the Company Directors Disqualification Act 1986 and the regime for giving relief from 'unfairly prejudicial conduct' under s 459 of the Companies Act 1985.[91] However, neither of these has, in fact, great potential for contributing towards the juridification of corporate governance. As to the former – disqualification – ss 6 and 8 of the 1986 Act permit disqualification of those whose conduct makes them 'unfit to be concerned in the management of the company'.[92] When determining a director's unfitness, a court could *choose* (although it is not compelled)[93] to place some weight upon a director's compliance, or otherwise, with the Code.[94] However, in practice it is likely to be fairly rare that a court will be called upon to disqualify a director of a listed company for unfitness, given that the overwhelming majority of such actions arise in relation to smaller companies.[95]

---

88 For an examination of some of these arguments in the context of the courts' development of 'default rules' in contract law, see Riley 'Designing Default Rules in Contract Law: Consent, Conventionalism, and Efficiency' (2000) 20 OJLS 367.

89 See, for example, *Bolam v Friern Barnet Hospital Management Committee* [1957] 1 WLR 582; M Lunney and K Oliphant *Tort Law: Text and Materials* (Oxford, OUP, 2000) at pp 164–70.

90 See n 49 above.

91 See further the Lowry essay below at p 229.

92 On the disqualification regime generally, see A Walters and M Davis-White *Directors' Disqualification: Law and Practice* (London, Sweet & Maxwell, 1999).

93 Unsurprisingly, there is no reference to the Combined Code in Schedule 1 to the Company Directors Disqualification Act 1986 (matters to which the court *must* have regard in determining unfitness). Schedule 1 is clearly not exhaustive of the matters to which the court can have regard, however, since s 9 merely requires the court to have regard 'in particular' to the matters referred to in Schedule 1 to the Act.

94 There is, so far as I have been able to find, no case in which a court has expressly so chosen or, equally, refused to do so.

95 But compare, for example, *Re Barings plc and Others (No 5)* [2000] 1 BCLC 523.

Doubts also surface in relation to unfair prejudice actions.[96] It seems unlikely that a shareholder would be able to use s 459 to insist on his company adopting a particular governance structure for the company, or to complain about the company's failure to follow the Code. For one thing, exit from listed companies is relatively easy, enabling a shareholder to escape from the conduct of which he complains. If the price at which he can sell his shares is a reasonable one, then the court might well deny that he is being treated unfairly.[97] In any case, to succeed in the action a shareholder must show that his *interests* have been unfairly prejudiced. Whilst the courts did initially expand the notion of shareholders' interests to include their 'legitimate expectations',[98] they also adopted a rather narrower construction of the scope of these interests in public companies.[99] This limiting of the scope of legitimate expectations, moreover, has been continued in relation to *all* companies by more recent case law. So, in *O'Neill v Phillips*, Lord Hoffmann emphasised the importance of what the parties had actually agreed.[100] However, any actual agreement that a company would comply fully with the Code will be rare indeed.[101] Finally, even if, as the Law Commission asserts 'the codes can at the very least constitute benchmarks by which the courts can determine whether conduct is unfairly prejudicial',[102] the weight to be attached to the Combined Code would have to reflect the non-prescriptive form of many of its norms and the plea for toleration of 'the diversity of circumstances and experience amongst companies'.[103]

5 IS FURTHER REFORM DESIRABLE?

A clearer picture is now emerging of the extent – and the limits – of current moves towards the juridification of corporate governance. The State is to assume, through the proposed Standards Board, a greater role both in the rule-making (Code-making) process and in the disclosure regime that underpins the Combined Code's norms. Moreover, the switch to a more objective duty of care and skill means that some of the matters now within the compass of the Combined Code may become subject to review by the courts as they come to define the appropriate role of a director.

---

96 For a brief discussion of some of the case law here, see Law Commission Consultation Paper No 153, *Company Directors: Regulating Conflicts of Interests and Formulating a Statement of Duties* (London, TSO, 1998) at para 1.40 ff.

97 See *O'Neill v Phillips* [1999] 1 WLR 1092 at p 1107D.

98 See, for example, *Re A Company (No 00477 of 1986)* [1986] BCLC 376; *Re A Company (No 008699 of 1985)* [1986] BCLC 382; and *Re A Company (No 003160 of 1986)* [1986] BCLC 391. Later cases, such as *Re BSB Holdings Ltd (No 2) Ltd* [1996] 1 BCLC 155, reaffirmed this expansive interpretation of s 459.

99 See, for example, *Re Blue Arrow plc* [1987] BCLC 585. See also *Re Astec (BSR) plc* (1998) unreported, 7 May, Jonathan Parker J, cited in Law Commission Consultation Paper, above n 96, at para 1.40.

100 [1999] 1 WLR 1092 at p 1101F; see further the Lowry essay below at p 229. Note also *Re Guidezone Ltd* [2000] 2 BCLC 321, in which it was suggested that subsequent informal (albeit express) agreements would not be enforceable, in equity, if there had not been actual reliance on such agreements by the claimant.

101 There has been a good deal of academic discussion around the relationship between s 459 and the parties' actual or hypothetical agreements. See, for example, Riley 'Contracting Out of Company Law: Section 459 of the Companies Act 1985 and the Role of the Courts' (1992) 55 MLR 782.

102 See Law Commission Consultation Paper, above n 96, at para 1.43. In support, the Law Commission cited *Re Macro (Ipswich) Ltd* [1994] 2 BCLC 354 at p 407d.

103 See the *The Hampel Report*, above n 29, at para 1.13.

However, this remains a limited intrusion into the substance of governance norms. The Combined Code itself remains non-prescriptive in its content, compliance with its norms remains voluntary, and courts *might* maintain this spirit of non-juridification by offering only a minimalist role for directors. Given all that, I want to conclude this chapter by considering the case for three further reforms that would, indeed, go to the substance of a company's governance system, but which have been rejected (at least for the time being)[104] by the Steering Group. They are:

(a) A fuller specification could be provided, either in the Combined Code or in legislation, of the *role* of the board as a whole, and of the particular role of NEDs.[105] Such a specification could both describe, at a general level, the distinctive contribution expected of different types of director, as well as offering something akin to job descriptions for directors, spelling out more fully the activities which would constitute these different roles. Such roles would, of course, then be enforced through actions for breach of a director's duty of care and skill.

Such a reform is modest. It may do little more than accelerate a development that will occur anyway, even in the absence of any detailed specification of the roles of directors, as courts come to apply the 'open-ended' obligations of the duty of care and skill. Moreover, it focuses only on role, and says nothing *directly* about the proper governance structure that companies must adopt. It is certainly the case, as was argued above, that structure might be implicated indirectly, insofar as directors are held to be in breach of their duty of care and skill for their failure to ensure that a proper structure is in place. But that is itself less likely to occur insofar as the norms on structure remain only vaguely specified.

(b) The second reform, then, moves beyond the *role* of directors, and attends directly to structural governance rules. It seeks to strengthen – in the sense of making more detailed, prescriptive and rule-like – those norms within the Combined Code which address these matters (without yet making them legally enforceable).[106] A good example of how this might operate is in relation to the requirement that companies have 'independent' directors. The Code currently declares that '[t]he majority of non-executive directors should be independent of management and free from any business or other relationship which could materially interfere with the exercise of their independent judgment'.[107] But under this second reform, such a provision might be recast so as to spell out a range of relationships that would be taken as

---

104 See *The Final Report*, above n 5, at para 3.49.

105 I have sought, elsewhere, to distinguish, on the one hand, this specification of the activities required of any given director from, on the other hand, the standard of liability to be imposed when that director fails to fulfil those activities. The former could be done in some rigorously demanding way (and by reference to what a 'reasonable' director might do if he occupied that position in that company), whilst simultaneously employing a subjective standard of liability (say only holding this particular director liable if he was himself capable of performing those activities). Nothing I am arguing for in this chapter undermines that distinction. See further Riley 'The Company Director's Duty of Care and Skill: The Case for an Onerous but Subjective Standard' (1999) 62 MLR 697.

106 This retention of the voluntary status of the Code's norms reflects the point that even if non-statutory regulation is not working well enough, there are still intermediate measures falling short of formalising the specific requirements of a code into legal rules that can be considered; see further Ferran 'Corporate Law, Codes and Social Norms – Finding the Right Regulatory Combinational and Institutional Structure' (2001) 1 *Journal of Corporate Law Studies* 381.

107 See Combined Code, Part 2, section 1, provision A.3.2.

precluding independence.[108] Likewise, more detailed rules might be introduced on the qualifications (or other qualities) required of directors, the precise rights of directors to take independent professional advice,[109] on the 'back room' support to which directors are entitled,[110] and the like.

(c) The third proposed reform entails giving legal force to some or all of the structural norms of the Code – in the sense of making such provisions enforceable by injunction. Those with *locus standi* to sue, then, would not have to wait until a failure to comply with such norms had resulted in loss; precisely in the hope of avoiding such loss, steps could be taken *ex ante* to compel compliance with the relevant governance norms.[111] The norms might be left in the Code, or might be contained in some statutory restatement thereof.

5.1 Enforcement versus flexibility

In considering (and rejecting) these further reforms, the Steering Group addresses two considerations which underpin much of the debate here, namely the achievement of effective enforcement and the preservation of 'flexibility'.[112] Critics of the status quo challenge the level of compliance likely for a vaguely drafted and voluntary Code. Defenders of the status quo, on the other hand, argue that market forces and shareholder voice already secure sufficient compliance with the Combined Code and, further, point to the loss of flexibility that strengthening the Code, or increased legal intervention, would produce.

At first sight, scepticism that juridification would significantly improve enforcement seems to be supported by the apparent success of the existing voluntary regime. A report by PIRC Ltd,[113] for example, suggested fairly high compliance rates for a number of the Combined Code's provisions. The report examined a sample of 468 companies, drawn from the FTSE 100, the MidCap 250 and the FTSE SmallCap, together with 44 investment trusts. Examples of these high compliance rates included the following. Of the 468 companies surveyed, 406 reported that they had separated out the roles of Chairman and Chief Executive Officer ('CEO') (with 45 of the remainder offering a justification for their decision not to separate the roles). In 432 companies, NEDs constituted one-third of the board. Independent NEDs were identified by 428 companies, and 413 companies claimed that a majority of their NEDs were independent. And 296 out of 376 companies examined had nomination committees with a majority of NEDs.

---

108 For attempts to define independence, see the joint formulation of the National Association of Pension Funds and Association of British Insurers, set out (and discussed) in The Company Law Committee of the Law Society *Company Law Review – Developing the Framework* (Memorandum number 401) (London, The Law Society, August 2000) at pp 37–38; the American Law Institute, above n 21, at para 1.34 (defining independence in terms of the absence of a 'significant relationship' with the corporation's senior executives).

109 See Combined Code, Part 2, section 1, provision A.1.3.

110 See Combined Code, Part 2, section 1, provision A.1.4.

111 *Locus standi* might be conferred either on individual shareholders or, with a view to avoiding vexatious litigation, only on a shareholder, or group of shareholders, together holding some specified minimum. See further at n 134 below and the main text thereat.

112 See *The Final Report*, above n 5, at para 1.20.

113 See PIRC Ltd *Compliance with the Combined Code* (London, PIRC, September 1999).

As impressive as such statistics may initially seem, however, they fall well short of negating the case for the three further reforms set out above. First, these data deal only with the structural aspects of governance – board composition, existence and make up of board sub-committees and the like. They tell us very little about how well directors fulfil the *roles* that these structures in turn entail – whether NEDs carry out their responsibilities diligently and effectively, whether boards brief their members fully, and so on.[114] Of course, it might be that market forces are also securing effective compliance with the role-based aspects of governance, at least so far as NEDs are concerned. However, this seems unlikely. The market provides an incentive to non-executives to do their job effectively by threatening underperformers with removal from office and the resultant loss of benefits. However, for non-executives (and especially those who are full-time executives elsewhere), the threatened loss of the relatively modest fees payable are unlikely to cause too many sleepless nights. Equally, the threatened loss of reputation is unlikely to be overtroubling to those whose future careers hardly depend upon their reputation as good non-executive material.

Law, by contrast, operates not only by denying future benefits but also by threatening liability. In that regard, it seems likely to constitute a more cogent threat to non-executives. Further, even if market forces would in fact be much more effective in securing appropriate behaviour by directors than the foregoing suggests, still such forces will typically do little to secure *corrective* justice – compensation for any losses suffered by whatever breaches of the Code the market still fails to deter.[115] Given these limitations in the extent to which market forces are likely to secure compliance with the role-based aspects of governance (or to secure compensation for past non-compliance), law must have a continuing role to play here. Of course, it will indeed do so precisely through the duty of care and skill discussed earlier. But the limitations in that action, even under its more objective formulation, were also noted, limitations which the first reform described above was designed to address.

Secondly, even in relation to compliance with the structural aspects of the Combined Code, the statistics cited above still reveal very many non-compliant companies, as a more recent report by PIRC makes clear.[116] So, whilst it sounds impressive to note that fully 73% of companies have an audit committee with a majority of independent directors, that still leaves over a quarter of companies lacking that basic structural check on managerial power. Moreover, there is the further danger that compliance with some of the structural aspects of the Code is sometimes little more than the 'box ticking' so condemned by Hampel itself.[117] So, 'headline' changes such as separating the role of CEO

---

114 See Combined Code, Part 2, section 1, provision A.4.1. Note that the Government has announced its intention to set up an independent review of the role and effectiveness of non-executive directors; see DTI Press Release 128 of 2002 (27 February 2002).

115 This is not to suggest that market forces never result in redress for harm already caused. Sometimes thinking about the future may require compensation for the past. But in the context of board structures, it seems unlikely that market forces would compel directors to compensate their companies (and thereby their shareholders) for their past choice of an inappropriate board structure.

116 See PIRC Ltd *Corporate Governance 2000: Annual Review of Corporate Governance Trends and Structures in the FTSE All Share Index* (London, PIRC, November 2000). I am grateful to PIRC for providing me with a copy of this report.

117 See *The Hampel Report*, above n 29, at paras 1.12–1.14.

and Chairman achieve apparently high levels of compliance. Nevertheless, where the Code is vague in its demands, real substantive compliance may be much reduced. Take the requirement that '[t]he majority of non-executive directors should be independent of management and free from any business or other relationship which could materially interfere with the exercise of their independent judgement'.[118] When PIRC measured compliance against its own, reasonably demanding definition of 'independence', it found that 'nearly one-third of companies still do not have a majority of independent directors among their non-executives'. It also found that 'only one-third of remuneration committees are fully independent' and 'only 43% of nomination committees have a majority of independent directors'.

Even if the foregoing points are persuasive, however, defenders of the status quo can argue that these shortcomings are an acceptable price to pay for the flexibility inherent in the current regime. Why, however, is 'flexibility' so important, and precisely what sort of regulatory regime does it necessitate?

We can begin by dismissing one familiar, but unpersuasive, argument for flexibility. It invokes the value of autonomy, claiming that even when we know what is best for another person, still we should avoid the temptations of paternalism and allow others to make their own, possibly bad, choices. We should be *free* to live our lives badly, not *forced* to live our lives well. Now, such an argument is often advanced in favour of freedom of contract,[119] and against the heavy hand of State regulation, but it carries little weight in relation to the Combined Code. For probably few defenders of flexibility in relation to the Code would want to argue that shareholders are likely, but should be free, to live their investment lives badly. As we shall see, the claim here is more typically that market actors know better than rule-makers what is best for their companies, not that market actors have a right to be stupid.[120]

A seemingly more persuasive argument for flexibility concerns limitations in our knowledge of the comparative merits of different governance systems. Authors such as Bhagat and Black have shown convincingly the difficulty in establishing empirically the relationship between board composition and firm performance.[121] If we do not know whether, say, independent directors actually have a negative or positive effect on corporate wealth, how can we possibly introduce mandatory rules regarding the number of such directors companies must have?[122]

However, such an argument is self-contradictory when used to *support* a 'flexible' Code of Practice. For if our ignorance were as complete as this argument suggests, then there would be no case for the Code to offer its recommendations at all (*even* in their

---

118 See Combined Code, Part 2, section 1, provision A.3.2.

119 For a discussion of this argument, and of its difficulties, see MJ Trebilcock *The Limits of Freedom of Contract* (Cambridge, Massachusetts, Harvard University, 1993).

120 Further, insofar as we were concerned merely with strengthening the Code by making it more rule-like, the restriction on autonomy looks pretty modest.

121 See Bhagat and Black 'The Uncertain Relationship between Board Composition and Firm Performance' (1999) 54 *The Business Lawyer* 921, providing a good overview of existing literature, and the results of the authors' own empirical study.

122 Such concerns have been particularly forcefully expressed in the international context, and been used to counter moves towards the harmonisation of different national systems. See, for example, Mayer 'Corporate Governance, Competition, and Performance' (1997) 24 JLS 152.

voluntary form). In a world in which we know nothing of the consequences of different governance regimes, a voluntary code might admittedly be less offensive than mandatory legal rules. But, in such a world, it would be even better to abandon the Code as well, with its soft, but unfounded, prescriptions of good governance.[123]

In any case, there are good reasons for doubting that we can really say so little about the comparative merits of competing governance systems. Certainly, the empirical evidence is inconclusive.[124] However, that, in part, is a reflection on the difficulties of gathering meaningful empirical data here.[125] Moreover, empirical studies by their nature try to measure the wealth effects of existing governance systems; they do not tell us (directly) what would be the effects of some idealised system.[126] They also, of necessity, focus on the effects of different *structures*. If, as has been argued throughout this chapter, improving governance depends upon improving the enforcement of governance *roles*, then structure-based studies will inevitably be inconclusive. In the absence of conclusive empirical data on these matters, much of the debate rightly focuses on theoretical arguments. We favour remuneration committees because we think that allowing a person to set his own remuneration is probably a dangerous thing to do, given familiar assumptions about self-interest. Such reasoning and the recommendations it seems to warrant might be thrown into doubt by clear and conclusive empirical evidence. However, until that happens, theoretical arguments provide an acceptable guide for our actions.

Where, then, does that leave the argument for flexibility? The most plausible argument in its favour, it seems, is based neither on a strong commitment to autonomy, nor on a strong claim about our ignorance of the merits of different governance systems. It is, rather, an acknowledgment that what we *do know* is that one size of governance system does not fit all companies well. Any single set of rules might be right for many companies, but will still be both under- and over-inclusive.[127] Such rules will fail to demand enough of some directors, or some companies, and yet demand too much of others.

---

123 Admittedly, if our ignorance were so complete, then it is difficult to see how the market could make any sensible judgment about companies' governance systems either. But it might be thought preferable to let shareholders make their own mistakes with their own money, rather than having government, or the Code-setting body, making their mistakes for them.

124 Some of it is indeed supportive of the positive effects of independent directors on company performance. See Millstein and MacAvoy 'The Active Board of Directors and Performance of the Large Publicly Traded Corporation' (1998) 98 *Columbia Law Review* 1283. For a positive discussion of this article, see Parkinson, above n 46, at pp 243–44. For a much more critical appraisal of that article, and of the wealth effects of independent boards more generally, see Romano 'Less is More: Making Institutional Investor Activism a Valuable Mechanism of Corporate Governance' (2001) 18 *Yale Journal of Regulation* 1 at pp 18–22.

125 For a good account of these difficulties, see Bhagat and Black above n 121.

126 See G Stapledon and J Lawrence *Corporate Governance in the Top 100* (Melbourne, Centre for Corporate Law and Securities Regulation, 1996) at pp 6–9.

127 For theoretical elaboration on the nature of rules, and their likely under- and over-inclusiveness, see J Black *Rules and Regulations* (Oxford, OUP, 1997), especially at chapter 1.

5.2 Flexibility and the three proposed reforms

How far do the three proposed reforms set out above fall foul of these twin dangers of over- and under-inclusiveness? The first point to stress is that none of the three reforms necessarily entails the imposition of a single governance system on all companies. Much flexibility can be retained, even within the more rigorous systems the reforms envisage. For one thing, insofar as the reforms do entail relying on more detailed rules, flexibility can be retained by promulgating not a single rule applicable to all alike, but instead a number of rules 'tailored' to different companies or to different directors. In relation to the specification of directors' roles, for example, we can offer different job descriptions for different types of directors, in different types of company. We might, for example, tailor structural rules to reflect different patterns of share ownership within the company, such as the proportion of shares held by directors themselves,[128] the age of the company, and so on. Of course, there are limits here. Writing different menus of rules suitable for different companies raises the costs of drafting and updating these rules.[129] Moreover, the rule-maker may struggle to predict in advance the different situations of different directors that might warrant different specifications of their roles.[130] Finally, there is a cost in terms of the increasing complexity of the system. Thus, the practice of offering multiple, tailored rules is unlikely to provide a complete solution, but it can, nevertheless, substantially mitigate the problems of inflexibility that the three reform proposals are said to encounter.

Secondly, although it is commonplace to see 'self-regulation' as inevitably characterised by reliance upon broad principles, and legal regulation as necessarily dependent upon narrowly drawn rules, neither necessarily follows. Indeed, there is a strong case (which cannot be fully defended here) that more specific rules are appropriate for a voluntary code designed to trigger the operation of market forces, whilst generalised standards can more easily be employed where some body has the authority to enforce *ex post* interpretations of those standards. So, just as the second proposed reform envisages making (still voluntary) norms more rule-like, in respect of the third reform the norms that are to be legally enforceable might be drafted as general standards. Courts would then have to interpret those standards in the light of the particular fact situation now before them, maintaining much flexibility in their application. Of course there is nothing new in company law relying on general standards in this way. It has been argued that it is precisely through the promulgation of these general standards, and the body of reliable precedent that builds up around their repeated application and interpretation in the

---

128 See, for example, the ALI's Principles of Corporate Governance, whose recommendations on board composition vary according to ownership patterns; ALI, above n 21, at para 3A.01. For arguments in favour of presumptions of compliance with legal duties where directors own substantial shares, see Bhagat, Carey and Elson 'Director Ownership, Corporate Performance and CEO Turnover' (1999) 54 *The Business Lawyer* 885 and Balotti, Elson and Laster 'Equity Ownership and the Duty of Care: Convergence, Revolution or Evolution' (2000) 55 *The Business Lawyer* 661.

129 For a consideration of the issues raised by the optimum degree of tailoring, see Ayres 'Preliminary Thoughts on the Optimal Tailoring of Contractual Rules' (1993) 3 *Southern Californian Interdisciplinary Law Journal* 1.

130 For a useful and broader perspective on the problems raised by creating rules today to ease decision making tomorrow, see Sunstein and Ullmann-Margalit, 'Second-Order Decisions' in CR Sunstein (ed) *Behavioral Law and Economics* (Cambridge, CUP, 2000).

courts, that company law can score over private ordering.[131] Furthermore, although there are concerns about the reliance on standards – especially the lack of certainty and predictability from those who need to adjust their behaviour in response thereto – that particular concern looks misplaced here. This is because the third proposed reform does not threaten to make directors compensate their companies for their failure to comply with some governance standard. It simply permits the courts to compel compliance for the future.

The third point to note is that the concerns over 'box ticking', of which Hampel made so much, also look misplaced in relation to all three of the proposed reforms. For one thing, note again how these proposed reforms do not entail the reduction of all governance norms to limited and narrowly defined rules. Even as we juridify the substance of our governance norms, reliance on some open-ended standards look set to remain. Further, whilst box ticking is itself used in a pejorative sense, it is important to remember the important safeguards that box ticking can generate. Suppose the role of a NED were broken down into a series of (rule-like) activities required of directors. These activities might not cover all that would be expected of a NED, but they would help to disaggregate a complex role into more easily identifiable tasks, thereby aiding transparency and so on. Finally, it is difficult to see how promulgating more rule-like norms (whether in the Code or in legislation) would, in any event, *detract* from whatever pressures the Code, in its existing form, mobilises to enforce high governance standards. Suppose a NED had done all that some more detailed (rule-like) specification of his activities required, but it were still felt that his conduct was unsatisfactory. Or, suppose that a company appointed a person as an 'independent' director who was able to meet some detailed rule defining 'independence', but who ought nevertheless to be regarded as not independent (for some reason not covered by the rule). In each case the director or the company would, in Hampel's terms, have ticked all the right boxes, but would not have met the 'substance' of good governance standards. In each case, however, shareholders and the market would have as much power as they currently enjoy to express their displeasure at such a state of affairs. 'Lazy' shareholders or directors might be happy to take compliance with the specific rules as adequate, but it seems unlikely that such parties would be any less indolent under the current form of the Code.

Fourthly, insofar as the second reform is concerned (retaining, but strengthening, the Code), the problem of over-inclusiveness looks much less significant, for its norms will remain *voluntary*. By strengthening the Code we are likely to raise a stronger presumption that a certain practice is desirable, and that presumption might regrettably be wrong in some particular case. However, this still looks a modest problem to overcome, given that the norms remain voluntary.

This argument does not, admittedly, apply to the first and third reforms, where the law is to be employed to enforce governance norms. Even here, however, the dangers of overprescription and the loss of flexibility seem exaggerated, and for several reasons. For one, legal actions would still likely be rare. Legal proceedings would be a gloss to the other means of self-help that shareholders enjoy.[132] If shareholders are unhappy about

---

131 See Ayres 'Making a Difference: The Contractual Contributions of Easterbrook and Fischel' (1992) 59 *University of Chicago Law Review* 1393 at p 1403 ff.

132 Contrast this with actions under s 459 of the Companies Act 1985, where the minority shareholder is often trapped inside a quasi-partnership with little chance of exit from the company.

their directors' performance or the governance structure they have chosen for their company, then such shareholders have other means of pressing that dissatisfaction.[133] If market forces do indeed exert the strong pressure for compliance their proponents claim, then we should expect legal action to be seen as a rarely used last resort. The apparently impressive figures for compliance rates cited above are usually used to deny the need for legal intervention. Nevertheless, they also suggest that such legal intervention, even if available, would be infrequently employed. Legal resources would then be concentrated on the relatively few cases of 'hardcore' non-compliance.

This 'last resort' quality of legal enforcement would be buttressed by maintaining existing *legal* restrictions on the *locus standi* for bringing enforcement actions. So, for example, allegations of a breach of the directors' duty of care and skill would remain corporate (or derivative) actions, and nothing said in this chapter would lower the hurdles which shareholders currently face in relation thereto.[134] It should also be borne in mind that the UK does not seem to suffer from a problem often alleged in relation to the US, namely overly litigious shareholders. On the contrary, UK shareholders seem fairly reluctant to use whatever modest causes of action company law gives them. This may in part be because of economic considerations that suggest that apathy is rational. It may also be because of some social norm against too ready a reliance on litigation to settle intracorporate disputes. Whatever its source, such a reluctance should go some way towards allaying fears of vexatious litigation here.

Admittedly, courts must beware the dangers of judging directorial behaviour with the perfect vision of hindsight. Such dangers can be lessened, however, by the courts focusing upon the process by which directors arrived at their decisions (rather than upon the substantive consequences of whatever decisions they made).[135] Did they, for example, collect appropriate expert evidence touching on the issue (say from management consultants about the likely suitability of a particular person acting as a director despite his apparent lack of independence), did they appropriately weigh competing considerations, and so on?

Moreover, there is an important point to be made here about the interrelationship of legal and market judgments. In defence of continued reliance upon a voluntary code, the Steering Group has stressed its 'self-limiting' nature: 'if a Code requirement is introduced which does not command the respect of the markets then habitual non-compliance, with acceptable explanations, will establish that the norm is ineffective.'[136] However, courts will also sometimes have the market's judgment to guide them. Suppose a court is asked to decide if a particular director was at fault in approving (or failing to challenge) the governance structure adopted by his company. By the time proceedings come before the

---

133 Of course, other actions (such as procuring the removal of underperforming directors) would not ensure that such directors compensated the company for past losses.

134 For separate proposed reforms in respect of derivative actions, see *The Final Report*, above n 5, at paras 7.46–7.51. Note also the comments above at n 111.

135 Davies makes the point that our experience of the UK judiciary in relation to actions against directors suggests that they would likely be quite sensitive to the dangers here; see Davies 'Notes of a Talk Delivered at a Conference on Developments in Company Law, Conflicts of Interest and Duty' (Institute of Advanced Legal Studies, London, 20 November 1998, unpublished manuscript) at pp 3–6.

136 See *The Final Report*, above n 5, at para 3.64.

court, the market will probably have passed its own (individual) judgment on the company's governance structure. Courts can, in such a case, follow the market.[137] Moreover, the courts can also defer heavily to industry insiders in evaluating departures from governance norms. Finally, the courts' traditional reluctance to become involved in intracorporate disputes[138] suggests the courts are unlikely to be overenthusiastic in overturning managerial decisions.

6 CONCLUSIONS

Despite the best efforts of the Hampel Committee, corporate governance in the UK seems subject to a clearly discernible trend towards further juridification. Public control over the future updating of the Combined Code is likely to be consolidated by the creation of the proposed Standards Committee, and its 'taking ownership' of the Combined Code. Moreover, whilst the Code's norms remain ostensibly voluntary, subject only to disclosure, still the law is set to play an increasing role in specifying, and enforcing, such disclosure. In terms of substance, less movement seems to have been seen towards the law's involvement, but even this perception needs careful qualification. We have seen a range of proposals, some well advanced, for introducing greater legal regulation in matters of corporate governance covered by, or closely related to, the subject matter of the Code. Of considerable importance here is the movement towards an objective duty of care and skill. An objective duty at least opens up the possibility of actions in respect of board structure, as well as the ongoing 'monitoring' obligations of NEDs which the traditional, subjective formulation of the duty kept hidden.

Critics of juridification may accept the picture painted above, but lament its appearance, pointing to the apparently high levels of compliance produced under the existing regime, together with the need to retain flexibility. This essay has taken a rather different line, arguing that much here depends upon the precise form that juridification takes. Stressing the importance of attention to behaviour (or 'role'), the essay has argued for an intensified, *ex post*, review of directorial behaviour, through a more richly delineated duty of care and skill. It has also advocated a strengthening of the Combined Code itself, in the sense of making at least some of its structural provisions more rule-like. Finally, it has suggested that even the most ambitious, far reaching proposal – to permit some parts of the Code to become enforceable, *ex ante*, by injunction – is unlikely to be as disruptive of corporate life, or as an unsuitable a job for the judiciary, as many critics of juridification seem to assume.

---

137 This is an important difference between *ex ante* action to enforce a particular governance system, and *ex post* action to penalise directors for their failure to instigate changes which, by the time the matter comes to court, the market will likely have forced upon the company anyway. In the latter case, the court works with the market, deciding only if the directors were at fault for failing to make the change that the market eventually forced upon the company. In the former case, the court is asked to trump the market's choice.

138 For a discussion of the case law demonstrating such reluctance, see Drury 'The Relative Nature of the Shareholder's Right to Enforce the Company's Articles' [1986] CLJ 219; Baxter 'The Role of the Judge in Enforcing Shareholder Rights' [1983] CLJ 96. See also the Neuberger essay, above at p 70.

CHAPTER 9

THE DISQUALIFICATION OF COMPANY DIRECTORS IN THE MANAGEMENT OF INSOLVENT COMPANIES

Stephen Griffin

1 INTRODUCTION

The principle of law established in *Salomon v A Salomon Ltd*[1] deems that a company registered with a limited liability status is, as a separate legal entity, *prima facie* responsible for its own actions and liable for its own debts. At common law, other than where a company is incorporated to impugn an existing contractual obligation or where it is otherwise considered a sham or agent of another company,[2] the principle in *Salomon* will prevail. Accordingly, in pursuing business activity through the medium of a limited liability company, the company's shareholders and directors will *prima facie* be shielded from the incursion of personal liability should the enterprise fail.[3] The medium of the limited liability company therefore minimises risk and encourages entrepreneurs to invest capital in business projects. The said investment also serves to benefit the public interest in so far as it stimulates the growth and prosperity of the national economy.

However, while a solvent company may serve to benefit the public interest, a company's insolvency may cause irreparable harm.[4] Where, as is frequently the case, a company's demise is caused by the delinquent conduct of its management, a failure to penalise managerial wrongdoing may inadvertently encourage the exploitation of the concept of the limited liability company. To this end, the disqualification process aims to protect the public interest from the future activities of delinquent directors by temporarily removing them from participating in the future management of a company. The imposition of a disqualification order affords a significant commercial penalty in so far as it may hamper a director's future income earning capacity, cause personal and

---

1   [1897] AC 22.
2   See: *Adams v Cape Industries* [1990] Ch 433; and *Ord v Belhaven Pubs* [1998] BCC 607.
3   Specific statutory provisions, for example, Insolvency Act 1986, ss 212–14 will, following a company's liquidation, also have the effect of disturbing the limited liability status of a company by imposing a personal liability on company directors to contribute towards the company's assets. However, such provisions are rarely invoked; see further, Griffin *Personal Liability and Disqualification of Company Directors* (Oxford, Hart, 1999).
4   A company may be viewed as insolvent when its liabilities exceed its assets (known as balance sheet insolvency; see Insolvency Act 1986, s 123(2)). However, for the purposes of a winding-up petition, a company may be viewed as insolvent where it can no longer pay its debts as they fall due (known as cash flow insolvency; see Insolvency Act 1986, s 123(1)). For the purposes of a disqualification order made under the Company Directors Disqualification Act 1986, s 6, an insolvent company is defined in broader terms in the sense that it also includes any situation where an administrative receiver has been appointed to the company or where an administration order has been made in relation to the company.

professional humiliation, and in cases where a director fails to successfully defend an action, may result in the incursion of substantial costs.[5]

The objective of this essay is to critically examine the effectiveness of the disqualification process in the context of insolvent companies. Accordingly, the paper is primarily concerned with ss 6 and 10 of the Company Directors Disqualification Act 1986 and ss 216 and 217 of the Insolvency Act 1986. In analysing these provisions, the paper will consider whether the regulation of the disqualification process should be subject to some future reform.

2 SECTION 6 OF THE COMPANY DIRECTORS DISQUALIFICATION ACT 1986

The vast majority of all disqualification orders are imposed under s 6 of the Company Directors Disqualification Act 1986.[6] The primary purpose of this provision is to protect the public interest by disqualifying directors who have exploited the limited liability status of companies through their unfit trading practices.[7]

2.1 Identifying a company director

For the purposes of s 6, of the Company Directors Disqualification Act 1986, a person is identified as a director of a company where he is formally appointed to hold office (a *de jure* director) or, in accordance with s 22(4) of the Act, where a person occupies the position of a director, by whatever name called (a *de facto* director). Alternatively, in accordance with s 22(5) of the Act a person may be classified as a shadow director.[8] A person who is classified as a *de facto* or shadow director may, for the purposes of the Company Directors Disqualification Act 1986, be liable and/or culpable in respect of the mismanagement of a company's affairs in a manner akin to a *de jure* director.

---

5   However, the deterrent effect of a disqualification order may vary depending upon the personal circumstances of a director. Obviously, disqualification may be very detrimental to the economic well being of the professional director whose income will be dependant upon securing a managerial position, but will be less so in relation to the small businessman who, following disqualification, may decide to continue to operate a business through the medium of a business partnership or as a sole trader.

6   Statistics taken from Table D1 of the Department of Trade and Industry publication *Companies in 1999–2000* (London, TSO, 2000) at p 37 reveal that over 90% of all disqualifications imposed under the Companies Directors Disqualification Act 1986, were made under s 6.

7   Company Directors Disqualification Act 1986, s 6(1) provides that the court is under a duty to impose a mandatory disqualification order against any person in circumstances where:
    (a) that person is or has been a director of a company which has at any time become insolvent (whether while the person was a director or subsequently); and
    (b) that person's conduct as a director of the company (either taken alone or taken together with the person's conduct as a director of another company or companies) makes the person unfit to be concerned in the management of a company.

8   Company Directors Disqualification Act 1986, s 22(5) provides that a shadow director is a person:
    '... in accordance with whose directions or instructions the directors of a company are accustomed to act ... a person is not deemed a shadow director by reason only that the directors act on advice given by him in a professional capacity.'

In the case of *Re Kaytech International plc*[9] the Court of Appeal (in approving the respective decisions of Judge Cooke in *Secretary of State for Trade and Industry v Elms*[10] and *Secretary of State v Tjolle*[11]) held that a person's standing as a *de facto* director should not be determined by the application of a single decisive test but in all cases a number of factors should be considered in a manner akin to a jury question. Such factors include whether there was a holding out by the company of the individual as a director, whether the individual described himself as a director, whether the individual had proper information (for example, management accounts) on which to base decisions, and crucially, whether the individual had a capacity to participate in the decision making process of the company.[12]

Until recently a person was considered to have acted as a shadow director in circumstances where that person, albeit outside the formal management structures of a company, was in a position to exert dominance and control over the company's formally appointed directors, to the extent that he was capable of engineering or directing corporate activity through what in effect was a 'puppet board of directors'.[13] However, following the decision of the Court of Appeal in *Secretary of State v Deverell*,[14] this interpretation must now be viewed with caution. As a result of *Deverell* a person will act as a shadow director where that person exerts a 'real influence' over management issues. According to the Court of Appeal in *Deverell*, influence may be exerted where a person provides mere advice as opposed to a direction or instruction, in so far as a direction, instruction or the giving of advice all share the common characteristic of an act of guidance. Further, the Court of Appeal considered that a person may be defined as a shadow director where he takes a visible role in the management of the company exerting considerable influence from inside or outside formal management structures. Finally, the Court of Appeal opined that it was unnecessary, in seeking to establish a person as a shadow director, to prove that the board had been cast in a subservient role, that is, that the board was a mere 'puppet'.

While the distinguishing characteristics of a *de facto* and shadow director are not always clear cut, it is suggested that the interpretation afforded to a shadow director in *Deverell* further blurs the distinction. Contrary to the Court of Appeal's judgment, it is submitted that a person who has an open and active role in the management of a company's affairs should properly be regarded as a *de facto* as opposed to a shadow director. Further, in respect of the Court of Appeal's assertion that a shadow director need not always have a dominant lead in directing corporate policy, it is submitted that s 22(5) of the Company Directors Disqualification Act 1986 implies that a direction or instruction of a shadow director will ordinarily be followed, that is, it would be unusual if the

---

9   [1999] BCC 390.
10 16 January 1997, unreported.
11 [1998] BCLC 333.
12 See further, Griffin 'The Characteristics and Identification of a *De Facto* Director' [2000] *Company Financial and Insolvency Law Review* 126.
13 See generally: *Re Lo-Line Electric Motors Ltd* [1988] 2 All ER 692; *Re Unisoft Group Ltd (No 3)* [1994] 1 BCLC 609; *Re Hydrodam (Corby) Ltd* [1994] 2 BCLC 180; *Secretary of State v Laing* [1996] 2 BCLC 324; and *Re Kaytech International plc* [1999] 2 BCLC 351.
14 [2000] 2 All ER 365.

direction or instruction was not followed.[15] As a result of *Deverell* it may be observed that the distinction between the characteristics attached to a *de facto* and shadow director is now a distinction without little difference and as such it is important to note that the ability to label a person or other entity as a shadow director will now be less arduous than had previously been the case.

2.2 Unfit conduct

In assessing whether a director is unfit to act in the management of a company, the court will[16] have particular regard to the matters set out in both Part 1 and Part 2 of Sched 1 to the Company Directors Disqualification Act 1986.[17] However, as s 9 of the Company Directors Disqualification Act 1986 directs the court to have *particular regard* to the matters contained in Sched 1, it is possible to establish unfit conduct in circumstances other than those governed by that Schedule.[18]

In so far as s 6 invokes no criminal liability, the assessment of whether a director's managerial activities amount to conduct of an unfit nature will be determined by the civil standard of proof.[19] As s 6 cases are not of a criminal nature it follows that hearsay evidence and findings of primary and secondary fact are more readily admissible.[20]

---

15 It is to be noted that the Company Law Review Steering Group has not recommended that this definition be altered; see *Modern Company Law for a Competitive Economy – Final Report* (London, DTI, June 2001) at para 6.7; hereafter *The Final Report*.

16 In accordance with the Company Directors Disqualification Act 1986, s 9.

17 Schedule 1 contains a detailed list of matters for the court to consider and merits individual inspection by the reader.

18 Such matters may include: a director's connection with other failed companies, a failure to take positive steps to correct management errors, a failure to resign from office where that step was the only viable option open to him, a failure to co-operate with a liquidator; see *Secretary of State for Trade and Industry v McTighe and Egan* [1997] BCC 224, and a director's potential culpability under the Insolvency Act 1986, s 216; see *Re Migration Services International Ltd* (1999) *The Times*, 2 December.

19 However, because allegations made in the course of disqualification proceedings may invoke very serious insinuations of personal misconduct, the courts have occasionally failed to interpret the civil standard in its purest form, interpreting the provision as one whereby a director's culpability must be established at a standard which is reasonably conclusive of a finding of unfitness, see *Re Polly Peck International plc* [1994] 1 BCLC 574. See further Griffin 'The Burden of Proof in Disqualification Proceedings' (1997) 18 *Company Lawyer* 24.

20 See *Re Barings plc (No 5)* [1999] BCLC 433.

Further, as s 6 proceedings are of a regulatory as opposed to criminal nature, Art 6 of the European Convention on Human Rights[21] will have a limited application.[22]

In determining whether to impose a disqualification order under s 6 the court is solely concerned with the nature, extent and degree of the director's past conduct to the point whereby mitigating factors indicative of a director's potential to reform his future conduct will be ignored. For example, in *Secretary of State v Gray*[23] although Hoffmann LJ conceded that extenuating circumstances may affect the court's consideration of whether a director's past conduct had reached an appropriate standard of unfitness to justify disqualification, his Lordship stressed that any decision to impose a disqualification order would not be influenced by considering a director's capacity to reform his past activities. Accordingly, unlike s 6's predecessor, namely s 300 of the Companies Act 1985, the court is not possessed of a general discretion to consider the likelihood of a director's ability to refrain from committing any future malpractice in the exercise of his managerial responsibilities. Under s 6, following a finding of unfitness, liability is strict and as such the provision promotes consistency and certainty in respect of a positive requirement on the part of the courts to disqualify directors in circumstances where their conduct in the management of a company is deemed to be unfit.

In seeking to identify conduct which, for the purposes of s 6, may be justified to be of an unfit nature, the courts have expressed an unwillingness to impose disqualification orders in a situation where the degree of fault attached to a director's act or omission is attributable to business practices of an improper but nevertheless naive and imprudent standard. The courts have explained the necessity of establishing a serious degree of misconduct on the basis that a disqualification order may dramatically infringe upon the commercial liberty of a director in respect of his ability to pursue future employment in the management of a company. For example, in *Re Bath Glass Ltd*,[24] Peter Gibson J

---

21   The Human Rights Act 1998 gives effect to the rights and freedoms guaranteed under the European Convention of Human Rights (ECHR). According to ECHR, Art 6(1), 'In the determination of his civil rights and obligations or of any criminal charge against him, everyone is entitled to a fair and public hearing within a reasonable time by an independent and impartial tribunal established by law'. Following *Saunders v United Kingdom* (1996) 23 EHRR 313 Art 6(1) will be especially pertinent to self-incrimination, where statements made under compulsion under the Companies Act 1985 to Department of Trade and Industry inspectors are used in a later criminal trial against the person making the statement. The European Court of Human Rights ruled such to be an infringement of the right to a fair trial. Disqualification cases have not been found to be within the ambit of Art 6(1), largely because disqualification has been regarded by both the domestic courts as a civil regulatory matter, and not a criminal charge, see: *R v Secretary of State for Trade and Industry ex p McCormick* [1998] BCC 379; *DC, HS and AD v United Kingdom* [2000] BCC 710; and *Re Westminster Property Management Ltd* [2001] BCC 121.

22   See, *DC, HS and AD v UK* [2000] BCC 710 and *WGS and MSLS v UK* [2000] BCC 719. However, as observed in the latter case, the fact that disqualification proceedings are to be treated as regulatory civil proceedings and not criminal proceedings for the purposes of Art 6(1) will not remove from the applicants a right to a fair hearing. Following *EDC v United Kingdom* [1998] BCC 370, delays in the prosecution of civil proceedings against a director under the Company Directors Disqualification Act 1986 may constitute a violation of Art 6(1). In *EDC* the disqualification proceedings began on 28 August 1991 when the proceedings were issued and terminated on 22 January 1996 when the High Court ordered a stay by a consent order. It was held that the UK authorities had allowed delay to occur without any convincing explanation. By the time the disqualification proceedings were stayed in January 1996, approximately seven years had elapsed from the date of the events which gave rise to the proceedings. While the disqualification proceedings were pending they would have had a considerable impact on the applicant's reputation and ability to practice his profession. However, see *Re Abermeadow Ltd* [2001] BCC 724.

23   [1995] 1 BCLC 276.

24   [1988] BCLC 329.

concluded that two directors, having been party to the company's wrongful trading, should not be disqualified under s 6, because although imprudent, their misconduct had not been undertaken with an intention to benefit themselves at the expense of the company's creditors. This finding as to the directors' honesty in the conduct of the company's affairs had been substantiated, in part, by their willingness to make a firm financial commitment to the company by, for example, taking shares in the company in return for repaying the company's overdraft. In addition, the two directors had sought to act upon professional advice, had drawn up regular and meticulous (albeit inaccurate) business plans and genuinely and reasonably believed that the company would be able to trade itself out of its difficulties.

In effect, the courts seek to equate unfit conduct with conduct of a commercially culpable nature, that is, conduct which is viewed to be harmful to the public interest so as to exhibit a clear exploitation of the privileges attributable to the limited liability status of a company. In reality, the ability to determine whether a director's conduct is of an unfit nature will always be a question of fact, ascertained from the individual circumstances of a given case. The seriousness of a particular course of conduct will be measured in accordance with its perceived prejudicial effect on the public interest which for the purposes of disqualification, may be tentatively defined as incorporating the interests of corporate creditors, the company's existing and future customers, company employees, company shareholders and the regional and national economy.

Ordinarily, the requisite degree of exploitation will be portrayed by evidence of a wanton[25] or reckless[26] disregard and abuse of the interests of creditors, an obvious and serious (if not persistent) failure to comply with provisions of the companies legislation,[27] gross negligence in the management of a company,[28] or a combination of any of the above failings. In respect of managerial abuse, the culpability required to establish unfit conduct may often be expected to exceed conduct exhibiting a breach of fiduciary duty.[29] Accordingly, it is unlikely whether a disqualification order will be imposed in circumstances where a breach of fiduciary duty results in but a marginal decline in the company's financial position.[30] A disqualification order will be more readily imposed where a breach of fiduciary duty prevents the repayment of corporate debts in

---

25 See generally: *Re T & D Services (Timber Preservation & Damp Proofing Contractors) Ltd* [1990] BCC 592; *Re Melcast (Wolverhampton) Ltd* [1991] BCLC 288; and *Re Moorgate Metals Ltd* [1995] BCC 143.

26 See generally: *Re GSAR Realisations Ltd* [1993] BCLC 409; *Re New Generation Engineers Ltd* [1993] BCLC 435; and *Re Hitcho 2000 Ltd* [1995] 2 BCLC 63.

27 See: *Re Firedart Ltd* [1994] 2 BCLC 340; and *Secretary of State v Arif* [1996] BCC 586.

28 See generally: *Re Linvale Ltd* [1993] BCLC 654; *Re Continental Assurance Co Ltd* [1997] BCLC 4; and *Re Park House Properties Ltd* [1997] 2 BCLC 530.

29 In *Re Barings plc (No 5)* [1999] 1 BCLC 433 at p 486, Jonathan Parker J observed that it may be possible to find unfit conduct where, for example, a director is responsible for trading at the risk of creditors notwithstanding that the conduct did not involve a breach of duty or an act of wrongful trading under the Insolvency Act 1986, s 214. Further, he also remarked that, in addition to finding unfitness in a situation where a director made a negligent mistake, it may also be possible to find unfit conduct in a situation where he erred in his judgment. However, with the greatest respect, such observations must be considered doubtful in accordance with the accepted judicial interpretation of conduct, which may be considered to be of an unfit nature.

30 See generally: *Re Time Utilising Business* [1990] BCLC 568; *Re CSTC Ltd* [1995] BCC 173; *Secretary of State v Van Hengel* [1995] BCLC 545; *Re Dominion International Group plc (No 2)* [1996] 1 BCLC 572; *Secretary of State v Cleland* [1997] 1 BCLC 437; and *Secretary of State v Lubrani* [1997] 2 BCLC 115.

circumstances where it causes a company to fall into an insolvent state or where the breach exacerbates a company's already insolvent position.

While negligent conduct may also justify the imposition of a disqualification order under s 6 of the Company Directors Disqualification Act 1986, the degree of negligence must be substantial. In assessing a requisite standard of competence to be expected of a director, the standard is measured in accordance with the expectations of a reasonable diligent person as opposed to the standards expected of a professional businessman. While such an assessment may be regrettable, in so far as it ignores the fact that a director is, indeed, a professional businessman and as such is likely to possess business skills in excess of those to be expected from a reasonable diligent person, it should be observed, following the judgment of Jonathan Parker J in *Re Barings plc (No 5)*,[31] that the court will consider the specific role and duties of the respondent director in respect of the management of the company in which he held office. He explained the position as follows:

> ... while the requisite standard of competence does not vary according to the nature of the company's business or to the respondent's role in the management of that business – and in that sense it may be said there is a universal standard – that standard must be applied to the facts of each particular case. Hence to say that the Act envisages a universal standard of competence applicable in all circumstances takes the matter little further since it says nothing about whether the requisite standard has been met in a particular case. What can be said is that the court, whilst taking full account of the demands made upon a respondent by his management role, will recognise incompetence in whatever circumstances and at whatever level of management it occurs, from the chairman of the board down to the most junior director. In that sense, there is an element of universality in the court's approach.[32]

Therefore, in accordance with this statement, the expectations of the reasonable diligent person will, in effect, become the expectations of a reasonable diligent person occupying a position akin to that held by the respondent. Accordingly, the standard against which a director's competence will be measured is similar to that stipulated by s 214 of the Insolvency Act 1986[33] and indeed, the general standard applicable to determine a director's breach of a duty of care as advocated in *The Final Report* of the Company Law Review Steering Group.[34]

While the measure of competence required to substantiate a finding of negligence for the purposes of disqualification under s 6 of the Company Directors Disqualification Act 1986 may share similar characteristics to that required in respect of s 214 of the Insolvency Act 1986,[35] it must be stressed that the minimum degree of incompetence deemed

---

31 [1999] 1 BCLC 433.

32 See [1999] 1 BCLC 433.

33 Section 214(4) provides that: '... the facts which a director of a company ought to know or ascertain, the conclusions which he ought to reach and the steps which he ought to take are those which would be known or ascertained, or reached or taken, by a reasonably diligent person having both:

   (a) the general knowledge, skill and experience that may reasonably be expected of a person carrying out the same functions as those which were carried out by that director in relation to the company; and

   (b) the general knowledge, skill and experience of the director.'

34 See *The Final Report*, above n 15, Annex C at p 346.

35 See further, Walters 'Directors' Duties: The Impact of the Company Directors Disqualification Act 1986' (2000) 21 *Company Lawyer* 110.

necessary to justify disqualification will be in excess of negligent conduct which would found a charge of wrongful trading under s 214. For negligent conduct to validate the imposition of a disqualification order, the negligence must substantiate a finding of unfitness, it must be of a gross standard.

Factors and circumstances to be equated with gross negligence will naturally extend beyond matters which substantiate a mere breach of a duty of care.[36] However, the case law pertinent to this area would appear unclear in respect of the extent and degree of negligence deemed necessary to substantiate a finding of gross negligence. The inconsistency in seeking to define the hallmarks of gross negligence may, in part, be illustrated by the language adopted by the courts to describe the requisite level of negligence deemed necessary to warrant a finding of unfit conduct. To this end, gross negligence has been described as, 'total incompetence',[37] 'incompetence in a very marked degree',[38] 'really gross incompetence'[39] and, 'incompetence of a very high degree'.[40] While such expressions indicate a standard which far exceeds an act of mere negligence, the extent by which conduct may be defined at a level in excess of mere incompetence is unclear. Indeed, as in all cases involving the determination of unfit conduct, the matter will be left to the subjective perceptions of the trial judge. The question to be tried will be one of fact rather than formula. While the standard of culpability under s 6 of the Company Directors Disqualification Act 1986 may be criticised on the basis that the conceptual boundaries of 'unfitness' are vague and, although the precise definition of the degree of misconduct which is required to warrant a finding of unfitness is far from certain, the term 'unfit conduct' does at least serve to reinforce the provision's intention of seeking to penalise only the most serious instances of managerial malpractice.

3 THE PROSECUTION OF SECTION 6 ACTIONS

In accordance with s 7(3) of the Company Directors Disqualification Act 1986, insolvency practitioners are under a statutory obligation to report to the DTI any director who is suspected of conducting the affairs of a company in an unfit manner.[41] The Insolvency Service, a department of the DTI, is, through its Disqualification Unit, responsible for determining whether to commence proceedings under s 6.[42]

---

36 See *Re Westmid Packing Services Ltd* [1998] 2 All ER 124.
37 See *Re Lo-Line Electric Motors Ltd* [1988] Ch 477 at p 486 *per* Browne Wilkinson V-C.
38 See *Re Sevenoaks Stationers (Retail) Ltd* [1991] Ch 164 at p 184 *per* Dillon LJ.
39 See *Re Dawson Print Group Ltd* [1987] BCLC 601 at p 604 *per* Hoffmann J.
40 See *Re Barings plc (No 5)* [1999] 1 BCLC 433 at p 483 *per* Jonathan Parker J.
41 For these purposes, the insolvency practitioners are: the official receiver; the liquidator; the administrator; or the administrative receiver.
42 See Company Directors Disqualification Act 1986, s 7(1) (as amended).

At present, the Disqualification Unit's success rate in the prosecution of actions is most creditable, as 94% of all cases prosecuted under s 6 result in the imposition of a disqualification order.[43] However, this figure may overstate the unit's achievements given that the prosecution of s 6 cases is clearly influenced by financial restrictions. As with all government departments, the unit's funding is limited to the extent that only prosecutions which are virtually certain to result in the imposition of a disqualification order are likely to be pursued.[44] Accordingly, it is probable that many instances of commercially culpable conduct will go unpunished. To this end, the disqualification process is a slave to economic pressures and constraints.[45]

If the Disqualification Unit was financially unfettered in its prosecution of s 6 cases, it is most probable that there would be a substantial increase in the imposition of disqualification orders. Nevertheless, it should be stressed that an increase in the number of prosecutions under s 6 would inevitably collapse an already overburdened court system. Evidence of the strain on the court system may be illustrated by the number of s 6 actions currently pending trial. For example, DTI statistics confirm for the period 1997–2001, that as an annual average, in excess of 1,000 cases were awaiting prosecution. Further, for the period 2000–01, 58% of disqualification cases under s 6 were not concluded within two years from the commencement of proceedings and as such exceeded the two-year limit specified by s 7(2) of the Company Directors Disqualification Act 1986.[46]

However, had it not been for the court's willingness to adopt a summary form of procedure, the 'Carecraft Procedure', the strain on the system would have been radically more transparent. The Carecraft Procedure, which in the period 2000–01 was employed in approximately 30% of all s 6 cases, allows a director to reach an agreement with the Secretary of State to proceed to court on the understanding that a disqualification order

---

43 For the period 2000–01, the number of disqualification proceedings issued under s 6 totalled 1,456. As a result of these proceedings, 1,548 disqualification orders were imposed. Obviously, in some cases, disqualification proceedings would have been commenced in circumstances where more than one delinquent director was involved in the management of the insolvent company. Of the 1,548 disqualified directors, 887 were disqualified for a period of between two and five years. Only 47 directors were disqualified for a period of between 11 and 15 years; see *The Insolvency Service Annual Report and Accounts 2000–01* available at www.insolvency.gov.uk.

44 This is despite an improvement in the working practices of the Insolvency Service. The improvements were prompted as a result of an investigation by the National Audit Office into the workings of the Insolvency Service, see *Company Director Disqualification* (London, HMSO, 1993). The improved performance of the Insolvency Service was highlighted in a follow-up report by the National Audit Office, see House of Commons Papers, Session 1998–99 Paper No 424. The Insolvency Service more than doubled the resources spent on its disqualification unit from £9m in 1993–94 to £22m in 1997–98. Further, it allocated more high-grade and support staff to improve the vetting, targeting and processing of cases. For 1999–2000, approximately £22m was spent on the Disqualification Unit. As such, spending was not increased between 1998–2000. See The *Quinquential Review of the Insolvency Service* (London, DTI, September 2000).

45 The public costs involved in respect of the disqualification process include the costs of the Disqualification Unit, the provision of legal aid, social security benefits payable to directors unemployed as a consequence of disqualification, and the costs of the courts. See, further, Wheeler 'Directors Disqualification: Insolvency Practitioners and the Decision Making Process' (1995) 15 LS 283.

46 See *The Insolvency Service Annual Report and Accounts 2000–01*, above n 43.

will be made (subject to the agreement of the court) for a predetermined period.[47] The Carecraft Procedure was approved by the Court of Appeal in *Secretary of State v Rogers*.[48] Here, the court welcomed the procedure as one which would save the court and the parties involved in the proceedings the time and expense which would otherwise have been incurred by a full trial of the proceedings. In approving the Carecraft Procedure, the court emphasised that although it would be wrong for a judge to pursue allegations other than those contained in the agreed facts[49] it was essential for the judge to retain a discretion to overturn the findings of the agreement in respect of the agreed facts and an agreed disqualification period.

3.1 Section 17 CDDA 1986 – sidestepping mandatory disqualification

Given that evidence to establish a director's culpability under s 6 must be of an exacting nature, it is perhaps surprising to discover that the mandatory nature of a s 6 order may be disturbed by the application of s 17 of the Company Directors Disqualification Act 1986. The objective of s 17 is to allow a director to be granted leave[50] to continue to act in the management of a specified company or companies in circumstances where he is successfully involved in the management of that company or companies.[51]

In reality, the effect of a s 17 order pulls the public interest consideration in two quite distinct directions. While the practical effect of s 17 is one which offends against the mandatory nature of s 6, the purpose and justification of the provision is one which serves to benefit the public interest, because s 17 will only be invoked in circumstances where the effect of a disqualification order would adversely affect the interests of the specified company, causing prejudice to that company's employees and creditors.[52]

---

47 This type of summary procedure was first sanctioned by Ferris J in *Re Carecraft Construction Co Ltd* [1994] 1 WLR 172. Following the *Practice Direction No 2 of 1995* [1996] 1 WLR 170 at p 172D–F whenever a Carecraft application is made, the applicant must:

(a) except in simple cases where the circumstances do not merit it or when the court otherwise directs, submit a written statement containing in respect of each respondent any material facts which (for the purposes of the application) are either agreed or not opposed (by either party); and

(b) specify in the written statement, or a separate document, the period of disqualification which the parties will invite the court to make or the bracket (ie, 2–5 years; 6–10 years; 11–15 years) into which they will submit that the case falls; see also below at n 54.

48 [1996] 2 BCLC 513.

49 See *Secretary of State v Rogers* [1996] 2 BCLC 513. Here the Court of Appeal found that the trial judge was wrong to speculate on the effect disputed facts may have had (here the disputed facts related to the director's honesty) on a finding as to the seriousness of the director's conduct. As it is important for a court, in applying the Carecraft Procedure, to restrict itself to the alleged statement of facts, it is imperative that any facts which are advanced by the applicant should be precise in the sense that they should leave no room for any form of speculative interpretation. Accordingly, where, for example, a director's conduct was of a dishonest nature, it is inappropriate for the agreed statement of facts to allege that the director knew or ought to have known of the impropriety of his conduct. This statement would be far too ambiguous for the court to conclude that the director's admission of misconduct was based upon the acceptance that his conduct had been of a dishonest nature; see *Re PS Banarser & Co (Products) Ltd* [1997] BCC 425.

50 The power to grant leave is alluded to by the Company Directors Disqualification Act 1986, s 1.

51 The courts have an absolute discretion in determining whether to grant leave. The grant of leave is not, in any way, reserved for exceptional cases; see *Secretary of State for Trade and Industry v Rosenfield* [1999] BCC 413.

52 See: *Re Gibson Davies Ltd* [1995] BCC 11; *Secretary of State v Barnett* [1998] 2 BCLC 64; and *Secretary of State v Baker* (No 4) [1999] 1 BCLC 262.

Clearly, the courts must strike a delicate balance between two conflicting public policy considerations, always mindful that in invoking s 17 and thereby allowing an unfit director a 'second chance' in respect of the management of the specified company, the public interest could be further prejudiced where the director fails to sustain a commitment to the nominated company or, worse still, is a party to future delinquent acts of mismanagement.[53]

Indeed as a matter of future reform, it is suggested that in cases involving disqualification periods in excess of five years, the power to grant leave to act under s 17 should be abrogated. This suggestion is born from the fact that disqualification periods set in the upper disqualification brackets[54] will obviously represent very serious instances of unfit conduct, to the extent that in such cases it is unlikely whether the economic advantages of permitting a director to continue to act in respect of a nominated company will outweigh the need to protect the public interest from a potential re-occurrence of managerial misconduct.[55]

---

53 Where a director is granted leave to act under s 17 and acts in contravention of any conditions imposed under the leave agreement, it is probable that he will be severely penalised. For example, in *Secretary of State v Davies* (6 March 1998, unreported) a director who was subject to a five year disqualification period (see *Re Gibson Davies Ltd* [1995] BCC 11) breached conditions of a leave agreement and, in addition, committed further delinquent acts in the management of the nominated company. As a consequence of his conduct, the director was disqualified for 12 years. Had the director not been in breach of the leave agreement, the penalty would, it is assumed, have been significantly less severe.

54 In *Re Sevenoaks (Retail) Ltd* [1991] Ch 164, the Court of Appeal, in an attempt to alleviate any potential for inconsistency in the setting of disqualification periods, gave the following guidelines. The top bracket of disqualification for periods of over 10 years should be reserved for particularly serious cases. Disqualification in this bracket could include those cases where a director who had been previously disqualified was the subject of a further disqualification order. The middle bracket of disqualification for a period of six to 10 years should apply in serious cases but cases which did not merit the attention of the top bracket of disqualification. The minimum bracket of two to five years should be applied in cases where a director was found to be unfit to be concerned in the management of a company, although the misconduct was not of a particularly serious nature.

55 However, see *Re TLL Realisations Ltd* [2000] 2 BCLC 223 which involved a director (X) who was disqualified for a period of eight years for conduct in relation to his role as a finance director. The company was wound up in 1995 with a substantial deficiency. From 1993, X and the company's other directors knew that there was no reasonable prospect of avoiding insolvency but nevertheless continued to trade. X also acted in breach of other duties, including an involvement in diverting payment of insurance moneys to another company and the payment of a preference. Before being made subject to the disqualification order, X commenced employment as a senior manager with another group of companies. The director subsequently sought leave under s 17 to be concerned in the management of specified companies within this group. At first instance, Park J granted the s 17 application on the basis that the dishonesty of the director had never been established and that there was no real risk that the public would be insufficiently protected if the director remained in his position with the group subject to the conditions imposed. The said conditions included that the director should be subordinate to and report to a specified non-directorial member of staff, that he should only carry out specified duties and that the leave only applied to the identified group of companies and not to any other unidentified companies that might be acquired by the group in the eight-year period of the disqualification. The Secretary of State appealed on the basis that the grant of leave was inappropriate in a case involving a lengthy disqualification period. In dismissing the appeal, the Court of Appeal concluded that it was not open to the court to interfere with the judge's exercise of discretion except on limited and well-recognised grounds. Although the court took a serious view of a finance director being party to the trading of an insolvent company over a significant period and on the facts may have refused to have granted leave, the judge had nevertheless considered the relevant factors and his decision was not plainly wrong. The conditions attached to the order, defining X's functions and providing for supervision, were not unworkable and therefore granting leave would not undermine the purposes of the disqualification order.

4 REFORMING THE PROSECUTION OF DISQUALIFICATION CASES UNDER SECTION 6 OF THE COMPANY DIRECTORS DISQUALIFICATION ACT 1986

In respect of s 6 of the Company Directors Disqualification Act 1986, the disqualification system has been stretched to a point of optimum capacity to the extent that its reform is an essential prerequisite in seeking to safeguard its future efficiency. Clearly, a fundamental requirement for the reform of the disqualification system is to devise a more competent mechanism for the prosecution of s 6 cases and to this end the enactment of the Insolvency Act 2000 affords a viable means of attaining this goal.[56] In accordance with the amending provisions of the Insolvency Act 2000, a new s 1A is incorporated into the Company Directors Disqualification Act 1986,[57] so as to permit the Secretary of State to accept a disqualification undertaking as an alternative to the imposition of a disqualification order.[58] By virtue of the introduction of a new s 2A into the Company Directors Disqualification Act 1986 the Secretary of State may now accept an undertaking if it appears to him expedient in the public interest to do so.[59] In respect of the statutory undertaking procedure, a defendant will agree for a specified period to refrain from acting as a director or in any other capacity specified by s 1A (1)(a) and (b) of the Act.[60] As with a disqualification order, the minimum duration for an undertaking is two years[61] and the maximum period, 15 years.[62]

---

56 On 11 February 1998, the Minister for Competition and Consumer Affairs announced that legislation would be passed to introduce a statutory procedure regulating formal undertakings. This procedure was introduced into the Insolvency Bill 1999 as subsequently enacted by the Insolvency Act 2000. Note that an alternative mode of reform was proposed advancing the creation of a special Director Disqualification Tribunal, see Hicks 'Disqualification of Unfit Directors: No Hiding Place for the Unfit?' Association of Chartered Certified Accountants (1998) Research Report 59 at Chapter 15 (London, ACCA, 1998). Hicks considered that a tribunal would offer a more accessible and efficient means of hearing disqualification cases and given its more informal setting, business failures would not be unduly stigmatised. Hicks proposed that the tribunal should consist of a legally qualified chairperson and one or two other persons with business-related expertise and that a number of tribunals should be set up on a regional basis. Although this proposal would have had the effect of reducing costs otherwise incurred in court proceedings, it is submitted that the proposed informality and efficiency of the proceedings may have become illusory in cases involving disputed facts and contentious legal issues.

57 Inserted by the Insolvency Act 2000, s 6.

58 The new undertaking procedure only applies to disqualification cases falling within the terms of the Company Directors Disqualification Act 1986, ss 6 and 8. Section 8 provides that following a DTI investigation a person may be disqualified as a director on the ground that the person is unfit to be concerned in the management of a company and that the disqualification order would be in the public interest. The maximum period of disqualification under s 8 is 15 years.

59 In determining whether to accept a disqualification undertaking, the Secretary of State may take account of matters other than criminal convictions, notwithstanding that the defendant may potentially be criminally liable in respect of those matters, see the Company Directors Disqualification Act 1986, s 1A(4), inserted by the Insolvency Act 2000, s 6(2).

60 Company Directors Disqualification Act 1986, s 1A(1)(a) and (b) contains exactly the same restrictions as those contained in the Company Directors Disqualification Act 1986, s 1, as amended by the Insolvency Act 2000, s 5.

61 The minimum period does not apply to undertakings or disqualification orders in respect of Company Directors Disqualification Act 1986, s 8.

62 Company Directors Disqualification Act 1986, s 1A(2) as inserted by the Insolvency Act 2000, s 6(2). A person who agrees to an undertaking may, in accordance with the Company Directors Disqualification Act 1986, s 17, still apply for leave to continue to act in a capacity specified by Company Directors Disqualification Act 1986, s 1A(1)(a).

Although, prior to the Insolvency Act 2000, the courts had tentatively adopted an informal undertaking procedure as an alternative to the imposition of a disqualification order, the deployment of such a procedure was limited to a handful of cases.[63] In *Practice Direction No 2 of 1985*, Sir Richard Scott V-C pronounced that in circumstances where both the Secretary of State and the respondent agreed that the respondent's conduct warranted a prescribed period of disqualification, it would be sensible for the period of disqualification to be imposed by way of a formal undertaking, as opposed to a court order. His Lordship confirmed his view in *Secretary of State v Rogers*.[64]

The court undertaking procedure was primarily used in circumstances where the defendant was unlikely to have a physical capacity to act in the future management of a company, for example, where ill health and/or age precluded his future participation in the management of a company. In such cases, the duration of the undertaking was always set for the lifetime of the director. Following the decision of the Court of Appeal in *Re Blackspur Group plc*,[65] the ability of the courts to agree to an undertaking for life was restricted to a situation where the defendant was willing to agree to make a full admission to the effect that his misconduct had been of a commercially culpable nature. Lord Woolf MR, in delivering the judgment of the court, observed that the factual basis for making disqualification orders, whether in the contested context or in the summary uncontested procedure (sanctioned in *Re Carecraft Construction Co Ltd*), ensured that orders, determined on findings or admissions of unfitness, had a real deterrent effect and, in that way, afforded public protection against the threat of persons who were unfit to enjoy the privileges of limited liability.[66]

The principal objective of the new statutory undertaking procedure is to significantly reduce the need for disqualification actions to proceed by way of a full trial and accordingly it will promote the advantages of the Carecraft Procedure in a most logical way.[67] Indeed, it is most probable that the merits of the undertaking procedure will completely extinguish any future need for disqualification proceedings under s 6 to be determined by way of the Carecraft Procedure. In the light of an ever-expanding number of disqualification cases, it is to be expected that the statutory undertaking procedure will significantly reduce the pressure on the court system and considerably reduce the costs incurred by the parties involved in disqualification proceedings.

The statutory undertaking procedure will also permit the resources of the Insolvency Service to be more effectively taken up with the prosecution of cases in which there is a

---

63 See, for example: *Re Homes Assured Corporation plc* [1996] BCC 297; and *Secretary of State v Cleland* [1997] BCC 473.

64 [1996] 2 BCLC 513.

65 [1998] 1 WLR 422.

66 It is pertinent to observe that Lord Woolf MR considered that the appellant's real dispute was with Parliament. Parliament had failed to provide the legislative machinery for consent undertakings as a means of summarily disposing of cases against directors who were unwilling to contest the proceedings or to concede any of the allegations made against them. The Court of Appeal confirmed the first instance judgment of Rattee J at [1997] 1 WLR 710. Here, Rattee J refused to agree to stay disqualification proceedings by way of a formal undertaking on the premise that an undertaking did not (at present) have the effect of a disqualification order.

67 In relation to the undertaking procedure and general reforms to disqualification procedures, the Insolvency Act 2000, ss 5, 6, 7, 8 and Schedule 4 were brought into force on 2 April 2001 by the Insolvency Act 2000 (Commencement No 1 and Transitional Provisions) Order SI 2001/766.

real dispute between the parties, either in relation to the extent and nature of the alleged misconduct, or to a disputed period of disqualification. Further, it may be assumed that the efficiency of the statutory undertaking procedure will permit the Insolvency Service to prosecute disqualification cases with greater speed and possibly in greater numbers. However, such enthusiasm may be subject to some caution. Although in one sense the statutory undertaking procedure will reduce the pressure on the financial and human resources of the Disqualification Unit, the additional financial and human resources involved in managing and administrating disqualification undertakings may negate some part of any of the expected economic gains.

Although it may be expected that the statutory undertaking system will improve the efficiency of the present disqualification system, conversely, it is possible to contend that it may also serve to cause prejudice to the public interest. For example, as a result of the statutory undertaking procedure, matters relating to the accountability of delinquent directors will largely be dealt with in the absence of judicial and public scrutiny. While a new s 18(2A) is inserted into the Company Directors Disqualification Act[68] to provide that the Secretary of State shall include in the register of disqualified directors such particulars as he considers appropriate of disqualification undertakings accepted by him, the extent and nature of 'such particulars' are not defined. Not only will disqualification cases be dealt with 'behind closed doors' but once an undertaking is agreed, the courts will only be called upon to consider the merits or otherwise of the undertaking in a situation where a defendant applies to have its duration varied. The power of the court to vary the duration of an undertaking is provided for by a new s 8A of the Company Directors Disqualification Act.[69]

Therefore, in contrast with the Carecraft Procedure, other than where a director makes an application under s 8A of the Company Directors Disqualification Act 1986, the statutory undertaking procedure will provide no means of judicial scrutiny as to the nature and extent of an agreed disqualification period. In the majority of cases the courts will play a muted role in the disqualification process and as such will cease to operate as the guardian of justice and the protector of the public interest. Further, as the statutory undertaking system provides an attractive and far less expensive alternative to court proceedings, its expediency may serve as an economic incentive for the prosecution and defence to agree to an undertaking, the duration of which may be fixed for a period which is disproportional to the nature and extent of the defendant's conduct. As the factual circumstances surrounding the terms of a disqualification undertaking may not always be in the public domain, the existence of this economic incentive may prove to be no more than conjecture, but as the primary justification for the undertaking procedure is, itself, coloured by economic necessity, the concern may, in terms of the public interest, be viewed with some anxiety. Apprehension may be especially prevalent in the more serious instances of commercially culpable conduct where both the Disqualification Unit and defence may, in an attempt to save time and reduce costs, accept a disqualification undertaking, the duration of which may have been for a more extensive period had the case proceeded by way of a full trail. While the adoption of the statutory undertaking

68 Inserted by the Insolvency Act 2000, s 58 and Schedule 4 para 13(3). However, following the decision of the Court of Appeal in *Re Blackspur plc* (13 September, unreported), a decision confirming the judgment of Patten J [2001] 1 BCLC 653, the Secretary of State may, if he so decides, only accept an undertaking to which is attached a Statement of Facts indicating instances of the unfit conduct.

69 Inserted by the Insolvency Act 2000, s 5.

procedure represents an essential reform in maintaining the efficiency of the disqualification system, it may nevertheless be viewed with some degree of consternation, given its availability in all uncontested disqualification cases.

In seeking to capitalise on the advantages of the statutory undertaking procedure, but in an attempt to minimise its potential prejudice to the public interest, it is suggested that its availability should have been restricted to cases warranting a disqualification period of up to a maximum of five years, that is, cases involving less serious instances of unfit conduct and falling within the lower bracket of the disqualification periods set out in *Re Sevenoaks Stationers Ltd*.[70] In an attempt to mitigate costs, the Carecraft Procedure could have been employed in all other undisputed cases. While the Carecraft Procedure saves the court and the parties involved in disqualification proceedings the time and expense that would otherwise have been incurred had the application proceeded to a full trial, unlike the statutory undertaking procedure, it retains the advantage of permitting the courts (albeit in exceptional circumstances) to overturn or adjust the findings of any agreement made between the defendant and the Secretary of State. It is suggested that in maintaining the prominence of the Carecraft Procedure the courts would, in cases involving more serious instances of commercially culpable behaviour, have been able to retain a visible, albeit muted role in the enforcement of disqualification proceedings, thereby conferring some nominal form of safeguard in respect of the public interest.

5 SECTION 10 OF THE COMPANY DIRECTORS DISQUALIFICATION ACT 1986

While the introduction of the statutory undertaking procedure will reduce the number of s 6 cases which have hitherto been determined by the courts and accordingly reduce the pressure on the financial resources of the Disqualification Unit in respect of the preparation and prosecution of such cases, it is questionable whether the new procedure will result in a significant increase in the number of disqualification orders imposed. The effectiveness of the disqualification process would be improved if a far greater number of disqualification cases could proceed via s 10 of the Company Directors Disqualification Act 1986.[71] Section 10 provides that the court may, if it thinks fit, impose a disqualification order in circumstances where, following an application from a company's liquidator, a person is found liable to make a contribution to the company's assets under ss 213 or 214 of the Insolvency Act 1986. Although the principal sanction under both these provisions is one whereby a director may be made subject to a personal responsibility for the repayment of corporate debts,[72] the court may, at its discretion, impose a disqualification order for up to a maximum period of 15 years. While s 10 provides no guidance as to when a disqualification order should be imposed, it may be assumed that the fraudulent

---

70 [1991] Ch 164.
71 At present, s 10 is rarely invoked. Statistics taken from Table D1 of *Companies in 1999–2000*, above n 6, show that between 1992–2000 only 17 directors were disqualified under s 10.
72 The contribution order is paid into the company's general assets for the benefit of the company's unsecured creditors. Although the payment becomes a part of the company's general assets, a holder of a floating charge will not take priority over the assets in so far as the sum of the contribution order is not regarded as a property right; see *Re Oasis Merchandising Services Ltd* [1998] Ch 170.

or wrongful trading would need to exhibit the hallmarks of unfit conduct akin to that which is required for the purposes of establishing culpability under s 6 of the Act.[73]

In respect of establishing liability under s 213 of the Insolvency Act 1986, it must be shown that a person was knowingly a party to the carrying on of the company's business being aware that the company had no reasonable prospect of being able to repay its debts.[74] Although fraudulent trading may be committed by any person who was actively involved in the commission of the fraud, in practice, liability will ordinary fall on a person involved in the management of a company's affairs. The essential requirement of the provision is, quite simply, to establish that there was an intention to perpetrate the fraudulent act, an intention confirmed by proving that the respondent acted in a dishonest manner. Dishonesty will be ascertained on the basis of whether, at the time of the incursion of a corporate debt, the respondent was aware that the debt would not be met on the date it was due, or shortly after that date.[75]

Section 214 of the Insolvency Act 1986 was introduced following the recommendations of the Cork Committee's report.[76] *The Cork Report's* proposal for a wrongful trading provision sought to provide a more efficient and accessible mechanism by which directors of insolvent companies could be held accountable for conduct prejudicial to the interests of corporate creditors. The report's underlying criticism of the fraudulent trading provision was its failure to provide an effective means of penalising and discouraging the culpable behaviour of irresponsible directors other than in instances where a director had acted in a dishonest manner. Section 214 seeks to penalise a director in circumstances where the director allows the company to continue to trade at a date up to the commencement of the company's winding up when he knew or ought to have concluded that there was no reasonable prospect of the company being able to avoid insolvent liquidation.[77] Where a director is liable under the terms of s 214, the director will, at the discretion of the court, be liable (as under s 213) to pay a contribution order into the general assets of the company. The potential beneficiaries of the contribution

---

73 See *Re Brian D Pierson (Contractors) Ltd* [1999] BCC 26. Here, Hazel Williamson QC, sitting as a deputy judge in the Companies Court, disqualified two directors, a husband and wife, under the Company Directors Disqualification Act 1986, s 10 for a period of five and two years, respectively. The company in which they had held office had an estimated deficiency for creditors in the sum of £1.18m. In addition to being found liable for wrongful trading, the husband and wife were also held liable for contributions to preferences under the Insolvency Act 1986, s 239 and for damages in respect of misfeasance/breach of fiduciary duties. See also *Secretary of State v Creegas* [2002] 1 BCLC 99.

74 Proceedings may only be commenced by a liquidator in circumstances where the company carried on its business with the intent to defraud its creditors or creditors of any other person, or for any fraudulent purpose. The liquidator may apply to the court for an order that those responsible should, where they were knowing parties to the carrying on of the business, be liable to make such contributions to the company's assets as the court sees fit.

75 In determining whether a person's participation in the fraudulent trading activities of a company was of a dishonest nature, the courts employ a subjective test to determine the state of mind of the respondent at the time of the alleged fraudulent trading; see *Re Patrick Lyon Ltd* [1933] 1 Ch 786. Although a person's culpability for fraudulent trading will be dependent upon whether he formed an intention to commit the fraudulent act, the definition of an intention to defraud has been stretched to the point whereby, in reality, it resembles a test based upon recklessness, albeit that recklessness will be measured in a subjective as opposed to an objective sense; see: *R v Grantham* [1984] QB 675; and *Aktieselskabet Dansk v Brothers* [2001] 2 BCLC 324.

76 *The Report of the Review Committee into Insolvency Law and Practice* (1982) Cmnd 8558 (London, HMSO, 1982) at paras 1781–1806; hereafter *The Cork Report*.

77 The essential requirements for determining a person's liability for wrongful trading are contained in the Insolvency Act 1986, s 214(1)–(3).

order are the company's unsecured creditors. In effect, the introduction of s 214 has impliedly negated the necessity for s 213, although contrary to the recommendations of *The Cork Report*, s 213 is retained as a distinct provision.

However, while the objective of s 214 seeks to penalise the delinquent trading activities of directors[78] without a need to establish fraud or dishonesty, procedural barriers have severely restricted the provision's application. Evidence indicative of the provision's ineptitude may be found from the diminutive number of reported cases involving actions under s 214. While a lack of reported cases may not, in itself, be conclusive of the provision's failure to achieve a more efficient regulation of the wrongful trading activities of directors, it is clearly a strong indicator of the provision's inadequacy.[79]

The principal difficulty in respect of s 214 relates to a liquidator's inability to reclaim the costs incurred in pursuit of the action. Although s 115 of the Insolvency Act 1986 provides that all the expenses incurred in the winding up of a company are payable out of the company's assets in priority to all other claims, such expenses relate to the realising or getting in of any of the assets of the company rather than expenses incurred in relation to pursuing an action which may result in an addition to the company's assets.[80] Accordingly, although a s 214 action may result in a contribution being made to the company's assets, such a contribution will obviously have had no existence prior to the commencement of the action and cannot, therefore, be classed as a corporate asset for the purposes of s 115.

---

78 See Prentice 'Creditor's Interests and Director's Duties' (1990) 10 OJLS 265.

79 See further Doyle 'Ten Years of Wrongful Trading' [1996] *Insolvency Lawyer* 10. It has been argued that s 214 may be having a positive effect on curbing wrongful trading in that directors who may otherwise have been liable under the provision have sought to settle their liability out of court; see Hicks 'Wrongful Trading – Has it been a Failure?' (1993) 8 *Insolvency Law and Practice* 134. Nevertheless, given that the liquidator's ability to establish liability under s 214 may be both an arduous and expensive task, it is unlikely whether such settlements will be commonplace; see Williams and McGhee 'Curbing Unfit Directors – Is Personal Liability an Empty Threat?' [1993] *Insolvency Lawyer* 2.

80 See: *Re MC Bacon Ltd (No 2)* [1990] BCC 430; and *Re Oasis Merchandising Services Ltd* [1998] Ch 170. In *Katz v Mcnally* [1999] BCC 291, the Court of Appeal doubted the standing of *Re MC Bacon Ltd (No 2)* in relation to the conclusion that contributions which do not form a part of the company's property at the commencement of its winding up cannot be properly regarded as assets of the company. The Court of Appeal considered (albeit without the benefit of in depth argument in relation to the issue) that the statutory scheme for determining the identification of liquidation expenses was permissive of a liquidator's ability to claim expenses in respect of financing an action to recover assets of the company, irrespective of whether or not those assets were derived from part of the company's property. Phillips LJ, in delivering the leading judgment of the court, considered that Rule 12.2 of the Insolvency Rules 1986 put the matter beyond any doubt.
Yet while the Court of Appeal's common sense approach to the determination of liquidation expenses is to be applauded, a literal interpretation of the Insolvency Act 1986, s 115, when read in conjunction with Rule 4.218 of the Insolvency Rules 1986, would seem to infer that the 'realising or getting in of any of the assets of the company' is indicative of the fact that the term 'assets' refers to assets which form a part of the company's property at the commencement of its winding up. Accordingly, it is submitted that Rule 12.2 should not be construed in isolation but rather in conjunction with s 115 and Rule 4.218. Indeed, a more recent decision of the Court of Appeal, namely *Re Floor Fourteen Ltd; Lewis v Commissioners of Inland Revenue* [2001] 3 All ER 499, confirms that the costs of proposed wrongful trading proceedings under the Insolvency Act 1986, s 214 cannot be recouped by the liquidator from the assets of the company as a liquidation expense in priority to preferential creditors. The court also came to the same conclusion in respect of preference proceedings under the Insolvency Act 1986, s 239. The Court of Appeal held that moneys recovered in proceedings under the Insolvency Act 1986, ss 214 or 239 could not be classed as assets of the company.

6 REFORMING THE PROSECUTION OF SECTION 214 CASES

In the majority of cases a liquidator's capacity to pursue a s 214 action will be dependant upon the potential sum of the company's realised assets and the extent to which such assets are capable of financing the action after all other prior debts have been paid. Following the payment of such debts the company's assets will often be severely depleted to the extent that they are insufficient to finance a s 214 action.[81]

In an attempt to create a more efficient means of penalising the wrongful trading activities of delinquent directors, it is submitted that there is an obvious need to reform the method by which s 214 proceedings are financed. Reforming the method by which s 214 proceedings are financed would clearly suspend the future trading activities of many a delinquent director by accelerating the court's ability to disqualify under s 10 of the Company Directors Disqualification Act 1986. As many cases pursued under s 6 of the Act involve instances of wrongful trading, the pressure and burdens placed on the Disqualification Unit would be eased if, instead of pursuing such cases via s 6, they were dealt with under s 10. Yet despite such an obvious need for reform, it is to be noted that neither the Company Law Steering Group or the Insolvency Review Group[82] have as yet sought to address this issue.

In seeking to advance reform, it is suggested that an obvious and quite simple method of restructure would be to amend the insolvency legislation to provide that the proceeds of any litigation instigated at a time subsequent to a company's liquidation could, in the context of s 15 of the Insolvency Act 1986, be treated as corporate assets. However, such proceeds would need to be reserved to the claims of unsecured creditors. A more radical method of reform would be to create a central fund from which selected actions could be financed. Under such a scheme, the ability of a liquidator to apply for central funds to aid an action under s 214 could, for example, be determined by a vetting procedure to establish the viability of the proposed litigation. Following a successful action under s 214 the central fund could be reimbursed from any costs awarded against the director. In addition, a percentage of any contribution order could also be paid over to the central fund, thereby enabling it to sustain any losses incurred as a result of funding unsuccessful actions or in cases in which a director defaulted on the payment of costs.

---

81 Although a liquidator may be unwilling or unable to commit corporate assets for the purpose of funding an application under s 214, the liquidator may nevertheless proceed with the application where a creditor(s) of the company decides to fund the action. Obviously, a creditor, in considering whether to fund an application, must carefully determine whether the pursuit of the s 214 action would be financially sustainable in relation to the probable cost of the proceedings. Yet even where the action is successful, there can be no guarantee that a director will be able to meet the costs of the action, let alone the terms of any contribution order made against him; see further: Griffin 'Protecting the Interests of Unsecured Creditors: Section 214 of the Insolvency Act 1986' (1999) 4 *Scottish Law & Practice Quarterly* 193; Parry 'Funding Litigation in Insolvency' [1998] *Company Financial and Insolvency Law Review* 121. Note, however, that a company may, by virtue of Companies Act 1985, s 310(3)(a), take out insurance, on behalf of a director, to protect the director against the imposition of personal liability in circumstances where he is in breach of his duty to the company. It is suggested that a director will be in breach of his duty in circumstances where he is found liable under s 214, ie, the director will have acted contrary to the interests of corporate creditors.

82 The issue was not raised in a recent consultation exercise by the Insolvency Review Group. The consultation exercise led to a White Paper, entitled *Productivity and Enterprise – Insolvency – A Second Chance* (2001) Cm 5234 (London, TSO, 2001). It is disappointing that the issue was not considered, given that an objective of the White Paper was to promote collective insolvency procedures, providing unsecured creditors with a greater say in the process and the outcome.

7 SECTIONS 216 AND 217 OF THE INSOLVENCY ACT 1986 ('PHOENIX COMPANIES')

Section 216 of the Insolvency Act 1986 incorporates an implied form of disqualification in so far as it seeks to prohibit a director or shadow director of a company which is in liquidation (the section applies to a director who held office up to 12 months before the company's liquidation) from being involved for five years from the date of the company's liquidation, in the management of another company (the successor company) which adopts the name or a name closely associated with the name of the insolvent company.[83] As with a breach of a disqualification order, a contravention of s 216 constitutes a criminal offence. A person guilty under s 216 in respect of a successor company (but not an unincorporated business) is automatically, by virtue of s 217 of the Insolvency Act 1986, deemed jointly and severally liable with the successor company and any other person who may be also deemed liable in respect of the debts of the successor company.[84] Under s 217, liability is not dependant upon an actual conviction under s 216; albeit for liability to accrue, the constituent elements of s 216 must be met.

In part, s 216 attempts to regulate what is commonly referred to as the 'phoenix syndrome'. The phoenix syndrome describes a situation in which the controllers of a company place the company into liquidation with the objective of seeking to continue its business activities under the banner of a newly constituted company or unincorporated business concern (the successor company or business) but without the debts or other liabilities of the former company. Although not all phoenix companies will be incorporated with the intention of dishonestly exploiting the concept of limited liability, the effect of such conduct may be prejudicial to the public interest in so far as the successor company or business will be devoid of any responsibility or accountability in respect of the corporate debts of the first company.[85] Further, the creditors of both the first company and the successor company or business may be mistakenly induced into advancing credit facilities to the successor company or business in the mistaken belief that it is but an extension of the first company, when in reality, the two enterprises are legally distinct.

While examples of reported cases involving ss 216 and 217 are few,[86] in practice, it is probable that there are many examples of phoenix companies.[87] The extent and degree of prejudice which the effect of the phoenix syndrome may cause will vary but it is likely to

---

83 See, Insolvency Act 1986, s 216(1).

84 A person will be personally liable to discharge the debts of a corporate creditor under s 217, irrespective of the fact the creditor was aware of and possibly aided and abetted the commission of the criminal offence under s 216; see *Thorne v Silverleaf* [1994] BCC 109.

85 The prejudicial effect of the phoenix syndrome was severely criticised by *The Cork Report*, above n 76, at para 1813.

86 See, *The Final Report*, above n 15, at para 15.61. According to the report the reason why there are so few cases may, in part, be explained by the fact that liquidators often pursue other remedies in respect of the exploitation of creditors' interests. The said remedies would include actions for fraudulent or wrongful trading, misfeasance, preferences and transactions at an undervalue. However, notwithstanding the logic of this reasoning, it is to be observed that the alternative remedies are employed in but only a very small percentage of liquidations.

87 Both *The Cork Report*, above n 76, at paras 18.26–18.30 and the *The Final Report*, above n 15, at paras 15.58–15.59, considered the phoenix syndrome to be prejudicial to the public interest and to represent a real and significant problem.

be especially harmful in two circumstances. First, where, prior to its liquidation, the controllers of the liquidated company were able to purchase the assets of the company at a significant undervalue and then employ the assets for the benefit of the successor company or business. Secondly, where the successor company attempts to benefit from any goodwill which remains from the business activities of the liquidated company by adopting a name which is the same as, or closely associated with the name of the liquidated company. The effect of adopting a like name may dupe creditors into believing that the first and successor companies were one in the same. Although s 216 regulates the latter activity it does not specifically regulate the former.[88] However, s 320 of the Companies Act 1985 does seek to prohibit a company from entering into an arrangement where a director or connected person[89] acquires, or is to acquire, one or more non-cash assets of the requisite value from the company.[90] Nevertheless, the protection afforded by this provision may be negated where, at a general meeting, the company's shareholders approve the transaction.[91] Therefore, s 320 will, in respect of phoenix cases, be of little worth, in so far as any party who has an interest in the transaction will be allowed to vote on the matter. Accordingly, an interested party commanding over 50% of the votes will be able to secure the transaction's approval.[92]

7.1 Exemptions to the incursion of liability under s 216 of the Insolvency Act 1986

The prohibitive effect of s 216 may be excluded where, in accordance with s 216(3) of the Insolvency Act 1986, one of the exceptions prescribed by Rules 4.228, 4.229 and 4.230 of

---

88 However, had *The Cork Report*, above n 76, proposals been adopted in full; see at Chapter 44, paras 1813, 1826–37, civil liability (but not criminal liability) would have been incurred by any person involved or concerned in the management (whether directly or indirectly) of a liquidated company during the period of two years prior to the commencement of the company's insolvency, in a situation where that person had also been a participant in or been concerned in the management of a successor company (whether directly or indirectly) which had a paid-up share capital of less than £50,000 and which, after commencing or continuing trading within 12 months after the commencement of the insolvent winding up of the first company, had, itself, within a period of three years from the winding up of the first company, been placed into insolvent liquidation. A person would have been deemed personally liable (unless the court otherwise directed) for the unpaid liabilities of the successor company in circumstances where those liabilities were created or incurred within two years after the commencement of the winding up of the first company.

89 A connected person is defined by the Companies Act 1985, s 346(2) and includes amongst others, the director's spouse, child or step-child and a company with which the director is associated.

90 The requisite value is currently set at £100,000 or 10% of the company's net assets; transactions of less than £2,000 are not included.

91 Where the general meeting does not approve an arrangement involving a substantial property transaction, the transaction will become voidable at the company's option; Companies Act 1985, s 322.

92 Further, although the creditors of the first company may be entitled to prove for their debts in liquidation, the assets against which they can lay claim may have been depleted. For example, the controllers of the first company may have undertaken a policy of disposing of the assets, or may have run down the company's most viable assets; this problem is related to a practice known as centrebinding, so called after the case of *Re Centrebind Ltd* [1967] 1 WLR 377. To some extent this practice has been restricted by the introduction of legislative controls designed to render directors and liquidators more accountable for their actions in respect of the disposal of corporate assets; see Insolvency Act 1986, ss 98, 99, 114, 166 and 388. Alternatively, the controllers of the first company may have held prior-ranking security interests over the company's assets so as to defeat the claims of other corporate creditors.

the Insolvency Rules 1986 apply.[93] Further, a person may apply to the court under s 216(3) of the Act for leave to be associated with the management of a successor company or business.[94] The circumstances which may give rise to a successful leave application are not alluded to by the provision and accordingly the method by which leave will be determined is left to the discretion of the court.[95]

The manner by which the courts have dealt with s 216(3) leave applications has been conflicting. For example, in *Re Bonus Breaks Ltd*,[96] Morrit J held that, in determining whether to grant leave, it was necessary to consider the successor company's ability to avoid the pitfalls which had resulted in the liquidated company's demise. Accordingly, Morrit J considered that it was necessary to examine the manner in which the successor company was structured and its potential to avoid the commercial difficulties which had befallen the liquidated company. Morrit J was particularly anxious in respect of the manner in which the successor company's share capital had been structured, in so far as it comprised 98% of redeemable shares. The learned judge feared that if the shares were redeemed within a short period, then the company would be left undercapitalised and heavily dependant upon bank borrowings. The concern expressed by Morrit J was undoubtedly driven by the learned judge's desire to protect creditor interests in respect of the successor company, a justifiable anxiety given that the liquidated company's insolvency had been of a serious nature. However, in so far as the applicant was willing to give an undertaking to the court, the effect of which was to alleviate a threat of an immediate reduction of the company's capital base, Morrit J approved the leave application.

---

93 Rule 4.228 of the Insolvency Rules 1986 operates where a person to whom s 216 would otherwise apply, seeks to be associated with the management of a successor company which acquires the whole or substantially the whole of the business of the insolvent company, under arrangements made by an insolvency practitioner acting as its liquidator, administrator or administrative receiver, or as a supervisor of a voluntary arrangement under Part 1 of the Insolvency Act 1986. Rule 4.229 of the Insolvency Rules 1986 provides a transient period during which a person will be allowed to continue to be associated with a successor company. The exception operates where, in accordance with s 216(3), an application for leave is made not later than seven days from the date on which the company went into liquidation. The transient period commences from the beginning of the day on which the company went into liquidation and ends either on the day falling six weeks after that date, or on the day on which the court disposes of the application for leave, whichever of those days occurs first. Rule 4.230 of the Insolvency Rules 1986 provides that a person who is associated with the management of a successor company which traded under a name by which it was known for the whole of the period of twelve months ending with the day before the liquidating company went into liquidation, may be exempted from the prohibitive effect of s 216, providing that the successor company was not, at any time in the said period, dormant within the meaning of Companies Act 1985, s 250(3).

94 Other than where a case falls under one of the exceptions provided by the Insolvency Rules, or alternatively where leave is obtained under the Insolvency Act 1986, s 216(3), the effect of s 216 is to create a strict liability offence; see *R v Cole, Lees & Birch* [1998] BCC 87.

95 However, in respect of an application for leave, the Insolvency Act 1986, s 216(5) provides that the Secretary of State or the Official Receiver may appear and call the court's attention to any matters which may have a bearing on the application. The court may call on the liquidator (or former liquidator) of the liquidating company for a report into the circumstances surrounding the liquidated company's insolvency and the extent by which the applicant's conduct may have contributed to the company's demise.

96 [1991] BCC 546. This was the first reported case in which a court had to consider application for leave.

Nevertheless, a different approach was taken by Chadwick J in *Penrose v Official Receiver*.[97] Here, Chadwick J disapproved of an investigation into the applicants' competence to conduct the affairs of a limited company and the business merits of the successor company. He considered that such an investigation was unnecessary, given that the applicants' participation in the management of the liquidated company had never been viewed to be unfit so as to warrant disqualification proceedings under the Company Directors Disqualification Act 1986. Further, although Chadwick J pointed to similarities between s 216(3) and the leave procedure under s 17 of the Company Directors Disqualification Act 1986, he observed that the leave procedure under s 216(3) was quite distinct from an application under s 17 in so far as under the latter provision the court would be compelled to instigate a thorough investigation of the applicant because, in seeking leave, the applicant would have been doing so in a situation where his previous conduct had already been adjudged as unfit. In the context of a leave application under s 216(3), Chadwick J concluded that it was patently wrong for a court to refuse an application on the basis that the applicants' involvement in a subsequent corporate venture would carry a degree of commercial risk. He pointed out that the creation of any corporate enterprise always entailed an element of risk.[98]

In a desire to protect the public interest it may be contended that the approach for determining leave as adopted by Morrit J in *Re Bonus Breaks* should be preferred to that advocated by Chadwick J in *Penrose*. However, an examination of s 216 reveals that the former approach portrays the provision's construction as one which attempts to prohibit the phoenix syndrome in a manner far removed from the actual terms of s 216. Section 216 does not seek to preclude the creation of a phoenix company other than in a situation where it adopts a corporate name which is the same as, or similar to, the liquidated company. The provision sets no standard as to the fitness or otherwise of a director in the context of the successor company.

While in the context of s 216(3) the reasoning adopted in *Penrose* implies that leave will only be refused if an applicant's conduct in the affairs of a liquidated company justified the imposition of a disqualification order under the Company Directors Disqualification Act 1986, the said approach would nevertheless appear to be more logical in the context of a literal construction of s 216. Nevertheless, such logic fails to recognise, given the difficulty of establishing unfit conduct for the purposes of s 6 of the Company Directors Disqualification Act 1986, that an applicant's conduct in the affairs of the liquidated company may still have been of such a poor standard so as to raise a serious question mark over his future ability to conduct business through the medium of a limited liability company, especially in circumstances where the successor company adopted a name which was the same as or similar to that of the liquidated company.

---

97 [1996] 1 WLR 482.

98 The reasoning adopted by Chadwick J to resolve the leave application in *Penrose v Official Receiver* was subsequently affirmed by the decision of EW Hamilton QC (sitting as a deputy judge of the Chancery Division) in *Re Lightning Electrical Contractors Ltd* [1996] BCC 950. See further Wilson 'Delinquent Directors' (1996) 47 *Northern Ireland Quarterly* 344.

8 REFORMING SECTION 216 OF THE INSOLVENCY ACT 1986

In attempting to curb the potentially prejudicial effect of the phoenix syndrome, s 216 must be viewed as an unmitigated failure. The provision is inept in two material respects. First, in so far as s 216 is only concerned with phoenix companies which adopt the same or similar name as the liquidated company, a phoenix company which adopts a name unrelated to the liquidated company will escape the consequences of both ss 216 and 217 of the Insolvency Act 1986. This is notwithstanding the fact that it may have the potential to cause as much harm to the public interest as a phoenix company which adopts the same or a similar name to that of the liquidated company. Secondly, following the reasoning adopted by Chadwick J in *Penrose* a major flaw in s 216 may be identified as the ease in which a person may successfully apply under s 216(3) for leave to be associated with the management of a successor company or business.

To a large extent, the aforementioned difficulties were considered in *The Final Report* of the Company Law Review Steering Group, where it was acknowledged that the present regulation of the phoenix syndrome failed to significantly disturb the syndrome's potential to prejudice the public interest.[99] However, the Steering Group did not recommend an alteration of the provision in the context of extending s 216 beyond its present ambit of regulating the corporate names of successor companies. Instead, the Steering Group sought to widen the regulation of the phoenix syndrome by recommending an extension to the present scope of s 320 of the Companies Act 1985.[100] The effect of this amendment would be that a company which is insolvent (or becomes insolvent in consequence of a transaction to which s 320(1) applies) and goes into liquidation within 12 months of a motion to approve a transaction to which s 320(1) applies, would have the resolution to approve the transaction declared invalid in circumstances where the successor company was a person connected to any of the directors of the liquidated company and where the resolution would not have been passed without the votes of the director in question or any person connected to that director. Alternatively, the resolution would be declared invalid where notwithstanding unanimous shareholder approval for the transaction, the director in question or together with any of his connected persons held over 50% of the company's issued share capital carrying a right to vote on the motion to approve the transaction. However, in all cases a transaction would retain its validity where it was supported by an independent valuation of the assets which were sold in accordance with terms of that valuation.

Where, in accordance with the aforementioned recommendations, the resolution was declared invalid, the company would be able to set the transaction aside and sue the directors in question for an account of their profit or an indemnity against the loss which the company suffered. To prevent the shareholders from subsequently approving the otherwise invalid transaction,[101] the Steering Group recommended that any affirmation of the transaction should be subject to the same requirements as the revised s 320, namely that the votes of the director in question or any of his connected persons should be discarded in respect of the motion to affirm the transaction.

---

99 See *The Final Report*, above n 15, at paras 15.55–15.77.
100 See *The Final Report*, above n 15, at paras 15.66–15.70.
101 In accordance with the Companies Act 1985, s 322(2)(c).

Although in seeking to extend the ambit of s 320 the Steering Group's proposal would appear to accommodate many of the criticisms concerning the restrictive circumstances in which s 216 of the Insolvency Act may currently be applied, it is submitted that the objective of such amendments would be better employed by specifically targeting them at reforming s 216. In addition to its current form it is suggested that s 216(2) could be strengthened by providing that a director of a liquidated company, or a person connected to that director, would be precluded, prior to the company's liquidation, from purchasing assets of the company for the benefit of a successor company or other business in circumstances where the purchase of such assets was at an undervalue and where the director or a connected person was involved or subsequently involved in the management of the successor company or business. As a result of this amendment liability would extend to the successor company or unincorporated business even though it was not linked by the use of the same or a similar corporate name as that of the liquidated company. As with the Steering Group's proposed amendment to s 320 of the Companies Act 1985, it is suggested that it would be possible for a director to evade liability under this revised version of s 216(2) in circumstances where it was established, in accordance with an independent valuation, that the assets of the liquidated company had been sold at a fair value.

The advantage of amending s 216(2) in the aforementioned manner would be that liability under s 216 extends to a successor company or unincorporated business whereas under s 320 of the Companies Act 1985, liability would only extend to the former. In addition, the amended s 216 would provide a more compelling deterrent than s 320 in so far as persons who were instrumental in exploiting the phoenix syndrome would, in the case of a successor company, be subject to both a criminal sanction (via s 216) and also a civil sanction (via s 217 of the Insolvency Act 1986). Finally, it is contended that the suggested amendment to s 216 would be potentially less complex to implement than the alteration to s 320 of the Companies Act 1985 as advanced in *The Final Report* of the Company Law Review Steering Group.

In respect of a grant of leave to act under s 216(3) of the Insolvency Act 1986, the Steering Group recommend that the courts should not ordinarily grant leave to the director of a liquidated company if, within the twelve months prior to its liquidation, there was a material transfer of assets from the liquidated company to a successor company in which the director was also interested. However, the Steering Group recommended that leave should be permissible in circumstances where a transaction complied with the terms of their suggested amendments to s 320 of the Companies Act 1985.[102] While in the context of s 216(3), the recommendations of the Steering Group are to be welcomed in setting some form of prohibitive standard against which an application for leave could be refused, it is worth pointing out that where the formation of a successor company contravenes the terms of the amended s 320 of the Companies Act 1985, the transaction in question would not necessarily be caught by the terms of the presently constituted s 216, because the latter is only applicable where the successor company was incorporated with a name which was the same as or similar to the liquidated company. Therefore, it would not be possible to apply for leave in cases falling within the ambit of

---

102 See *The Final Report*, above n 15, at paras 15.70–15.72.

the amended s 320 of the Companies Act 1985 but falling outside the terms of the currently constituted s 216.

Finally, in the context of phoenix companies, the Steering Group concluded that a contravention of s 216 should not result in the automatic disqualification of a director. The Steering Group considered automatic disqualification to be an inappropriate penalty because a breach of s 216 did not necessarily involve a course of conduct justifying a director's exclusion from management, other than, that is, the exclusion from a successor company having adopted the name or a similar name to that of the liquidated company. Indeed, as culpability under s 216 may be established without any evidence to establish a director's past failings in the management of the liquidated company, any suggestion that the provision should warrant the automatic disqualification of the director would seem completely unjust. However, akin to ss 213 and 214 of the Insolvency Act 1986, it is submitted that the court, in determining s 216 proceedings, could, in circumstances establishing the conduct of a director as unfit, be afforded a discretion to impose a disqualification order up to a maximum of 15 years.

9 CONCLUSIONS

While economic stability is in part reliant upon an enterprise culture which readily encourages entrepreneurs to risk capital in the pursuit of profit through the medium of the corporate entity, it is essential, in seeking to safeguard the public interest, that company directors should be made subject to efficient penalties in cases where the advantages afforded to a limited liability company are abused.[103]

While the imposition of a disqualification order under s 6 of the Company Directors Disqualification Act 1986 represents a potent and potentially effective form of penalty, the utilisation of the provision has hitherto been restricted by the procedural constraints of the disqualification process. Indeed, the totality of disqualification orders, in comparison with, for example, the annual number of company liquidations, suggests that the disqualification process is merely skimming the surface in relation to its objective of removing unfit directors from the future management in limited liability companies. For example, during the period 1995–2000 there were over 70,000 insolvent company liquidations; however, it is remarkable that during the same period there were only 5,808 recorded disqualification orders imposed under s 6.[104]

While the introduction of the statutory undertaking procedure will be expected to increase the efficiency of the disqualification process, it is questionable whether it will produce a more successful means of curbing the activities of delinquent directors. Further, given that the majority of disqualification proceedings under s 6 of the Act will, as a result of the undertaking procedure, be devoid of any judicial or public scrutiny, it may be uncertain whether disqualification periods will accurately reflect the extent of the unfit conduct in question.

---

103 See further Hicks 'Director Disqualification: Can it Deliver?' [2001] *Journal of Business Law* 433. Note also Bradley 'Enterprise and Entrepreneurship: The Impact of Director Disqualification' (2001) 1 *Journal of Corporate Law Studies* 53.

104 The statistics are taken from the DTI *Statistics Directorate* (August 2001) available at www.dti.gov.uk.

In an attempt to increase the value of the disqualification process by enhancing its ability to penalise and deter the activities of unfit directors, there must, given the limited resources of the Insolvency Service, be an alternative means of effective disqualification other than by proceedings under s 6 of the Company Directors Disqualification Act 1986. To this end, it is suggested that there must be a reform of the procedural restrictions attached to s 214 of the Insolvency Act 1986. Following such reform it is highly probable that an expansion of disqualification proceedings under s 10 of the Company Directors Disqualification Act 1986 will follow. Likewise, directors who exploit the practice of forming phoenix companies and so abuse the interests of corporate creditors must be subject to more stringent controls. Accordingly, s 216 of the Insolvency Act 1986 should be reformed to afford the public interest a far more stringent form of protection than is currently the case. Further, following a breach of s 216, the courts should be given a discretion as to whether to impose a general disqualification order against an offending director in circumstances where managerial misconduct is deemed to have been of an unfit nature. To this end, it is submitted that the creation of a more effective and far reaching disqualification system will not deter or discourage corporate enterprise but, on the contrary, will promote, enhance and protect the stability of the present order.

CHAPTER 10

MAPPING THE BOUNDARIES OF UNFAIR PREJUDICE

John Lowry

1 INTRODUCTION

If the sheer weight of case law generated since the unfair prejudice remedy was first introduced by the Companies Act 1980 were to be taken as the yardstick, it might be concluded that the effect of unshackling minority shareholders from the judicial restrictions imposed on the old oppression remedy has been a resounding success in terms of strengthening the position of 'oppressed' minority shareholders.[1] However, the flip side of this prevalence of minority shareholder litigiousness is the destructive effect it has on profitable owner-managed small private companies. A major anxiety of the law reform bodies which have been examining the issue of shareholder remedies over the last five years or so, and one that is mirrored in recent judicial pronouncements on s 459, is how best to construct a regime which, first, affords minority shareholders in small private companies effective avenues for redress for conflicts with the majority owners,[2] and, secondly, reduces the length, complexity and costs of litigation under the provision.[3] In respect of the latter, the Woolf reforms have largely addressed many of these concerns,[4]

---

1   The unfair prejudice remedy is now found in s 459 of the Companies Act 1985 (as amended), which provides: 'A member of a company may apply to the court by petition for an order under this part on the ground that the company's affairs are being or have been conducted in a manner which is unfairly prejudicial to the interests of its members generally or some part of the members (including at least himself) or that any actual or proposed act or omission of the company (including any act or omission on its behalf) is or would be so prejudicial.' This replaced the 'oppression' remedy contained in s 210 of the Companies Act 1948, which was expressly stated to be only available where the facts of the case justified a winding-up order.

2   In public limited companies and large private companies the unfair prejudice provision is of limited effect; see *Re Blue Arrow plc* [1987] BCLC 585, considered below at n 64.

3   The Law Commission's Consultation Paper No 142, *Shareholder Remedies* (London, TSO, 1996) notes at para 1.7 n 16, that in one case, *Re Elgindata Ltd* [1991] BCLC 959, the hearing lasted 43 days, costs totalled £320,000 and the shares, originally purchased for £40,000, were finally valued at only £24,600. Judicial concern was expressed by Harman J in *Re Unisoft Ltd (No 3)* [1994] BCC 766 at 767: 'Petitions under s 459 have become notorious to the judges of this court – and I think also the Bar – for their length, their unpredictability of management, and the enormous and appalling costs which are incurred upon them particularly by reason of the volume of documents liable to be produced. By way of example, on this petition there are before me upwards of 30 lever-arch files of documents. In those circumstances it befits the court, in my view, to be extremely careful to ensure that oppression is not caused to parties ...'

4   See the Woolf Report, *Access to Civil Justice, Final Report to the Lord Chancellor on Civil Justice in England and Wales* (1996) (London, TSO, 1996). See the Civil Procedure Act 1997 and the Civil Procedure Rules 1998, SI 1998/3132. Rule 1.1(1) lays down the overriding objective:

1.1.1 These rules are a new procedural code with the overriding objective of enabling the court to deal with cases justly. 2 Dealing with a case justly includes so far as is practicable: (a) ensuring that the parties are on an equal footing; (b) saving expense; (c) dealing with the case in ways which are proportionate: (i) to the amount of money involved; (ii) to the importance of the case; (iii) to the complexity of the issue; and (iv) to the financial position of each party; (d) ensuring that it is dealt with expeditiously and fairly; and (e) allotting to it an appropriate share of the court's resources, while taking into account the need to allot resources to other cases.

and in the context of s 459 actions, the new Civil Procedure Rules have received an unequivocal welcome by the Law Commission.[5]

On the substantive level much is also afoot. Since the Law Commission completed its work on shareholder remedies, and during the course of the Department of Trade (DTI)'s fundamental review of company law,[6] the first case on s 459, *O'Neill v Phillips*,[7] reached the House of Lords. As will be seen, *O'Neill* marks the culmination of the process (embarked upon principally by Lord Hoffmann who has contributed much to the shaping of the remedy during the course of his judicial career) for adopting a principled and pragmatic approach to the scope of the unfair prejudice provision. Although the DTI initially expressed some disquiet about the likely impact of *O'Neill* on the expansive proposals put forward by the Law Commission,[8] the Company Law Review Steering Group now endorses the approach taken by the House of Lords.[9]

This essay will first review the history of s 459 and the early judicial approach towards framing the scope of the remedy. Secondly, it will survey the recent reform proposals promulgated by the Law Commission and the DTI. In this respect, obvious emphasis will be given to the approach adopted by Lord Hoffmann to the determination of unfair prejudice in *O'Neill v Phillips*.[10] The jurisprudential background to the decision in *O'Neill* will be considered with the aim of identifying the origins and the theoretical basis of the current move towards restricting the scope of the concept of 'fairness'. It will be concluded that the future of the remedy now lies confined to three categories of breach: (a) a breach of the corporate contract or some collateral shareholders' agreement; (b) a breach of a fundamental understanding between shareholders (noted in the *The Final Report* as 'some sort of agreement that makes it inequitable to confine the member to his strict legal rights under the constitution');[11] and/or (c) some other breach of duty. It will be seen that such categorisation itself has the potential to give rise to inherent uncertainties which, at the minimum, should be addressed by precise drafting of the successor provision to s 459.

---

5   See the Law Commission's Consultation Paper No 142, *Shareholder Remedies*, above n 3, and the ensuing Law Commission Report No 246, *Shareholder Remedies* (1997) Cm 3769 (London, TSO, 1997), which is considered further below.

6   See *Modern Company Law for a Competitive Economy* (London, DTI, March 1998).

7   [1999] 1 WLR 1092; see Payne and Prentice 'Section 459 of the Companies Act 1985 – The House of Lords' View' (1999) 115 LQR 587.

8   See, *Modern Company Law for a Competitive Economy: Developing the Framework* (London, DTI, March 2000) at paras 4.108–4.110; hereafter *Developing the Framework*.

9   See *Modern Company Law for a Competitive Economy: Completing the Structure* (London, DTI, November 2000); hereafter *Completing the Structure*, at paras 5.77–5.79; confirmed in *Modern Company Law for a Competitive Economy: Final Report* (London, DTI, July 2001); hereafter *The Final Report*, at para 741.

10 [1999] 1 WLR 1092.

11 See *The Final Report*, above n 9, at para 2.26. As will be seen, this stems from Lord Hoffmann's reliance in *O'Neill* on the speech delivered by Lord Wilberforce in *Re Westbourne Galleries Ltd* [1973] AC 360, considered further below. In aligning the unfair prejudice remedy with the equitable principles underlying Lord Wilberforce's approach towards the just and equitable winding-up provision, it seems that the DTI is tacitly fusing s 459 with the concept of equitable estoppel.

2 THE GENESIS OF SECTION 459 OF THE COMPANIES ACT 1985

It is instructive to consider briefly the role which the architects of the unfair prejudice provision had in mind for the remedy as a means of setting the current DTI proposals for its continued role in their historical context. The origins of the provision can be traced to the Cohen Committee.[12] The Committee, which took the 'internal management principle'[13] as the background for its deliberations, found that shareholders frequently considered themselves impotent when seeking to institute an action challenging the conduct of the majority. The only real means of outflanking the rule in *Foss v Harbottle*[14] was to petition the court for the winding up of the company. Yet, as far as the petitioner was concerned, the deterrent value of this course of action was inherent in its very nature for, '[I]n many cases ... the winding up of the company will not benefit the minority shareholders, since the break-up value of the assets may be small, or the only available purchaser may be that very majority whose oppression has driven the minority to seek redress'.[15] The Committee, therefore, went on to recommend that the court should be given unfettered discretion to impose upon the parties to a dispute whatever settlement it considered just and equitable.[16] This was translated into the so-called 'oppression' remedy contained in s 210 of the Companies Act 1948. It provided a discretionary remedy but which, by virtue of its drafting, was expressly stated to be only available where the facts of the case justified a winding-up order.[17] As a result of the inadequacies of its drafting and of the unimaginative approach adopted by the judges to its interpretation, only two cases were successfully brought under the section.[18] The term 'oppression' was restrictively construed as covering acts which were 'burdensome, harsh and wrongful'.[19] Unfairness was, of itself, insufficient. Consequently, petitions brought, *inter alia*, on the basis of directors awarding themselves excessive remuneration,[20] and mismanagement,[21] were unsuccessful.

---

12 *Report of the Committee on Company Law Amendment* (1945) Cmnd 6659 (London, HMSO, 1945); hereafter *The Cohen Report*.

13 Also known as the rule in *Foss v Harbottle* (1843) 2 Hare 461. See further Wedderburn 'Shareholders' Rights and the Rule in *Foss v Harbottle*' [1957] CLJ 154 and [1958] CLJ 219. See also Sealy 'Problems of Standing, Pleading and Proof in Corporate Litigation' in BG Pettet (ed) *Company Law in Change* (London, Stevens, 1987) at p 1.

14 (1843) 2 Hare 461.

15 See *The Cohen Report*, above n 12, at para 60.

16 See *The Cohen Report*, above n 12, at para 60.

17 It has been argued that in summarising its recommendation, the Cohen Committee used language which misled the DTI of the time into the belief that the Committee intended the new provision to be coextensive with the court's power to make a winding-up order. See Instone 'Unfair Prejudice to Shareholders' (1981) 131 NLJ 1316.

18 See: *SCWS Ltd v Meyer* [1959] AC 324 and *Re HR Harmer Ltd* [1959] 1 WLR 62. For a full analysis of s 210 see Prentice 'Protection of Minority Shareholders – Section 210 Of The Companies Act 1948' [1972] *Current Legal Problems* 124. See also, Prentice 'Winding up on the Just and Equitable Ground: The Partnership Analogy' (1973) 89 LQR 107.

19 See *SCWS v Meyer* [1959] AC 324 at p 342, *per* Lord Simonds.

20 See *Re Jermyn Street Turkish Baths Ltd* [1971] 1 WLR 1042.

21 See *Re Five Minute Car Wash Service Ltd* [1966] 1 WLR 745.

Given the failure of the oppression remedy to provide adequate relief, the Jenkins Committee,[22] when reviewing the operation of s 210 of the 1948 Act, identified a number of defects which had to be addressed if it was 'to afford effective protection to minorities in circumstances such as those with which it is intended to deal'.[23] More particularly, the Committee felt that the section 'must extend to cases in which the acts complained of fall short of actual illegality'.[24] It therefore recommended its amendment to cover complaints that the affairs of the company were being conducted in a manner unfairly prejudicial to the interests of the petitioner.[25] Somewhat belatedly, this was put into effect by the Companies Act 1980,[26] now re-enacted in Part XVII of the Companies Act 1985.

An initial problem, resulting from judicial timidity in interpreting the provision, as originally drafted, was that s 75 and subsequently s 459 of the Companies Act 1985 (prior to its 1989 amendment) stated that a petition could only be brought where the company's affairs were being conducted in a manner unfairly prejudicial to the interests of 'some part' of the members. This was construed to mean that a petitioner had to show discrimination.[27] Consequently, in Re A Company (No 0370 of 1987),[28] for example, Harman J held that the board's failure to declare a dividend was not discriminatory between shareholders given that all members were affected equally. He therefore refused an interlocutory application for leave to amend the s 459 petition; however, the judge allowed the amendment in relation to a claim for just and equitable winding up. The amendment of s 459 of the Companies Act 1985, which was effected by the Companies Act 1989,[29] directly reversed the requirement of discrimination. This gave statutory effect to the decision of Peter Gibson J in Re Sam Weller & Sons Ltd[30] who, in refusing to follow Harman J, held that the failure to declare adequate dividends could amount to unfairly prejudicial conduct notwithstanding that all of the company's shareholders were affected. While Parliament showed itself willing to intervene on this limited ground, it left unresolved the fundamental question of what is meant by 'unfairly prejudicial' conduct. It was, therefore, left to the courts to determine the scope of the remedy. As will be seen, notions of what should constitute 'unfairness' and 'prejudice' has ebbed and flowed between an expansive view being adopted towards the scope of the remedy and, more recently, a determination to confine the basis of a claim within fixed parameters.[31]

---

22 *Report of the Company Law Committee* (1962) Cmnd 1749 (London, HMSO, 1962); hereafter *The Jenkins Report*.

23 See *The Jenkins Report*, above n 22, at para 201.

24 See *The Jenkins Report*, above n 22, at para 203.

25 See *The Jenkins Report*, above n 22, at para 204.

26 See Companies Act 1980, s 75.

27 See *Re Carrington Viyella plc* [1983] 1 BCC 98, in which it was held that a breach of directors' duties could not support a s 459 petition because the conduct in question affected all of the company's shareholders.

28 [1988] 1 WLR 1068.

29 See Companies Act 1989, s 145 and Schedule 19 at para 11, which came into force in 1991.

30 [1990] Ch 682.

31 The Company Law Steering Group in *The Final Report*, above n 9, at para 7.41 stated that although the majority of responses to *Developing the Structure* were in favour of extending the scope of the remedy, 'after careful consideration we came down against this'. Citing *O'Neill v Phillips*, the Steering Group concluded, at para 7.41, that 'the basis for a claim should be a departure from an agreement, broadly defined, between those concerned, to be identified by their words or conduct'.

3 REFORMING SECTION 459 OF THE COMPANIES ACT 1985

The proposals for legislative reform of s 459 of the Companies Act 1985 framed by the Law Commission, and which have been the subject of two consultation exercises: first, by the Law Commission itself,[32] and second, by the DTI's Company Law Review Steering Group,[33] were formulated with the new Civil Procedure Rules standing at centre stage in the deliberations.[34] The principal concern of the Law Commission was not directed towards the substantive remedy itself, but to the length and cost of typical unfair prejudice actions and the destructive effect such proceedings had on small private companies. As noted above,[35] the consultation paper gave a number of examples from the case law to highlight this problem, including *Re Macro (Ipswich) Ltd*[36] where the hearing of the petition and a related action lasted 27 days and the costs claimed came to some £725,000, excluding appeal costs. The Law Commission, in accordance with the Woolf reforms, therefore, recommended that the difficulties of length, cost and complexity of s 459 proceedings should be addressed by active case management by the courts. More particularly, the Law Commission took the view that the courts should make greater use of the power to direct that preliminary issues be heard, or that some issues be tried before others; to impose costs sanctions; and to have the power to dismiss any claim or part of a claim or defence thereto which, in the opinion of the court, had no realistic prospect of success at full trial.[37]

In terms of substantive reform, the Law Commission noted, from its statistical survey, that the majority of petitions were brought by minority shareholders in small private companies seeking to have their shares purchased on the basis of their exclusion from management. In order to attain the objectives of providing such petitioners with a speedy and economical exit route, the Law Commission recommended that ss 459–61 of the Companies Act 1985 should be amended so as to raise rebuttable presumptions that, where a shareholder had been excluded from participating in management, then:

(a) the affairs of the company will be presumed to have been conducted in a manner which is unfairly prejudicial to the petitioner; and

(b) if the presumption is not rebutted and the court is satisfied that it ought to order a buy out of the petitioner's shares, it should do so on a *pro rata* basis.[38]

The presumption would only apply where the company was a private limited company in which the petitioner held shares in his sole name giving him not less than 10% of the rights to vote at general meetings, and all, or substantially all of the members of the company were directors. The petitioner must have been removed as a director or had been prevented from carrying out all or substantially all of his functions as a director. Further, to avoid the risk of introducing some inadvertent limitation into the scope of

---

32 See n 3 above.
33 In relation to *Developing the Framework*, see n 8 above.
34 See n 4 above.
35 See n 3 above.
36 [1994] 2 BCLC 354.
37 See Law Commission Report *Shareholder Remedies*, above n 5, at Part 2.
38 See Law Commission Report *Shareholder Remedies*, above n 5, at para 3.30.

s 459,[39] the Law Commission recommended that the general wording of the provision should be left as it now stands so that the term 'unfairly prejudicial' should not be defined.[40]

It is also recommended that Table A[41] should be amended so as to include an exit article whereby shareholders would be encouraged from the outset to provide for what was to happen in the event of a dispute.[42] It was envisaged that an exit article would enable a shareholder to leave a company without necessarily having to resort to s 459 proceedings. As with Table A generally, such an article could be excluded by the parties. The Law Commission stated that the exit regulation would be conferred by an ordinary resolution and that every shareholder who was to have or be subject to exit rights must be named in the resolution and must consent to it. Such a resolution would have to stipulate first, the events in which exit rights were to be exercisable; secondly, that the shareholder entitled to the right required the other shareholders named in it to buy his shares at a fair price; and finally, how the 'fair price' was to be calculated. The company would not be permitted to amend either the resolution or the exit article without the consent of the named shareholders. It was envisaged that the purchase would need to be completed within three months. The Law Commission went on to conclude that at the minimum the exit provision would at least prompt registration agents to advise their clients to consider entering into a shareholders' agreement as an alternative means of providing for dispute resolution.[43] The effect of this would be that the current burgeoning case load would be significantly reduced.

While noting that the remedies available under s 461 are very wide, the Law Commission considered that shareholder remedies would be streamlined if winding up was added to the array of orders available to the court under the provision. To avoid the risk of reputational damage and loss of confidence among its customers and suppliers which a company may suffer in the event of an unjust claim for winding up, a petitioner who sought such an order under ss 459–61 would first have to obtain the court's leave to do so. Further, a petitioner who sought a winding-up order under s 122(1)(g) of the Insolvency Act 1986 in conjunction with an application under s 459 would also be required to first obtain the leave of the court before making such an application.[44]

The Company Law Review Steering Group supported the Law Commission's emphasis on case management which is now largely in place as a result of the Woolf reforms.[45] The so-called 'guiding principles' which the Law Commission formulated with the object of striking a balance between the need to protect shareholder interests while

---

39 The fear being that the guidelines laid down by the Court of Appeal in *Re Saul D Harrison & Sons plc* [1995] 1 BCLC 14, considered below, for the determination of when conduct would be considered unfairly prejudicial might have the effect of restricting the availability of s 459.

40 See Law Commission Report *Shareholder Remedies*, above n 5, at paras 4.12–4.13.

41 See generally the Companies Act 1985, s 8 and SI 1985/805 (as amended).

42 See Law Commission Report *Shareholder Remedies*, above n 5, at para 5.4 onwards.

43 See Law Commission Report *Shareholder Remedies*, above n 5, at para 5.31.

44 See Law Commission Report *Shareholder Remedies*, above n 5, at para 4.40.

45 See generally n 4 above.

nevertheless preventing litigation inhibiting the proper operation of companies,[46] were adopted by the Steering Group as being the paradigm.[47] However, with respect to other specific Law Commission proposals, the Company Law Review Steering Group's consultation paper, *Developing the Framework*,[48] considered that the proposed exit article was unlikely to be used much in practice because of its inherent inflexibility – 'it was impossible to prescribe in advance, and for the full diversity of companies, what would be a fair exit regime'.[49] The case for the proposed presumptions of unfair prejudice was also doubted,[50] as was the desirability of including winding up as a remedy under s 459.[51] Of greater import, for present purposes, was the Steering Group's endorsement of Lord Hoffmann's most recent pronouncement on s 459. The November 2000 Consultation Paper stated that the provision should be retained in its present form,[52] but 'subject to the focus laid down' by the House of Lords decision in *O'Neill v Phillips*.[53] This position was emphatically confirmed in the July 2001 document *The Final Report*,[54] on the basis that it 'is necessary in the interests of certainty and the containment of the scope of s 459 actions'.[55]

The Steering Group's conclusion is significant. Future legislative amendment of s 459 is now unlikely, at least in substantive terms, and therefore the decision in *O'Neill* will have lasting impact on the scope of the concept of unfair prejudice. The Steering Group took the view that the effect of the decision is that for a petitioner 'to sustain an action for unfair prejudice in reliance on some claim other than a breach of the articles or some other breach of duty, he must show breach of some sort of agreement, based on words or conduct, which makes it inequitable to confine him to his strict rights under the articles or constitution of the company'.[56] In assessing the impact of *O'Neill* on s 459 and how the concept of fairness is likely to be viewed in future cases, it is instructive to view Lord Hoffmann's reasoning against the background of the case law which rapidly burgeoned following the demise of the old oppression remedy[57] and its replacement with the current remedy found in s 459 of the Companies Act 1985.

---

46 See Law Commission Report *Shareholder Remedies*, above n 5, at para 1.9. Six principles are listed under the following headings: (i) Proper plaintiff; (ii) Internal management; (iii) Commercial decisions; (iv) Sanctity of contract; (v) Freedom from unnecessary shareholder interference; (vi) Efficiency and cost-effectiveness.

47 See: *Developing the Framework*, above n 8, at paras 4.70–4.71; *Completing the Structure*, above n 9, at para 5.106.

48 Above n 8.

49 See *Developing the Framework*, above n 8, at para 4.103.

50 See *Developing the Framework*, above n 8, at para 4.104.

51 See *Developing the Framework*, above n 8, at para 4.105.

52 See *Completing the Structure*, above n 9, at para 5.108. The Steering Group stated, at para 5.78, that: 'After careful consideration, our conclusion is that the *O'Neill* ruling ought not to be reversed. The effect of the unfair prejudice claim being unlimited is to lead to all manner of factual allegations being potentially admissible, which encourages the widest possible range of evidence being adduced to assemble a case of unfairness. This makes proceedings lengthy and undisciplined and means that there is little guidance for those operating companies as to what is and is not acceptable conduct ...'

53 [1999] 1 WLR 1092.

54 See n 9 above.

55 See *The Final Report*, above n 9, at para 7.41.

56 See *Completing the Structure*, above n 9, at para 5.77. See also *The Final Report*, above n 9, at para 7.41.

57 Contained in the Companies Act 1948, s 210; see nn 17–21 above and the main text thereat.

4 THE JURISPRUDENTIAL LANDSCAPE: THE ROAD TO *O'NEILL*

Prior to the amendment of s 459 by the Companies Act 1989,[58] a petition could only be brought where the company's affairs were being conducted in a manner unfairly prejudicial to the interests of 'some part' of the members. This was construed to mean that a petitioner had to show discrimination.[59] As noted above, in *Re A Company (No 0370 of 1987)*,[60] Harman J held that the board's failure to declare a dividend was not discriminatory between shareholders; all members were affected equally. The judge, therefore, refused an interlocutory application for leave to amend the s 459 petition; however, he allowed the amendment in relation to a claim for the draconian remedy of just and equitable winding up. The amendment introduced by the Companies Act 1989, by way of inserting the phrase 'of its members generally' into the provision, directly reversed the requirement of discrimination. This, as we have seen, gave statutory effect to the decision of Peter Gibson J in *Re Sam Weller & Sons Ltd*.[61] Although the legislature was willing to intervene on this limited ground, the more fundamental question of how the concept of unfairly prejudicial conduct should be determined was left unresolved notwithstanding the considerable differences of judicial opinion which had been expressed on this issue.[62] It therefore fell to the courts to address this issue on a case-by-case basis.

Since its introduction the unfair prejudice remedy has been typically deployed as a device by petitioners for enforcing their so-called legitimate expectations arising in addition to, but outside of, their strict legal rights. Thus, in the small private company context, frequently owner-managed (commonly termed quasi-partnerships), petitions have traditionally been resolved by balancing the expectation interests of the minority member when forming or investing in the company,[63] with the rights of the majority and the board of directors to exercise strict legal powers conferred by the company's constitution and the companies legislation.[64] Where a petitioner's legitimate expectation

---

58   See n 29, above.
59   See *Re Carrington Viyella plc* (1983) 1 BCC 98 at p 751, in which it was held that a breach of directors' duties could not found the basis of a s 459 petition since this breach affected all shareholders in the company.
60   [1988] 1 WLR 1068.
61   [1990] Ch 682.
62   See the examples cited in nn 66–70 below, and the main text thereat.
63   For example, to participate in management as a director.
64   For example, to remove a director by ordinary resolution under the Companies Act 1985, s 303. In *Re Ringtower Holdings plc* (1989) 5 BCC 82 at p 90, Peter Gibson J stated that: '... the [relevant] conduct must be both prejudicial ... to the relevant interests and also unfairly so: conduct may be unfair without being prejudicial or prejudicial without being unfair and in neither case could the section be satisfied ... the test is unfair prejudice, not of unlawfulness, and conduct may be lawful but unfairly prejudicial ...' The concept of thwarted shareholder expectations is limited in widely held companies, where the expectations of members do not generally extend beyond the hope of receiving a return on investment; see, for example, *Re Blue Arrow plc* [1987] BCLC 585.

has been frustrated so as to amount to unfairly prejudicial conduct on the part of the majority, the court is given wide powers under s 461 to provide a remedy.[65]

The concept of unfair prejudice has resulted in marked differences of approach amongst the judiciary towards the determination of its scope. For example, Arden LJ has been at pains to maintain the widest possible discretion which the scope of the legislative language seemingly confers. In *Re Macro (Ipswich) Ltd*,[66] the first case where an allegation of mismanagement has succeeded under s 459, she stressed that 'the jurisdiction under s 459 has an elastic quality which enables the courts to mould the concepts of unfair prejudice according to the circumstances of the case'.[67] Lord Hoffmann, on the other hand, has been at the forefront in seeking to lay down clearly defined criteria to guide the court in its determination of 'fairness'. Lord Hoffmann's approach is hallmarked by his declared objective of restricting the ambit of s 459 so as to inhibit the adoption of a case-by-case approach unhindered by settled categories of unfair prejudice. This is evident in cases decided by him while still sitting in the Chancery Division. It came to the fore in his judgment delivered in the Court of Appeal in *Re Saul D Harrison*[68] and, following *Arden* J's remarks in *Re BSB Holdings (No 2)*[69] to the effect that it was not open to the Court of Appeal to limit the general words used in the section, he took the opportunity from the vantage point of the House of Lords in *O'Neill v Phillips*[70] to at last settle the point. In so doing, he reinforced the need, so often expressed by him before, that the remedy should be viewed from an orthodox contractarian standpoint that does not permit the court to simply grant an order to an aggrieved shareholder on the basis of unguided notions of justice or fairness.

In a series of cases culminating in *O'Neill v Phillips*, Lord Hoffmann stressed that the concept of 'unfairness' in s 459 runs parallel to the 'just and equitable' ground on which a company may be wound up.[71] In framing this approach the reasoning of Lord Wilberforce in *Re Westbourne Galleries Ltd*[72] is enlisted in order to demonstrate that although equitable considerations should underlie the court's determination of unfair prejudice, nevertheless it should not result in decisions unfettered by principle. Lord Wilberforce had stated that:

---

65 Section 461(1) provides that: 'If the court is satisfied that a petition is well founded, it may make such order as it thinks fit for giving relief in respect of the matters complained of.
   (2) Without prejudice to the generality of sub-s (1), the court's order may:
      (a) regulate the conduct of the company's affairs in the future,
      (b) require the company to refrain from doing or continuing an act complained of by the petitioner or to do an act which the petitioner has complained it has omitted to do,
      (c) authorise civil proceedings to be brought in the name and on behalf of the company by such person or persons and on such terms as the court may direct,
      (d) provide for the purchase of the shares of any members of the company by other members or by the company itself and, in the case of a purchase by the company itself, the reduction of the company's capital accordingly.
66 [1994] 2 BCLC 354. See further Lowry 'Stretching the Ambit of Section 459 of the Companies Act 1985: The Elasticity of Unfair Prejudice' [1995] *Lloyd's Maritime and Commercial Law Quarterly* 337.
67 [1994] 2 BCLC 354 at p 404.
68 [1995] 1 BCLC 14.
69 [1996] 1 BCLC 155 at p 243.
70 [1999] 1 WLR 1092.
71 See Insolvency Act 1986, s 122(1)(g).
72 [1973] AC 360.

The words ['just and equitable' contained in the Insolvency Act 1986, s 122 (i)(g)] are a recognition of the fact that a limited company is more than a mere legal entity, with a personality in law of its own: that there is room in company law for recognition of the fact that behind it, or amongst it, there are individuals, with rights, expectations and obligations *inter se* which are not necessarily submerged in the company structure. The structure is defined by the Companies Act [1985] and by the articles of association by which shareholders agree to be bound ... The 'just and equitable' provision does not ... entitle one party to disregard the obligation he assumes by entering a company, nor the court to dispense him from it. It does, as equity always does, enable the court to subject the exercise of legal rights to equitable considerations; considerations, that is, of a personal character arising between one individual and another, which may make it unjust, or inequitable, to insist on legal rights, or to exercise them in a particular way.[73]

Lord Wilberforce went on to observe that in most companies, irrespective of size, a member's rights under the articles of association and the Companies Act could be viewed as an exhaustive statement of his or her interests as a shareholder. However, he went on to list three situations in which equitable considerations could be 'superimposed', namely, where there is a personal relationship between shareholders which involves mutual confidence, or, secondly, an agreement that some or all should participate in the management, or, thirdly, where there are restrictions on the transfer of shares which would prevent a member from realising his or her investment.[74] In examining the scope of shareholders' obligations, therefore, the courts will look beyond the articles of the particular company. For example, in the absence of a specific undertaking that the petitioner will participate in management, the court may imply or infer such an obligation from the conduct of the parties.[75]

Given that the force of the decision in *Re Westbourne Galleries* has long pervaded the s 459 case law, Lord Hoffmann's return to it in *O'Neill* is by no means surprising. Going back across the case law spanning some 15 years or so, it is clear that Lord Wilberforce's reasoning has been a central point upon which the remedy pivots despite the fact that he was considering the just and equitable winding up under what is now s 122(1)(g) of the Insolvency Act 1986.[76] For example, in *Re A Company (No 00477 of 1986)*[77] Hoffmann J considered that the language of s 459 facilitated the exercise by the Court of its residual equitable jurisdiction. He observed that the interests of a member are not necessarily limited to the strict legal rights conferred by the constitution of a company. Accordingly, a member's interests can encompass the legitimate expectation that he or she will continue to participate in management. However, it is important to bear in mind the type of

---

73 [1973] AC 360 at p 379.
74 See [1973] AC 360 at p 379 cited by Hoffmann J in *Re A Company (No 00477 of 1986)* [1986] BCLC 376 at p 379.
75 See *Tay Bok Choon v Tohansan Sdn Bhd* [1987] 1 WLR 413 (PC). See also *Re Fildes Bros Ltd* [1970] 1 WLR 592 at p 596 where Megarry J said that: 'It cannot be just and equitable to allow one party to come to the court and require the court to make an order which disregards his contractual obligations. The same, I think, must apply to a settled and accepted course of conduct between the parties, whether or not cast into the mould of a contract.'
76 See, for example, his analysis of *Re Westbourne Galleries* in *Re Posgate & Denby (Agencies) Ltd* [1987] BCLC 8 which has been approved in a series of cases; see: *Re Elgindata Ltd* [1991] BCLC 959, *Jaber v Science and Information Technology Ltd* [1992] BCC 596 and *Re Estate Acquisition and Development Ltd* [1995] BCC 338.
77 [1986] BCLC 376. On the facts of the case, the petitioner failed to establish unfair prejudice.

corporate enterprise which has given rise to the bulk of litigation under the provision. In this regard, the courts pay heed to the reality which lies behind the corporate veil.[78] For example, in *Re A Company (No 003160 of 1986)*,[79] Hoffmann J observed that s 459:

> ... enables the court to protect not only the rights of members under the constitution of the company but also the 'rights, expectations and obligations' of the individual shareholders inter se. In the typical case of the corporate quasi-partnership, these will include the expectations that the member will be able to participate in the management of the company.[80]

The weight of this approach is also discernible in Commonwealth jurisdictions with comparable provisions covering unfairly prejudicial conduct. For example, in *Thomas v HW Thomas Ltd*[81] Richardson J observed that it was not necessary for a complainant to point 'to any actual irregularity or to an invasion of his legal rights or to a lack of probity or want of good faith towards him on the part of those in control of the company'.[82] The Canadian courts also recognise that a shareholder's interest in a company can extend beyond his or her immediate financial returns. Section 241 of the Canadian Business Corporations Act 1988 (as amended) provides for minority protection against both 'oppressive' and 'unfairly prejudicial conduct' which 'unfairly disregards the interests of any security holder, creditor, director or officer ...'. Petitions brought under this provision are increasingly resolved by balancing the expectation interests of the shareholders against the rights of the board to exercise its strict legal powers. For example, in *Re Mason and Intercity Properties*,[83] the petitioner, a director, was granted relief because she was able to establish that her 'interests' had been disregarded as a result of her exclusion from any meaningful participation in the management of the company. Similarly, in *Miller v F Mendel Holdings*,[84] a case also involving exclusion from management, the court reached a finding of oppression 'by putting the action in its proper perspective and judging it in the context of the overall relationship between the parties'.[85]

However, to counter any tendency that could lead to the misconception that s 459 equipped the courts with a fluid remedy capable of being moulded to achieve justice on

---

78 In *Re A Company (No 004475 of 1982)* [1983] Ch 178, Lord Grantchester QC, citing what is now *Gore-Browne on Companies* (Bristol, Jordans, loose-leaf, 44th edn, 1986) at para 28.14, stated: 'It is obvious that in a small private company it is legalistic to segregate the separate capacities of the same individual as shareholder, director or employee. His dismissal from the board or from employment by the company will inevitably affect the real value of his interest in the company expressed by his shareholding.'

79 [1986] BCLC 391.

80 [1986] BCLC 391 at p 396. In seeking to define the limits of legitimate expectation, some assistance can be derived from other legal disciplines, notably public law and the flexible concept of estoppel that pervades our legal system. For, in those areas as opposed to its use in company law, such phrases have become terms of art, skilfully used by judges and practitioners. There are distinct analogies that can be drawn. For example, see Lord Diplock's analysis in *Council of Civil Service Unions v Minister for the Civil Service* [1985] AC 374 at p 408.

81 [1984] 1 NZLR 686. See also *Re Norvabron Pty (No 2) Ltd* (1987) 11 ACLR 279.

82 [1984] 1 NZLR 686 at p 693; cited with approval by Brennan J in *Wayde v New South Wales Rugby League Ltd* (1985) 10 ACLR 87 at p 94.

83 (1987) 59 OR (2d) 631.

84 (1984) 26 BLR 85.

85 (1984) 26 BLR 85 at p 96.

an ad hoc basis,[86] Lord Hoffmann in *O'Neill* adopted a resolute stance. While recognising that the legislative intent behind the adoption of fairness in s 459 was to 'free the court from technical considerations of legal right', he went on to stress that the concept of fairness 'must be applied judicially and the content which is given by the courts must be based upon rational principles'. Citing Warner J in *Re JE Cade & Son Ltd*[87] Lord Hoffmann observes that: 'The court ... has a very wide discretion, but it does not sit under a palm tree.'[88]

5 A PRINCIPLED APPROACH TO FAIRNESS

The concept of unfairness was considered by the Jenkins Committee to be 'a visible departure from the standards of fair dealing and a violation of the conditions of fair play on which every shareholder who entrusts his money to a company is entitled to rely'.[89] While s 459 itself does not define the meaning of unfairly prejudicial conduct, early case law suggests that it should be determined objectively. In *Re Bovey Hotel Ventures Ltd*[90] Slade J formulated the test for determining the issue in the following terms:

> The test of unfairness must, I think, be an objective, not a subjective, one ... [T]he test, I think, is whether a reasonable bystander observing the consequences of their conduct, would regard it as having unfairly prejudiced the petitioner's interests.[91]

The application of this test can be seen in *Re RA Noble & Sons (Clothing) Ltd*[92] where the petitioner, a founder member of the business, in essence a quasi-partnership, alleged that he had been excluded from the running of the company. In fact, the respondent had not set out to deliberately oust him, but had simply proceeded to manage the company's business in the belief, based on the petitioner's conduct, that he was uninterested in its affairs. It was held, applying the objective test, that a reasonable man might well have thought that the conduct complained of was prejudicial but would not have regarded it as unfair, for the petitioner, by his lack of interest, had partly brought it upon himself. However, objective determination of unfairness was questioned by Hoffmann LJ in *Re Saul D Harrison*. He doubted whether such an approach is necessarily 'the most illuminating way of putting the matter'.[93] In this vein he went on to add:

---

86 Arguably discernible in, for example, *Re Macro (Ipswich) Ltd* [1994] 2 BCLC 554; and *Re BSB Holdings (No 2)* [1996] 1 BCLC 155; see nn 66 and 69 above, and the main text thereat.

87 [1992] BCLC 213 at p 227.

88 [1999] 1 WLR 1092 at p 1098.

89 See *The Jenkins Report*, above n 22, at para 204 – adopting the view expressed by Lord Cooper in *Elder v Elder & Watson Ltd* [1952] SC 49 at p 55.

90 31 July 1981, unreported, cited by Nourse J in *Re RA Noble & Sons (Clothing) Ltd* [1983] BCLC 273 at p 290.

91 Citing this passage, Prentice has noted that: '[T]he focal point of the court's enquiry in determining whether conduct has been unfairly prejudicial is its impact and not its nature.' See 'The Theory of the Firm: Minority Shareholder Oppression: Sections 459–61 of the Companies Act 1985' (1988) 8 OJLS 55 at p 78.

92 [1983] BCLC 273.

93 [1995] 1 BCLC 14 at p 17. This line of thought can be traced to Hoffmann J's judgment in *Re A Company (No 008699 of 1985)* [1986] BCLC 382 at p 388, where he stated that: 'Unfairness is a familiar concept employed in ordinary speech, often by way of contrast to infringement of legal right. It was intended to confer a very wide jurisdiction upon the court and I think it would be wrong to restrict that jurisdiction by adding any gloss to the ordinary meaning of the words.'

For one thing, the standard of fairness must necessarily be laid down by the court. In explaining how the court sets about deciding what is fair in the context of company management, I do not think that it helps a great deal to add the reasonable company watcher to the already substantial cast of imaginary characters which the law uses to personify its standards of justice in different situations. An appeal to the views of an imaginary third party makes the concept seem more vague than it really is.[94]

Given the complexity of the relationships found within owner-managed companies, the rejection of yet another objective test based upon the hypothetical bystander is no doubt sensible. Many of the petitions brought under s 459, and its predecessors, involve a breakdown of relationships within families. Accordingly, in a series of cases Lord Hoffmann has drawn the analogy between s 459 petitions and divorce petitions, and alluded to the difficulties experienced by judges when called upon to apportion fault.[95] In this respect, he has commented that in the event of a breakdown in relations it is frequently clear which member should go. The choice is obvious in a situation involving an elderly member/employee who lacks business acumen, and for whom there was never any prospect of assuming a decisive role in the management of the company.[96] Simply because the petitioner is innocent, it does not follow that the respondent is presumed to have been guilty of culpable conduct. Lord Hoffmann has remarked that:

> There are many cases in which it becomes in practice impossible for two people to work together without obvious fault on either side. They may have come together with a confident expectation of being able to co-operate but found that insurmountable differences in personality made it impossible. In those circumstances the only solution is for them to part company. If one of them asks the other to leave the business, I cannot accept that the former must automatically be regarded as having acted in a manner unfairly prejudicial to the interests of the latter.[97]

However, Lord Hoffmann takes the view that there are limits to the concepts of unfairness and shareholder expectations, and he has emphatically warned against taking a fanciful approach to Lord Wilberforce's reasoning in *Westbourne Galleries*. Any notion that Lord Wilberforce was seeking to provide some equitable vehicle to ride rough shod over commercial undertakings is clearly misplaced. Indeed, Lord Wilberforce himself recognised that where in a commercial enterprise the relationship between the members is governed by comprehensively drafted articles of association,[98] then 'the "superimposition" of equitable considerations would require something more'.[99] In this respect, Lord Hoffmann's anxiety that the courts should maintain a balanced perspective towards the determination of unfairness manifested itself long before *O'Neill*. For example, in *Re A Company (No 004377 of 1986)*[100] he stressed that:

---

94 [1995] 1 BCLC 14 at p 17.
95 See, for example, *Re A Company (No 004377 of 1986)* [1987] BCLC 94 at p 101.
96 See *Re A Company (No 007623 of 1986)* [1986] BCLC 362 at p 366.
97 [1986] BCLC 362 at p 366.
98 To this, shareholder agreements and service contracts should now be added, see *Re Ringtower Holding plc* [1989] 5 BCC 82, *sub nom Re A Company (No 005685 of 1988) ex p Schwartz (No 2)* [1989] BCLC 427.
99 See [1973] AC 360 at p 379.
100 [1987] BCLC 94.

Section [459] was a valuable and overdue reform of the law which conferred on the court a wide and useful discretion. Nothing that I say in this judgment is intended to (or could) reduce the ambit of that discretion. But the very width of the jurisdiction means that unless carefully controlled it can become a means of oppression.[101]

It has thus long been recognised that the scope for the courts to find legitimate expectations which go beyond strict contractual rights under the company's constitution, yet which nevertheless fall within the protection of s 459, is subject to limitation and in this respect *O'Neill* merely reaffirms what has long been the case. The process of drawing clear demarcation lines surrounding a petitioner's equitable expectations has been evolving since the provision first came into being in the 1980 Act.[102] In *Re A Company (No 004377 of 1986)*,[103] for example, the majority, including the petitioner, voted for a special resolution to amend the company's articles so as to provide that a member, on ceasing to be an employee or director of the company, would be required to transfer his or her shares to the company. To remedy a situation of management deadlock, the petitioner was dismissed as director and was offered £900 per share. When he declined, his shares were valued by the company's auditors in accordance with the preemption clauses. He petitioned the court under s 459 to restrain the compulsory acquisition of his shares, arguing that he had a legitimate expectation that he would continue to participate in the management of the company which, he argued, was in essence a quasi-partnership. Hoffmann J held that there could be no expectation on the part of the petitioner that should relations break down the article would not be followed. In a vigorous judgment, he stated:

> I am satisfied that, having regard to the articles, the petitioner could have no legitimate expectation that in the event of a breakdown of relations ... they would not be relied on to require him to sell his shares at fair value. To hold to the contrary would not be to 'superimpose equitable considerations' on his rights under the articles but to relieve him from the bargain he made.[104]

The approach taken by Hoffmann J presaged his more recent attempts to constrain the concept of legitimate expectations when in the Court of Appeal in *Re Saul D Harrison & Sons plc*[105] and subsequently in the House of Lords in *O'Neill*. The question is how best to strike the optimum balance in the ostensible conflict between a company's constitution on the one hand, and a member's extraneous expectations on the other. The difficulty lies in the proper determination of at which point a member's interests or expectations become totally subsumed in the company's constitution. The solution emerged in the Court of Appeal in *Re Saul D Harrison*, and is driven home in *O'Neill v Phillips*.[106]

---

101 [1987] BCLC 94 at p 103. A warning which he first issued in *Re A Company (No 007623 of 1986)* [1986] BCLC 362.

102 See the Companies Act 1980, s 75.

103 [1987] BCLC 94.

104 [1987] BCLC 94 at p 103. In a similar vein, Hoffmann J stated in *Re Posgate & Denby (Agencies) Ltd* [1987] BCLC 8 at p 14, that: 'Section 459 enables the court to give full effect to the terms and understandings on which the members of the company become associated but not to rewrite them.'

105 [1995] 1 BCLC 14.

106 [1999] 1 WLR 1092.

In *Re Saul D Harrison*,[107] the petitioner complained that the prospects for the company's business had, for a number of years, been so poor that any reasonable board would have gone into voluntary liquidation and distributed the not inconsiderable assets to the shareholders. The essence of the petition was that the directors, in allowing the company to continue trading, dissipated its assets so as to preserve their inflated salaries and perquisites. The Court of Appeal recognised, of course, that the personal relationship between a petitioner and the controlling members may be such that a legitimate expectation may be inferred which will effectively estop the exercise of a legal power by the majority. However, Hoffmann LJ, as he then was, stressed that in the absence of 'something more', there can be no basis for finding a legitimate expectation which goes beyond the articles. On the facts of the case, it was found that the petitioner's rights were exhaustively laid down in the articles of association. Consequently, her legitimate expectations did not extend beyond the expectation that the board would manage the company in accordance with their fiduciary duties, the Companies Act and the articles.[108]

Lord Wilberforce's 'something more' test was also the decisive factor in denying the petitioner's claim in *O'Neill*. The dispute, as is typical in s 459 petitions, involved allegations of broken promises. Pectel Ltd provided asbestos stripping services to the construction industry. In 1983 the issued share capital of the company, 100 £1.00 shares, was owned entirely by Mr Philips (P). Mr O'Neill (O) was employed by the company in 1983 as a manual worker. P was favourably impressed by O and he received rapid promotion. In early 1985 O received 25% of the company's shares and he was made a director. In May 1985 O was informed by P that he, O, would eventually take over the running of the company's business and at that time would receive 50% of the profits. In December 1985 P retired from the board and O became sole director and effectively the company's managing director. For a while the business enjoyed good profitability. However, its fortunes declined during the recession of the late 1980s and in August 1991, disillusioned with O's management of the business, P used his majority voting rights to appoint himself managing director and he took over the management of the company. O was informed that he would no longer receive 50% of the profits but his entitlement would be limited to his salary and dividends on his 25% shareholding. Early discussions about further share incentives when certain targets were met were aborted. O thereupon issued a petition alleging unfairly prejudicial conduct on the part of P.

The trial judge, Judge Paul Baker QC, dismissed the petition, holding that P had not made an unconditional and permanent undertaking to share the profits equally. O's appeal to the Court of Appeal was successful. Nourse LJ found that O had a legitimate

---

107 [1995] 1 BCLC 14.
108 See also the judgment of Neill LJ in the case who concluded: 'Like Hoffmann LJ I can see no adequate basis for the allegation that the directors have carried on business with no or no substantial expectation that they will succeed in making a profit which will reflect the value of the assets employed ... As Hoffmann LJ has pointed out, the petitioner's evidence pays scant regard to the obligations imposed on the board by s 309 of the 1985 Act to take account of the interests of the employees of the company, of whom there are over a hundred' [1995] 1 BCLC 14 at p 33. It is noteworthy that the shares in this case were inherited by the petitioner. In such a situation, the scope for finding legitimate expectations is severely limited. See also *Jackman v Jackets Enterprises Ltd* [1977] 4 BCLR 358, where the petitioner's claim that her exclusion from participating in the company's management constituted oppression was dismissed. The court, in finding no such expectation on her part, had regard to the fact that she had acquired her shares by way of gift.

expectation that he would receive additional shares and an equal share of profits. P appealed to the House of Lords. The central issue was whether P's conduct was 'unfairly prejudicial' for the purposes of s 459 of the Companies Act 1985. Lord Hoffmann's reasoning is instructive in providing detailed insight into the legal nature of the relationship existing between members of small private companies and the court's jurisdiction under the unfair prejudice provision. First, the incorporation of a company gives rise to the creation of a legal relationship between the members which is contractual in nature.[109] The written terms of this contract are contained in the company's formal constitution, which binds the members and the company alike. Thus, where an issue arises which falls within the company's constitution, a petition under s 459 is not the appropriate vehicle for redress. However, where a term of the constitution is broken, a member may be able to launch a petition under the statutory provision. A majority shareholder will not, therefore, normally be able to establish a claim because his voting power will enable him to determine the membership of the board of directors and exert significant influence over the conduct of the company.

Secondly, in quasi-partnerships there may be a duty on members to act in good faith. This duty will be broken, and the conduct in question will be considered unfair where, for example, there is a breach of the company's constitution. In such cases the court has the power to superimpose equitable considerations onto the exercise of strict legal rights. Accordingly, in order to satisfy the requirements of 'unfairness' and 'prejudice' a petitioner must establish that the conduct complained of is both prejudicial (in the sense of causing prejudice or harm) to his interests and also unfairly so. Conduct may, therefore, be unfair without being prejudicial or prejudicial without being unfair and in neither case would the criteria be satisfied.[110]

Applying the above principles to O's petition, the House of Lords found that P's conduct would have been unfair had he used his majority voting power to exclude O from the business. This he had not done, but had simply revised the terms of O's remuneration. P's refusal to allot additional shares as part of the proposed incentive scheme was not unfair as the negotiations were not completed and no contractual undertaking had been entered into by the parties. For Lord Hoffmann, delivering the principal speech,[111] the issue could be simply dispensed with:

> The real question is whether in fairness or equity Mr O'Neill had a right to the shares. On this point one runs up against what seems to me the insuperable obstacle of the judge's finding that Mr Phillips never agreed to give them. He made no promise on the point. From which it seems to me to follow that there is no basis, consistent with established principles of equity, for a court to hold that Mr Phillips was behaving unfairly in withdrawing from the negotiation. This would not be restraining the exercise of legal rights. It would be imposing upon Mr Phillips an obligation to which he never agreed.[112]

---

109 See generally the Companies Act 1985, s 14.

110 See *Re A Company ex p Schwartz (No 2)* [1989] BCLC 427 at p 437 *per* Peter Gibson J. Note also, *Re Macro (Ipswich) Ltd* [1994] 2 BCLC 354.

111 Lord Jauncey of Tullichettle, Lord Clyde, Lord Hutton and Lord Hobhouse of Woodborough concurring.

112 [1999] 1 WLR 1092 at p 1103.

Nor was P's decision to revise O's profit-sharing arrangement unfair conduct. O's entitlement to 50% of the company's profits was never formalised and it was, in any case, conditional upon O running the business. That condition was no longer fulfilled as P had to assume control over the running of the business. Although O argued that he had lost trust in P, that alone could did not form the basis for a petition under the unfairly prejudicial conduct provision. To hold otherwise would be to confer on a minority shareholder a unilateral right to withdraw his capital. O's petition therefore failed. He did not prove that P's conduct was both unfair and prejudicial.

The effect of *Re Saul D Harrison* and *O'Neill* is that a petitioner under s 459 must establish a breach of the bargain between him, the other shareholders and the company;[113] or, at the minimum, a breach of some fundamental understanding which has the effect of estopping the majority from insisting upon exercising a strict legal right.

6 CONCLUSIONS

The essential core of Lord Hoffmann's reasoning in *O'Neill* seems to be based upon the objective of achieving 'legal certainty' by giving content to the concept of unfair prejudice.[114] Recognising the force of Lord Wilberforce's words that it would be impossible and, in any case, undesirable to define the circumstances when the application of equitable principles might make it unjust for a party to insist on exercising a legal right in a particular way, he added:[115]

> But that does not mean that there are no principles by which those circumstances may be identified. The way in which equitable principles operate is tolerably well settled and in my view it would be wrong to abandon them in favour of some wholly indefinite notion of fairness.[116]

The tenor of Lord Hoffmann's approach seen both here and in *Re Saul D Harrison*[117] that notions of fairness are founded upon settled principles referable to the commercial undertakings of the parties connects solidly with the idea that contract is the cohesive force underlying corporate relationships.[118] On this view, the role of the judiciary in s 459 proceedings is to distil what the terms of the petitioner's bargain are. 'Bargain' here is not limited to the constitutional contract which falls within the province of s 14, but encompasses informal agreements not incorporated into the articles of association. In *Re Saul D Harrison* Lord Hoffmann went to considerable lengths to stress that if the conduct

---

113 This may include a breach of the directors' fiduciary duties. See, for example, *Re London School of Electronics* [1986] Ch 211.

114 See [1999] 1 WLR 1092 at p 1099. The point is picked up by the DTI in the *The Final Report*, above n 9, at para 7.41, which emphasises the desirability of restricting the scope of s 459 actions 'in the interests of certainty'.

115 See [1973] AC 360 at p 380.

116 See [1999] 1 WLR 1092 at p 1099H. This was a decisive factor in the approach adopted by Jonathan Parker J in *Re Guidezone Ltd* [2000] 2 BCLC 321.

117 [1994] 1 BCLC 14. This approach is also discernible in some of his earlier judgments in the Chancery Division; see, for example, *Re Posgate & Denby (Agencies) Ltd* [1987] BCLC 8.

118 See further Sugarman 'Is Company Law Founded on Contract or Public Regulation' (1999) 20 *Company Lawyer* 162. See also Riley 'Contracting Out of Company Law: Section 459 of the Companies Act 1985 and the Role of the Courts' (1992) 55 MLR 782.

complained of is in accordance with the company's constitution it cannot, as a general rule, be viewed as unfair since 'there is no basis for a legitimate expectation that the board and the company ... will not exercise whatever powers they are given by the articles of association'.[119] Hoffmann LJ did, however, provide guidelines for determining unfairness. Reaffirming the sanctity of the statutory contract,[120] he stressed that fairness for the purposes of s 459 must be viewed in the context of a commercial relationship and that the articles of association are the contractual terms which govern the relationships of the shareholders with the company and each other:

> Since keeping promises and honouring agreements is probably the most important element of commercial fairness, the starting point in any case under s 459 will be to ask whether the conduct of which the shareholder complains was in accordance with the articles of association.[121]

To this he added two exceptions by virtue of which the court's jurisdiction under s 459 will be triggered. First, where the petitioner can demonstrate that a personal relationship exists with the controlling members of the company which has given rise to a legitimate expectation that a constitutional power will not be exercised. Secondly, where a power contained in the articles is exercised for an improper purpose. In these situations it will be just and equitable for the court to grant a remedy. Lord Hoffmann's analysis therefore aligns the notion of 'interests' as used in the section more closely with legal rights.[122] He returns to the point again in *O'Neill* in which he expresses the view that in determining whether the alleged conduct is unfairly prejudicial, a 'useful cross-check' is to 'ask whether [it] ... would be contrary to what the parties, by words or conduct, have actually agreed'.[123] However, although stopping short of confining the scope of unfairness to promises enforceable as a matter of law, he concluded that legitimate expectation 'should not be allowed to lead a life of its own, capable of giving rise to equitable restraints in circumstances to which the traditional equitable principles have no application'.[124]

From this reasoning, and the Company Law Review Steering Group's adoption of it as forming the proper basis for the future development of the remedy, two general observations can be made. First, the restrictive stance taken towards the scope of the unfair prejudice remedy arises from its alignment by Lord Hoffmann with Lord Wilberforce's determination of the circumstances when a petitioner will be entitled to a just and equitable winding-up order. It can be questioned whether this is necessarily the best way forward, given the fundamental differences between the nature of the two remedies. Secondly, it puts beyond doubt that even in the exercise of constitutional rights, the majority shareholders are subject to equitable limitations along the lines postulated by Foster J in *Clemens v Clemens Bros Ltd*.[125] The view expressed by Plowman J in *Bentley-*

---

119 *Re Saul D Harrison* [1995] 1 BCLC 14 at p 20.
120 See the Companies Act 1985, s 14.
121 [1995] 1 BCLC 14 at p 18.
122 Cf *Re Sam Weller & Sons Ltd* [1990] Ch 682.
123 [1999] 1 WLR 1092 at p 1101.
124 [1999] 1 WLR 1092 at p 1102.
125 [1976] 2 All ER 268. In so holding, Foster J cited *Re Westbourne Galleries* [1973] AC 360. See, further, R Hollington QC *Minority Shareholders' Rights* (London, Sweet & Maxwell, 3rd edn, 1999), at paras 2-007–2-012.

Stevens v Jones[126] to the effect that *Westbourne Galleries* should be confined to its statutory context, must now be doubted.

From the wider practical perspective, the decision in *O'Neill* can be viewed as underpinning, for the purposes of s 459, the Woolf objectives of constructing a system of civil litigation that is accessible, speedy and certain. It also serves to reinforce the guiding principles which the Law Commission and the DTI see as serving to underpin the development of the remedy.[127] In this respect, it is particularly noteworthy that the fourth principle, 'Sanctity of contract' states that:

> A member is taken to have agreed to the terms of the memorandum and articles of association when he becomes a member, whether or not he appreciated what they meant at the time. The law should continue to treat him as so bound unless he shows that the parties have come to some other agreement or understanding which is not reflected in the articles or memorandum. Failure to do so will create unacceptable commercial uncertainty. The corollary of this is that the best protection for a shareholder is appropriate protection in the articles of association.[128]

This dovetails neatly with the renewed focus taken by the courts towards determining the particulars of shareholder undertakings and understandings. From the policy perspective, the desirable goal here is that 'lawyers should be able to advise their clients whether or not a petition is likely to succeed'.[129] It remains to be seen whether this will be achieved. However, for the trial judge confronted with multifarious allegations of unfairly prejudicial conduct, the attraction of Lord Hoffmann's principled approach towards the delineation of the content of fairness is compelling.

---

126 [1974] 1 WLR 638.
127 See Law Commission Report *Shareholder Remedies*, above n 5, at para 1.9.
128 See Law Commission Report *Shareholder Remedies*, above n 5, at para 1.9.
129 [1999] 1 WLR 1092 at p 1099, *per* Lord Hoffmann.

CHAPTER 11

THE COMPANY LAW REVIEW AND MULTINATIONAL CORPORATE GROUPS

Peter Muchlinski

1 INTRODUCTION

This essay considers a specific question that has been highlighted in recent years by the growing concern over the operations of multinational enterprises (MNEs). How and to what extent should MNEs be subject to specialised regulation through laws and rules relating to their activities as cross-border corporate groups? In particular, should parent companies be directly responsible for the acts of their overseas subsidiaries by reason of specific rules of liability for those acts? Furthermore, should MNE groups be more accountable for their operations by reason of disclosure and governance systems that are adapted to the transnational nature of those operations? Such questions would appear to be exactly of the kind that a comprehensive review of company law should be addressing, if it is to be rooted in the realities of increased international economic integration encouraged by the transnational business practices of MNEs. In the event, and rather surprisingly, the Company Law Review Steering Group had little to say on these very important questions. Indeed, the issue of corporate groups was introduced only at a later stage in the Review process and consisted of a single chapter in the November 2000 Consultation Document *Modern Company Law for a Competitive Economy – Completing the Structure*.[1] In that chapter, there is little said by the Steering Group on the specific question of group liability for tortious acts of affiliates, let alone on the specific problems surrounding MNE accountability. More strikingly, *The Final Report* of the Steering Group, published on 26 July 2001, contains nothing on corporate groups. Neither the Foreword, nor the opening chapter on 'Guiding Principles, Methods and Output', offer any explanation for this omission.[2] In the meantime, litigation involving the liability of UK-based parent companies for the acts of their overseas subsidiaries has been instituted, and was until recently continuing, before the English courts, raising precisely the kinds of issues outlined above. The principal cases, which involved Cape plc and Thor Chemicals as defendants, arose out of the operations of the subsidiaries of these English-based parent companies in South Africa. In the *Cape* case, the litigation arose out of the exposure of large numbers of employees and local residents to asbestos mining and milling operations undertaken by the subsidiaries of Cape, with attendant consequences to the health of the claimants.[3] In the *Thor* case, the parent company was pursued for the exposure of employees in its South African subsidiaries to highly toxic chemical processes

---

1 (London, DTI, November 2000) at chapter 10; hereafter *Completing the Structure*.
2 See The Company Law Steering Group *Modern Company Law for a Competitive Economy: Final Report* (London, DTI, 2001) Vol 1; hereafter *The Final Report*.
3 See further Muchlinski 'Corporations in International Litigation: Problems of Jurisdiction and the United Kingdom Asbestos Case' (2001) 50 ICLQ 1.

that are in fact unlawful in the United Kingdom, but which were moved out of the English jurisdiction to South Africa.[4]

The question of holding MNEs to legal account for the consequences of their unlawful actions has been a recurring theme in litigation over the past two decades. MNEs, in common with all advanced enterprises, whether national or multinational, have the potential to harm very large numbers of people through the use of hazardous technologies. However, unlike national enterprises, MNEs apply such technologies in their worldwide operations. Where such a technology injures people in the overseas location in which it is used, this may lead to transnational mass tort litigation, as was the case in relation to the Bhopal accident in India in 1984. Indeed, the consequences of this litigation have yet to be finally resolved some 17 years on.[5]

It is the aim of this essay to analyse the principal legal and policy issues raised by such cases, as seen in the context of the business and industrial organisation of MNEs.[6] It is in the context of this analysis that the work of the Company Law Review Steering Group will be considered. Though, as already noted, the wider discussion of corporate governance and accountability in relation to groups was rather limited, the Steering Group did offer a view on the question of group liability in tort and also considered the question of accountability, in particular, by suggesting some new methods of group governance based on the concept of an 'elective' regime for groups. These matters will be examined more closely in the third section of the chapter, as will the likely reasons for the Steering Group's reticence on these important issues.

Before that is done, the essay will begin with an overview of the conceptual issue of MNE parent company liability for the tortious acts of its affiliates, with a view to the development of possible arguments concerning the existence of a duty of care on the part of parent companies of an MNE for the infliction of personal injuries upon claimants at the hands of their overseas subsidiaries. This demands an excursus into the literature on the organisation of MNEs. That literature is vast. Furthermore, there is no single definitive theory of the growth and operation of MNEs, whether in economics, business studies or economic and business history. However, certain general themes can be identified and these can be used to structure an argument for the existence of the abovementioned duty of care.

Attention will then turn to the issues raised by the recent United Kingdom litigation. Thus far judicial decisions have dealt with only one of the two principal issue areas around which MNE group liability is determined, namely, jurisdiction over the parent to answer for the acts of its overseas subsidiary in the host country where the alleged harm is suffered. The second question, that of the existence of a duty of care and of group liability for harm caused by overseas subsidiaries to overseas claimants, has yet to be decided, at least under English law. A decision on this issue of substance is unlikely in the

---

4   See Richard Meeran 'Liability of Multinational Corporations: A Critical Stage in the UK' in Menno Kamminga and Sam Zia-Zarifi (eds) *Liability of Multinational Corporations under International Law* (The Hague, Kluwer Law International, 2000) at p 251.

5   For regular updates on the current legal situation in the continuing Bhopal litigation see www.bhopal.net/legal.html.

6   See further PT Muchlinski *Multinational Enterprises and the Law* (Oxford, Blackwell, revised paperback edition, 1999) at chapters 3, 9 and 10. Note also Gobert 'Corporate Killing at Home and Abroad – Reflections on the Government's Proposals' (2002) 118 LQR 72.

near future. The Cape litigation, due to be heard on the merits in April 2002, has since been settled.[7] Indeed, such cases rarely come to a final decision on the merits as, once jurisdiction is accepted, the case will often go to settlement. This occurred in the Bhopal litigation and in Thor Chemicals. Accordingly there is a dearth of judicial pronouncement on this matter,[8] and much remains in the realm of speculation based on the existing state of the law, and on what that law should be. Thus, in the third part of this essay, the wider questions of MNE accountability will be examined in the light of the general question posed above and, as mentioned, in the light of the views of the Steering Group.

2 THE CONCEPTUAL FRAMEWORK: THE BUSINESS ORGANISATION OF MNEs

In order to determine whether a parent company should be liable for the tortious acts of its subsidiary, it is necessary to prove that, on the basis of the relationship between them, the parent can *justifiably* be held so liable. In legal terms that requires proof, either that the parent has acted as a joint tortfeasor with its subsidiary,[9] or that the subsidiary acted as the agent or *alter ego* of the parent when committing the alleged tort. In either case the evidential basis for such a finding will emerge from the actual business organisation of the MNE. Thus, in order to develop a clear theory of parent company responsibility, it is first necessary to understand something of that organisation.

A good starting point is to review certain common definitions of MNEs.[10] These have moved from a simple definition of MNEs as 'corporations ... which have their home in one country but which operate and live under the laws and customs of other countries as well'[11] to a more economic conception as any enterprise which 'owns (in whole or in part), controls and manages income generating assets in more than one country'.[12] This definition distinguishes an enterprise that engages in *direct investment*, that is investment

---

7 See 'Date set for South African miners' battle with UK firm' *The Observer* 27 May 2001 at p 6. Settlement was reached in January 2002, with Cape agreeing to a £21 million sum to be placed in a trust fund to be administered by two South African government officials and a Cape nominee. Each victim will receive up to £5,250. Though not a large sum, this was considered to be a realistic settlement given Cape's precarious financial position and the risks involved in bringing the case, which involves 'cutting edge' issues. The payment is to be made in two tranches of about £10 million. Claimants to the fund will forfeit their rights to bring a court action. For further details of the settlement and its surrounding circumstances see Richard Meeran 'Cape pays the price as justice prevails' *The Times* 15 January 2002, Law Section at p 5. See too 'Asbestos miners in battle for compensation' *Financial Times* 10 December 2001.

8 But see, for an exceptional decision finding the MNE parent liable for the acts of its overseas subsidiaries: *The Amoco Cadiz* [1984] 2 Lloyd's Rep 304; for a decision holding that the parent cannot be liable due to its separate corporate existence from the subsidiary see *Briggs v James Hardie & Co Pty* (1989) 16 NSWLR 549.

9 See, for example, *The Amoco Cadiz* [1984] 2 Lloyd's Rep 304.

10 See further Muchlinski, above n 6, at pp 12–15.

11 See the definition of David Lilienthal, quoted in DK Fieldhouse 'The Multinational: a Critique of a Concept' in A Teichova *et al* (eds) *Multinational Enterprise in Historical Perspective* (Cambridge, CUP, 1986) at p 10.

12 See N Hood and S Young *The Economics of the Multinational Enterprise* (London, Longmans, 1979) at p 3. See too JH Dunning *Multinational Enterprises and the Global Economy* (Wokingham, Addison-Wesley, 1993) at pp 3–4. Richard Caves Multinational *Enterprise and Economic Analysis* (Cambridge, CUP, 2nd edn 1996) at p 1.

which gives the enterprise not only a financial stake in the foreign venture but also managerial control, from one that engages in *portfolio investment*, which gives the investing enterprise only a financial stake in the foreign venture without any managerial control. Thus the MNE is a firm that engages in *direct investment outside its home country*. The term 'enterprise' is favoured over 'corporation' as it avoids restricting the object of study to incorporated business entities and to corporate groups based on parent/subsidiary relations alone. International production can take numerous legal forms. From an economic perspective the legal form is not crucial to the classification of an enterprise as 'multinational'.[13]

The most recent general definition of MNEs can be found in the *OECD Guidelines for Multinational Enterprises*, revised in June 2000. According to this definition such enterprises:

> ... usually comprise companies or other entities established in more than one country and so linked that they may co-ordinate their operations in various ways. While one or more of these entities may be able to exercise a significant influence over the activities of others, their degree of autonomy within the enterprise may vary widely from one multinational enterprise to another. Ownership may be private, state or mixed.[14]

The crucial characteristic of an MNE is, according to this definition, the ability to co-ordinate activities between enterprises in more than one country. Other factors are not decisive. The definition is, therefore, broad enough to encompass both equity and non-equity-based direct investment, regardless of the legal form, or ownership structure, of the undertakings. It also reflects the more recent trend in academic literature to move away from a simple, classical model of the MNE as a hierarchical 'pyramid' with the parent as the directing 'brain' of the company and the subsidiaries as its subordinate organs, and with emphasis on line management though divisionalised corporate structures, towards a more flexible organisational form where subsidiaries are given more initiative over major decisions and to which significant strategic functions may be devolved.[15] In addition, these more recent models stress the trend in more modern industries, that are not so dependent on economies of scale in manufacturing, to develop

---

13 See Muchlinski, above n 6, at p 12.

14 *OECD Guidelines For Multinational Enterprises* 27 June 2000 I 'Concepts and Principles' at para 3 available at www.oecd.org/daf/investment/guidelines/mnetext.htm at p 3. For the old version of this paragraph see *OECD Guidelines 1991 Review* (Paris, OECD, 1992) at p 104; also reproduced in *The OECD Guidelines for Multinational Enterprises* (Paris, OECD, 1994, 1997) and Muchlinski, above n 6, at p 13. The old version of this definition, which stressed control even more strongly by way of reference to the ability of one company to control the activities of another company located in another country, had been substantially adopted in the final version of the proposed text of the now shelved United Nations Draft Code of Conduct on Transnational Enterprises: See UN Doc E/1990/94 12 June 1990 para 1 at p 5.

15 For a general overview of the early and more recent thinking on MNE business organisation see: Muchlinski, above n 6, at pp 57–61; Dunning *Multinational Enterprises and the Global Economy*, above n 12, at chapters 8 and 9; Caves, above n 12 at chapter 3. As an example of the early approach see further D Channon and M Jalland: *Multinational Strategic Planning* (London, MacMillan Press, 1979) at chapter 2. A leading statement of the more recent 'heterarchical' approach is C Bartlett and S Ghoshal *Managing Across Borders: The Transnational Solution* (London, Random House Business Books, 2nd edn, 1998) Part I. Also useful is Hedlund 'The Hypermodern MNC: a Heterarchy?' (1986) 25 *Human Resource Management* at pp 9–36, which some see as the first paper to use this term. Julian Birkinshaw stresses a new 'Internal Market' perspective on MNE management in his new work *Entrepreneurship in the Global Firm* (London, Sage Publications, 2000) especially at chapters 1 and 8.

more open 'heterarchical' management structures and more readily to establish strategic alliances with other firms as and where necessary.

This trend towards more open types of business organisation has given rise to two further developments in thinking on the business organisation of MNEs. First, the earlier theories of MNE growth have tended to explain the growth of the hierarchically integrated MNE.[16] They emphasise the ownership of specific competitive advantages by firms, the locational advantages of investment destinations and the 'internalisation' of markets into the corporate group of the MNE on the basis of the lower transaction costs that such a strategy offers.[17] Such theories are being modified so that they can be made more useful in explaining the emergence of co-operative relationships between firms. Thus, for example, according to Professor Dunning, strategic alliances arise so that the competitive advantages of the participating firms can be combined through the new co-operative form of the enterprise, which then behaves much like a single integrated business, taking advantage of its collectively internalised advantages in global markets.[18] Secondly, both among economists and business management experts, there is now a shift in emphasis away from theories of why MNEs develop in the first place, and how they tackle the problems of managing an evolving multinational business, to questions of how already established MNEs further develop and manage their operations.[19]

How is this knowledge to be used when constructing arguments for and against the creation of duties of care incumbent on parent companies for the acts if their subsidiaries? From the perspective of the United Kingdom litigation in *Cape*, the business organisation of this firm at the time relevant for the contested claims would have been that of a hierarchical parent-subsidiary group, typical of early MNEs operating in high-risk, capital intensive extraction industries where economies of scale are important.[20] *Cape* thus appears to fit into the theoretical model of the closely controlled, managerially centralised, MNE. On the other hand, the defendants have maintained that their operations were devolved to their South African affiliates in 1948. Thus, they may wish to argue that their corporate structure fitted more into the 'heterarchical' model of more

---

16 General overviews of the various early theories of MNE growth can be found in: Muchlinski, above n 6 at chapters 2 and 3; Dunning, above n 12, at chapters 3 and 4; Hood and Young, above n 12, at chapters 1 and 2; Caves, above n 12, at chapters 1–3. For a very useful discussion of the major trends in economic theory concerning the growth of MNEs that is accessible to non-economists see: C Pitelis and R Sugden *The Nature of the Transnational Firm* (London, Routledge, 1991) especially John Cantwell: 'A Survey of Theories of International Production' at p 17. Also useful is Geoffrey Jones *The Evolution of International Business* (London, Routledge, 1996) at chapter 1.

17 These approaches have been brought together into the so called 'eclectic paradigm' of MNE growth by Professor John Dunning. The 'eclectic paradigm' is explained by Professor Dunning in his textbook above at n 12. For further readings see: J Dunning *International Production and the Multinational Enterprise* (London, Allen and Unwin, 1981) at chapters 1 and 2; J Dunning *Explaining International Production* (London, Unwin Hyman, 1988) especially at Introduction and chapters 2 and 12.

18 Professor Dunning has adapted the 'eclectic paradigm' in relation to strategic alliances in *Alliance Capitalism and Global Business* (London, Routledge, 1997) of which chapter 3 provides a useful summary.

19 Thus Mark Casson emphasises the need for a new research agenda that looks at the flexibility of MNEs in relation to global economic stimuli in chapter 1 of his edited book *Economics of International Business: A New Research Agenda* (Cheltenham, Edward Elgar, 2000). See too Birkinshaw, above n 15, at chapter 7.

20 See further Jones, above n 16, at chapter 3. The corporate organisation of Union Carbide Corporation in the *Bhopal* case displayed similar characteristics. See further Muchlinski 'The *Bhopal* Case: Controlling Ultrahazardous Industrial Activities Undertaken by Foreign Investors' (1987) 50 MLR 545.

recent literature, with considerable autonomy being granted to local managers.[21] Although such an argument may not be historically accurate, it may impress a court.

Against this background, caution needs to be exercised on how contemporary ideas on the business organisation of MNEs should be used when constructing legal duties of care. First, much of the more recent literature on open and flexible forms of corporate organisation relates primarily to newer high-technology industries such as information technology or advanced product manufacture. It does not relate to older forms of MNE organisation, which might still appear before the court. Thus, when reviewing evidence of the business organisation of the defendant MNE, sweeping generalisations, based on a literal reading of the academic literature, about the 'general' organisation of MNEs should be avoided. At most such literature can offer models of business organisation against which the defendant enterprise's actual organisation may be compared. Secondly, none of the more recent literature predicts the imminent end of the hierarchical multinational corporate group, just that this form of enterprise has a specific application to specific industries.[22] Thirdly, even if it can be shown that the defendant MNE operates a devolved management system, or is part of a wider alliance of co-operating companies, this does not, of itself, deny the existence of a duty of care on the part of the MNE parent towards employees of its subsidiaries (or of co-operating firms in an alliance), or to members of the local community in the host country adversely affected by the operations of the enterprise. A direct duty of care may exist on the part of the parent (or the controlling enterprise(s) in an alliance) on the basis of general principles of tort, regardless of the precise business organisation of the enterprise, where, as a matter of policy, it is thought important for the duty to exist. Equally, liability for certain ultrahazardous activities may be strict and the need for proving the existence of a duty of care may be unnecessary.[23]

Thus it is not possible to offer wide and absolute concepts of MNE organisation. On the other hand, the law may develop through the use of presumptions as to the nature of corporate organisation, which may be rebutted on the provision of evidence to the contrary. For example, it may be presumed that a parent company which owns 100% of the stock in its subsidiary controls that subsidiary and may therefore be further presumed to direct its activities unless there is evidence to the contrary. Equally, the law could presume strict liability on the part of the parent for the acts of its subsidiary unless it can be shown that the chain of causation has been broken in some way. Such approaches are not unproblematic. In particular, they challenge the advantage of limited liability implicit in the corporate separation between parent and subsidiary.[24] However, as will be shown below, when the existence of a duty of care is considered further, such an argument may, in fact, misapprehend the true meaning, and legitimate boundaries of, limited liability in a group enterprise context.

---

21 See further Birkinshaw, above n 15.
22 See: Birkinshaw, above n 15; and Muchlinski, above n 6, at p 60.
23 As in the Indian doctrine of absolute enterprise liability for ultrahazardous activities; see Muchlinski, above n 20.
24 See further Muchlinski, above n 6, at pp 331–32.

3 THE CONTEXT: THE *CAPE* AND *THOR CHEMICALS* LITIGATION

Two main issues arise in relation to litigation involving alleged breaches of a duty of care on the part of a parent company for the acts of its overseas subsidiaries: first, does the forum before which the case has been brought have jurisdiction to hear the case, and, secondly, is the parent company liable for the alleged breach of the duty of care? As noted in the introduction, the current English litigation has been concerned mainly with the first question, while the second question awaits a judicial pronouncement in future litigation. Each issue will now be considered in turn.

3.1 Jurisdiction[25]

The first issue to be dealt with in all the recent cases involving English-based parent companies has been that of jurisdiction: were the English courts the proper place for the litigation on the merits of the case to be heard? In all of these cases jurisdiction before the English courts was available 'as of right' because all the defendant companies are domiciled in England.[26] In the *Thor Chemicals* litigation, jurisdiction was accepted by the English courts prior to the settlement of the case for £1.3 million in 1997.[27] However, in the *Cape* litigation, the matter proved to be more problematic. Cape argued that, as South Africa was the place where the alleged harm had occurred, it was the correct forum for the case to be heard. Thus, the main issue was whether England or South Africa was the more appropriate forum under the doctrine in the *Spiliada* case.[28] The '*Spiliada* Doctrine' has two limbs: First, taking account of all the circumstances and, especially, the nature of the subject matter and the convenience of the parties, which forum is the more appropriate for the action to be heard? Secondly, notwithstanding that a forum other than the English forum may be the more appropriate, will substantive justice be achieved by the hearing of the case in that other forum?

Different courts involved in these claims arrived at different conclusions. In the first set of claims, that were brought in 1997 by Rachel Lubbe and five others, South Africa was held to be the proper forum at first instance, though this was overturned on appeal to the Court of Appeal.[29] Then in January 1999, Hendrik Afrika and 1,538 others commenced their claims. In July 1999 Buckley J reopened the jurisdiction issues in *Lubbe et al* while hearing the Afrika class action cases. He found for a South African forum.[30] In November 1999 a second Court of Appeal upheld Buckley J on the South African forum and on his approval of US public interest criteria in US case law on forum issues.[31] On 20 July 2000 the House of Lords overturned the second Court of Appeal decision and upheld the first Court of Appeal decision under the second limb of the *Spiliada* Doctrine:

---

25 For a more detailed and extensive discussion of this issue see Muchlinski, above n 3.

26 That is: *Cape, Thor Chemicals* and *Rio Tinto Zinc*. See also *Connelly v RTZ plc* [1998] AC 854, which has had a significant bearing on the *Cape* litigation.

27 See *Ngcobo et al v Thor Chemicals Holdings* [1995] TLR 579. A further 21 claims are now in progress against Thor. Again jurisdiction was accepted; see *Sithole et al v Thor Chemicals Holdings* [1999] TLR 110.

28 See *Spiliada Maritime Corporation v Cansulex Ltd* [1987] AC 460.

29 See *Lubbe v Cape plc* [1999] International Litigation Procedure 113 (CA).

30 See [2000] 1 Lloyd's Rep 139 at p 141 (QBD).

31 See [2000] 1 Lloyd's Rep 139 (CA).

substantial justice could not be done in South Africa, even though there were factors that could point to the South African forum.[32]

In arriving at its decision the House of Lords was asked to consider three sets of questions: first, what was the scope of the *Spiliada* Doctrine in the context of MNE operations; secondly, should the Brussels Convention on Civil Jurisdiction and Judgments,[33] with its emphasis on the principle of jurisdiction over corporations based on domicile, be mandatory in all cases, including cases brought by claimants from on-convention countries, as in the present case; and, thirdly, should the English courts take into account public policy considerations when determining whether jurisdiction should be exercised over English-based parent companies for the alleged torts committed by their subsidiaries in another country.

As to the first question, the House of Lords did not go so far as to accept enterprise analysis under the first limb of *Spiliada*, and conclude that, as an integrated MNE, Cape plc was a proper party to the proceedings as a result of its actual or potential control over the health and safety activities of its overseas subsidiaries. Instead, the House of Lords came to its conclusion by relying on the second limb of *Spiliada* and finding that, in the light of the evidence submitted by the claimants, and by the Government of South Africa in its special submission to the House of Lords, the claimants' case was very unlikely ever to be heard in South Africa due to, in particular, the absence of legal aid and of lawyers expert enough and willing to take on such a complex mass tort action. That would, in effect, take away the claimants' right to a hearing. In this their Lordships were following the approach taken in the earlier case of *Connelly v RTZ plc*[34] where the absence of legal aid in the foreign forum (Namibia) was held to have been a significant factor pointing to the conclusion that substantial justice could not have been achieved there, notwithstanding that the foreign forum may have been more appropriate on the basis of the first limb test. Therefore, it would appear that the House of Lords is developing a 'due process' approach to the second limb of the *Spiliada* Doctrine. As to the second question, the House of Lords did not feel it necessary to deal with this point, in view of its finding under the *Spiliada* Doctrine. As to the third question, the House of Lords expressly rejected the US approach, evident in cases such as *Bhopal*, of weighing the public interests of the home and foreign forums in conducting the litigation.

3.2   The existence of a duty of care

As noted in the introduction to this essay, none of the recent English cases involving MNE parent companies has yet determined the substantive question of liability for the acts of their overseas subsidiaries. Until it settled, the *Cape* litigation would have been the first

---

32 See [2000] 1 WLR 1545 (HL).
33 See now Council Regulation (EC) 44/2001 of 22 December 2000 on Jurisdiction and the Recognition and Enforcement of Judgments in Civil and Commercial Matters [2001] OJ L 12/1. The Regulation supersedes the Convention for Member States. It entered into force on 1 March 2002.
34 [1998] AC 854.

instance of this question to reach an English court for decision. It follows that the question of MNE group liability remains an open and speculative one.[35]

In Part I of this essay it was argued that a presumption of parent company liability for the acts of its owned and controlled overseas subsidiaries could be established in principle, subject to rebuttal by evidence negating control. It was further said that the main objection to this presumption is that it effectively undermines the vital principle of limited liability. In reply, it is arguable that too much is made of the need for limited liability between parent and subsidiary when they form part of an integrated economic entity. As has been pointed out by Professor Philip Blumberg, in his seminal work *The Multinational Challenge to Corporation Law*:[36]

> Under entity law and limited liability, each higher-tier company of the multitiered corporate group is insulated from liability for the unsatisfied debts of the lower-tier companies of which it is a shareholder. In the multitiered group, there are, thus, as many layers of limited liability as there are tiers in corporate structure. Limited liability for corporate groups thus opens the door to multiple layers of insulation, a consequence unforeseen when limited liability was adopted long before the emergence of corporate groups.[37]

When applied to involuntary creditors of the group, such as the victims of an alleged tort committed by the enterprise in the course of its operations, this extension of limited liability does little more than shift the risk of liability onto them and away from the group. Can this be a justifiable result when the victims are uninsured, as was the case with the *Cape* claimants? Even where the claimants are insured, can such a transfer of risk from corporation to involuntary creditor be justifiable, given the risk of moral hazard implicit in such a policy? In relation to the *Cape* case, it is not immediately obvious why the cost of dealing with asbestos-related injuries should be borne by the local subsidiary alone, especially where it does not have the assets from which to compensate the claimants, given that Cape closed down its asbestos operations in South Africa in 1979. On the other hand Cape has enjoyed the profit stream from those overseas investments, and it would seem proper to make those proceeds available to compensate involuntary creditors where they can show that the parent controlled the operations in South Africa, and so could be held responsible for them. In any case direct liability might be possible on the ground that as Cape was aware of the dangers of asbestos mining and milling, given the state of knowledge at the time these activities were being carried on, and so any failure on its part to follow established safe practices, and, in particular, to require its South African subsidiaries to do so, would amount to a breach of a duty of care by omission.[38]

Therefore, the issues relating to the existence of a duty of care and of its breach could be kept separate from the wider issue relating to the extent to which the parent company could benefit from the principle of limited liability as a means of insulating itself against tort claims arising out of the actions of its subsidiaries. However, that is a position entirely

---

35 On which see further M Kamminga and S Zia-Zarifi (eds), above n 4 at Part III on US, English and Dutch approaches to such litigation. See too *The Amoco Cadiz* [1984] 2 Lloyd's Rep 304.
36 Philip I Blumberg *The Multinational Challenge to Corporation Law* (Oxford, OUP, 1993).
37 See Blumberg, above n 36, at p 139.
38 See further *Lubbe et al v Cape plc* House of Lords Claimants Final Served Case Papers at pp 43–50.

dependent on the particular facts of the case, and on whether there is sufficient proof of parental complicity in the alleged tort. It does not remove the broader question of whether the economic entity of the group as a whole should act as a source of funds for the compensation of involuntary creditors, and of whether there should be such a thing as 'multinational enterprise liability' based on the integrated nature of the transnational system of economic activities carried on by the MNE.[39] This matter will now be considered further in the light of the views of the Company Law Review Steering Group.

4 THE COMPANY LAW STEERING GROUP AND GROUPS OF COMPANIES

The Steering Group's treatment of corporate group matters will be analysed under three sub-headings. First, the Group's views on corporate group liability in tort will be considered, followed by an assessment of the wider governance proposals for groups in the light of their likely impact on the risk of negligent action being taken by the company and its officers. Thirdly, the possible reasons behind the silence of *The Final Report* on group issues will be discussed.

4.1 Group liability in tort

The Steering Group accepts that the arguments for permitting parent companies to take advantage of limited liability in relation to tort liability are less strong than in the case of liability to creditors, given that the latter can exact a price for the credit to reflect the risk, while in cases of tort liability the parent can externalise the risk without the need to compensate. Furthermore, it is recognised that torts may protect very important interests such as freedom from wrongful personal injury.[40] However, the Steering Group also notes that the British courts are unwilling to 'lift the corporate veil' in such cases, citing the case of *Adams v Cape Industries* in support.[41] The Steering Group continues:

> However, there are circumstances in which we regard it as entirely proper for a holding company to segregate an activity in a subsidiary with the risks of liability, including tortious or delictual liability, in mind. Many torts are closely linked with contractual liabilities, for example liability for professional services and misrepresentation and product liability. We are also not aware of any jurisdiction providing for parent companies to be automatically liable for the torts or delicts of their subsidiaries. Defining the circumstances in which the use of limited liability in this way should be regarded as abusive would be difficult. Nor are we aware of cases where parent companies have engaged in such abuse. The undercapitalisation of subsidiaries, and their operation in a way which creates undue risks of insolvency, are matters best dealt with by insolvency law. We do not propose any reforms in this regard.[42]

---

39 See, for example, *The Amoco Cadiz* [1984] 2 Lloyd's Rep 304 at p 338 paras 43–46. See further Muchlinski, above n 6, at pp 328–33. See too Halina Ward 'Governing Multinationals: The Role of Foreign Direct Liability' Royal Institute of International Affairs *Briefing Paper* New Series No 18, February 2001.

40 See *Completing the Structure*, above n 1, at para.10.58.

41 [1990] Ch 433.

42 See *Completing the Structure*, above n 1, at para 10.59.

That is all the Steering Group says. There are many shortcomings in this approach. First, reliance on the hesitation of judges to 'lift the corporate veil' seems overcautious for a law reform committee. A review of the validity, in policy terms, of the approach taken in *Adams v Cape Industries*[43] would be entirely proper for such a body.

The main issue in the *Adams* case was whether a US personal injuries court award that used quantification techniques regarded as contrary to principles of justice in England should be recognised here. By emphasising the legal separation between Cape and its US sales subsidiary, and the independently owned associated sales company that replaced it, such recognition could be avoided on the ground that the English-based parent company was not present in the US through its subsidiary, or through the independent sales company with which it had business links. It is likely that the refusal by the Court of Appeal to 'lift the corporate veil', or to see the apparently independent sales company that replaced the sales subsidiary in the US as *de facto* controlled by Cape, was motivated by a desire to prevent recognition of an award that was tainted in the eyes of English principles of justice. If so, then the case turned on issues of private international law, to which the corporate separation between Cape, its overseas subsidiary and subsequent associate company was a convenient justification for non-recognition. As such, the case did not turn on the issue of substantive liability in tort, where, given the seriousness of the risk that Cape could externalise its liability in negligence through the interposition of a separate corporate entity, the very question of whether the corporate veil should be lifted is central. Yet, at the hands of the Steering Group, *Adams v Cape Industries* has grown into a device for the avoidance of a full discussion as to whether that case went too far in protecting the legal separation between parent and subsidiary, and, indeed, in accepting an apparently deliberate interposition of a seemingly independent company between the English parent and its US customer for asbestos, this having been done in anticipation of the claims that Cape Industries was going to face there from employees of the customer, who alleged that they had been injured by the asbestos.

Secondly, the Steering Group conflates torts committed in breach of contract with other types of tort. Clearly, this fails to appreciate some very fundamental distinctions between different types of torts. While the trend in commercial law has been to control the rise of tort liability by means of contractual provisions so as to return to the contracting parties a degree of control over their allocation of risks on the transaction, this cannot be taken to represent good policy across all types of torts. In particular, not all contractual regimes are appropriately seen as the outcome of an equal bargain. In such cases, the law accepts that some protection is needed for the weaker party. Thus, the specific mention of product liability cases seems rather puzzling. The deliberate use of a subsidiary to insulate the parent against liability for a negligently manufactured product would appear to be a good case for considering the lifting of the veil and making the parent responsible, at least so far as private consumer claimants are concerned. The case of commercial consumers may be different on the grounds of more equal bargaining power, which should lead such consumers to require guarantees from the parent or to accept their own risk in purchasing the goods, though even here complex questions as to the distribution of knowledge of risks may require some protection for the business consumer. Equally, in the case of employment contracts, the reasoning implicit in the

43   [1990] Ch 433.

opinion of the Steering Group would be inapplicable given the demise of doctrines such as those of 'common employment' or of voluntary assumption of risk by employees.

Furthermore, when liability for hazardous industrial processes is in question, as in the *Cape* and *Thor Chemicals* cases, the potential seriousness of the foreseeable harm caused by the negligent operation of industrial processes on the part of subsidiaries to employees and third parties goes beyond contract. Here the public policy of the law will dictate the nature and extent of the duty of care. It is here that the interposition of separate corporate entities may be used in an excessive or abusive manner. However, instead of examining this question the Steering Group shies away from it on a number of indefensible grounds. First, it says that no other jurisdiction has accepted automatic parent liability for the torts of its subsidiary, ignoring the development, in India, of a concept of absolute enterprise liability for injury caused by the conduct of ultrahazardous industrial processes.[44] While this doctrine may not be the answer to the problems under discussion, it nonetheless warrants an examination. Furthermore, the Steering Group's assertion appears to equate the absence of a particular rule of law in any other legal system with the desirability of that situation. That flies in the face of the way in which company law has grown, as a response to problems perceived at any particular time with the governance and operations of companies.[45] Perhaps it is only now that the problem of the abuse of the corporate legal form by groups to insulate against the legitimate application of tort liability is coming to be seen as a problem. Perhaps, too, no legal system has tried to take a lead, given the fear of undermining the competitive position of its economy if it is seen as creating increased operating risks for groups subject to its laws. That, however, is an argument for a co-ordinated international policy on group liability in tort in hazardous industries, on which the Steering Group could have taken a lead.

Secondly, the Steering Group says that defining the circumstances where the abuse of limited liability occurs would be difficult. If difficulty were a bar to legal reform then very little of it would ever occur! In any case, is it so difficult to see that it is morally repugnant for a large, profitable, corporate group to hide behind the legal fiction of corporate separation in order to externalise risks onto involuntary creditors, who may not be able to bear those risks, especially in poorer communities and/or in developing countries? Perhaps it is, if one's focus is too much on making company law as cost-free as possible for corporations to improve their 'competitiveness'. Thirdly, the Steering Group asserts that it is unaware of cases where parent companies have engaged in such abuse. Three points can be made in response: first, if the Steering Group is referring to the lack of any judicial findings of such abuse then it has been made clear above why this is so – cases mostly settle out of court; secondly, at the very least, the Steering Group could have expressly considered such evidence of abuse as might be available from claimants, their lawyers and pressure groups engaged in this field; thirdly, an abuse remains an abuse even if it is, thankfully, a rare event, a fact that is not to be doubted in relation to the vast majority of responsible corporate groups.

---

44 See *Mehta v Union of India* AIR 1987 SC 965 at p 1,086 and see, for a discussion of the problems associated with this doctrine, Muchlinski, above n 6, at pp 326–28.

45 See DTI *Modern Company Law for a Competitive Economy* (London, DTI, March 1998) at para 2.5; hereafter *Competitive Economy*.

4.2 Governance of groups and risk reduction

In the light of the foregoing discussion it should be remembered that litigation ought to be the last resort as a means of ensuring that MNE groups comply with standards and duties of care in relation to their hazardous operations. A better approach is to provide corporate governance structures that help reduce the risk of negligent corporate behaviour from arising in the first place.

In this regard the Steering Group offers a suggestion for reform of the parent/subsidiary relationship by means of an 'elective' regime for groups.[46] The suggestion is that, 'in exchange for a guarantee by the parent company of the liabilities of a subsidiary and satisfaction of certain publicity requirements, the subsidiary shall be exempted from the requirements under the [Companies] Act relating to annual accounts and audit'.[47] The Steering Group saw no merit in a more integrated regime for corporate groups as this would detract from flexibility in the way businesses organised themselves and would strike at the limited liability basis for company law.[48] To be a member of an 'elective' group an 'elective subsidiary' must be wholly owned and exclusively controlled by the elective parent. The administering group should be free to decide which wholly owned subsidiaries make the election. Third parties must be informed of the election by means of clear information.

The elective parent's guarantee applies to all the liabilities of the elective subsidiary, including liabilities in tort or delict,[49] but there is no reciprocal guarantee of the parent's liabilities by the subsidiary. The guarantee is a 'simple bilateral guarantee' making the assets of the elective parent and subsidiary available to settle liabilities. The Steering Group rejected a 'pooling' of liability across the group as a whole. Such a wider pooling of assets would, in the Steering Group's opinion, raise some significant difficulties for overseas parents in particular, in that an elective parent located in another EU Member State might have to be sued there by a creditor, subject to the rules of the Brussels Convention.[50]

The Steering group's proposal is significant in that for the first time consideration is being given to the question whether English law should have a specialised regime for group liabilities, though the proposal expressly falls short of the types of regime found in the German Stock Corporations Act of 1965 or the now shelved draft Ninth Directive on Company Law of the EU. However, the proposal appears to offer little that might help to avoid the kind of mass tort litigation seen in *Cape* or *Thor Chemicals*. Though an express election by the parent to guarantee the liabilities of its subsidiary is a means of avoiding the use of corporate separation as a defence to direct claims against the parent, the proposal fails to address other very important matters. First, there is no compulsion on the parent to make an election. Thus, it would be perfectly legitimate to leave out subsidiaries undertaking high-risk operations, where full limited liability would continue.

---

46 See *Completing the Structure*, above n 1, at paras 10.19–10.57.
47 See *Completing the Structure*, above n 1, at paras 10.19–10.57.
48 See *Completing the Structure*, above n 1, at para 10.20.
49 See *Completing the Structure*, above n 1, at para 10.28.
50 See *Completing the Structure*, above n 1, at paras 10.34–10.36. The 'elective' regime would only be available to EU-based parent companies on the basis of the non-discrimination rule in EU law, but not to parents based outside the EU; see at para 10.37.

Secondly, the proposal is silent on whether election could extend to any subsidiary, including an overseas subsidiary of an English-based parent company. It may be presumed that it extends to UK-based subsidiaries only as otherwise the proposal will have an extraterritorial dimension that would be inconsistent with earlier case law.[51] On the other hand, as the House of Lords decision in *Lubbe v Cape plc*[52] shows, an English-based parent can be taken to court to determine whether it is liable for the acts of its overseas subsidiaries. If the elective regime were to be unavailable in such cases, a difference would arise in the legal regime applicable to English domestic groups and English-based multinational groups. The former would be subject to greater potential liabilities than the latter should they choose to confer elective status on their English-based subsidiaries as compared to the liabilities faced by English-based parents for their overseas subsidiaries upon whom such an election could not be made. Why such a difference of treatment between domestic and overseas subsidiaries might arise is not explained by the Steering Group. Indeed, the proposal as a whole is remarkable for the absence of any serious consideration of the jurisdictional matters it raises, save for the point that the elective regime would apply only to other EU-based parent companies, but not to groups whose parent company was from outside the EU.[53]

Thirdly, the rejection of a 'pooling' approach to the delineation of the 'capital boundary'[54] of assets available to claimants ignores a basic problem in mass tort litigation: where the economic activity of the group as a whole is involved in the hazardous processes that lead to the harm causing the claims, then the entire asset base of the group should be available on the ground that the group as a whole is involved in the harm. Furthermore, as in the Bhopal litigation, the sheer number of claimants may be so great that the assets of the entire group may be needed to meet their claims. Moreover, as in *Cape*, the subsidiaries that are alleged to have caused the claimants' injuries may no longer be in operation but the assets of the group, which have been enhanced by the operation in the past of those subsidiaries, still exist.

Fourthly, even where the parent does elect to cover the liabilities of its subsidiary, this means very little if it is not asset rich. It would be relatively easy to insulate the parent from liability by removing its assets offshore, rather as in the *Multinational Gas* case[55] where the assets of the joint venture company in question were located in Liberia, while the main business operations occurred in England through a services-only company. In the absence of clear minimum asset requirements on the part of the elective parent and subsidiary the election would be meaningless. Furthermore, as pointed out by respondents to the proposal, unless the guarantee is contained in a standardised statutory form, it could be rendered ineffective given that guarantees offered by a parent on behalf of its subsidiary are notoriously difficult to enforce unless they are very clearly worded.[56]

---

51 See: *Adams v Cape Industries* [1990] Ch 433; *Multinational Gas and Petrochemical Services Co v Multinational Gas and Petrochemical Services Ltd* [1983] Ch 258 (CA).

52 [2000] 1 WLR 1545.

53 See *Completing the Structure*, above n 1, at para 10.37.

54 On which see further Collins 'Ascription of Legal Responsibility to Groups in Complex Patterns of Economic Integration' (1990) 53 MLR 731.

55 [1983] Ch 258.

56 See *Company Law Review: Responses to the Consultation Document Completing the Structure* at chapter 10 question 10.1; hereafter *Responses*. See too: *Re Augustus Barnett* [1986] BCLC 170; *Kleinwort Benson Ltd v Malaysia Mining Corporation* [1989] 1 WLR 379; *Amalgamated Investment and Property Co Ltd (In Liq) v Texas Commerce International Bank Ltd* [1982] QB 84.

Thus the capacity of the 'elective group' concept to deal with the issues underlying mass tort litigation in England against English-based parent companies is limited. However, there is one further aspect of the Steering Group's proposal that needs to be mentioned. Elective group membership does not obviate the need, on the part of an elective subsidiary, to comply with the proposed new operating and financial review (OFR).[57] According to the Steering Group the OFR is a pillar of the new approach to corporate governance, alongside the proposed statement of directors' duties which includes not only a duty to take account of shareholder interests but also those of others.[58] The OFR is to be published by all public and very large private companies (defined as having an annual turnover of more than £500 million) as part of the Annual Report. It is to give an account by the directors of:

> ... the performance and direction of the business, including in all cases a fair review of achievements, trends and strategic direction, and covering other matters, including wider relationships, risks and opportunities and social and environmental impacts where these are relevant to an understanding of the performance of the business.[59]

The aim of the OFR is to 'account for and demonstrate stewardship of a wide range of relationships and resources which are of vital significance to the success of modern business, but often do not register effectively, or at all, in financial accounts'.[60] The question arises, how far can the OFR be used as a vehicle for ensuring more responsible corporate practice, especially in relation to the operation of overseas subsidiaries in areas prone to the creation of risks of personal injury such as health and safety, employment and environmental practices? In principle the OFR should provide a more transparent and accountable approach to these matters. However, the directors retain considerable discretion in relation to how they report the wider issues of corporate performance. The Steering Group has recognised that this discretion must be exercised in good faith on the basis of a test as to the materiality of the information to be disclosed.[61] Equally it accepts that certain matters will need more detailed and mandatory treatment. Thus, the Steering Group recommends that requirements on disclosure of risk should be made a matter for mandatory disclosure standards under the aegis of the proposed new Companies Commission.[62] This offers some scope for clear requirements as to the disclosure of high-risk practices. In the process it might be possible to hold parent company directors to account on how those risks are being dealt with as, for example, through the health and safety practices of overseas subsidiaries.

4.3   Why are these ideas not developed in *The Final Report*?

As noted in the introduction to this chapter, *The Final Report* does not contain any further development of the above ideas. This can be explained by reference to two main factors: first the whole philosophy underlying the Review was unlikely to lead to a

---

57 See *Completing the Structure*, above n 1, at para 10.42.
58 See *Completing the Structure*, above n 1, at para 3.2. See further *The Final Report*, above n 2, at chapter 8.
59 See *Completing the Structure*, above n 1, at para 3.2. See further *The Final Report*, above n 2, at chapter 8.
60 See *Completing the Structure*, above n 1, at para 3.4.
61 See *Completing the Structure*, above n 1, at para 3.7.
62 See *Completing the Structure*, above n 1, at para 3.35.

comprehensive reconsideration of group liability, and, secondly, the 'elective' regime for groups is a weak idea that is unlikely to offer any significant overall benefit to the development of modern company law. Each of these two matters will now be considered in more detail.

(1) The philosophy of the Review and group liability

The Company Law Review was initiated in 1998 with the aim of creating 'a more effective, including cost-effective, framework of law for companies to improve their competitiveness and so contribute to national growth and prosperity'.[63] In addition, the new framework had to compare favourably with the company law frameworks of other developed economies and avoid any disincentives to inward investment into the UK by foreign firms caused by the obsolescence of parts of the existing law.[64] As part of this review, the question was raised whether the rights and duties of companies and their directors should extend to a wider range of 'stakeholders' going beyond shareholders and encompassing employees, creditors and other participants. However, this issue would be bounded by a presumption against interventionist legislation, and in favour of facilitating markets, and by the overriding concern with law reform and not the wider ethical or managerial issues about the behaviour and standards of participants in companies, except to the extent that this could be reflected in company law.[65] Therefore, the basic framework of analysis did not envisage a wholesale reconsideration of the ethical foundations of company law, nor of the nature and role of the company in society. Indeed, the Steering Group made clear in their March 2000 Consultation Document that a wider 'pluralist' approach to governance issues, requiring directors to take into account wider stakeholder interests, would not be the basis for the reform proposals. At most they felt that the best way to achieve the objective of ensuring that companies contributed to the overall health and competitiveness of the economy was to have a shareholder-orientated, inclusively framed, duty of loyalty, in the context of significant public policy-oriented mandatory provisions on care and skill, conflict of interest and extended disclosure.[66] The thinking of the Steering Group does not appear to have been strongly influenced by concerns such as those of involuntary creditors who have suffered personal injuries at the hands of the overseas subsidiaries of UK-based MNEs. Rather, it was orientated towards the traditional, shareholder-based, model of company law and towards a cost-effective, pro-business, approach to regulation.

This view is strongly restated in *The Final Report*, which stresses three 'core policies' over all others: a 'think small first' approach, which places the interests of small companies in a simple, less burdensome system of company law at the fore, an inclusive, open and flexible regime of company governance and a flexible and responsive institutional structure for rule-making and enforcement.[67] Against such a backdrop, there

---

63 See *Competitive Economy*, above n 45, at para 3.1.
64 See *Competitive Economy*, above n 45, at para 4.4.
65 See DTI Consultation Document *Modern Company Law for a Competitive Economy – The Strategic Framework* (London, DTI, 1999) at para 5.1.2.
66 See DTI Consultation Document *Modern Company Law for a Competitive Economy – Developing the Framework* (London, DTI, 2000) at chapter 3, especially at para 3.22.
67 See *The Final Report*, above n 2, at para 1.52.

would have been little room for the re-regulation of group liability, a policy mainly aimed at large corporations and one which increases the 'burden on business'.

Yet if one examines more closely the terms used by the Steering Group in *The Final Report*, there would, in fact, be little incompatibility between the Steering Group's aims and the development of a stronger regime for national and multinational group liability. In particular, *The Final Report* (while accepting that in many cases the result of the Steering Group's scrutiny has been deregulation) asserts that where patterns of abuse exist, which disrupt and add cost to effective economic activity, rules have been recommended which restrict economic freedom to the extent necessary to prevent such abuse.[68] *The Final Report* continues:

> We also recognise that abuse may lead to a more indirect and intangible threat to our economic system – the loss of public confidence in the legitimacy of the exercise of the huge economic powers which are involved. It is right and in the longer-term interests of the economy that the law should respond to these concerns ...[69]

Sadly, this sentiment does not extend to the issue of MNE group liability for the tortuous acts of overseas subsidiaries. Surely, in a world where the legitimacy of global capitalism is being increasingly questioned, such an approach is unacceptable. Clearly, if the avoidance of group liability for mass torts does not lead to a loss of 'public confidence in the legitimacy of the exercise of huge economic powers', what does?

Furthermore, *The Final Report* asserts that the effective management and control of resources requires taking into account a wide range of factors, including 'the need to manage relationships with employees, with suppliers of all kinds of resources ... and with customers, both direct and indirect'.[70] *The Final Report* continues:

> They include the need to manage wider impacts on consumers, the community and the environment. Reputational assets are also of critical importance in a world where external perceptions can transform business prospects for better or worse.[71]

The Final Report concludes on this point by noting that many of these resources and assets are not reflected fully in the rules relating to corporate accountability.[72] This would suggest, again, that the governance questions raised by the transnational operations of MNEs need to be reconsidered. Not least of these is group liability, which, perhaps more than most areas of group action, will affect the firm's reputational assets.

(2) The weakness of the 'elective regime' for groups

Apart from the specific criticisms offered above as to the unsuitability of the 'elective regime' to deal with risk reduction, other criticisms of a more general kind have been voiced against this proposal. In particular, responses received by the Steering Group highlighted two further matters of concern: first, that the proposal would lead to an overall reduction in the transparency of group activities which would be damaging to

---

68 See *The Final Report*, above n 2, at para 1.16.
69 See *The Final Report*, above n 2, at para 1.16.
70 See *The Final Report*, above n 2, at para 1.23.
71 See *The Final Report*, above n 2, at para 1.23.
72 See *The Final Report*, above n 2, at para 1.24.

shareholder accountability and, secondly, that the proposal was probably dead in the water unless the Inland Revenue ceased to require each company in the group to submit individual accounts for tax purposes. Otherwise, any apparent cost saving arising from the reduction of reporting requirements under the elective regime would be neutralised by the need to continue to draw up accounts for revenue purposes.[73] In the light of such wide criticisms it is safe to assume – though *The Final Report* does not say anything on the matter, not even in a footnote – that the idea has been quietly dropped. No other inference can be made on the basis of the publicly available information from the Steering Group.

5 CONCLUSIONS

From the above it can be said that English law still has a long way to go before a comprehensive doctrine of parent company liability for the acts of overseas subsidiaries or affiliates is in place. So far, the outcome of litigation has clarified some of the issues relating to jurisdiction. It is now possible for an English-based parent company to be sued before the English forum for the acts of those subsidiaries or affiliates, even where a more appropriate foreign forum in the host country of the subsidiary/affiliate may be said to exist, if it can be shown that the foreign forum in question is unable to provide an environment for the litigation such that substantive justice can be done. However, English law has not yet gone so far as to accept a mandatory rule of jurisdiction over English-domiciled parent companies for torts or other unlawful acts committed abroad by their affiliates.

As regards substantive liability, it remains to be seen whether, given the settlement in *Cape*, a future English court will be moved by the kinds of policy-based arguments put forward in this essay for an extension of the duty of care to parent companies for the acts of their affiliates. These policies can be summarised as follows: first, limited liability was never intended to be used as a means of insulating succeeding layers of corporate group organisation from liability. Only the ultimate shareholders were to enjoy this protection. Acceptance of this wide interpretation of limited liability allows for an illegitimate shifting of risk to the involuntary creditors of the company among whom the most conspicuous category are victims of personal injury caused by the negligent acts of affiliates. Secondly, in mass tort cases, the assets of the entire group may be needed to ensure a sufficient capital fund from which to satisfy claims. This is especially justifiable where it can be shown that the group acts as an integrated economic entity which together creates the wealth of the group enterprise. Thirdly, there is a growing expectation of public policy that corporations, including MNEs, should act in a socially responsible way. This may require *inter alia* acceptance of group liability for cases of gross corporate negligence leading to mass tort claims. In response to such an extension of the duty of care, the parent company may be able to rebut the allegation of liability by showing that, in the conduct of its management of the overseas affiliates involved, it acted reasonably in all the circumstances or that the chain of causation leading to the alleged harm was broken in a way that indicated the non-involvement of the parent. An alternative solution

---

73   See *Responses*, above n 56.

might be to impose strict liability on the parent for the acts of its subsidiaries, though such an outcome is unlikely in future litigation and legislation to this effect is not forthcoming.

As regards the contribution of the Company Law Review Steering Group to the question at hand, this chapter must end with a strong expression of dissatisfaction. The Steering Group has inexplicably avoided a proper analysis of the wider issue of parent company liability in tort for the acts of its affiliates, it has put forward a weak proposal for an 'elective regime' of group liability and the extent of the accountability obligations to be placed on directors when drawing up the OFR remains obscure. Furthermore, it might be added that a legal reform process of this importance must be sufficiently transparent for any interested person to be able to determine the precise course of the analysis without having to resort to any sources other than those made publicly available. This is not a case in which 'insider information' should be needed to complete the picture. Unfortunately, it cannot be said with confidence that the public record offers a clear picture of what, precisely, the Steering Group thinks now about the 'elective regime' or of its other views on corporate groups. It is simply unacceptable for such a high-level review process to end with the omission, from its *Final Report*, of a major question addressed in earlier consultation papers. To plead, as *The Final Report* does, that certain matters had to be left out to avoid an unmanageably large document[74] appears to be disingenuous. In all a missed opportunity, though, perhaps, a not unexpected outcome given the aims of the Company Law Review process.

This leaves a final question – in which direction could the law develop? As it stands the Review process has defended the status quo. However, it may be necessary, at some future date, to return to the issues raised in this chapter as part of a wider ranging review of basic principles of corporate social responsibility. In this connection, a possible starting point may be to refer to the *OECD Guidelines for Multinational Enterprises*[75] as the background for a new UK Code of Conduct for corporate groups to be undertaken by the proposed Companies Commission, should this beast ever be born. Such a Code could form the basis of guidance for directors as to the content of OFRs and of the general statement of directors' duties. This is not to say that the *OECD Guidelines* are, in themselves, a comprehensive or sufficient statement of principles. However, they do offer a minimum of agreed international standards of corporate social responsibility from which a developed body of national principles can emerge. This is significant, in that following the agenda set by the *OECD Guidelines* takes care of the argument that greater regulation acts as a competitive disadvantage for the regulating system, given that the *Guidelines* represent an international consensus among the major capital exporting countries as to the proper conduct of MNEs, domiciled therein, in their global operations.

Such an international orientation should also reduce the power of any objection based on the notion that developing countries may become disadvantaged by the raising of corporate responsibility standards, enforced through litigation in the home country against the parent, in that they will become less attractive as locations for foreign investors given the rise in labour costs, and regulatory costs, that may follow. This argument cannot stand, as the observance of international minimum standards in developing country locations would still leave much room for competition over labour

---

74   See *The Final Report*, above n 2, at para 1.7.
75   See n 14 above.

costs among countries and firms. The point is that, in observing such standards, MNEs would ensure that their activities do not amount to violations of fundamental labour and human rights standards that are condemned by the *OECD Guidelines* and, indeed, by other international standard-setting instruments. Furthermore, the risk of litigation would be much reduced, as observance of international minimum standards by MNEs would provide evidence of practice that is in conformity with general legal standards, even where the host country fails to regulate by way of national legislation and/or adequate monitoring and enforcement.

This approach should also weaken arguments to the effect that litigation in the home country amounts to an illegitimate extraterritorial extension of home country standards to host countries. The issue would not revolve around the existence of lower labour and regulatory standards in the host country, and whether these can be ignored in favour of higher home country standards, but on whether international standards have been violated. It may well be that a dual system of standards could eventually emerge – higher-level standards contained in the domestic law of the home (or indeed host) country which would normally apply, and lower-level international minimum standards that can be applied in cases where the home/host country fails to apply such standards in its own law. It may be the only way to accommodate the needs of justice for foreign claimants who allege they have suffered harm at the hands of the local affiliate of a foreign MNE, and the freedom for countries, whose major comparative advantage lies on lower labour and regulatory compliance costs, to develop their economic policy in a way that exploits such an advantage. On the other hand, the significance of such an advantage should not be overstated. Competition over labour and regulatory costs is not a viable long-term strategy in the modern global economy, where capital-intensive production continues to displace unskilled and semi-skilled labour. The real objective must be to add value to the productive process and this requires development in skills and technology.[76] Thus, too much heed should not be given to claims that the adequate provision of health, labour and human rights standards undermine the competitive advantages of developing countries. It is an argument in support of failure and should be treated with the suspicion it deserves, especially when it comes from countries where the real problem is not underdevelopment but authoritarian and elitist government which does not place high value on equity and fairness towards its population. One way around such problems is to place a higher responsibility on MNEs to use their cross-border management network as a conduit for higher standards. Indeed, such firms generally apply higher than local standards in their treatment of workers in developing countries. Cases of lower local standards being applied are rare, but, as cases like Bhopal show, the results can be catastrophic. The real problem lies mainly in the treatment of local populations by local institutions, whether private businesses or public bodies, and in the effectiveness of local regulation. Imposing new responsibilities of MNEs cannot substitute for good governance by local institutions, but it can be of use in extreme cases where MNEs themselves allow their local operations to fall below acceptable minimum standards.

Finally, in relation to the question of standards of liability, should the parent company, in the conduct of its management of a subsidiary in a foreign country, have acted in a

---

76 See further UNCTAD *Foreign Direct Investment and Development* UNCTAD Series on issues in international investment agreements (New York and Geneva, United Nations, 1998).

manner that violates its home country standards, then is it not unreasonable to hold it to those higher standards, even if they go far beyond what might be acceptable in the foreign host country, at least so far as liability is concerned? Differences in earning capacity and cost of living between the developed home country and the developing host country can then be taken into account at the compensation stage.

Also of importance in this connection is a review of the functions and uses of limited liability, which must be reconsidered in the light of the realities of corporate group power and risk allocation. After all, the aim of the Company Law Review has been to reconsider a company law that it has described in places as being Victorian, stuffy and obsolete. What could be more obsolete in a world economy dominated by extensive networks of interconnected group enterprises – based on both equity and contractual links – than a rigid, formalistic, doctrine of limited liability that is out of touch with the ability of MNEs to absorb risk and to take responsibility for any risk to third parties that they have created?

CHAPTER 12

THE REGULATION OF INTRA-GROUP TRANSACTIONS

Mike Lower

1 INTRODUCTION

This essay is concerned with the ways in which UK company law regulates transactions between a parent company and its partly owned subsidiary. One example of such a subsidiary is the corporate joint venture where one party has a majority interest; the joint venture in *Scottish Co-operative Wholesale Society Ltd v Meyer*[1] was just such a subsidiary. The common law fiduciary duties which directors, shadow directors and, arguably, controlling shareholders owe to the subsidiary company are one source of such regulation; Part X of the Companies Act 1985 is another. When it comes to enforcement of this regulation by minority shareholders in the subsidiary, the derivative action and s 459 of the Companies Act also come into play. It is argued that company law ought to impose fiduciary duties on the majority shareholder in the corporate joint venture. UK company law does not impose this duty in clear terms. This essay will consider whether or not recent reform proposals of the Company Law Reform Steering Group (the Steering Group) improve matters in this respect. The reform proposals under consideration are principally those set out in *Modern Company Law for a Competitive Economy – Final Report*[2] which largely refers to the proposals made out in the earlier documents issued by the Steering Group *Modern Company Law for a Competitive Economy – Completing the Structure*[3] and *Modern Company Law for a Competitive Economy – Developing the Framework.*[4]

2 PROBLEMS OF INTRA-GROUP TRANSACTIONS

In essence, a corporate group exists when one company has control over another.[5] In the absence of contractual rights of veto for the minority shareholder or shareholders, the majority shareholder controls decision making in the partly owned subsidiary; this control creates the risk that the majority shareholder will, for example, ensure that the terms of any transactions between it and its subsidiary are unduly advantageous to the majority shareholder. Tunc neatly summarised the difficulty to which commonly accepted principles of company law give rise:

> Companies of a group are often linked by frequent contracts either long term or short term. Under the traditional view, it is not only the right, but the duty of the parent's directors to

---

1   [1959] AC 324.
2   July 2001 (London, DTI, 2001); hereafter *The Final Report*.
3   November 2000 (London, DTI, 2000); hereafter *Completing the Structure*.
4   March 2000 (London, DTI, 2000); hereafter *Developing the Framework*.
5   See the definitions of 'subsidiary' and 'holding company' in Companies Act 1985, s 736(1).

consider only the parent's interests; they may impose on the subsidiary unfair contracts, the only limit on unfairness being an economic one, ie, the need to let the subsidiary survive.[6]

If this is, indeed, how the law stands then it is manifestly inadequate. It is submitted that an important element of the law governing intra-group relationships is a full acknowledgment of the power that the parent company wields. There is a case to be made for the imposition, at least in some cases, of some type of fiduciary duty on the parent company. The incorporated joint venture is the classic example of the sort of partly owned subsidiary whose governance is being considered. A number of jurisdictions recognise that the parties to an unincorporated joint venture owe fiduciary duties to each other.[7]

Our company law in this area would be strengthened and simplified were it to recognise that parent companies owe fiduciary duties to the partly owned subsidiary and to the minority shareholders in it. As Tunc pointed out, English law is very close to recognising the fiduciary duties of a dominant shareholder; it should go one stage further and actually recognise them.[8]

3 THE GENERAL DUTIES OF NOMINEE DIRECTORS WHEN CONSIDERING INTRA-GROUP TRANSACTIONS

Responsibility for the negotiation of contracts will usually be vested by the subsidiary company's constitution in the hands of its directors. Their role is to do the best they can for the company's shareholders.[9] This requirement finds expression in a number of fiduciary obligations imposed on directors. *Developing the Framework* provides a list of the general obligations of directors.[10]

The Steering Group proposed that a new Companies Act should include a statement of directors' duties which would replace the corresponding equitable and common law rules[11] but would be declaratory of existing law[12] rather than a source of new legal principles. A new Companies Act would also be exhaustive in the sense that further judicial development of the law in this area would be expected to take place within this new statutory framework.[13] The Steering Group also recommended that there be a

---

6   See Tunc 'The Fiduciary Duties of a Dominant Shareholder' in C Schmitthoff and F Wooldridge (eds) *Groups of Companies* (London, Sweet & Maxwell, 1991) at p 5. See also Yeung 'Corporate Groups: Legal Aspects of the Management Dilemma' [1997] *Lloyd's Maritime and Commercial Law Quarterly* 208 at p 237.

7   See Loke 'Fiduciary Doctrine and Implied Duties of Good Faith in Contractual Joint Ventures' [1999] *Journal of Business Law* 538, which provides an account of some of the major decisions and a review of the basis upon which fiduciary duties are imposed.

8   See Tunc, above n 6, at p 3.

9   See Grantham 'New Zealand – Reforming the Duties of Company Directors' (1991) 12 *Company Lawyer* 27 for historical and conceptual justifications of the notion that when the law says that fiduciary duties are owed to 'the company', it actually means that the directors have to act in the shareholders' collective interest.

10 See *Developing the Framework*, above n 4, at para 3.12.

11 See *The Final Report*, above n 2, Schedule C, s 17(1).

12 See *Developing the Framework*, above n 4, at para 3.43.

13 See *Developing the Framework*, above n 4, at para 3.12; and *Completing the Structure*, above n 3, at para 3.12.

provision in the main body of the new Companies Act incorporating a duty to comply with the new legislative code of directors' duties; the code itself will be in a schedule and a draft of this was contained in *The Final Report*.[14] Some of the provisions in the code have accompanying notes which will also have legal force.[15]

Often the subsidiary's directors are appointees or nominees of the parent company. The Australian Companies and Securities Law Review Committee have defined 'nominee directors' as:

> .... persons who independently of the method of their appointment, but in relation to their office, are expected to act in accordance with some understanding or arrangement which creates an obligation or mutual expectation of loyalty to some person or persons other than the company as a whole.[16]

The problem that faces nominee directors arises out of the loyalty that they owe 'to some person or persons other than the company as a whole' which could conflict with the fiduciary duties that they owe to the company. How, for example, can this loyalty be made consistent with compliance with their duty to act *bona fide* in the interests of the company and not for any collateral purpose?[17] In *Scottish Co-operative Wholesale Society Ltd v Meyer*, Lord Denning was of the view that nominees could not subordinate the interests of the subsidiary to those of the parent.[18] In *Boulting v Association of Cinematograph Television and Allied Technicians*, he went further and denied the lawfulness of an agreement whereby nominees agreed to act in the interests of a third party.[19] The difficulties facing nominee directors have received their fair share of comment.[20]

The law requires nominee directors to act exclusively in the interests of the subsidiary's shareholders when they are negotiating contractual terms with the parent company.[21] In doing so, they may take into account the fact that the well-being of the company depends to some extent on the well-being of the group. The judgments in *Charterbridge Corporation Ltd v Lloyds Bank*[22] and *Nicholas v Soundcraft Electronics Ltd*[23] recognise the benefits that accrue to a subsidiary by virtue of its membership of a group. It may be, for example, that some head office costs (such as the costs of providing accounting and secretarial services) can be shared between all the members of a group. If a company left the group it would probably see an increase in the cost to it of procuring

---

14 See *The Final Report*, above n 2, at Annex C.

15 See *The Final Report*, above n 2, at Annex C, Explanatory Notes at para 3.

16 See *Nominee Directors and Alternate Directors Report*, Report No 8, 2 March 1989 at para 3 available at www.takeovers.gov.au/Content/Resources/CASES/08-NomineeDirectorsAndAlternateDirectors.asp.

17 See *Re Smith & Fawcett Ltd* [1942] Ch 304 at p 306 *per* Lord Greene MR.

18 See [1959] AC 324 at pp 366–67.

19 See [1963] 2 QB 606 at pp 626–27.

20 See, for example: Crutchfield 'Nominee Directors: The Law and Commercial Reality' (1991) 12 *Company Lawyer* 136; Boros 'The Duties of Nominee and Multiple Directors (Part I)' (1989) 10 *Company Lawyer* 211 and Boros 'The Duties of Nominee and Multiple Directors (Part II)' (1990) 11 *Company Lawyer* 6.

21 See Grantham 'The Content of the Director's Duty of Loyalty' [1993] *Journal of Business Law* 149 at p 152.

22 [1970] Ch 62.

23 [1993] BCLC 360.

these services. Nevertheless, the subsidiary's director should have an exclusive focus on the company's interests and not those of the group.

UK company law allows directors of a subsidiary to have regard to the benefits of group membership, but strictly from the perspective of the subsidiary's own interests; it does not allow directors to subordinate the interests of the subsidiary to those of the group;[24] the Steering Group expressed approval of this approach.[25]

On the face of it, New Zealand's company law offers greater latitude to nominee directors than does English company law. In New Zealand, where the subsidiary's constitution permits it, directors may substitute the interests of the holding company for those of the subsidiary.[26] Where the subsidiary is partly owned, a statement to this effect in the company's constitution and the prior agreement of shareholders (other than the holding company) is required.[27] If the company has been incorporated to carry out a joint venture, a statement in the company's constitution suffices.[28] One imagines that this provision must have given rise to concerns since the company's constitution might have been altered to make use of s 131(3) or 131(4) of the New Zealand Companies Act 1993 against the wishes of a sizeable majority of the company's shareholders.

The Steering Group's proposed restatement of directors' duties gives primacy to compliance with the company's constitution and decisions taken under it.[29] But it is submitted that this does not mean that the constitution can override the duty of good faith since the intention is that the proposed legislative statement should merely be declaratory of existing law;[30] this requires directors of the subsidiary to act in the company's best interests.

The duty of good faith will require that a director 'act in the way he decides, in good faith, would be most likely to promote the success of the company for the benefit of its members as a whole'.[31] Directors would be required to take account of all material factors including the need to foster business relationships, the impact of the company's operations on the communities affected (including the environment), the need to maintain a reputation for high standards of business conduct and fairness as between members.[32] The duty of good faith would cease to bind directors if there was no reasonable prospect of avoiding insolvent liquidation; directors would be under an obligation to minimise creditors' losses instead.[33] The Steering Group were unsure as to

---

24 See *Charterbridge Corporation Ltd v Lloyds Bank* [1970] Ch 62 at p 74 *per* Pennycuick J and *Nicholas v Soundcraft Electronics Ltd* [1993] BCLC 360 at pp 366–67 *per* Fox LJ.

25 See *Developing the Framework*, above n 4, at para 3.84.

26 See New Zealand Companies Act 1993, s 131(2).

27 See New Zealand Companies Act 1993, s 131(3). See further Thomas 'The Role of Nominee Directors and the Liability of their Appointors' in F MacMillan Patfield (ed), *Perspectives on Company Law Volume 2* (London, Kluwer Law International, 1997) at p 235, for a defence of the New Zealand approach.

28 See New Zealand Companies Act 1993, s 131(4).

29 See *The Final Report*, above n 2, at Annex C, Schedule 2, para 17(1).

30 See *Developing the Framework*, above n 4, at para 3.5 which included the statement 'we are proposing only minor changes of substance (but major ones of form)'.

31 See *The Final Report*, above n 2, at Annex C, Schedule 2 para 2(a).

32 See *The Final Report*, above n 2, Annex C, Schedule 2 at para 2(b) and notes.

33 See *The Final Report*, above n 2, at Annex C, Schedule 2 para 9.

whether the duty of good faith should also be displaced where insolvency was 'more likely than not'[34] but they kept an open mind on this in their *Final Report*.[35]

The rule that directors must not entertain a conflict of interests places nominees who are also directors or shareholders of the parent on the horns of yet another dilemma. The nominee must be alert to the risk that the creation of a contractual relationship between the parent and the subsidiary will breach the no conflict rule established by the House of Lords in *Aberdeen Railway Co v Blaikie Bros*.[36] Where two companies contract with each other and they have common directors or the director of one is a major shareholder of the other then the transaction is voidable at the instance of the company whose director has failed to observe the no conflict rule.[37] The director will also be liable to account for any gain made by him as a result of the transaction.

Unlike the duty to act in good faith, the no conflict rule is easily circumvented. Article 85 of Table A validates transactions caught by the no conflict rule provided that the director affected has disclosed his interest to the board of the subsidiary.[38] The effectiveness of Article 85, despite the fact that it seems to conflict with s 310 of the Companies Act 1985, was confirmed in *Movitex Ltd v Bulfield*.[39]

The no conflict rule in the Steering Group's newly proposed legislative statement of directors' duties would read:

A director of a company must not:

(a) in the performance of his functions as a director, authorise, procure or permit the company to enter into a transaction, or

(b) enter into a transaction with the company, if he has an interest in the transaction which he is required by this Act to disclose to any persons and has not disclosed the interest to them to the extent so required.[40]

Although these words seem to cast the net fairly wide, the Steering Group's intention in using them was to narrow the scope of the no conflict rule. The intention was to require the director to take some positive part in a decision before the no conflict rule could come into play.[41] Disclosure would allow the no conflict rule to be circumvented; the disclosure 'required by this Act' refers to the disclosure requirement in what is now s 317.[42] Clearly, the duty of good faith offers, at least potentially, a far higher degree of protection to the minority shareholder than the no conflict rule does. This is particularly so because the no conflict rule can be overcome by disclosure.

---

34 See *The Final Report*, above n 2, at Annex C, Schedule 2 para 8.

35 See *The Final Report*, above n 2, at Annex C, Explanatory Notes para 26.

36 (1854) 2 Eq Rep 1281.

37 See *Transvaal Lands Co v New Belgium (Transvaal) Land and Development Co* [1914] 2 Ch 488 at p 503 *per* Swinfen Eady LJ.

38 For a discussion concerning the nature of the disclosure to be made see Griffiths 'Interlocking Directorships and the Danger of Self-Dealing: The Duties of Directors with a Conflict of Interest' (1999) 10 *International Company and Commercial Law Review* 280.

39 [1988] BCLC 104.

40 See *The Final Report*, above n 2, at Annex C, Schedule 2 para 5.

41 See *Developing the Framework*, above n 4, at para 3.62.

42 See *The Final Report*, above n 2, at Annex C, Explanatory Notes para 23.

Currently, nominee directors are in a difficult position because their fiduciary duties to the company require them to disregard the interests of the parent where they do not further the interests of the subsidiary. Whilst this ambiguity may be unwelcome to nominee directors it is, in principle at least, a safeguard for the subsidiary company and its nominee directors. Of course, the existence of directors' duties is only helpful to minority shareholders if they have some means of enforcing them. The reforms that the Steering Group proposed in the area of minority protection are discussed below.

4 PART X OF THE COMPANIES ACT 1985 AND NOMINEE DIRECTORS

Directors' fiduciary duties offer some protection to the company against managerial depredation and provide directors with useful ethical guidance, albeit of a very general nature. Part X of the Companies Act 1985 supplements the broad-brush approach of these judicially fashioned rules.

Part X is directed specifically at situations in which there is the risk of a conflict of interest between a director (or a person connected with the director) and the company on the board of which he or she serves. The provisions of Part X overlap with the directors' fiduciary duties but are more specific than them in at least three respects. First, many of the provisions declare with great precision the range of transactions to which they apply. The definition of a substantial property transaction, for example, makes use of financial thresholds as the core of the definition of the type of transaction caught by the relevant rule.[43] As a result, there can rarely be any doubt as to whether or not a given transaction is caught by the requirement to obtain shareholder approval for a given transaction. Secondly, the provisions of Part X state very clearly what they require of directors who have an interest in a transaction conflicting with that of the company. Thirdly, the consequences of breach of the provisions of Part X are very clearly stated. One shortcoming of Part X, it could be argued, is that it is of limited practical use to the minority shareholder; in effect, parent companies of partly owned subsidiaries have obligations of disclosure imposed upon them but (if they are in the majority at the general meeting) they can be certain of obtaining any approvals required by Part X.

Part X is directed principally at transactions between a company and one or more of its directors. However, its provisions are quite capable of catching intra-group transactions. The parent company might be 'connected'[44] with one or more directors of the subsidiary. The effect of this would be that the director, or directors, in question would have to comply with the relevant rules in Part X when transactions between the parent and the subsidiary are in contemplation. Part X makes extensive reference to the concept of 'connected persons' and some of its provisions are deemed to apply not only to transactions between a company and its directors but also to transactions between a company and persons who are connected with its directors. In particular, the substantial property transaction rules in s 320 of the Companies Act and the prohibitions affecting

---

43 See Companies Act 1985, s 320.
44 See Companies Act 1985, s 346 for the definition of 'connected person'.

relevant companies[45] on the making of quasi-loans[46] and entering into credit transactions[47] catch transactions with, or in favour of, connected persons. A parent company is connected with a director of the subsidiary if the director is interested in at least one-fifth of the company's shares or is entitled to exercise or control the exercise of more than one-fifth of the voting power in the subsidiary's general meeting.[48]

Parent companies dealing with their subsidiary might find that the provisions of Part X apply directly to them if they are shadow directors of the subsidiary. The concept of a shadow director will be discussed below. Many of the provisions of Part X apply to shadow directors as they do to directors but, because of the special provision made for parent companies in s 741(3) of the Companies Act (discussed at section 5 below), parent companies will not usually be shadow directors of their subsidiaries for the purposes of many of the provisions in Part X. As Millett J pointed out in *Re Hydrodam (Corby) Ltd*, however, it is possible for individual directors of a parent company to be shadow directors of the subsidiary by individually and personally giving directions to the directors of the subsidiary.[49] In any event, parent companies can be shadow directors for the purposes of s 317 of the Companies Act 1985.

Three aspects of the code in Part X are especially likely to be relevant to intra-group transactions. Section 317 requires directors who have an interest in a transaction with their company to disclose that fact to the company's board. This provision also applies to shadow directors[50] and, since s 741(3) of the Companies Act does not mention s 317, a parent company can be a shadow director for this purpose. Secondly, s 320 requires the approval of the company in general meeting in respect of any substantial property transaction between the company and its directors or connected persons. Finally, s 330 prevents companies from making loans to their directors; extra prohibitions apply to 'relevant companies' and these extra prohibitions also apply to transactions with or on behalf of connected persons. The impact of these provisions, and of any reforms proposed by the Company Law Review, will now be examined.

Section 317 will be relevant to transactions between companies in the same group. On its face, s 317 requires disclosure to the board of any transaction in which a director has a direct or indirect interest. There is no judicial guidance as to when a director could be said to have an indirect interest in the transaction but the concept of indirect interest is one way in which an intra-group transaction might come to be caught by s 317. Section 317 applies to shadow directors, and because the restriction in s 741(3) is not applicable here, the parent company/shadow director will also have to disclose its interest.

The Steering Group proposed that s 317 should only apply to 'material interests'.[51] An interest would be immaterial if the board could not reasonably have felt constrained in its decision if it had been aware of the interest.[52] Whilst the introduction of a 'materiality'

---

45 Defined in Companies Act 1985, s 331(6).
46 Defined in Companies Act 1985, s 331(3).
47 Defined in Companies Act 1985, s 331(7).
48 See Companies Act 1985, ss 346(2) and 346(5).
49 See [1994] 2 BCLC 180 at p 184.
50 See Companies Act 1985, s 317(8).
51 See *Developing the Framework*, above n 4, at Annex C para 11.
52 See *Developing the Framework*, above n 4, at Annex C para 11.

test is attractive in principle, it is not without its difficulties. In particular, how is the broad test proposed by the Steering Group to be applied in practice? For good reasons, the Steering Group rejected any suggestion of a monetary limit below which interests would be immaterial.[53] If the proposed amendment is made, the likelihood is that directors will disclose their interest in any transaction even if it is immaterial; compliance is easy and cheap and so it would never be worth taking any time or trouble to consider whether or not a particular interest is material. The practical importance of the amendment would be that it would give the courts a discretion to pardon, after the event, any failure to disclose under s 317. However, judicial relief is, in any event, available under s 727.

Directors and connected persons would have no obligation to disclose in a situation where the directors already knew of the nature and extent of the director's interest.[54] This would cover group contracts[55] (where the obligation of disclosure might arise because the same person is a director of two companies in the same group which are contracting with each other, or because one group company is a shadow director of the other, or is connected with a director of the company with which it is contracting). The burden of proof would be on the director to show that the rest of the board knew of his interest and the burden would be discharged by proof that he had, in due time, notified his fellow directors of this fact in writing.[56] As far as intra-group transactions are concerned, this appears to be a sensible provision since the boards of both companies will be aware, without any need for disclosure, that they are dealing with another company in the same group. Provided, then, that the rest of the board know of the relationship between a director and the parent company, s 317 would become inapplicable to intra-group contracts.

Section 320 regulates 'substantial property transactions'. Essentially, these are transactions between the company and one of its directors (including a shadow director) or a person connected with a director. Because of s 741(3), parent companies are not shadow directors for this purpose, but intra-group transactions will be caught if the parent is connected with a director of the subsidiary. Transactions which fall within the s 320 prohibition have to be approved in advance by ordinary resolution. The regulatory scheme in s 320 is adapted to the group context in three ways. First, where the company in question is a subsidiary, arrangements between its directors and the holding company are also caught by s 320.[57] Secondly, the approval of the shareholders of a wholly owned subsidiary is never needed;[58] where the director of a wholly owned subsidiary is a party to such a transaction, approval will be given by the shareholders of the holding company instead. Thirdly, there is an exemption for intra-group transactions where the only subsidiaries involved are wholly owned.[59] The primary sanction for breach of s 320(1) is that the transaction is voidable.[60] The transaction ceases to be voidable, however, if:

---

53 See *Completing the Structure*, above n 3, at para 4.11.
54 See *Developing the Framework*, above n 4, at Annex C para 11.
55 See *Completing the Structure*, above n 3, at para 4.12.
56 See *The Final Report*, above n 2, at para 6.8.
57 See Companies Act 1985, s 320(1)(a).
58 See Companies Act 1985, s 321(1).
59 See Companies Act 1985, s 321(2)(a).
60 See Companies Act 1985, s 322(1).

restitution is no longer possible; if the company has been indemnified in respect of its loss; if the rights of those who acquired rights in good faith and without notice of the breach would be affected; or if the necessary approval is obtained within a 'reasonable period' after the entering into of the arrangement.[61] The director who entered into the offending arrangement, and any other director who authorised it, is liable to account to the company for any gain and is to indemnify it for any loss.[62]

The requirement of shareholder approval for substantial property transactions affords little protection when the director dealing with the company controls the general meeting of a partly owned subsidiary or is the nominee of the controlling shareholder. This control can be used to secure approval for a transaction which is to the subsidiary's disadvantage. To address this problem, the Steering Group suggested that the s 320 sanctions should apply to transactions between a company (C1) and another company connected with a director of C1 (C2). This would apply where:

(a) C1 is insolvent at the time of the transaction (or became insolvent as a result of it); and

(b) C1 goes into insolvent liquidation within 12 months of the s 320 resolution approving the transaction; unless

(c) either

    (i) the resolution approving the transaction would have been passed even without the votes of the director and any persons connected with him; or

    (ii) the transaction is supported by the valuation of an independent valuer.[63]

In other words, if the subsidiary is threatened by insolvency at the time of the transaction, or as a result of it, the transaction will need to be supported either by the approval of an independent majority or by independent evidence that the transaction was on terms which were fair to the subsidiary. This proposal seems to favour minority shareholders because it dilutes the control of the majority shareholder and allows transactions which are to the manifest disadvantage of the subsidiary to be challenged unless the approval of an independent majority of the subsidiary's shareholders has been obtained. Nevertheless, the degree of comfort that the proposal gives to minority shareholders is, in fact, extremely limited because it only comes into play in the event of insolvency. If the subsidiary is insolvent, it is unlikely that there will be any funds available for shareholders.

The Steering Group proposed a number of amendments to the substantial property transactions provisions.[64] These recommendations included a proposal that a company should be able to enter into a transaction contingent on shareholder approval. Their later recommendation that the remedies for breach of Part X should be codified[65] would also be relevant.

---

61 See Companies Act 1985, s 322(2).
62 See Companies Act 1985, s 322(3).
63 See *The Final Report*, above n 2, at para 15.66.
64 See *Developing the Framework*, above n 4, at Annex C para 26.
65 See *Completing the Structure*, above n 3, at para 13.74.

Section 330 prohibits a company from making a loan to one of its directors or to a director of its holding company or providing a guarantee in connection with a loan to a director.[66] Relevant companies are also barred from making quasi-loans[67] to, or entering into credit transactions for, their directors or directors of their holding company, or persons connected with them.[68] Nor may relevant companies provide guarantees or security in respect of loans or quasi-loans between directors or connected persons and third parties.[69] The Steering Group proposed that the prohibitions which currently apply only to relevant companies should apply to all companies.[70] Breach of s 330 means that the transaction is voidable at the instance of the company unless restitution is no longer possible, or the company has been indemnified in respect of its loss or the rights of third parties acquired in good faith and without notice of the breach would be affected.[71] In addition, directors and connected persons are liable to account for any gain that they have made and to indemnify the company for any loss which it has suffered.[72] There are also criminal sanctions where relevant companies enter into prohibited transactions.[73]

It is important to note that the prohibitions contained in s 330 are largely inapplicable to loans and quasi-loans made by a subsidiary to its parent company.[74] Similarly, subsidiary companies are free to enter into credit transactions as creditor for their holding company or to provide security in respect of any such transaction.[75] Clearly, this puts the subsidiary, and the minority shareholders in it, at risk that the terms of the loan, quasi-loan or credit transaction will be unfavourable to the subsidiary.

The major reform proposal from the Steering Group, so far as ss 330 to 344 are concerned, is that transactions which have the prior approval of the general meeting should be excepted from the prohibition.[76] The remedial regime for breach of the prohibitions might be affected by the proposed codification of the remedies for breach of Part X.[77]

It is interesting to note that Part X of the Companies Act is peppered with references to intra-group transactions. A sensible, deregulatory approach is taken with regard to transactions involving wholly owned subsidiaries. The proposed reforms to Part X will not have a significant impact on the position of minority shareholders. From their perspective, it would be helpful if some means could be devised to allow them to challenge transactions which infringe Part X. The difficulty that they face is that the parent company's voting power can be used to procure any clearances that may be needed for the purposes of ss 320 and 330. In dealing with contracts between the subsidiary and the parent company, company law could leave minority shareholders at

---

66 See Companies Act 1985, s 330(2).
67 See Companies Act 1985, s 330(3).
68 See Companies Act 1985, s 330(4).
69 See Companies Act 1985, ss 330(3)(c) and 330(4)(b).
70 See *Developing the Framework*, above n 4, at Annex C para 28.
71 See Companies Act 1985, s 341(1).
72 See Companies Act 1985, s 341(2).
73 See Companies Act 1985, s 342.
74 See Companies Act 1985, s 336(a).
75 See Companies Act 1985, s 336(b).
76 See *Completing the Structure*, above n 3, at para 4.21.
77 See *Completing the Structure*, above n 3, at para 13.74.

the mercy of the majority. At the other end of the regulatory spectrum, the assent of a majority of disinterested shareholders could be required. Part X steers a middle course; it ensures that certain intra-group transactions are publicised and discussed. However, the parent company can force its will on the subsidiary.

5 SHADOW DIRECTORS

The Companies Act defines a shadow director as 'a person in accordance with whose directions or instructions the directors of the company are accustomed to act' but it excludes from this definition a person where 'the directors act on advice given by him in a professional capacity'.[78] A parent company that gives directions or instructions to the board of its subsidiary falls within this definition. However, parent companies benefit from a statutory exemption for certain purposes and, as a result, even an interventionist parent company will escape many (but not all) of the Companies Act consequences of being a shadow director.

Parent companies which are found to be shadow directors of their subsidiaries must make disclosure of their interest in the transaction to the subsidiary's board for the purposes of s 317 of the Companies Act 1985. A further consequence of being a shadow director is that the parent company will, in that capacity, probably owe the fiduciary duties that company law imposes on directors; this is because it is strongly arguable that shadow directors are subject to the general duties that directors owe to their companies[79] (and the Steering Group propose to put this question beyond doubt by expressly providing that the statutory statement of directors' duties applies to shadow directors as it does to directors).[80] Those who believe that the parent company is (or should be) the real fiduciary in a closely held, partly owned subsidiary can take great encouragement from the possibilities offered by the shadow directorship provisions; they offer a means by which duties can be imposed on the controlling shareholder who may wield far greater levels of power over the subsidiary's affairs than do the formally appointed directors.

Part X of the Companies Act 1985 and the disciplines that it imposes on directors with a personal interest in a transaction with their company are discussed elsewhere in this essay.[81] Many of the provisions of Part X are expressed to apply to shadow directors as they do to directors.[82] But parent companies will rarely be shadow directors of their subsidiary for the purposes of the Companies Act 1985 because s 741(3) of the Act provides that for the purposes of most of the provisions of Part X:

> ... a body corporate is not to be treated as a shadow director of any of its subsidiary companies by reason only that the directors of the subsidiary are accustomed to act in accordance with its directions or instructions.

---

78 See Companies Act 1985, s 741(2).
79 Shadow directors are also subject to a number of provisions of the Insolvency Act 1986 as though they had been formally appointed directors of the subsidiary (and in this context there is no statutory exemption in favour of parent companies).
80 See *The Final Report*, above n 2, at para 6.7.
81 See section 4 above.
82 Including Companies Act 1985, ss 317, 320 and 330.

Insolvency Law does not fall within the scope of the Company Law Review. It is worth noting in passing, however, that the Insolvency Act 1986 also contains a definition of 'shadow director'[83] but the Insolvency Act definition does not include the s 741(3) exemption for parent companies. As a result, parent companies of insolvent subsidiaries face liability under, for example, the wrongful trading provisions in s 214 of the Insolvency Act 1986.

It is also thought that the general duties of directors, including their fiduciary duties, also apply to shadow directors. For instance, in *Yukong Line v Rendsburg Investments Corporation (No 2)*, Toulson J was of the opinion that a shadow director owes a fiduciary duty to the company of which he is a director.[84] As mentioned above, the Steering Group propose to put the matter beyond doubt by a clause which applies the proposed statutory statement of directors' duties to shadow directors as well as directors.[85]

The Law Commission envisaged that the new statutory derivative action would be available to pursue claims against shadow directors.[86] It would be very convenient if this were the case since it would afford the minority shareholder a way of enforcing the statutory duty. For obvious reasons, it is unlikely that the subsidiary itself will pursue the parent for breach of its duties contained in the statutory statement of directors' duties. If the statutory derivative action is not available, the minority will be forced to rely on a s 459 petition.[87] Unfortunately, although the Steering Group referred fleetingly to the Law Commission's view in this regard,[88] they did not consider it nor make any recommendation one way or another.

If, as seems likely, the new statutory code of directors' duties applies to shadow directors, parent companies will need clear guidance as to when they will be categorised as shadow directors of their subsidiary. The Steering Group consulted on whether it would be enough to exercise the necessary influence over just one director.[89] Although the Steering Group did not rule this out, they reported that a slight majority of respondents were against it.[90] Even where only a single director follows the parent company's directions or instructions, there is an argument in favour of treating the parent as a shadow director. It is appropriate to fix liability on the source of the mischief rather than the nominee who is merely a puppet.

It is clear that making the controller of a single director (or even of any number of directors who, together, are in the minority) the key to parent company liability would require a change in the law. The definition includes the phrase 'the directors' which indicates that there is a need to control the board as a whole. The matter was considered

---

83 See Insolvency Act 1986, s 251.
84 See [1998] 1 WLR 294 at p 311.
85 See *The Final Report*, above n 2, at para 6.7.
86 See Law Commission Report No 246 *Shareholder Remedies* (1997) Cm 3769 (London, TSO, 1997) at para 6.36.
87 *Scottish Co-operative Wholesale Society v Meyer* [1959] AC 324 is most convincingly viewed as a case in which breach of a controlling shareholder's duty of good faith was enforced by means of what is now the unfair prejudice remedy.
88 See *Developing the Framework*, above n 4, at para 4.130.
89 See *Developing the Framework*, above n 4, at para 3.11.
90 See *Completing the Structure*, above n 3, at para 4.6.

in *Kuwait Asia Bank v National Mutual Life Nominees Ltd*[91] and it was held that a shareholder with a right to appoint two directors to a board of five members could not be a shadow director. There are *dicta* of Harman J in *Re Unisoft Group Ltd (No 3)* which speak of the need for a shadow director to control a 'governing majority' at board level.[92]

The parent is only a shadow director if its subsidiary is 'accustomed' to act in accordance with its directions or instructions. This seems to preclude 'one-off' directions or instructions. Beyond that, it is difficult to know when the line will have been crossed. In *Re Unisoft Group Ltd (No 3)*, Harman J opined that 'accustomed' refers to acts 'not on one individual occasion but over a period of time and as a regular course of conduct'.[93] In *Re Hydrodam (Corby) Ltd*, Millett J said that there needed to be 'a pattern of behaviour in which the board did not exercise any discretion or judgment of its own, but acted in accordance with the directions of others'.[94]

The judgment of the Court of Appeal in *Secretary of State for Trade and Industry v Deverell*[95] offers important guidance on what must be proved to substantiate an allegation that someone is a shadow director. It looks at how extensive the parent's involvement in the subsidiary's affairs must be before the parent becomes a shadow director. Morritt LJ reviewed the earlier authorities on the meaning of the term 'shadow director' and concluded that:

> The purpose of the legislation is to identify those, other than professional advisers, with real influence in the corporate affairs of the company. But it is not necessary that such influence should be exercised over the whole field of its corporate activities.[96]

The test is that of 'real influence'. How far a controlling shareholder can go in seeking to control a subsidiary before it will be a shadow director remains problematical. Prudence suggests that if a parent company lays down policy (including policy concerning the terms of intra-group transactions) in any non-trivial respect, then it should accept that it may be a shadow director with all that follows from that.

The judgment also explains that the label attached to the 'communication' does not matter. 'Advice' can still amount to 'directions or instructions'.[97] There does not seem to be a requirement that the directors be, or feel themselves to be, under any compulsion to comply with the directions or instructions; it is enough that they do so.[98]

The judgment of Millett J in *Re Hydrodam (Corby) Ltd*[99] is especially relevant since it looks at the circumstances in which a parent company itself, as well as individual directors of the parent company, might be shadow directors of the subsidiary (as explained earlier, this is not possible so far as most of Part X of the Companies Act 1985 is concerned). Where the parent's board, acting as such, gave directions to the subsidiary's

---

91 [1991] 1 AC 187.
92 See [1994] BCC 766 at p 775.
93 See [1994] BCC 766 at p 775.
94 See [1994] 2 BCLC 180 at p 183.
95 [2001] Ch 340.
96 See [2001] Ch 340 at p 354.
97 [2001] Ch 340 at p 354.
98 [2000] Ch 340 at p 354.
99 [1994] 2 BCLC 180.

directors then the parent company might be a shadow director. The mere fact that the parent company is a shadow director, however, does not mean that the individual members of the parent company's board are necessarily shadow directors of the subsidiary. Individual directors of the parent may be shadow directors of the subsidiary if they personally give the necessary directions or instructions.[100]

6 DOES THE PARENT COMPANY OWE A FIDUCIARY DUTY TO THE SUBSIDIARY?

Elsewhere in this essay the circumstances in which the parent company might be categorised as a shadow director were discussed. There is authority for the view that, in that capacity, the parent company owes the duties of a director to the subsidiary. The same might be said of individual directors of the parent company. But does the parent company, in its capacity as controlling shareholder, owe any fiduciary duty to the subsidiary?

One context in which this question arises is that of the exercise by the parent company of its voting rights in the subsidiary. Shares, and the voting rights attached to them, are items of property and members are free to cast their votes as they wish and, if they so desire, to cast their votes in their own selfish interests.[101] This is the received wisdom and must be the starting point for a discussion of equitable constraints imposed on the exercise by a controlling shareholder of its voting rights.[102]

It is clear that parent companies, in their capacity as majority shareholders, have to exercise their voting power in good faith when altering the company's articles of association.[103] Foster J's judgment in *Clemens v Clemens Bros Ltd*[104] shows that a majority shareholder has to act in good faith when voting in favour of an increase in the company's share capital. The requirement of the majority shareholder to act in good faith when considering an alteration of the company's constitution is also considered in *Greenhalgh v Arderne Cinemas Ltd*.[105] The judgments in both *Clemens* and *Greenhalgh* have been criticised on the basis that they fail to make clear whether the equitable restraint on the exercise of voting rights apply to all shareholders or merely to majority shareholders.[106]

Whether or not there is any restriction on the exercise of the parent company's voting rights when it is asked to consider an intra-group transaction in which it has an interest is unclear. Substantial property transactions require shareholder approval even though the board has the authority to commit the company to the transaction.[107] Is the controlling

---

100 [1994] 2 BCLC 180 at p 184.
101 See *Pender v Lushington* (1877) 6 Ch D 70 at pp 75–76 *per* Jessel MR.
102 See the review of the English authorities emphasising the freedom of shareholders to vote in their own selfish interests by Xuereb 'Voting rights: a comparative review' (1987) 8 *Company Lawyer* 16 at pp 16–17.
103 See, for example, the well known words of Lord Lindley MR in *Allen v Gold Reefs of West Africa Ltd* [1900] 1 Ch 656 at p 671.
104 [1976] 2 All ER 268.
105 [1951] Ch 286.
106 See Xuereb, above n 102, at pp 18–19.
107 See Companies Act 1985, s 320.

shareholder subject to a good faith requirement when considering whether or not to approve the transaction?

Xuereb has argued that majority shareholders are under a general duty to act in good faith for the benefit of the company as a whole.[108] He believes that this principle can be derived from the decision in *Estmanco (Kilner House) Ltd v Greater London Council*.[109] This may be a possible reading of this decision but, on the face of it, that decision seems to govern the controlling shareholder's ability to prevent the company from pursuing a remedy against it for breach of contract. It may not be authority for the broader proposition put forward by Xuereb. It might be argued that the decision turns on the fact that the shareholder was exercising a power usually vested in the board.

The decision of the House of Lords in *SCWS v Meyer*[110] can plausibly be viewed as authority for the proposition that a parent company can be called to account if it misappropriates corporate opportunities of the subsidiary or that it owes a duty of good faith to the subsidiary. So, for example, Viscount Simonds said:

> The truth is that whenever a subsidiary is formed ... with an independent minority of shareholders, the parent company must ... accept as a result of having formed such subsidiary an obligation so to conduct what are in a sense its own affairs as to deal fairly with its subsidiary.[111]

It seems likely that the same facts would give rise to a successful s 459 petition.[112]

The decision of the House of Lords in *O'Neill v Phillips*[113] establishes that s 459 does not create rights and duties which do not already exist as a matter of law or equity. So the duty that Viscount Simonds speaks of must be one which exists in its own right and cannot be seen merely as a 'creature' of s 459. Admittedly, Viscount Simonds is referring to a duty which applies to decisions taken by the board of the parent company but which affect the subsidiary. However, if there is a duty to act fairly in this context, it is logical to assume that the same duty affects the parent company's exercise of its voting rights as a member of the subsidiary.

There seems to be no reason why the principle laid down by Viscount Simonds should not apply to intra-group transactions. Suppose that a subsidiary's articles of association allow the shareholders to give directions to the board by special resolution. If the parent company owns 75% of the voting rights in the subsidiary, it might direct the subsidiary to contract with the parent on terms which are very much to the advantage of the latter. If it controls more than half of the voting rights it might authorise a substantial property transaction which is manifestly unfair to the subsidiary. Why should this not be said to be a breach of the duty to deal fairly with the subsidiary?

---

108 See Xuereb 'An Enterprise Theory of Company Law and Judicial Control' in R Drury and P Xuereb (eds) *European Company Laws: A Comparative Approach* (Aldershot, Dartmouth, 1991) at p 185.

109 [1982] 1 WLR 2.

110 [1959] AC 324.

111 See [1959] AC 324 at p 343.

112 See Milman 'Groups of companies: the path towards discrete regulation' in D Milman (ed) *Regulating Enterprise Law And Business Organisation In The UK* (Oxford, Hart, 1999) at pp 233–34.

113 [1999] 1 WLR 1092.

The Steering Group considered whether, apart from the cases of resolutions to alter the company's constitution or vary class rights, 'there should be any other limits on the powers of the majority to exercise control over the company, for whatever purpose, selfish or not, they choose'.[114] They suggested that a limit exists where the effect of the resolution would be to enable or facilitate the commission by the voting members, or by persons with substantial influence over those members, of a wrong on the company, or to prevent the company from pursuing the remedy for such a wrong. In these circumstances, the 'tainted' votes would be invalidated.[115] This seems to be the principle established in *Estmanco*. It obviously falls far short of an acceptance of a general duty of good faith owed by the parent company/controlling shareholder to its subsidiary.

The Steering Group proposed to retain the principle that decisions to alter the company's constitution must be taken in the best interests of the company as a whole.[116] They further advocated the codification of the equitable restraint on the exercise of shareholders' voting rights to ensure that the 'benefit of members as a whole' test was in line with the same test when applied to directors' duties.[117]

7 MINORITY SHAREHOLDER PROTECTION

As matters stand, nominee directors who give excessive weight to the interests of the parent or the group are in breach of their duty to act in good faith. They must be careful to abide by the no conflict principle. If the parent company is a shadow director then it may be possible to argue that it owes the same duty of good faith to the subsidiary.

In practical terms, however, will the minority shareholder benefit from the imposition of fiduciary duties on the parent or from the duties currently imposed on nominee directors and, possibly, shadow directors? It is trite law that directors owe their duties to the company[118] and that only in exceptional circumstances do they owe any duty to individual shareholders.[119] The effect of the rule in *Foss v Harbottle*[120] is that, as a general rule, minority shareholders cannot enforce the duties owed to the company.[121] Minority shareholders seem to derive no benefit from any strengthening or rationalisation of the law on directors' duties because of the absence of a mechanism for enforcing the duty.

It is well known, however, that the courts have a discretion to give a shareholder leave to bring a derivative action to pursue certain claims of the company. This discretion

---

114 See *Completing the Structure*, above n 3, at para 5.91.
115 See *The Final Report*, above n 2, at para 7.60.
116 See *The Final Report*, above n 2, at paras 7.53–7.56.
117 See *The Final Report*, above n 2, at paras 7.57–7.59.
118 *Percival v Wright* [1902] 2 Ch 421.
119 See: *Allen v Hyatt* (1914) 30 TLR 444; *Coleman v Myers* [1977] 2 NZLR 225; *Re Chez Nico (Restaurants) Ltd* [1992] BCLC 192 and *Heron International Ltd v Lord Grade* [1982] BCLC 244.
120 (1843) 2 Hare 461.
121 As for the difficult issues to be faced when a company and its shareholders have overlapping claims, see the decision of the House of Lords in *Johnson v Gore Wood & Co* [2001] 2 WLR 72 (HL); note the discussion on this point in the Neuberger essay above at pp 72–73.

arises when there has been fraud on the minority and the wrongdoers are in control of the company.[122]

The Law Commission Report on *Shareholder Remedies*[123] advocated that the existing common law derivative action should be replaced by a statutory derivative action which would be available where it could be shown:

> ... that, if the company were the applicant, it would be entitled to any remedy against any person as a result of any breach or threatened breach by any director of the company of any of his duties to the company.[124]

The Steering Group endorsed this view.[125]

Then there is the question of the criteria to be applied by the courts in the exercise of their discretion. The Steering Group proposed that the test should be whether it was in the best interests of the company in accordance with the criterion set out in the principles on directors duties, and in that context, paying particular regard to the views of the majority of members who were not party to, and had no personal interest in, the wrong complained of.[126] The Law Commission suggested that the statutory derivative action should be available to pursue claims against shadow directors;[127] this would undoubtedly be helpful to minority shareholders.

Section 459 of the Companies Act 1985 is the principal remedy available to minority shareholders and it could be used to fashion a fiduciary standard to evaluate intra-group transactions.[128] As is well known, it entitles members to petition for relief on the grounds that the company's affairs are being, or have been, conducted in an unfairly prejudicial manner.[129]

Tunc makes the point that:

> Section 459 ... may be considered as a statement in the negative of the duty of directors and dominant shareholders alike to conduct the company's affairs with fairness which is another way of expressing their fiduciary duties.[130]

A number of points can be made about the operation of the unfair prejudice remedy.

First, the petitioner's grievance must arise out of the conduct of the company's affairs. In the normal course of events, the conduct of the company's affairs is vested in the board. However, as we have seen, a parent company may play a major role in setting policy for the subsidiary even if it is left to its nominees on the subsidiary's board to carry

---

122 For a general discussion see J Farrar and B Hannigan *Farrar's Company Law* (London, Butterworths, 4th edn, 1998) at pp 435–41.

123 Above n 86.

124 See *Shareholder Remedies*, above n 86, at para 6.5.

125 See *Completing the Structure*, above n 3, at para 5.82.

126 See *The Final Report*, above n 2, at para 7.48.

127 See *Shareholder Remedies*, above n 86, at para 6.36.

128 For a discussion of the Canadian equivalent and its potential use in this way see Anisman 'Majority-Minority Relations in Canadian Corporation Law: An Overview' (1986–87) 12 *Canadian Business Law Journal* 473.

129 Companies Act 1985, s 459(1). See further on this area the Lowry essay, above at p 229.

130 See Tunc, above n 6, at p 8.

that policy into effect. The decision of the Court of Appeal in *Nicholas v Soundcraft Electronics Ltd*[131] shows that the courts will treat the exercise of control by a parent company over its subsidiary as conduct in the affairs of the subsidiary for the purposes of s 459.

It can be argued that when a parent company makes decisions concerning the allocation of resources or opportunities within the group then it is conducting the affairs of the subsidiary for the purposes of the unfair prejudice remedy.[132] Although this is by no means an obvious reading of s 459, this approach would allow the court to focus on the nature of the relationship between the members of the subsidiary. This, it is submitted, is desirable in the case of a quasi-partnership. It also avoids the need to look for artificial instances of unfairly prejudicial behaviour on the part of nominee directors as occurred in the House of Lords judgment in *SCWS v Meyer*.[133] But there is no need to enter further into this question for present purposes.

The second point is that the conduct of the subsidiary's affairs must unfairly prejudice the petitioner. Authoritative guidance on the meaning of 'unfair prejudice' is found in the judgment of the House of Lords in *O'Neill v Phillips*.[134] Giving the main judgment, Lord Hoffmann emphasised that the question as to whether or not conduct is unfairly prejudicial has to be answered by reference to the terms of the bargain between the parties and established principles of equity. Section 459 does not give the court a discretion to do whatever seems fair. Applying this approach to the facts, Lord Hoffmann held that O'Neill had no right in equity to enforce the transfer of further shares to him nor to a continuation of the equal sharing of profits. The importance of the judgment in *O'Neill* is that it creates a relatively clear framework for the application of the concept of unfair prejudice. The Steering Group considered reversing the decision in *O'Neill v Phillips* but decided against this in the interests of shorter and cheaper legal proceedings.[135]

Earlier in this essay the point was made that the scope of the directors' duties of good faith is adapted to take the peculiarities of the group context into account; the board of the subsidiary are entitled to have regard to the need for the group to survive where this has an effect on the interests of the subsidiary. It is to be hoped that the courts will take such opportunities as may come their way to develop this body of doctrine. Similarly, decisions concerning parent-subsidiary relations under s 459 ought to offer guidance to parent companies. This should clarify the principles to be applied by the parent when deciding on, for example, the terms of intra-group transactions, the allocation of business opportunities within the group and so on.[136]

Yeung has suggested that s 459 could be amended to include an additional provision which creates a presumption of unfair prejudice where the company in question is a subsidiary and the parent obtains a pecuniary benefit from the subsidiary on terms more

---

131 See [1993] BCLC 360 at p 364 *per* Fox LJ.
132 See Lower 'Good Faith and the Partly Owned Subsidiary' [2000] *Journal of Business Law* 232 at pp 246–47.
133 [1959] AC 324.
134 [1999] 1 WLR 1092. See further the Lowry essay, above at p 229.
135 See *The Final Report*, above n 2, at para 7.41.
136 See Yeung, above n 6, at pp 264–65.

favourable than those which could be expected to apply between parties dealing at arm's length. This principle would not arise where disinterested shareholders had ratified or authorised the transaction.[137] One difficulty with this proposal is that, as Yeung herself points out, it would be very difficult to find transactions which are truly comparable to those which occur in the group context. Afterman made the point that attempts to formulate standards of fairness to be applied to intra-group transactions 'generally fail to take account of the unique arrangement between the corporations and the reality of their economic unity'.[138] In any event, the Steering Group have rejected the concept of introducing presumptions into s 459.[139]

It is highly likely that disgruntled minority shareholders will rely on s 459 for a remedy. As the speech of Lord Hoffmann in *O'Neill v Phillips*[140] makes clear, petitioners will have to demonstrate either a breach of contract or a failure to observe some equitable principle.[141] Thus, it is all the more important that the courts should develop clear principles as to the requirements that good faith imposes on controlling shareholders.

8 CONCLUSIONS

So ubiquitous is the group relationship that it is sensible to ensure that it is properly catered for in our system of company law. This does not mean that there should be a separate statute or part of a statute dealing simply with corporate groups.[142] It is argued, however, that there should be an effort to ensure that those areas of company law which are of particular importance in the group context, such as those mentioned in this essay, cater adequately for corporate groups. The Steering Group propose that a Companies Commission should be created whose role would be to keep company law under review.[143] It is submitted that this body should keep the development of the law of groups under review.

The role of nominee directors in negotiating intra-group transactions is quite heavily regulated; some argue that the law ought to allow nominee directors to subordinate the interests of the subsidiary to those of the parent where this is sanctioned by the company's constitution. Parliament and the courts have been unwilling to allow directors to subordinate the interests of the company to those of some other person or group.[144] It remains to be seen whether the expected reforms will make it possible for the

---

137 See Yeung, above n 6, at p 267.

138 See Afterman 'Directors' Duties in Joint-Venture and Parent Subsidiary Companies' (1968) 42 *The Australian Law Journal* 168 at p 173.

139 See: *Developing the Framework*, above n 4, at para 4.104; and *Completing the Structure*, above n 3, at para 5.76.

140 [1999] 1 WLR 1092.

141 See [1999] 1 WLR 1092 at pp 1101–02.

142 Though some commentators have called for this; see Milman, above n 112, at p 240.

143 See *Completing the Structure*, above n 3, at paras 12.59 and 12.62. The Steering Group received representations to the effect that the title 'Companies Commission' is inappropriate and a possible alternative title is 'the Company Law and Reporting Commission' (see *The Final Report*, above n 2, at para 5.21).

144 See the discussion in section 3 above, especially at nn 18 and 19 and the main text thereat.

constitutions of subsidiary companies to give priority to, for example, parent company or group interests over those of the subsidiary itself.

A theme running through this essay is that greater attention should be paid to the legal duties of the controlling shareholder. In this respect, the proposal that the statutory statement of directors' duties should include a declaration that these apply to shadow directors is to be welcomed; it remains to be seen whether or not the relevant definition of a shadow director will specifically exclude parent companies. Should an ability to give directions or instructions to at least a governing majority of the board be an essential part of the definition of a shadow director also remains to be determined.

Parent companies, as controlling shareholders, should be subject to a duty to act in good faith towards partly owned subsidiaries. For the time being the most likely routes by which this might be secured are by categorising parent companies as shadow directors or by making use of the unfair prejudice provisions. It may be that, in certain circumstances, parent companies owe a fiduciary duty to their partly owned subsidiary. There are plain indications to this effect in *Scottish Co-operative Wholesale Society v Meyer*.[145] However, it is submitted that it would be sensible to allow the courts to explore this area further before creating a statutory duty to this effect.

Domestic company law has to consider the role that good faith has to play in the group setting and in general. On the assumption that there is a place for fiduciary duties, however labelled and enforced, it becomes important to consider the detail of the rules for ensuring compliance with a view to securing a fair deal for the minority shareholder. As has been shown, traditional fiduciary duties imposed on directors and equitable constraints on the majority shareholder's freedom to vote in its own interests vie with s 459 for consideration as the primary source of these rules.

Traditional fiduciary rules are imperfect in this regard because of their failure to come to grips with the nominee director's dilemma, uncertainty as to how they apply to controlling shareholders and the procedural obstacles facing minority shareholders. Arguably, the difficulty facing s 459 has been the lack of coherent principles to guide decision making. But the decision in *O'Neill*[146] has strengthened a movement towards the development and application of such principles. In theory at least, the unfair prejudice regime is free of the procedural obstacles that face the minority shareholder as a result of *Percival v Wright*[147] and *Foss v Harbottle*.[148]

It is clear that our company law will be improved if it develops clear standards to guide directors and controlling shareholders when they set the terms of intra-group transactions. This will mean developing consistent standards to be applied whether the route chosen is the enforcement of fiduciary duties (by means of the derivative action) or an unfair prejudice petition. Courts have primary responsibility but commentators and, as suggested earlier, the Companies Commission (or Company Law and Reporting Commission), will have a role to play in keeping judicial developments under review and suggesting ways in which the UK law of groups should develop.

---

145 [1959] AC 324.
146 [1999] 1 WLR 1092.
147 [1902] 2 Ch 421.
148 (1843) 2 Hare 461.

CHAPTER 13

THE REFORM OF CORPORATE CRIMINAL LIABILITY

Celia Wells

1 INTRODUCTION

Companies, as legal persons, are subjects of criminal law just as natural persons are. However, this simple picture is complicated by changes in the nature and role of business corporations in modern economies and by a number of conceptual difficulties. A conventional account would emphasise the conceptual challenges involved in applying criminal laws to the corporation. Vicarious liability, the device deployed in civil law to render a company liable for the acts of its employees, is of limited application in criminal law. Routes over and around this obstacle have taken two main forms: the introduction of regulatory offences specifically directed at businesses and, secondly, the development of new tools to bridge the conceptual gap between the actions of individual managers and employees and the idea of the 'company'. In recent times, corporate manslaughter has been the main focus of debate but it is important not to lose sight of the significance of criminal sanctions in the regulatory and supervisory schemes, many dating back to the 19th century, addressed specifically to business enterprises.

In this essay I first sketch the wider international context before introducing the 'conceptual tool kit' for corporate liability. From this broad base, I narrow my concentration on the legal regime in England and Wales, with a general account of the development of corporate criminal liability, followed by discussion of the more specific topic of corporate manslaughter. I conclude with a summary of proposals for reform.

2 THE INTERNATIONAL LEGAL CONTEXT

Globalisation, leading to pressures for convergence and harmonisation of laws, constitutes an important factor influencing the modern debate. Concerns about the reach and power of global corporations, their involvement in fraud, economic crimes, corruption, health and safety breaches and environmental depredations are reflected in the recent appearance of corporate criminal liability on national and international law reform agendas.[1] The growth of transnational corporations, the product of the dismantling of nationalistic anti-competitive measures and the general deregulation movements in the US and other major economies from the 1980s onwards has transformed the entire architecture of legal control of business activities. National, international and supra-national political institutions and legal regimes are all implicated.

---

[1]   See further C Wells *Corporations and Criminal Responsibility* (Oxford, OUP, 2001) at chapter 7.

This complex environment cannot be properly captured in a short essay yet provides the fast moving background to the debate.

Many European jurisdictions have, until recently, made no provision for the criminal liability of non-human agents, and some still do not. Even in England and Wales where corporate bodies have long been subject to the criminal law, it has been a Cinderella topic, rarely appearing for discussion at the appellate level, largely ignored by the major writers and theorists and regarded as of marginal interest in legal education generally. In all jurisdictions, and at the supra-national level such as the European Union, there are provisions specifically to regulate business (health and safety at work, trading standards, control of financial institutions and so on). What differs between jurisdictions is the legal mechanism selected. In some jurisdictions this is a branch of criminal law, perhaps enforced by a specialist agency pursued through the normal criminal courts or in separate courts; while in others, the institutional sanctions are found in administrative codes.[2] In those jurisdictions adopting the former solution, there has often been the parallel development that enterprises have been held liable for the 'classic' offences as well. Those that have adopted the administrative route do so in the main because criminal liability for corporate groups has been historically unacceptable as a matter of principle. Criminal law in these jurisdictions addresses individual human agents. Nonetheless, it is not uncommon for individual directors of corporations to be held accountable for negligently caused deaths; Italy provides an example here.

Whether the criminal, quasi-criminal or administrative model is adopted, the regulatory system will form part of a larger four-part institutional structure.[3] On one side, there are controls intrinsic to technology: such matters as design, safety procedures, and worker training. While many such regimes are not specifically legal they are nonetheless regulated through scientific and technological practices. Secondly, there exist administrative controls including health and safety regulatory regimes as well as specific legislative provisions. These national differences form part of the business considerations determining the best location for the manufacture and production of goods, although moves towards convergence and harmonisation of business regulation are gradually reducing these differences. Public institutions for absorbing and spreading losses, health care systems and welfare services comprise the third layer, and private law the fourth.

The aversion to corporate criminal liability in the European penal codes is fast being eroded. The debate is no longer whether to have such liability but what form it should take. Not that the aversion was ever shared by all European countries; it was strongest amongst Germany, Italy and Spain. Northern European jurisdictions such as the Netherlands and Denmark have adopted a pragmatic approach for some time. National legal systems increasingly subject themselves to international conventions (such as those emanating from their membership of the Council of Europe or the OECD), or supra-national bodies (such as the EU). These bodies exert pressures to harmonise or approximate responses to matters such as fraud, corruption and occupational safety.

---

2   See G Heine 'New Developments in Corporate Criminal Liability in Europe: Can Europeans Learn from the American Experience – or Vice Versa?' (1998) *St Louis – Warsaw Transatlantic Law Journal* 173.

3   See Galanter 'The Transnational Traffic in Legal Remedies' in S Jasanoff (ed) *Learning from Disaster* (Philadelphia, University of Pennsylvania Press, 1994) at pp 133–57.

3 THE CONCEPTUAL TOOL KIT

Three different theories of corporate blameworthiness have competed for attention in the common law: the Agency Principle (also known as vicarious liability or *respondeat superior*); the Identification Doctrine (sometimes known as *alter ego* or direct liability) and the Holistic Model.[4] The first theory is based on the principle that a corporation's employees are its agent.[5] The second theory of blame attribution identifies a limited layer of senior officers within the company as its 'brains'; the company is liable for their individual culpable transgressions on the basis that their acts are also the acts of the company. Since agency and identification theories both seek, in different ways, to equate corporate culpability with that of an individual they can be characterised as derivative forms of liability. The third Holistic Theory, on the other hand, exploits the dissimilarities between individual human beings and group entities, by locating corporate blame in the procedures, operating systems or culture of a company. English law[6] draws on the first theory only in relation to strict liability (mainly regulatory) offences; for crimes requiring proof of a mental element, the much more restricted liability identified in the second theory has applied.[7] In the United States the federal courts broke away at the turn of the century to a more general reliance on the first theory. In neither jurisdiction has the history been straightforward. Other common law jurisdictions, including many American states, mainly follow the English bifurcated approach although some have adopted a rather broader interpretation of identification liability. The third way, the Holistic Theory, is deployed for Commonwealth (federal) offences in Australia,[8] and is seen also in the proposed corporate killing offence in England.[9] Table 1 maps the broad application of these somewhat fluid categories in selected common law jurisdictions.

---

4   See Note 'Corporate Crime: Regulating Corporate Behaviour through Criminal Sanctions' (1979) 92 *Harvard Law Review* 1227 at p 1243.

5   This includes so called 'personal' liability under duty-based legislation such as the Health and Safety at Work Act 1974.

6   Used here as a shorthand for English, Welsh and Northern Irish. Gordon implies that Scottish law follows the same principles, although there is little authority outside the vicarious category; see G Gordon *The Criminal Law of Scotland* (Edinburgh, W Green and Sons, 1978) at p 322. Canada and New Zealand both rely on a form of this theory as do some state jurisdictions in the United States.

7   The one exception being *Mousell Bros Ltd v London and NW Rlwy* [1917] 2 KB 836.

8   See, for example, Criminal Code Act (Commonwealth) 1995, s 12.

9   See Home Office Consultation Paper *Reforming the Law of Involuntary Manslaughter: The Government's Proposals* (London, Home Office, 2000), draft Involuntary Homicide Bill.

Table 1: Common law variations – a broad typology

Agency Principle	Identification Doctrine		Holistic Theory
	Pure Form	Modified Form	
US – federal offences (including *mens rea*) South Africa	Selected US state offences	US Model Penal Code states	
England and Wales – regulatory (strict liability and hybrid offences)	England and Wales – all other offences		England and Wales – proposed corporate killing offence
Australian states– strict liability offences	Australian states		Australia – Federal Law
New Zealand – regulatory strict liability offences	New Zealand – other offences	New Zealand – regulatory non-strict liability offences	

4 THE DEVELOPMENT OF CORPORATE CRIMINAL LIABILITY IN ENGLAND AND WALES

Corporate criminal liability is woven from a number of interweaving strands and the resulting cloth is uneven.[10] Contemporary principles of corporate criminal liability mainly owe their history to two parallel developments, in both cases transplants from private law.

4.1 Vicarious liability

Vicarious liability (which incidentally is not peculiar to corporations since it applies also to unincorporated associations or sole traders), was first deployed against corporations in relation to statutory non-feasance and to the common law offence of nuisance. In the early years of the 20th century it was increasingly common to visit vicarious liability on a corporation for statutory offences. These were mainly, but not exclusively, offences of strict liability. Especially where the offence was drafted using verbs such as 'selling' or 'supplying' there was a neat logic in concluding that the employee's act was in truth (and civil law) an act on behalf of the master (or corporation).[11] The notion that a corporation might commit a conventional criminal offence, such as manslaughter, was firmly rejected in the 1920s[12] and gradually the idea that a corporation could not commit an offence

---

10 See generally L Leigh *The Criminal Liability of Corporations in English Law* (London, Weidenfeld and Nicolson, 1969).
11 See *Pearks, Gunston and Tee Ltd v Ward* [1902] 2 KB 1.
12 See *R v Cory Bros* [1927] 1 KB 810.

requiring proof of any form of *mens rea* held firm until the 1940s.[13] Ironically, the emergence of the identification doctrine to deal with such offences not only complicated matters but also contributed to a pincer effect enabling corporations to evade criminal liability for a narrower range of regulatory offences than before. It was only towards the end of the 20th century that the smokescreen of conceptual objections preventing the application of vicarious liability to a broader range of offences began to dissipate.

4.2　Identification liability

A trio of cases in the 1940s established the corporate liability principle for *mens rea* offences which is known in English law today.[14] None of these cases gave any clear idea as to how far this doctrine, whereby the *mens rea* of certain company officers could be imputed to the company, should extend. It was not until 1971 that guidance emerged as to who, for the purposes of criminal liability, might be regarded as a company's *alter ego*. When the House of Lords came to consider the issue in *Tesco Supermarkets Ltd v Nattrass*,[15] the question was not whether the company was guilty of an offence because of the acts of its store manager, but whether it could evade liability through a due diligence defence. The company was charged with a trade descriptions offence[16] because it had indicated that goods would be sold at a lower price than in fact they were sold. A defence of due diligence was provided where the defendant could show that the offence was due to the act or default of 'another person'.[17] The company claimed that the misleading price arose through the default of the manager at the particular branch where the offence was committed. The manager was not regarded as an embodiment of the company and, therefore, despite being the employee whose job it was to display the offending offer, he was 'another person'.

What elevates someone who works *in* and *for* a company to the position of acting *as* the company? For the House of Lords in *Tesco v Nattrass* the answer clearly derived from a conception of the company in which there existed a nerve centre of command. Only the transgressions of those who belong to this nerve centre could be imputed to the company. Some assistance with this came from Lord Pearson who explained:

> There are some officers of a company who may for some purposes be identified with it, as being or having its directing mind and will, its centre or ego, and its brains ... The reference in section 20 of the Trade Descriptions Act 1968 to 'any director, manager, secretary or other similar officer of the body corporate' affords a useful indication of the grades of officers who may for some purposes be identifiable with the company, although in any particular case the constitution of the company concerned should be taken into account.[18]

The word 'manager', he added, only referred to someone in the position of managing the affairs of the company, and would not cover the manager of a store.[19]

13　Discussed in detail in section 4.2 below.
14　See: *DPP v Kent and Sussex Contractors* [1944] KB 146; *R v ICR Haulage* (1944) 30 Cr App R 31; and *Moore v Bresler* [1944] 2 All ER 515.
15　[1972] AC 153.
16　See Trade Descriptions Act 1968, s 11(2).
17　See Trade Descriptions Act 1968, s 24(1).
18　[1972] AC 153 at pp 190G–191A.
19　See [1972] AC 153 at p 191A *per* Lord Pearson.

The idea that some people within a corporation act as that corporation while others do not is fundamentally flawed. While the company is regarded as a fiction, it is nonetheless real. Whatever the managing director does as an individual will be entirely different in its scope and effect from anything a managing director does within the company. The same goes for other workers. Whatever the branch manager of Tescos did with special offers (the subject of this prosecution) he was only able to do because the company had invested and maintained the shop, the supplies to it, and the the posters advertising the offer. The limitations of the doctrine are summed up by Gobert: 'One of the prime ironies of *Nattrass* is that it propounds a theory of corporate liability which works best in cases where it is needed least and works least in cases where it is needed most.'[20]

The impact of *Tesco v Nattrass* has been diluted in part by decisions in the 1990s removing its application in some reverse-onus regulatory offences.

4.3 Waking from the big sleep

Corporate criminal liability had been a subject undeveloped in theory and little explored in practice. This changed in the 1990s after which developments fell into two broad categories: judicial or legal changes in corporate liability generally and, secondly, proposals for the reform of corporate manslaughter. The judicial changes themselves fall into two divisions: those concerning the 'classification' of offences, and moves to extend identification liability.

Clearly the categorisation of any particular offence between these two types of liability is critical: identification liability attributes to the company only the wrongdoing of directors or top managers; vicarious extends liability for the actions of all employees. Yet this important element, in considering corporate responsibility, remained largely hidden. Most accounts of the subject seemed to assume that there were only two types of offence. Only if the offence were one of strict liability (that is, no mental element was required) would the corporation's liability be determined on the vicarious route. If the offence required proof of a mental element such as intention, or recklessness, then the identification principle applied. However, this left a large number of offences out of consideration. Many regulatory offences have a hybrid nature. They are similar to strict liability offences in the sense that the prosecutor does not have to prove knowledge, intention or recklessness. But, for the purposes of corporate liability, they were treated as *mens rea* offences because they contain a reverse onus of proof defence which allows the defendant to prove that they exercised all due diligence in avoiding the offence, or took all reasonable precautions or some similar formulation. An additional characteristic of some offences, for example those under the Health and Safety at Work Act 1974, is that they are duty-based. For example s 3 of the Act provides:

> It shall be the duty of every employer to conduct his undertaking in such a way as to ensure, so far as is reasonably practicable, that persons not in his employment who may be affected thereby are not thereby exposed to risks to their health and safety.

---

20   See Gobert 'Corporate Criminal Liability: Four Models of Fault' (1994) 14 LS 393 at p 401.

Until very recently *Tesco v Nattrass* was assumed to be the appropriate route to liability for corporate defendants for this and other 'hybrid' offences. However, in *R v British Steel plc*,[21] the Court of Appeal held that s 3 imposed a strict, or vicarious, liability. The company could not escape liability by showing that, at a senior level, it had taken steps to ensure safety if, at the operating level, all reasonably practicable steps had not been taken. The company, in other words, falls to be judged not on its words but on its actions, including the actions of all its employees.

A number of other cases have taken a similar line.[22] There remains some debate about the appropriateness of the term 'vicarious' liability because the liability is a personal one owed by the employer.[23] However, this is largely a distinction without a difference. Whether it is a personal or a vicarious liability (that is, whether the company is liable because it has breached its duty personally or because an employee has done a wrongful act), the breach has to come about through human agency. As Coffee has stated: 'the difference seems highly formalistic: one did not impute liability from agent to principal; rather, one decided that agent and principal were the same person.'[24] Courts have not been consistent in their interpretation of the extent of the duty imposed on employers but they have been consistent in rejecting *Tesco v Nattrass* as the governing principle.[25] The law was summarised in 1998 as follows:

> If persons not in the employment of the employer are exposed to risks to their health or safety by the conduct of the employer's undertaking, the employer will be in breach of section 3(1) ... unless the employer can prove on a balance of probability that all that was reasonably practicable had been done by the employer *or on the employer's behalf* to ensure that such persons were not exposed to such risks.[26]

These cases all point in the direction of the appellate courts taking a far stricter approach than was evidenced in the years following *Tesco v Nattrass*.[27] Of the many reasons why the issue came to the fore 25 years later, the most prominent include the trend towards blaming of corporations, consequent increased levels of enforcement, and higher maximum penalties. All this promotes a culture in which lawyers are more critical and in which corporations wish to defend health and safety prosecutions more vigorously. Both regulators and the regulated have a heightened interest in the form that liability takes in an increasingly deterrence-orientated enforcement culture. In defending themselves rigorously corporate employers have in fact subjected themselves to broader liability principles. While British Steel may have rued the day it appealed a conviction for a negligently caused workplace death which had attracted a meagre £100 fine,[28] the fact

---

21 [1995] 1 WLR 1356.
22 See: *R v Associated Octel* [1996] 1 WLR 1543; *R v Gateway Foodmarkets* [1997] IRLR 189 (a case under the Health and Safety at Work Act 1974, s 2).
23 See *R v Gateway Foodmarkets* [1997] IRLR 189.
24 See Coffee 'Corporate Criminal Liability: An Introduction and Comparative Survey' in A Eser, G Heine and B Huber (eds) *Criminal Responsibility of Legal and Collective Entities* (Freiburg, Iuscrim, 1999) 1 at p 15.
25 See, for example, *R v Nelson Group Services* [1998] 4 All ER 331.
26 See *R v Nelson Group Services per* Roch LJ [1998] 4 All ER 331 at p 351c–d (emphasis added).
27 [1972] AC 153.
28 Even Steyn LJ was moved to remark that this punishment was 'derisory' and regretted the fact that it could not be increased; see [1995] 1 WLR 1356 at p 1364E.

that they did appeal perhaps tells us something both about the impact of a criminal record on a corporate offender and about corporate arrogance.

There have been signs too of a broader interpretation of the identification rule, even where it does apply. The decision of the Privy Council in *Meridian Global Funds Management Asia Ltd v Securities Commission*[29] heralded a more modern, organisational concept of liability. In this case an alleged breach of securities legislation turned on whether the company had knowledge of the activities of its investment managers. Lord Hoffmann showed an appreciation of the need for a more sophisticated and flexible approach to the problem of attributing knowledge (or other *mens rea*) to a corporate body. Admitting that attribution of knowledge raised difficult philosophical questions, he suggested that the directing mind model was not always appropriate. It was relevant to examine the language of the particular statute, its content and policy. Since, in this case, the policy was to compel disclosure of a substantial security holder, the relevant knowledge should be that of the person who acquired the relevant interest. The Court of Appeal has said that this statement of principle is of general application, applying it to assist in determining when perjured evidence will be attributed to the company on whose behalf it is given.[30]

Yet the broader *Meridian* rule was firmly rejected in the corporate manslaughter case against Great Western Trains,[31] confirming once again that corporate criminal law is far easier to apply when there is an identified individual's act to be attributed rather than a negligent failure to take appropriate safety measures.

5 THE RISE, RISE AND FALL OF CORPORATE MANSLAUGHTER

The appeal courts in this country have had very few opportunities to think about corporate manslaughter or even about corporate liability more generally. The trial of P&O on charges of manslaughter following the 1987 *Herald of Free Enterprise* disaster was a landmark in this bare picture. Although the prosecution of P&O was ultimately unsuccessful, as was that of Great Western Trains almost a decade later, *the idea* of corporate manslaughter now has a clear place in popular vocabulary. This cultural recognition was reflected in the Law Commission's 1996 *Report on Involuntary Manslaughter*, almost half of which was occupied by this issue.[32]

The indictment against P&O was not the first attempt to prosecute a company for manslaughter. Cory Brothers had been indicted in 1927,[33] and there was an isolated trial in 1965 which attracted little publicity.[34] P&O's trial in 1991 marked the first judicial

---

29 [1995] 2 AC 500.

30 See *Odyssey and Alexander Howden Holdings v OIC Run-Off Ltd*, unreported (CA), 13 March 2000; available on Westlaw.

31 See *Attorney General's Reference (No 2 of 1999)* [2000] QB 796.

32 Law Commission *Legislating the Criminal Code: Involuntary Manslaughter*, Report No 237 (1996) HC 171 (London, HMSO, 1996).

33 See *R v Cory Bros* [1927] 1 KB 810.

34 *R v Northern Strip Mining*; see *The Times* 2, 4 and 5 February 1965. Presumably, a conviction would have attracted more notice.

ruling that a charge of manslaughter against a corporation was recognised in law.[35] In confirming this Turner J followed an earlier Queen's Bench Division ruling arising from the inquests into the *Herald* deaths.[36] When a car ferry capsized as a result of leaving Zeebrugge harbour with its bow doors open, 188 people had drowned. The trial ended when the judge directed acquittals. Since there is no appeal from acquittal in the Crown Court, the only possible avenue for further action would have been a reference by the Attorney General to the Court of Appeal on a point of law, but this was not taken.[37] When Great Western Trains was prosecuted in 1999 for the manslaughter of seven passengers in the Southall rail crash that case also resulted in directed acquittals. However, the Attorney General on this occasion referred the legal issues to the Court of Appeal, making history as the first time that an appellate court had considered the law relating to corporate manslaughter.[38]

A train, operated by the Great Western Train Company (GWT), en route from Swansea to London ran through red lights and collided with a goods train on the last leg of its journey.[39] GWT's procedures had allowed a high-speed train with a malfunctioning Automatic Warning System to be driven by one man. The new safety device for trains, Automatic Train Protection System, promised after earlier rail crashes,[40] was not in use because this particular driver had not been trained to operate it. Seven passengers were killed. The company pleaded guilty to a charge under s 3(1) of the Health and Safety at Work Act 1974. The evidence disclosed that the company encouraged drivers to depart their trains on time even if safety devices were not working. The company was fined a record £1.5 million. However, the manslaughter prosecution against the company proved to be much more difficult.

As has already been noted, the period between these two transport disasters bears witness to a 'quiet revolution' in corporate liability.[41] The first stage was the side-lining of the *Tesco v Nattrass* identification doctrine in relation to some regulatory offences.[42] Secondly, the Privy Council in *Meridian* laid the foundations for a broader conception of the 'directing mind' in offences still subject to the identification rules.[43] In their case against GWT, the prosecution sought to exploit these changes, arguing that it was unnecessary to pursue an individual director of GWT. Instead, the prosecution argued that the company's liability should be established by proving that the company's management policies had resulted in the failure to have a proper warning system which led directly to the crash. This attempt to forge a route to liability independent of an individual director's negligence was rejected. The trial judge ruled that a non-human defendant (that is, the company) could only be convicted via the guilt of a human being with whom it could be identified; it was a condition precedent to a conviction for

---

35 See *R v P&O European Ferries (Dover) Ltd* (1991) 93 Cr Ap R 72 at p 83.

36 See *R v HM Coroner for East Kent ex p Spooner* (1989) 88 Cr Ap R 10.

37 See Criminal Justice Act 1972, s 36.

38 See *Attorney General's Reference (No 2 of 1999)* [2000] QB 796.

39 See Cullen *The Ladbroke Grove Rail Inquiry, Part 1 Report* (London, HSE Books, 2001).

40 Specifically after the inquiry into the Clapham Junction crash in 1988; see the Hidden Report *Investigation into the Clapham Junction Railway Accident* (1989) Cm 820 (London, HMSO, 1989).

41 See further Wells 'A Quiet Revolution in Corporate Liability for Crime' (1995) 145 NLJ 1326.

42 Following cases such as *R v British Steel plc* [1995] 1 WLR 1356 and the cases listed at n 22 above.

43 See n 29 above and the main text thereat.

manslaughter by gross negligence for a guilty (human) mind to be proved. The case therefore collapsed. The Court of Appeal ruled that this was the correct approach; the narrow identification doctrine of *Tesco v Nattrass*[44] still applied. The quiet revolution was in reverse. The conclusion was that 'unless an identified individual's conduct, characterisable as gross criminal negligence, can be attributed to it, the company is not, in the present state of the common law, liable for manslaughter'.[45] Given that few directors are involved in operational roles (they do not actually drive trains), the suggestion that this includes the *actus reus*[46] would add an additional burden in a corporate prosecution.

An opportunity has been lost to establish the law of corporate manslaughter on a sound basis. Instead, a series of cases ranging from the prosecution of supermarket for misadvertising a sales offer,[47] the conviction of a company for failing to ensure the health (and life) of one of its workers,[48] the conviction of a company for failing to notify a shares acquisition,[49] to the conviction of an anaesthetist for the manslaughter of a patient,[50] has been used to define the common law on corporate manslaughter, a subject central to none of them. The court showed no inclination at all to consider the issue from a point of first principle. It is widely accepted that *Tesco v Nattrass*[51] relies on an outdated and shallow theory of organisational behaviour in assuming that only directors make decisions. It also fails to see companies as an organic whole or to capture the 'corporateness' of their conduct. Given that the case was decided 30 years ago, had no direct bearing on manslaughter, and had been diluted by a number of decisions since, and given the development of theories in relation to corporate attribution in the ensuing period, such uncritical reliance on it in the *GWT* case[52] was disappointing.

Only two companies have been convicted of manslaughter since the *P&O* case; both were small, effectively one-person companies, in which the identification doctrine for attributing fault to a company can work very easily. There was no problem in saying that the documented disregard for safety by Peter Kite, the managing director of the leisure company (OLL Ltd) responsible for the deaths of three teenagers in the Lyme Bay canoeing tragedy, could be imputed to OLL Ltd.[53] On the other hand, it is difficult to argue that the company's conviction added much to that of Mr Kite. After all, no-one had heard of OLL Ltd before the tragedy and it is unlikely that it continued trading after it. Nevertheless, the big corporate names, invariably large plcs, are those which people will most likely want to blame and are also the most difficult to target under the identification rule (or possibly any other). The larger the company is the harder it will be to secure a conviction for corporate manslaughter.

---

44   [1972] AC 153.
45   See *Attorney General's Reference (No 2 of 1999)* [2000] QB 796 at p 815E *per* Rose LJ.
46   See n 45 above.
47   *Tesco v Nattrass* [1972] AC 153.
48   *R v British Steel plc* [1995] 1 WLR 1356.
49   *Meridian Global Funds Management Asia Ltd v Securities Commission* [1995] 2 AC 500.
50   *R v Adomako* [1995] 1 AC 171.
51   [1972] AC 153.
52   See [2000] QB 796.
53   See *R v Kite and Others Ltd* (1994) *The Independent,* 9 December.

6 CORPORATE KILLING – A NEW OFFENCE

The prosecutions of P&O and GWT arose from high-profile public transport disasters. However, there were several other well-publicised disasters in the 1980s and 1990s which gave rise to public demands for corporate manslaughter prosecutions. At the same time, there was pressure from some campaign groups for workplace deaths to be taken more seriously in the criminal justice system.

Between 1996 and 1998, 510 people died in accidents and 47,803 suffered major injuries from work-related accidents.[54] In some industrial sectors the number of major injuries has actually increased in the last two decades.[55] During the last 10 years 3,555 people have lost their lives at work.[56] Many of these deaths were preventable according to the Health and Safety Executive (HSE), which concluded that 75% of maintenance accidents in the chemical industry were either partly or wholly the result of site management's failure to take reasonably practicable precautions.[57] Studies of other industries reveal similar startlingly high rates of both regulatory violations and reckless endangerment of workers' lives.[58] It has been stated that: '[I]n at least two out of three fatal accidents, managements were in violation of the Health and Safety at Work Act 1974 ... Popular definitions of an 'accident' are called into question by such data.'[59] Between 1981 and 1985 there were 739 deaths in the construction industry 70% of which (over 500) could have been avoided by 'positive action by management'.[60] Yet there has been only a handful of prosecutions of company directors for manslaughter following a workplace death and these resulted in only two convictions.[61] Prosecutions of companies are also rare. Workplace deaths are automatically investigated by the HSE who do not have the power to bring manslaughter prosecutions and have only since 1998 agreed a protocol with the police and the Crown Prosecution Service (CPS) for co-ordinating investigations in such cases. Of the 59 cases referred to the CPS by the HSE in the period 1992–98, only 18 prosecutions for manslaughter were brought, mostly against individuals. Prosecutions under the Health and Safety at Work Act 1974 are brought in only 20% of workplace deaths and in only 1% of reported major injuries. Between 1996–98, the HSE did not prosecute any managers or directors in relation to over 500 workplace deaths and 47,000 major injuries reported to it.[62] The Home Office suggests that these low numbers 'do not

---

54 Centre for Corporate Accountability Memorandum to the House of Commons' Environment Sub-Committee of the Select Committee on Environment, Transport and the Regions (1999) HC 828 (London, TSO, 1999).

55 See Pearce and Tombs 'Ideology, Hegemony, and Empiricism: Compliance Theories of Regulation' (1990) 30 *British Journal of Criminology* 423 at p 426. Recent figures are even more alarming and by the end of 2001 it is estimated that 295 workers will have been killed during the course of their employment, a figure up by 75% on the year 2000; see 'Rise in Workplace Deaths' (2001) 151 NLJ 1631.

56 See Centre for Corporate Accountability, n 54 above.

57 See Health and Safety Executive *Dangerous Maintenance* (London, HMSO, 1987).

58 See Health and Safety Executive: *Deadly Maintenance. Plant and Machinery. A Study of Fatal Accidents at Work* (London, HMSO, 1985); *Agricultural Blackspot* (London, HMSO 1986); *Blackspot Construction* (London, HMSO 1988).

59 See Pearce and Tombs, n 55 above.

60 See HSE *Blackspot Construction*, n 58 above.

61 See G Slapper and S Tombs *Corporate Crime* (London, Longman, 1999); Centre for Corporate Accountability, Written Evidence, n 54 above.

62 See Centre for Corporate Accountability, Written Evidence, n 54 above.

reflect any unwillingness on the part of the health and safety enforcing authorities to refer such cases to the CPS and the police but result principally from shortcomings in the existing law on corporate manslaughter'.[63]

This analysis is not convincing. Although indirectly aided and abetted by restrictive doctrine, the systemic reluctance to press for conviction either of companies or their senior managers is far more complex and the underlying arguments in favour of corporate manslaughter are not straightforward. There is flux between the desire to pin blame on *anyone*, on *someone*, and on *no-one* in particular (when the company can be a useful surrogate); in addition there may be an unrealistic expectation that criminal prosecution after the event will have a safety-enhancing instrumental effect in the future. But perhaps I get ahead of myself here.

In 1997, shortly after the Southall rail crash (which gave rise to the *GWT* prosecution), the Government announced its intention to legislate the Law Commission's proposed offence of corporate killing.[64] The Government's consultation paper was not however published until May 2000, coinciding with the failure of the manslaughter charges against GWT. The Paddington (Ladbroke Grove) crash in October 1999, in which 31 people died, had earlier served as a reminder that the promise to legislate had not been fulfilled.[65] There was further talk of manslaughter prosecution against Railtrack following the HSE inquiry into the causes of the Hatfield crash in October 2000.[66] This is a very long lead time and a reasonable inference is that the Government is not as interested in introducing this legislation as it sometimes claims.[67]

The Law Commission proposed three offences to replace the current single offence of manslaughter.[68] For individual offenders two offences were proposed: reckless killing and killing by gross carelessness (which would replace manslaughter by the gross negligence route). It was also envisaged that a corporation could be indicted for these offences through the existing identification rules. In addition, however, the Law Commission Report proposed a separate offence of corporate killing which could only be committed by a corporation. This new offence was intended to be the corporate equivalent of killing by gross carelessness, but the Report sought to overcome the problems of the identification principle by introducing a tailor-made test of corporate culpability based on 'management failure'.[69]

The key to the Law Commission's thinking lay in the collapse of the prosecution for manslaughter against P&O Ferries. The law applicable at the time presented three potential hurdles to a successful prosecution of P&O (the judge directed an acquittal

---

63　See Home Office paper, n 9 above, at para 13, n 4.

64　Draft Involuntary Homicide Bill, cl 4, n 32 above.

65　Under pressure from the injured and bereaved relatives, the CPS has been reconsidering its decision not to bring manslaughter prosecutions in respect of the Paddington crash. The HSE meanwhile has announced that it will bring health and safety charges; see *The Guardian* 14 March 2002; 'Railtrack in dock over Paddington crash' (2002) 146 *Solicitors Journal* 252.

66　See *The Guardian* 30 July 2001. However, it now appears as if no prosecutions will result from the Hatfield crash; see 'Railtrack prosecution for Hatfield unlikely' *The Financial Times* 1 November 2001.

67　These claims were asserted again by Home Office minister Keith Bradley in June 2001; see Hickman 'Corporate Killing Reforms' (2001) 151 NLJ 912.

68　Draft Involuntary Homicide Bill, in Law Commission Report No 237, above n 32, at clauses 1, 2 and 4.

69　See draft Involuntary Homicide Bill, in Law Commission Report No 237, above n 32, at clause 4(2).

before the prosecution had presented all its evidence). First, could a corporation commit manslaughter? That question was resolved as an initial point of law.[70] Secondly, the restrictive, anthropomorphic identification doctrine of corporate liability meant that the company could be liable only through its directing mind, in this case represented by some of its directors. Thirdly, the substantive law of manslaughter, which relied on a test of whether the defendant (here one or more of the directors) had realised that there was an 'obvious and serious risk' of such an event occurring, gave rise to problems. Before the Law Commission Report was published the last difficulty was removed by the re-introduction of 'gross negligence' as the legal test for manslaughter; juries are now asked to consider 'whether the extent to which the defendant's conduct departed from the proper standard of care incumbent upon him ... was such that it should be judged criminal'.[71]

The Law Commission recognised that it is difficult to apply the identification principle especially to large corporations with diffuse management structures. Rather than recommend any change to that rule, a separate offence of corporate killing was proposed. This offence adopts a 'holistic' theory of attribution, that is, a theory that does not derive from the actions of one individual in the company. As adapted by the Home Office in the draft Involuntary Homicide Bill in its 2000 Consultation Paper,[72] the clause for the new styled offence reads:

(1) A corporation is guilty of corporate killing if:

    (a) a management failure by the corporation is the cause or one of the causes of a person's death; and

    (b) that failure constitutes conduct falling far below what can reasonably be expected of the corporation in the circumstances.

(2) For the purposes of sub section (1) above:

    (a) There is a management failure by the company if the way in which its activities are managed or organised fails to ensure the health and safety of persons employed in or affected by those activities; and

    (b) Such a failure may be regarded as a cause of a person's death notwithstanding that the immediate cause is the act or omission of an individual.

Apart from being somewhat circular, a major weakness in the new formulation of corporate killing is that 'management' is not defined. This could lead to problems when the courts are called upon to interpret the scope of 'management'. It could be that either an exceptionally broad test is applied or one which is interpreted very narrowly. John Coffee, the leading US commentator on corporate liability, puts it well:

This standard if adopted could make the corporation a virtual insurer for any accidental killing. In any event, this ... proposal suggests a high degree of cognitive dissonance within the British legal community; on the one hand, the prevailing legal rule on corporate criminal liability is understood to be very narrow and, on the other hand, the appropriate legal standard proposed by the leading law reform group is extremely broad.[73]

---

70 See *R v P&O European Ferries (Dover) Ltd* (1991) 93 Cr App R 72.
71 See *R v Adomako* [1995] 1 AC 171 at p 187C *per* Lord Mackay of Clashfern LC.
72 See n 9 above.
73 See Coffee, above n 24.

Given the judicial aversion to corporate liability as evidenced in the *GWT* and *P&O* trials it is more likely that the cognitive dissonance will be resolved in favour of a narrow interpretation. The judge in the aborted *P&O* trial gave as his reason for directing an acquittal that evidence had been heard from P&O's own employees that no-one had thought that there might be a risk of the ferry sailing with an open door:

> I do not understand that the statements of any of these witnesses condescend to criticism of the system employed by the defendants in this case as one which created an obvious and serious risk, *except to the extent that any legitimate deduction may be made from the fact that they took precautions other than those employed by any of these defendants.*[74]

Yet the official shipping inquiry into the disaster had concluded that all concerned in the company's management shared responsibility for the failure in their safety system.[75] The Law Commission argued that its new culpability test based on management failure would allow a jury to conclude that:

> ... even if the immediate cause of the deaths was the conduct of the assistant bosun, the Chief Officer or both, another of the causes was the failure of the company to devise a safe system for the operation of the ferries; and that that failure fell far below what could reasonably have been expected.[76]

The reasons given for the failure of the prosecution (that there was no obvious and serious risk perceptible to a prudent master that the ferry might sail with its doors open), suggests that we cannot regard it as a management failure that no system was devised to avoid it. The two tests (obvious and serious risk and management failure to ensure safety) reduce to very similar ways of putting the same question. We can either say 'the company's failure to provide a safe system fell far below what was reasonably expected' or 'the company [that is, the management] failed to realise that there was an obvious risk that a ship might sail with its doors open'. If the risk were not obvious, as the judge concluded, why should we expect the company to devise a safe system to prevent it?

In endorsing the Law Commission's proposals, the Government has extended the application of the new offence beyond incorporated bodies to cover 'undertakings'. It is usually assumed that corporate liability will extend at least to incorporated business enterprises, local authorities, charities, and incorporated clubs. It does not, however, cover unincorporated associations such as partnerships, trusts (including hospital trusts), registered Friendly societies and registered trade unions. Since many unincorporated bodies are, in practice, indistinguishable from corporations, the Government extended the application of corporate killing to cover 'undertakings', that is, 'any trade or business or other activity providing employment'.[77] This [would] mean that three-and-a-half million enterprises now subject to the Health and Safety at Work Act 1974 would additionally be

---

74 See *Stanley and Others* 10 October 1990 (CCC) transcript, at p 17D–F, quoted in Law Commission Report No 237, above n 32, at para 6.54 (emphasis added).

75 See The Sheen Report *MV Herald of Free Enterprise Report of the Court No 8074* (London, HMSO, 1987) at para 14.1.

76 See Law Commission Report No 237, above n 32, at para 8.50.

77 See Home Office, above n 9, at para 3.2.2. This relies on the term used in the Health and Safety at Work Act 1974 as defined in Local Employment Act 1960.

potentially liable for corporate killing.[78] Nor would the proposed offence cover a foreign subsidiary of an English parent company.[79]

It is time to return to the argument I introduced earlier that we need to think more deeply about why corporate manslaughter is important and why it has so far failed. A test based on 'management failure' begins to address some of the shortcomings. However, the belief that the new test would entirely solve the problems inherent in corporate manslaughter cases may be misplaced. The major difference is that the new test allows us to speak of 'management' rather than look to individual directors. In some cases, looking to 'management' may well involve a more effective method of capturing the essence of a company's decision making framework than the identification theory allows. Yet the conundrums lurking behind corporate liability remain, in particular that tricky question 'who is the company?' It would be churlish not to concede that speaking of management and failures of systems is an advance on the identification doctrine. It will undoubtedly be easier in many cases to address corporate culpability through 'management failure' than through the directing mind notion. But it is not enough to speak of 'management' or 'the way [the company's] activities are managed or organised' to resolve the real difficulty in determining which employees and which systems can be said to be those of the company. If there is one lesson from the P&O and other corporate killing sagas, it is that corporate defendants are highly motivated and well placed to exploit the metaphysical gap between 'the company' and its members. Two recent examples illustrate some of the confusions in the corporate manslaughter debate. Acquittals were directed in a trial of two companies following the death of a 12-year-old boy under the wheels of a lorry reversing unaided out of the companies' premises. The operations director, who was also charged, could not be said to have *caused* the death even if the jury had been convinced that he had permitted unaided reversing, in disregard of advice given by the Health and Safety Executive some years earlier.[80] This should have been a simple case of corporate manslaughter on either the existing or the proposed new law. If judges continue to resist the very idea that there is a connection between decisions at the top of companies (whether by directors or management) and accidents on the ground, it is difficult to see how legal reforms will lead to the change desired by some. Campaign groups such as the Centre for Corporate Accountability epitomise the conflicting forces. A company recently pleaded guilty to a manslaughter charge. The CCA was highly critical that the CPS promptly dropped all charges against a director of the company.[81]

7 CONCLUSIONS

Even though the conceptual problems surrounding the attribution of liability to corporations can be overcome, awkward questions will still be asked about the efficacy of corporate punishment. Corporate prosecutions, it could be said, allow guilty individuals

---

78   See Home Office, above n 9, at para 3.2.5.
79   See further Gobert 'Corporate Killing at Home and Abroad – Reflections on the Government's Proposals' (2002) 118 LQR 72.
80   See *R v HJ Lea Oakes Ltd, Oakes Millers Ltd and Jepson* Chester Crown Court, 16 July 2001.
81   See *R v English Brothers Ltd* Northampton Crown Court, 3 August 2001.

to escape penalty, and the target is misdirected because 'innocent' shareholders, employees, and so on bear the real costs. One simple answer to the suggestion that corporate liability is ineffective is to point to the extraordinary efforts corporations frequently employ to avoid conviction. But the real question is 'ineffective' at what? Especially in the field of health and safety, it is the major disaster that the high-profile company is anxious to prevent as much as the manslaughter conviction which possibly follows. This is especially so once manslaughter convictions lose their rarity value. This does not mean that we should not hold reckless companies to account. It means that we need to think carefully about why we do so and what it will achieve. Rather than seek to argue in favour of a regime of corporate liability, in this chapter I have outlined and discussed the shortcomings of the various mechanisms adopted by the common law to hold corporations responsible in criminal law. I have also analysed proposals for a specific offence of corporate homicide. The Government's preoccupation with reforming the law of corporate manslaughter is unfortunate, for a debate on the general principles of corporate liability for crime is long overdue.

CHAPTER 14

COMPANY INVESTIGATIONS BY THE DTI

Andrew Lidbetter

1 INTRODUCTION

Any system which prohibits certain conduct on the part of companies and those who control companies requires an effective policing mechanism. The purpose of placing restrictions on specified activities and imposing sanctions for breach of those restrictions would largely be undermined if no such mechanism were in place. The companies legislation, with its restrictions upon the activities of companies and those who operate them including, for example, the requirement of an external auditor's report on the annual accounts,[1] provides a framework which, to an extent, acts as an internal policing mechanism. However, this is incomplete and UK company law has entrusted the public policing mechanism to the Department of Trade and Industry (DTI). The company investigations regime administered by the DTI therefore fulfils a crucial role in relation to policing the activities of companies and those individuals who run companies. It primarily concerns the interaction of companies, directors and shareholders on the one hand and the State in the form of the Secretary of State for Trade and Industry, inspectors appointed by him and the Financial Services Authority on the other.[2]

Although the recent DTI company law review has seen a far reaching examination of many aspects of company law, the investigations regime was not covered in *The Final Report* and was effectively treated as being outside the terms of reference of the review, however, the DTI is proposing to look separately at the investigations regime and has published a consultation document in this regard.[3]

The investigations regime had its genesis in legislation in the mid-19th century. The Joint Stock Companies Act 1856 provided that the Board of Trade could appoint inspectors to examine the affairs of a company and produce a report upon the application of a proportion of shareholders and the inspectors could require officers and agents to produce documents and be examined on oath.[4] Thus, the regime of inspections has been part of company law for around 150 years albeit that the powers have changed in subsequent Companies Acts. For example, the Companies Act 1947 introduced a power for the Board of Trade to appoint inspectors of its own volition rather than simply responding to applications by a proportion of shareholders. In addition to inspections, Parliament, over the course of time, gave other powers to the Board of Trade, most

---

1 Companies Act 1985, s 235.
2 See in particular Companies Act 1985, Part XIV and, more generally, A Lidbetter *Company Investigations and Public Law* (Oxford, Hart, 1999).
3 See Company Law Review Steering Group *Modern Company Law For a Competitive Economy: Final Report* (London, DTI, July 2001). Although I was a member of a working party concerning sanctions for the review, the views expressed in this essay are entirely my own. Note also *Company Investigations: Powers for the 21st Century* (London, DTI, 2001); the latter document was published too late to be incorporated in this essay.
4 Joint Stock Companies Act 1856, ss 48–52.

importantly, in the Companies Act 1967 the power for the Secretary of State to require the production of documents and to require an explanation of them.[5]

Although the investigations regime has been refined gradually over a period of the last 150 years it is now time to reconsider whether the present powers and practices are appropriate. The last major consideration of the regime took place in 1990 when the Trade and Industry Committee produced a report[6] to which the Government issued a White Paper in response.[7] Business activity is becoming increasingly complex and the scope for fraudulent conduct in relation to shareholders and the public is increasing. The policing mechanism of the investigations regime has to be effective to detect and deter wrongdoing but, at the same time, the cost to the business community and the public purse should not be disproportionate. Also, the regime must operate in a way that does not unduly infringe the civil liberties of those involved with companies. This essay explores the investigations regime against that background.

The essay concentrates on the power to appoint inspectors under s 432 of the Companies Act, since that is the power invoked in the most high-profile major investigations, and the more limited document-based investigation under s 447, because that is the most widely used power. In each of the years from 1996–97 to 1999–2000 the number of investigations completed under s 447 ranged from 167 to 218 whilst in the whole of the period only two investigations were completed under s 432.[8] The DTI does, however, have other rarely used powers[9] and the Financial Services Authority also has wide investigatory powers[10] whilst other regulatory authorities have powers to

---

5 Companies Act 1967, s 109 implementing the recommendations of the Report of the Company Law Committee (1962) Cmnd 1749 (London, HMSO, 1962) *The Jenkins Report*. See now Companies Act 1985 s 447.

6 *House of Commons, Trade and Industry Committee's Third Report: 'Company Investigations'*, Session 1989–90 HC 36 (London, HMSO, 1990).

7 *Company Investigations. Governments Response to the Third Report of the House of Commons Trade and Industry Committee: 1989–90 Session* (1990) Cm 1149 (London, HMSO, 1990).

8 See *Companies in 1999–2000* (London, TSO, 2000).

9 Other Companies Act powers which are very rarely used are to appoint inspectors upon an application by a company or a certain number or proportion of its members (s 431); to appoint inspectors to investigate the ownership of a company (s 442); to obtain information as to the beneficial ownership of shares, etc (s 444); to appoint inspectors to investigate whether there have been any contraventions of provisions imposing restrictions on share dealings by directors and their families and imposing disclosure requirements on directors (s 446); and to seek a court order requiring books and papers to be produced for inspection where it is suspected that a company officer has committed an offence in connection with the management of the company's affairs (s 721). The Secretary of State also has some other specific powers in other legislation including to assist overseas regulatory authorities (Companies Act 1989, ss 82–91), to investigate insurance companies (Insurance Companies Act 1982, s 84), and to investigate a possible offence by a company's officer or member when it is reported to the Secretary of State by a liquidator (Insurance Companies Act 1982, s 84).

10 Prior to the coming into force of the relevant provisions of the Financial Services and Markets Act 2000, the Financial Services Authority (FSA) has various investigation powers by virtue of the Financial Services Act 1986 – investigations into the operations of authorised unit trusts and collective schemes, etc (s 94); investigations into the affairs of anyone carrying on investment business (s 105); and investigations into insider dealing (s 177). Under the Financial Services and Markets Act 2000 (the main provisions of which came into force on 30 November 2001), the FSA has specific and formal powers to gather information and conduct investigations in order to execute its statutory functions. Some of these powers are held concurrently with the Secretary of State. Under s 167, the FSA or Secretary of State will be able to initiate a general investigation into a business, any particular aspect of that business, or the ownership or control of it, if they believe that there is a just cause for doing so. Either the FSA or the Secretary of State also has the power to appoint competent individuals to carry out an investigation on their behalf. Under s 168, the FSA is able to appoint investigators [cont]

investigate particular aspects of a company's affairs, for example, the Inland Revenue, Customs and Excise, Competition Commission, etc.

The next part of this essay, part 2, considers whether the statutory powers are appropriate to achieve their objective of identifying any illegitimate activity on the part of companies and those individuals who run companies. In particular, it focuses on whether the investigators have sufficient statutory powers to initiate investigations and then whether, once an investigation has been initiated, the investigators have adequate statutory powers to require the production of documents and answers to questions. It is only by the investigators having adequate powers that there can be any degree of confidence that they will be able to identify any wrongdoing. Part 3 briefly considers the interplay between the need for adequate powers on the one hand and the public law constraints on their exercise. Investigations must be carried out with due regard for procedural fairness and investigators must also bear in mind the impact of the Human Rights Act 1998 particularly in relation to search powers.[11] There is inevitably a tension between exercising powers in a rigorous and thorough manner and the individual rights of those who are subject to the investigation and it will be argued that the current balance is about right.

Parts 4 and 5 of the essay consider the action that can be taken in the light of investigators' findings. The policing mechanism can only be effective it if is backed up by adequate criminal, civil or regulatory sanctions. Part 4 looks at the existing range of follow-up actions and, in particular, identifies the possible need for a new power to apply for injunctive relief to restrain particular types of conduct on the part of a company – a remedy which could be used more sensitively than existing sanctions such as winding-up proceedings. Part 5 concentrates on the use of evidence obtained by investigators in follow-up action. The need for an in-depth analysis of this topic springs from the European Court of Human Rights' judgment in *Saunders v United Kingdom*[12] and then the subsequent introduction of the Human Rights Act effectively placing restrictions on the use of evidence in criminal trials. The case law in the area is not straightforward, but it will be argued that the balance between effective follow-up action and the procedural rights of individuals has not been upset.

The final discussion in part 6 considers the present law and practice concerning the publication of reports and, in particular, revisits the approaches advocated in 1990 by the House of Commons Trade and Industry Committee and the then Government. The importance of this debate is obvious: reports are paid for from the public purse and their

---

10 [cont] in a number of specific circumstances to investigate possible contraventions of both a criminal and civil nature, including circumstances suggesting that insider dealing or market abuse have taken place. The Secretary of State shares some of these powers with the FSA. Those appointed to investigate in specific circumstances have wider powers than those appointed under s 167. The FSA has a specific information gathering power in respect of persons authorised by the FSA (Financial Services and Markets Act 2000, s 166). Under s 169, the FSA also has a similar power to the Companies Act 1989, s 83, ie, the power to assist foreign regulators in obtaining information and investigating matters. The numbers of investigations completed each year under the Companies Act 1989, s 84 in the period 1996–97 to 1999–2000 ranged from three to 15 and the numbers of inspectors' reports submitted under Financial Services Act 1986, s 177 ranged from 13 to 21; see *Companies in 1999–2000*, above n 8.

11 See: *Re Pergamon Press Ltd* [1971] Ch 388; *Maxwell v DTI* [1974] QB 523. The most significant of the Articles of the European Convention on Human Rights incorporated by the Human Rights Act 1998 are Arts 6 (right to a fair hearing) and 8 (right to respect for private and family life).

12 (1996) 23 EHRR 313.

publication can teach valuable lessons but the value of publication cannot override the need to ensure that, in particular, defendants in criminal cases receive a fair trial.

2 THE DTI INVESTIGATIVE POWERS

Under the Companies Act 1985, the Secretary of State has two main powers pursuant to which he may initiate an investigation. These powers are to be found in ss 432 and 447 of the Act. The power under s 432 to appoint inspectors to investigate suspected malpractice is invoked where there are complex factual issues and there is a strong public interest in recognising and reporting upon them. It will usually be used where there is already public debate in relation to a company and it is envisaged that a report will be published. The Secretary of State does, however, have the power to appoint inspectors on the basis that their report will not be published.[13] Given the expense of major investigations under s 432 and the length of time they can take to complete it is not surprising that they are rare.

Conversely, the more limited powers under s 447 to obtain documents and require an explanation of them are used far more widely. This is because s 447 can be used to trigger a more limited confidential fact finding exercise which, depending on its findings, can lead to follow-up action. By carrying out the investigation in a confidential manner this should not unnecessarily affect public confidence in the company. Whether follow-up action is appropriate and, if so, the nature of that action will obviously depend on what is uncovered by the investigation.

Although s 447 permits the Secretary of State to require the production of documents and to apply to a Justice of the Peace for a warrant to search premises,[14] the powers to interrogate those involved in running a company are limited. The Secretary of State can only require a person who produces documents or any other past or present officers or employees of the company 'to provide an explanation' of any of the documents[15] or, where documents are not produced, require the person who had been required to produce them to state where they are.[16] By contrast, the powers of interrogation in s 432 are not limited to explanations of documents but are more widely framed to include the power to require any persons to attend before the inspectors and otherwise give them all assistance in connection with the investigation which they are reasonably able to give.[17]

Although the purpose of the s 447 powers is more limited[18] than the purpose of inspections under s 432 they are both aimed at uncovering the relevant facts surrounding the company's affairs. Therefore, the powers under both routes of enquiry must be sufficient to achieve this common aim. Also, investigations under s 432 have long been criticised for the delay taken to produce the final reports and this has encouraged the

---

13 See Companies Act 1985, s 432A.
14 See Companies Act 1985, s 448.
15 See Companies Act 1985, s 447(5)(a).
16 See Companies Act 1985, s 447(5)(b).
17 See Companies Act 1985, ss 434(1) and (2).
18 Section 447 also applies to companies incorporated in other jurisdictions but which conduct business within the United Kingdom.

greater use of s 447 powers.[19] Given the use made of s 447 investigations and the need to prevent and track down corporate wrongdoing there is an argument that greater powers should be given to the DTI to strengthen s 447 to make them more akin to the powers available to inspectors appointed under s 432.

However, rather than amending s 447, if it is felt that greater investigation powers are needed in a particular case but without warranting the appointment of outside inspectors under s 432 (most typically a QC and an accountant from a large firm), a slightly different approach could be adopted. There is no reason why the DTI could not appoint their own officers as inspectors under s 432 (as often happened with investigations into alleged insider dealing under s 177 of the Financial Services Act 1986) and then conduct a focused investigation. Although an appointment can only be made under s 432 if one of the criteria for an appointment is satisfied, the criteria are widely drawn and there would be few cases in practice where the DTI would be able to commence an investigation under s 447 but not fulfil one of the criteria for appointing inspectors under s 432.[20] There would be no need for the inspectors to conduct an inspection on the same scale as some of the major inspections such as House of Fraser plc,[21] Guinness plc[22] and Mirror Group Newspapers plc.[23] There would even be no need to publish a report if an appointment were made on the basis that any report produced was not for publication.[24]

Therefore, when considering any reform of the statutory powers available to the DTI, particularly in view of the usefulness but limitations of s 447, serious consideration should be given to whether s 432 might, in practice, be used to conduct investigations on a smaller scale rather than used only in those few cases where that section is currently invoked. Thus, simply by changing the balance as to when s 432 is invoked rather than s 447, and ensuring that any s 432 investigation is appropriately focused, the investigation powers can be strengthened in practice without the need for any legislative change.

---

19 See, for example, the outcome of the review announced by the then Secretary of State for Trade, on 19 May 1980 and note the criticism of this approach by Sugarman 'DoT System of Inspections and Prosecutions is Streamlined' (1981) 2 *Company Lawyer* 79.

20 The Secretary of State may appoint inspectors to investigate a company's affairs under s 432 of the Companies Act if it appears that there are circumstances suggesting the company's activities are or have been conducted with the intention of defrauding its creditors or creditors of any other person or for any other fraudulent or unlawful purpose or in a manner which unfairly prejudices some part of its members; or an actual or proposed act or omission of the company or done on its behalf is or would be prejudicial to it; or the company was formed for a fraudulent or unlawful purpose; or the individuals involved with a company's creation or management have been guilty of fraud, misfeasance or other misconduct towards the company or its members; or a company's members have not been given all the information with respect to its affairs which they might reasonably expect. Section 432(1) also provides that the Secretary of State must appoint inspectors if the court orders that a company's affairs ought to be investigated.

21 *DTI Report into House of Fraser Holdings plc* (London, HMSO, 1988).

22 *DTI Report into Guinness plc* (London, TSO, 1997).

23 *DTI Report into Mirror Group Newspapers plc* (London, TSO, 2001).

24 See Companies Act 1985, s 432(2A). As to publication generally see section 6 below.

3 THE CONDUCT OF INVESTIGATIONS AND PROCEDURAL AND SUBSTANTIVE FAIRNESS

It is well established that procedural fairness or the rules of natural justice apply to the conduct of investigations at least where a report is to be published[25] but that the content of the obligation of fairness is limited. The need to put intended criticisms to witnesses and give them an opportunity to respond will inevitably lead to delay in completing any reports but a consideration of those witnesses' responses serves the useful function of enabling the investigators to correct any errors they may otherwise make in their conclusions and this step is also an important procedural safeguard for the rights of the individual. Thus, someone who may be criticised is entitled to know the gist of the criticism and have an opportunity to make written submissions to rebut the criticism but the person is not, for example, entitled to demand to cross-examine anyone who may have given evidence adverse to the version of events put forward by the person who may fall to be criticised.[26]

Similarly public law principles and the general principle that witnesses should not be treated oppressively are applicable to investigations. In *R v Secretary of State for Trade and Industry ex p Perestrello*,[27] Woolf J took the view that notices which required an individual to produce at the DTI's offices various categories of documents including 'all accounting records of the company such as to disclose the financial position of the company' and 'all files of correspondence relating to the affairs of the company including ...' were 'unreasonable and excessive'[28] in circumstances where the person concerned had been co-operating with the investigation. However, generally a significant degree of latitude is given to those investigators examining potential corporate wrongdoing before a court will conclude that requests made by investigators are in breach of public law principles or are oppressive.[29]

However, the position needs to be re-assessed in the light of two developments. The first is the recent case of *Re an Inquiry into Mirror Group Newspapers plc*[30] and is of importance because of the approach of Sir Richard Scott V-C towards the inspectors' treatment of Kevin Maxwell. In this case the DTI inspectors had certified to the court Kevin Maxwell's refusal to answer questions and his refusal to enter into a confidentiality undertaking not to disclose information which they had put to him during the course of their enquiries. Maxwell argued that the inspectors' questioning was oppressive and that they had no power to require him to give the confidentiality undertaking. Sir Richard Scott V-C agreed that there was no power to impose a confidentiality undertaking. He

---

25 See: *Re Pergamon Press Ltd* [1971] Ch 388; *Maxwell v DTI* [1974] QB 523; Lidbetter, above n 2, at chapters 5 and 7.

26 See the material at n 25 above.

27 [1981] 1 QB 19.

28 [1981] 1 QB 19 at p 31A. Note by analogy the approach taken by the courts when faced with claims that Inland Revenue notices seeking documents were unduly wide in *R v O'Kane ex p Northern Bank* [1996] STC 1249, *R v Inland Revenue Commissioners ex p Ulster Bank Ltd* [1997] STC 832 and *R v Commissioners of Inland Revenue ex p Banque Internationale a Luxembourg SA* [2000] STC 708.

29 See, for example, *R v Secretary of State for Trade and Others ex p Perestrello* [1981] 1 QB 19. Note also Lidbetter, above n 2, at pp 93–106.

30 [2000] Ch 194.

said that a witness could not be required to sign an undertaking although a witness who used the contents of documents or other information for a purpose other than that for which it had been given to him may commit a breach of duty to those from whom information or documents had been obtained. In relation to the obligation under s 434 to give assistance to inspectors, this extended only to the assistance that the witness was reasonably able to give, whether as to the time he would have to expend, or the expense he would have to incur in preparation for the questions or in any other respect.

Prior to the inspectors' questions, Kevin Maxwell had already been questioned by administrators, liquidators, the Serious Fraud Office and at a criminal trial in relation to the collapse of the Maxwell group of companies in 1991 run, primarily, by his late father, Robert Maxwell. Sir Richard Scott V-C said that the inspectors should do their best to avoid questioning Kevin Maxwell on topics on which he had been questioned before and, so far as possible, should rely on answers given in previous interrogations. However, he said that there was nothing unreasonable in the DTI refusing to assure him that his answers would not be used as the basis of further civil or criminal proceedings. In what Sir Richard Scott V-C described as a 'highly unusual case' he put forward steps to limit the questioning, for example, requiring inspectors to identify answers in earlier transcripts that fairness to Kevin Maxwell required to be drawn to his attention.

The central message from *Re Mirror Group Newspapers plc* is that the powers of investigators are not untrammelled and that, in practice, inspectors may be restrained by the courts. However, the case was unusual in that Kevin Maxwell had already been questioned by various other agencies and Scott V-C did not rule out the possibility of the inspectors being able to ask him further questions. There is nothing to suggest that the result of *Re Mirror Group Newspapers plc* should lead to the conclusion that the powers of inspectors, or other investigators, need strengthening by statute and, in any event, statute could not exclude the court's powers to apply public law principles when considering the discretionary exercise of powers.[31] Equally, the approach in *Re Mirror Group Newspapers plc* demonstrates that courts will have some regard for the rights of individuals required to assist in an investigation.

The second development is the incorporation into domestic law of the European Convention on Human Rights through the Human Rights Act 1998. Section 6 of the Human Rights Act provides that it is unlawful for a public authority to act in a way which is incompatible with a Convention right. The DTI and inspectors constitute a public authority and must not therefore, contravene any articles of the European Convention on Human Rights.[32] In the light of this it is necessary to consider the extent to which the investigation process could fall foul of the Convention.

Although the investigation process has been characterised as one which does not involve a determination of civil rights, and therefore Art 6 of the Convention concerning

---

31 See *Anisminic v Foreign Compensation Commission (No 2)* [1969] 2 AC 147.
32 Prior to the Human Rights Act 1998 coming into force, the European Convention on Human Rights could only be relied on in domestic law in limited circumstances, such as to resolve an ambiguity in the common law or to assist in an argument that a public authority was behaving in an irrational manner, eg, *R v Secretary of State for the Home Department ex p McQuillan* [1995] 4 All ER 400.

the right to a fair trial is not engaged by the investigations process itself,[33] nonetheless Art 8 may still be engaged in the evidence gathering process. The question arises as to how Art 8 impacts upon the exercise of investigators' powers given the existing restrictions that investigators must not act in breach of public law principles or otherwise act oppressively. Article 8 provides:

1   Everyone has the right to respect for his private and family life, his home and his correspondence.

2   There shall be no interference by a public authority with the exercise of this right except such as is in accordance with the law and is necessary in a democratic society in the interests of national security, public safety or the economic well-being of the country, for the prevention of disorder or crime, for the protection of health or morals, or for the protection of the rights and freedoms of others.

There is some debate as to whether a company rather than individuals can rely on Art 8 of the Convention.[34] However, it is clear that a request for material or a search of business premises can engage Art 8. In *Niemietz v Germany*[35] the European Court of Human Rights held that the search of a lawyer's office infringed Art 8 as the interference was not necessary in a democratic society and there were no legal safeguards in relation to how the search was to be carried out which would prevent an abuse of power. The notion of 'private life' could extend to activities of a professional or business nature and 'home' can, in principle, extend to an office.[36] Thus, in *Miailhe v France*[37] where French customs officers seized around 15,000 documents from the applicant's head office (registering 9,478 and returning the remainder as being of no relevance) there was found to be an infringement of Art 8. The Strasbourg Court noted, for example, the absence of a requirement of a judicial warrant and that the seizures made were 'wholesale and, above all, indiscriminate', to such an extent that the customs considered several thousand documents to be of no relevance to their enquiries and returned them to the applicants.[38]

Notwithstanding the *Niemietz* and *Miailhe* cases the application of Art 8 should have only a marginal impact on the exercise of search and seizure powers. This is because even where Art 8(1) is engaged, the search is likely to be justified under Art 8(2). The search will be 'in accordance with law' in view of the statutory powers permitting searches[39] and the purpose of the search should fall within one of the objectives in Art 8(2) – most

---

33   See *Fayed v United Kingdom* (1994) 18 EHRR 393. Note also in the context of *R v Hertfordshire County Council ex p Green Environmental Industries Ltd* [2000] 2 AC 412. Cf *Heaney and McGuinness v Ireland* (REF00002127) and *Quinn v Ireland* (REF00002128). The use of evidence obtained by DTI investigators in subsequent proceedings can engage Art 6 (see below).

34   Note that in *R v Broadcasting Standards Commission ex p BBC* [2000] 3 WLR 1527, it was held that a company could rely upon the concept of privacy in the BSC's Code but the judges gave no clear guidance as to whether a company could rely upon Art 8 of the Convention.

35   (1993) 16 EHRR 97.

36   Were this not the case there would effectively be discrimination against home-workers if their home did not engage the protection of Art 8.

37   (1993) 16 EHRR 332.

38   See (1993) 16 EHRR 332 at para 39. Note the more restrictive approach of the European Court of Justice in *National Panasonic (UK) Ltd v Commission of the European Communities* [1980] ECR 2033 and *Hoechst AG v Commission of European Communities* [1989] ECR 2859.

39   See Companies Act 1985, s 448.

obviously the interests of 'the economic well-being of the country' or 'the prevention of ... crime'. The legality of the search will then depend on whether it is 'necessary in a democratic society' in the sense of it being for a 'pressing social need' and proportionate. The fact that a search warrant is required from a magistrate before a search can be carried out[40] will assist in demonstrating that the search is proportionate because there will be independent scrutiny of the decision to carry out a search.[41] Also, the domestic law concerning the exercise of statutory powers places limits on the exercise of powers in any event.[42]

Therefore, Art 8 heightens the scrutiny of the reasons for a search and the manner of its exercise to ensure that the search is proportionate. It does not, however, have the effect that significant numbers of requests for evidence and searches which would previously have been regarded as lawful are now vulnerable to successful challenge by those required to produce material to the investigators or to undergo a search of their premises. The balance which is struck in applying Art 8 should not unduly inhibit the exercise of powers by investigators. However, the requirement to obtain a warrant serves a useful function in helping to demonstrate the need for the search in any particular case. Therefore, although the requirements of Art 8 place emphasis on the rights of the individual, there is unlikely to be a case where the DTI would be complying with domestic law with its strictures against substantive unfairness and oppression and yet at the same time be in breach of the Human Rights Act.

4 FOLLOW-UP ACTION

Once an investigation has been completed various follow-up actions are available. These are:

(a) commencing civil proceedings in the name of the company;[43]

(b) presenting a winding-up petition where it appears to the Secretary of State that it is expedient in the public interest that the company investigated should be wound up;[44]

(c) presenting a petition to the court if it appears to the Secretary of State that the affairs of a body corporate that is liable to be wound up are being or have been conducted in a manner that it is unfairly prejudicial to its members;[45]

(d) commencing directors disqualification proceedings;[46]

(e) criminal prosecutions including for insider dealing[47] and money laundering, etc, and from November 2001 proceedings leading to possible penalties for market abuse under the Financial Services and Markets Act;[48]

---

40 See Companies Act 1985, ss 448(1) and (2).
41 See *Birse v HM Advocate* 2000 JC 503.
42 *R v Secretary of State for Trade and Industry ex p Perestrello* [1981] 1 QB 19.
43 See Companies Act 1985, s 438.
44 See Insolvency Act 1986, s 124A.
45 See Companies Act 1985, s 460.
46 See Company Directors Disqualification Act 1986, s 8.
47 See Criminal Justice Act 1993, Part V.
48 See Financial Services and Markets Act 2000, s 123.

(f) action by other regulators such as professional disciplinary proceedings against solicitors and accountants when information is passed to those regulators by the DTI under the gateways in the Companies Act which provide statutory exceptions to the restriction on the disclosure of information obtained during the course of investigations.[49]

Therefore, there are a range of steps that can be taken consequent upon the production of a report,[50] and the power to seek a winding up of a company or the disqualification of a director are of particular importance in protecting the public. However, there is inevitably a delay in obtaining the final court orders winding up a company or disqualifying directors and there is usually a significant delay, even from the completion of an investigation to the appointment of a receiver, because of the need to assemble evidence to show the risk to the public.[51]

Although the DTI can apply to the court for an interim injunction to restrain the conduct of a company pending the winding up on public interest grounds[52] a further possibility would be to permit the Secretary of State to apply for a restraining injunction in circumstances where it was not intended that there would be winding up or disqualification proceedings. This would meet a concern that companies will, at times, engage in activities which are harmful and which should be stopped in the public interest but where there is no need to go so far as to wind up the companies concerned. Such an injunction could initially be on an interim basis and then made final to restrain a particular type of activity or a particular individual in the public interest. The evidence in support of the injunction would be the material gathered in the course of the company investigation. It would then be for the court to consider whether or not to grant an injunction in the public interest.

This remedy would have the advantage of being able to restrain behaviour in a more targeted way. For example, an individual could be restrained from acting in a particular way or in a particular business area without going so far as to prevent him from acting as a director.[53] This would have some similarities with the power of the Secretary of State, under s 61 of the Financial Services Act, to apply to the court to obtain an injunction to prevent the contravention of certain sections of the Act and rules of self-regulating organisations or recognised professional bodies, or an order requiring a person knowingly concerned in a contravention to take steps to remedy it. However, the power in s 61 linked to specific statutory sections or rules, whereas a proposed new injunctive power in the public interest would be a potentially powerful weapon in relation to consumer protection but could be open-ended. The difficulty, therefore, with such a new remedy is that it may initially be vague in practice but the position would become clearer

---

49 See Companies Act 1985, s 449.
50 Note the possibility of a challenge to the decision of the DTI to take follow-up action; see *R v Secretary of State for Trade and Industry ex p Lonrho plc* [1992] BCC 325.
51 Note *Re Senator Hanseatische Verwaltungs GmbH* [1997] 1 WLR 515 and particularly the comments of Millett LJ at pp 526H–27A in relation to the advantages of appointing a provisional liquidator as against granting temporary injunctions.
52 See for example *Re Senator Hanseatische* [1997] 1 WLR 515.
53 As an analogy, note the powers of some professional regulators to impose particular restrictions on particular certificates or licences, eg, the power to prohibit solicitors from handling clients' monies.

once the courts have dealt with a number of contested applications and it could then be seen how the public interest test would operate in different types of cases.

The approach towards applying a test of whether an activity is or is not in the public interest would be similar to that adopted in relation to a petition to wind up a company in the public interest under s 124A of the Insolvency Act 1986 because it is clear that courts may order that a company be wound up in the public interest even though the company is not engaged in any unlawful activity.[54] Indeed, protecting those who deal with companies underlies the jurisdiction to wind up companies. As Millett LJ stated in *Re Senator Hanseatische*:

> I reject [the submission] that the Secretary of State has no business to intervene in a case where no illegal activity is being carried on. The expression 'expedient in the public interest' is of the widest import; it means what it says. The Secretary of State has a right, and some would say a duty, to apply to the court to protect members of the public who deal with the company from suffering inevitable loss, whether this derives from illegal activity or not. A common case in which he intervenes is where an insolvent company continues to trade by paying its debts as they fall due out of money obtained from new creditors. The insolvency is the cause of the eventual loss, but it is the need to protect the public, not the insolvency, which grounds the Secretary of State's application for a winding up order in such cases.[55]

It is also necessary to consider the court's approach towards the DTI's view of what is in the public interest. In the context of winding up in the public interest it is for the court when weighing the factors for and against a winding-up order to carry out a balancing exercise. In doing so it will note that the DTI's submissions are made by a government department charged by Parliament with wide-ranging responsibilities in relation to the affairs of companies and that the DTI has expertise and can be expected to act with a proper sense of responsibility. The court will, however, consider the cogency of the DTI's submissions in the same way as any other submissions.[56] The approach requires the court 'to identify for itself the aspect or aspects of public interest which, in the view of the court, would be promoted by making a winding-up order in the particular case'.[57] A similar approach to the DTI's views on what the public interest requires could be adopted to applications for injunctive relief either on an interim or final basis in cases where the DTI considers that, in the public interest, certain activities by companies or individuals should be restrained short of winding up the company or disqualifying directors.

Care would be needed to ensure that the form of any injunction granted was one which could realistically be policed and enforced. The problem of enforcement is, however, no more difficult than where the court decides to accept undertakings on the part of those controlling companies. For example, in *Re Forrester & Lamengo Ltd*[58] Carnwath J considered the case of an application for the appointment of a provisional liquidator in the context of a petition to wind up a company where the DTI argued that the company, which was carrying on business as a broker of champagne and wine, was being run irresponsibly and with a lack of probity. Carnwath J stated:

---

54 See, for example *Re Senator Hanseatische* [1997] 1 WLR 515. The Company Directors Disqualification Act 1986, s 8 also necessitates a consideration of what the public interest requires.

55 [1997] 1 WLR 515 at p 526 B–D.

56 See *Re Walter L Jacob & Co Ltd* [1989] BCLC 345 at p 353 F.

57 See *Re Walter L Jacob & Co Ltd* [1989] BCLC 345 at p 353 F *per* Nicholls LJ.

58 [1997] 2 BCLC 155.

Undoubtedly the company has made exaggerated and misleading claims for its products, but it is open to argument whether that fact by itself affects the public interest so seriously as to require the drastic remedy of winding up if other less drastic remedies are available. On the evidence, there are arguable issues in response to the petition which it would be wrong to prejudge at this stage.[59]

Carnwath J said it would be wrong to allow the company to be presented as independent specialist advisers competent to recommend products as investments but it was not a case where the whole business of the company was based on a lie or where investors' funds were at risk because records were lacking. His approach was that:

... provided that there are acceptable undertakings to ensure that the marketing stays within the bounds of fair dealing and the assets are protected ... on balance ... it is right to allow it to continue at least pending the hearing of the petition.[60]

In relation to the problems in policing the undertakings Carnwath J said:

Clearly they are not as convenient as having the matter under the control of an independent provisional liquidator. But I am not persuaded that it is unworkable. The advertising methods are, by their nature, open and can be checked by random telephone calls to the salesmen. Those difficulties are not so great, in my view, as to justify the extreme course of, in effect closing down the business pending the hearing of the petition.[61]

The case of *Re Forrester & Lamengo Ltd* is instructive in that the court was prepared to proceed on the basis of undertakings which would require some careful policing by the DTI. There is no reason why a court order with similar content to the undertakings could not also be policed. Any difficulty in policing an injunction would be something to be considered when deciding whether or not to grant an injunction and, if so, the terms of that injunction. However, the potential difficulty in policing an interim or final injunction in some cases should not mean that it is inappropriate to have the remedy available for use in other cases.

Finally, the question as to whether the DTI would be required to give a cross-undertaking in damages as a condition for the grant of an interim injunction to restrain certain activities would need to be addressed. Courts will not normally impose cross-undertakings on a public authority seeking to enforce the law unless the defendant shows a strong *prima facie* case that its conduct is lawful.[62] This principle led to the conclusion in *Re Highfield Commodities Ltd*[63] that the Secretary of State, in seeking the appointment of a provisional liquidator under a petition to wind up the company in the public interest, was not required to give a cross-undertaking and also in *Securities and Investments Board v Lloyd-Wright*[64] that the Securities and Investments Board should not have to give a cross-undertaking when obtaining a Mareva injunction in relation to proceedings under ss 6 and 61 of the Financial Services Act 1986 to restrain the conduct of unauthorised

---

59 [1997] 2 BCLC 155 at p 159 G–H.
60 [1997] 2 BCLC 155 at p 160 A.
61 [1997] 2 BCLC 155 at p 160 B–C.
62 See *Hoffman-La Roche & Co AG and Others v Secretary of State for Trade and Industry* [1975] AC 295.
63 [1985] 1 WLR 149.
64 [1994] 1 BCLC 147.

investment business.[65] However, the proposed remedy is a potentially far reaching one and is based on a more general public interest test than enforcing specific laws and in these circumstances there might be a stronger case for requiring the DTI to give a cross-undertaking, notwithstanding *Re Highfield Commodities Ltd*.[66]

5 THE USE OF EVIDENCE, *SAUNDERS* AND ARTICLE 6 OF THE CONVENTION[67]

Although Art 6 of the Convention is not engaged by DTI investigations, an important issue arises in relation to the extent to which Art 6 inhibits the use that can be made of information obtained during the course of an investigation. This issue is of importance because when an investigation is launched one purpose will usually be to enable follow-up action to be taken. That follow-up action might well involve a determination of civil rights or a criminal charge such that Art 6 will be engaged. Such follow-up action could be frustrated if the evidence obtained in the course of the DTI investigation and the investigators' findings could not be used.

Generally, sworn and unsworn statements given to those conducting investigations will be admissible in evidence against the statement-maker.[68] Also, the reports of investigators will be admissible as evidence of the investigators' opinions in subsequent proceedings, albeit that they contain hearsay, and are admissible in disqualification proceedings as evidence of any fact.[69] However, a limitation arises in respect of statements which tend to incriminate the statement-maker. The starting point for this limitation is that although legislation enables investigators to require a witness to attend to give evidence, for example, s 434(1) and (2) of the Companies Act 1985, the legislation is silent in relation to whether a person can be required to answer questions which would tend to incriminate them. However, the legislation was interpreted in such a way as to override the right not to answer incriminating questions in *Re London United Investments plc*.[70] Building on this approach, the Court of Appeal in *R v Seelig, R v Spens*[71] refused to exclude answers given to DTI inspectors from a criminal trial. It had been argued that the answers should be excluded on the basis that to admit any confession was contrary to s 76 of the Police and Criminal Evidence Act 1984[72] because it was oppressive and that it

---

65　But note that in *Customs & Excise Commissioners v Anchor Foods Ltd* [1999] 3 All ER 268 a cross-undertaking in damages was required from Customs & Excise to support a Mareva injunction.

66　[1985] 1 WLR 149.

67　Generally see P Davies 'Self-Incrimination, Fair Trials, and the Pursuit of Corporate and Financial Wrongdoing' in B Markesinis (ed) *The Impact of the Human Rights Bill on English Law* (Oxford, Clarendon, 1998).

68　See Companies Act 1985, s 434(5) and s 447(8) in respect of sworn statements. In *London and County Securities v Nicholson* [1980] 1 WLR 948 Browne-Wilkinson J held that sworn and unsworn evidence are admissible in evidence against the statement-maker.

69　See Companies Act 1985, s 441(1) and note *Re Rex Williams Leisure plc* [1994] Ch 350 concerning the use of investigators' reports in support of applications to wind up companies in the public interest. See generally Lidbetter, above n 2, at pp 234–40.

70　[1992] Ch 578. See also: *Bank of England v Riley* [1992] Ch 475; and *Styr v HM Advocate* 1994 SLT 5.

71　[1992] 1 WLR 148.

72　Section 76 restricts the admissibility of confessions which may have been obtained by oppression or are likely to be unreliable.

would be contrary to s 78 of that Act[73] as being unfair, and that the answers should therefore be excluded in the exercise of the court's discretion under s 82(3)[74] but these submissions were rejected. A similar approach was adopted in *R v Saunders and Others*.[75]

Consequently, the extent to which evidence given to inspectors appointed under the Companies Act 1985 may be used in criminal proceedings was considered by the European Court of Human Rights in *Saunders v United Kingdom*,[76] where the applicant, Ernest Saunders (who had been convicted of various criminal offences arising out of his tenure as Chairman and CEO of the company Guinness during its takeover of the company Distillers in 1986), argued that he had been denied a fair trial in breach of Art 6(1) in relation to the use of statements obtained by the DTI inspectors during the criminal proceedings against him. The court accepted this argument pointing out that 'the right to silence and the right not to incriminate oneself, are generally recognised standards which lie at the heart of a fair procedure under Art 6'.[77] The majority stated:

> 68   ... [the] right not to incriminate oneself ... presupposes that the prosecution in a criminal case seek to prove their case against the accused without resort to methods of coercion or oppression in defiance of the will of the accused ...
>
> 69   The right not to incriminate oneself is primarily concerned, however, with respecting the will of an accused person to remain silent. As commonly understood in the legal systems of the contracting parties to the Convention and elsewhere, it does not extend to the use in criminal proceedings of material which may be obtained from the accused through the use of compulsory powers but which have an existence independent of the will of the suspect such as, inter alia, documents acquired pursuant to a warrant, breath, blood and urine samples and bodily tissue for the purposes of DNA testing ...

The majority concluded that the procedural safeguards contained in the Companies Act 1985 and the provisions of the Police and Criminal Evidence Act 1984 did not operate to prevent the use of the statements in criminal proceedings and accordingly there was a violation of Art 6. *Saunders* was, not surprisingly, followed by the European Court of Human Rights in *IJL, GMR and AKP v United Kingdom*[78] which upheld a challenge by three other individuals also convicted as a result of the Guinness share price support affair in 1986 and who had complained of use by the prosecution of transcripts of their interviews with DTI inspectors.[79]

The effect of the Strasbourg Court decision in *Saunders* was considered in *R v Morrisey, R v Staines*[80] where the appellants challenged their convictions for insider dealing, arguing that answers obtained by inspectors appointed under s 177 of the Financial Services Act 1986 using coercive powers should have been excluded. However, Sir

---

73   Section 78 gives the court a power to exclude evidence where to admit the evidence would have such an adverse effect on the fairness of the proceedings that the court ought not to admit it.

74   Section 82(3) gives the court a general power to exclude evidence in the exercise of its discretion.

75   [1996] 1 Cr App R 463. Note also *R v Lyons, Parnes, Ronson & Saunders* [2001] EWCA Crim 2860.

76   (1996) 23 EHRR 313. See also: *Funke v France* (1993) 16 EHRR 297; and *Orkem v Commission* [1989] ECR 3283.

77   (1996) 23 EHRR 313 at pp 337–38.

78   (2001) 33 EHRR 225.

79   A separate argument that there had been improper collusion between the DTI and the prosecuting authorities was rejected by the European Court of Human Rights.

80   [1997] 2 Cr App R 426.

Thomas Bingham MR was concerned that if the courts were to use their discretion under s 78(1) of the Police and Criminal Evidence Act to override the admission of such evidence, then they would be obliged to exclude such evidence in all similar cases which, he concluded, would amount to a repeal, or a substantial repeal of an English statutory provision, namely s 177(6) of the Financial Services Act. Nevertheless, the decision in *Saunders*[81] prompted an announcement by the Attorney General on 3 February 1998 of the Government's intention 'to bring forward legislation when a suitable opportunity arises' to ensure the full compatibility of domestic law with the United Kingdom's obligations under the European Convention. As an interim measure he set out guidelines for prosecuting authorities to the effect that where the evidence available to the prosecution included answers obtained by the exercise of compulsory powers, subject to limited exceptions, these answers should not be used in evidence by the prosecution as part of its case.

The next development was *R v Faryab*[82] which concerned an appeal against a conviction for handling stolen goods where the principal ground for the appeal was that the conviction was rendered unsafe by reliance on answers given by the defendant in the course of his examination by an officer on behalf of the official receiver in accordance with the Insolvency Act 1986.[83] The court noted that *Bishopsgate Investment Management Ltd (In Provisional Liquidation) v Maxwell*[84] established that the privilege against self-incrimination was overridden by the provisions of ss 235 and 236 of the Insolvency Act. The Court of Appeal considered the Attorney General's 1998 Guidelines and *R v Morrisey, R v Staines*.[85] The latter case was distinguished on the basis that in *Faryab* the answers obtained by compulsion had formed a significant plank in the prosecution's case at trial and the Court of Appeal therefore quashed the conviction.

Notwithstanding the approach in *Faryab* which was consistent with Strasbourg's approach to Art 6, new legislation was enacted in the form of the Youth Justice and Criminal Evidence Act 1999 which made amendments to the various pieces of legislation requiring compulsory answers to questions by limiting the use which could be made of the answers.[86] For example, a new s 434(5A) was added to the Companies Act 1985 and provides that, where a person is charged with a criminal offence, no evidence relating to an answer given under compulsory powers may be adduced and no question relating to it may be asked by or on behalf of the prosecution unless the evidence has already been adduced, or a question relating to it has been asked in those proceedings by or on behalf of the accused person.[87] A new s 434(5B) provides that this section applies to all offences in England except perjury.[88] A similar approach is adopted in relation to the compulsory

---

81 At the time of the European Court of Human Rights' judgment in *Saunders* the law of the European Convention was not directly part of the United Kingdom. See now the Human Rights Act 1998.

82 [1999] BPIR 569.

83 In s 433 of the Insolvency Act 1986 it is provided that answers obtained by compulsion during the course of interview are admissible in all proceedings.

84 [1993] Ch 1.

85 [1997] 2 Cr App R 426.

86 See s 59 and Schedule 3.

87 See Youth Justice and Criminal Evidence Act 1999 at Schedule 3, para 5.

88 See also Schedule 3, at para 5. Similar amendments were also made to various other statutory provisions including Companies Act 1985, s 447; Companies Act 1989, s 83; and Financial Services Act 1986, ss 105 and 177.

powers in s 174 of the Financial Services and Markets Act 2000. Various issues, however, remain to be considered.

5.1 The limits of *Saunders*

In considering the approach towards the use of evidence obtained under compulsory powers it is interesting to note that the UK courts, in contexts other than the investigation of companies, have interpreted *Saunders* flexibly. This, combined with the amendments to the relevant legislation in the Youth Justice and Criminal Evidence Act 1999, has had the effect that there will now be circumstances where compulsorily obtained evidence will now be admissible in criminal trials in some contexts where it would be inadmissible in criminal trials following company investigations.

For example in *Brown v Stott (Procurator Fiscal, Dunfermline) and Another*[89] the Privy Council rejected an appeal against a drink driving conviction under the Road Traffic Act 1988, where the police had required the defendant to inform them as to the identity of the driver of her vehicle at the time of the incident and this had been argued by the defendant to infringe her right not to incriminate herself. The Privy Council distinguished *Saunders* on the ground that whilst Art 6 guaranteed the overall fairness of a criminal trial, the constituent rights comprised within Art 6, whether expressly or impliedly, were not themselves absolute. Therefore, limited qualification of those rights, including the right against self-incrimination, would be acceptable if reasonably directed by national authorities towards a clear and proper public objective, and so long as it represented no greater qualification than the situation called for. Lord Bingham of Cornhill concluded that the Scots court had interpreted *Saunders* as laying down a more absolute standard than the European Court intended, and that the court had not given any consideration to the need to balance the general interests of the community against the interests of the individual.[90]

Similarly, in *R v Hertfordshire County Council ex p Green Environmental Industries Limited*[91] the House of Lords held that the privilege against self-incrimination did not entitle a person to refuse to provide information about his activities which had been requested pursuant to a statutory power by a local waste regulation authority and added that whether potentially incriminating answers should be excluded from the evidence in subsequent criminal proceedings was a matter for the judge's discretion under the Police and Criminal Evidence Act 1984. Thus, in these other regimes we see a greater flexibility in relation to the use that can be made of compelled evidence at a subsequent criminal trial.[92]

In addition to this flexibility in the domestic courts, the Court in Strasbourg itself is now interpreting *Saunders* restrictively in the context of incriminating statements, in that only where there is shown to be unfairness will the evidence be excluded. We see this approach when the case of *R v Morrisey, R v Staines* was taken to Strasbourg. At

---

89 [2001] 2 WLR 817.

90 See [2001] 2 WLR 817 at p 838A–B.

91 [2000] 2 AC 412.

92 But note the approach towards compulsory questioning by the Serious Fraud Office in excluding self-incriminating statements from the criminal process; see Criminal Justice Act 1987, s 2(8).

Strasbourg, in the case now known as *Staines v United Kingdom*,[93] the applicant argued that she had not received a fair hearing in the UK since her right not to incriminate herself had been undermined where the prosecution evidence produced at trial included answers and a statement she had been compelled to give to DTI inspectors. However, the applicant had previously attended the DTI inspectors on a voluntary basis and had voluntarily provided the inspectors with a written statement and answered questions while not under oath. The Strasbourg Court noted that the compulsorily obtained statement and answers served in the main to confirm the previous statement and answers. After considering all the circumstances, the European Court of Human Rights was able to distinguish the *Staines* case from their earlier decision in *Saunders*, because (a) the applicant had already provided inspectors with written and oral statements before she was compelled to do so; (b) unlike Mr Saunders, the applicant had not objected to the prosecution relying on the statements obtained under compulsion but had herself sought to rely on them; and (c) the prosecution had not sought to impugn the applicant's credibility by comparing and contrasting what she had said under oath before the inspectors with her other statements. The court therefore, concluded that there had been no violation of Art 6. This approach can be seen to be more flexible than the statutory restriction on the use of evidence in the amendments made by the Youth Justice and Criminal Evidence Act 1999 and s 174 of the Financial Services and Markets Act 2000.

Although the *Saunders* case has implications for criminal trials following company investigations it does not appear to have implications for any follow-up action falling short of criminal proceedings. In *R v Secretary of State for Trade and Industry ex p McCormick*[94] the applicant sought to challenge the exercise of discretion by the Secretary of State to use transcripts of evidence in director disqualification proceedings where the evidence had been compulsorily obtained under s 434(5) of the Companies Act 1985. The Court of Appeal held that disqualification proceedings were not criminal proceedings under domestic law and nor were they for the purposes of Art 6. If disqualification proceedings were regarded as civil proceedings then, the court held, questions concerning the privilege against self-incrimination did not arise. This approach is consistent with that of the European Court of Human Rights in *DC, HS and AD v United Kingdom*.[95] Here, the European Court distinguished directors disqualification proceedings from the ambit of *Saunders* on a number of grounds: the proceedings in *Saunders* were criminal whereas the present case concerned regulatory, civil proceedings; the applicant in *Saunders* vigorously attacked the use of the contested statements whereas here there was no challenge; and in *Saunders* the compulsorily obtained statements formed a 'significant part' of the prosecution case whereas in the present case the statements were relevant but did not play a predominant part.[96]

---

93   Application no 41552/98 (16 May 2000).

94   [1998] BCC 379. See also *Official Receiver v Stern* [2000] 1 WLR 2230.

95   [2000] BCC 710.

96   See also *WGS and MSLS v United Kingdom* 38172/97 (23 November 1999). The restriction on the use of statements given in directors disqualification proceedings in subsequent criminal proceedings introduced by the Youth Justice and Criminal Evidence Act 1999 has, however, influenced the court in finding that there would be no unfairness in allowing disqualification proceedings to proceed in circumstances where the police had indicated an intention to prosecute the defendants in respect of closely related matters; see *Secretary of State for Trade and Industry v Crane* [2001] All ER (D) 148.

A further possibility of follow-up action relates to disciplinary proceedings where DTI investigators rely on the exceptions to the restrictions on the disclosure of information in the Companies Act to pass information to other regulatory bodies for them to take action. Disciplinary proceedings are regarded by Strasbourg as civil rather than criminal for the purposes of Art 6. In *R (Fleurose) v The Securities and Futures Authority Ltd*,[97] although Morrison J observed that SFA disciplinary proceedings were subject to the fair trial provisions of Art 6(1) which could include elements of the Art 6(2) and 6(3) rights under the requirement of fairness, he held that the right to a fair hearing was not infringed by the use of evidence given under compulsion in SFA disciplinary proceedings.[98]

5.2   Documentary and derivative evidence

It is important to distinguish between primary evidence, that is evidence which is produced directly by the suspect via the application of compulsory powers against him and derivative evidence. The latter concept applies in a situation where compelled evidence leads the prosecuting authorities to independent evidence that they may wish to use in proceedings to establish the guilt of the suspect. However, the approach of the courts towards derivative evidence has influenced the approach towards the compulsory production of documents.

The European Court of Human Rights in *Saunders*[99] was faced with the use of incriminating statements rather than the question of whether incriminating documents obtained under compulsory powers should be admitted. However, the approach of the majority in that case[100] indicates that the privilege against self-incrimination is primarily concerned with the right to remain silent and so would not extend to material which exists independently of the will of the accused, such as documents. This is, however, inconsistent with the earlier Strasbourg authority of *Funke v France*,[101] where the court had held that a conviction for failing to produce documents to French customs authorities infringed the right to a fair trial.[102]

The question of whether documents obtained under compulsory powers should be admitted in evidence was considered by the Court of Appeal in *Attorney General's Reference (No 7 of 2000)*[103] in the context of documents compulsorily delivered up to the Official Receiver. Rose LJ referred, in particular, to relevant Canadian authorities including *Thomson Newspapers Ltd and Others v Director of Investigation and Research and Others*[104] where La Forest J drew a distinction between compelled testimony and derived testimony:

---

97 [2001] IRLR 764, upheld at [2001] EWCA Civ 2015.
98 Note also the suggestion that by being a member of a professional body the member agrees to abide by its rules and if that includes an obligation to provide evidence then the privilege against self-incrimination is effectively waived; see *R v Institute of Chartered Accountants in England and Wales ex p Taher Nawaz* [1997] PNLR 433, at p 453C *per* Sedley J; note also 25 April 1997, CA (unreported).
99 (1996) 23 EHRR 313.
100 See the main text following n 77 above.
101 (1993) 16 EHRR 297.
102 But the *Saunders* approach was followed in *L v United Kingdom* [2000] FLR 322.
103 [2000] EWCA Crim 888.
104 (1990) 67 DLR (4th) 161.

... the difference between evidence which the accused has been forced to create (the compelled testimony), and the independently existing evidence he or she has been forced to assist in locating, identifying or explaining (evidence derived from compelled testimony), will be readily discernible ...

The fact that derivative evidence exists independently of the compelled testimony means ... that it could also have been discovered independently of any reliance on the compelled testimony. It also means that its quality as evidence does not depend on its past connection with the compelled testimony. Its relevance to the issues with which the subsequent trial is concerned, as well as the weight it is accorded by the trier of fact, are matters that can be determined independently of any consideration of its connection with the testimony of the accused.[105]

The Court of Appeal adopted this approach and concluded that insofar as there was a conflict between *Funke*[106] and *Saunders*,[107] the approach in *Saunders* would be followed.

Most recently, however, the question of documents supplied pursuant to compulsory powers has been considered by the European Court of Human Rights in *JB v Switzerland*.[108] In the context of Swiss tax evasion proceedings the applicant failed to supply to the relevant authority all the documents which he had concerning certain companies and then to explain the source of income invested. Consequently, disciplinary fines were imposed upon him. The applicant successfully raised the privilege against self-incrimination. The European Court concluded:

... the [Swiss] Federal Court referred to various obligations in criminal law obliging a person to act in a particular way in order to be able to obtain his conviction, for instance by means of a tachograph installed in lorries, or by being obliged to submit to a blood or a urine test ... However, the present case differs from such material which, as the court found in the *Saunders* case, had an existence independent of the person concerned and was not, therefore, obtained by means of coercion and in defiance of the will of that person.[109]

This approach by the European Court of Human Rights suggests some inconsistency between Strasbourg and the UK domestic courts. In *JB* the court appears to have regarded the compulsory production of documents as being by coercion and in defiance of the applicant's will whereas in *Attorney General's Reference (No 7 of 2000)*[110] a clearer distinction was drawn between compelled testimony and the production of documents. The latter case, with a more understandable distinction being drawn as to what constitutes the will of the person required to produce documents, appears preferable in that it will not lead to the almost certain exclusion of relevant pre-existing documents. This is, however, subject to appropriate limits being placed on the use of derivative evidence so that a balance is maintained between the necessity of prosecuting wrongdoing and procedural fairness to the accused.

---

105 (1990) 67 DLR (4th) 161 at p 253.
106 (1993) 16 EHRR 297.
107 (1996) 23 EHRR 313.
108 Application No 31827/96, 3 May 2001.
109 At para 68.
110 [2000] EWCA Crim 888.

The European Court in *Saunders* did not deal with the issue of derivative evidence but in *Ferreira v Levin*[111] the South African Constitutional Court considered analogous provisions to UK law albeit in the context of insolvency.[112] The court balanced the public interest in investigating insolvent companies and protecting the constitutional guarantee of freedom and security of the person. In the court's view this balance could be achieved by giving the trial judge a discretion to exclude evidence to which the prosecution was led by the compelled testimony, but evidence that could not have been obtained, or the significance of which would not have been appreciated, without the compelled testimony should normally be excluded. The approach adopted by the South African Supreme Court, following the Canadian authorities,[113] strikes the appropriate balance but it is to the hoped that *JB*[114] does not lead to investigating authorities being unduly hampered in their work and that a principled distinction can be maintained between requiring and subsequently using compulsorily obtained explanations on the one hand, and obtaining and using pre-existing documents on the other.

The question of whether either the Companies Act 1985 or the Police and Criminal Evidence Act 1984 could be re-interpreted to have the effect that domestic law can be regarded as compatible with the Convention has been superseded by the enactment of s 59 and Schedule 3 to the Youth Justice and Criminal Evidence Act 1999. It now seems clear that the approach in *Saunders* will not have such a far reaching impact as might, at the time of the European Court's judgment, have seemed possible for various reasons. The investigations regime as a whole, including investigations into insider dealing, will not be regarded as determining civil rights for the purposes of Art 6 of the Convention. The application of the privilege against self-incrimination in the context of follow-up action which does engage Art 6 will then depend on the facts of the particular case and it will be open to the courts to distinguish *Saunders*,[115] as was done in *Staines*.[116] This will give the courts some flexibility in relation to the evidence concerned. Further, the principle will only apply to criminal proceedings and not to other possible follow-up action such as director disqualification proceedings. Finally, it seems that the courts will be reluctant to exclude documentary evidence.

It is now clear that the post-*Saunders* cases have had a limited impact on follow-up action after DTI investigations. This effect is primarily in relation to the use of transcripts of oral interviews of the accused in subsequent criminal trials. Whilst prosecutors will need to consider the gathering and presentation of evidence carefully, *Saunders* should not unduly hinder proper follow-up action after an investigation. In the light of the importance of fundamental human rights it would not be appropriate for the UK courts to cut back on the Convention protections. The approach in *Saunders* provides a safeguard in the interest of citizens' rights and subsequent court decisions have balanced this carefully against the need to deal effectively with wrongdoing although it is to be hoped

---

111 1996 1 (SA) 984. See also in the context of the Canadian Charter: *Thomson Newspapers Ltd v Director of Investigation and Research* (1990) 67 DLR (4th) 161 at p 204; *RJS v The Queen* (1995) 121 DLR (4th) 589; and *British Columbia Securities Commission v Branch* (1995) 123 DLR (4th) 462.

112 See South African Companies Act 61 of 1973 s 417(2)(b).

113 See n 104 above.

114 See n 108 above.

115 (1996) 23 EHRR 313.

116 Application No 41552/98, 16 May 2000.

that the *JB* case will not lead to the work of investigators in obtaining and using documents being unduly hampered.

6 PUBLICATION OF REPORTS

It is the DTI's practice to announce the appointments of inspectors under the Companies Act and to publish reports 'if it considers that it is in the public interest to do so'.[117] The DTI's policy is, however, that enquiries under s 447 of the Companies Act (and into insider dealing) are not announced and the reports are not published. The fact that investigations under s 447 are not announced reflects the fact that the Companies Act does not envisage the publication of a report. Also, as explained above, the policy of not announcing investigations under s 447 reflects a concern not to unnecessarily undermine public confidence in a company. Information about the reports under s 447 can only be disclosed under defined circumstances, for example, to regulatory authorities or for criminal proceedings.[118]

A question arises as to the operation of the DTI's policy to publish reports of inspections under s 432 'in the public interest'. As a preliminary point it is clear that it is very difficult to attack the exercise of discretion by the DTI as to whether or not to publish a report. In *R v Secretary of State for Trade and Industry ex p Lonrho plc*[119] the House of Lords upheld the Secretary of State's decision not to publish the report on House of Fraser plc where the Secretary of State had been concerned that any publication might prejudice any possible future prosecutions by the Serious Fraud Office arising in relation to matters contained in that report.[120]

The policy on publication of reports was considered by the House of Commons Trade and Industry Committee in 1990,[121] which recommended that publication should be delayed only in cases where a criminal investigation had begun before completion of the report, or where it would be hindered by publication.[122] However, the then Government's response was that whether to publish at a particular time had to be considered on the facts of the individual case, having regard to the risk of prejudice to possible criminal proceedings.[123] The Government pointed out that in cases where criminal investigations are commenced after completion of the report, the DTI must take the same factors into consideration in deciding whether publication would prejudice any eventual proceedings as are relevant in cases where investigations have been commenced earlier.[124]

---

117 See *Companies in 1999–2000* (London, TSO, 2000) at p 12. The second edition of the DTI's *Investigation Handbook* (London, HMSO, 1990) (and no longer usually referred to in DTI literature) explains (at para 48) that reports by inspectors relating to private companies are not normally published unless they raise issues of general public interest. See generally Lidbetter, above n 2, at pp 185–91.

118 See Companies Act 1985, s 449.

119 [1989] 1 WLR 525.

120 In the event there was no prosecution and the report was subsequently published.

121 See *House of Commons, Trade and Industry Committee's Third Report: 'Company Investigations'*, above n 6.

122 Above n 121 at para 88 and recommendation 18.

123 See (1990) Cm 1149, above n 7, at p 13.

124 Above n 123, at p 13.

The debate in front of the House of Commons Trade and Industry Committee was affected by taking place at the time when the Secretary of State had held back publication of the report into House of Fraser plc (completed in 1988 and published in 1990). However, the approach of the Government at that time, even now, appears preferable. There is a strong argument that reports should be published, particularly if the fact of an investigation has been announced. It is only through publication that those cleared of any allegations of wrongdoing will be publicly vindicated. Also, publication may enable lessons to be learned for the future and informed debate as to good practice and/or law reform may take place against the background of a particular case. However, the DTI should not be put in a position where the publication of a report should prejudice follow-up action, particularly criminal proceedings. Once there is no risk of prejudicing follow-up action, however, the policy reasons in favour of publishing reports are such that reports should normally be published as soon as possible. Also, it should be incumbent on the relevant authorities to decide expeditiously whether or not there will be follow-up action and then act accordingly if publication of the report is being delayed pending that decision.

The requirements of procedural fairness which the investigators should follow should not be affected by whether or not the report will be published. The cases of *Re Pergamon Press Ltd*[125] and *Maxwell v DTI*[126] demonstrate that where someone is to be criticised in a DTI report they should be given a fair opportunity for correcting or contradicting what is said against them. This has led to a practice (which goes further than was required by the court) of giving those criticised in a draft report a copy of the relevant extracts for them to comment upon – a process commonly referred to as 'maxwellisation'. However, in requiring that the rules of natural justice be followed in the production of a report, it is not entirely clear whether the judges in *Re Pergamon Press Ltd* were basing their conclusions on (a) the fact that an adverse report could lead to serious follow-up action being taken or (b) that publication of the report could seriously affect reputations. Buckley LJ[127] relied on (a), whereas Sachs LJ[128] appeared to rest his conclusion on (b) and Lord Denning MR[129] referred to both (a) and (b). Thus, although the point is not free from doubt, it seems that the requirements of natural justice do not depend on whether or not the report will be published[130] and it is, therefore, strongly arguable that whether or not a report will be published makes no difference to the application of the rules of procedural fairness.

Finally, it is suggested above that s 432 could be invoked in some of those cases where investigations are currently carried out under s 447. If, however, there is continued reliance on s 447 rather than s 432 then consideration should be given to reforming the

---

125 [1971] Ch 388.
126 [1974] QB 523.
127 See [1971] Ch 388 at p 407A–D.
128 See [1971] Ch 388 at pp 402H–03A.
129 See [1971] Ch 388 at p 399F–G.
130 See generally Lidbetter, above n 2, at pp 126–28. Note also the DTI's *Investigation Handbook*, n 117 above. Appendix C, para 55 states in the context of inspections under s 177 of the Financial Services Act 1986 that 'where criticism of individuals is contemplated it is suggested that inspectors inform the individual of the criticism intended and the evidence for it with a fixed period of, for example, 21 days for response'.

law to enable the publication of reports produced under s 447. This would be with a view to reports being published if, before or during the course of the investigation, it is clear that the level of publicity which the company is attracting (notwithstanding that any investigation under s 447 will not have been announced) makes it in the public interest for a report to be published. Alternatively, it might be that the findings of the investigation are such that it would be in the public interest for the report to be published in order to draw attention to a particular practice or to assist in the debate as to what appropriate policy should be or to assist in the consideration of law reform.

7 CONCLUSIONS

It can be concluded that the DTI has, in general, appropriate powers with which to investigate corporate wrongdoing. Nevertheless, the current powers need rationalising and it is submitted that s 432 rather than s 447 should be invoked more often such that it would strengthen the hand of investigators who are currently limited by the constraints of s 447. The s 432 power should be used in a targeted way to avoid the investigations becoming unwieldy or unduly expensive. Effectively s 432 would be used to fill the gaps in the s 447 powers such that the investigators were not restricted to asking for explanations of documents but could also ask witnesses other relevant questions. The aim of this suggested change in practice would not be to cause more large-scale investigations to take place.

One area where the powers could, however, be amended by primary legislation is in relation to follow-up action. The present follow-up actions, such as director disqualification proceedings or winding up in the public interest, lack flexibility. This leads to the proposal that a new injunctive power should be introduced to restrain particular activity or the conduct of particular individuals in the public interest, a power which would enable more sensitive action to be taken to protect the public from aspects of corporate wrongdoing. The latter remedy could protect shareholders and those who deal with companies without the draconian impact of a measure such as the winding up of the company.

Recent case law developments, particularly *Re Mirror Group Newspapers plc*, have not upset the balance between effectiveness of the investigations on the one hand and procedural fairness on the other. A similar analysis applies in relation to the European Convention on Human Rights. The decision of the European Court in *Saunders* has now been around for a few years, and although the implications of it are still being worked out, it has not unduly tipped the balance against investigators. Similarly, Art 8 rightly has the effect that there should be increased sensitivity in relation to the carrying out of searches but, as in many other areas of domestic law, the incorporation of the Convention has not had a major impact on the investigations regime but has instead affected it in significant but marginal ways.

There are still outstanding issues in relation to DTI investigations which should be given further consideration. Notable amongst these is the scope for invoking s 432 more often but then applying it in a more targeted way than is currently done under s 432. Nevertheless, the main reform needed is the introduction of a new, more sensitive remedy, of a restraining injunction to operate in the public interest. That these proposed legislative changes are of a relatively limited ambit reflects the modest way in which the investigations regime has evolved and been refined over the last 150 years.

PART 4

CORPORATE SECURITY AND INSOLVENCY

REFLECTIONS ON THE AMBIT AND REFORM OF PART 12 OF THE COMPANIES ACT 1985 AND THE DOCTRINE OF CONSTRUCTIVE NOTICE

John de Lacy

1 INTRODUCTION

In many respects the completion of the work by the Company Law Review Steering Group[1] has marked the end of the formal review of company law and all that remains is for the Government to legislate on these matters. However, the subject of company charges has proved the exception to this and the work of the Steering Group on this subject[2] has been but a preliminary measure pending further review and consultation. Indeed, the main finding of the Steering Group in this area is that the Law Commission should look into this subject and make recommendations on how it should be reformed, taking into account the very much 'provisional conclusions' of the Steering Group as expressed in *The Final Report*.[3] It has to be said that this represents a most unfortunate outcome of what has been an otherwise comprehensive review of company law. Given that the subject has already been dealt with by three separate reviews, the publication of *The Final Report* amounting to the fourth review, a fifth review by the Law Commission is a daunting prospect. Nevertheless, the subject is of enormous significance to all companies and it is important that when reforms are eventually enacted that we get it right. Secured finance is an essential and well-used tool by today's companies, large and small.[4] Whilst some may care to debate the legitimacy[5] or efficiency[6] of an economic and legal system that permits financiers or credit providers to take security in consideration for their services, it remains a simple fact that this system is here to stay.[7] The acceptance of security, whether good or bad, leads us to address other related regulatory areas. This chapter looks at the area contained in Part 12 of the Companies Act 1985, which provides

---

1 See generally *Modern Company Law for a Competitive Economy: Final Report* (London, DTI, 2001), hereafter *The Final Report*.

2 See generally *The Final Report*, above n 1, at chapter 12.

3 See *The Final Report*, above n 1, at para 12.8.

4 At the end of the period 1999–2000 there were 1,361,000 companies registered in Great Britain of which 12,400 were public companies and 213,000 mortgage documents (ie, company charges) were filed for public registration with the Registrar of companies; see DTI *Companies in 1999–2000* (London, TSO, 2000) at pp 24–25, Tables A1 and A2 and at p 43 Table F1.

5 See further Goode 'Is the Law too Favourable to Secured Creditors?' (1983–84) 8 *Canadian Business Law Journal* 53.

6 See further Shupak 'Solving the Puzzle of Secured Transactions' (1989) 41 *Rutgers Law Review* 1067.

7 Indeed, the Report by Professor AL Diamond *A Review of Security Interests in Property* (London, HMSO, 1989), hereafter *The Diamond Report*, was to conclude that 'security was a fact of life' (at para 8.1.5) such that its abolition could not be countenanced. The Report also noted the vigorous academic debate that had raged (chartered by Shupak, above n 6) concerning the utility and efficiency of security but remarked that it was inconclusive and it would, therefore, be wrong to base any recommendations for the reform of UK law on security interests over personal property on these arguments; at para 8.1.8.

for the establishment of a registration system for company charges, and, in particular, the gloss placed on this statutory measure by the courts when fusing the doctrine of constructive notice onto this system.[8] The chapter will assess some of the more important principles underlying the operation of Part 12 and offer suggestions on how this scheme should be reformed taking into account the work of the Steering Group.

2 THE PURPOSE AND AMBIT OF THE PUBLIC REGISTER OF CHARGES

Part 12 of the Companies Act 1985 requires the particulars of certain types of security interests,[9] referred to by the Act as 'charges',[10] to be delivered to the registrar of companies for registration within 21 days of their creation. Should this not happen then the charge is rendered void against prescribed parties.[11] Ever since the introduction of a centralised public register, maintained by the registrar of companies, in 1900,[12] only certain specified categories of charge have required registration.[13] The reason for what might be seen to be a limited[14] approach is that, historically, it represented a compromise between the expert opinion that favoured the registration of all charges[15] and that which was against even limited registration due to the complexities it would introduce to

---

8   It should be noted that Part 12 of the Act is divided into two chapters – Chapter 1 covering companies registered in England and Wales and Chapter 2 covering Scotland; on the inter-relationship between these two Chapters see *Arthur D Little Ltd v Ableco Finance LLC* (2002) *The Times*, 22 April. This essay is only concerned with Chapter 1 of the Act covering England and Wales. The Companies Act 1989, Part 4, would, if brought into force, bring about a new integrated Part 12. However, it appears as if the Companies Act 1989 will not be brought into force and further reforms will have to be brought about by fresh legislation; see DTI Consultative Document 'Proposals for Reform of Part 12 of the Companies Act 1985' (1994) URN 94/635 (London, DTI, 1994) at p 8 para 8.

9   See Companies Act 1985, s 396(1) for the list of charges that require registration.

10 See Companies Act 1985, ss 395–96. For these purposes charge is deemed to include mortgage; s 396(4).

11 These parties are: a liquidator, administrator, or any creditor of the company; Companies Act 1985, s 395(1). For the meaning of avoidance in this context see *Smith v Bridgend County BC* [2001] 3 WLR 1347. The rationale of avoidance against these parties is discussed at section 5 below.

12 See Companies Act 1900, s 14.

13 This can be readily contrasted with the company's internal register of charges which applies to all charges created by the company, discussed at section 6 below.

14 Cf the Report by Professor LCB Gower (which reviewed the state of company law in Ghana in 1961, the system in Ghana being based upon that then found in the UK, and made recommendations on the shape and form of a new system of company law), The Ghana Report (1961) at p 87 comment 6 (all company charges should be registrable 'in the interests of brevity and simplicity' other than certain stated exceptions); this policy was later adopted by the Ghana Companies Code 1963. The US Uniform Commercial Code, Art 9, goes even further and requires the registration of all transactions (other than stated exceptions) that perform a security function if such interests are to achieve priority over competing interests; see Art 9-102 and official comment.

15 See, for example, the views of Lord Justice Lindley before the House of Lords' Select Committee on the Companies Bill, Reports Committees (1897) Vol X at para 31.

everyday practice.[16] This rationale has been continually supported[17] and when what was to become the Companies Act 1989 was being debated in Parliament it was stated that:

> The principle behind the new section 396, which it has in common with the 1985 Act, is that we should make registrable only specified categories of charge. We should not embrace all types of charges because we could catch charges which arise in the ordinary course of day-to-day business and which it would be impractical to register ... We must be certain that we do not impose impossible duties which could damage commercial transactions by, for example, preventing people from taking certain types of charge which are currently common.[18]

Although the relevant provisions of the Companies Act 1989[19] which were intended to amend the 1985 Act have never been brought into force, this statement does represent an accurate summation of the policy underlying Part 12 of the 1985 Act (unamended). Therefore, it has always been provided that only the specified categories of charge which it was felt would cause the most problems left undisclosed should be made registrable under the Act.[20]

The purpose of establishing a public register of charges in 1900 was to ensure that persons dealing with companies had a reliable method of ascertaining whether a company's property was the subject of a charge security interest. Prior to 1900 those dealing with companies had to make do with the unsatisfactory private register maintained by the chargor company.[21] This register suffered from a number of defects, not least from the fact that it was seldom maintained in the first place or, where it was, it was only open to inspection by existing creditors or members of the chargor company.[22] Nevertheless, by 1900 it had been recognised that the continued growth of companies[23] and the supply of finance to support them depended upon the availability of a sound and reliable system of public information for those minded to invest. This was particularly the case as sources of corporate finance were beginning to develop from external institutions such as the banks who were keen to ensure that their potential investments were adequately protected via the taking of security over unencumbered assets. No longer

---

16 See the evidence of Francis Palmer before the House of Lords' Select Committee on the Companies Bill 1898, Reports Committees Vol IX at para 655, who described the introduction of the registration requirement coupled with invalidity for failure to register as 'a most frightful complication' (although he did favour the introduction of a quarterly return stating the outstanding indebtedness held by secured parties). HB Buckley QC was also against wholesale registration which 'would be a very great error'; at para 1616, but favoured the general approach taken by what was to become s 14 of the Companies Act 1900 (see now Companies Act 1985, s 396(1)).

17 See: *Company Law Amendment Committee Report* (1926) Cmnd 2657 (London, HMSO, 1926) at para 65; *Report of the Company Law Committee* (1962) Cmnd 1749 (London, HMSO, 1962) at para 301, hereafter *The Jenkins Report*; a similar position was also adopted in Australia by The Eggleston Report, *Registration of Company Charges*, 1972 Parliamentary Paper No 230 (Canberra, Commonwealth Government Printing Office, 1973) at para 34.

18 *Per* the Under Secretary of State Official Reports Standing Committee D (Companies Bill), 10th Sitting (20 June 1989) at 404; see also *The Diamond Report*, above n 7, at para 23.1.6 for a similar finding.

19 See Companies Act 1989, Part 4.

20 See s 396(1) for these categories of charge.

21 See Companies Act 1862, s 43.

22 See Companies Act 1862, s 43.

23 See DTI *Companies In 1999–2000*, above n 4, at p 26 Table A4 where it is stated that during the period 1862–69, 5,000 companies were incorporated, however by the period 1890–99 the figure had risen to 36,600; from 1870–89 there were 27,900 incorporations.

could companies rely solely on their internal membership as the exclusive source of capital injection.[24] The growth of external financing went hand in hand with the need for independent and reliable sources of corporate information. Indeed, the whole philosophy of the Companies Act 1900 had been described, by the then President of the Board of Trade, as being 'to ensure the fullest information being available to all those who desire to take part in companies or invest their capital'.[25] This was particularly appropriate with regard to what he termed the 'evil'[26] of unregistered charges.

Whilst one can readily agree with the disclosure philosophy underlying the public register of charges it becomes apparent from inspecting the classes of charge that require registration that 'the fullest information'[27] is currently not being made available to those minded to deal with companies. Part 12 of the Act requires the following interests[28] to be registered: charges for securing any issue of debentures;[29] charges on uncalled share capital;[30] charges which would require registration as bills of sale if executed by an individual;[31] charges on land;[32] charges on book debts;[33] floating charges;[34] charges on calls made but not paid;[35] charges on ships (including a share therein)[36] and aircraft;[37] charges on goodwill[38] or intellectual property.[39] It can be seen that the list of registrable

---

24 See also *Insolvency Law and Practice* (1982) Cmnd 8558 (London, HMSO, 1982) at paras 1474–77, hereafter *The Cork Report*.

25 (1900) *Hansard* HC 4th Series vol 84 at 1141. The courts have also interpreted the purpose of charge registration under the Companies Act in this way; see: *Re Jackson & Bassford Ltd* [1906] 2 Ch 467 at p 476; *Re Cardiff Workmen's Cottage Co Ltd* [1906] 2 Ch 627 at p 629; *Esberger & Sons Ltd v Capital & Counties Bank* [1913] 2 Ch 366 at p 374; *Dublin City Distillery Ltd v Doherty* [1914] AC 823 at p 854; *Re Wallis & Simmons Ltd* [1974] 1 WLR 391 at p 404H; *Re Bond Worth Ltd* [1980] Ch 228 at p 274C; *Re Brightlife Ltd* [1987] Ch 200 at p 215A–D; *Smith v Bridgend County BC* [2001] 3 WLR 1347 at p 1354D *per* Lord Hoffmann.

26 See (1900) *Hansard* HC 4th Series vol 84 at 1143.

27 Above n 25 and the main text thereat *per* the President of the Board of Trade.

28 See s 396(1)(a)–(j).

29 First made registrable by virtue of Companies Act 1900, s 14. In the evidence presented to the Company Law Review Steering Group it was stated that this type of charge is 'no longer in practice given to secure issues of debentures' and, as a consequence it is proposed that it no longer be registrable; see *The Final Report*, above n 1, at paras 12.59 and 12.60(ii).

30 First made registrable by virtue of Companies Act 1900, s 14.

31 First made registrable by virtue of Companies Act 1900, s 14. The Steering Group were of the view that this category of registrable charge 'clearly needs updating' and should be replaced by a provision requiring all charges on goods to be registrable unless the chargee was in possession of the goods; see *The Final Report*, above n 1, at paras 12.55 and 12.57.

32 First made registrable by virtue of Companies Act 1907, s 10.

33 First made registrable by virtue of Companies Act 1907, s 10.

34 First made registrable by virtue of Companies Act 1900, s 14. The Steering Group were 'firmly of the view' that floating charges should have to be registrable after any reforms to the current system; see *The Final Report*, above n 1, at para 12.54. See further on this topic the McCormack essay below at p 389.

35 First made registrable by virtue of Companies Act 1928, s 43.

36 First made registrable by virtue of Companies Act 1928, s 43.

37 First made registrable by virtue of Mortgaging of Aircraft Order 1972, SI 1972/1268.

38 First made registrable by virtue of Companies Act 1928, s 43.

39 The term 'intellectual property' is defined by s 396(3a) as: any patent, trade mark, registered design, copyright, design right or any licence under or in respect of any such right. These intellectual property rights were first made registrable by virtue of the Companies Act 1928, s 43, with the exception of registered designs and design rights which were made registrable by virtue of the Copyright Designs and Patents Act 1988, s 303(1) and Sched 7 para 31(1)(2).

charges which started in 1900 had effectively crystallised by 1928. This is highly significant and means that our conception of 'the fullest information' being available to searchers of the charges' register is effectively shaped by the conceptions of those persons responsible for the creation and development of the register during the first part of the 20th century. If commercial activity had stood still then, assuming that we could agree with the form of the register as it existed in 1928, all might now be well. Of course this was not to be the case and there have been numerous developments in the world of secured financing throughout the whole course of the 20th century. It is unfortunate that the present register remains confined to a snap shot of the picture as it stood in 1928.

There are two clear policies underlying the public register established by Part 12. These are: first, that it is only charge security interests created by the company over its property that require registration, if – secondly, that charge security interest covers a category of charge listed by s 396(1). Therefore, any security interest arising by operation of law is automatically excluded from the register since it does not come into existence by virtue of any act of creation on the part of the company.[40] Whilst it might be argued that since the purpose of the public register is to disclose the existence of charge security interests however they might have come into existence and, therefore, it follows that interests arising by operation of law should be included on the register,[41] the acceptance of such an argument would be misplaced. This is because, despite the commendable simplicity of this argument, it would not appear to be practical to render non-consensual security interests registrable. It is necessary to bear in mind why the law recognised these interests in the first place. Two reasons can be advanced:

(a) The underlying commercial activity which benefitted from this type of security interest might be frustrated if consensual security was the only mechanism by which security could come into existence, since in many situations it would be impractical to require the creditor to contract for security before undertaking the relevant transaction.

(b) As a consequence of (a) the law recognised the vulnerability of certain classes of creditor and imposed a security interest in their favour when the relevant transaction was undertaken. This recognition was demanded in the public interest in that it served to support and encourage the business/activity in question, such business/activity being perceived to be in the interests of the general community due to the valuable service provided.

It follows that the policy of only requiring the registration of consensual security charges can be supported.[42]

Even if a charge can be said to have been created by the chargor company the second policy underlying the public register means that if the charge does not fall within one of

---

40 See generally: *Brunton v Electrical Engineering Corp* [1892] 1 Ch 434; *Re Overseas Aviation Engineering (GB) Ltd* [1963] 1 Ch 24; *Capital Finance Co Ltd v Stokes* [1969] 1 Ch 261; *London & Cheshire Insurance Co Ltd v Laplagrene Property Ltd* [1971] 1 Ch 499.

41 See *London & Cheshire Insurance Co Ltd v Laplagrene Property Co Ltd* [1971] 1 Ch 499 at p 514C *per* Brightman J who was 'tempted' by this argument.

42 This is not to say, however, that a review of security interests arising by operation of law is not demanded. It might well be that certain types of security interest might require reform in the light of modern conditions which might have changed beyond all recognition from the days in which the law sought to protect certain classes of creditor.

the specified categories of registrable interest it will be exempt from registration. This is a significant limitation on the effectiveness of the register and means that many common forms of security interest are currently excluded. For example, charges over shares are not registrable.[43] It has remained a moot point over the years whether or not charges on shares should be added to the categories of registrable security interest. *The Jenkins Report* recommended that charges created by a parent company over the shares of any subsidiary company should be made registrable since it was anomalous that if a company carried on its business via branches and raised a loan by giving security over the branch assets that would require registration; however, by charging the shares of a subsidiary to secure a loan, the company could escape from the registration requirement.[44] In 1982 *The Cork Report* simply recommended that all charges on shares should be made registrable.[45] Nevertheless, both *The Diamond Report* of 1989 and the legislature were to reject both these recommendations for reform. The recommendation that charges on shares over a subsidiary be made registrable was rejected due to difficulties over ascertaining the exact status of being a subsidiary company and the consequent uncertainty that would be caused in deciding whether or not registration would be necessary.[46] Also it was perceived to be a potential source of injustice in circumstances where a charge was granted over shares at a time when the company was not a subsidiary, but subsequently became such, which might mislead a potential searcher of the register (after the company had become a subsidiary) into believing that no such charge existed.[47]

---

43 See *Re Sugar Properties (Derisley Wood) Ltd* [1988] BCLC 146. It should be noted that the taking of security over shares is a potentially risky venture dependent upon the market's support for the value of the shares and, more importantly, the continued solvency of the company since otherwise the shares are worthless; see, by way of analogy: *Standard Chartered Bank v Walker* [1992] 1 WLR 561; *China & South Sea Bank Ltd v Tan* [1990] 1 AC 536; *Worwood v Leisure Merchandising Services Ltd* [2002] 1 BCLC 249.

44 See *The Jenkins Report*, above n 17, at paras 301, 306(f). This proposal was later adopted by the ill-fated Companies Bill 1973 cl 83 and Sched 2 cl 1(2). However, it should be noted that Jenkins was against wholesale registration of charges on shares.

45 See *The Cork Report*, above n 24, at para 1520.

46 See *The Diamond Report*, above n 7, at para 23.8.8. See generally Companies Act 1985, ss 736, 736A and 736B concerning the meaning of 'subsidiary company'.

47 See *The Diamond Report*, above n 7, at para 23.8.7. This misapprehension could, of course, only be induced by fraud on the part of the chargor. *The Diamond Report* was also to reject the obligation being placed on the chargor to register upon the company achieving subsidiary status, which would have cured the problem raised in the main text, because 'it would not seem sensible' to require registration at a later time than that of the charge's initial creation. Apart from being against the general principle that charges are registrable within 21 days of creation, any change in favour of registration from the date of achieving subsidiary status would severely prejudice the interests of the first chargee because: a) at the date subsidiary status was achieved this might not have been clear to the parties involved; b) even if the date was clear, the chargee might not know that there had been a change in status since he would not be privy to such information and would therefore be unable to ensure compliance with the registration requirement. Curiously, the reason given by the Government against registering shares on subsidiaries was that it would be the first chargee who would be thereby prejudiced in the situation where the company was not a subsidiary at the time the charge was created; see (1989) *Hansard* HL vol 504 at 122 *per* Lord Strathclyde. This was because it was said upon the company becoming a subsidiary the charge would then become void against the parties specified in s 395(1) (assuming at least 21 days had passed between these events). This argument would appear to be erroneous because in this situation the duty to register does not arise at the date of the charge's creation and therefore the Act can never apply in the absence of a retro-active provision which is not a feature of the present Act, or the proposals in favour of registration of shares.
It should be noted that charges over shares do require registration on the companies' internal register of charges.

The recommendation that all charges on shares be made registrable was rejected due to the inconvenience and demands it would place upon those routinely interested in such dealings. As has been explained:

> First, companies will often own a changing portfolio of shares. It would place an impossible duty on companies if they had to register a charge every time they acquired shares. Secondly, those dealing in shares in the market take charges over such shares in respect of payments due to them. The thought that particulars should have to be delivered on the occasion of each acquisition of shares to prevent their becoming void under the Companies Act is beyond contemplation. The operation of the market could be severely undermined.[48]

It can be doubted whether this rationale is as convincing as at first sight it might appear. With regard to the point that there might be a high volume of turnover transactions relating to share dealings so that it would be impractical to register, this may well be the case in some situations. However, the Act appears to have already catered for this eventuality by providing for a 21-day period of grace in which the chargor (or indeed chargee) has to deliver the prescribed particulars for registration.[49] This effectively means that if any particular batch of shares that have become subject to a charge security interest are likely to be disposed of within 21 days of the date in which the security interest is created then no registration is in fact needed to ensure that the charge is not avoided. A three-week period of grace would appear adequate to compensate for any inconvenience that might potentially arise from day-to-day dealings. Should enforcement become necessary, provided the security was realised within the 21-day period, the lifespan of the security interest would have been immune from invalidation because of non-compliance with the registration requirement.[50] If enforcement and realisation could not be concluded within that period the chargee could simply send the prescribed particulars of the charge to the Registrar and his priority would be assured.

A chargee, in these circumstances, is, therefore, given a 21 day period in which to evaluate the probability that enforcement of the security interest might become necessary. It does not appear unreasonable in these circumstances to extend the registration requirement so as to cover shares. The chargee who neglects to register within 21 days must run the risk that other parties might gain the protection afforded by the Act.[51] On this approach it hardly seems an undue burden to require registration in these circumstances such that 'the market could be severely undermined' if this were done, for the Act already appears to have catered for the short-term expedient that the omission is

---

48 *Per* the Under Secretary of State for Industry and Consumer Affairs, Official Reports Standing Committee D (Companies Bill) 10th Sitting (10 June 1989) at 404; cf the company's internal register of charges, which would require registration in such circumstances.

49 See s 395(1). It should be noted that although the 21 day period under the present Act would serve to protect the chargee, the chargor would still be liable for a criminal penalty for a failure to register the charge.

50 See, by way of analogy, *Mercantile Bank of India Ltd v Chartered Bank of India* [1937] 1 All ER 231 at p 241 *per* Porter J.

51 See above n 11 and the main text thereat.

allegedly designed to protect.[52] Nevertheless, the Steering Group recommended that shares should be exempt from a registration requirement.[53]

A further category of consensual charge security interest which does not require registration is a charge granted over an insurance policy.[54] It has been argued that such an interest should be registrable as being a charge upon book debts.[55] However, this argument was rejected by the courts[56] for two reasons. First, an insurance policy would not be entered on the company records as a book debt[57] before the admission of liability and the ascertainment of the amount due under the policy and therefore could not be classified as a 'book debt' for the purposes of the Act.[58] Secondly, the liability to pay out under an insurance contract is contingent upon the specified conditions being fulfilled of which there is no certainty that they might ever be met. As Pennycuick J has explained:

> Looking at the matter for a moment apart from authority, I do not think that in ordinary speech one would describe as a 'book debt' the right under a contingency contract before the contingency happens ...
>
> It seems to me that, in order to ascertain whether any particular charge is a charge on book debts within the meaning of the section, one must look at the items of property which form the subject matter of the charge at the date of its creation and consider whether any of those items is a book debt. In the case of an existing item of property, this question can only be answered by reference to its character at the date of creation. Where the item of property is the benefit of a contract and at the date of the charge the benefit of the contract does not comprehend any book debt, I do not see how that contract can be brought within the section as being a book debt merely by reason that the contract may ultimately result in a book debt.[59]

Although the reasons given by Pennycuick J have a logical basis, they do appear to draw a fine divide between the charge on an insurance contract and a charge which extends (or

---

52 Cf Australian Corporations Law, s 262(1)(g), which would require all charges upon shares to be registrable except where the charge involved the deposit of a document of title to the shares or where the shares were registered in the chargee's name upon the company's own share register. This Australian scheme would appear to be a sensible rationalisation of the English provisions (from which it originally derived). If similar provisions were introduced into English law then it has been stated that the 'vast majority' of security interests over shares would be exempt from registration since it is standard practice to take a deposit of the chargor's share certificate which, according to s 186 of the Companies Act 1985, is *prima facie* evidence of title to the shares; see *The Diamond Report*, above n 7, at para 23.8.5. Nevertheless, if this position were to be achieved here then share certificates would have to be made into documents of title since it is now established that a share certificate is neither a negotiable instrument nor a document of title and the title evidenced by the share certificate will be liable to be defeated by a person with superior title; see *Longman v Bath Electric Tramways Ltd* [1905] 1 Ch 646. The Australian Corporations Law overcomes this problem by defining 'document of title' so as to embrace a share certificate; see s 261(1)(g).

53 See *The Final Report*, above n 1, at para 12.60(iv).

54 Indeed, a security interest over any type of contingency contract is also not registrable, eg, a guarantee or indemnity contract.

55 See *Paul & Frank Ltd v Discount Bank (Overseas) Ltd* [1967] Ch 348.

56 See *Paul & Frank Ltd v Discount Bank (Overseas) Ltd* [1967] Ch 348.

57 The expression 'book debts' is not defined by the Act, contrary to a recommendation of *The Diamond Report*, above n 7, at para 23.9.25 and we are thus left with the common law definition; on which see: Gough, *Company Charges* (London, Butterworths, 2nd edn, 1995) at pp 677–89; *Palmer's Company Law* (London, Sweet & Maxwell, 25th edn, 1992) Vol 2 at para 13.317 and the cases there cited.

58 See s 396(1)(e).

59 *Paul & Frank Ltd v Discount Bank Ltd* [1967] Ch 348 at pp 360B, 362C–E.

even solely covers) future acquired property. Just as in the latter case equity will enforce the security agreement the moment the chargor acquires an interest in the property if the parties have done all they can upon execution of the security to give effect to their intention,[60] there is surely no reason why the law (in the sense of requiring registration) should not take a similar view with respect to a current asset that may not be realised. After all, the chargor is placing a fetter upon his contractual entitlement to deal with the payment should the contingency occur. When the security interest over an insurance policy is granted there is nothing left for either party to do to render the security interest effective and it is, therefore, submitted that the decision to exclude these interests might well be open to review before a higher court. However, even if this argument were to be accepted, commercial practice would still have to regard the insurance policy (prior to the contingency being fulfilled) as a book debt in order for the Act to apply. These circumstances should be distinguished from a situation where the transaction provides for the creation of a charge should certain events occur. In the latter situation no security interest arises at all until the charge is actually created and the potential chargee has a merely personal right to insist upon performance if and when the stipulated event occurs.[61]

In order to meet these difficulties the only sensible solution would be to add the insurance policy (and other types of contingency contract) to the list of registrable categories. This, however, presupposes that the insurance policy is an interest that should be disclosed via registration. It cannot be doubted that insurance policies are routinely used as security and *The Diamond Report* was to comment that 'it could be of some importance to persons dealing with the company to ascertain whether it was entitled to the benefit of a policy and whether the asset was charged'.[62] *The Diamond Report* noted that there was support for the view that the insurance contract be made registrable and indeed recommended as such,[63] subject to minor exceptions.[64] It would seem that the *Diamond* proposals are a sound and rational extension to the registration requirement providing necessary information to those who would seek to use the register. Unfortunately, this recommendation was omitted from the reforms which were intended to be brought about by the Companies Act 1989[65] although no clear reasons were given.[66]

---

60 *Tailby v Official Receiver* (1888) 13 App Cas 523; the charge would, of course, be registrable at the date the security was created rather than the subject matter thereof acquired; see *Independent Automatic Sales Ltd v Knowles & Foster* [1962] 1 WLR 974.

61 See: *Williams v Burlington Investments Ltd* (1977) 121 Solicitors Journal 424 (HL); *Re Gregory Love & Co* [1916] Ch 203; *Re Jackson & Bassford Ltd* [1906] 2 Ch 467 at p 477 *per* Buckley J.

62 Above n 7, at para 23.5.3.

63 Above n 7, at paras 23.5.3–23.5.4.

64 The exceptions being with regard to marine insurance and goods to be exported (which would preserve the result in *Paul & Frank Ltd v Discount Bank Ltd* [1967] Ch 348).

65 See Part 4 of that Act.

66 See Official Reports Standing Committee D (Companies Bill) 10th Sitting (20th June 1989) at 403–04 where it is stated that there was 'no clear view at present among those affected' by the proposals in favour of the reform. Also the reasoning given in favour of exempting shares, above n 48 and the main text thereat, appears to have been deemed equally applicable. The exclusion of the insurance policy from Art 9 of the US Uniform Commercial Code was similarly 'politically inspired' and not based on any arguments relating to the inconvenience of such an extension; see G Gilmore *Security Interests in Personal Property* (Boston, Little, Brown & Co, 1965) Vol 1 at p 315. The various Canadian Personal Property Security Act schemes appear to have accepted the legitimacy of the exemption without question, merely following the Art 9 model.

The *Diamond* proposals were recently adopted in a slightly extended form in *The Final Report*.[67]

Another potentially significant category of charge which does not require registration is a charge over a bank account.[68] It remains to be settled whether a charge taken over a company's bank account is a registrable interest amounting to a charge on book debts under the Act. Although it is clear that upon depositing money at the bank the relationship of debtor-creditor arises between the bank and the company[69] so that there appears to be no reason why the debt should not be classified as a book debt, generally speaking 'it would not be a natural usage for a businessman or accountant to describe it in that way rather than as "cash at bank"'.[70] Although current commercial practice would appear to dictate against the charge being recognised as covering book debts, it also appears that many commercial documents purporting to charge such accounts are more appropriately classified as floating charges[71] due to the wide autonomy given to the chargor company.[72] Nevertheless, it remains a possibility that an appropriately drafted document could still be recognised as amounting to a charge on book debts. As Hoffmann J was at pains to point out in his judgment in *Re Permanent Houses*:

> But I should perhaps take this opportunity to say, if it was not sufficiently clear, that *Re Brightlife Ltd* did not decide that a credit balance at a bank could not in any context be a 'book debt' or 'other debt'. In particular, I did not and do not express any opinion on whether a credit balance is a 'book debt' for the purpose of section 396(1)(e) of the 1985 Act. *Re Brightlife Ltd* and this case are concerned with the construction of particular debentures.[73]

The vexed status of the charge over a bank account has also caused confusion at the companies' registry with the registrar's viewpoint having 'fluctuated'[74] over the years between refusing to accept these charges as being registrable and accepting them for registration. Such resultant uncertainty is surely a cause for concern under a system designed, in so far as is reasonably possible, to ensure certainty in the registration process.[75] In this respect it is unfortunate that our understanding of the term 'book debts' is not as certain and defined to a standard as would remove all doubts.[76] Any future problems would be removed by simply adding the category of bank account to the list of

---

67 See *The Final Report*, above n 1, at paras 12.60(v) and 12.65–12.66.
68 Such charges are very common in banking circles to secure a customer's indebtedness to his bank; see *Re BCCI (No 8)* [1998] AC 214.
69 *Foley v Hill* (1848) 2 HL Cas 28.
70 *Re Permanent Houses (Holdings) Ltd* [1988] BCLC 563 at p 566g *per* Hoffmann J; see also *Northern Bank Ltd v Ross* [1990] BCC 883 at p 885E *per* Hutton LCJ.
71 It should be noted that this type of charge would be registrable in its own right. However, the book debts charge controversy has arisen out of the fact that a fixed charge on debts would assure priority over other creditors, in particular those creditors that are given preferential status, on which see Insolvency Act 1986, ss 175, 386 and Sched 6; see *Re Permanent Houses Ltd* [1988] BCLC 563.
72 See: *Re Brightlife Ltd* [1987] Ch 200; *Re Permanent Houses Ltd* [1988] BCLC 563; *Re Brumark Investments Ltd* [2000] 1 BCLC 353; *Agnew v Commissioner of Inland Revenue* [2001] 2 AC 710.
73 [1988] BCLC 563 at pp 566i–567a. Note also *Re BCCI (No 8)* [1998] AC 214 at p 227E–F *per* Lord Hoffmann to like effect.
74 See *The Diamond Report*, above n 7, at para 23.4.8. Prudence would appear to dictate that such an interest should be registered as a matter of course.
75 See also above n 18 and the main text thereat.
76 See above n 57.

registrable interests. It is submitted that in accordance with the principle that the present scheme is (or rather should be) designed to disclose the 'fullest information'[77] in relation to consensual security interests, then the charge on bank accounts should be added to the list to remove any doubts.[78]

Despite this critique concerning the limited nature of the list of registrable charges it might be thought that we at least had the benefit of a simple and predictable system. The *numerus clausus* approach to registration would appear to suggest that the issue of registration could be addressed by simply looking at the list of registrable charges[79] and then comparing it with the relevant transaction at hand in order to discover whether that transaction was registrable or not. Nothing could be further from the truth and, as Professor Gower once noted, the issue of registrability concerning any particular transaction remains 'a fruitful source of litigation'.[80] For example, prior to 1985 it was never considered that the long-established shipowner's lien on sub-freights to secure performance of the master time charter payments over a ship could operate as a registrable charge. However, suddenly such interests were challenged in the courts and found to be void for non-registration.[81] This was despite the fact that it was acknowledged that 'great practical difficulties'[82] would be caused by requiring such interests to be registered. Similar problems have also accrued with respect to other forms of transaction.[83] Nevertheless, the importance of cases such as *Re Welsh Irish Ferries Ltd* for our purposes lies in the fact that they threaten to undermine the certainty and predictability of the registration system by introducing the elements of chance and surprise. Whatever criticisms might be levelled at the registration system for excluding certain types of security interest the bottom line is that one should at least know the type of transactions that are within the scheme. Indeed the rationale for the present scheme, based on a *numerus clausus* of registrable security interests, was to ensure that 'impossible duties'[84] were not imposed upon security holders which could 'damage commercial transactions'[85] by preventing the use of certain types of security interest due to the

---

77 See above n 25 and the main text thereat.

78 *The Cork Report*, above n 24, recommended, at para 1520, that a charge over any type of debt or liability owing to the company should be registrable. *The Diamond Report*, above n 7, was against registration, at para 23.4.10, but only in the context of imposing registration as a short term measure. It was in favour of imposing registration of charges on bank accounts as part of a new and reformed personal property registration system; at para 18.2.2. Under the proposals contained in *The Final Report*, above n 1, at para 12.60 charges on bank accounts would become registrable unless covered by exemption (vii).

79 On which see s 396(1).

80 See LCB Gower *Modern Company Law* (London, Stevens, 4th edn, 1979) at p 479.

81 See: *Re Welsh Irish Ferries Ltd* [1986] Ch 471; *Annangel Glory Compania Naviera SA v Golodetz Ltd* [1988] PCC 37.

82 See *Re Welsh Irish Ferries Ltd* [1986] Ch 471 at p 481C *per* Nourse J. The difficulties involved in requiring these interests to be registered was recognised in the Companies Act 1989, s 93 substituting a new s 396(2)(g) into the Companies Act 1985 so as to exclude the shipowner's lien as a registrable interest. Of course, the latter provision has never been brought into force. See also *The Final Report*, above n 1, at para 12.60(vi), where it is recommended that this type of charge be exempt from registration. However, in *Agnew v Commissioner of Inland Revenue* [2001] 2 AC 710 at pp 727E–728D (PC) the decision in *Re Welsh Irish Ferries* was doubted as to its correctness.

83 See *Smith v Bridgend County BC* [2001] 3 WLR 1347 at p 1359C–D *per* Lord Hoffmann and note also the cases below at n 128.

84 See above n 18 and the main text thereat.

85 See above n 18 and the main text thereat.

impracticalities of compliance with a general registration requirement. This rationale was recently supported by *The Diamond Report* whose author, in rejecting the proposal that all charges be made registrable noted that: 'I am not confident that all charges that might possibly be used in the future have been identified'.[86] Although the latter remark is undoubtedly correct the problem is, as *Re Welsh Irish Ferries* serves to demonstrate, that the present list of registrable charge interests is not identified by those whom the scheme serves with all the situations in which it has the potential to apply. Thus, the thesis presented[87] against a blanket coverage of registrable charge interests appears to be equally applicable to the present scheme based on a *numerus clausus*. In short, the present scheme contains a latent potential for unpredictability.[88] This problem is compounded by the fact that it is not only chargees who have difficulty in ascertaining whether a charge is registrable or not. The registrar of companies inspects charge documents before entering the prescribed details on the public register and if he believes that a charge is not covered by the scheme then he will refuse to register it.[89] Because s 395 only avoids a charge if the prescribed particulars are not delivered to the registrar within 21 days of the charge's creation this means that once the particulars have been delivered to the registrar the charge is, from that point onwards, immune to the avoidance power contained in s 395.[90] Therefore, if the registrar decides to reject a charge which is submitted to him on time for registration there will be no public record of the charge meaning that third parties might be misled but the chargee will be safe since he has complied with s 395.[91] Given the difficulty presently faced in deciding whether a particular transaction creates a registrable interest it is hardly surprising to learn that the attitude of the registrar is prone to fluctuations[92] over time regarding certain types of transaction and whether he will accept them for registration or not.

A further category of charge that requires registration arises in a situation where the company acquires property which is already encumbered by a charge at the time of the acquisition and the charge is of a type which would have required registration under Chapter 1 of Part 12 if it had been created by the acquiring company.[93] If such charges are not registered within 21 days of the acquisition then the company is liable to a fine, but the charge is not liable to avoidance.[94] This is a curiously drafted section since it imposes

---

86 Above n 7, at para 23.1.6.

87 See above n 18 and the main text thereat.

88 See below at n 128.

89 See *The Diamond Report*, above n 7, at para 22.2.5. The Steering Group recommended that the duty to deliver the original instrument creating the charge along with the prescribed particulars to the Registrar of companies should be removed; see *The Final Report*, above n 1, at para 12.82.

90 See *Slavenburg's Bank v Intercontinental Natural Resources Ltd* [1980] 1 WLR 1076 at p 1086B–D *per* Lloyd J.

91 The only possible disadvantage to a chargee in this situation is that he might not be able to rely on the doctrine of constructive notice since his charge has not become a public document such that third parties could be taken to have notice of it due to their ability to inspect the public register of charges; see section 7 below.

92 See *The Diamond Report*, above n 7, at para 23.4.8 (referring to the ability to register charges over bank accounts).

93 Section 400(1).

94 Section 400(2)(4).

a registration obligation linked to consensual charges[95] but applies it to charges generally under Part 12 rather than linking it to the *numerus clausus* established by s 396(1).[96]

3 LIMITATIONS ON THE AMBIT OF REGISTRABLE CHARGE SECURITY INTERESTS

Our discussion so far on the ambit of the public register has been confined to illustrating limitations in relation to the list of registrable charges. A more fundamental concern relates to the ambit of the concept of the 'charge'[97] security interest. The public register of security interests only requires security interests arising by way of specified types of 'charge' to be registered. Thus, it is only interests arising by way of the grant[98] of a proprietary interest, that is to say the creation of a consensual charge, that can be classified as a security interest for the purposes of the registration requirement.[99] This serves to highlight a wider problem of English law concerning the meaning and ambit of the phrase 'security interest'.[100] Our law only recognises consensual security interests as arising when a party (the debtor) creates an interest over his property in favour of another party[101] (the creditor) in order to secure the debtor's performance[102] of some duty or obligation (usually the repayment of money).[103] Therefore, if the debtor fails to perform the duty or obligation the creditor will be free to enforce his security, via the realisation of the property that was assigned to him, in order to discharge that duty/obligation.[104] As a

---

95 Section 400(1) speaks of charges *'created* by the company ...' (emphasis added).

96 The requirement to register such charges was originally introduced by the Companies Act 1928, s 43 introducing a new s 93(1A) to the Companies Act 1908. However, at this time the registration duty was confined to the numerus clausus of charges listed in s 93(1). When the Companies Act 1908 was replaced by the Companies Act 1929, s 81(1) of the latter Act extended the duty to register such charges to the entire part (ie, covering the internal register of charges as well). This has remained the position.

97 Note for these purposes 'charge' includes mortgage; see s 396(4).

98 Section 395(1) uses the language '... a charge *created* by the company ... ' (emphasis added).

99 See *Clough Mill Ltd v Martin* [1985] 1 WLR 111.

100 See further: Allan 'Security: Some Mysteries, Myths and Monstrosities' (1989) 15 *Monash Law Review* 337; Goode 'Security: A Pragmatic Conceptualist's Response' (1989) 15 *Monash Law Review* 361; RM Goode *Legal Problems of Credit and Security* (London, Sweet & Maxwell, 2nd edn, 1988) at pp 1–26; Oditah *Legal Aspects of Receivables Financing* (London, Sweet & Maxwell, 1991) at pp 4–14; E Sykes and S Walker *The Law of Securities* (Sydney, The Lawbook Co, 5th edn, 1993) at pp 3–27.

101 For these purposes a declaration of trust by a debtor that he holds property as a trustee in order to secure his performance of a duty or obligation towards the secured creditor/beneficiary would also create a security interest operating by way of an equitable charge; see *Re Bond Worth Ltd* [1980] Ch 228 at p 250B *per* Slade J.

102 It should be noted that the security interest can also be created by a third party over his property in favour of the creditor, despite the fact that the third party is under no liability for the performance of the original duty/obligation the debtor undertakes to perform; see *Re Wallis & Simmonds Ltd* [1974] 1 WLR 391 at p 398E–H *per* Templeman J. This position is expressly recognised by the US Uniform Commercial Code Art 9-105(d) which defines the scope of the term 'debtor' to include such a third party who undertakes this type of liability and see also Art 9-112 (third party debtor's rights against secured party).

103 See generally *Armour v Thyssen Edelstahlwerke AG* [1991] 2 AC 339.

104 Realisation in this context can take a number of different forms, depending on the type of security interest we are dealing with. In the case of a mortgage the mortgagee may become the unfettered owner of the property via the extinguishing of the mortgagor's equity of redemption or, more usually, he will simply sell the property and apply the proceeds thereby realised to discharge the debt. [cont]

matter of practice, a 'security interest' will function as just described but will operate in terms of its formal contractual adoption by the parties as a transaction by way of mortgage; charge; pledge or lien. It follows that under general law there are only four types of recognised security interest.[105] This means that when we speak about registrable corporate security interests the wording of s 395 effectively limits itself to security interests arising by way of mortgage[106] and charge. Therefore, a pledge[107] or lien[108] over goods created by the company will not require registration.[109]

This definition of 'security interest' is important because it assumes a formal significance when assessing a whole host of commercial financing transactions that have developed which might, without more, have been assumed by the casual observer to have been naturally grouped together under the heading of 'security interests'. The casual observer could be forgiven for thinking that a 'security interest' would arise in any situation where property was appropriated, via a transaction, to the discharge of a debt upon the default of a debtor. In other words into thinking that the creditor would be secure under a transaction, should his debtor default, if he could look to some form of property to compensate him (in whole or in part) for that default. However, although this definition poses no difficulties from an informal conversational standpoint, particularly as we have used the word 'secure' to describe the effects of the transaction, it would, nevertheless, pose difficulties for the legal theorist. This is because at law a security interest must either arise by force of law[110] or, by grant of a proprietary interest intended to operate by way of security. The law is concerned with the method by which property is appropriated to the discharge of debt. Such an analysis is not an exercise in semantics but of considerable practical significance. From our particular standpoint it makes the difference between being able to differentiate a registrable transaction from a transaction that is not registrable.

---

104 [cont] In the case of a charge the property will be sold by the chargee and the proceeds applied to discharge the debt. The latter will also apply where the security interest is a pledge of goods. Where the security interest operates as a lien then the holder will only have a right to retain possession of the property against the debtor until the relevant debt is settled. However, as a matter of practice many transactions which establish a lien security will now include a contractual right of sale in the event of the debtor's default. Cf *Worwood v Leisure Merchandising Services Ltd* [2002] 1 BCLC 249.

105 See *Re Cosslett (Contractors) Ltd* [1998] Ch 495 at p 508F *per* Millett LJ.

106 See s 396(4).

107 *Barrett & Co Ltd v Livesey* (1981) 131 NLJ 1213.

108 See: *Re Cosslett (Contractors) Ltd* [1998] Ch 495; *Re Hamlet International Ltd* [1999] 2 BCLC 506; *Trident International Ltd v Barlow* [2000] BCC 602.

109 Historically, our law has generally only been hostile to non-possessory security interests since it was felt that the separation of possession and ownership of goods would cause ostensible ownership problems leading to fraud; see: *Twyne's* Case (1601) 3 Co Rep 80b; de Lacy 'Reflections on the Ambit of the Rule in *Dearle v Hall* Part 1' (1999) 28 Anglo-Am L Rev 87 at pp 95–110. This was not generally perceived to be a problem where the secured party took possession of the debtor's goods because other creditors could not be misled by the debtor's apparent wealth; see *Re Hall* (1884) LR 14 QBD 366 at p 391 *per* Cave J, although such a view ignored the possible effects of possession on the potential creditors of the secured party. In *The Final Report*, above n 1, at para 12.57 it is recommended that an exemption to registration should occur when the chargee has possession of the encumbered assets. *The Diamond Report*, above n 7, also rejected the need for a public register of possessory security interests; at para 11.5.7. It should be noted that in the modern world of corporate financing possessory security is not very common since it would remove productive assets from the marketplace.

110 This would be either at common law or by virtue of a statutory provision.

A good example of this distinction is provided by the leading case of *Armour v Thyssen Edelstahlwerke AG*.[111] The case concerned a dispute between a seller of goods and the receiver of an insolvent buyer as to the ownership of goods in the receiver's possession which had not been paid for by the buyer. The goods had been supplied by the seller subject to a retention of title clause in the contract of sale which provided that title to the goods would not pass until the buyer had paid 'all debts' owing to the seller. The case turned on whether the use of this retention of title clause amounted at law to a security interest or not.[112] It is clear that the purpose of the clause was to secure the position of the seller in the event of the buyer failing to pay him 'all debts' via allowing the seller to recover the goods in the buyer's possession. In other words the buyer's default would allow the seller to have recourse to identified goods in order to secure his position. But did this transaction amount to the creation of a security interest? The House of Lords was unanimous in holding that the use of such a retention of title clause could not be recognised by the law as a security interest, since there was no element of creation in the transaction whereby a proprietary interest was created in favour of the seller by the buyer. Property in the goods had at all times remained with the seller and it followed that the buyer had no interest in the goods to convey by way of security. The leading speech was given by Lord Keith who explained the position as follows:

> I am, however, unable to regard a provision reserving title to the seller until payment of all debts due to him by the buyer as amounting to the creation by the buyer of a right of security in favour of the seller. Such a provision does in a sense give the seller security for the unpaid debts of the buyer. But it does so by way of a legitimate retention of title, not by virtue of any right over his own property conferred by the buyer.

In all cases where a right of security is conferred the debtor retains an ultimate right[113] over the subject matter in question. The creditor, having realised out of that subject matter a sufficient sum to meet the debt, is obliged to account to the debtor for any surplus. Where, however, the seller of goods retains title until some condition has been satisfied, and on failure of such satisfaction repossesses them, then he is not obliged to account to the buyer for any part of the value of the goods. Where the condition is to the effect that the price of the goods shall have been paid and it has not been paid, then in the situation where the market price of the goods has risen so that they are worth more than the contract price, the extra value belongs to the unpaid seller. That is clearly the position where the condition relates to payment of the price of the actual goods, and goes to show that the retention of title provision is not one creating a right of security, forming an exception to the general rule requiring possession by the creditor.[114] The same is true, in my opinion, where the provision covers not only the price of the very goods which are the subject of the particular contract of sale, but also all debts due to the seller under other contracts.[115]

---

111 [1991] 2 AC 339.

112 The point was important because under Scottish law a security interest is void if possession of the goods (ie, the subject matter of the alleged security interest) is not given to the secured creditor (which had not taken place in this case); see further de Lacy 'All Sums Retention of Title: The Scottish Approach' [1989] *The Conveyancer* 364.

113 Ie, the equity of redemption. See also: *Re Bond Worth Ltd* [1980] Ch 228 at p 248E–F *per* Slade J; *Re George Inglefield Ltd* [1933] 1 Ch 1 at p 27 *per* Romer LJ; *Curtain Dream plc v Churchill Merchanting Ltd* [1990] BCC 341 at pp 351F and 352H *per* Knox J.

114 See above n 112.

115 See [1991] 2 AC 339 at p 353A–E (emphasis added). Note also: *Bristol Airport plc v Powdrill* [1990] Ch 744 at p 760C–D *per* Browne-Wilkinson VC; *The Manchester, Sheffield & Lincolnshire Railway Co v The North Central Wagon Co* (1888) 13 App Cas 554 at p 567 *per* Lord Macnaghten.

This debate highlights the antiquated language of Part 12 requiring the registration of charges rather than of security interests.[116] It is more common to speak of a creditor taking a security interest than of a creditor taking a charge. A prospective creditor of the modern corporation should be entitled to expect that a public register of security interests would reflect the full sense of that term rather than a narrow sub-division of transaction operating by way of consensual charge,[117] as currently exists. Nevertheless, even if we were to amend the definition of registrable interest so that it was 'security interests' rather than 'charges' that required registration this act alone would not advance the issue to any great extent. This is because the Act currently catches two out of the four types of transaction[118] that are recognised by our law as security interests and the two interests that do not require registration are generally regarded as legitimate exemptions.[119] However, there still exist a whole host of other types of transaction that are intended to secure the position of corporate creditors and are not recognised as security interests and would, therefore, still escape the registration requirement. In short, our conception of 'security interest' has become too narrow and legalistic, divorced from the wider expectations associated with the term.

The limited nature of our legal concept of 'security interest' means that a whole host of transactions designed to secure the position of the creditor, in the event of the debtor's default, escape from the current registration regime. So, for example, transactions involving: retention of title clauses;[120] hire-purchase;[121] leases; or *Quistclose* trust provisions;[122] are all immune from registration. These transactions, although involving varying legal incidents, can be unified in that they involve the supply of goods or finance[123] to a debtor and allow the creditor a right of recovery in the event of default by the debtor. In short they all involve the retention of title[124] to an asset or fund by the creditor. Nevertheless, there also exist transactions which seek to utilise the above types of arrangement in reverse. By this we mean that title to the goods was originally located in the debtor who then 'sells' the goods to a 'buyer' (in reality the financier/creditor) who

---

116 Cf Companies Act 1989, s 93 which would have introduced a new s 395(2), whereby a registrable charge 'means any form of *security interest* (fixed or floating) over property, other than an interest arising by operation of law' (emphasis added).

117 Or mortgage; s 396(4).

118 Ie, the mortgage and charge. The other two types of recognised security interest are the pledge and lien.

119 Ie, possessory security interests; see above n 109.

120 *Clough Mill Ltd v Martin* [1985] 1 WLR 111. See further de Lacy '*Romalpa* Theory and Practice under Retention of Title in the Sale of Goods' (1995) 24 *Anglo-American Law Review* 327. The Steering Group recently recommended that it be made clear that simple retention of title clauses are not registrable charges and more complex clauses be left to the courts to determine the issue; see *The Final Report*, above n 1, at paras 12.58 and 12.60(i).

121 *Stoneleigh Finance Ltd v Phillips* [1965] 2 QB 537.

122 *Carreras Rothmans Ltd v Freeman Mathews Treasure Ltd* [1985] Ch 207; the label '*Quistclose* trust' is derived from the case of *Barclay's Bank Ltd v Quistclose Investments Ltd* [1970] AC 567. See further Bridge 'The *Quistclose* Trust in a World of Secured Transactions' (1992) 12 OJLS 333.

123 In the case of the *Quistclose* trust.

124 Retention of beneficial title via a trust in the case of the *Quistclose* trust.

then resupplies those goods to the 'seller', now known as the 'buyer'[125] subject to a title retention arrangement allowing the 'seller' (that is, creditor) the right of repossession in the event of default. Under this form of arrangement a debtor is able to manipulate the concept of title to utilise his assets to generate 'secured' finance without having to comply with any registration designed to disclose the true nature of his encumbered assets. This is a problem which the legal community has not been slow to appreciate but has been unable to satisfactorily resolve. Thus, a debate has continued to rage seeking to chart the dividing line between a sale and resupply of goods to the debtor and a transfer by way of security.[126] It is unnecessary to enter into this debate; suffice it to say that once again it serves to highlight the pedantic approach of the English common law in its promotion of form over substance according to the location of title when addressing the existence of security. What is surprising is that the debate was ever necessary since it only arose when some courts balked at the prospect of adopting a formalistic approach in this type of situation.[127] Clearly the courts' refusal to uphold certain transactions expressed to be absolute in form involved a substantive approach to contractual construction. Unfortunately, in a domain where title is supreme (and generally allocated via contractual stipulation), it is hardly surprising that the attempt to promote substance over form was productive only of uncertainty.[128] A rigid adherence to the location of title does at least have the benefit of producing simple solutions to often complex transaction problems, which, in turn, leads to the greater certainty in relationships, which is the hallmark of successful commercial activity.[129] Nevertheless, that this approach has not been exclusively pursued by the courts perhaps illustrates that simplicity is not always to be equated with equity or the perceived wider interests of justice and accountability.[130]

The problems associated with Part 12 and, in particular, the limitations of the common law concept of 'security interest' were first highlighted as an area for reform by

---

125 Or lessee etc, depending on the form of the supply transaction.

126 See, for example: Goode *Legal Problems of Credit and Security*, above n 100; Oditah, above n 100, at pp 35–40; Gough, above n 57, at pp 569–600; Diamond 'Hire Purchase Agreements as Bills of Sale, Part 2' (1960) 23 MLR 516.

127 See, by way of example: *Re Watson* (1890) 25 QBD 27; *Madell v Thomas & Co* [1891] 1 QBD 230; *Polsky v S & A Services* [1951] 1 All ER 185, affirmed [1951] 1 All ER 1062; *Curtain Dream plc v Churchill Merchanting Ltd* [1990] BCC 341; cf *Yorkshire Railway Wagon Co v Maclure* (1882) 21 Ch D 309; *British Railway Traffic & Electric Co v Khan* [1921] WN 52; *Ashby, Warner & Co v Simmons* [1936] 2 All ER 697; *Welsh Development Agency v Export Finance Co Ltd* [1992] BCC 270.

128 See, for example, *Clough Mill Ltd v Martin* [1984] 1 WLR 1067 (unpaid vendor's claim to recover goods subject to a retention of title clause void for want of registration) overturned on appeal at [1985] 1 WLR 110; *Welsh Development Agency v Export Finance Ltd* [1990] BCC 393 (purported sale of goods to financier to be then resold as financier's agent, in reality a registrable charge transaction to secure loans) overturned on appeal at [1992] BCC 270.

129 An approach graphically illustrated by the House of Lords' decision in *Armour v Thyssen* [1991] 2 AC 339. As Dillon LJ has explained: 'Indeed the similarity in result between a loan and a sale ... would make it virtually impossible to decide which the transaction was if it was not possible to have regard to the words the parties had used in their agreement in describing the transaction on which they had agreed. There is nothing illegal in a party raising finance by a sale of book debts or goods, rather than by a mortgage or charge, if he chooses to do so'; *Welsh Development Agency v Export Finance* [1992] BCC 270 at p 281A–B.

130 This is especially the case with respect to the courts' rejection of the *Romalpa* case [1976] 1 WLR 676; see especially: *Tatung (UK) Ltd v Galex Telesure Ltd* (1989) 5 BCC 325 at p 337D–E *per* Phillips J; and note: *Modelboard Ltd v Outer Box Ltd* [1992] BCC 945; *Compaq Computer Ltd v Abercorn Group Ltd* [1991] BCC 484; *Re Weldtech* [1991] BCC 16; *Pfeiffer GmbH v Arbuthnot Factors Ltd* [1988] 1 WLR 150; *Re Andrabell Ltd* [1984] 3 All ER 407.

The Crowther Report of 1971.[131] The need for reform was again pressed for by *The Diamond Report* of 1989.[132] Sadly, nothing has been done to implement either of these Reports' recommendations in so far as they affect corporate security interests.[133] This has meant that the scheme has continued to be beset with fundamental problems in relation to the ambit of the registration requirement. What is now needed is a reversal in the current policy requiring a *numerus clausus* of interests to be registered and its replacement with a new policy requiring all consensual security interests to be registered. The new policy would exempt certain transactions from registration and these would be listed in the new statute. Of course, given the deficiencies associated with the term 'security interest' the reforms would have to include a revised and new statutory definition of this term. Such a definition should be based upon that found under Art 9 of the US Uniform Commercial Code.[134] The latter makes it clear that it is the substantive nature of the transaction (that is, is it designed to perform the function of giving the creditor security in the event of the debtor's default?) rather than its descriptive form that is the important factor in determining whether the transaction should be registered or not.[135] Under this approach the types of transaction which have been mentioned as being immune from the current public register established under Part 12 of the Act would all be caught. If such reforms were to be implemented then for the first time creditors would have available to them the 'fullest information'[136] in relation to security interests covering the corporate debtor's estate. Unfortunately, although the Steering Group have recommended fundamental reform to this area (based on the adoption of the notice file principle)[137] they did not address the issue of the need for a new concept/definition of 'security interest'.

4 THE REGISTRATION DUTY

A duty is placed upon the company creating the charge to comply with the registration requirement subject to the imposition of a criminal financial penalty against the company and any of its officers responsible for failing to deliver the particulars of the charge to the

---

131 *Consumer Credit* Report of the Committee on Consumer Credit (1971) Cmnd 4596 (London, HMSO, 1971), hereafter *The Crowther Report*. See generally Part 5 of this Report at p 182 onwards.

132 See generally: Diamond 'The Reform of the Law of Security Interests' (1989) 42 *Current Legal Problems* 231; Goode 'The Modernisation of Personal Property Security Law' (1984) 100 LQR 234.

133 A small qualification to this statement is to be found in the Companies Act 1989, Part 4, which would, if brought into force, make minor amendments to Part 12 of the Act, based in part on *The Diamond Report*, above n 7. However, it is unlikely that these provisions will ever be brought into force.

134 See Art 9-102.

135 See the Official Comment to Art 9-102. One important qualification should be noted in respect of the Art 9 scheme. Although it has introduced a new and unified concept of security interest, the scheme goes further in respect of sales of accounts (ie, book debts/receivables) which are also covered. The reason for this extended coverage is that it is not easy, as a matter of practice, to distinguish between a genuine sale of accounts and an assignment of them intended to operate by way of security. In order to simplify matters, Art 9 applies equally in respect of both types of assignment in so far as imposing a perfection requirement in order to secure the priority of the assignment against other creditors of the assignor. This policy should also be incorporated into any reform of Part 12; see generally *The Diamond Report*, above n 7, at para 18.2.

136 See above n 25 and the main text thereat.

137 See generally below at section 11.

registrar of companies.[138] It is important to note that the Companies Act has always made registration a mandatory requirement for the company creating the charge in the sense that it is required to deliver the prescribed particulars[139] relating to the charge to the registrar of companies. It might be questioned whether the imposition of this positive duty is warranted. For example, no comparable registration system goes so far as to impose a duty to register. Registration in the non-corporate sphere has remained a voluntary matter.[140] Nevertheless, although the act of registration has remained voluntary as a matter of law in the non-corporate domain, as a matter of practice the need to maintain priority against competing security interests has served to render registration the prudent course of action in the majority of cases.

It is strange that the Companies Act imposes the duty to register upon the chargor alone when for most practical purposes it is the chargee who is the interested party in ensuring that registration is effected.[141] This is because registration is made to perform a perfection function meaning that unregistered charges may become void against prescribed parties thereby diluting the value of the chargee's interest.[142] Indeed, the Act recognises the practical realities of the situation since 'any person interested in the charge'[143] may also see that the registration is effected.[144] Therefore, the chargee is not dependent upon the chargor's good faith in order to obtain maximum protection for his security, which is just as well in many cases,[145] since the chargor may have no incentive to signal the encumbered status of his property via public disclosure at the companies registry.[146]

---

138 See Companies Act 1985, s 399(1) and (2). However, no offence will be committed if the particulars of the charge are delivered to the registrar of companies by another party interested in it; s 399(1) and (3). The duty to register is reinforced by the Company Directors Disqualification Act 1986, s 9(1) and Sched 1 Part 1 para 4(n), which makes the company's failure to comply with s 399 a matter for the court to take into account when considering a person's conduct as a director in the context of director disqualification proceedings.

139 On which see s 401(1).

140 See, generally: Bills of Sale Act 1878, s 8; Mortgaging of Aircraft Order 1972, SI 1972/1268 para 4(1); Land Charges Act 1972, s 2(1). Cf Land Registration Act 1925, s 120; Local Land Charges Act 1975, s 5 (both of which impose a duty to register, although these Acts raise a different policy issue, since they are concerned with registers of title to property rather than registers of claims against property, and there is no criminal sanction for non-compliance). In the US, Art 9 of the UCC also operates on a voluntary basis.

141 See *Capital Finance Co Ltd v Stokes* [1969] 1 Ch 261 at p 282D *per* Sachs LJ. The only substantive justification for imposing a registration duty backed by criminal sanction is that it is deemed necessary that information regarding security interests must be brought to the public's attention, irrespective of any issue of priority between competing creditors of the debtor. Because the debtor will, short of altruism, have no incentive to voluntarily disclose such information the criminal sanction becomes the only method by which the law can attempt to enforce compliance. Nevertheless, it is submitted that the security interest register is ill-suited to employing criminal sanctions to enforce mandatory duties (see main text below) and registration should remain a purely civil matter. Any requirements mandating the supply of security interest information should be kept in the context of more general company information duties which can be actively enforced and which provide a more convenient single point of reference; see below n 163 and the main text thereat.

142 See s 395(1).

143 Section 399(1).

144 Such a party is entitled to recover any fees paid to the registrar as a consequence from the chargor company, which reinforces the mandatory duty placed upon the chargor; see s 399(2).

145 See generally: *Re RM Arnold & Co Ltd* (1984) 1 BCC 99,248; *Re Braemar Investments Ltd* (1988) 4 BCC 366; *Re Chantry House Developments plc* [1990] BCC 646; *Re Fablehill Ltd* [1991] BCC 590; *Re Telomatic Ltd* [1993] BCC 404; *Re Mistral Finance Ltd* [2001] BCC 27; *Barclays Bank plc v Stuart Landon Ltd* [2001] 2 BCLC 316.

146 See, by way of analogy: *Re Ashpurton Estates Ltd* [1983] Ch 110 at p 121D–E; *Horsley v Style* (1893) 69 LT 222.

The reason why the chargor remains under a duty to register appears to be the legacy of history. Registration of security interests was first introduced into the corporate world by virtue of the Companies (Clauses) Act 1845.[147] This Act requires companies[148] incorporated by Special Act of Parliament (incorporating the standard clauses the Act of 1845 laid down) to keep a register of mortgages and bonds over their property. It was thought desirable at this time that such interests be publicised and that this could only be achieved by placing the company under a positive duty to maintain such a register. However, no sanctions were imposed for a failure to comply with this duty; it was simply assumed that compliance would be made. This Act was quickly superseded however as modern company law, as we would now recognise it, emerged in the shape of the Companies Act 1862, the 'magna carta'[149] of company law which established the first modern and comprehensive system for the incorporation of companies via registration. A similar policy underlay s 43 of the latter Act, which imposed a duty on companies to maintain a register of 'all mortgages and charges'[150] specifically affecting their property. However, in an attempt to ensure that a register was maintained by the company a criminal sanction was added rendering every director, manager or officer of the company who was responsible for non-registration liable to a fine. Despite this development the duty was widely ignored[151] and it was to take the introduction of the penalty of invalidation for unregistered security interests by virtue of the Companies Act 1900[152] before the registration requirement became widely respected. The centralised and, for the first time, public register[153] of charges set up in 1900 adopted two sanctions to ensure registration was made. First, reflecting the origins of company security interest registration, it adopted the principle of requiring the chargor to deliver the prescribed particulars for registration upon sanction of a criminal penalty. Secondly, it attempted to

---

147 See s 45. It should be noted that this Act is still in force although, for most purposes, it is now an irrelevance since in 2000 there were only 123 companies registered by Special Act of Parliament to which the Act applies; see DTI Companies In 1999–2000, above n 4, at p 42 Table E3.

148 As a matter of fact, the Act imposes the duty on the company secretary.

149 See *Palmer's Company Law*, above n 57, Vol 1 at para 1.110.

150 Note the change from the register established under s 45 of the 1845 Act which required bonds to be registered. The change is accounted for on the basis that the bond created a purely personal obligation to repay the loan, which lenders were increasingly reluctant to accept, wanting more specific forms of security giving them a proprietary interest.

151 This fact was recognised by the courts who developed what was to become known as the equitable rule against directors in an attempt to counter the prejudice that a creditor of the company might encounter when faced with an unregistered charge of which he had no notice. This rule was a crude attempt to invalidate charges held by directors of insolvent companies due to the fact that they had breached their duties to the company in failing to have their charge registered and therefore they should not be allowed to benefit from their default to the detriment of the general creditors of the company. However, this judge-made rule did not apply to non-director chargees and so no reliance could ever be placed on the register as a result. Indeed, the arbitrariness of the position was recognised by the House of Lords when reviewing the rule in the case of *Wright v Horton* (1887) 12 App Cas 371 who were forced to overrule the cases that had established the rule on the basis that the Act did not contemplate such a remedy and a financial penalty was all that could be imposed against errant directors of the chargor company.

152 See s 14.

153 It should be noted that the register of charges established by the Companies Act 1862, s 43 was not only maintained by a private body (ie, the chargor company) but it was also only open to inspection by members of the company and creditors. Therefore, a potential creditor or other party contemplating dealing with the company had no means of ascertaining the state of charges against the company's property. The register established under the Companies (Clauses) Act 1845, s 45 appears to be wider since it is open to shareholders, chargees and 'any person interested'.

neutralise the effects of non-compliance by avoiding the enforceability of the unregistered security interest against certain parties. In 1907 a third sanction was added in that if a charge became void for non-registration then the money secured by the avoided charge became payable immediately.[154] The latter provision was brought in to avoid the perceived injustice that might befall the chargee if the charge were to be avoided but yet the chargee forced to wait until the contractually appointed time for repayment. The latter position was unjust because the registration duty was on the chargor and therefore it was their fault if, through non-registration, avoidance came into play.[155] These three sanctions have remained in force ever since.

It can be seen that the use of both civil and criminal penalties under Part 12 of the Act is an attempt to ensure that company charge information is disclosed on the public register maintained by the Registrar of companies. Nevertheless, it can be questioned whether the imposition of a positive duty coupled with a criminal penalty for default upon the chargor company aids the process of disclosure. Indeed, it appears as if it does nothing of the sort. Companies have no real incentive to comply with the duty since the act of registration does not directly benefit them and in many cases may be viewed as a detrimental requirement.[156] The criminal sanction is no avail since there do not appear to have been any prosecutions under the various provisions over the years.[157] This is not to say that the duty could not be made to work via active enforcement of the criminal sanction. For example, in the context of companies, duties to send annual returns[158] and accounts[159] to the Registrar, it has been stated that 'companies ... are deplorably dilatory in delivering returns'.[160] However, as a result of a 'blitz'[161] by the Registrar the number

---

154 See Companies Act 1907, s 10(1) and see now Companies Act 1985, s 395(2).

155 The Steering Group have recommended that this provision should be repealed if chargees were given the ability to register charges out of time without recourse to the High Court as under the present regime (on which see s 404); see *The Final Report*, above n 1, at paras 12.77 and 12.75–12.76. They were influenced in this when consultation revealed that the provision was used by chargees 'primarily to ensure that chargors agree to the reconstitution of any charge not registered in time'; at para 12.77. However, it is submitted that this recommendation could only be justified in the context of a scheme which did not place a duty upon the chargor to register such that it could not be said to be the chargor's fault if the charge were to be avoided for non-registration pursuant to s 395(1). If the latter feature is not present such that fault can be attributed to the chargor then a chargee would suffer in a situation where a third party gained and registered a charge over the assets at a time the avoidance power was in force due to non-registration and this would mean that late registration would be of no avail to the first chargee. The chargee might also suffer if the company were to go into administration and the encumbered assets were sold by the administrator; see below at n 196. The acceleration of repayment provision serves to keep the chargor on his toes. It should be noted that there is nothing to prevent the chargee contracting for such accelerated repayment in any event.

156 See above n 146. One possible benefit to the chargor in ensuring that registration is made is that if it is not then the sum secured by the unregistered charge 'immediately becomes payable' should the charge become void to any extent; see s 395(2).

157 *The Diamond Report*, above n 7, was to comment: '[p]rosecutions are so rare that the threat can be ignored', at para 24.1.1; echoing the findings of *The Loreburn Report* (Report of the Company Law Amendment Committee) which had stated in 1906 'the penalty for non-compliance with this section [Companies Act 1862, s 43] was rarely exacted, and practically, therefore, little reliance could be placed in the register thus provided for' (1906) Cd 3052 (London, HMSO, 1906) at para 35. The latest DTI statistics confirm this position; see *Companies in 1999–2000*, above n 4, at p 39 Table D3.

158 See s 363.

159 See s 242.

160 PL Davies Gower's *Principles of Modern Company Law* (London, Sweet & Maxwell, 6th edn, 1997) at p 509.

161 See Davies, above n 160.

of defaulting companies has been cut nearly in half[162] due to a policy of active enforcement and prosecution.[163] Nevertheless, there are two qualifications which can be placed upon this contrast. First, in the case of annual accounts and returns the registrar is in a position to know whether or not the duty to submit returns has been complied with. The company is registered with the registrar and if no returns are received appropriate action can be taken. However, the creation of security interests remains essentially a private contractual matter which the registrar will be unaware of and cannot possibly be expected to discover or police. The only time action could be reasonably contemplated would be upon an application for late registration of an unregistered charge[164] or the winding up of the chargor company. Secondly, the effects of non-disclosure are different. The failure to submit annual returns will mean that third parties have no independent method of assessing the financial position of the company. Such a position could obviously have serious repercussions for those dealing with a company that has failed to submit returns and was later to go into insolvent liquidation. Those attempting to deal with companies have the right to assess the worthiness of the company via its financial history as revealed by the annual returns. The non-availability of this information is an obvious cause of potential prejudice to those minded to deal with companies. By way of contrast, the effects of non-registration of company security interests are different. Because registration is made to perform a perfection function unregistered security interests are routinely avoided. Therefore, the secured creditor who assumes this status upon reliance of an unencumbered register will not be prejudiced since the non-disclosed interest is avoided against him.[165] The unsecured creditor also avoids prejudice since, should the company subsequently collapse, any undisclosed interest will also be avoided against the liquidator.[166] It can be seen, therefore, that the practical consequences of non-compliance with a registration duty differs fundamentally between the submission of annual returns and security interests. Criminal penalties are the only sanction that can be employed in the former case whilst in the latter situation their use appears to be cosmetic.

The only substantive benefit that is achieved by imposing a duty to register security interests (assuming that the chargor was minded to comply with the duty) is that these interests are disclosed at a much earlier stage than the information contained in the annual returns which, by their very nature, are only disclosed once a year.[167] The chargor company is required, at present, to send the prescribed particulars to the registrar within

---

162 See DTI *Companies in 1997–98* (London, TSO, 1998) at p 45 Table F3, where it is stated that in June 1992 15.2% of companies were in default but by June 1994 the figure had fallen to 9.4%. The latest figures in *Companies in 1999–2000*, above n 4, at p 45 Table F3 show further falls, namely 6.6% of companies in default for late filing of annual returns and 4.9% in default for late filing of accounts.

163 See DTI *Companies in 1999–2000*, above n 4, at p 39 Table D3 where it is stated that in 1999–2000 there were 1,806 prosecutions for a failure to deliver annual accounts and 683 prosecutions for a failure to deliver annual returns. See also s 242A which renders companies liable to a civil penalty for a failure to deliver accounts to the Registrar; this penalty is in addition to any criminal sanctions. The latter penalty has brought in millions of pounds in revenue; see DTI Report, above n 4, at p 46 Table F4.

164 See s 404. Prosecution at such a stage might well act as a deterrent to late registration and prove to be counter-productive.

165 See s 395(1).

166 See s 395(1).

167 See s 226(3) and Sched 4 which set out the information to be contained in the annual accounts, note especially para 48(4) which requires the balance sheet to state the aggregate amount of any debts in respect of which any security has been given by the company and an indication of the nature of any security so given.

21 days of the creation of the charge security interest. It follows that this information is more likely to enter the public domain at an earlier stage than the annual returns. Nevertheless, it is submitted that given the practical realities of the present situation in that the registration duty is not enforced and the fact that other comparable systems omit[168] any such requirement, the duty to register should be abolished. The information function of registration is best served by an articulated policy of limited avoidance for unregistered security interests in the context of a comprehensive scheme of priorities. Any wider demands for disclosure would be best served by amending the general provisions relating to annual returns or accounts[169] so that more explicit information is required in relation to security interests.[170] Registration of security interests should be an optional requirement,[171] but if registration is not made the chargee will have to bear the consequences.[172]

5 THE LEGITIMACY OF CHARGE AVOIDANCE

If a charge is not registered within 21 days of its creation then it is void against a liquidator, administrator or any creditor of the chargor company 'so far as any security on the company's property or undertaking is conferred by the charge'.[173] The avoidance of the unregistered charge will relegate the chargee to the status of an unsecured creditor. However, in the absence of intervention by one of the parties protected by the avoidance power, as between the chargor and chargee, the charge is valid and fully enforceable and the chargor cannot challenge the security interest on the grounds of non-registration.[174] The latter position logically follows because the purpose of establishing the public register of charges was to disclose potentially prejudicial information to the wider community of third party interests against the chargor company. This prejudice cannot apply to the chargor since it is a party to the information that the Act seeks to disclose. The point is reinforced by the fact that the duty to register charges is actually placed on the chargor[175] and, therefore, avoidance against the chargor would act as a deterrent to registration. Whilst non-avoidance against the chargor can readily be supported, it is

---

168 See above n 140.

169 See above at nn 158–59 and 167.

170 It should be noted that the annual accounts are required to be independently audited; see s 235.

171 *The Final Report*, above n 1, at para 12.48 states that it is 'unnecessary' to have a criminal penalty for non-registration of a charge and goes on to recommend the abolition of this penalty, at para 12.73. Both *The Crowther Report*, above n 131, at para 5.7.48 and *The Diamond Report*, above n 7, at para 11.5.17 were also in favour of voluntary registration.

172 As a matter of practice the chargee's legal advisors would come under a duty to ensure registration was made and contract/tort liability would inevitably flow against the negligent adviser; see: *Foster v Crusts* [1986] BCLC 307; *Midland Bank Trust Co Ltd v Hett, Stubbs & Kemp* [1979] Ch 384; *Bell v Peter Browne & Co* [1990] 2 QB 495. Cf *Ladenbau (UK) Ltd v Crawley & De Reya* [1978] 1 WLR 260.

173 See s 395(1). In the context of a liquidator or administrator 'void' means that the charge is void against a company in liquidation or administration since there is 'little value' in distinguishing between the company and the liquidator/administrator for these purposes; see *Smith v Bridgend County BC* [2001] 3 WLR 1347 at pp 1355A and 1357A *per* Lord Hoffmann.

174 *Independent Automatic Sales Ltd v Knowles & Foster* [1962] 1 WLR 974; *Bank of Scotland v Neilson & Co* 1991 SLT 8 at p 11A *per* Lord Maclean. Note also *Re Ayala Holdings Ltd* [1996] 1 BCLC 467.

175 See s 399(1).

appropriate to examine the other categories of party in favour of whom avoidance does operate.

The avoidance of unregistered charges against the liquidator is based on his role as the person responsible for winding up the debtor company. His role is to ascertain liabilities and realise, in so far as there exist, the assets of the company pending its formal dissolution.[176] The avoidance mechanism recognises this function and is designed to reflect his 'agency'[177] on behalf of the unsecured creditors who might have been prejudiced by the undisclosed charge. Avoidance is founded upon a collectivist[178] efficiency rationale based upon the hypothetical creditor who inspects the register prior to advancing credit to the company and then makes his advance according to the information disclosed.[179] Although such a party is not entitled to the preservation of the status quo at the time of advancing credit to the company, the creditor is entitled to rely upon the information as then disclosed or would have been subsequently disclosed were a charge to have been created later but not registered. The assumption here is that the creditor bases his decision to advance credit and then maintain credit in favour of the company, at least in part, upon the strength of the information revealed by the register.[180] Registration is therefore made to perform a mirror function[181] in that it reflects the charges in existence over the property of the debtor company.[182] The avoidance power serves to reflect the register as the exclusive arbiter of information since those that enter into relationships with the debtor company in reliance thereof cannot be prejudiced as a result of non-disclosure. The hypothetical nature of the unsecured creditor in this context is designed to remove complex factual inquiries that would otherwise occur at considerable expense to the liquidation process thereby prejudicing creditors as a whole.

---

176 See Insolvency Act 1986, s 143.

177 The agency label is used in this context merely to reflect the idea that the liquidator acts on behalf of the unsecured creditors when the avoidance mechanism is triggered by his appointment; see *Re Lambert* (1991) 2 PPSAC 2d 160 at p 162 *per* Farley J. Prior to liquidation the unsecured creditors have no proprietary rights against the debtor company and no *standi* to complain about the company's general dealings; see *Re Ehrmann Bros Ltd* [1906] 2 Ch 697. Upon liquidation the unsecured creditor has a right to see that the company's property is applied towards the *pari passu* satisfaction of creditor claims; Insolvency Act 1986, s 107 (voluntary winding up), Insolvency Rules 1986, r 4.181 (compulsory winding up), and see *Re Ashpurton Estates Ltd* [1983] Ch 110 at p 123E–F *per* Lord Brightman.

178 See T Jackson *The Logic & Limits of Bankruptcy Law* (Cambridge Massachusetts, Harvard University Press, 1986) at chapter 1.

179 It should be noted that reliance on the register is not always direct and a creditor may indirectly rely upon the register in advancing credit via the medium of a credit reference, or other third party, agency; cf *Horsley v Style* (1895) 69 LT 222. The notion of 'hypothetical' status is also found under US Bankruptcy Code 1978, s 544.

180 *Searles v Scarlett* [1892] 2 QB 56 at pp 59–61 *per* Lord Esher MR; *Re Abrahams & Sons* [1902] 1 Ch 695 at p 700 *per* Buckley J. In *Salomon v Salomon & Co Ltd* [1897] CA 22 at p 40 Lord Watson was to remark of the then registration system that it placed unsecured creditors under a 'duty' to inspect the register prior to advancing credit to the company. Under the present Companies Act the 21 day period of grace can serve to undermine the effectiveness of the register with regard to the quality of the information conveyed since a charge may be in existence at the time a potential creditor inspects but has yet to be registered, the chargee relying on his 21 day grace; see, by way of analogy: *Re Middleton* (1870) 11 Eq 209; *Marples v Hartley* (1861) 3 El & El 610. Note also *The Final Report*, above n 1, at para 12.13.

181 The term 'mirror' is normally associated with land registration schemes; see Ruoff, *An Englishman Looks at the Torrens System* (1957) at p 8.

182 This is subject to the inherent limitations concerning the nature and list of registrable charge security interests that has already been discussed.

Indeed the concept of reliance in this context would be exceedingly difficult to establish or refute were it to be made fact specific.[183]

Despite this rationale[184] it should be noted that the arguments in favour of avoidance against the liquidator are not all one way. If one accepts that the basic principle of insolvency law is that pre-insolvency entitlements will, as a general rule,[185] be respected[186] then avoidance against the liquidator appears unjustifiable. The reason for this is that pre-insolvency an unregistered charge could be enforced against the company and the unsecured creditors would have no grounds of complaint since they would have no proprietary interest over the company's assets nor any interest over the company's everyday business decisions.[187] The only relationship between the unsecured creditors and the company is the purely personal relationship of debtor/creditor – if the company debtor does not pay the debt at the appointed time the creditor can seek judgment against them, but nothing more. This argument therefore raises the question as to why insolvency should change matters. The basic answer to this question is that post-insolvency the unsecured creditors can only look to the assets of the company to realise their outstanding claims;[188] the company is no longer a trading concern able to meet its day-to-day liabilities. However, this alone is not enough to justify priority for the unregistered chargee freely bargained for his right of priority in this eventuality, why should the unsecured creditor now receive a belated form of protection? The reason for this protection is the prejudice that might have befallen the hypothetical creditor whose relationship with the company was based (albeit only partially) upon the absence of the relevant charge upon the public register. This party is entitled to assume the integrity of the register and the avoidance mechanism serves to reinforce that expectation.

It is important to stress that this rationale is founded exclusively upon the concept of the hypothetical creditor who has relied upon the state of the register before dealing with the company. Although this has been justified upon the basis that reliance in this context would be difficult to either establish or refute, there is also another powerful reason for basing avoidance against a hypothetical, rather than real, reliance interest (assuming that

---

183 Cf *Midland Bank Trust Co Ltd v Green* [1981] AC 513 at p 530A–E *per* Lord Wilberforce.

184 It should be noted that this rationale has never been expounded by any legislature despite avoidance against creditors being universally recognised; see also: UCC Art 9–301(1)(b), (3); and note the Canadian approach seen in Uniform Personal Property Security Act, s 19(1)(b); Ontario Personal Property Security Act, s 20(1)(b). The fact that the policy of the avoidance mechanisms under both the Companies Act and North American Personal Property Security schemes appear to be 'ambiguous' has not gone without comment; see McCoid 'Bankruptcy, the Avoiding Powers and Unperfected Security Interests' (1989) 59 *American Bankruptcy Law Journal* 175. For a further rationale of the present Companies Act avoidance mechanism, see Goode, *Principles of Corporate Insolvency Law* (London, Sweet & Maxwell, 2nd edn, 1997) at pp 419–21.

185 For exceptions to this rule see Insolvency Act 1986, ss 238, 239, 244, 245, 423.

186 Goode, above n 184, at p 54.

187 See: *Re Ehrmann Bros Ltd* [1906] 2 Ch 697 at p 709 *per* Cozens-Hardy LJ; *Mercantile Bank of India Ltd v Chartered Bank of India* [1937] 1 All ER 231 at p 241 *per* Porter J; *US Shoe Corp v Cudmore-Neiber Shoe Co* (1976) 419 F Supp 135.

188 See also: Goode, above n 184, at p 421 who describes unsecured creditor rights in this context as being 'converted [upon insolvency] from purely personal rights into rights more closely analogous to that of beneficiaries under an active trust'; *Re Ashpurton Estates Ltd* [1983] Ch 110 at p 123F *per* Lord Brightman. Cf *Kinsela v Russell Kinsela Pty Ltd* (1986) 4 ACLC 215 at p 223 *per* Street CJ.

reliance could be established).[189] The reason for this is that if reliance could be established by a creditor so that the unregistered security interest thereby became void against that party (but remained valid against the other non-reliance creditors) this party would be promoted fortuitously to secured status due to the event of non-registration. Such a promotion of status would be unjustified because it was unbargained for and would serve to defeat the *pari passu* rule of distribution of the company's assets.[190] In effect one undisclosed interest would merely be substituted for another. If this position were to be accepted it would also add the element of arbitrariness to the insolvency process since the reliance creditor's monetary return would be dependent upon the size and value of the unregistered secured creditor's debt and security. The only way to avoid these difficulties is to avoid the unregistered security against all the unsecured creditors if one of them can establish reliance, but this raises the question as to why the 'non-reliance' element in their midst should benefit from avoidance? Perhaps the answer to this question is that the only 'right' of the reliance creditor in this context is to be included in a *pari passu* distribution of the company's assets minus registered charge entitlements since this is the sole basis on which he entered into a relationship with the company. Nevertheless, whatever the merits of these arguments, it is submitted that the best justification for the avoidance mechanism is based upon the hypothetical creditor reliance interest theory since it produces a simple and efficient solution thereby reinforcing the integrity of the register and the priority of interests which are subject to it.

Although the hypothetical reliance creditor status justifies the avoidance mechanism it should be noted that avoidance *per se* will not achieve creditor satisfaction upon liquidation. There may be hundreds of unsecured creditors among whom the liquidated company's assets have to be distributed *pro rata* resulting in any actual return being a mere fraction of the original debt. It is probably a fact that the majority of creditors will advance credit upon the perceived trading strength of the company[191] of which the existence of charge security interests will probably only form a small ingredient of the

---

189 Cf Companies Act 1989, s 97 which (if brought into force) would bring in a new s 402(4) thereby introducing a fact-specific concept of reliance in the context of omissions or errors in the registered particulars of a charge so that the charge may, at the court's discretion, remain valid against a liquidator or administrator if no unsecured creditor was 'misled materially to his prejudice' or that no person assumed unsecured status at the time the registered particulars contained omissions or errors. By virtue of the new (if brought into force) s 402(5) the court is also given a discretion to order that a registered charge (which is incomplete or inaccurate) is valid against a person acquiring an interest in or right over property subject to the registered charge if it is satisfied that person did not rely upon the state of the register at the time of his acquisition of that right or interest. This limited concept of reliance is distinguishable from the arguments in the main text on the basis that here we are dealing with registered particulars such that some information, at least, is conveyed by the public register. Nevertheless, it is submitted that these measures are contrary to the general avoidance power contained in what is now s 395(1), which contains no qualification based upon actual detrimental reliance. If the concept of reliance is to be admitted into the scheme then logic would appear to suggest that it should also apply in the latter situation. Nevertheless, it is submitted that the concept of actual reliance should have no place within the registration system due to the difficult fact-based inquiries that it might cause.

190 See Insolvency Act 1986, s 107 (voluntary winding up) and Insolvency Rules 1986, SI 1986/1925 r 4.181(1) (compulsory winding up).

191 This reliance interest is recognised by Insolvency Act 1986, ss 213, 214 which make it an offence to carry on a business with an intent to defraud creditors or for a director to allow the company to continue trading when he ought to have realised the company could go into insolvent liquidation. See also Companies Act 1985, s 458 (punishment for fraudulent trading).

equation.[192] Nevertheless, the disclosure function of the public register should not be underestimated and, although it has been suggested that registration should no longer be enforced by criminal sanctions,[193] invalidation will inevitably follow liquidation despite the fact that actual prejudice may not have occurred in many situations.

The second category of party to benefit from the present avoidance provisions is the administrator. Avoidance against the administrator is based upon similar policies justifying the avoidance as against the liquidator. In the majority of cases administration serves as the only alternative to liquidation and this is reflected by many of the situations recognised by the Insolvency Act 1986 in which the court may make an administration order.[194] Once again there is a collectivist ideal underpinning the avoidance mechanism since it prevents prejudice to the creditors of the company.[195] Upon the conclusion of the administration order the company will either have been restored to its financial health and management autonomy, in which case the charge will become enforceable once again,[196] or the company will be wound up, whereby the secured creditor will be relegated to unsecured status.[197]

The final beneficiary of the avoidance power are creditors of the chargor company. There are two types of creditor, the secured creditor and the unsecured creditor. Unfortunately, the Act fails to distinguish between them or to elaborate on why they should benefit from the avoidance power. Nevertheless, secured creditors are the largest and most obvious category of beneficiary from the avoidance power. After all, it is the free availability of security to creditors minded to take it that necessitates the existence of the registration system in the first place. It has been officially recognised that the interests of secured creditors lie at the heart of the system:

> The register is there to disclose as comprehensively as possible the details of charges created by companies. *The fundamental intention is to allow a company's prospective creditors to find out*

---

192 The annual returns and accounts will give the potential creditor a more accurate reflection of the company's financial strength, although by their very nature such accounts may be stale; the consent of the debtor would be required for the latest information; cf *Thomas Witter Ltd v TBP Industries Ltd* [1996] 2 All ER 573.

193 See above n 171 and the main text thereat.

194 See especially s 8(1)(a), (3)(d).

195 Prejudice in this context is based upon the hypothetical reliance interest as outlined above. Indeed, the special interests of creditors (contingent or prospective) is expressly recognised by s 9(1); see *Re Gallidoro Trawlers Ltd* [1991] BCC 691. It should be noted that even registered and non-registrable security interests are affected by the making of an administration order; see Insolvency Act 1986, ss 10(1)(b), 10(4), 11(3)(c), 15(1).

196 It should be noted that in some cases the administrator might have realised the property which was subject to the charge as part of the rehabilitation of the company. Because the charge is rendered void against the administrator there is nothing the chargee could do to prevent this. When the company comes out of administration the chargee would have to rely upon s 395(2) and demand repayment of the debt.

197 There is one important qualification to this under the present law since the holder of an unregistered floating charge can prevent the grant of an administration order by appointing an administrative receiver; see ss 9(3), 29(2). The floating chargeholder must be given notice of any petition for the grant of an administration order; s 9(2), which will allow him to appoint an administrative receiver; s 10(2)(b), thereby causing the petition to be dismissed by the court pursuant to s 9(3). It might be questioned whether this exposes a lacuna in the law since s 9(3)(b) denies certain categories of floating chargeholder the ability to prevent the grant of an administration order, although unregistered floating chargeholders are not one of them. However, this would change if Companies Act 1989, s 107 and Sched 16 para 3 were brought into force introducing a new Insolvency Act 1986, s 9(3)(b)(i), [cont]

whether property offered to them as security is unencumbered. The degree of assurance that these persons can obtain from the register allows them to lend with confidence to companies, which is of advantage to companies themselves.[198]

Although one might express reservations about the accuracy of this statement when applied to Part 12 of the Act it is certainly an admirable statement of the policy which should underlie the public registration system. However, even accepting the limitations of the present system based on a *numerus clausus* of registrable interests, we can see how the avoidance of unregistered charges benefits the secured creditor. The public register at least allows the prospective secured creditor to learn if certain categories of property/charge[199] are already in existence.[200] If no registration entry is found then the creditor can take a charge and register it safe in the knowledge that he will be assured of priority against any interest which is not disclosed. Public registration is highly efficient in this regard by eliminating what would otherwise be a difficult if not impossible task in soliciting reliable information about companies prior grants of charge security interests.

The rationale for avoidance would be even more beneficial if Part 12 were to be amended along the lines already advocated for above.[201] Under this approach all security interests would require registration such that prospective secured creditors could be confident in taking security having searched the register prior to dealing with the company. This problem is compounded under the present system because Part 12 does not impose any rules of priority thereby regulating the competition of registered charges against one another. Part 12 is purely negative in its effects rendering unregistered charges liable to avoidance but nothing more; it does not tell us about the status of registered charges. This highlights the limitations of principle which underlie public registration under Part 12. It is submitted that the public register should be based upon two cardinal principles which would serve primarily to benefit the secured creditor. First, the register should be a reliable source of information consisting of the degree to which security interests exist over company property. Secondly, the secured party should be given a guarantee of his own priority ranking once the decision to advance secured credit has been made (after a search of the register) and registration effected to protect that interest. Any efficient registration system will ensure as a matter of first principle that both these requirements are met. A system which identifies 'security interests' according to a functional criterion and then imposes a perfection and priority rule according to the date of a registration entry will achieve this result. Part 12 of the Companies Act has sadly failed in this respect, but in Canada where these principles have been adopted in the form of modern Personal Property Security statutes the financial institutions (the largest category of secured creditor) have been among the keenest supporters of these new schemes.[202] In effect modern computerised registration systems allow, via the notice file

---

197 [cont] which would remove the ability of an unregistered floating charge holder to appoint an administrative receiver in these circumstances, in order to block the granting of an administration order by the court.

198 *Hansard* (1989) vol 504 HL at 128 *per* Lord Strathclyde (emphasis added). The quoted extract was taken from the debates surrounding the passage of what was to become the Companies Act 1989, Part 4, which was never brought into force. However, the policy quoted is reflective of the theory underlying the current Companies Act 1985, Part 12 (unamended).

199 See s 396(1) for these interests.

200 Subject to the black hole caused by the 21-day period of grace given to chargees in which an undisclosed interest can lurk undetected before the avoidance power comes into play.

201 See above at pp 349–50.

202 See Ziegel 'The New Canadian PPS Legislation' [1986] *Lloyd's Maritime and Commercial Law Quarterly* 160 at p 170.

principle,[203] a secured creditor to stake a claim[204] against a respective debtor. A single registration entry enables the secured party to obtain a guaranteed priority against listed categories of asset which are/may be held by a debtor. Subject only to the debtor having a right in the appropriate assets, the register is the sole source of priority entitlements at any given time.[205]

It cannot be denied that the prime beneficiaries of the avoidance power are secured creditors,[206] but it would be wrong to limit avoidance to this class of creditor alone. Unsecured creditors also benefit from the avoidance power. Any sensible creditor will, prior to dealing with the company, make a credit assessment of the company's worth. The method and practice of such an assessment will obviously vary, depending upon the circumstances, but whatever form that assessment takes it will involve the acquisition of information concerning the financial health of the company. Much of the regulation of the English company is founded upon the establishment of effective disclosure of information relating to every aspect of the company from creation,[207] to general trading[208] and ultimately the death of the company.[209] The public register of charges is but an extension of the trend in disclosure. The assumption is that creditors will utilise the register as part of their assessment of the creditworthiness, and the continuation thereof, of the company. Obviously, if company assets are heavily encumbered then the real value of the company will be reduced in proportion to the value of the secured debt. Nevertheless, if the company is solvent and able to meet its obligations, the existence of secured debt by itself is not an indication that the company cannot/should not be dealt with,[210] but it may well be an indication to proceed with caution prior to dealing such that further inquiries are made.[211]

The state of the register is of vital importance to the potential secured creditor because if certain charges are listed on the register no priority can be gained by the later party and such a result will largely determine the decision as to whether to advance credit. In the context of the US Uniform Commercial Code Art 9 (which regulates security interests),

---

203 Notice filing is a system which allows a prospective secured creditor to register an interest against a debtor before the actual security interest has materialised. It is a pragmatic device to enable priority to be given to the creditor in advance of any financial commitment to the secured relationship. The system originated in North America and is integral to the various personal property security registration schemes to be found in the US and Canada. This can be contrasted to Part 12 of the Companies Act which only allows the registration of actual security interests. However, the Steering Group have recommended that this principle should now be adopted by Part 12; see below at section 11.

204 See Baird 'Notice Filing and the Problem of Ostensible Ownership' (1983) 12 *Journal of Legal Studies* 53 at p 60.

205 In other words, we are not dealing with a register of title, but instead a register of transactions operating by way of security against a named entity be it an individual or corporation.

206 It also follows that the interests of the debtor will also benefit from this since it will promote the availability of security and, therefore, the provision of finance/credit in their favour. The grant of a security interest is, after all, a bilateral transaction; see above n 198 and the main text thereat.

207 See Companies Act 1985, s 10 and Sched 1.

208 See Companies Act 1985, ss 190, 242 and 363, 288, 352.

209 See Insolvency Act 1986, s 130(1).

210 Those responsible for the trading company are under an obligation to ensure that the company remains solvent if it continues to trade; see Insolvency Act 1986, ss 213, 214.

211 This assumption underlies the decision in *Salomon v Salomon & Co Ltd* [1897] AC 22, especially at p 40 *per* Lord Watson.

the latter position has been used to advance the thesis that the register 'provides virtually no assistance to unsecured creditors' and is almost exclusively the prerogative of the secured creditor.[212] Other justifications for this viewpoint[213] include the propositions that unsecured creditors: rarely check the register; even if they did they would gain little information; any information gained would not affect their decision to advance credit since the nature of unsecured status is the decision not to acquire proprietary rights; reliance on the register is of no use since the debtor can still create security interests at a later date. Such a thesis could be applied by way of analogy to the present public register of charges. If the proposition that unsecured creditors did not use the register was justified then it could be argued that the avoidance power should not operate in their favour since no prejudice would have resulted from the existence of unregistered charges.

There is force to this argument but, it is submitted, if it is applied outside the specific context of Art 9 then it does not offer any legitimate focus for limiting the avoidance power to the interests of secured creditors alone. English company law has always been geared towards providing a reliable source of information for all categories of creditor (existing/potential; secured/unsecured) based upon good practice. Therefore, the fact that many, if not the majority, of unsecured creditors might not utilise a public register is not determinative. The fact that the register would provide a creditor with reliable information concerning the company if that creditor were minded to use it is a more satisfactory rationale for the existence of the avoidance power for unregistered charges. Indeed, this rationale formed the very basis for the foundation of the present company charge register back in 1900.[214]

The avoidance rule for unregistered charges ensures that creditors of all varieties can rely upon the state of the register at any given time. Registration is an ongoing process which contemplates a fluctuating state of affairs as new entries appear and old entries become stale.[215] Although an unsecured creditor, who assumes this status after inspecting the register, is not entitled to preserve the status quo at the time of achieving his status,[216] by making regular inspections of the register the unsecured creditor can police the company. For example, should an entry later appear on the register the unsecured creditor can adjust his relationship with the company accordingly.[217] Also, a registered security interest might cause the unsecured creditor to renegotiate his interest rates or terms of supply or, indeed, he might even terminate his relationship with the company. If the unsecured relationship includes negative pledge type covenants, the register would be the prime method of ensuring that the covenants were complied with. Although an unsecured creditor may not actively seek a proprietary right against the company, the

---

212 See Baird, above n 204, at p 55 onwards.

213 See Baird, above n 204, at p 55 onwards.

214 See above at pp 335–36.

215 There is no provision in the Companies Act to remove spent charges (however, there is a power to register a memorandum of satisfaction when the debt is paid or property released from the charge in whole or in part; see s 403). A search against a company will therefore reveal the entire history of its secured relationships insofar as they involved the creation of registrable charges. A search of the company's internal register of charges pursuant to s 408(2) should, however, reveal the entire charge history of the company since it applies to all charges affecting the company's property. The latter register is discussed below at section 6.

216 Ie, he cannot prevent the debtor from creating security interests subsequently in priority.

217 See Re Abrahams & Sons [1902] 1 Ch 695 at p 200 per Buckley J.

register does provide him with important information about the existence of creditors who do possess such rights. The general credit assessment of the company would involve receipt of such information and therefore a wider reliance interest is promoted.[218] Linked to this point is the fact that unsecured creditors are potential proprietary claimants against the company in two situations. First, should the company neglect to pay the debt or meet judgment then the creditors' remedy will be to levy execution against company assets. In this situation it is vital that the creditor knows exactly what assets, that is unencumbered assets, he can deal with, otherwise he would be liable to those holding a security interest over the relevant 'asset'.[219] Secondly, should the company become insolvent then its assets would have to be realised to meet the claims of creditors. At this time it is the true net worth of the company that is vital for it is only unencumbered assets that can be realised for the benefit of general creditors. The register enables the true net worth of the company to be assessed both at the time of insolvency and, more importantly, at the date the creditor assumed that status. The avoidance power protects that reliance interest and ensures that the creditor need have no fear of the holder of an unregistered charge materialising to enforce his proprietary interest in priority to the unsecured creditor.

So much for the theoretical legitimacy of avoidance against creditors. On a more practical level the use of the word 'creditors' in the context of avoidance has been unfortunate.[220] It has prompted debate concerning the context in which the avoidance power can be invoked. The mere fact that there coexist both an unregistered chargeholder and a creditor of the company does not mean that the unregistered charge is thereby avoided. If that creditor is an unsecured creditor then he will have to have some form of proprietary right against the subject matter of the unregistered charge in order to be granted *standi* by the courts to invoke the avoidance power of s 395(1).[221] It is only upon the insolvency of the company that the unsecured creditors can object to the enforcement of an unregistered charge since at that time enforcement would take away a company asset that could be used to pay off, *pari passu*, the claims of general creditors. Until the company becomes insolvent there is no competition between the unregistered chargeholder and the creditor relating to the charged assets. Prior to insolvency an unsecured creditor will only be able to invoke the avoidance power if he reduces his debt claim to judgment and levies execution against the subject matter of the charge.[222]

With regard to secured creditors, the application of the avoidance power is straightforward when a competition arises with the unregistered chargee in a situation where the secured creditor holds either a registered charge[223] or a charge which does not require registration.[224] In both situations the secured creditor defeats the unregistered

---

218 That is a wider interest than Baird's thesis of purely proprietary security interest acquisition reliance; above n 204.

219 See: *National Provincial & Union Bank of England v Charnley* [1924] 1 KB 43; *Re Ferrier* [1944] Ch 295; *Marples v Hartley* (1861) 3 El & El 610. Cf *Observer Ltd v Gordon* [1983] 1 WLR 1008; *Cave v Capel* [1954] 1 QB 367.

220 See s 395(1).

221 See: *Re Ashpurton Estates Ltd* [1983] Ch 110 at p 119A–B *per* Lord Brightman; *Re Ehrmann Bros Ltd* [1906] 2 Ch 697 at p 708 *per* Romer LJ.

222 *Re Ashpurton Estates Ltd* [1983] Ch 110 at p 123E *per* Lord Brightman.

223 See *Re Monolithic Building Co* [1915] 1 Ch 643.

224 See *Re Abrahams & Sons* [1902] 1 Ch 695.

chargee whose interest is avoided under s 395(1). This result promotes the integrity of the register and applies even if the secured creditor took his interest with notice of the unregistered charge.[225] The courts have sought to uphold the integrity of the registration process so that the public register of charges is the sole source of information.[226] Equitable doctrines will not be applied so as to undermine the effectiveness of the statutory avoidance power.[227]

Things become more complicated when dealing with a conflict between two secured creditors who both hold unregistered charges. This is reflected in the academic literature and at least three viewpoints have emerged as to the priority solution in this situation. Professor Goode tells us that the second unregistered chargee will prevail in this situation because '[r]egistration serves no purpose in relation to prior parties, for their interests have already been acquired.'[228] A different view is taken by Gough,[229] who suggests[230] that the conflict would be resolved according to the general law rules of priority. Under this approach the holder of a first unregistered charge would prevail in the majority of situations unless the second chargee held a legal charge and could invoke the purchaser for value without notice rule.[231] A third view is advanced by Professor Pennington,[232] who states that neither interest has priority since they are both void against each other pursuant to s 395(1). However, this impasse will be broken by the creditor who is the first to gain a court order allowing registration out of time[233] for his charge, thereby gaining retroactive perfection of the charge, meaning that s 395(1) can no longer be invoked by the other creditor.[234]

It should be noted that the problem of priority conflict between the holders of unregistered charges is not a common one and has not featured in case law despite the fact that it has remained a possibility for the past 100 years. The real problem with this seemingly theoretical conflict is that we cannot provide a satisfactory answer by looking at s 395(1). Reform is now needed and the categories of 'creditor' who should benefit

---

225 *Re Monolithic Building Co* [1915] 1 Ch 643.

226 See *Re Monolithic Building Co* [1915] 1 Ch 643.

227 See *Midland Bank Trust Co Ltd v Green* [1981] AC 513.

228 See RM Goode *Commercial Law* (London, Penguin, 2nd edn, 1995) at p 721.

229 See *Company Charges*, above n 57, at p 744(2).

230 A note of caution needs to be added to the equation due to the decision of the Court of Appeal in *Re Monolithic Building Co* [1915] 1 Ch 643. In that case Lord Cozens-Hardy MR, at p 662, interpreted 'creditor' in the context of what is now s 395(1) as meaning 'exactly what it says, that is to say [an unregistered charge] is void against *any creditor who has a registered charge* on the company's property' (emphasis added). If this interpretation is given general effect then it lends substance to Gough's priority solution. Unfortunately, s 395(1) is not so circumscribed and it can be argued (as Gough acknowledges) that avoidance also applies to other types of secured creditor (ie, the holder of an unregistered charge), meaning that both charges are void against each other in the case posed in the main text above. This viewpoint is taken by Professor Pennington, see below at nn 232 and 233 and the main text thereat.

231 See *Pilcher v Rawlings* (1872) 7 Ch App 259.

232 See RR Pennington *Pennington's Company Law* (London, Butterworths, 8th edn, 2001) at p 625(c).

233 See Companies Act 1985, s 404.

234 Pennington notes an exception to this, above n 232, in the case where the second charge was created within 21 days of the first charge such that the second chargee cannot utilise s 404 to achieve priority following the case of *Watson v Duff Morgan & Vermont Holdings Ltd* [1974] 1 WLR 450. This so called exception is, however, out of date and is no longer applicable; see *Palmer's Company Law*, above n 57, at paras 13.334–13.335.

from avoidance needs to be spelt out by the Act. It is submitted that a reformed avoidance power should operate in favour of: the liquidator; administrator; the holder of a registered charge; the holder of an unregistrable charge; an execution creditor or holder of similar process; and unsecured creditors in the event of the company going insolvent. A further reform is needed in that at present avoidance does not operate to protect the interest of a purchaser of the encumbered property.[235] The latter category should also gain the protection of the avoidance power. Unfortunately, this area was not addressed by the Steering Group in *The Final Report*.[236]

6 THE COMPANY'S INTERNAL REGISTER OF CHARGES

Part 12 of the Act establishes not one but two registers for company charges. A second register is also required to be kept by the chargor company.[237] The latter register is immediately distinguishable from the public register of charges maintained by the Registrar of companies in two respects. First, unregistered charges are not liable to avoidance and remain fully enforceable against the company and third parties.[238] Secondly, the internal register is not limited by any *numerus clausus* of the type found under s 396(1). Therefore, as long as any charge[239] exists over the company's property, it will require entry on the company's internal register of charges. Failure to maintain this register renders any company officer responsible liable to a fine.[240] The register is open to public inspection.[241]

It is immediately clear that the internal register is of considerably greater ambit than that maintained by the Registrar of companies. Thus, for example, charges arising by operation of law will require registration.[242] Other significant examples of charges caught by the s 407 register include charges on: shares;[243] insurance policies;[244] annuities; and even an equitable lien on sub-freights.[245] It can be doubted whether the extended remit of s 407 serves any great public policy function and can rather be termed a historical relic of

---

235 See *Stroud Architectural Systems Ltd v John Laing Construction Ltd* [1994] BCC 18 at p 24A. Cf Companies Act 1989, s 95 which, if brought into force, would introduce a new s 399(1)(b) rendering unregistered charges void against a person who acquires an interest for value in the encumbered property.

236 On which see generally below at section 11.

237 See s 407(1). By virtue of s 407(2) the register maintained by the company is required to provide the following details in relation to each charge: a short description of the property charged; the amount secured by the charge; and the names of the persons entitled to the charge (except in the case of securities issued to bearer).

238 See *Wright v Horton* (1887) 12 App Cas 371 at pp 376–77 *per* Lord Halsbury LC.

239 For these purposes charge includes mortgage, see s 396(4).

240 See s 407(3).

241 See s 408(2).

242 See also above at p 337.

243 See, for example, Table A Art 8 which provides: 'The company shall have a first and paramount lien on every share (not being a fully paid share) for all moneys (whether presently payable or not) payable at a fixed time or called in respect of that share ...' By virtue of Art 9 the company is given the power to sell any share subject to this lien. Although Table A uses the word 'lien', the security in fact operates as an equitable charge; *Re General Exchange Bank* (1871) 6 Ch App 818; see also Companies Act 1985, s 150 (prohibitions on charges over shares by public companies). See also above at pp 338–40.

244 See further above at pp 340–42.

245 See further above at pp 343–44.

its forbear in the shape of s 43 of the Companies Act 1862.[246] Failure to appreciate the full scope of s 407 could have dire consequences for those company officers who fail to comply with its terms since they commit a criminal offence.[247] Indeed, cases such as *Re Welsh Irish Ferries Ltd*[248] illustrate the potential for a 'double whammy' effect relating to the criminal penalties for non-compliance with the Part 12 registration requirements. Although the latter case provides an example of the inherent unpredictability of the public register of charges already referred to,[249] it also demonstrates the impracticalities of registering certain types of charge, particularly in respect of certain proprietary rights which are frequently changing and of relatively short-term duration.[250] This has been the main justification for keeping s 396, which limits the categories of registrable charge, as it is today and has been a policy underlying successive Companies Acts since 1900.[251] It is submitted that such a policy rationale should also be applicable to the s 407 register.

As presently constituted, the internal register of charges established by s 407 presents major compliance problems to companies. The most obvious problem of compliance is actually determining whether a charge exists in the first place, as the case of *Re Welsh Irish Ferries Ltd*[252] so graphically illustrated. This is compounded by the fact that compliance with s 395 is obviously the more important registration requirement, since failure results in invalidation of the charge and not just a financial penalty against the officers of the company. Invariably it is the chargee who effects registration so that s 395 will not be breached, since he is obviously the main party to suffer from any breach due to the effects of the avoidance power. However, there is the danger that the categories of charge laid down by s 396(1) become equated with those registrable under s 407 despite its expanded wording such that the s 407 register is made to duplicate the categories established by s 396(1). History has demonstrated that s 407 in its various guises was a 'dead letter'[253] and compliance was more observed as the exception than the rule.[254] Indeed there is no reason to suppose that things have radically altered in this respect since it is clear that the public register established in 1900 has become and was intended to be the most important

---

246 See above n 21 and the main text thereat.

247 See s 407(3).

248 [1986] Ch 471.

249 See above at pp 343–44.

250 Eg, over shares, see above n 48 and the main text thereat.

251 See above n 18 and the main text thereat; see also *London & Cheshire Insurance Co Ltd v Laplagrene Property Co Ltd* [1971] 1 Ch 499 at p 514D–E *per* Brightman J, who speaks of the 'profound inconvenience' that would be caused if an unpaid vendor's lien were registrable under the Act; discussed above at p 337.

252 [1986] Ch 471.

253 *Per* Sir Albert Rollit, commenting on Companies Act 1862, s 43; *Hansard* (1900) HC vol 87 at 111. Lord Williams was to point out at the committee stage, of what was to become the Companies Act 1989, that the 'fact is that company registers are not kept up to date and everybody who has been in the real world and dealt with the matter will know this' (*Hansard* (1989) HL vol 504 at 163). Indeed the *Report of the Departmental Committee to Inquire what Amendments are Necessary in the Acts Relating to Joint Stock Companies Incorporated with Limited Liability*; commonly known as *The Davey Report* (1895) c 7779 (London, HMSO, 1896) at para 47 was to state that 'many companies, even amongst the largest and best-managed, keep no register at all'. More recently it was stated that 'compliance with this requirement is poor'; see *The Final Report*, above n 1, at para 12.68. The *New Zealand Macarther Report: Final Report of the Special Committee to Review the Companies Act* (Wellington, Government Printer, March 1973) at para 185, was to remark that the obligation on each company to maintain a charge register was 'an unnecessary burden'.

254 See above at pp 335–36.

reference point for those desiring information. However, it always has been a criminal offence not to comply with what is now s 407 despite the fact that the financial penalty never appears to have been imposed.[255]

A more significant criticism of s 407 is that, in theory, it establishes a register of company charge security interests operated by a private, partisan body, that is of wider scope than that maintained by the State under the management of the registrar of companies, a public official. The history of company charge registration has demonstrated the need for independent public disclosure with the sanction of invalidation as the main weapon for compliance. Although, the present s 407 register is open to inspection by any member of the public[256] the fact that it is maintained and operated by the chargor company itself must remain a significant impediment to the general policy of disclosure. Even if one were to ignore the inherent conflicts in the role assigned to the chargor company, any register established pursuant to s 407 would prove of scant use to creditors (actual, or aspiring) of the company for the following reasons:

(a) There is no invalidation of unregistered charges which is the 'potent' method of ensuring compliance.[257]

(b) There is no prescribed time period for entering details of existing charges on to the register.

(c) Generally creditors do not use the internal company register, preferring the public register maintained by the registrar of companies.

(d) Generally, companies do not maintain their own register in the first place.

(e) The scope of s 407 security charge interests remains unclear and is wider than s 396.

(f) Section 407 is rarely, if ever, enforced and therefore there is no incentive for the company (or, indeed, the chargee)[258] to comply with its terms.

(g) There are no safeguards as to the accuracy of the s 407 register.[259]

(h) In many cases companies may desire to keep secret the state of encumbrances against their property,[260] and the tacit policy of non-enforcement of s 407 aids that process.

Despite this critique it is possible that the s 407 register may have some benefits (although extreme caution would have to be maintained by any user).[261] As a matter of practical convenience it may prove of some use to the potential searcher who, perhaps, was at the companies' registered office pursuant to a transaction in which his status as a (potential)

---

255 *The Diamond Report*, above n 7, at para 24.1.1, was to state: 'Prosecutions are so rare that the threat can be ignored'; echoing the earlier findings of *The Loreburn Report*, above n 157, at para 35.

256 See s 408(2).

257 See *The Diamond Report*, above n 7, at para 24.1.2.

258 Cf the possible application of the constructive notice doctrine to the internal register; see below at section 9.

259 Cf an amendment proposed at the committee stage of what is now the Companies Act 1989 by Lord Williams, which would have rendered the companies' register open to inspection by auditors to ensure that it was up to date and adequately maintained; *Hansard* (1989) HL vol 504 at 162, however, this amendment was rejected because it was thought to serve 'little purpose'; *Hansard* (1989) HL vol 504 at 162 *per* Lord Strathclyde; cf below n 267.

260 See, for example: *English & Scottish Mercantile Investment v Brunton* [1892] 2 QB 700; *Re Jackson & Bassford Ltd* [1906] 2 Ch 467; *Re Ashpurton Estates Ltd* [1983] Ch 110 at p 121D–E.

261 Ie, a countercheck made of the public register established by s 401.

creditor might be affected. This is linked to the fact that companies are also required to keep copies of every instrument creating a charge requiring registration under either of the registers established by Part 12 at their registered office.[262] Therefore, a person desiring further information relating to a specific charge identified on the public register would be forced to visit the companies' registered office. However, at present only an existing creditor or member of the company has a right to inspect charge instruments as opposed to the internal register of charges.[263] Whilst this may not prove an insurmountable obstacle to the determined inquirer[264] it is submitted that these documents should now be made available to the general public.[265]

By way of conclusion to this issue it is appropriate to note the comments of *The Diamond Report*:

> In the nature of things it is highly desirable that companies should keep registers of charges and copy documents, and I recommend no change to these statutory provisions.[266]

Although some may find it possible to share the desires of Professor Diamond that companies should maintain their own registers of charges and copy documents, if only as a convenient aid to disclosure (however inherently unreliable such a system is at present), it is surely disturbing that, in theory at any rate, s 407 promotes a wider policy of disclosure than the main public register. It may be possible to dismiss this as a mere quirk of history and of no practical significance, since no general importance is attached[267] to the s 407 register, but such remarks do little to improve the public confidence and aid the promotion of sound policy objectives behind the system of company charge registration. It would be far simpler to abolish the internal register and promote the external register, maintained by the registrar of companies as the sole source of public information.[268] Happily, the Company Law Review Steering Group have recently recommended that the

---

262 See s 406.

263 See s 408(1).

264 If the company was a listed plc, a single share could be purchased to qualify for inspection. If the inquirer was a potential creditor then it would be in the company's interest to volunteer access to charge instruments.

265 Cf Companies Act 1989, s 101 which (if brought into force) would introduce a new s 412 providing for such a right.

266 Above n 7, at para 28.3.5.

267 *The Diamond Report*, above n 7, at para 28.3.4, noted that 'auditors sometimes have recourse to the register and to copy charges in the course of their duties'. Lord Strathclyde was to remark at the committee stage of what is now the Companies Act 1989: 'I am aware that, as part of their audit, some auditors regard it as best practice to inspect the register of charges'; *Hansard* (1989) HL vol 504 at 162. The Irish Republic removed the duty upon the individual company to maintain a register of charges when their company law was consolidated under the Companies Act 1963 (as amended). This change has been described as an 'important omission'; Keane, *Company Law* (Dublin, Butterworths, 3rd edn, 2000) at p 243; however, in the light of the points raised here it is difficult to endorse this comment since Irish law was a derivative of the earlier English company legislation and subject to the same deficiencies. If anything the Irish approach is more consistent with the policy of independent, centralised disclosure. Indeed *The Macarther Report*, above n 253, at para 125 recommended that New Zealand abolish a similar requirement since 'no great harm' would be done by such a measure.

268 Indeed, the DTI has stated that it is 'seriously considering' the abolition of this register on deregulation grounds; see DTI letter (November 1995) issued in respect of the public responses to consultation document URN 94/635, above n 8. However, no action has been taken on this matter.

internal register of charges be abolished, although members and creditors of the chargor company would still have the right to inspect copies of instruments creating charges.[269]

7 THE INFILTRATION OF CONSTRUCTIVE NOTICE INTO PART 12

One of the most noticeable features of the public register of charges, from the chargee's point of view, is that its effects are purely negative. We are told that if a prescribed category of charge is not registered within 21 days then it is liable to be avoided.[270] However, we are not told about the actual status of a registered charge other than being left to infer that it is an interest which is no longer liable to avoidance. This issue is of considerable importance because the essence of any security interest is the ability to enforce that interest against a debtor in priority to other creditors. It is remarkable that Part 12 has nothing to say on the issue of priorities. Part 12 is concerned with establishing registers of public information for those minded to utilise them; it is not concerned with the priority of those interests it seeks to disclose.[271]

From a modern standpoint this is a remarkable omission and serves to demonstrate the one-dimensional perspective of the legislature in 1900 which was concerned only with establishing a public register of information relating to charges. Disclosure was the sole philosophy underlying the establishment of the charges register. Effective registration statutes should be about producing a balanced trade-off between the financial community's desire for information about the company (that is, relating to security interests) and the chargees' desire for effective priority. Both these interests can only be achieved via a statutory priority rule based upon the date of registration.[272] Unfortunately, the legislature has so far declined to accept this principle.[273] This leaves us then with a potential problem. What is the status of a registered charge when a priority competition arises with a third-party interest over the charged asset?

---

269 See *The Final Report*, above n 1, at paras 12.68–12.69. However, they did not go so far as to recommend that these documents be made open to public inspection as the Companies Act 1989 would have done; see above at n 265.

270 See s 395(1).

271 Subject only to the fact that unregistered interests are liable to avoidance pursuant to s 395(1) and, indirectly thereby, a loss of priority against prescribed third-party interests.

272 See, for example: Bills of Sale Act 1878, s 10; Land Registration Act 1925, s 29; Law of Property Act 1925, s 97; Merchant Shipping (Registration) Act 1993, s 6 and Sched 1 para 8(1); The Mortgaging of Aircraft Order 1972 (SI 1972/1268) para 14(2); all to the effect that the date of registration is the priority point for competing security interests. Cf Companies Act 1985, s 464 (which regulates the priority of floating charges in Scotland).

273 It should be noted that it was at one time envisaged that the Companies Act should have a priority rule based upon the date of registration; see Companies Bill 1896 (HL) Bill No 23, Clause 20(11). However, this provision was eventually dropped on the basis that it would contradict the policy of having a period of grace in which to effect registration such that a second chargee might intervene and register his interest in priority over the first chargee; see the evidence of HB Buckley QC before the House of Lords' Select Committee on the Companies Bill (1898) Reports Committees Vol IX at para 1642. Cf *The Diamond Report*, above n 7, at para 26.2: 'The most important of my recommendations [in respect of the reform of Part 12] ... is to fix priorities as between charges by reference to the date of registration.' However, the Steering Group have recently proposed that company charge priorities should now be determined according to the date of registration; see *The Final Report*, above n 1, at para 12.19(b).

Part 12 of the Act does not provide an answer to this question and, without more, one might have expected the answer to be found by applying the common law to resolve the problem. That is to say, the act of registration has no bearing on the issue of priority; it is merely a preliminary measure in order that the chargee has an interest capable of assertion against the third party in the first place. This means that the normal general law rules of priority then apply. Although this argument is commendable in its simplicity, the position has become complicated by the addition of the constructive notice doctrine into the equation so as to engraft onto Part 12 a priority mechanism.

Conventional wisdom now tells us that the act of registration pursuant to s 395 operates so as to impose upon secondary chargees constructive notice of the prior registered charge.[274] This mechanism therefore operates so as to deny the holder of a subsequent legal interest priority over a prior (registered) equitable interest. Although it now appears to be accepted that registration does operate in tandem with constructive notice, an analysis of the judicial antecedents of this principle reveals a paucity of sound judgment in support of this. The main case which is used to support the doctrine of constructive notice is *Wilson v Kelland*.[275] This case involved a priority conflict between the holder of a first registered floating charge covering the entire property of the company (the charge containing a restrictive clause preventing the chargor from granting other security interests without the permission of the chargee) and a second chargee holding a mortgage over a property sold by them to the company, the mortgage being given to secure the outstanding purchase price. The later mortgage did not require registration at this time.[276] The court held that the interest of the mortgagee must prevail in this conflict since the company only acquired the property subject to the obligation to create a first-ranking mortgage security interest over it. In other words the company could not have acquired the property without giving priority to the mortgagee who had provided the purchase monies upon credit subject to the condition of obtaining a first security.[277] Because the holder of the prior floating charge was asserting an interest through the company, it followed that his security was subject to the overriding interest of the mortgagee. This was enough to dispose of the case. However, Eve J went on to express an *obiter* opinion that the act of registering the floating charge, under what is now s 395, 'amounted to constructive notice of a charge affecting the property but not of any special provisions contained in that charge restricting the company from dealing with their

274 See: *Gore-Browne On Companies* (Bristol, Jordans, 44th edn, 1986 as updated) Vol 1 at para 18.13 n 6 and the main text thereat; *Palmer's Company Law*, above n 57, at paras 13.325 and 13.326 point 2; Gough, above n 57, at pp 809–10; Goode, above n 228, at p 717 n 114 and the main text thereat; McCormack *Registration of Company Charges* (London, Sweet & Maxwell, 1994) at p 133 point 5.

275 [1910] 2 Ch 306.

276 Being granted in 1905; see above n 32.

277 This type of arrangement would now be referred to as a purchase money security interest and received the approval of the House of Lords in *Abbey National BS v Cann* [1991] 1 AC 56; see further: de Lacy 'The Purchase Money Security Interest: A Company Charge Conundrum?' [1991] *Lloyd's Maritime and Commercial Law Quarterly* 531; and de Lacy 'Retention of Title Company Charges and the Scintilla Temporis Doctrine' [1994] *The Conveyancer* 242.

property in the usual manner when the subsisting charge is a floating security.'[278] On the facts of the case, the mortgagee had no actual notice of the prior floating charge and it followed that they had no notice of the restrictive clause such that the application of the constructive notice doctrine would not have prejudiced them in any event.[279] It will be immediately noticed that the 'decision' in *Wilson v Kelland*, in so far as it concerned the effects of registration as giving constructive notice of the existence of a charge, was purely *obiter*. Although Eve J purported to follow the earlier case of *Re Standard Rotary Machine Co*,[280] (another case sometimes cited as an authority on this issue) when expressing this opinion, that case did not decide that the act of registration gives constructive notice of the existence of the charge. In the case of *Re Standard Rotary Machine* Kekewich J had assumed, for the sake of argument, that the holder of a second fixed charge had notice of an earlier registered floating charge but, following earlier cases,[281] found that notice of the floating charge was not notice of any restriction contained therein and the later chargee was under no obligation to make inquiries concerning the ambit and nature of the prior floating charge. It followed that the later fixed charge took priority.

The second main case which is used to support the constructive notice principle is that of *Earle v Hemsworth RDC*.[282] This case concerned an action brought by a mortgagee, holding security by virtue of an assignment of a chose in action over a money retention fund, against the fundholder[283] who had wrongfully paid the fund to the assignor beneficiaries' receiver appointed by the holders of a prior floating charge over the beneficiaries' assets. The fundholder alleged that the floating charge had priority, being a

---

278 [1910] 2 Ch 306 at p 313. The classic theory of the floating charge tells us that the chargor remains free to deal with the charged assets in the ordinary course of his business. This freedom will include the ability to create subsequent security interests which have priority over the existing floating charge; *Wheatley v Silkstone & Haigh Moor Coal Co* (1885) 29 Ch D 715. However, the position has now changed and most floating charges will contain restrictive clauses forbidding the chargor from granting security in priority to the floating charge. The latter development has not been enough, however, to alter the accepted theoretical basis of the floating charge which contains no such limitation, and therefore a third party is under no duty to inquire as to the precise terms of a floating charge and can presume that no restrictions are present; see *Welch Ltd v Bowmaker Ltd* [1980] IR 251 at p 256 *per* Kenny J. This position would change when the floating charge crystallised via the appointment of a receiver and the registrar was notified of this appointment pursuant to s 405(1). The latter event should also attract the application of constructive notice if registration of the primary security does; see Gough, above n 57, at p 846. If the recommendations of the Steering Group are implemented then it will be possible to register restrictive clauses such that the doctrine of constructive notice will apply to them; see below at nn 378 and 379 and the main text thereat.

279 It being established law that a fixed charge defeats an earlier floating charge so long as the fixed chargee has no notice of any special restriction contained in the floating charge even though he has notice of the existence of the floating charge itself; *English & Scottish Mercantile Investment Co Ltd v Brunton* [1892] 2 QB 700; *Re Valletort Sanitary Steam Laundry Co Ltd* [1903] 2 Ch 654. Since a restrictive clause is not a prescribed particular for the purposes of the public register of charges (on which see s 401(1)) then constructive notice could not apply since it is not information that a potential searcher of the register could expect to find; see *Re Standard Rotary Machine Co Ltd* (1906) 95 LT 829 at p 834 *per* Kekewich J. The position is otherwise in Scotland; see s 417(3)(e). Cf Companies Act 1989, s 103, which, if brought into force, would introduce a new s 415(2)(a) allowing restrictive clauses to become prescribed particulars for the purposes of the legislation. See below at nn 378 and 379 and the main text thereat for the views of the Steering Group on this question.

280 (1906) 95 LT 829.

281 Above n 278.

282 (1928) 44 TLR 605.

283 The fundholder had been given notice of this assignment, which complied with Law of Property Act 1925, s 136.

prior created interest which contained a restrictive clause preventing the creation of subsequent interests in priority and, therefore, was not liable. At first instance the fundholder was found liable by Wright J on the basis that although the assignee must be taken to have constructive notice of the floating charge, he did not have actual notice of the restriction contained therein and it followed that the assignment by way of mortgage must have priority.[284] In reaching this conclusion Wright J was doing no more than follow *Wilson v Kelland*.[285] Although the outcome of this decision is plainly correct,[286] it must be stated that the finding that registration amounted to constructive notice of the floating charge was once again purely *obiter* and unnecessary to the actual decision in the case. In this respect it is useful to note that the decision was appealed on a technical ground relating to the nature of a legal assignment, Scrutton LJ there remarking that the appeal did not concern the 'extremely interesting and intricate question of equitable priorities'.[287]

Apart from these cases there is no substantive English authority for the proposition that registration pursuant to s 395 gives constructive notice of the charge. On the contrary, where the issue has subsequently arisen the courts have been rather circumspect in their treatment of the matter.[288] For example, in the case of *Channel Airways Ltd v Manchester Corp*[289] Forbes J was to state:

> I do not find that the mere registration of a debenture [pursuant to what is now section 395] amounts to notice to all the world, still less that it of itself prefers the debenture holder to any subsequent encumbrancer.[290]

In the case of *Siebe Gorman & Co Ltd v Barclays Bank Ltd*,[291] the case of *Wilson v Kelland* was cited as authority for the constructive notice principle but Slade J was cautious in accepting the authority, stating that registration '*may* by itself serve to give subsequent mortgagees constructive notice ...'.[292]

Whilst the academic texts now universally accept the doctrine of constructive notice,[293] this was not always the case. For example, *Gore-Browne* was once cautious about the doctrine, telling us '[i]t is not yet fully decided whether registration is notice to all the world of the existence of the debentures or charge'.[294] *Palmer's Company Law*, on the other

---

284 (1928) 44 TLR 605 at p 608.

285 [1910] 2 Ch 306.

286 Ie, in line with the authorities cited above at n 279 and with *Wilson v Kelland* in so far as it applied the latter authorities.

287 (1928) 44 TLR 758 at p 760.

288 Reference should be made to the case of *Abbey National BS v Cann* [1991] AC 56 at pp 91B–C and 92C–D *per* Lord Oliver, where there are *dicta* which might appear to suggest that there is constructive notice of a registered charge. However, this *dicta* is unclear and given in the context of an unrelated dispute and therefore fails to address the substantive issue. It is submitted that this case can be safely ignored as an authority on the matter; cf Gough, above n 57, at p 811.

289 [1974] 1 Lloyd's Rep 456.

290 [1974] 1 Lloyd's Rep 456 at p 459 (emphasis added).

291 [1979] 2 Lloyd's Rep 142.

292 [1979] 2 Lloyd's Rep 142 at p 160 (emphasis added).

293 Above n 274.

294 *Handbook on the Formation, Management & Winding Up of Joint Stock Companies* (London, Jordan and Sons, 41st edn, 1952) at p 328 (emphasis added).

hand, took until the 1960 edition[295] to tell us that it would 'appear' that registered charges are public documents such that the doctrine of constructive notice should apply in the same manner as it did to the corporate constitutional documents.[296] It is remarkable that there is no case authority intervening between these statements and those given in the latest editions and yet the latest editions no longer contain any cautionary language. Constructive notice has crystallised into a principle of law in the eyes of the textbook writers.

The weakness of the two main authorities which allegedly support the constructive notice doctrine becomes even more apparent when it is realised that not only are the statements *obiter* but also that they are unreasoned. In neither case does the judge attempt to justify or support the assertion that constructive notice applies to registered charges. Even in the pre-*Pepper v Hart*[297] world, there is no evidence that Parliament intended such a doctrine to apply to the charges register when introducing it in 1900. Gough has speculated that the doctrine emerged as an adjunct to the established constructive notice principle regarding the corporate constitutional documents which addressed the issue of the capacity of the company to contract.[298] The analogy is a touch ironic given the legislature's relatively recent intervention to abolish such limitations on corporate capacity.[299] However, it is submitted that the real element of 'speculation'[300] comes, not from the origins of constructive notice, but in accepting the principle itself when applied to the charges register. It is remarkable that three relatively obscure cases have been propelled to the fore in support of a doctrine that has in related areas been rejected out of hand.[301]

8 THE AMBIT OF CONSTRUCTIVE NOTICE

If we accept, for one moment, that the doctrine of constructive notice does apply to registered charges, it is instructive to pursue the implications of the doctrine. Looking at the three cases which are used to support the doctrine, we would deduce that the act of registration gives constructive notice to the world of the existence of the charge and of the

---

295 See 20th edn, 1960 (London, Sweet & Maxwell) at p 243 n 6 and the main text thereat.

296 On the latter see *Mahony v East Holyford Mining Co* (1875) LR 7 HL 869 at p 893 *per* Lord Hatherly.

297 [1993] AC 591.

298 Above n 57 at pp 820–34.

299 See Companies Act 1985, ss 35, 35A and 35B. Note also the proposed s 711A (introduced by Companies Act 1989, s 142(1)) which, if brought into force, would abolish the doctrine of notice insofar as it affects public documents registered by the Registrar of companies with the exception of the charges register; see s 711A(4)(a).

300 See Gough, above n 57, at p 823.

301 Note in particular *Re Monolithic Building Society* [1915] 1 Ch 643; and see also: *Midland Bank Trust v Green* [1981] AC 513; *Edwards v Edwards* (1876) 2 ChD 291. On a more general level the courts have shown hostility to the doctrine of constructive notice when applied to commercial transactions, see: *Manchester Trust v Furness* [1895] 2 QB 539 at p 545 *per* Lindley LJ; *Greer v Downs Supply Co* [1927] 2 KB 28 at p 36 *per* Scrutton LJ; *Feuer Leather Corp v Johnstone* [1981] Com LR 251 at p 252 *per* Neill J.

particulars required for registration, but no more.[302] A third party is not to be affected by details which do not appear, or are not required to appear, on the register. The effects of this would be to protect the holder of a registered charge (legal or equitable) against all subsequent third parties who sought to acquire an interest in the encumbered assets in priority.[303] The justification for such a priority would, presumably, be the theory that the third party could (if they had made a search of the register) have discovered the existence of the prior charge.[304]

As a matter of practice it is here that the conventional textbook writers begin to differ. *Gore-Browne on Companies* tells us that registration gives 'constructive notice to all those affected'.[305] Unfortunately, the text then fails to elaborate on exactly who are 'all those affected' such that the reader is none the wiser as to the ambit of constructive notice. *Palmer's Company Law* tells us that a registered charge will bind a subsequent purchaser who will be taken to have constructive notice of it.[306] Gough goes further and presents the thesis that a registered charge gives notice to the entire world[307] such that, in the absence of consent or reprehensible conduct on the part of the registered chargee, no subsequent third-party interest can ever achieve priority.[308] Professor Goode, on the other hand, is more cautious in his approach to the matter. Whilst Goode accepts the general principle of constructive notice, he limits the doctrine with the words:

> ... registration [pursuant to section 395] fixes a [third] party with notice ... if and only if the dealing between him and the debtor [ie, chargor company] with respect to the asset is of such a kind that it would be reasonable to expect the [third] party in question to search [the public register of charges].[309]

According to this approach the 'court must be free to adopt a flexible approach, and consider the circumstances of the particular facts before it'[310] when considering whether a third party should be affected by constructive notice of a prior registered charge. Therefore, on Goode's approach, registration would generally only give constructive notice to subsequent chargees or other forms of security interestholder who could have

---

302 In *Wilson v Kelland* [1910] 2 Ch 306 at p 313 Eve J tells us, *obiter*, that the second chargee had constructive notice of the prior registered floating charge, but in *Earle v Hemsworth RDC* (1928) 44 TLR 605, 608 Wright J tells us, *obiter*, that 'all the world' is deemed to have constructive notice of a registered charge as well as the subsequent chargee. In *Re Standard Rotary Machine Co Ltd* (1906) 95 LT 829 at p 834 Kekewich J tells us, *obiter*, that a searcher of the public register of charges would discover the existence of a registered floating charge but not of any restrictive clause contained therein and so constructive notice could not apply to the latter restriction.

303 Unless the registered charge is a floating charge which will lose out to a subsequent fixed chargeholder or other purchaser unless that person has actual notice of a restrictive clause in the prior floating charge; *Re Standard Rotary Machine Co Ltd* (1906) 95 LT 829 at p 834 *per* Kekewich J.

304 See, by way of analogy, *Ernest v Nichols* (1857) 6 HL Cas 401 at pp 418–20 *per* Lord Wensleydale explaining that those dealing with companies will be taken to have notice of the companies' publicly registered memorandum and articles of association and must be taken to have notice of any restrictions upon the powers of directors contained therein.

305 Above n 274.

306 Above n 57, at para 13.326 point 2.

307 Following the cases cited above at n 302.

308 Above n 57, at pp 834–47.

309 Above n 228, at pp 719–20.

310 Above n 228, at p 719.

been expected to search the register prior to taking their interest over the encumbered assets. A similar view is adopted by Professor McCormack.[311]

We therefore see at least two very different formulations concerning the application of constructive notice to registered charges. Which view then represents English law? There is no answer to this question since there is no case authority. If one took the *obiter* statement of Wright J in the case of *Earle v Hemsworth RDC* seriously, then constructive notice operates against 'all the world'.[312] This would mean that Gough's formulation of the doctrine would be an accurate statement of the law. The latter position was certainly that which the then Government believed to be the position during the passage of the Companies Act 1989[313] which, if brought into force, would introduce a new statutory version of the doctrine of constructive notice such that:

> A person taking a charge over a company's property shall be taken to have notice of any matter requiring registration and disclosed on the register at the time the charge is created.
>
> Otherwise, a person shall not be taken to have notice of any matter by reason of its being disclosed on the register or by reason of his having failed to search the register in the course of making such inquiries as ought reasonably to be made.[314]

It will be noticed immediately that the statutory formulation of the doctrine is in harmony with Goode's suggested version currently pertaining to the unamended Act.

There would certainly appear to be no major obstacles in the way of the courts adopting Goode's formulation of the doctrine. The words of Parke J in the Irish case of *Welch Ltd v Bowmaker Ltd* come readily to mind: 'The doctrine of constructive or implied notice, like that of public policy, may be an unruly horse and it should be ridden with a firm hand.'[315] Indeed, it can be doubted whether constructive notice can apply to the 'whole world'. For example, although Gough has stated that registration of a charge over a chose in action is enough to comply with the rule in *Dearle v Hall*[316] such that the fundholder (that is, debtor) will be taken to have notice of an assignment of the fund by way of charge security,[317] this is not received wisdom. Only actual notice to the fundholder of the assignment will be enough to comply with the rule in *Dearle v Hall*.[318] It would be stretching credibility to think that the cases used to advance the constructive notice theory could alter this. If constructive notice does apply to registered charges then there is no reason to suppose that its contours cannot be shaped by the courts. The fact that the legislature intervened to curb the doctrine in the context of the corporate constitutional documents and their effects on the corporations' capacity should serve as

---

311 Above n 274, at pp 133–34 point 6 and 142–45.

312 (1928) 44 TLR 605 at p 608.

313 Lord Strathclyde stated, on behalf of the Government, that the 'prevailing view' was that a registered charge gave constructive notice to the 'whole world'; (1989) *Hansard* HL vol 505 at 1216.

314 See Companies Act 1989, s 103, introducing a new s 416(1) and (2) to the Companies Act 1985, provisions which have yet to be brought into force.

315 [1980] IR 251 at p 262.

316 (1828) 3 Russ 1. See generally de Lacy 'Reflections on the Ambit of the Rule in *Dearle v Hall* Parts 1 and 2' (1999) 28 *Anglo-American Law Review* 87 and 197.

317 Above n 57, at p 835 point 5.

318 See: *Lloyd v Banks* (1868) LR 3 Ch App 488 at p 490 *per* Lord Cairns LC (expressly rejecting constructive notice for this purpose); *Browne v Savage* (1859) 4 Drewry 635 at p 640 *per* Kindersley VC; *Ipswich Permanent Money Club Ltd v Arthy* [1920] Ch 257 at pp 268–69 *per* Lawrence J.

ample encouragement to a court faced with a problem concerning a registered charge given the lack of the doctrine's development in the latter situation.[319] Certainly, the effects of applying a doctrine of constructive notice to 'all the world' are not edifying. Can we really expect purchasers in the ordinary course of business to search the register prior to dealing? A literal adoption of an obscure *obiter dictum*[320] would lead to much inconvenience and an increase in transaction costs for all those dealing with companies. As a matter of practice such difficulties have not presented themselves before the courts but they do remain a real threat since the 'law' as stated in the texts[321] would lead to problems if it were ever to be applied in practice.

Despite this, it is submitted that the courts should reject the theory of constructive notice underpinning the registration of charges. An analysis of the basis for constructive notice reveals a paucity of theory to support it and, indeed, the application of constructive notice raises even more problems than it solves.[322]

9 CONSTRUCTIVE NOTICE AND THE INTERNAL REGISTER OF CHARGES

Our discussion so far has concerned the possible effects of constructive notice on the public register of charges maintained by the registrar of companies. It is interesting to note that no-one appears to have considered the possibility that constructive notice should also apply to the separate public register of charges maintained by the chargor company itself.[323] Although it has been stated that constructive notice should not apply to the register of charges maintained by the registrar of companies, it is instructive, if only to confirm this statement, to pursue the logic of constructive notice in the context of the companies' internal register of charges.

If we return to the general theory of constructive notice then we would say that persons are obliged to take notice of public documents before they deal with companies and if they do not then they will be taken to have dealt with the company on the basis that they had knowledge of the information that they should have received had they inspected the register of public documents prior to dealing.[324] Therefore, in respect of company charges, persons are taken to have notice of all the information required to be kept on the public register of charges maintained by the registrar of companies.[325] Accepting, for one moment, the general validity of constructive notice when applied to the charges register it is remarkable that the textbook writers[326] appear to have ignored

---

319 In the area of corporate capacity constructive notice was an unyielding doctrine where the concept of reasonableness was never an issue; see: *The Diamond Report*, above n 7, at para 24.4.3 and note *Re Jon Beauforte Ltd* [1953] Ch 151.

320 See *Earle v Hemsworth RDC* (1928) 44 TLR 605 at p 608 *per* Wright J.

321 At least insofar as is represented by *Palmer's Company Law*, above n 306 and Gough, above n 308.

322 On this point, note also the application of constructive notice to the companies internal register of charges, discussed below at section 9.

323 See ss 407 and 408(2).

324 See above n 304 and the main text thereat.

325 On which see ss 396, 401(2) and note the cases cited above at n 302.

326 Above n 274.

the application of the doctrine to the companies internal register of charges.[327] The latter register is equally a public register[328] of charges and should therefore, as a matter of logic, also be subject to the doctrine of constructive notice. Indeed, historically, the internal register of charges predates that maintained by the registrar of companies.[329]

It is submitted that if one accepts that constructive notice applies to the register of charges maintained by the registrar of companies then it must also apply to that maintained by the company. That is to say that constructive notice applies to Part 12 as a whole or not at all. The point is significant because the internal register of charges is much wider in scope and requires all charges to be entered on it.[330] As a matter of practice it appears as if the internal register of charges is often neglected by the company[331] and this perhaps explains why the register has received little analysis or academic commentary. However, if the doctrine of constructive notice was applied to it then it would serve as a powerful incentive to the holders of charges which were not caught by s 396 to ensure that registration was made on the internal register, particularly if constructive notice applied to 'all the world'.[332]

Further, it is not only a public register of charges that is required to be kept by the chargor company. Pursuant to s 406, the company is required to keep a copy of every instrument creating a charge requiring registration under Chapter 1 of Part 12[333] at its registered office.[334] These copies of instruments are open to inspection by any creditor[335] or member of the company so long as they relate to a charge requiring registration with the registrar of companies.[336] The latter restriction is curious, given that companies are required to keep copies of all instruments relating to charges they create irrespective of whether they require registration with the registrar of companies.[337] It follows that certain charge instruments will not be available for inspection to anybody except the relevant officer of the company who ensures compliance with s 406.[338] The latter point is a curious drafting anomaly.[339]

---

327 See s 407.

328 See s 408(2).

329 See generally above at pp 335–36. The internal register of charges was first established by the Companies Act 1862, s 43 but was only open to inspection by the members and creditors of the chargor company. It was only by virtue of the Companies Act 1907, s 17 that the latter register became open to public inspection.

330 See generally above at section 6.

331 See above n 253.

332 Above n 320.

333 Ie, in relation to companies registered in England and Wales.

334 Note that the section applies to all charges created by the company, there is no *numerus clausus* as is found under s 396.

335 For these purposes creditor does not include a prospective creditor; *Wright v Horton* (1887) 12 App Cas 371 at p 376 *per* Lord Halsbury LC.

336 See s 408(1).

337 See s 406(1) which also covers charges requiring registration on the companies' internal register.

338 Eg, an instrument creating a charge on shares or over an insurance policy.

339 It should be noted that the original internal register of charges established by the Companies Act 1862, s 43 did not require the company to maintain copies of the instruments creating the charge such that the modern legislation re-enacting this provision has not removed any pre-existing entitlement to this information. Rather the drafting error appears to have occurred in stating that companies maintain copies of instruments requiring registration under the entire Part 12 Chapter 1 (ie, including the internal register of charges) rather than limiting it to those charges covered by s 396 (ie, the [cont]

The importance of companies being required to keep copies of instruments is the fact that, once we admit the doctrine of constructive notice into Part 12, its application becomes all pervasive. Therefore, we would apply the doctrine to bind all creditors and members of the chargor company in respect of relevant instruments creating charges which were available for inspection at the time they acquired rights over the encumbered property. Because the legislature has deemed these two parties worthy of special information rights then they should also be expected to utilise such rights or proceed at their peril. Therefore, we see a more limited application of the doctrine of constructive notice but the logic remains the same; the creditor or member of the company proposing to deal with encumbered assets is expected to search both the external and internal register of charges and should also be expected to search for copies of instruments in relation thereto[340] because the legislature has deemed that such information should also be available to them.

The significance of applying constructive notice to creditors and members of the company becomes clear when dealing with priority conflicts involving first-registered floating charges with restrictive clauses. We have already seen that constructive notice can only apply (if at all) to give a subsequent fixed chargee notice of the floating charge but not of the restrictive clause such that the fixed chargee will take priority.[341] If, however, that fixed chargee is a creditor (the likely scenario) or member of the chargor company at the time he takes his interest then he will be fixed with constructive notice of the restrictive clause by virtue of s 408(1). Unlike the common law cases holding to the contrary, the chargee comes under a duty to investigate the nature of the floating charge because he is given the ability to discover it via the copy of the charge instrument being made available to him by force of law.[342] At common law no such right exists, nor does it under Part 12 in respect of any party other than a creditor or member of the chargor company. Thus, cases such as *Re Standard Rotary Machine Co Ltd*[343] would be decided differently today if one were prepared to accept constructive notice as a legitimate feature

---

339 [cont] register of charges maintained by the registrar of companies). Cf Companies Act 1989, s 101, which, if brought into force would introduce a new s 412(1) allowing any person to inspect the copies of instruments creating charges of all types requiring registration under Part 12. The Steering Group recommended that only members and creditors of the chargor company should have the right to inspect copies of instruments creating charges since a potential creditor refused access would simply withhold their loan/credit to the company; see *The Final Report*, above n 1, at paras 12.68 and 12.68(b). However, the Steering Group did not consider the possible effects of the constructive notice doctrine applying to the internal register of charges or to the duty to maintain copies of instruments.

340 Subject to their availability; see above n 338 and the main text thereat. An analogy might be drawn here with the rule in *Turquand's Case* (1856) 5 E & B 248 and the fact that it generally only applies to protect outsider rights (that is, the rights of persons who have no access to inside corporate information) such that insiders (who do have access to inside information relating to corporate activities) cannot invoke the rule in their dealings with the company; see *Morris v Kanssen* [1946] AC 459 at pp 475–76 *per* Lord Simonds.

341 Above n 279.

342 Ie, by virtue of s 408(1). Note this inspection right is not available to other persons since s 408(2) only grants a general right to inspect the companies' internal register of charges; it does not extend to the grant of a right to inspect copies of instruments creating a charge.

343 (1906) 95 LT 829.

of the present charges registration system. The point was never taken in that case[344] and Kekewich J refused to go into the issue of notice in any detail.[345] We see then that the application of constructive notice to Part 12 is a much more complicated and extensive exercise than would be believed if we were to accept the main texts at face value.

10 THE FUTURE OF CONSTRUCTIVE NOTICE

The above discussion has raised serious doubts concerning the validity and ambit of the constructive notice doctrine when applied to Part 12. It is submitted that there is no sound legal precedent for allowing constructive notice to operate in this context and if the issue should ever arise for determination then the courts should reject the doctrine as being inapplicable. As a matter of practice the doctrine does not appear to have caused too many problems and its relevance to secured finance/credit appears more theoretical than real. Secured financing in the corporate domain is for professionals and may involve the advance of many millions of pounds in financing corporate ventures. In such an environment, risk management is at a premium resulting in credit assessment and extensive inquiries becoming par for the course. A potential secured party will search the public register of charges as a matter of routine. Depending on the information revealed, extensive follow-up inquiries will generally also result. For example, should a search reveal the existence of a prior floating charge, the potential secured party will then contact the chargee and seek assurances about his potential dealings with the debtor. In this way restrictive clauses will be revealed as a matter of routine resulting in secured creditors negotiating mutually beneficial arrangements with the debtor company. A secured party will not see a registered floating charge and then proceed in a cavalier fashion making an advance secured by a fixed charge safe in the knowledge that floating charge theory will guarantee him priority if no further inquiries are made.

However, although established practice would appear to dictate that there are no substantive problems with the existing regime,[346] it is disappointing to note that this merely serves to mask the substantive theoretical weaknesses behind it. A rejection of the constructive notice doctrine serves to focus attention on the absence of a simple priority rule integral to the system of charge registration established by Part 12. It is high time the statute recognised this and imposed a simple priority rule according to the date of registration for all security interests.[347] In the meantime it would follow that the common

---

344 The Companies Act 1900, s 14(9) did impose a similar requirement on chargor companies to maintain copies of instruments creating charges (such copies being available to creditors and members) and a floating charge did require registration at this time; s 14(1)(d). However, it may well be that the chargor neglected the duty and as such the later chargee creditor could not be affected with constructive notice in any case.

345 (1906) 95 LT 829 at p 834.

346 See also Law Society Memorandum No 311 (London, Law Society, February 1995) 'Proposals for the Reform of Part 12 of the Companies Act 1985' at p 1 para 1.1: 'We have no reason to believe that the retention of the present law would give rise to any unacceptable risks. The present system of registration has worked tolerably well in the past and it is not in urgent need of reform.'

347 This recommendation would be coupled with the removal of the mandatory registration duty placed upon the chargor and the 21 day period of grace presently found in s 395. The Steering Group have recently recommended that the date of registration should become the priority point for registered charges; however, they have also favoured the continuation of the doctrine of constructive notice in this area; see below at section 11.

law alone would resolve priority matters without the aid of the constructive notice doctrine. Part 12 would only apply, as originally intended, so as to invalidate unregistered charges against prescribed parties.[348]

11 THE STEERING GROUP'S REFORM PROPOSALS

It has to be stated that the proposals of the Company Law Review Steering Group, in respect of company charges, are disappointing. Whilst the Steering Group acknowledged that this subject 'is highly technical'[349] and of 'real importance to the capital markets',[350] it was dealt with almost as an afterthought in the Review process. That process started in March 1998[351] and the final results were published in July 2001. However, it was not until October 2000 that company charge reform formally entered into the equation.[352] Even then the task of reform was thought to be a relatively modest endeavour, since the presumption was that more fundamental reforms[353] would not be popular with the general commercial community. Nevertheless, following consultations on the October 2000[354] document which had revealed 'convincing arguments in favour of more radical change',[355] it was decided to adopt a new approach which was 'very different'[356] from that envisaged when the reform issue was first raised. This new approach was to recommend[357] the adoption of a new registration system for company charges based upon the notice file principle.[358]

Nevertheless, although this recommendation was largely unexpected, it did still come in a highly qualified format. The recommendation was only 'provisional'[359] and coupled with a second recommendation that the subject of company charge reform be linked with the wider issue of a wholesale reform of the law on personal property security assignments and referred to the Law Commission for further work.[360] The latter issue

---

348 On which see s 395(1).

349 See *The Final Report*, above n 1, at para 12.10.

350 See *The Final Report*, above n 1, at para 12.1.

351 See *Modern Company Law for a Competitive Economy* (London, DTI, 1998).

352 See consultation document *Modern Company Law for a Competitive Economy: Registration of Company Charges* (London, DTI, 2000); hereafter *Registration of Company Charges*.

353 Based upon the notice file principle as found under Art 9 of the US UCC.

354 See *Registration of Company Charges*, above n 352. Note also the Rickford essay above at pp 33 and 39.

355 See *The Final Report*, above n 1, at para 12.7. Half the respondents to the consultation document *Registration of Company Charges*, above n 352, were in favour of a new notice file scheme being brought in and opposition from other respondents 'was much weaker than in previous consultations'; see *The Final Report*, above n 1, at para 12.15.

356 See *The Final Report*, above n 1, at para 12.7.

357 See *The Final Report*, above n 1, at para 12.2.

358 See above n 203 for the meaning of notice file. It should be noted that the Steering Group also made a proposal for more limited reforms to the current system which would apply in the event that their main recommendations in respect of the adoption of a notice file principle were to be rejected. These alternative proposals are considered incidentally in this text; see *The Final Report*, above n 1, at pp 271–74 for full details of these alternative proposals.

359 See *The Final Report*, above n 1, at paras 12.2 and 12.8.

360 See *The Final Report*, above n 1, at para 12.8. At the time of writing it has yet to be decided whether the Law Commission will undertake a formal review of this area; see generally Law Commission Eighth Programme of Law Reform (2001) HC 227 (London, TSO, 2001) at para 1.11.

was stated to be 'outside our remit' and merited a separate inquiry which would take account of the 'provisional' findings of the Steering Group.[361] In any case the 'provisional' recommendations of the Steering Group had not been tested widely and 'further consultation would be needed before they could be adopted'.[362]

So what were the 'provisional' recommendations of the Steering Group? As has just been mentioned, the main recommendation was that the basis of company charge registration should be changed from a register of actual charges to a new system based on notice filing (that is, covering intended/prospective charges).[363] Under this system registration would be effected by the filing of a financing statement with the registrar of companies giving notice that a charge over a designated asset or class of assets had been taken or was about to be taken by the chargee from the chargor.[364] Charges would then be accorded priority according to their respective dates of registration/filing.[365] In this respect the date of registration/filing would be the date that details of the charge were entered on the register at Companies House and that date would be 'conclusive'.[366] Coupled with this priority rule would be the doctrine of constructive notice which would bind all subsequent creditors taking registrable security charges and apply in respect of all the information (that is, mandatory and voluntary) filed at Companies House.[367] In respect of other third parties, the doctrine of constructive notice would not apply and any conflicts involving the interests of registered chargees would be resolved according to general law.[368]

It should be open to either the chargee or chargor to file the particulars of the charge.[369] However, given the fact that it will invariably be the chargee who files the particulars for registration, protection would need to be given to the chargor since details might be registered of non-existent potential charges (which never in fact materialised) to the prejudice of the chargor's general credit rating. This protection would take the form of requiring a chargee presenting particulars for filing to 'verify' the consent of the chargor.[370] A second protection would come from the fact that it would be an offence to knowingly or recklessly submit inaccurate particulars for filing.[371] In the event that inaccurate particulars were entered on the register then the chargor would be given the ability to get the details cancelled.[372] Should inaccurate particulars appear on the register

---

361 See *The Final Report*, above n 1, at para 12.8.
362 See *The Final Report*, above n 1, at para 12.7.
363 See *The Final Report*, above n 1, at para 12.2.
364 See *The Final Report*, above n 1, at para 12.19(a).
365 See *The Final Report*, above n 1, at para 12.19(b).
366 See *The Final Report*, above n 1, at para 12.20. The Steering Group noted that there would be no need to issue a certificate of this date to the chargee. However, they went on to note that further provision 'might be needed to address the relative priority of charges for which Companies House received particulars on the same day'; at para 12.20.
367 See *The Final Report*, above n 1, at paras 12.50–12.51.
368 See *The Final Report*, above n 1, at para 12.52.
369 See *The Final Report*, above n 1, at para 12.21.
370 See *The Final Report*, above n 1, at para 12.23. No details were given as to the form this verification might take. However, it was stated that the chargor would not be required to sign the particulars form presented for filing as happens under Art 9 of the US UCC; at para 12.23.
371 See *The Final Report*, above n 1, at paras 12.29 and 12.33.
372 See *The Final Report*, above n 1, at paras 12.34–12.36.

then the substantive charge would be void to the extent of any inaccuracy but would otherwise be valid and enforceable.[373] Liability for inaccurate particulars appearing on the register would lie with the chargee irrespective of who actually filed those particulars for registration.[374] The registrar of companies would not be liable for any inaccuracy in the information filed.[375]

With regard to the information disclosed by the register of charges, the Steering Group proposed two main extensions to the information already required from those seeking to register a charge.[376] This was in respect of automatic crystallisation clauses contained in floating charges which would in future need to be registered[377] and, on a voluntary basis, that chargees should be able to register any negative pledge clause contained in their security agreement with the chargor.[378] The latter change would be significant since the doctrine of constructive notice would then apply to those registered particulars.[379] Further recommendations in this area included provision to be made for the voluntary filing of any assignment of the chargee's interest in the security[380] and also that a chargee's signature be required if the chargor attempted to file a memorandum of satisfaction in respect of the registered charge interest signifying its extinction.[381]

The Steering Group noted that the sanction of invalidity for non-registered charges was an 'essential feature'[382] and 'underpins'[383] the current system. They proposed that this sanction should continue under a notice file regime.[384] Under the new regime (as under present law)[385] an unregistered charge would be void against a liquidator, an administrator and the creditors of the chargor under these respective proceedings.[386] Curiously, no mention was made of the need to avoid an unregistered charge against an execution creditor or purchaser for value of the encumbered goods.[387] It was also recommended that a late registered charge would be void if registered after the beginning of insolvency proceedings against the chargor company.[388]

---

373 See *The Final Report*, above n 1, at paras 12.29–12.30. However, this invalidity would not apply if the subject matter of the charge was also covered by another specialist registry. In the latter situation priority would be governed solely by that other registry; at para 12.31.

374 See *The Final Report*, above n 1, at para 12.32.

375 See *The Final Report*, above n 1, at para 12.32.

376 See now Companies Act 1985, s 401(1)(b) and SI 1985/854 Form No 395 for the information on the public register of company charges.

377 See *The Final Report*, above n 1, at para 12.28(g). They also recommended that this be adopted by the current provisions in any case; at para 12.79(h).

378 See *The Final Report*, above n 1, at para 12.28(k). They also recommended that this provision be adopted by the current provisions in any case; at para 12.79(j).

379 See *The Final Report*, above n 1, at para 12.51.

380 See *The Final Report*, above n 1, at para 12.38.

381 See *The Final Report*, above n 1, at para 12.42. This would also apply in respect of a partial satisfaction of a charge; at para 12.43.

382 See *The Final Report*, above n 1, at para 12.3.

383 See *The Final Report*, above n 1, at para 12.17.

384 See *The Final Report*, above n 1, at para 12.44.

385 See generally above at section 5.

386 See *The Final Report*, above n 1, at paras 12.44 and 12.45.

387 See also above at pp 364–65.

388 See *The Final Report*, above n 1, at para 12.46. In the context of a notice file regime, 'late', presumably, must be taken to mean that an interest is registered after the substantive obligation/security interest has been executed in favour of the chargee.

One feature of the avoidance power for unregistered charges that troubled the Steering Group was its compatibility with the European Convention on Human Rights (The Convention)[389] which was incorporated into UK law by the Human Rights Act 1998. It was put to them that the avoidance power may breach Article 1 of the First Protocol to The Convention as it might operate as a disproportionate 'deprivation' of the chargee's property rights.[390] The Steering Group made no attempt to examine the force of this argument but simply accepted that the present avoidance power needed amending and, therefore, recommended that the chargee be given the right to apply to a court for relief from the invalidity.[391] Under this new right the court would be given the power to validate the avoided charge against a liquidator, administrator or any future secured creditor but would not be able to validate the charge against a competing charge that had already been registered at the time of the chargee's application to the court for such an order.[392]

The simple acceptance of the avoidance power as being contrary to The Convention is disappointing and potentially worrying should this view lead to a successful challenge of the existing provisions which will continue in force for some time to come. However, on reflection, it can be doubted whether the avoidance power is susceptible to this challenge. The Convention First Protocol only applies if the deprivation of property by the relevant law is not in the public interest and the State cannot justify the deprivation in the general interest. More recently, when this test came under scrutiny by the Court of Appeal in 'an analogous situation',[393] the test of whether a law would be compatible with the Convention was expressed as 'it is necessary to ask whether the statutory inhibition is proportionate to the aim. Is there a proper balance between the ends and the means?'.[394] To answer this question one needed to look at the policy behind the relevant law and whether that policy was legitimate, and if so then judge whether the law applies that policy in a proportionate manner. If it does, then the law is compatible; if it does not, then it will be incompatible.[395]

When applied to the avoidance power of s 395 of the Companies Act 1985, it is submitted that the avoidance power is legitimate, proportionate and justifiable in the general interest as required under The Convention. The rationale for the avoidance power has already been dealt with at length and need not be repeated in any detail.[396] Suffice to say that the purpose of avoidance is to ensure that publicity is given to defined categories of charge security interest via the act of registration on a public register. The avoidance power operates to ensure that an unregistered charge cannot be enforced to the detriment of creditors of the chargor company who might have been misled by the non-appearance of the charge on the public register. The power is proportionate because it does not automatically apply upon a failure to register the charge but only effectively applies when

---

389 (1953) Cmd 8969.
390 See *The Final Report*, above n 1, at para 12.16.
391 See *The Final Report*, above n 1, at para 12.17. They also recommended such a change in the context of the present regime; at para 12.71.
392 See *The Final Report*, above n 1, at paras 12.18–12.19 and 12.44.
393 See *The Final Report*, above n 1, at p 250 n 188.
394 See *Wilson v First County Trust Ltd* [2001] 3 WLR 42 at p 53G *per* Sir Andrew Morritt VC.
395 See *Wilson v First County Trust Ltd* [2001] 3 WLR 42 at p 58D–E *per* Sir Andrew Morritt VC.
396 See generally above at section 5.

the company is insolvent or a creditor levies execution against the assets subject to the unregistered charge. In all other respects the charge is enforceable against the company and should it become void then the company will be under a duty to repay the sums secured by the charge immediately.[397] The chargee would still be able to prove the secured debt in the insolvency of the chargor in any case. Given these facts, the avoidance power can easily be distinguished from the case the Steering Group had in mind when considering this issue.[398] In any case it is difficult to see how the proposed power to apply to the courts for validation of the unregistered charge would ever be granted since it would be extremely prejudicial to the insolvency process and involve many difficult, if not impossible, fact-finding inquiries into the state of mind of the insolvent company's creditors (at the time they assumed that status or extended credit) to determine which, if any, had been misled by the non-registered charge such that belated validation of the unregistered charge could be justified against the liquidator or administrator.

The current regime duplicates the registration requirement in respect of certain types of asset-based charge which are also required to be registered in separate registries. A charge over an interest in land or over a ship or aircraft are good examples of this.[399] The latter registries are different from (and more important than) the Companies Act regime in that they govern matters relating to the title to the relevant asset rather than merely claims against the company holding that asset.[400] It might have been reasonably thought that the current review would have removed this superfluous additional registration requirement but 'the clear majority of consultees'[401] were in favour of its retention. This was because a single search of the companies registry could then be undertaken by the casual inquirer[402] to determine the range of securities granted by a particular company.[403] Therefore, the Steering Group recommended that the double registration

---

397 See Companies Act 1985, s 395(2).

398 See *Wilson v First County Trust Ltd* [2001] 3 WLR 42. The *Wilson* case concerned the compatibility of certain highly technical sections of the Consumer Credit Act 1974 which purported to render a loan and security agreement unenforceable and also to prevent the creditor getting the court's assistance to enforce those agreements (contrary to Art 6(1) of The Convention). Due to the fact that the policy behind these sections was unclear other than via recourse to those sections directly (ie, *Hansard* was of no avail), and in any case the policy manifested by the wording of these sections was wholly disproportionate to the ends they sought to achieve, the Court of Appeal found the sections incompatible with The Convention, both Art 6(1) and the Art 1 of the First Protocol. At the time of writing the decision of the Court of Appeal in *Wilson* is under appeal; see [2001] 1 WLR 22–38E.

399 See generally: Land Registration Act 1925 (registered land); Land Charges Act 1972 (unregistered land); Merchant Shipping (Registration) Act 1993 (ships); Mortgaging of Aircraft Order 1972 (aircraft).

400 See *The Final Report*, above n 1, at para 12.56.

401 See *The Final Report*, above n 1, at para 12.56.

402 The potential chargee would be forced to search the other register in any case in order to establish the chargor's title to the asset and then register under that other register (in addition to under Part 12 of the Act) to establish his own new title to the asset after the charge had been created.

403 See *The Final Report*, above n 1, at para 12.56. This appears to ignore the fact that under a notice file regime most of the particulars on the register will be in respect of possible future charges which have yet to be created at the time of registration. Therefore, the person inspecting the register will be unsure whether the charge did in fact materialise other than by way of inference that it did, otherwise the chargor would have had the entry cancelled to preserve his credit rating. Given the fact that the Steering Group recommended that criminal penalties for non-registration were to be removed (see above at n 171) and possibly (*The Final Report* is not clear on this) that invalidation would not apply in respect of charges requiring dual registration where the other registry governed priority matters (see above at n 373), then it might be questioned whether the registration 'duty' (it must be presumed that the Steering Group intended that the duty to register charges would remain on the chargor, although *The Final Report* is not explicit on this point) to continue registering such charges would be complied with in any event since there would appear to be no incentive to do so.

requirement be retained but hoped that technological improvements might lead to a single submission of information by a chargee to achieve the double act of registration in the appropriate registers.[404] However, the question of conflicting priority rules was not addressed directly by the Steering Group. They did recommend that registered charges under the Companies Act scheme be accorded priority according to the date of registration[405] but did not consider this in the context of other registration schemes which imposed a similar rule of priority.[406] This serves to highlight the folly of attempting to preserve abstract information functions divorced from priority issues.[407]

12 CONCLUSIONS

This discussion has shown that Part 12 is an outmoded and ill-fitting regulatory scheme for company charges. Although the Steering Group have recognised this and gone some way to rectifying matters via the recommendation of a new notice file-based registration system, much of their work on this area was constrained by their terms of reference and limited time, such that their work can best be regarded as a step in the right direction.[408] It is now high time that the core principles highlighted in *The Crowther Report* in 1971[409] and reinforced by *The Diamond Report* of 1989[410] were put into practice. However, this need not mean that we implement a comprehensive personal property security scheme applying to all categories of debtor, be they a corporation or an individual.[411] A more selective approach can be recommended. This would involve the creation of a new computerised security interest register requiring all company[412] security interests[413] to be registered other than defined exceptions. Registration would be based on the notice file principle[414] and would be optional in the sense that there would be no duty or criminal sanctions for registration against either the company or the holder of the security interest.

---

404 See *The Final Report*, above n 1, at para 12.56.

405 See *The Final Report*, above n 1, at para 12.19(b).

406 Presumably the improvements in technology, referred to above at n 404, would solve this problem such that simultaneous registration could happen. In the context of inaccurate particulars, the Steering Group recommended that the invalidity penalty should not obstruct other registration systems' priority rules; see above at n 373.

407 The question of whether the Companies Act invalidation power should be applied in respect of non-registered charges registered under another system also applies in this context.

408 For example, there is no discussion in *The Final Report* about the need for a new statutory definition/concept of 'security interest' which is a principle which goes hand in hand with the adoption of the notice file system under personal property security systems such as Art 9 of the UCC.

409 Above n 131.

410 Above n 7.

411 There is always the danger that if the question of company charge reform is dealt with in the context of a wholesale reform of personal property security law involving both companies and individual debtors (currently covered by the Bills of Sale Acts 1878–90, which require major revision/reform), then the issue might be bogged down for years to come and meet the same fate as both the *Crowther* and *Diamond Reports*.

412 The Steering Group recommended that the registration provisions be extended to unregistered companies; see *The Final Report*, above n 1, at para 12.67(b). A new statutory system might also be extended to cover all forms of business organisation, eg, partnerships.

413 On the meaning of this term see above nn 134 and 135 and the main text thereat.

414 On which see above n 203.

The sole purpose of registration would be to perfect the security interest against defined categories of interest[415] and to gain a priority point according to the date of registration. The system would be self-financing, generating income via fees from registration and inspection services.[416] In order to simplify the main body of company law, these suggestions should be implemented via a new and separate piece of legislation removed from the Companies Act.[417] We could have a new Companies Security Interest Registration Act as the vehicle for this reform. A further point that should be implemented is the removal of the categories of security interest already covered by other registration systems which purport to govern priority from the Companies Act scheme.[418] The land registration system is the most significant example of this and has become a major obstacle to the reform of Part 12.[419] This is surprising given the unnecessary duplication of resources and costs that is involved in maintaining dual registration systems at no obvious gain to the commercial community. Why should a chargee have to make two searches of different registers in relation to the same property and then have to make two separate acts of registration in order to be protected? These other registers are specialised and generally govern title matters in relation to certain types of property, meaning that they are the more important sources of information and regulation. It is submitted that these registers should be given sole responsibility for governing security interests when the debtor is a company.

Given the increasing global nature of our economy and the central role played by companies, it is appropriate to note that these recommendations have been largely adopted, in one form or another, by the USA,[420] Canada[421] and New Zealand[422] and it is probably only a matter of time before all the common law world follows suit. As a former President of the Board of Trade explained, when setting up the Company Law Review in 1998:

> [W]e are determined to ensure that we have a framework of company law which is up to date, competitive and designed for the next century, a framework which facilitates enterprise and promotes transparency and fair dealing.[423]

---

415 See generally above at section 5 for these categories of interest.

416 Such fees would include an insurance premium for the benefit of the registrar of companies, or other public official given responsibility for the new system, who could indemnify users of the new register who were prejudiced due to defects in the operation of the registry.

417 Even the Steering Group were aware of the need to have legislation that could be quickly amended to meet changing commercial expectations and developments; see *The Final Report*, above n 1, at para 12.10 and chapter 5. Cf Sealy, *Company Law and Commercial Reality* (London, Sweet & Maxwell, 1984) at chapter 4.

418 See generally: Land Registration Act 1925 (registered land); Land Charges Act 1972 (unregistered land; although this Act is becoming of less importance now that land registration is mandatory); Merchant Shipping (Registration) Act 1993 (ships); Mortgaging of Aircraft Order 1972 SI 1972/1268 (aircraft). The Steering Group also acknowledged the difficulties caused by specialist registers; see *The Final Report*, above n 1, at paras 12.6, 12.31, 12.56. However, they failed to deal with this problem in an adequate manner.

419 See DTI consultative document, above n 8, at para 8 where it is explained that the Companies Act 1989, Part 4, which reforms Part 12 was not brought into force due to the problems associated with its interaction with the Land Registry.

420 See Uniform Commercial Code, Art 9.

421 Each of the Canadian provinces has adopted their own version of a Personal Property Security Act; see for example Ontario Personal Property Security Act 1990 (as amended).

422 See Personal Property Security Act 1999.

423 See *Modern Company Law for a Competitive Economy* (London, DTI, 1998) at p 1.

Applying this test to Part 12 we see a spectacular failure. Part 12 is neither up to date; competitive; modern; facilitating in promoting the availability of security; transparent or fair in the results it promotes. It is high time that fundamental reforms along the lines advocated for here were introduced. Although in the past bodies such as the Law Society[424] and others[425] have felt that such reforms are not needed, it is time to overrule these voices. The principles of Art 9 of the US Uniform Commercial Code have proven successful in replacing a system similar to that which currently exists in England and has been successfully exported.[426] The recent conclusion of the Company Law Review has presented us with a third major opportunity, via the Law Commission, to institute fundamental overhaul and reform of company charge law. Given the fact that this subject has now been through four separate review/consultation processes in the past 30 years[427] without any substantive reforms resulting, it is to be hoped that the Law Commission will be able to successfully complete the work of both the *Crowther* and *Diamond Reports* at least insofar as they apply to company security interests.[428]

---

424 See above n 346. The Law Society have recently confirmed that they believe that there is no demand for fundamental reform to Part 12 however, they do support further work by the Law Commission about how Part 12 might be reformed along the lines of Art 9 of the UCC so that comparisons and further judgments can be made; see Law Society Memorandum No 409 'Registration of Company Charges' (London, Law Society, January 2001) at pp 1–2.

425 See DTI letter, above n 268, where it is stated that, after consulting on the reform of Part 12 (on which see DTI document URN 94/633, above n 8), support for a new system 'was very low'. However, it should be noted that the DTI only received 60 replies from this consultation exercise. Cf the Canadian experience, see above n 202 and the main text thereat.

426 Eg, to Canada and New Zealand; see above n 202 and the main text thereat. This is not to say that a reformed Part 12 system should slavishly copy the US/Canadian approach, merely that they offer some guiding principles of how a new scheme should look in the UK; cf McCormack 'Personal Property Security Law Reform in England and Canada' [2002] JBL 113.

427 Ie, *The Crowther Report*, above n 131, in 1971; *The Diamond Report*, above n 7, in 1989; DTI Consultation Document, above n 8, in 1994; and by the Steering Group in *The Final Report*, above n 1, in 2001.

428 On the general question of the need for reform of our commercial law see Goode 'Insularity or Leadership? The Role of the UK in the Harmonisation of Commercial Law' (2001) 51 ICLQ 751 especially at pp 759–60 and 764–65.

CHAPTER 16

THE FLOATING CHARGE IN ENGLAND AND CANADA

Gerard McCormack

1 INTRODUCTION

The floating charge has been the mainstay of bank finance in England for over a century – so much so that it has been described as the workhorse of the banking industry.[1] It permits the entirety of a company's business operations to be charged by the use of a simple formula and, moreover, the security can extend to later advances made by the creditor as well as covering property subsequently acquired by the debtor. Not all common law jurisdictions, however, are still under the embrace of the floating charge. The Canadian common law provinces, including Ontario, the most populous and economically the most important, have adopted a personal property security regime along the lines of Art 9 of the US Uniform Commercial Code.[2] The same applies with respect to New Zealand though, at the time of writing, the New Zealand legislation is not in force.[3] An Art 9-type security regime is based around two fundamental principles; namely, a comprehensive register of security interests with a statutory definition of 'security interest' and secondly, a principle of 'notice' rather than 'transaction' filing with priorities between competing security interests generally determined by the application of a 'first-to-file' priority rule. Given that these leading common law jurisdictions have abandoned their English law roots in this area, this chapter addresses the question whether there is a continued place for an English-style floating charge in a security regime based on Art 9?[4]

Certainly, the Canadian experience would tend to suggest that this question should be answered in the negative.[5] It will become apparent from the essay, however, that I am sceptical about the merits of an Art 9-type system in English conditions but it is not my purpose in writing the essay to canvass the merits and demerits of Art 9. Rather the essay proceeds on the assumption that England will go over to an Art 9-type system and, assuming that to be the case, then asks the question whether there is still a place for the

---

1   See Ziegel 'The New Provincial Chattel Security Regimes' (1991) 70 *Canadian Bar Review* 681 at p 712.
2   Article 9 has been recently revised but the revision does not really affect the points at issue in this article. For reference to the revised version of Art 9 see the National Conference of Commissioners on Uniform State Laws website – www@nccusl.org – and for discussion see the special issue of the *Chicago-Kent Law Review* (1999) 74 *Chicago-Kent Law Review* No 3. See also Corinne Cooper (ed) *The New Article 9* (Chicago, American Bar Association, 2nd edn, 2000).
3   For information concerning the implementation schedule of the New Zealand PPSA see the following New Zealand government website – www.ppsr.gov.nz.
4   See generally A Abel 'Has Article 9 scuttled the floating charge?' in JS Ziegel and WF Foster (eds) *Aspects of Comparative Commercial Law* (Montreal, McGill University, Dobbs Ferry, 1969); FM Catzman *Personal Property Security Law* (Toronto, Carswell, 1976) at pp 62–66.
5   Canada is a more fertile testing ground for the theory than the United States for pre-Art 9 US law did not recognise any equivalent of the floating charge; see *Benedict v Ratner* (1925) 268 US 354.

floating charge. My answer to the latter question is 'no'.[6] Of course some pragmatists might draw the conclusion that if the answer to the question is 'no' then Art 9 in English conditions is not a good idea. The floating charge has been an engine of commerce for over a century and it should not be scrapped, they might say. On the other hand, Art 9 enthusiasts might respond by saying that Art 9 is a more logical and conceptually coherent system and you would still have the functional equivalent of the floating charge. Be that as it may, the response might be – if this is not too cheap a shot – the life of the law has been logic rather than experience and experience shows the wisdom of retaining the floating charge.

The Company Law Review team passed the buck when it came to the general issue of company charges, including floating charges, suggesting that the whole area of security interests over property should be considered by the Law Commission.[7] A possible harbinger of more immediate legislative change comes in the shape of an almost simultaneously published DTI/Insolvency Service White Paper, *Insolvency – A Second Chance*.[8] This White Paper proposes an integrated package of measures with the aim of enhancing the culture of rescuing ailing businesses. It suggests curtailing the right of a floating chargeholder to appoint an administrative receiver; removing the floating chargeholder's power of veto over the appointment of an administrator and as a counterbalancing measure, abolishing Crown preference in all insolvencies. In order to ensure that the benefits of the abolition of Crown preference are enjoyed by all creditors and not just creditors secured by a floating charge, it is proposed that a certain proportion of floating charge realisations should be set aside for unsecured creditors.[9] Nevertheless, while curbing some of the advantages enjoyed by floating chargeholders, the White Paper does not propose the abolition of the floating charge.

This chapter has a slightly different focus examining, as it does, the continued viability of the floating charge in Art 9-type conditions. Canada is used as the focus of analysis rather than the US for the simple reason that the US never had the floating charge. It is hoped also that the chapter will serve to sharpen our understanding of the conceptual foundations of the floating charge and its key features. First, however, it is necessary to look at the basic aspects of the floating charge. Then the proposals for reform will be examined. Attention will then switch to the essential attributes of the Canadian

---

6 In New Zealand, while the floating charge has not been abolished as such and while commercial debentures may continue to use the expression 'floating charge', floating charges are made subject to the general rules on attachment and perfection of security interests; see Personal Property Securities Act 1999, s 40. In this connection see the comments of Lord Millett when giving the judgment of the Privy Council in *Agnew v Commissioner of Inland Revenue* [2001] 2 AC 710 at p 716D: 'A curiosity of the case is that the distinction between fixed and floating charges, which is of great commercial importance in the United Kingdom, seems likely to disappear from the law of New Zealand when the Personal Property Act 1999 comes into force.'

7 See Company Law Review Steering Group *Modern Company Law For a Competitive Economy: Final Report* (London, DTI, July 2001) at para 12. 8; hereafter *The Final Report*. For a detailed treatment of company charges see the essay by de Lacy above at p 333.

8 (2001) Cm 5234 (London, TSO, July 2001).

9 (2001) Cm 5234 at para 2.19. The White Paper goes on to say that '[t]he preferential status of certain claims by employees in insolvency proceedings, such as wages and holiday pay within certain limits, will remain, as will the rights of those subrogated to them'. For more details on the government's reform proposals see www.insolvency.gov.uk. See now Enterprise Bill 2002.

system.[10] Ontario will serve as the centrepiece of the Canadian analysis since it is the commercial centre of Canada.

2 FUNDAMENTALS OF THE FLOATING CHARGE

The floating charge owes its origins to the skill and originality of English 19th century Chancery lawyers.[11] The *locus classicus* on the definition of a floating charge is to be found in the judgment of Romer LJ in *Re Yorkshire Woolcombers Association Ltd*[12] where the following ingredients of such a charge were identified:

> [If] a charge has the three characteristics that I am about to mention it is a floating charge. (1) If it is a charge on a class of assets of a company present and future; (2) if that class is one which, in the ordinary course of the business of the company, would be changing from time to time; and (3) if you find that, by the charge, it is contemplated that, until some future step is taken by or on behalf of those interested in the charge, the company may carry on business in the ordinary way as far as concerns the particular class of assets I am dealing with.[13]

Re Yorkshire Woolcombers Association Ltd was appealed to the House of Lords where it is reported under the name of *Illingsworth v Houldsworth*.[14] There Lord Macnaghten drew a distinction between the fixed charge and the floating charge in the following terms:

> A specific charge [ie, fixed charge], I think, is one that without more fastens on ascertained and definite property or property capable of being ascertained and defined; a floating charge, on the other hand, is ambulatory and shifting in its nature, hovering over and so to speak floating with the property which it is intended to affect until some event occurs or some act is done which causes it to settle and fasten on the subject of the charge within its reach and grasp.[15]

The essence of the floating charge is that it does not inhibit a company from disposing of assets within the category covered by the charge in the ordinary course of its business without reference to, or the consent of the person entitled to the benefit of the charge. A fixed charge, on the other hand, prevents a company from disposing of an unencumbered title to the assets, the subject matter of the charge.[16]

---

10   For a detailed exposition on the Ontario PPSA see Ziegel and Denomme *The Ontario Personal Property Security Act: Commentary and Analysis* (Aurora Ontario, Canada Law Book, 2nd edn, 2000). See also McLaren *The Ontario Personal Property Security Act* (Toronto, Carswell, 1994).

11   A floating charge was first mapped out by the Court of Appeal in Chancery in *Re Panama, New Zealand and Australian Royal Mail Co* (1870) 5 Ch App 318. See generally on the history and development of the floating charge Pennington 'The Genesis of the Floating Charge' (1960) 23 MLR 630.

12   [1903] 2 Ch 284.

13   [1903] 2 Ch 284 at p 295. It should be noted that it is the members of the class rather than the class itself which is changing. A floating charge may be described as a charge over a pool of assets.

14   [1904] AC 355.

15   [1904] AC 355 at p 358. The characteristics of a floating charge were also recently considered by the House of Lords in *Smith v Bridgend County BC* [2001] 3 WLR 1347.

16   One commentator has spoken of the 'mental block experienced by the courts in the early floating charge cases when they were quite unable to fathom the idea of a fixed mortgage or charge over trading assets coupled with a licence to dispose of those assets in the ordinary course of business ...' – see McLauchlan 'Fixed Charges Over Book Debts: *New Bullas* in New Zealand' (1999) 115 LQR 365 at p 367.

The floating charge represents a legal response to the needs of a rapidly industrialising society for effective security interests in order to generate loan capital to finance business expansion. As a result of the Industrial Revolution, only a small proportion of an enterprise's wealth might consist of land and fixed plant and equipment with the bulk consisting of raw materials, manufactured articles or articles in the course of manufacture, stock-in-trade (inventory) and debts owing to the business (receivables). The fixed charge forms of security meant that only a small proportion of a company's wealth-generating capacity could be used to secure loans made to it. Lending on an unsecured basis to companies became even more hazardous as far as banks were concerned after the passage of the Limited Liability Act 1855. The position of the lender was, however, alleviated by two main legal developments. First, in *Holroyd v Marshall*[17] the House of Lords held that it was possible to create fixed charges over after-acquired assets and secondly, the floating charge was given the judicial sanction – most notably in the landmark decision *Re Panama, New Zealand and Australian Royal Mail Co*.[18]

Floating charges have been the subject of parliamentary regulation as well as judicial consideration for many years. Hoffmann J in *Re Brightlife Ltd*[19] reviewed the various legislative interventions.[20] Legislation in 1897 gave priority to preferential debts over the floating charge. While the precise boundaries of the category of preferential debts have waxed and waned over time basically the category covers certain unpaid taxes and employee claims. Provision was made in the Companies Act 1907 for the invalidation of floating charges granted within three months prior to the commencement of winding up; which period now, generally speaking, stands at 12 months as laid down by s 245 Insolvency Act 1986. The Companies Act 1900 in s 14 introduced the requirement of registration of floating and certain other types of charge. The floating charge is normally enforced through the mechanism of the appointment of a receiver over the assets covered by the charge and in 1907 the Companies Act laid down that the appointment of a receiver be registered.[21]

With a floating charge, the company creating the charge has management autonomy. In other words, it has freedom to carry on business in the ordinary way as far as the class of assets charged is concerned until some event occurs to bring that autonomy to an end. Such an event is referred to as a crystallising event. On the occurrence of such an event, the floating charge then becomes fixed on those assets within the category referred to in the instrument of charge and which are under the control of the debtor. As traditionally understood a floating charge crystallised or, to use non-technical terminology, converted into a fixed charge, where the debenture-holder appointed a receiver or upon the commencement of winding up. In *Re Woodroffes (Musical Instruments) Ltd*[22] Nourse J decided that the cessation of a company's business brought about the crystallisation of a floating charge. This occurred because cessation removed the *raison d'être* of the floating charge which was to permit the company to carry on business in the ordinary way insofar

---

17 (1862) 10 HL Cas 191.
18 (1870) 5 Ch App 318. See generally Pennington, above n 11.
19 [1987] Ch 200.
20 [1987] Ch 200 at pp 214–15. See also *Re Permanent Houses (Holdings) Ltd* [1988] BCLC 563.
21 See section 11.
22 [1986] Ch 366.

as the class of assets charged was concerned. Then in *Re Brightlife Ltd*[23] Hoffmann J held that notice given by the chargee to the chargor could convert a floating charge into a fixed charge. He said it was not open to the courts to restrict the contractual freedom of parties to a floating charge. He pointed to the limited and pragmatic interventions by the legislature in the area and suggested that these rendered it wholly inappropriate for the courts to impose additional restrictive rules on grounds of public policy.

The decision in *Re Brightlife Ltd* paves the way for clauses that provide for crystallisation on the happening of events such as the company's borrowings exceeding a certain amount or its assets falling below a specified level. These events may take place at a time unknown to the chargee who is, therefore, unaware that crystallisation has taken place. The objective of widely drafted crystallisation clauses is to advance the position of the chargee in the queue of creditors. The Insolvency Act 1986 has, however, shorn automatic crystallisation clauses of some of their advantages in this respect. According to ss 40 and 175 preferential debts are payable in priority to the claim secured by a floating charge in a receivership or liquidation. A floating charge is defined in s 251, for these purposes, as a charge which, as created, was a floating charge.[24] So even if a floating charge has crystallised automatically prior to receivership or liquidation, it still ranks after the preferential creditors. A crystallised floating charge will still, however, take priority over a prior ranking floating charge, a subsequently created equitable fixed charge and execution creditors.[25]

Section 251 of the Insolvency Act has the effect of diverting attention to other ways whereby secured lenders may outrank preferential creditors. One obvious way is for the lender to try to obtain fixed security over assets that traditionally fall within the domain of the floating charge such as future trade debts payable to the borrower. The theoretical possibility of creating such a fixed security was acknowledged in *Siebe Gorman v Barclays Bank*.[26] In the main the courts have been prepared to uphold a fixed charge characterisation applied by the lender to such security provided that the borrower is restricted from assigning the debts to anybody else and provided that the debts, once collected, are paid into a bank account that is under the control of the lender.

The Privy Council has recently considered in *Agnew v Commissioner of Inland Revenue*[27] the fixed/floating charge distinction in the context of a charge over book debts.

---

23 [1987] Ch 200.

24 See also the Insolvency Act 1986, s 29(2).

25 There is however, at least one caveat to this statement. It is strongly arguable that a person dealing with a company prior to crystallisation, and aware of the existence of the floating charge, is entitled to assume the continuance of the company's managerial autonomy until cessation of that autonomy by crystallisation has been brought to his attention; see generally RM Goode *Legal Problems of Credit and Security* (London, Sweet & Maxwell, 2nd edn, 1988) at pp 70–71. Also worth mentioning perhaps are the observations of McGarvie J in an Australian case *Horsburgh v Deputy Commissioner of Taxation* (1984) 54 ALR 397 who doubted whether 'modern equity would be forced to run in such established grooves that if employees received pay and customers bought goods from a company, while reasonably unaware that the property of the company had become subject to a fixed equitable charge, they would be losers.'

26 [1979] 2 Lloyd's Rep 142. See also: *Re Brightlife Ltd* [1987] Ch 200; and *Re Keenan Bros Ltd* [1986] BCLC 242.

27 [2001] 2 AC 710. See further: Watts 'The Rending Of Charges' (2002) 118 LQR 1; Berg 'Brumark Investments Ltd and the Innominate Charge' [2001] *Journal of Business Law* 532; Wood 'Fixed and Floating Charges' [2001] CLJ 472.

The court reiterated the point that 'labelling' and 'non-assignment' clauses in the debenture are insufficient to constitute a charge over book debts a fixed charge. Lord Millett said categorically:

> A restriction on disposition which nevertheless allows collection and free use of the proceeds is inconsistent with the fixed nature of the charge; it allows the debt and its proceeds to be withdrawn from the security by the act of the company in collecting it.[28]

The court appeared to approve *Siebe Gorman* subject to the caveat that the restrictions on withdrawals of the proceeds of debts, once collected, were real and substantial in practice. In other words, a charge on book debts could be a fixed charge if the proceeds of the debts collected by the chargor were required to be paid into a blocked account with the chargeholder. It was said:

> ... such an arrangement is inconsistent with the charge being a floating charge, since the debts are not available to the company as a source of its cash flow. But their Lordships would wish to make it clear that it is not enough to provide in the debenture that the account is a blocked account if it is not operated as one in fact.[29]

As was explained however, in *Agnew v Commissioner of Inland Revenue*, lenders wanted to have the best of both worlds. Lenders wanted to have a fixed charge on the book debts while, at the same time, allowing the company the same freedom to use the proceeds that it would have if the charge were a floating charge. With this objective in mind the drafter of the charge which came before the court in *Re New Bullas Trading Ltd*[30] adopted a different approach.

In that case the debenture did not treat book debts indivisibly. The debenture purported to create a fixed charge over book debts while uncollected coupled with a floating charge over the proceeds of the debts. This meant that if the borrower became insolvent, and went into liquidation or receivership, but with large amounts owing to it from trade debtors, the lender could step in and intercept payment from the debtors before it reached the hands of the borrower. In the normal course of events however, pre-insolvency the borrower would continue to collect the debts and use the proceeds in the ordinary course of business operations. The debenture was endeavouring to combine the advantages of fixed and floating security in the same instrument. The borrower was in a state of servitude, so to speak, while insolvent yet, while solvent, had freedom to conduct business and make use of cash flow in the standard way.

The Court of Appeal took the view that there was nothing inherently objectionable in this state of affairs. Nourse LJ said:

> He who lends money to a trading company neither wishes nor expects it to become insolvent. Its prosperous trading is the best assurance of the return of his money with interest. But against an evil day he wants the best security the company can give him consistently with its ability to trade meanwhile. Hence the modern form of debenture which, broadly speaking, gives the lender a fixed charge over assets that the company does

---

28 [2001] 2 AC 710 at p 726H.
29 [2001] 2 AC 710 at p 730A–B.
30 [1994] 1 BCLC 485.

not need to deal with in the ordinary course of its business and a floating charge over those that it does not.[31]

The court concluded by stating that there were no considerations of public policy which prevented lender and borrower from making whatever contract they chose. Just as it was open to contracting parties to provide for a fixed charge on future book debts, so it was open to them to provide that they shall be subject to a fixed charge while they were uncollected and a floating charge on realisation.

The decision has the effect of downgrading the claims of preferential creditors for, by recognising an expanded sphere of operation for the fixed charge, this has the result of siphoning off assets that would otherwise be available to satisfy preferential creditors. Moreover, the decision has been criticised on conceptual grounds. The burden of the criticism is that the proper characterisation of a charge over book debts cannot be divorced from a consideration of contractual provisions relating to the application of proceeds of the debts.[32] Ultimately a debt is worth nothing unless and until it is turned into money.[33] To use the language of Millett LJ in *Royal Trust Bank v NatWest Bank*[34] it was impossible 'to separate a debt or other receivable from the proceeds of its realisation'.

The Privy Council, upholding the decision of the New Zealand Court of Appeal, has now in *Agnew v Commissioner of Inland Revenue*,[35] refused to follow *Re New Bullas Trading Ltd*. The Privy Council, having examined the old authorities, took the view that the designation of a charge over book debts as fixed or floating traditionally turned on the extent of the freedom that the borrower enjoys in relation to collecting the debts and using the proceeds of the same. Relatively untrammelled freedom to use debt proceeds in the ordinary course of business, as in this case, meant that the charge was a floating charge. Lord Millett added:

> While a debt and its proceeds are two separate assets ... the latter are merely the traceable proceeds of the former and represent its entire value. A debt is a receivable; it is merely a right to receive payment from the debtor. Such a right cannot be enjoyed in specie; its value can be exploited only by exercising the right or by assigning it for value to a third party. An assignment or charge of a receivable which does not carry with it the right to the receipt has no value. It is worthless as a security. Any attempt in the present context to separate the

---

31 See [1994] 1 BCLC 485 at p 487.

32 See, for example, the comments of Hoffmann J in *Re Brightlife Ltd* [1987] Ch 200 at p 209: 'But a floating charge is consistent with some restriction upon the company's freedom to deal with its assets. [F]loating charges commonly contain a prohibition upon the creation of other charges ranking prior to or *pari passu* with the floating charge. Such dealings would otherwise be open to a company in the ordinary course of its business. In the debenture, the significant feature is that *Brightlife* was free to collect its debts and pay the proceeds into its bank account. Once in the account, they would be outside the charge over debts and at the free disposal of the company. In my judgment a right to deal in this way with the charged assets for its own account is a badge of a floating charge and is inconsistent with a fixed charge.'

33 See generally Goode 'Charges over Book Debts: a Missed Opportunity' (1994) 110 LQR 592 who points out that 'the distinctive feature of debts as an object of security is that they are realised by payment, upon which they cease to exist.'

34 [1996] 2 BCLC 682 at p 704.

35 [2001] 2 AC 710; for discussion see McLauchlan '*New Bullas* in New Zealand Round Two' (2000) 116 LQR 211. The case is reported in the New Zealand courts under the name of *Re Brumark Investments Ltd*.

ownership of the debts from the ownership of their proceeds (even if conceptually possible) makes no commercial sense.[36]

3 POSSIBLE LEGISLATIVE CHANGES

The Privy Council judgment in *Agnew v Commissioner of Inland Revenue* is of major significance in clarifying the boundaries of the floating charge. The judgment, however, does not alter the fact that the floating charge is a very versatile tool which permits assets to be used as security with the minimum of restrictions and the maximum flexibility. Moreover, while legislation has curbed some of the perceived advantages associated with the floating charge, in other respects, statute has strengthened the position of the floating chargeholder. In the corporate rehabilitation and re-organisation context, Part 11 of the Insolvency Act 1986 permits a floating, but not a fixed chargeholder, to block the appointment of an administrator to an ailing company.[37] In short, the floating charge has a valued place in English lending practice.

The floating charge is under partial threat at the moment, however, as a result of the proposals contained in the DTI/Insolvency Service White Paper, *Insolvency – A Second Chance*.[38] The White Paper recommends that floating chargeholders should lose the unilateral right to appoint an administrative receiver over a company's assets and also the power to block the appointment of an administrator. As a balancing measure, Crown preference but not employee preference would be abolished, with a certain proportion of floating charge realisations being set aside for unsecured creditors so as to ensure that the fruits of the abolition of Crown preference were enjoyed by all creditors.[39] These proposals, if implemented, would seriously detract from the status of the floating charge.

Potentially an even greater threat comes from the recommendation by the Company Law Steering Group in its *Final Report* that the Law Commission should examine in a more fundamental way the whole issue of security interests over property other than land.[40] *The Final Report* recommends that, as far as company charges are concerned, English law should go over to a system of notice filing and that registration should be used as a reference point for settling priorities.[41] These proposals point in the direction of

---

36   [2001] 2 AC 710 at p 729D–E.
37   See further the Milman essay below at p 419. A floating charge given in such a context is often referred to as a 'lightweight floating charge' because the instrument of charge may lack the onerous covenants typically found in such documents. Such floating charges were given the judicial imprimatur in *Re Croftbell Ltd* [1990] BCLC 844; on which see Oditah 'Lightweight Floating Charges' [1991] *Journal of Business Law* 49.
38   (2001) Cm 5234, above n 8.
39   See the statement at para 2.20 of the White Paper: 'Where there is no floating chargeholder, the benefit of abolition will be available for the unsecured creditors. Where there is a floating chargeholder (in relation to a floating charge created after the coming into force of the legislation), we would ensure that the benefit of the abolition of preferential status goes to unsecured creditors. We will achieve this through a mechanism that ringfences a proportion of the funds generated by the floating charge.' For current information pertaining to the reform proposals see www.insolvency.gov.uk.
40   See *The Final Report*, above n 7, at para 12.8.
41   It is stated at para 12.8 of the *The Final Report*, above n 7: 'Although charges created by companies over their assets other than land must far outnumber similar charges created by other debtors, it would not be sensible to consider a notice filing system for company charges without at the same time considering a similar system for all charges over property other than land and for functionally equivalent legal devices (often termed 'quasi-security' devices).

Art 9 and it should be noted that the Steering Group advisory team included Professor Sir Roy Goode who is an influential advocate of Art 9.[42] The question arises what role does the floating charge play in jurisdictions that have embraced fundamental reform and adopted a more functional approach towards security interests – modelled on Art 9 of the United States Uniform Commercial Code? Let us now turn our attention to the Ontario Personal Property Security Act (OPPSA).

4 ATTACHMENT AND PERFECTION OF SECURITY INTERESTS UNDER THE OPPSA

The OPPSA is centred around the concepts of attachment and perfection of a security interest.[43] The basic premise of the legislation is to permit lenders and sellers to register their interest in the personal property of a debtor so as to secure payment of the debt and to mark out their priority position in the collateral (secured property). A security interest attaches when it becomes enforceable vis à vis creditor and debtor. The expression 'attachment' therefore identifies the process whereby a proprietary right is attached to a personal obligation in order to secure performance of the latter. 'Perfection' signifies the enforceability of the security interest against third parties, that is, it is regarded as having created a property right and perfection will generally occur as a result of registration. Section 11 of the OPPSA sets the cases in which attachment is deemed to have occurred. There are three conditions which must be satisfied. First, the secured party (or a person on behalf of the secured party other than the debtor or the debtor's agent) obtains possession of the collateral or, more usually, when the debtor signs a security agreement that contains a description of the collateral sufficient to enable it to be identified. Secondly, value must be given. 'Value' is defined as meaning any consideration sufficient to support a simple contract and includes an antecedent debt or liability. The third condition is that the debtor must have rights in the collateral. Section 12 of the OPPSA explicitly provides that a security agreement may cover after-acquired property but, of course, the security agreement will not attach unless and until the debtor 'has rights in the collateral'. Floating charges are specifically referred to in s 11 and made subject to the general rules on attachment. It should be noted however, that the parties may agree to postpone the time for attachment, in which case the security interest attaches at the agreed time.

---

42 The recommendations in *The Final Report* on company charges come as something of a surprise for in the earlier consultation document *Registration of Company Charges* (London, DTI, October 2000) it was suggested that the best way forward would be to retain the essentials of the present system rather than to move over to a brave new world of notice-filing, etc. See the comments by Roy Goode in 'The Exodus Of The Floating Charge' in D Feldman and F Meisel (eds) *Corporate and Commercial Law: Modern Developments* (London, Lloyd's of London Press, 1996) 193 at p 203: 'I shall mourn the passing of the floating charge, which has done so much to facilitate large-scale secured financing and, in the process to enrich English doctrine and jurisprudence. English law can take pride in having fashioned through the ingenuity of its equity judges an instrument of great power and even greater mystery. But the world moves on, and we must move with it. As we enter the next millennium it is time for the unified personal property security interest to take hold in these islands.'

43 The references are to the 1990 Ontario Personal Property Security Act RSO 1990 cP10 (as amended). The first Personal Property Security Act was enacted in Ontario in 1967 but this did not come into force until 1976. Revisions of the statute were recommended by the Catzman Committee – see Report of the Minister's Advisory Committee on the Personal Property Security Act (Toronto, June 1984); on which see Ziegel 'Recent and Prospective Developments in the Personal Property Security Law Area' (1985) 10 *Canadian Business Law Journal* 131.

In the case of non-possessory security interests, PPSA systems generally make the issue of priorities turn on a 'first-to-register' principle. The OPPSA is no exception and revolves around the notion of notice-filing. A creditor may file a financing statement before a security agreement has actually been executed and this may cover the entire credit relationship of the parties. The creditor may state simply that he is taking security in certain collateral to cover advances made to the debtor including future advances, irrespective of whether or not there is any commitment on the part of the creditor to make the advance. The secured party who firsts registers a financing statement achieves priority even though he is not the first in terms of executing a security agreement with a debtor or indeed acquiring an attached security interest in the collateral. Professors Cuming and Wood have described the policy underlying this approach as being quite simple:

> Once a financing statement is registered, any person who is planning to deal with someone named as debtor in the financing statement has the ability to determine whether or not the interest he intends to acquire will be subject to a security interest having a prior status. If such a person goes ahead and acquires an interest in the personal property described in the financing statement without making some accommodation with a registering party or without obtaining a discharge of the financing statement, there is no reason to give his interest priority over a subsequent security interest acquired by the registering party.[44]

If the Canadian system is based on notice-filing then the English system may be described as one of transaction-filing – details of certain prescribed transactions must be recorded.[45]

5 ATTACHMENT VERSUS CRYSTALLISATION

The OPPSA adopts the generic concept of a security interest applying to transactions irrespective of form which secure the performance of an obligation and irrespective of where title is located.[46] The Act does not distinguish between legal and equitable security interests nor between fixed and floating charges.[47] It is important to note, however, that security agreements may continue to use the old terminology. The memory of yore and lawyers' precedent banks are not easily erased. Priority between competing security interests is generally determined by the order of registration and not by whether or not the security interest is a fixed or, alternatively, a floating charge. Notwithstanding the language used in the Personal Property Security legislation judges were initially reticent about reaching the result that a security agreement creating what seemed, under

---

44 See Cuming and Wood 'Compatibility of Federal and Provincial Personal Property Security Law' (1986) 65 *Canadian Bar Review* 267 at p 285.

45 See Companies Act 1985, at Part 12.

46 Section 2 OPPSA applies the legislation to '(a) every transaction without regard to its form and without regard to the person who has title to the collateral that in substance creates a security interest including, without limiting the foregoing (i) a chattel mortgage, conditional sale, equipment trust, debenture, floating charge, pledge, trust indenture or trust receipt, and (ii) an assignment, lease or consignment that secures payment or performance of an obligation; and (b) a transfer of an account or chattel paper even though the transfer may not secure payment or performance of an obligation'.

47 See the decision of the Supreme Court of Canada in *Royal Bank of Canada v Sparrow Electric Corp* (1997) 143 DLR (4th) 385 which is discussed below; on which see Davis 'Priority of Crown Claims In Insolvency' (1998) 29 *Canadian Business Law Journal* 145.

traditional taxonomy, to be a floating charge attached upon execution of the agreement.[48] A case in point is *Canadian Imperial Bank of Commerce v Otto Timm Enterprises Ltd.*[49]

This is a case where a bank had provided finance to a farm equipment dealer and taken a general security agreement covering existing and future property, registering financing statements in respect of the agreement. Under the terms of the security agreement the dealer was expressly authorised to sell inventory in the ordinary course of business but it was also stated in the agreement that the security interest attached when it was signed and delivered to the bank. Subsequently the dealer entered into conditional sale agreements with a supplier in respect of a number of deliveries of tractors. Financing statements were filed in relation in some of these deliveries. The question arose who had best claim to the proceeds of sale of the tractors – the bank or the conditional seller? At first instance it was held that the conditional seller prevailed.[50] According to Donnelly J the security interest attached when the agreement was signed and delivered to the bank, but only in the collateral then owned by the dealer. In his view the parties did not intend attachment upon delivery of future inventory to the dealer, because the agreement permitted sales in the ordinary course of business. Thus, as regards after-acquired inventory, the agreement contained a floating charge and since the bank's security had not attached, it could not be perfected by registering the financing statements. Perfection was impossible without attachment and therefore the bank could not invoke the priority protection of s 30(1)(a) of the OPPSA which provides:

> If no other provision of this Act is applicable, priority between security interests in the same collateral shall be determined:
>
> (a) by the order of registration, if the security interests have been perfected by registration.

The judge held that the bank's floating charge over after-acquired property did not crystallise until the bank appointed a receiver. By that stage the dealer had repossessed the tractors and consequently had priority.

A completely different analysis was adopted in the Ontario Court of Appeal.[51] The court held that in accordance with s 12 the bank's security interest attached when the tractors were delivered to the dealer, since the parties intended it to attach, the bank had given value and the dealer had rights in the collateral. The bank's security interest became perfected at that stage since previously it had registered a financing statement and maintained it in force. By way of contrast, the distributor's security interest was only perfected subsequently whether by filing an appropriate financing statement or by taking possession of the inventory. Doherty JA said that the first instance judge had erred in applying common law concepts referable to the crystallisation of floating charges. Instead

---

48 See: *Royal Bank of Canada v Mohawk* (1985) 49 OR (2d) 734; and *Re Standard Modern Technologies Corp* (1992) 6 OR (3d) 161; 87 DLR (4th) 44.

49 (1995) 130 DLR (4th) 91. See generally on the case Harason and Denomme, 'The PPSA and Floating Charges Again' (1997) 115 *Banking & Finance Law Review* 115.

50 (1991) 79 DLR (4th) 67.

51 (1995) 130 DLR (4th) 91.

he should have determined when attachment occurred by reference to the statutory provisions.[52]

The impact of Personal Property Security legislation on traditional conceptions of security interest has been well-nigh revolutionary.[53] The revolutionary impact of the legislation in this sphere was confirmed by the Supreme Court of Canada in *Royal Bank of Canada v Sparrow Electric Corp ('Sparrow')*.[54] Here the court acknowledged that for practical purposes the distinction between fixed and floating charges and between legal and equitable security interests had been swept away. The *Sparrow* case will now be examined in detail with particular reference to the nature of attachment.

6 THE *SPARROW* CASE

In *Sparrow* the Royal Bank of Canada made loan facilities available to Sparrow, a large electrical contractor, and security for this funding arrangement was obtained through the use of two mechanisms, one of which involved the taking of an assignment of the debtor's inventory pursuant to s 427 of the federal Bank Act 1991. The second mechanism entailed recourse to the registration procedure under the PPSA and the execution of a general security agreement covering the debtor's present and after-acquired property. The debtor experienced financial difficulties and a 'stand-still' agreement was drawn up under which the bank was entitled, on default, to appoint a receiver over the debtor's assets and enforce its security. A receiver was appointed and it was discovered that, both before and after the execution of the stand-still agreement, the debtor had in effect been using the revenue as an extra source of credit. Payroll deductions had been made for employee income taxes but these had not been remitted to the Revenue Canada as required by the federal Income Tax Act.

Section 227 of the Income Tax Code creates a statutory deemed trust in favour of Revenue Canada over unremitted income tax deductions. Section 227(5) provides that notwithstanding any provision of the insolvency legislation, in the event of any liquidation, assignment, receivership or bankruptcy of or by a person, an amount equal to unremitted tax deductions 'shall be deemed to be separate from and form no part of the estate in liquidation, assignment, receivership or bankruptcy, whether or not that amount has in fact been kept separate and apart from the person's own moneys or from the assets of the estate'.[55] According to the Supreme Court the statutory deemed trust lacked the

---

52 See also *Euroclean Canada Inc v Forest Glade Investments Ltd* (1985) 49 OR (2d) 769 and see generally Ziegel 'Recent and Prospective Developments in the Personal Property Security Area' (1985) 10 *Canadian Business Law Journal* 131 at pp 148–54.

53 For similar decisions in Saskatchewan and Manitoba, respectively, see: *Royal Bank v GM Homes Inc* (1984) 10 DLR (4th) 439 and *Roynat Inc v United Rescue Services Ltd* (1982) 2 PPSAC 49.

54 (1997) 143 DLR (4th) 385; on which see Davis (1998) above n 47.

55 It should be noted, however, that in the wake of the *Sparrow* decision the legislation was amended so as to bring about the substantive reversal of the decision; see Department of Finance Canada New Release 97-97-030, 'Unremitted Source Deductions and Unpaid GST' (April 7, 1997); see www.fin.gc.ca/. It appears however that the amendments may not have quite the effect that was apparently intended; on this see *Royal Bank v Tuxedo Transportation Ltd* (1999) 6 CBR (4th) 385 and Wood and Reeson 'The Continuing Saga of The Statutory Deemed Trusts' (2000) 15 *Banking & Finance Law Review* 515.

traditional attributes of a trust in that its subject matter could not be identified from the date of the trust's creation. The identification of the subject matter of the trust occurred *ex post facto* in that the Revenue was given a statutory right to access whatever assets the employer then had and then to realise from those assets the original trust debt. The statutory deemed trust however could not attach to assets which already belonged beneficially to third parties. To construe the statute in any other fashion would be to violate long-established principles of statutory interpretation in that it would be to permit the expropriation of the property of third parties who were not specifically mentioned in the statute.[56]

The crucial question was, therefore, did the debtor's secured property belong beneficially to the bank once the security agreement had been executed? The Supreme Court answered this question in the affirmative and in doing delved into the fundamentals of the PPSA. The general tenor of the PPSA was that, in the absence of an express intention to the contrary, a security interest in all present and after-acquired personal property will attach whenever that agreement is executed by the parties.[57] Upon attachment, the security becomes in law a fixed and specific charge over the collateral. The bank, therefore, had a fixed and specific charge and this was coupled with a licence to deal in that the debtor had expressly been granted permission to sell the encumbered inventory. The charge attached on execution of the security agreement. The court went on to say that the secured creditor becomes the legal owner of inventory as it comes into possession of the debtor; subject, however, to the debtor's right of redemption.

The court said that the critical significance of the characterisation of an interest as being fixed or floating was that it described the extent to which a creditor could be said to have a proprietary interest in the collateral. During the period in which a charge over inventory was floating the creditor possessed no legal title to that collateral. Therefore, if a statutory trust or lien attaches in this period, it attaches to the debtor's interest and thus takes priority over a subsequently crystallised floating charge. On the other hand, if the security interest was properly characterised as fixed or specific, it would take priority over a subsequent statutory trust or lien for all that the lien could attach to was the debtor's equity of redemption.

The court recognised that personal property security legislation had fundamentally changed the characterisation of security interests. While the position pre-PPSA was that a security agreement purporting to create a floating charge could be said to remain unattached to the collateral until crystallisation, this was no longer the case. The court approved academic commentary to the effect that once a floating charge has attached under the PPSA it has no floating attributes even though the security agreement, whether expressly or by implication, gives the debtor considerable powers to dispose of the collateral in the course of its business. The collateral might change its character because of

---

56 Reference was made in this connection to the following observations of Martland J in *Board of Industrial Relations v Avco Financial Services Realty Ltd* (1979) 98 DLR (3d) 695 at p 699: 'The property to which a [tax] lien attaches is not defined or identified. In the absence of a specific statutory provision to that effect, in my view it should not be construed in a manner which could deprive third parties of their pre-existing property rights.' Mention was also made of the statement of Twaddle JA in *Pembina on the Red Development Corp Ltd v Triman Industries Ltd* (1991) 85 DLR (4th) 29 at p 46 that '[I]t is a long-established principle of law that, in the absence of clear language to the contrary, a tax on one person cannot be collected out of property belonging to another'.

57 See s 11 of the Ontario PPSA.

the debtor's power of disposition but this did not change the nature of the security interest. Reference was made to an implicit legislative declaration that, as a matter of public policy, there was nothing objectionable to having a fixed charge on stock-in-trade of a debtor coupled with a licence to deal with the collateral in the ordinary course of business. The court went so far as to approve the statement by Professor Ron Cuming that 'there can be no such thing as a floating charge under a Personal Property Security Act'.[58]

7 ATTACHMENT AND CRYSTALLISATION OF A FLOATING CHARGE

The concept of attachment under the PPSA should be contrasted with the position that exists in England in equity and common law under the floating charge. Once an instrument of charge has been executed, the floating charge is a presently existing security interest even though it does not attach to any specific interest until crystallisation.[59] This seems a subtle distinction – presently existing but not attaching.[60] In one sense it seems to exist yet on the other hand, it does not. The 'present existence' of the floating charge is demonstrated by three factors. First, if the floating charge extends over land the security instrument must comply with the formality requirements laid down in the Law of Property (Miscellaneous Provisions) Act 1989 and the predecessor provisions in the Law of Property Act 1925 on the basis that the agreement creates an immediately subsisting 'interest in land'.[61] Secondly, the floating chargeholder can apply for an injunction to restrain the debtor from disposing of assets otherwise than in the ordinary course of business.[62] Thirdly, and this covers largely the same territory as the second point, the floating chargeholder has an inherent right to apply to the court for the appointment of a receiver if his security is in jeopardy.[63] Finally, the overall message is further reinforced by an analysis of the priority picture that arises when two floating charges containing after-acquired property clauses are in competition. Assuming that both have been duly registered, the first in point of time prevails,[64] whereas if there was no security agreement in existence until the property came into existence, one would assume that the two

---

58 The statement comes from 'Commercial Law ... Floating Charges and Fixed Charges of After-Acquired Property ...' (1988) 67 *Canadian Bar Review* 506 at pp 510–11.

59 See the comments of Buckley LJ in *Evans v Rival Granite Quarries Ltd* [1910] 2 KB 979 at p 999: 'A floating charge is not a future security; it is a present security which presently affects all the assets of the company expressed to be included in it ... A floating security is not a specific mortgage of the assets, plus a licence to the mortgagor to dispose of them in the course of his business, but is a floating mortgage applying to every item comprised in the security, but not specifically affecting any item until some act or event occurs or some act on the part of the mortgagee is done which causes it to crystallise into a fixed security.' See also the observations of Kekewich J in *Brunton v Electrical Engineering Corp* [1892] 1 Ch 434 at p 440.

60 Note the statement of Dixon J in *Barcelo v Electrolytic Zinc Co of Australasia Ltd* (1932) 48 CLR 391 at p 420 that 'some degree of abstraction is involved in this description of the operation of a floating charge as a present security over assets'.

61 *Driver v Broad* [1893] 1 QB 744; *Wallace v Evershed* [1899] 1 Ch 891.

62 *Re Woodroffes (Musical Instruments) Ltd* [1986] Ch 366 at pp 377–78 per Nourse J; *Tricontinental Corp Ltd v Commissioner of Taxation* [1988] 1 Qd R 474 at p 484.

63 See: *McMahon v North Kent Ironworks Co* [1891] 2 Ch 148; *Edwards v Standard Rolling Stock Syndicate* [1893] 1 Ch 574; *Re Victoria Steamboats Ltd* [1897] 1 Ch 158; *Re London Pressed Hinge Co Ltd* [1905] 1 Ch 576; *Norton v Yates* [1906] 1 KB 112 and see generally WJ Gough *Company Charges* (London, Butterworths, 2nd edn, 1996) at pp 132–34.

64 *Re Benjamin Cope & Sons Ltd* [1914] 1 Ch 800; but cf *Re Automatic Bottle Makers Ltd* [1926] Ch 412.

agreements would rank equally. The answer lies in the fact that from the very moment that the first security instrument is executed there is a presently existing security. As one commentator puts the matter:

> In other words, it creates an inchoate security interest which is waiting for the asset to be acquired so that it can fasten on to the asset but which, upon acquisition of the asset, takes effect as from the date of the security agreement.[65]

Yet the floating charge does not attach until crystallisation. This means that there are some significant differences between the position in England and that in Ontario under the OPPSA. These differences will be discussed under three heads: (1) effect on execution creditors; (2) dispositions of assets in the ordinary course of business; (3) priorities between security interests.

8 EXECUTION CREDITORS

Assets within the category embraced by the floating charge are liable to be seized by the debtor's judgment creditors up until the time that the floating charge crystallises.[66] So in a sense the debtor has a cushion of free assets that is liable to attack by judgment creditors. But this window of opportunity is quite small and as one commentator reasons is likely to benefit only 'an extremely nimble and fleetfooted unsecured creditor'.[67] The position of the unsecured creditor is, in this respect, even worse in Ontario for the 'window' is not open; even for a short period of time. An execution creditor is prejudiced in that, under the common law, assets subject to an uncrystallised floating charge would be available for payment of the debt but this is no longer the case under the OPSSA. Put another way, an unsecured creditor who seeks payment from the collateral takes subject to all prior perfected security interests, including those held in liquid or floating assets. This is because the floating charge is already statutorily deemed to have attached. Notwithstanding the wording of s 11(2) of the OPPSA, judges were at one stage hesitant in coming to this conclusion.[68] The reluctance has been explained on the basis that a secured party should not be allowed to blow hot and cold – to allow the debtor to continue to carry on business as before until there is a crystallising event and at the same time to deny execution creditors the right to enforce a judgment against the debtor's assets. The argument continues:

> The threat of execution creditor super-priority operated to significantly encourage closer monitoring as well as crystallization and enforcement on the first sign of cessation of the debtor's economic viability. Absent that threat, unsecured creditors can no longer rely on

---

65 RM Goode *Legal Problems of Credit and Security*, above n 25, at p 34.

66 See generally RJ Calnan 'Priorities Between Execution Creditors and Floating Charges' (1982) 10 *New Zealand Universities Law Review* 111.

67 Ziegel 'Canadian Perspectives on "How Far is Article 9 Exportable"' (1996) 27 *Canadian Business Law Journal* 226 at p 238.

68 See, for example, *Access Advertising Management Inc v Servex Computers Inc* (1994) 15 OR (3d) 635 and see generally Ziegel 'Recent and Prospective Developments in the Personal Property Security Law Area' (1985) 10 *Canadian Business Law Journal* 131 at pp 148–54.

the debtor's general secured lender to terminate the debtor's business dealings sufficiently early to minimize their losses.[69]

The reluctance could also be rationalised on legal grounds by using the argument that because the parties had employed the old terminology of the floating charge in their security agreement they had implicitly agreed to postpone the time for attachment until crystallisation had taken place in the traditional conception of things. This judicial view is, however, no longer in the ascendancy. The theory of implied contracting out has been abandoned. Courts now balk at the suggestion that a security party intended to forego the advantages of a presently attaching security interest merely by using, in a relatively carefree way, the old language of the floating charge.[70]

9 DISPOSITIONS IN THE ORDINARY COURSE OF BUSINESS

Under a floating charge the debtor has authority to dispose of assets within the class secured, in the ordinary course of business, until that authority is brought to an end by the process of crystallisation of the floating charge.[71] Under the OPPSA the old distinction between fixed and floating charges is swept away with the statute applying to every transaction, regardless of form, that secures payment or performance of an obligation.[72] The overarching notion of a security interest surely implies restrictions on the debtor's freedom to dispose of assets in the ordinary course of business – or does it? Section 28 of the OPPSA provides that a buyer of goods from a seller who sells the goods in the ordinary course of business takes them free from any security interest therein given by the seller even though it is perfected and the buyer knows of it, unless the buyer also knows that the sale constituted a breach of the security agreement.[73]

At common law a buyer of goods, which are subject to a fixed equitable charge (which would include a crystallised floating charge) will, in accordance with general principles, be adversely affected by the charge if he has actual as distinct from constructive knowledge of its existence.[74] The doctrine of constructive notice has been held not to apply to commercial transactions because of the speed with which business necessarily has to be conducted.[75] The difference with the position under the OPPSA is

---

69 See Bridge, Macdonald, Simmonds and Walsh 'Formalism, Functionalism, and Understanding the Law of Secured Transactions' (1999) 44 *McGill Law Journal* 567 at n 206 and the main text thereat.

70 See: *Canadian Imperial Bank of Commerce v Otto Timm Enterprises Ltd* (1991) 130 DLR (4th) 91; *Credit Suisse Canada v Yonge Street Holdings Ltd* (1996) 62 ACWS (3d) 497.

71 See generally Goode *Legal Problems of Credit And Security*, above n 25, at chapter 3.

72 Section 2 of the Act. Some commentators however, would assert that this apparent preoccupation with functionalism only goes so far – see generally Bridge, Macdonald, Simmonds and Walsh, above n 69.

73 For the position in Canada before modern personal property security legislation see Ziegel 'The Legal Problems of Wholesale Financing of Durable Goods in Canada' (1963) 41 *Canadian Bar Review* 54 at pp 76–96.

74 *Feuer Leather Corp v Frank Johnstone & Sons* [1981] Com LR 251.

75 See the celebrated comments of Lindley LJ in *Manchester Trust v Furness* [1895] 2 QB 539 at p 545: 'The equitable doctrines of constructive notice are common enough in dealing with land and estates, with which the Court is familiar; but there have been repeated protests against the introduction into commercial transactions of anything like an extension of those doctrines, and the protest is founded on perfect good sense. In dealing with estates in land title is everything, and it can be leisurely investigated; in commercial transactions possession is everything and there is not time to investigate title; and if we were to extend the doctrine of constructive notice to commercial transactions we should be doing infinite mischief and paralysing the trade of the country.'

that the buyer in that scheme of things will only be caught by the security interest not only if he actually knows of its existence but also he must know that the sale constitutes a breach of some restrictive provision in the security agreement.[76]

The Alberta equivalent of s 28 of the OPPSA was considered by the Supreme Court of Canada in *Sparrow*.[77] In this case a bank took a PPSA security interest which included an after-acquired property clause. The court was unanimous in holding that the security interest attached upon execution of the security agreement. There was substantial disagreement, however, in relation to the scope of the debtor's licence to deal with the assets, subject to the security, in the ordinary course of business. The minority took the view that as a result of this licence the bank's claim to the inventory must give way to any debts incurred in the ordinary course of business. In their opinion the debtor was permitted to sell its inventory in the ordinary course of its business and 'use' the proceeds generated therefrom. It was suggested that the licence in this case necessarily included a licence to sell inventory to pay wages, and remit wage deductions, in the course of the debtor's business. This view was grounded on the fact that the secured party had security over the majority of the assets of the debtor. Basically, the bank was a large-scale lender who permitted the debtor to use inventory sales to maintain the viability of its enterprise. In consequence, the licence must permit the debtor to sell the inventory and put it to the general use of its business, including towards the payment of wages. This necessarily included payroll deduction obligations. The minority judges were also of the opinion that to apply a licence theory in this particular context was not to produce undue uncertainty. In their view the licence operated narrowly and fairly and, in addition to providing certainty in disputes between consensual and non-consensual security interests, achieved fairness in commercial law. The bank was willing to accept the benefits of Sparrow's non-payment of statutory deductions and permitted the use of its collateral to pay these deductions but refused to accept the burden of Sparrow's unlawful action at the time of its receivership. The minority judges said that it should be the policy of the law to ensure that the bank was held responsible for the debtor's outstanding statutory obligations and the licence theory ensured that in appropriate circumstances this result would obtain.[78]

The majority, however, took a more limited view on the scope of the licence. In their conception of things the security interest in the inventory disappeared only if the debtor actually sells the inventory and applies the proceeds to the debt of a third party. According to s 28(1) of the PPSA, the effect of a sale of inventory was to give the purchaser an unencumbered interest in the inventory and the licensor a continuing security interest in the proceeds of sale. It was only where the debtor subsequently used the proceeds to satisfy an obligation to a third party that the proceeds were removed from the scope of the licensor's security interest in them. In a colourful expression it was said

---

76 The rationale of the Ontario provision has been described by McLaren *The Ontario Personal Property Security Act*, above n 10, at p 119: 'The Act acknowledges that it would be detrimental to the marketplace to force willing buyers to conduct a search of the registry in the ordinary course of business transactions, as this would dramatically increase the time which it would take to complete simple daily sales transactions. In this regard, s 28 represents the end result of the trading off of the ability of a secured party to continue a security interest in transferred collateral and permitting the marketplace to function unimpeded by transactional obstacles such as the Act. Section 28(1) is, thus, a marketplace certainty rule.'

77 (1997) 143 DLR (4th) 385 at p 422.

78 (1997) 143 DLR (4th) 385 at pp 422–23.

that the statute occupied the field and crowded out other possible interpretations of the licence. A number of policy considerations were invoked to support this conclusion. The court said that judicial innovation in this field risked legal uncertainty. Inventory financiers would have to provide against the risk that their security interest might be defeated by some rival claim and there was also a real possibility that recognition of a broad licence theory would obliterate the PPSA charge against inventory. If Parliament wished to do so, it could step in and assign absolute priority to the deemed trust but, in the absence of clear statutory language to that effect, the bank's general security agreement must prevail.[79]

The foundation stone of the licence theory is the judgment of McLachlin JA in *R v FBDB*.[80] In this case, at issue was a question of priority between a bank debenture and a provincial sales tax secured by a statutory lien over amounts that had been collected by the debtor following the sale of inventory but had not yet been remitted to the provincial government. The case was decided prior to the enactment of the British Columbia PPSA 1989 and a majority in the Provincial Court of Appeal took the view that even if the debenture created a fixed charge coupled with a licence to sell in the ordinary course of business, the provincial sales tax took priority.[81] This view was grounded on the proposition that the licence necessarily included a power to satisfy obligations that arose incidentally on sales such as the remission of sales tax to the provincial government. When the bank gave the debtor the power to sell the mortgaged goods in the ordinary course of business, the bank must be taken to have tacitly accepted that it would cede its priority not only to *bona fide* purchasers for value, but to other persons who might acquire rights incidental to such sales. McLachlin JA observed:

> [T]he licence to sell in the ordinary course of business must be taken as encompassing the ordinary incidents of business, including statutory liens arising as a result of sales tax, with the result that FBDB's charge is subject not only to the title of purchasers but to the lien for tax arising from sales.[82]

Perhaps it should be noted that McLachlin JA (since elevated to the Supreme Court of Canada) was part of the majority in *Sparrow* whose judgment was delivered by Iacobucci J.[83] Two grounds were given for distinguishing *FBDB* in *Sparrow*. First, Iacobucci J said that income taxes were not like sales taxes in that they were not as directly related to sales of inventory as sales taxes. Moreover, in his view, while the bank's charge was against the inventory, it did not extend so far as the sales taxes generated by a sale of inventory. It is submitted that this reasoning is somewhat unconvincing. A security agreement will

---

79 (1997) 143 DLR (4th) 385 at pp 431–33.

80 (1987) 43 DLR (4th) 188. The case is analysed in detail by Cuming 'Commercial Law – Floating Charges and Fixed Charges of After-Acquired Property' (1988) 67 *Canadian Bar Review* 506.

81 This is very much a 'but if' conclusion. The majority of the court were firmly of the view that a fixed charge coupled with a licence to sell in the ordinary course of business was a conceptual impossibility. This conclusion reflects the preponderance of judicial opinion in England. There was, however, a divergent line of authority in Canada which the court in *FBDB* firmly squashed; on which see Wood 'Floating Charges in Canada' (1989) 27 *Alberta Law Review* 191. In many ways the greatest change brought about by PPSA legislation has been to recognise that fixed security is not incompatible with a freedom on the part of the debtor to dispose of assets in the ordinary course of business.

82 (1987) 43 DLR (4th) 188 at p 227.

83 The majority in *Sparrow* consisted of Sopinka, McLachlin, Iacobucci and Major JJ with La Forest, Gonthier and Cory JJ dissenting. The minority judgment was delivered by Gonthier J.

normally embrace proceeds as well as inventory. The total purchase price paid by a buyer of inventory surely constitutes 'proceeds of sale' in the hands of the seller. Perhaps there is more merit in Iacobucci J's second ground which focuses on the fact that the *FBDB* case was decided before the British Columbia version of the PPSA was enacted. The British Columbia court, therefore, had greater latitude to interpret a licence to sell as a tacit consent to a reduction of the security interest in the inventory. In Iacobucci J's opinion, in the post-PPSA era something more than an unadorned licence to sell was needed to justify the conclusion that a creditor intended to abridge considerably its security interest in inventory. More generally, the judge was concerned about the ambit of an untramelled application of the licence theory. On the majority view, a licence to sell inventory necessarily included a power to satisfy obligations that would ordinarily be met from the proceeds of sale of inventory but which were not in fact met in the particular case. Iacobucci J considered that this would completely eviscerate the bank's general security agreement and turn the system of priorities established by the PPSA on its head. He said:

> The satisfaction of any legitimate debt or obligation, whenever incurred, is arguably 'in the ordinary course of business'. Certainly the payment of creditors is a permissible 'use' of the proceeds of a sale of inventory. Following my colleague's reasoning, this would mean that every subsequent claim should prevail over the respondent's general security agreement, because every rival claim might have been satisfied out of the proceeds of a hypothetical sale of the inventory. Moreover, the priority rules of the PPSA, whose general policy is to assign priority to the earliest registered security interest, would be turned on their head.[84]

It is now appropriate to consider the priority question.

10 PRIORITIES WITH RESPECT TO THE FLOATING CHARGE AND UNDER THE PPSA

In England, when a company becomes insolvent, the fixed chargeholders are paid ahead of floating chargeholders with preferential creditors coming in between the two. The categories of preferential creditors are set out in Sched 6 to the Insolvency Act 1986 and basically cover certain unpaid taxes and employee claims. The hierarchy of payment runs as follows; fixed charge creditors, preferential creditors, floating charge creditors and then unsecured creditors at the bottom of the pile. This order of priority for claims applies in the majority of situations. But there is a minor complication if the floating charge contains what is known as a negative pledge, or restrictive clause, that is, a clause prohibiting the creation of subsequent charges ranking in priority to or *pari passu* with the existing floating charge. It has been held that if a subsequent fixed chargeholder has actual notice, as distinct from constructive notice, of the restrictive clause, he will be postponed, priority-wise, to the floating charge. The law in this area was reviewed by the Irish Supreme Court in *Welch v Bowmaker (Ireland) Ltd*.[85] Here, the floating chargeholder argued that the subsequent fixed chargeholder should be fixed with constructive notice of the provision in the floating charge precluding the company from creating a mortgage which would have priority over the floating charge. Henchy J said that since such a prohibition was more or less common form in modern debentures, there was much to be

---

84 (1997) 143 DLR (4th) 385 at pp 427–28.
85 [1980] IR 251.

said for applying the doctrine of constructive notice in such a situation were it not settled law that there was no duty on the bank in these circumstances to seek out the precise terms of the debenture.[86] Actual or express notice of the prohibition must exist before the subsequent mortgagee could be deprived of priority.[87]

If a floating chargeholder has priority over a fixed chargeholder in a particular case because the fixed chargeholder has actual notice of a restrictive clause in the floating charge debenture, this gives rise to circularity problem. What about the preferential creditors who, in terms of priorities, are in between the fixed and floating charges? There has been some judicial disagreement on this issue. One view holds that by coming after the floating charge, the fixed charge should therefore come after the preferential creditors.[88] Another view is to apply the doctrine of subrogation, that is, that by virtue of the altered priorities between them, the floating chargeholder stands in the shoes of the fixed chargeholder to the extent of the amount secured by the fixed charge and therefore the floating chargeholder will be paid ahead of preferential creditors by the degree to which liabilities are secured by a fixed charge.[89]

If fixed and floating charges were statutorily assimilated, and no other legislative steps were taken, this would have the consequence that all secured creditors would be paid ahead of preferential creditors. The latter would lose out in a major way. A variety of arguments have been advanced for recognising claims by particular categories of creditors to preferential status.[90] As far as claims by governmental entities are concerned, such creditors are said to be involuntary and not consciously to have assumed the risk of the debtor's insolvency.[91] It is also arguable that they are not in a position effectively to monitor the debtor's behaviour and to assess the risk of default or insolvency. The recent DTI/Insolvency Service White Paper[92] proposes abolishing Crown preference but only as part of an 'integrated package of measures' whereby in return floating chargeholders would lose their veto over the appointment of an administrator and also their entitlement to appoint an administrative receiver would be removed. Moreover, it is proposed that a certain proportion of floating charge recoveries should be set aside for the benefit of unsecured creditors.[93] In the earlier report by a DTI and HM Treasury Review Group, *A Review of Company Rescue and Business Reconstruction Mechanisms*, it was stressed that the

---

86 [1980] IR 251 at p 256. The judge went on to say that it would be unfair to single out the bank for condemnatory treatment because of their failure to ascertain the full terms of the debenture when what they did was in accord with judicially approved practice and where such a precipitate change in the law would undermine the intended validity of many other transactions.

87 See also *Re Castell & Brown Ltd* [1898] 1 Ch 315. However, note the de Lacy essay above at p 378.

88 See *Re Portbase Clothing Ltd* [1993] Ch 388.

89 See *Re Woodroffes (Musical Instruments) Ltd* [1986] Ch 366.

90 See generally Keay and Walton 'The Preferential Debts Regime in Liquidation Law: In the Public Interest?' [1999] *Company, Financial and Insolvency Law Review* 84; and see also for a Canadian perspective Cantlie 'Preferred Priority in Bankruptcy' in Ziegel (ed) *Current Developments in International and Comparative Corporate Insolvency Law* (Oxford, Clarendon Press, 1994) at p 413.

91 See generally the report by the Department of Trade and Industry and HM Treasury Review Group *A Review of Company Rescue and Business Reconstruction Mechanisms* (London, TSO, 2000).

92 (2001) Cm 5234, above n 8.

93 See (2001) Cm 5234, above n 8, at para 2.19.

benefits flowing from any abolition or waiver of Crown preference should go to unsecured creditors rather than to the holders of floating charges.[94]

As far as claims to preferential status are concerned, employees, on the other hand, stand in a slightly different position. The main justification for according them such status rests on the proposition that employees effectively lose out in the struggle to be paid in an insolvency because they lack the economic muscle to bargain for security rights. The proposed insolvency reforms suggest the retention of employee preferential rights though the reason for this recommendation are not rehearsed in any detail or indeed at all.[95]

11 THE CANADIAN BANKRUPTCY JURISDICTION

What about the priority picture in Ontario? Well, Canada has been described as a secured creditor's heaven with 21st century personal property security law but 19th century bankruptcy law.[96] As we have seen, in Ontario it is very easy to create and perfect a security interest in all types of property including after-acquired property. Broadly based security interests, covering a wide range of debtor assets, seem now to be the norm for all types of business loans. Given the strengthening of the position of secured creditors one would expect some countervailing legislative response but, on the whole, the legislative reaction has been muted. In part this may be because of the federal/provincial jurisdictional divide in Canada. Bankruptcy and insolvency are matters within the domain of the Federal Government under the Canadian constitution but personal property security law is a provincial matter.[97] The provinces have authority over 'property and civil rights' which covers private commercial law including debtor-creditor relationships.[98] It has been argued by Professor Cuming that the federal legislature has adopted a 'hands-off' approach to bankruptcy law. This approach has had the effect of insulating secured creditors from policies enshrined in provincial law that were designed to protect the most vulnerable of unsecured creditors as well as protecting important

---

94 See *A Review of Company Rescue and Business Reconstruction Mechanisms*, above n 91, at p 26. While the report was actually delivered to the DTI and HM Treasury in May 2000 it was only published in November 2000.

95 See (2001) Cm 5234, above n 8, at para 2.20: 'The preferential status of certain claims by employees in insolvency proceedings, such as wages and holiday pay within certain limits, will remain, as will the rights of those subrogated to them.'

96 See Cuming 'Second Generation Personal Property Security Legislation in Canada' (1981–82) 46 *Saskatchewan Law Review* 5 at p 42.

97 See ss 91 and 92 of the Constitution Act 1867.

98 Also worth mentioning is the federal jurisdiction over banks which has led the Federal Government to devise a special security instrument available only to banks. The provision was first introduced in its modern guise in the Bank Act 1890, s 31, and is now to be found in s 427 of the Bank Act 1991. The rationale of these provisions has been judicially stated as follows: 'It is to be borne in mind that the Parliament of Canada has enacted these sections, not so much for the benefit of banks as for the benefit of manufacturers, but principally to provide a convenient and suitable means for the provision and application of capital to industry with the object that thus manufacturing and commercial enterprise in Canada may be encouraged ...' per Martin JA in *Bank of Montreal v Guarantee Silk Dyeing Finishing Co* (1935) 4 DLR 483 at p 490. It is arguable that the advent of modern personal property security legislation has diminished the need for Bank Act security; on which see generally Cuming and Wood 'Compatibility of Federal and Provincial Personal Property Security Law' (1986) 65 *Canadian Bar Review* 267 and Ziegel 'Harmonization of Section 427 of the Bank Act and the Personal Property Security Acts: Is there a Better Solution?' (1997) 12 *Banking and Finance Law Review* 425. Note also Wood 'The Nature and Definition of Federal Security Interests' (2000) 34 *Canadian Business Law Journal* 65.

sources of provincial revenue.[99] On the other hand, another distinguished commentator expresses the view that it would be a serious mistake to read the 'provincial PPS legislation in isolation from the many countermovements diluting or trumping the priorities established by the Acts'.[100]

One provision that is worth noting in this connection is s 244 of the Bankruptcy and Insolvency Act (BIA) which requires a secured creditor to give prior notice to the debtor of the intention to appoint a receiver over the debtor's assets.[101] The provision applies to secured creditors who intend to enforce a security interest over the whole or substantially the whole of a debtor's inventory, accounts receivable or other property. The effect of this provision is that enforcement of the security interest is not permitted to take place until 10 days after service of the notice on the debtor. The delay may enable the debtor to locate alternative sources of funding or alternatively to file a business re-organisation plan under the business rehabilitation provisions of the BIA which will result in an automatic stay on creditor enforcement proceedings.

Another important provision is the super-priority status accorded unpaid sellers of goods in certain circumstances under the BIA.[102] Such persons are entitled to repossess the goods from bankrupt business debtors provided that the demand is made within 30 days of delivery and the goods are still in an identifiable state and have not been resold in the meantime. The repossession right becomes exercisable if the debtor has become bankrupt or where a receiver has been appointed over the debtor's assets. Moreover, the right to repossess conferred by the section is said to rank above every other claim or right against the purchaser in respect of those goods, other than the right of a *bona fide* subsequent purchaser of the goods for value without notice that the supplier had demanded repossession of the goods.

12 THE DEEMED STATUTORY TRUST

What about provincial government claims for recovery of unpaid taxes and other levies from bankrupt businesses? There has been a whole gamut of provincial legislation awarding super-priority status to tax and other claims; usually by using the deemed trust device. Such claims include sales taxes collected at the point of sale by vendors and income taxes and unemployment insurance contributions collected from the wages and salaries of employees by employers. Provincial legislation would typically provide that every person who deducts or withholds any amount under the relevant legislation shall be deemed to hold the amount so deducted or withheld in trust for the Crown in right of

99 See generally Cuming 'Canadian Bankruptcy Law: A Secured Creditor's Heaven' in Ziegel (ed) *Current Developments in International and Comparative Corporate Insolvency Law* (Oxford, Clarendon Press, 1994) 379 at p 395.

100 See Ziegel 'Canadian Perspectives on "How Far is Article 9 Exportable"' (1996) 27 *Canadian Business Law Journal* 226 at p 244.

101 The legislative provision in fact reinforces some common law developments in Canada following on from the decision of the Supreme Court in *Lister Ltd v Dunlop Canada Ltd* (1982) 135 DLR (3d) 1.

102 Section 81 of the Act; on which see Klotz 'Protection of Unpaid Suppliers Under the New Bankruptcy and Insolvency Act' (1993) 21 *Canadian Business Law Journal* 161.

the province.[103] The statute might also go on to provide that the amount collected shall be deemed to be held separate from and form no part of the collector's money, assets or estate, whether or not the amount of the tax has in fact been kept separate and apart from the collector's own money, assets or estate.[104] The constitutionality of provincial deemed trusts provisions was considered in the *Henfrey Samson* case.[105] This is a case where a company charged its assets to a bank to secure a loan. The company collected provincial sales tax but instead of keeping the collections separate, as it was statutorily required to do, it mingled the amounts with its general accounts. The provincial government claimed that the relevant tax statute created a statutory trust over the company's assets with respect to the amount of the collected sales tax and that this statutory trust had priority over the bank's security. What is now s 67(1) of the Bankruptcy and Insolvency Act (BIA) includes the provision that the property of a bankrupt divisible among his creditors shall not comprise '... property held by the bankrupt in trust for any other person'. The word 'trust' is however not defined in the BIA. The question arises whether the provinces are free to define 'trust' for their own purposes or whether or not there is some conception of 'trust' in what might be referred to as federal common law that would override provincial statutory provisions. The matter is now dealt with in s 67(3) which provides that subject to certain specified exceptions and notwithstanding any federal or provincial legislative provincial, property shall not be regarded as being held on trust for the federal or provincial government unless it would be so regarded in the absence of the statutory provision. This provision, however, was not in force at the time of the *Henfrey Samson* decision.

In *Henfrey Samson* the Supreme Court held that to interpret the Bankruptcy Statute as encompassing statutory trusts created by the provinces that lacked the common law attributes of trusts, would be to permit the provinces to create their own priorities under the Bankruptcy Act and to invite a differential scheme of distribution on bankruptcy from province to province.[106] The provincial statute stipulated that tax collected shall be deemed to be held separate from and form no part of the collector's money, assets or estate. In the court's view, the deeming provision tacitly acknowledged that after conversion the statutory trust bears little resemblance to a true trust. There was no property which could be regarded as being impressed with a trust. The provinces could define 'trust' as they chose for matters within their own legislative competence, but they could not dictate to Parliament how it should be defined for purposes of the Bankruptcy and Insolvency Act.[107] A contrary interpretation, according to the court, would have the effect of permitting the provinces to determine priorities on a bankruptcy; a matter within exclusive federal jurisdiction.

In situations outside formal bankruptcy proceedings, provincial law continues to apply nevertheless. Secured creditors, therefore, have a perverse incentive to put debtors

---

103 See for example, the Ontario Employment Standards Act 1980, s 15.

104 See generally Anne E Hardy *Crown Priority in Insolvency* (Toronto, Carswell, 1986).

105 *British Columbia v Henfrey Samson Belair Ltd* (1989) 59 DLR (4th) 726. See also *Re Bourgault* (1979) 105 DLR (3d) 270; *Re Deloitte, Haskins & Sells Ltd and Workers' Compensation Board* (1985) 19 DLR (4th) 577; *Husky Oil Operations Ltd v MNR* (1996) 128 DLR (4th) 1.

106 (1989) 59 DLR (4th) 726 at p 740.

107 (1989) 59 DLR (4th) 726 at p 742.

into formal bankruptcy so as to avoid the operation of provincial laws.[108] Furthermore, such tactical moves by creditors have been given the judicial imprimatur as not amounting to an abuse of the bankruptcy process. In *Bank of Montreal v Scott Road Enterprises Ltd*[109] the British Colombia Court of Appeal reiterated the point that a provincial statute cannot override the scheme of distribution set out in the Bankruptcy Act. In the event of bankruptcy, priorities were exclusively a matter for federal jurisdiction. The fact that a secured creditor invoked the provisions of the Bankruptcy Act to establish its priority in accord with the scheme of distribution provided by that Act could not constitute 'sufficient cause' for refusing to make a bankruptcy adjudication. This state of affairs, however, was strongly criticised by one judge in the case:

> The circumstances of this case illustrate starkly the inequitable consequences which can flow from permitting the debenture-holder to employ the Bankruptcy Act to destroy the priority which would otherwise have been enjoyed by the Crown and wage-earners ... The difficulty thus created for wage-earners may be very serious because the extent to which the legislative scheme can be set at naught by the device employed here may be almost complete. Most businesses large enough to have employees carry on at the sufferance of their bankers in the sense that their loans may be called on demand ... It follows that, in most cases, the bank will be in a position to do what was done here, that is, to employ its security to make the debtor effectively bankrupt, and then to petition it into bankruptcy. Because of the inherent flexibility of its security, the bank in all such cases will be in a position to time the appointment of a receiver, as was done here, to arrange matters so that the undertaking will have the benefit of the employees' efforts for a maximum period.[110]

Varying views have been expressed on the merits or otherwise of deemed trust legislation; particularly, provincial deemed trust legislation. On the one hand, is the opinion of one Supreme Court justice that '[f]rom the point of view of fairness, there would seem to be no objection to the provincial government creating a lien or charge on the assets of the vendor for the amount of the sales tax (and the trust funds) which the vendor was responsible for collecting and remitting to the province'.[111] On the other hand, the contrary position has been argued strongly in a federal government position paper as follows:

> These Crown privileges have created significant disparities between the treatment of Crown claims in bankruptcy and other claims which cannot be justified either on grounds that the Crown is an 'unwilling creditor' ... or on the grounds that the Crown warranted privileged status as a representative ... of ... taxpayers as a whole and that it should not be obliged to finance other creditors, such as banks.[112]

The federal Bankruptcy and Insolvency Act now specifically tackles the subject of deemed trusts. Section 67(2) of the BIA renders all statutory deemed trusts invalid, whether created by federal or provincial legislation, though there is an exception for those

---

108 *Federal Business Development Bank v Quebec* (1988) 50 DLR (4th) 577.

109 (1989) 57 DLR (4th) 623.

110 (1989) 57 DLR (4th) 623 at p 631 *per* Esson JA.

111 See the comments of Cory J in *British Columbia v Henfrey Samson Belair Ltd* (1989) 59 DLR (4th) 726 at p 730.

112 The quote comes from a 1988 paper released by the Legislative Review Branch, Policy Co-ordination Bureau, Department of Consumer and Corporate Affairs which is quoted by Cuming 'Canadian Bankruptcy Law: A Secured Creditor's Heaven' in Ziegel (ed), above n 90, at p 399.

enumerated in sub-s (3), namely deemed trusts created by the Income Tax Code, under the Canada Pension Plan and by the Unemployment Insurance legislation. Provincial deemed trusts are also given the imprimatur in two situations. The first is where the provincial legislation imposes a tax similar to that imposed by the federal Income Tax Act and the deemed trust has, as its sole purpose, the ensuring of payment of amounts required by provincial legislation to be deducted or withheld. The second situation is where the province is providing a comprehensive pension plan and the provincial legislation creates a similar deemed trust to that envisaged in the Canada Pension Plan. It is necessary that the deemed trust should have as its sole purpose the ensuring of amounts required by provincial legislation to be deducted or withheld for the pension payment.

Given the fact that the tentacles of the provincial deemed statutory trust have been shorn, the position of employees is quite parlous in Canada. Section 136 of the BIA accords employees preferred status for wages that may have accrued in the six-month period immediately preceding bankruptcy. It is, however, explicitly stated in the section that preferred creditors are expressly subject to the rights of secured creditors. Originally, the federal government intended to protect unpaid employees in the event of employer bankruptcy by establishing an insurance fund. The necessary legislation, however, failed to pass because of the strength of opposition from the business lobby who saw the funding mechanism for the scheme as another tax, or burden, on business. Some provincial governments have taken up the baton, including Ontario, which has introduced a Wage Protection Programme.[113] This scheme is intended to compensate employees for unpaid wage claims including those which arise out of an employer's bankruptcy. The legislation also subrogates the programme administrator to an unpaid employee's rights. In England, as we have seen, preferential creditors including, unpaid employees, are paid after fixed charge creditors but before floating chargeholders. Unpaid employees in England also have the added protection of the National Insurance Fund which serves partly as a wage guarantee scheme in the event of employer insolvency.[114]

13 CONCLUSIONS

If England moves over to a new regime governing security interests along the lines of the OPPSA then that will spell the demise of the traditional floating charge. That much is clear from the experience in Ontario. Under English common law the floating charge covers a class of assets (both present and future) leaving the debtor creating the charge with managerial freedom over the class of charged assets until what is known as a crystallising event occurs to bring that managerial freedom to an end. The floating charge, however, does not attach to any specific assets until crystallisation. By way of contrast, the security interest under new PPSA legislation would attach as soon as the secured property came into existence. The distinction between fixed and floating charges is obliterated with the debtor having freedom to dispose of all categories of charged assets in the ordinary course of business. Statutory assimilation of fixed and floating charges

---

113 See Employment Standards Act 1990 (as amended); on which see generally Cantlie 'Preferred Priority in Bankruptcy' in Ziegel (ed), above n 90, at p 413.
114 See Employment Rights Act 1996, Part XII.

would have adverse consequences for execution creditors but the major detriment is likely to be felt by preferential creditors.[115] At the moment, preferential creditors are paid after claims secured by fixed charges but outrank floating chargeholders. Where would a new English Personal Property Security Act leave preferential creditors or execution creditors? If no measures were put in place to protect their position they would be a lot worse off under the new legislation. It is questionable to what extent this state of affairs would be socially or politically acceptable.[116] Nor are banks particularly pressing for reforms. While reform on a North American model might offer some theoretical improvements on the present position, it also risks reopening old controversies, long since resolved in favour of banks, on the scope of secured creditors' rights. The recent Insolvency White Paper proposes cutting back on some of the advantages enjoyed by floating chargeholders and it is unlikely that secured creditors would welcome any more legislative trenching on their privileges. English law through the mechanism of the floating charge provides for the possibility of taking security in the widest possible range of circumstances and with the minimum of restrictions and formalities. There are no obstacles to the taking of security over property that may subsequently be acquired by the debtor and moreover, security can be taken to cover future advances by the creditor. Looking at the matter from the perspective of banks, there are dangers that these advantages might be sacrificed in a new system. When the alternatives remain to be determined, the attractions of the 'tried and trusted' are obvious.[117] This being so, the floating charge seems destined to remain as the workhorse of the English credit industry for the foreseeable future. Nevertheless, a study of the Ontario experience and a comparison with England does offer some illuminating insights into both the theoretical foundations of the floating charge and its practical applications.

---

115 As has been noted already the DTI/Insolvency Service White Paper, *Insolvency – A Second Chance*, above n 8, proposes the abolition of Crown preference with a certain proportion of floating charge realisations being set aside for unsecured creditors so as to ensure that the benefits of abolition go to unsecured creditors and not to floating chargeholders. It is proposed to retain the preferential status of certain employee claims as well as the preferential rights of those subrogated to such employee claims.

116 It should be noted that in New Zealand where a Personal Property Securities Act was enacted in 1999, although not yet in force, preferential creditors are given priority over the holders of security interests in inventory or accounts receivable; see generally on this point McLauchlan, above nn 16 and 35.

117 See generally Bridge 'How Far is Article 9 Exportable? The English Experience' (1996) 27 *Canadian Business Law Journal* 196.

CHAPTER 17

REFORMING CORPORATE RESCUE MECHANISMS

David Milman

1 INTRODUCTION

The theme of this collection of essays is the reform of UK Company Law. That reappraisal process has largely manifested itself through the laudable efforts of the Company Law Review Project. However, it must not be assumed that this project has taken sole ownership of the revision of the entirety of company law. Many key areas, for better or for worse, fell outside its purview, as the initial terms of reference made clear. Financial services and corporate insolvency, key components in any modern system of companies regulation, are but two examples of excluded subject areas.[1] One can understand the pragmatic reasons for this ordinance of self-denial, but it is a fallacy to assume that the 'core' of companies regulation can be evaluated without reference to matters of corporate insolvency. Fortunately, the Company Law Review team has not taken a blinkered approach to its task and has kept a close eye on developments in corporate insolvency law reform. Conversely, even within the 'core' area the Law Commission has played a significant revising role (for example, with regard to directors' duties[2] and shareholder remedies[3]). In this chapter it is intended to review the progress of reform in the area of corporate rescue, a subject which has not been considered in either forum, over the past 20 years and to indicate where further change is likely.

Reform comes in a variety of guises. At the most visible level we have enacted changes in legislation. Allied to this is the more subtle process of judicial interpretation; the constructive (and occasionally destructive) contribution of the judiciary must never be underestimated.[4] Finally, we may have to address new professional perspectives, changes in social norms, increased sophistication of regulatory behaviour and evolutionary processes in entrepreneurial culture, before arriving at a rounded picture of a reform process.

---

1   See the initial terms of reference of the Company Law Review *Company Law for a Competitive Economy* (London, DTI, March 1998) at para 6.1. As the review progressed the Steering Group trespassed into areas directly relevant to insolvency law – see, for example, its proposals in *Modern Company Law for a Competitive Economy: The Final Report* (London, DTI, 2001) on schemes of arrangement at chapter 13 and, on the control of 'phoenix companies' at paras 15.55–15.77; hereafter *The Final Report*.

2   See Law Commission Report No 261, *Company Directors: Regulating Conflicts of Interest and Formulating a Statement of Duties* (1999) Cm 4436 (London, TSO, 1999). Any tightening up of the regime governing directors' duties might have a knock-on effect on corporate rescue in that the incentive to access these formal procedures is increased by a less relaxed climate for managers.

3   See Law Commission Report No 246, *Shareholder Remedies* (1997) Cm 3769 (London, TSO, 1997).

4   I touched upon this in my paper at the 1991 Hart Workshop; see 'Administration Orders and the Courts' in H Rajak (ed) *Insolvency Law: Theory and Practice* (London, Sweet & Maxwell, 1993) at p 369.

2 A LACUNA IN ENGLISH LAW?

The limited liability company arising out of a simple incorporation procedure based upon registration arrived finally on the scene in 1855.[5] Early companies legislation paid little attention to the rehabilitation of distressed companies. The assumption was that if a company fell into difficulties the problem would be terminal and the best solution would be liquidation. Companies were artificial legal entities, viewed with considerable suspicion in many quarters, and few persons would shed a tear about an untimely 'death'. It must be recalled that this cavalier approach was being taken at a time when the UK economy was generally buoyant and, in global terms, largely pre-eminent. Where economic fluctuations occurred and the fortunes of individual companies floundered these disappointments were more than matched by economic successes elsewhere. If workers lost their livelihoods through business failure that was not a major financial concern for the State because the State did not provide either redundancy payments[6] or guarantee payments.[7] Some paternalistic relief was offered by the Preferential Payments in Bankruptcy Acts 1888 and 1897 in treating a limited number of employee claims as preferential debts, but for the most part the economic burden of enterprise failure often fell upon the displaced workers, their families and the local community.

Although corporate rescue was largely a barren landscape as far as legislation was concerned there were some signs of limited statutory engagement. The best example is provided by schemes of arrangement. Under a scheme of arrangement a company experiencing difficulty could restructure its financial relationships with members and creditors on obtaining their approval and after securing the sanction of the court. This mechanism has been included in Companies Acts for over a century.[8] Schemes of arrangement and reconstruction (now provided for by s 425 of the Companies Act 1985) are available both to solvent and insolvent companies. The procedures for exploiting the statutory mechanism are complex and require the approval of each distinct 'class' of creditors and members. As stated above, the sanction of the court must then be obtained before the arrangement can proceed. By no stretch of the imagination could they be said to represent an emergency response to a company in distress. In practice, their utility is limited to the larger-type enterprise with complex corporate financing structures and requiring a long-term solution. In recent years they have been extensively exploited by insurance companies for want of a better alternative.[9]

---

5   See Limited Liability Act 1855. For comment on the significance of this change see Milman in D Milman (ed) *Regulating Enterprise* (Oxford, Hart Publishing, 1999) at p 10.

6   Mandatory redundancy payments were only introduced via the Redundancy Payments Act 1965.

7   State guarantee payments are a policy favoured by the European Union where Directive EEC/80/987 is a critical foundation. For the current law in the UK see Employment Rights Act 1996 ss 182–90.

8   Schemes of arrangement can be traced back in company law to the Joint Stock Companies Arrangements Act 1870, which allowed companies in liquidation to make compositions or arrangements with creditors. This provision was remodelled by the Companies Act 1900, s 24 to include members' participation. The facility was extended to companies outside liquidation by Companies Act 1907, s 38, and the current model is based upon the formulation first appearing in the Companies (Consolidation) Act 1908, s 120.

9   This is because insurance companies could not exploit the other rehabilitation models until the provisions of the Financial Services and Markets Act 2000, s 360, came fully into effect. Insurance companies have also sought to make creative use of the provisional liquidation procedure in the event of difficulties arising – see here *Smith v UIC Insurance Co Ltd* [2001] BCC 11 at p 20 onwards *per* Judge Dean QC. The Company Law Review *The Final Report*, above n 1, at chapter 13 has made a number of recommendations to enhance the utility of the scheme of arrangement procedure.

The courts, as is often the case, became more enlightened once their initial suspicions of the limited liability company had been allayed by the reassurance offered by the House of Lords in its epoch-making judgment in *Salomon v Salomon & Co Ltd*.[10] This may have been because they were often at the sharp end when it came to dealing with distressed businesses. Thus, where a creditor went to court to secure judicial assistance to complete an execution process or to present a petition to wind up a debtor company, the court might use its discretionary jurisdiction to delay matters if there was a prospect of the debtor company salvaging the situation.[11] In spite of these laudable and ad hoc attempts at offering solace to distressed businesses, the overriding impression was that English law was not interested in constructively engaging the problem.

The inadequacies of the law were thrown into sharp focus by what was happening on the ground level in the financial world. The City of London was aware of the need for the development of a rescue culture and that process materialised through the so-called London Approach[12] which was used to salvage large businesses owing substantial sums to a number of financial institutions. Under the London Approach, distressed businesses owing large sums of money to a number of banks can be nursed through their period of difficulty with one of the banks taking up a leading position in that rehabilitation process. The Bank of England has played a key facilitating role here in persuading the banking community to behave in a co-ordinated/utilitarian way and not to adopt a destructive policy based upon selfish reliance upon strict legal entitlements. In the years since this mechanism was launched the procedures have been modified and more formalised[13] but still remain outside the parameters of the law, relying instead upon social norms prevalent within the City of London to ensure their effectiveness.[14]

3 THE VIEWS OF THE CORK COMMITTEE

The Cork Committee on Insolvency Law and Practice[15] (which conducted a major review during the period between 1977 and 1982) felt that the law should contemplate the possibility of salvation for a distressed company and therefore should establish formal mechanisms to achieve that goal. The solution to the lacuna problem according to *The Cork Report* (at chapter 9) was to introduce dedicated corporate rescue procedures into English law and, in particular, the procedure which it called administration. Unfortunately, one distortion which the Cork Committee was responsible for was its

---

10 [1897] AC 22.

11 For examples of this exercise in judicial discretion see Hare and Milman 'Debenture Holders and Judgment Creditors – Problems of Priority' [1982] *Lloyd's Maritime and Commercial Law Quarterly* 57.

12 See Kent 'The London Approach' (1993) 33 *Bank of England Quarterly Bulletin* 110, Bird and Hunter 'The Nature and Functions of a Rescue Culture' [1999] *Journal of Business Law* 491 at p 508.

13 For the more recent developments see Kent 'Corporate Workouts – A UK Perspective' [1997] 6 *International Insolvency Review* 165.

14 On this issue of social norms see Armour and Deakin 'Norms in Private Bankruptcy: "The London Approach" to the Resolution of Financial Distress' (2001) 1 *Journal of Corporate Law Studies* 21. One problem with reliance upon social norms is that this strategy is capable of being knocked off course by new entrants to a market where those newcomers are not immersed in the prevailing social norms – witness the aggressive role of US 'vulture funds' in disrupting proposed rescues by relying upon their strict legal rights.

15 See *The Cork Report* (1982) Cmnd 8558 (London, HMSO, 1982).

perception of receivership as a corporate rescue mechanism. It cannot be denied that in some cases receivership based upon the enforcement of an all-embracing floating charge has, particularly through the hiving down procedure under which viable portions of a business are transferred to a new subsidiary company which is then sold on, lead to businesses, or merely parts of a business, being rehabilitated under new management. But receivership is not intended for that purpose and rescue is merely a by-product of the dominant aim of recovering debts due to the debenture holder. One consequence of this conservative preference for receivership was the fact that the new rehabilitation procedures recommended by *The Cork Report* were not (as is apparent from paragraphs 502–04 of the Report) primarily intended to operate in those situations where there was an extant floating charge and, therefore, the prospect of rescue (albeit partial) through receivership remained a possibility.

In making its recommendations for dedicated corporate rescue procedures to be introduced into the UK system the Cork Committee was fully aware that, in order to maximise their potential, directors would have to be given an incentive to have recourse to these new options. That incentive took a negative form in the shape of the harsher legal environment to be imposed on directors of struggling businesses through the agency of the wrongful trading sanction (now found in s 214 of the Insolvency Act 1986) and the revamped director disqualification regime embodied in the Company Directors Disqualification Act 1986 (as amended recently by the Insolvency Act 2000). In modern parlance, the Cork Committee strategy could be characterised as 'joined-up thinking' or 'carrot and stick' methodology.

4 THE ARRIVAL OF CORPORATE RESCUE 1985–86

The Cork Committee proposals, were, after some prolonged deliberation,[16] given statutory effect in modified form in 1985. Corporate rescue models first made their entrance via the Insolvency Act 1985, a piece of legislation that was immediately overtaken and replaced by the consolidating Insolvency Act 1986. In many senses this was the most radical feature of this new legislation.[17] Under the Insolvency Act 1986 two new rehabilitation models for distressed companies were enshrined in statute. They were the company voluntary arrangement regime and, secondly, the administration order procedure.

Part I of the Insolvency Act 1986 dealt with the company voluntary arrangement regime (CVA).[18] Under this consensual procedure a distressed company could, through the services of an insolvency practitioner acting as nominee, put a proposal for a composition or scheme of arrangement to its unsecured creditors. If accepted by the

---

16   See the 1984 White Paper *A Revised Framework for Insolvency Law* (1984) Cmnd 9175 (London, HMSO, 1984), which refined (some would say watered down) the proposals in *The Cork Report*.

17   The rehabilitation theme extended beyond corporate insolvency and encompassed personal insolvency, through the medium of the individual voluntary arrangement.

18   For reviews of the CVA procedure see: Pennells 'Rescued From Oblivion' (1993) 137 *Solicitors Journal* 824; Campbell 'Revised Proposals for CVAs' (1995) 139 *Solicitors Journal* 656; and Hermer 'CVAs and Insolvent Tenants: *Re Cancol Ltd*' (1996) 17 *Company Lawyer* 84.

required majority[19] the proposal would bind all those unsecured creditors who had notice of the relevant meeting and who were entitled to vote. Absenteeism could not, therefore, confer an opt-out right on unsecured creditors. The proposal could not, however, affect in a detrimental way the entitlements of secured creditors or preferential creditors without their assent.[20] The directors remained in control of the company (an important incentive for them) and their performance in fulfilling commitments made in the arrangement was to be overseen by the insolvency practitioner who was now designated 'supervisor' according to s 7(2) of the Insolvency Act 1986. The precise role of the supervisor in each particular arrangement would be mapped out in detail by the terms of the CVA (as supported by the Act). Essentially, the supervisor stood at a distance and collected periodic payments from the business profits of the company, sums which would then be applied under the terms of the arrangement. The day-to-day control of the business remained with the directors; thus the CVA regime could be characterised as an example of a 'debtor in possession' model. Although the supervisor, of necessity,[21] plays a peripheral role if things go well his input can be dramatic where matters do not go according to plan because the supervisor is expected to terminate the arrangement in such an eventuality by petitioning for administration or liquidation. His statutory power to do this is contained in s 7(4)(b) of the Act.

The other novel mechanism was administration, a court-based model that could be imposed upon hostile creditors. A common misconception is that the administration procedure is exclusively about rehabilitation. That is not correct because this procedure can be (and frequently is) used as a more economically efficient alternative to liquidation.[22] The administration order procedure is normally initiated by the company or its directors petitioning the court.[23] Section 10 of the Insolvency Act 1986 makes it clear that an immediate protective moratorium is triggered on presentation of the petition. This moratorium (which is firmed up on the making of the administration order, as s 11 makes clear) precludes most forms of hostile action against a company, but it is stressed by s 10(2)(b) of the 1986 Act that a floating chargeholder can frustrate it by appointing an administrative receiver. Indeed, this right of veto is facilitated by the requirement imposed by s 9(2)(a) of the Act that notice must be given to any debenture holder, who was entitled to appoint an administrative receiver, of an administration petition in order to avail it of this option. This effective right of veto was specifically written into the legislation in response to what (it is submitted) was the misguided Cork Committee perception of receivership as an alternative rescue model. If the court feels that an order will be likely (that is, there was a reasonable prospect) to achieve one of the specified purposes as contained in s 8(3) and referred to in the petition, such an order may be

---

19   Debt value of 75%, including the holders of 50% of the independent debt; see Insolvency Rules 1986, rr 1.19(1) and 1.19(4).

20   See Insolvency Act 1986, ss 4(3) and 4(4).

21   If the supervisor becomes too 'hands on' there is always the risk of being characterised as a shadow director (see Companies Act 1985, s 741) and then falling into the ambit of the wrongful trading or disqualification sanctions.

22   There are few official statistics on how often administration is used in this way. Administration can be a more efficient liquidation mode because the administrator has wider powers than a liquidator (eg, in dealing with title retention suppliers – see Insolvency Act 1986, s 15). See also the Neuberger essay above at pp 61–65.

23   Creditors can also petition under s 9(1), but this is a rarity.

made. On the making of the order an administrator would be appointed and charged with the task of developing a rescue package that would meet with the approval of creditors and then delivering on that package. The directors would not automatically lose office, but in reality they would have no control over the management of the company whilst in the hands of the administrators. This is one other significant point of contrast between this procedure and the CVA model.

The rescue theme (so fundamental to the 1986 Insolvency Act)[24] was also apparent in other parts of this legislation, most notably with regard to constraints imposed by s 233 on hostile actions by monopoly utility suppliers threatening to cut off essential supplies to distressed businesses now in the stewardship of office holders in order to secure payment of arrears.

5 REINFORCING CORPORATE TURNAROUND

There is one event more than any other that illustrated the changes in official attitudes to corporate rescue. The *Paramount Airways* affair[25] in the early 1990s was the stimulus. This company went into administration in August 1989 and the administrators retained the staff for several months to facilitate continued trading, though it was indicated through standard documentation that their contracts of employment were not being adopted. Several significant pieces of litigation ensued, the most controversial of which concerned liability for the wages and other accrued rights of employees retained by the administrators during this period of continued trading.

The Court of Appeal[26] ruled that, in behaving as they had done, the administrators had adopted the contracts of employment of the employees and had, therefore, become responsible for all accrued liabilities arising out of those contracts. This liability was, of course, covered by their indemnity and might ultimately reduce the sums available to the floating chargeholder. Where this was likely to be a significant cost item this in turn might persuade a floating chargeholder to exercise its statutory right to veto the administration. Thus, the whole rescue strategy was perceived to be endangered by this inconvenient decision.

The Court of Appeal judgment provoked howls of outrage from the community of insolvency practitioners who regarded the new burdensome rules on adoption of contracts of employment as an invitation to dismiss staff and to close down the business as quickly as possible. The decision was a surprise because it seemed to buck the judicial trend in favour of promoting rescue. The explanation seems to be that in so deciding the Court of Appeal gave priority to the powerful policy objective of protecting the rights of individual employees at the expense of wider economic considerations.

---

24   See Lord Browne Wilkinson in *Powdrill v Watson* [1995] 2 AC 394 at p 442.

25   For discussion of the background see the author's introductory note to the Current Law Statutes version of the Insolvency Act 1994.

26   *Re Paramount Airways Ltd* [1994] 2 All ER 513. For comment see Lawless 'Paramount 3 and Leyland DAF – The Story So Far (and What Next)' [1994] (October) *Insolvency Lawyer* 2.

Legislation was quickly passed in the form of the Insolvency Act 1994, a statute that unusually contained a retrospective element.[27] This legislation, which provides a perfect illustration of the political influence of a well-organised professional lobby, reduced the total of accrued liabilities that would have to be met where contracts of employment were adopted and thus made the retention of staff for the purposes of ongoing trading less economically burdensome. Ironically, after the legislation came into force the House of Lords[28] heard the case and came up with conclusions that were seen as less threatening to the burgeoning rescue culture by the profession. Nevertheless, the reverberations of *Paramount* continued to be felt for several years to come.[29]

This is the most graphic illustration of the growing importance of this new policy goal. More detailed study of the subject will also reveal changes in tax law[30] to encourage creditors to play ball and the extension of business rescue procedures to a wider range of undertakings such as banks[31] and insolvent partnerships.[32]

6 JUDICIAL SUPPORT FOR CORPORATE RESCUE

Notwithstanding what has been said about the *Paramount Airways* affair, the English courts[33] generally did their utmost to support the new rehabilitative strategy. This was particularly true in the context of administration where they imposed a low-probability test for the making of the order[34] and sought to maximise the impact of the protective

27 The legislation (and the partial relief from liability which it offered) was made retrospective until 15 March 1994 whereas the Royal Assent was dated 24 March 1994. Attempts by non-administrative receivers to secure the benefit of the legislation to offer protection against liabilities on adopted contracts of employment arising out of their activities met with no success. For analysis of the 1994 Act see: Mudd 'The Insolvency Act 1994 – Paramount Cured?' [1994] 10 *Insolvency Law and Practice* 38; and Pollard 'Adopted Employees in Insolvency – Orphans No More' [1995] 24 Industrial LJ 141.

28 See *Powdrill v Watson* [1995] 2 AC 394. By this stage there were three joined appeals that were being determined by their Lordships – *Powdrill v Watson* involving adoption by administrators and *Re Leyland DAF Ltd (No 2)* and *Re Ferranti International plc* (parallel cases involving the related issues arising where the adoption is effected by administrative receivers).

29 See, for example: *Re Maxwell Fleet Facilities Management Ltd* [2001] 1 WLR 323 and *Ramsey and Maclaine v Leonard Curtis (A Firm)* [2001] BPIR 389. *Paramount* has caused difficulties in Scotland where the statutory rules differ; see: *Jamieson Petitioners* 1997 SC 195 and *Lindop v Stuart Noble & Sons Ltd* [2000] BCC 747, discussed by Lewis '*Lindop* is Back!' [1999] *Insolvency Lawyer* 3.

30 See Finance Act 1994, s 144 (bad debt relief available for debts waived on a CVA).

31 See Banks (Administration Proceedings) Order 1987, SI 1987/1276. Insurance companies were not brought within the safety net until the enactment and implementation of the Financial Services and Markets Act 2000, s 360.

32 Insolvent Partnerships Order 1994, SI 1994/2421.

33 Although the administration order is available throughout the UK, one can detect regional variations in judicial attitudes. Thus the Scottish courts have added their refinements; see McKenzie-Skene and Enoch 'Petitions for Administration Orders Where There is a Need for Interim Measures: A Comparative Study of the Approach of the Courts in Scotland and in England and Wales' [2000] *Journal of Business Law* 103. In Northern Ireland the judiciary have been more circumspect; see Capper 'Administration in Northern Ireland' [1999] *Insolvency Lawyer* 283.

34 See *Re Harris Simons Construction* [1989] 1 WLR 368; this test invites the question whether there is a reasonable prospect of the stated aims of the administration (which might include a rescue) being achieved. In Ireland an even more generous approach was adopted in *Re Atlantic Magnetics Ltd* [1993] 2 IR 651 (where *any* prospect of success was deemed sufficient) but this was criticised by the banking community which felt that too many speculative court examinerships were being embarked upon and eventually the Irish moved over to a test that mirrored the English approach with the enactment of the Companies Amendment (No 2) Act 1999.

moratorium by including as many forms of hostile action as possible.[35] In recent years this supportive tradition has resurfaced in the courts' approach to emergency disposals by administrators. The problem is that when taking control of a distressed company opportunities may arise for immediate disposals of properties or businesses. If the administrator has to wait until the creditors have approved his general plan or have agreed to these particular sales the counterparty might drop out with disastrous results. Early decisions did not indicate much sympathy for the plight of the administrator faced with this scenario.[36] More recently, the courts have given the green light to administrators to proceed with despatch and have even offered constructive guidance on appropriate courses of action to adopt.[37]

Although the overwhelming preponderance of judicial decisions may be described as facilitative, there are inevitably exceptions which prove the rule. Apart from the inconvenience caused by the initial 'administration exit' ruling of Lightman J in *Re Powerstore Trading Ltd*[38] one could cite here the curious Court of Appeal ruling in *Re Coslett Contractors Ltd*, which seemed to limit the power of an administrator to sue in conversion before the House of Lords recently over-ruled it.[39] Equally there is the case of *IRC v Lawrence*[40] where the Court of Appeal indicated that certain tax liabilities run up during the course of the administration enjoy a super priority; this will hardly encourage banks to support the procedure as this will increase the risk of any floating charge security proving to be inadequate to protect the interests of the bank.

There has been less scope for judicial input into the evolution of the CVA model. This is because the court is not meant to be actively involved unless legal difficulties arise. The CVA regime is also more based upon consensus. Nevertheless, where the opportunity has arisen the courts have been prepared to lend a helping hand. First, they have allowed creditors to make their own mind up on this option by refusing to narrowly define what a company voluntary arrangement is or to look behind their decision, no matter how irrational it might appear to be.[41] No sign of paternalism here. Secondly, they have confirmed that although a secured creditor has the right to take protective steps prior to the CVA being agreed, once that arrangement has been agreed its right to lay claim to company assets is significantly marginalised because funds collected by the supervisor

---

35 See *Bristol Airport v Powdrill* [1990] Ch 744. For more recent authority see: *Re Axis Genetics plc* [2000] BCC 943 and *Environment Agency v Clark* [2000] BCC 653 which casts doubt upon the damaging authority of *Air Ecosse v Civil Aviation Authority* (1987) 3 BCC 492.

36 See *Re Consumer and Industrial Press Ltd (No 2)* (1988) 4 BCC 72.

37 See: *Re Montin Ltd* [1999] 1 BCLC 663; *Re Dana UK Ltd* [1999] 2 BCLC 239; *Re Osmosis Group Ltd* [1999] 2 BCLC 329; *Re T & D Industries plc* [2000] BCC 956 and *Re Harris Bus Co* [2000] BCC 1151. For further discussion see: Elboz 'T & D Industries plc – The Seven Principles: New Guidance for Administrators in Disposing of Assets' (1999) 15 *Insolvency Law and Practice* 183; and Roberts 'T & D Industries Revisited: Further Guidance for Administrators Disposing of Assets' (2000) 16 *Insolvency Law and Practice* 61.

38 [1997] 1 WLR 1280. Although this is undoubtedly an inconvenient authority it is difficult to contest the reasoning underpinning it. Clearly the court should not tie the hands of a future liquidator by corrupting strict priority rules on winding up. The issue of administration exits, and its attendant case law, will be revisited below.

39 [2000] BCC 1155 (CA) and see now *Smith v Bridgend County BC* [2001] 3 WLR 1347.

40 [2001] 1 BCLC 204.

41 See *IRC v Adam & Partners Ltd* [2000] BPIR 986.

become impressed with a trust for the benefit of the participating CVA creditors.[42] Finally, they have sought to maximise the freedom of manoeuvre enjoyed by supervisors when deciding whether to terminate a CVA and in deciding the fate of the CVA funds left in the hands of the supervisor.[43] As with administrations not all decisions handed down by the courts have been so accommodating. Thus in *Re Alpa Lighting Ltd*[44] the Court of Appeal refused to rewrite the terms of an arrangement; its supportive role in giving clarification in the form of directions did not permit it to go that far. The onus is on the parties to the arrangement to make provision for the unexpected.

7 CONCERNS WITH PROTOTYPE MODELS

As will be shown in the conclusion to this essay, statistical evidence shows a disappointing performance for both administration orders and CVAs in the years 1986–96. Commentators have speculated on the reasons for this lack of take up. As might have been expected, the initial attempt to provide effective models for corporate rescue were imperfect and technical problems were not fully anticipated. No one could seriously expect that such a radical change in corporate regulatory philosophy would be worked out successfully at the first attempt.[45]

The focus of criticism of the administration order scheme was the fact that the procedure involved an application to court, supported by financial documentation (especially the notorious Insolvency Rule 2.2 report which requires an independent expert to attest to the viability of what is being proposed in the petition), and this combination could prove expensive.[46] The courts quickly responded to these concerns by publishing a *Practice Direction*[47] designed to encourage a more economical approach. Rule 2.2 reports were to be kept as concise as possible and were not to be required in straightforward cases. Certainly, the experience of this commentator in interviewing practitioners is that cost is not seen as a major barrier to utilisation of administration orders these days.

Another perceived weakness was that the administration procedure could be vetoed by the bank enjoying the security of a floating charge. This commentator, although rejecting the idea of the existence of a right of veto in principle,[48] was somewhat sceptical of this thesis because it by no means followed that banks had in practice taken an obstructive view to rescues.[49] Indeed, research carried out by Rajak suggests that in half of the administrations studied this potential right of veto was not exercised.[50] Apart from

---

42 See *Re Leisure Study Group Ltd* [1994] 2 BCLC 65.

43 See here *Welsby v Brelec Installations* [2000] 2 BCLC 576 but compare *Re Maple Environmental Services Ltd* [2000] BCC 93. See also: *Souster v Carman Construction* [2000] BPIR 371; and *Re Kudos Glass Ltd* [2001] 1 BCLC 390.

44 [1997] BPIR 341.

45 See also the Neuberger essay above at pp 63–65 in relation to the moratoria provisions.

46 The figure of £20,000, which was often bandied around as a down payment needed to secure an administration order, may have been apocryphal but it seems to have been widely accepted.

47 See [1994] BCLC 347.

48 See D Milman and D Mond *Security and Corporate Rescue* (Manchester, Hodgsons, 1999).

49 See D Milman and F Chittenden, *CVAs and the Challenge of Small Companies* (London, Chartered Association of Certified Accountants Educational Trust, 1995).

50 This unpublished research was referred to in the Joint Report at para 71.

those atypical 'diplomatic' cases which impact upon the goodwill and image of the bank (such as where the distressed company owns the local football club) lending institutions will support rescue procedures if they feel that their security is adequate to protect them in the event of the rescue failing.

The moratorium, that characteristic feature of the administration procedure which is set forth in detail by ss 10 and 11 of the Insolvency Act 1986, also had its weaknesses. The most notable was the fact that landlords' traditional rights of re-entry were not apparently hindered,[51] nor indeed were damaging actions by regulatory authorities (such as the withdrawal of an essential trading or operating licence).[52]

In later years a new problem arose. This revolved around the technicalities of 'administration exit' routes where the administration was to be followed by immediate liquidation. Due to a quirk in the legislation the rights of preferential creditors were often maximised if liquidation was conducted by the compulsory winding-up mode because the preferential debts would be quantified from the date of the administration order, whereas in the case of exit by voluntary winding up the chosen date for computational purposes would be the much later date when the resolution for voluntary winding up was passed with the result that fewer debts would be treated as preferential. On the other hand, the most economically efficient method for all concerned would be via voluntary liquidation, but the legislation seemed to preclude use of this option without the support of the preferential creditors (who would be unlikely to give it). The judges were caught in a dilemma between observing the letter of the law and adopting a pragmatic approach.[53] Various inventive solutions were floated to solve this conundrum and certainly later court decisions indicate a more constructive line.[54]

Turning to the CVA model, most analysts suggested that potential CVAs were being frustrated by a lack of a moratorium.[55] Again this is a contentious proposition not established by any empirical data. Indeed, what research has been done suggests an increasingly co-operative attitude on the part of secured creditors.[56] There were also

---

51 See *Re Lomax Leisure Ltd* [1999] 2 BCLC 126 discussed in the Neuberger essay above at pp 64–65; and the general comments of Lord Millett in *Re Park Air Services plc* [2000] 2 AC 172 at p 186B–D as to the correct characterisation of the landlord's remedy of re-entry. The opposite view was taken by Harman J in *Exchange Travel Agency v Triton Property Trust* [1991] BCC 341. For a critique of this apparent Achilles heel in the business rescue strategy see Milman and Davey 'Debtor Rehabilitation – Implications for the Landlord-Tenant Relationship' [1996] *Journal of Business Law* 541. For further discussion see: Byrne and Doyle 'Administration – Can a Landlord Forfeit a Lease by Peaceable Re-Entry?' [1999] *Insolvency Lawyer* 167; and Shaw 'Peaceable Re-Entry by a Landlord Revisited' [1999] *Insolvency Lawyer* 254.

52 See *Air Ecosse v Civil Aviation Authority* (1987) 3 BCC 492.

53 See *Re Powerstore Trading Ltd* [1997] 1 WLR 1280, discussed by Fennessy 'What's in Store for Administrators and Creditors when Choosing Exit Routes from Administration?' [1998] 22 *Insolvency Lawyer* 11. The decision of Arden J in *Re Nordictrack (UK) Ltd* [2000] 1 BCLC 467 may also appear to be unhelpful but on closer examination the constructive features of the judgment are apparent.

54 See: *Re Philip Alexander Securities and Futures* [1998] BCC 819; *Re Mark One (Oxford Street) plc* [1998] BCC 984; *Re Dino Music Ltd* [2000] BCC 696 and *Re UCT (UK) Ltd* [2001] 1 WLR 436. For comment see Fennessy 'Reversal of Fortune for Creditors after Administration' [1999] *Insolvency Lawyer* 169.

55 This absence of a moratorium is well reflected by the ruling of Rimer J in *Alman v Approach Housing Ltd* [2001] 1 BCLC 530.

56 See Milman and Chittenden, 1995, above n 49. For further analysis of the data produced in this study see: Cook, Pandit and Milman 'Small Firm Rehabilitation and the Legal System: The Case of Great Britain' (2000) 38 *Journal of Small Business Management* 78; and also Pandit, Cook, Milman and Chittenden 'Corporate Rescue: Empirical Evidence on Company Voluntary Arrangements and Small Firms' (2000) 7 *Journal of Small Business and Enterprise Development* 241.

criticisms levelled at the relatively high threshold of creditor support required to get a CVA off the ground (that is, 75% creditor support) and the fact that members could effectively veto a proposal, a strange phenomenon in cases where the company was insolvent with the result that the members had no tangible interest in its assets.

Another, more fundamental, concern was that corporate rescue should not be viewed in isolation. The negative incentive of wrongful trading was not working in the sense that very few cases were coming before the courts and of those cases a number had proved unsuccessful. Having said that, the twin policy of disqualification was being used with increasing frequency and more than 1,000 directors every year were being banned,[57] though many others were escaping the crackdown and the delays in securing a disqualification were undermining confidence in the system. There was little point in having effective rescue procedures if directors were not inclined to pursue them because their exposure to risk was not considered by them to be too great.

8 CORPORATE RESCUE: BEYOND THE LEGAL PERSPECTIVE

To most insolvency practitioners working in the 1970s corporate turnaround was a minority specialism.[58] In the field of corporate insolvency the majority of professional fees were earned through the staple diet of winding up or receivership. Certainly, attitudes within professions are hard to change and it is significant that many of the early pioneers of corporate rescue, particularly where the preferred vehicle was the CVA, were small local practitioners rather than the large international accountancy firms. The success of these early pioneers, together with a realisation that the public climate towards corporate rescue had changed, impressed the larger firms who in recent years have embraced corporate rescue with the zeal of a convert. An indication of how things have moved on was provided by the change of name in 2000 of the Society of Insolvency Practitioners to the Association of Business Recovery Professionals (or 'R3').[59] Although one aim was to incorporate the growing number of turnaround specialists, there is no doubt that public perception of the profession was a key motivation behind this collective rebranding.

There are other professional sectors whose changing attitudes have assisted in the process of reform of corporate rescue. Foremost amongst these are the banks. Their initial response to the *Cork Report*-inspired reform was one of caution. The indications are that the preference for the tried and tested tool of receivership was hard to cast off, particularly at local branch level. However, after pressure from the Government the banks opted for self-regulation, presumably in the hope that this might stave off direct legislative dilution of their traditional rights. Thus, the Bankers' Code of Practice in 1997

---

57 See DTI Press Notice P/2000/249 – some 1,500 directors disqualified over the previous 12 months. As indicated the large numbers involved have caused logistical difficulties leading to the introduction of the director disqualification undertakings regime by s 6 of the Insolvency Act, 2000.

58 Generally in commerce this was virgin territory in the UK. It was only in the 1980s that it became a topic of serious study; for a key benchmark text see S Slatter *Corporate Recovery – A Guide to Turnaround Management* (Harmondsworth, Penguin, 1984).

59 This change of name was approved in January 2000. For the policy thinking behind this transformation see: Bloom 'R3 – Our Future' [2000] (March) *Recovery* 2; Gale 'Valediction' [2001] (February) *Recovery* 2; and Harris 'Turnaround Talk' [2001] (February) *Recovery* 20.

made explicit reference to the desirability of supporting rescue.[60] Some banks went even further and announced a policy of zero tolerance with respect to receiverships.

9 COMPARATIVE INSIGHTS

It is important to realise that the pattern of legal evolution which we have described was being replicated in most developed jurisdictions. With the exception of the USA[61] and South Africa,[62] corporate rescue was not an established feature of any major system of corporation law prior to 1980. The 1980s and 1990s witnessed an explosion of reform in this field on a global level. In the Commonwealth (and in other jurisdictions influenced by English law) various permutations of the models found in the UK were devised with mixed success. For example, Singapore adopted a model known as judicial management, which, on closer analysis, bore a remarkable resemblance to the UK administration order procedure.[63] English law does, however, stand out for the diversity of corporate rehabilitation options on offer. In Europe, in spite of a lack of EU-harmonised initiatives, corporate rehabilitation models have sprung up and been remodelled throughout the past two decades in the various national systems of company law and insolvency law.[64]

---

60 Note in particular Principle 9 of the Code which states that banks will aid rescue proposals which they believe will succeed. For comment see Hunter, above n 12, at p 507.

61 The chapter 11 corporate rescue mechanism in the US Bankruptcy Code was substantially remodelled in 1978. For background analysis see: Grenville 'An American Chapter: Is it Good Enough for Virtuous England?' (1986) 2 *Insolvency Law and Practice* 82; Donahue 'History and Application of Chapter 11 of the US Bankruptcy Code' (1988) 4 *Insolvency Law and Practice* 112; Moehlmann 'Supervising the Debtor Under Chapter 11 United States Bankruptcy Code' (1998) 14 *Insolvency Law and Practice* 165; and Broude 'How the Rescue Culture Came to the United States and the Myths that Surround Chapter 11' (2000) 16 *Insolvency Law and Practice* 194. For fierce debate over the pros and cons, the economic efficiency, and discussion of the wider morality of Chapter 11 see: Bradley and Rozenweig 'The Untenable Case for Chapter 11' (1992) 101 *Yale LJ* 1043; Warren 'The Untenable Case for Repeal of Chapter 11' (1992) 102 *Yale LJ* 437; Eisenberg 'Baseline Problems in Assessing Chapter 11' (1993) 43 *University of Toronto Law Journal* 633; Kordana and Posner 'A Positive Theory of Chapter 11' (1999) 74 *New York University Law Review* 161.

62 South Africa has had a system of judicial management since 1926. One reason for this early support for a discrete corporate rescue procedure was that the floating charge, and therefore the all-embracing species of receivership, was not accepted in South African law. For a critique of the South African model see Sealy 'The New Administration Procedure – Some Overseas Comparisons' (1986) 2 *Insolvency Law and Practice* 70. A contemporary review of the position in South Africa (coupled with an excellent comparative survey) is provided by Rajak and Henning 'Business Rescue for South Africa' (1999) 116 *South African Law Journal* 262.

63 For analysis of the judicial management system in Singapore under s 45 of the Singapore Companies Amendment Act 1987 (13 of 87) see Cheong 'Judicial Management in Corporate Insolvency' (1988) 30 *Malaya Law Review* 259. The similarity between the Singaporean model and UK administration is borne out by the review treatment adopted by Picarda 'Administration and Judicial Management Orders in the Nineties' [1994] 1 *Receivers, Administrators and Liquidators Quarterly* 29 and 115.

64 A useful summary of these is to be found in the study prepared by the Centre for Law and Business for the Company Law Review Project which is cited on page 7 of *The Final Report*, above n 1. This summary is to be found on the DTI website at www.dti.gov.uk/cld/review.htm. In western Europe, France would be a typical example of a jurisdiction where major rescue regimes were introduced in 1984 and 1985; see A Sorensen and P Omar *Corporate Rescue Procedures in France* (Kluwer Law International, 1996). For the more recent progress towards development of rescue regimes in central and eastern Europe see Rajak 'Rescue Versus Liquidation in Central and Eastern Europe' (1998) 33 *Texas International Law Journal* 157.

It is difficult to evaluate the relative strengths and weaknesses of other rehabilitation models. The problem, of course, may be that the critical contributing factor to success or failure is not be an inherent feature of the model but an obstruction in the underlying system of corporate law. However, some tentative observations are possible. The Irish court examiner model (which was introduced by the Companies (Amendment) Act 1990) has attracted a mixed response.[65] This procedure involves an application to the court and allows the directors considerable freedom of action during the course of the examinership. The main problem seems to be that it is perceived by banks as little more than a device whereby borrowing companies (and their controllers) can seek to evade their responsibilities to lenders.

The Australian scheme of voluntary administration[66] has many admirers. The great beauty of this mechanism (which first materialised in the Corporate Law Reform Act 1992) is that it is able to combine the merits of debtor in possession with the benefits of a moratorium facility. Critically, the procedure can be invoked by the filing of a notice with the court; a full court hearing is not required. Thus, it can be quickly invoked with the minimum of expense. The procedure is also robust in the face of traditional property rights enjoyed by secured creditors. Banks have not shown themselves to be unduly threatened by its advent.

A comparison of take-up rates produces mixed results. Schemes such as judicial administration in South Africa and the court examiner procedure in Ireland apparently have not been used extensively. Chapter 11 proceedings under the US Bankruptcy Code are much more prevalent, but that may owe much to the hostile nature of the litigation system in the US where even the most financially robust corporation can be bankrupted by those huge damages awards which so characterise US litigation. More significantly, voluntary administration under the Australian scheme has been widely exploited and, in view of the similarities with the culture of UK corporate law, that may well hold lessons for reformers in this jurisdiction. A perusal of the reforms introduced by the Insolvency Act 2000 may well detect an unseen Antipodean influence.

Not all corporate systems have progressed as far in the race to establish an effective rehabilitation regime. Certainly, in jurisdictions such as New Zealand and Hong Kong

---

65 On the Irish court examiner system see: Walshe 'The Irish Examinership Process – Not Just Administration under Another Guise' (1993) 9 *Insolvency Law and Practice* 150; Campbell and Garrett 'The Irish Examiner and Proposals for Reform of the Companies (Amendment) Act 1990' (1996) 10 *Insolvency Lawyer* 12; Linnane 'Ireland – Examinerships and the Company Law Reform Group: The Appointment of an Examiner' (1998) 19 *Company Lawyer* 286; Ensor 'Examinership in Ireland – Can the UK Learn Anything from the Experience of the Irish Examiner?' (1999) 15 *Insolvency Law and Practice* 53. It was in response to these concerns that the banks lobbied hard for reforms to be made to the examiner procedure to introduce more controls on its potential for abuse and to reassert some of their traditional security rights. This pressure paid off with the enactment of the Companies (Amendment) (No 2) Act 1999 (Ireland).

66 Voluntary administration was introduced into Australia in 1993 in the wake of the Australian Law Reform Commission recommendations in the 1988 Harmer Report *General Insolvency Inquiry* Report No 45 (Australia, ALRC, 1998). See: Chalkiadis 'Let's Talk Administration the Australian Way' (1994) 10 *Insolvency Law and Practice* 3; Campbell 'Company Rescue in Australia: Does the New Voluntary Arrangement Procedure Provide Guidance for Possible Reforms in the UK?' (1994) 10 *Insolvency law and Practice* 18; Keay 'Voluntary Administration in Australia – What Do the Courts Do?' (1995) 14 *Insolvency Lawyer* 12; Robinson 'Statutory Moratorium on Proceedings Against a Company' (1996) 24 *Australian Business Law Review* 429; Harmer 'The Experience of the Voluntary Administration Regime in Australia' (1998) 22 *Insolvency Lawyer* 18.

(where the banks wield considerable political influence), the route towards the integration of effective corporate rescue procedures has been painful.[67]

10 INSOLVENCY ACT 2000

The Insolvency Act 2000 represents part of the commitment of the Labour Government toward business. This statute runs to a modest 18 sections and it is only ss 1, 2, 4 and 9 that are of direct relevance to this discussion.[68]

The most significant change in the 2000 Act is the addition of a moratorium facility to support the CVA. In order to understand the reforms in the CVA process it is necessary to rehearse the painstaking deliberation that proceeded it. Throughout the 1990s consultative documents were emanating from the Insolvency Service designed to give the new corporate rescue mechanisms an additional cutting edge.[69] These documents produced mixed responses, but gradually a consensus developed that corporate rescue needed to be given a further helping hand from the law. That assistance is offered by the Insolvency Act 2000, and in particular by making available a moratorium to assist CVA usage.

In spite of this tortuous path to reform the advent of the CVA moratorium is a bold step when one realises that it involves a distressed company which is still being managed by the incumbent board being offered substantial protection from creditors wishing to exercise traditional enforcement rights. Thus, under paras 12–14 of Sched A1 of the Insolvency Act 1986 (which is inserted in Sched 1 to the 2000 Act), most hostile actions against the company, including the enforcement of a floating charge, are blocked. Indeed, existing crystallisation arrangements embodied in current floating charges which seek to pre-empt a CVA are rendered nugatory under para 43. The essential point to grasp about the CVA moratorium is that the company is not in the hands of an independent insolvency practitioner, which is the norm in other instances of such a moratorium.[70] Moreover, this protection is available without the need for a court order; all that is required by para 7 of Sched A1 is that specified documentation be filed with the court. For English law this is a significant psychological step. The boldness of this reform is matched by a cautious approach as to the availability of this facility. Thus, it is only available to

---

67 For discussion see: Bannister 'Staying Alive in Hong Kong: A Comparative Review' (2000) 16 *Insolvency Law and Practice* 17; Booth 'Hong Kong Corporate Rescue Proposals – Making Secured Creditors More Secure' (1998) 14 *Insolvency Law and Practice* 248; and Booth 'Hong Kong Insolvency Law – Preparing for the Millennium' [2001] *Journal of Business Law* 126. This slow progress may be linked to the political influence enjoyed by banks. This power is also reflected in the 1999 changes in the corporate rescue model in Ireland, reforms which were intended to reassure the banking community.

68 For full analysis of this legislation see the annotations by the author in the Current Law Statutes version of the 2000 Act. Note also Smith and Neill 'The Insolvency Act 2000' (2001) 17 *Insolvency Law and Practice* 84.

69 See, for example, the consultative documents: *CVAs and Administration Orders* (October 1993); *Revised Proposals for a New Company Voluntary Arrangement Procedure* (April 1995) and *A Review of Company Rescue and Business Reconstruction Mechanisms* (September 1999).

70 Where a company is subject to a winding-up petition the directors are subject to disabilities (eg, on dispositions of company property) but they are not automatically stripped of management powers unless the court appoints a provisional liquidator.

eligible 'small' companies (as defined by s 247(3) of the Companies Act 1985). The criteria governing eligibility can to some extent be modified by the Secretary of State using delegated powers.[71] Banks are also excluded from the benefit of this protection. Another key safety measure lies in the fact that the nominee is subjected to additional monitoring duties prior to the approval of the CVA by creditors. For example, it is made clear by para 24 of Sched A1 that the nominee must at all times be convinced that the proposal has a reasonable prospect of being approved by creditors and that the company is likely to have sufficient funds to keep its business going during the period of the moratorium. If either of these conditions is not satisfied, the nominee should withdraw consent to act in accordance with the terms of para 25.

During the period of the moratorium the directors are subject to considerable disabilities. Thus, para 17 of Sched A1 states that the obtaining of further credit in excess of £250 is prohibited unless the person providing the finance is informed of the moratorium. Equally, paras 18 and 19 emphasise that disposals and payments by the directors are not allowed unless there are reasonable grounds for believing that they will benefit the company and they have been approved either by the nominee or creditors' committee. Finally, new offences are created by para 41 to deal with abusive behaviour by directors (for example, concealing property). Creditors have a right of appeal to the court under para 40 of Sched A1 if the directors are behaving in a manner that is believed to be unfairly prejudicial to their interests. Balance, however, has to be maintained lest the business is paralysed thus precluding any prospect of rehabilitation.

This innovation merely provides an option. It is not mandatory that a company wishing to use the CVA procedure should also file for a moratorium. Where the creditors are in a co-operative mood there is no reason why the old-style CVA should not continue to be utilised. In view of the restrictions on availability of the new CVA model this is an important factor to bear in mind. Schedule 2 to the Insolvency Act 2000 fine-tuned the CVA model generally by dealing with the tricky problem of unknown creditors and the more remote scenario of obstructive shareholders.[72] The administration order regime did not originally feature in the provisions of the Insolvency Bill 2000, but a late amendment extended its moratorium to hostile actions by landlords.[73] This was a long-overdue development.

---

71   Although the new CVA model has not yet been brought into operation, these delegated powers were brought into effect by the Insolvency Act 2000 (Commencement No 2) Order 2001, SI 2001/1751. There may be an early use of these powers in that concerns have been raised in the City of London that to apply the CVA moratorium to special purpose vehicle companies used in syndicated loan agreements might seriously jeopardise the operation of syndicated loans business. Such companies may therefore have to be declared ineligible. For comment see Pawsey 'UK Securitisation Under Threat' *The Lawyer*, 16 July 2001 at p 3.

72   At present if a creditor was not alerted to the creditors' meeting that creditor would not be tied into the scheme but could instead rely on traditional enforcement rights (such as the option of presenting a winding-up petition) at some later date, thereby creating difficulties for the management of the CVA. Paragraph 5 of Sched 2 now ties in creditors who did not have notice of the meeting but offers special protection for their position under the arrangement. As a CVA as presently operated requires insolvency as a prerequisite, it is difficult to see why members (who by definition have no tangible stake in the company at this stage) should be involved in the process of approval. Paragraph 5 of Sched 2 makes it clear that in the event of a difference of opinion between the creditors and members it is the decision of the creditors' meeting (subject to a right of appeal to the court) that will prevail.

73   See Insolvency Act 2000, s 9. This change neutralised many of the cases cited in n 51 above. For comment see McIntosh 'Insolvency Act 2000 – Landlord's Right of Peaceable Re-Entry' (2001) 17 *Insolvency Law and Practice* 48.

Moving away from substantive modifications in corporate rescue mechanics the Insolvency Act 2000 does introduce a significant cultural change to the insolvency profession. Since the publication of *The Cork Report* in 1982 the dominant theme has been one of compulsory professional qualification backed by a strong system of self-regulation.[74] However, in recent years it has become apparent that a number of 'company doctors' or 'turnaround specialists' have been offering their services to distressed companies in spite of the fact that they were not licensed insolvency practitioners. This fact of life has presented both the profession and the Government with a dilemma. They have both responded by seeking to bring these individuals within the regulatory catchment so as to promote good standards. From the Government's perspective there is the added attraction of supplementing the pool of practitioners who can act in aid of distressed companies thereby increasing competition and possibly driving down professional fees. Accordingly, under s 4 of the Insolvency Act 2000, members of those groups which the Secretary of State recognises will be allowed to act as nominees and supervisors of company voluntary arrangements. It remains to be seen how this recognition exercise will be carried out.

11 FUTURE CHANGES

It was perhaps ironic (some would say unfortunate) that just as the Insolvency Bill 2000 was approaching its final parliamentary stages a major report should be published by the Joint DTI/Treasury Review Group on Company Rescue and Business Reconstruction Mechanisms.[75] This accident of timing must, however, be viewed in the context of a series of consultation documents emanating from the Insolvency Service in the 1990s, all of which concentrated on the question of optimising the prospects of business rescue.[76] The Review Group outlined proposals designed to upgrade the current model. First, the floating chargeholder's right of veto over administration (as conferred by s 9(3)(a) of the Insolvency Act 1986) is to be removed. This was not seen as a radical move because the evidence produced in Rajak's study (which has been referred to above) pointed to many floating chargeholders waiving their right of veto. That may be true, but the symbolic nature of the change – that is, the victory of rehabilitation over security rights – cannot be emphasised too highly.

There had been considerable criticism of the fact that preferential creditors could in effect veto business rescues using the CVA route by relying on the full extent of their vested rights under s 4(4) of the Insolvency Act 1986. A radical solution to this perceived difficulty would have been the complete abolition of preferential claims. In spite of teasing suggestions in the media that this solution might find favour, in the end the Review Group eschewed it. Observers have concluded that the Treasury's influence was decisive here. Instead, the Review Group contented itself with recommending new

---

74   See: Finch 'Insolvency Practitioners: Regulation and Reform' [1998] *Journal of Business Law* 9; Finch 'Controlling the Insolvency Professionals' [1999] *Insolvency Lawyer* 228, for an overview of this regime.

75   See 'A Review of Company Rescue and Business Reconstruction Mechanisms' (London, DTI, 2000). See DTI Press Notice P/2000/727 for an insight into official thinking. This report is the subject of the editorial in [2001] *Insolvency Lawyer* 1.

76   See n 69 above.

bureaucratic structures to foster a spirit of rehabilitation support on the part of the Revenue and Customs and Excise.[77] This change was coupled with an exhortation not to block rescues simply because preferential creditors would not receive 100 pence in the pound. In the light of later potential reforms noted below, this experiment in changing bureaucratic behaviour is likely to be of limited duration.

Turning to the professional constituency, the Review Group was at pains to foster the trend within the professions towards promoting business rescue. In the opinion of this commentator that bandwagon is already moving at a fast pace. One concern was noted by the Review Group and that centred upon the now notorious practice of investigating accountants being appointed subsequently as receivers of companies whose finances they had previously investigated. There is little to stop this happening at present and in a number of high-profile cases the firm of insolvency practitioners have come in for much criticism both in the media and in Parliamentary debates.[78] On the other hand, what empirical research that has been done has not been able to identify any wrongdoing.[79] The Review Group (at para 119) declined to support calls to outlaw this practice by means of legislation, though it was clearly sensitive to public perceptions. Instead, it recommended in para 121 of its Report that both banks and insolvency practitioners revisit their codes of practice and ethical statements to address the public relations downside of this practice. Whether this will resolve the problem is doubtful; one suspects that legislation will eventually have to be introduced to address the potential conflict of interest. Recent high-profile DTI investigation reports[80] and litigation on the use of the organisational device of 'Chinese Walls'[81] to minimise professional conflicts of interest between divisions of a single firm suggest that self-regulatory strategies are not effective in dealing with such problems. This is an issue that will continue to cause difficulties with the increased tendency of accountancy firms to merge.

The seemingly intractable issue of how the law might facilitate the financing of business rescues was touched upon. The mere fact that this question is now attracting serious official attention[82] illustrates the increased sophistication amongst policymakers in their awareness of the practicalities of business rescue. The first-generation rescue models focused almost exclusively on initiating rehabilitation procedures without giving adequate thought to the vital issue of how finance was to be obtained for a company that was undergoing a rehabilitation. Incentives must be given to those providing new finance. This idea however clashes with the old established principle of equality amongst creditors. The arguments for and against offering a 'super priority' for new funders were

---

77 The authorities are still in the process of firming up how this new Voluntary Arrangements Service system will work; see DTI Press Notice P/2000/727 and [2001] *Simon's Tax Weekly Intelligence* 165.

78 In 1999 Richard Page MP unsuccessfully introduced a Private Member's Bill to have the practice banned. See also the comments of Rudi Vis MP and the response by the Minister for Competition and Consumer Affairs (1999) *Hansard* HC vol 990 at cols 1268–72.

79 See the research done by Katz and Mumford – referred to in para 117 of the Joint Report. An outline of this research is to be found in the pieces by Katz and Mumford, 'Receivership Following Investigation' (1999) 15 *Insolvency Law and Practice* 135 and Katz and Mumford 'Should an Investigating Accountant be Permitted to Become a Receiver?' [1999] (November) *Recovery* 20.

80 See DTI Report on *Mirror Group Newspapers plc* (London, TSO, March 2001) (in two volumes) – see DTI Press Notices P/2001/217 and P/2001/218 for a useful summary.

81 The leading case here is *Bolkiah v KPMG* [1999] 2 AC 222.

82 See Company Rescue and Business Reconstruction Mechanisms (London, DTI, November 2000) at paras 122–39.

rehearsed and thrown open to wider debate. The outcome of this discussion will be a critical determining factor in the future of business rescue.

For once it is pleasing to report that the work of a consultative committee has not been allowed to gather dust. In February 2001 the Government reaffirmed its commitment to progressing the law on company rescue.[83] That commitment was redeemed in July 2001 with the publication of its radical White Paper, *Insolvency – A Second Chance*.[84] This White Paper in many senses goes beyond what was contemplated by the working party. For example, Crown preferential debts are to be abolished;[85] a long-overdue reform if there ever was one. The reason for the apparent *volte face* in the course of the year was that the Government was only prepared to surrender its preferential rights if secured creditors also made a sacrifice. This sacrifice lies in the fact that the remedy of administrative receivership is no longer to be permitted except in the case of enforcement of a market charge.[86] In future creditors enjoying the security of a floating charge will have to make do with administration, though the relevant procedure has been modified to allow secured creditors to make urgent and *ex parte* applications to protect their interests.[87] In a similar vein is the recommendation to abolish the floating chargeholder's right of veto over the administration process;[88] a clearer indication of the triumph of the alliance of collectivism and utilitarianism over the conservative forces supporting private property rights cannot be imagined. Finally, having recognised the utility of rescue regimes, the Government has indicated that it wishes to make the administration order procedure available to foreign companies.[89] In an era of increasing cross-border commerce, this is a sensible reform; at the moment this result can only be achieved through the circuitous route of judicial cooperation set out in s 426 of the Insolvency Act 1986.[90] These welcome reforms are to be implemented in the Enterprise Bill 2002.

12 CONCLUSIONS

It is now apparent that the corporate rescue strategy is firmly established in English law,[91] and, indeed, in most developed corporate systems across the globe. Looking at this trend

---

83 See: *Opportunity for All in a World of Change* (2001) Cm 5052 (London, TSO, 2001) at para 5.13; and DTI Press Notice P/2001/74.

84 See *Insolvency – A Second Chance* (2001) Cm 5234 (London, TSO, 2001).

85 See *Insolvency – A Second Chance*, above n 84, at para 2.19.

86 See *Insolvency – A Second Chance*, above n 84, at para 2.5. But see DTI Press Notice P/2001/629.

87 See *Insolvency – A Second Chance*, above n 84, at para 2.10 for details.

88 See *Insolvency – A Second Chance*, above n 84, at para 2.15.

89 See *Insolvency – A Second Chance*, above n 84, at para 2.17. The unavailability of administration to foreign companies was assumed by Hirst J in *Felixstowe Dock & Railway Co v US Lines Inc* [1989] QB 360 at p 367.

90 See *Re Dallhold Estates (Pty) Ltd* [1992] BCC 394 – at present the foreign company will have to apply to its local court to persuade it to issue a letter of request for support from the English courts under Insolvency Act 1986, s 426; a time-consuming and expensive process not geared to the needs of modern globalised commerce.

91 Another indicator of its significance lies in the fact of its incorporation in the new model for limited liability partnerships established under the Limited Liability Partnerships Act 2000 with effect from 6 April 2001.

from a purely European perspective the surprising element is the lack of EU input.[92] This is partly due to a European reticence to get involved in matters of insolvency. The evidence is that such reluctance is now being cast off, as attested to by the EU Insolvency Proceedings Regulation[93] which will be of considerable utility in managing cross-border insolvencies in the years to come.

Statistically the trend towards usage of the new procedures is a positive one, with the major change occurring only in recent years. Thus, by referring to official figures one can see that in 1988–89 in Great Britain there were 11,052 cases of liquidation/receivership with a mere 187 administrations and 52 CVAs agreed.[94] In 1992–93 (the worst year on record for corporate insolvencies) the figures were as follows – 32,840 (liquidations and receiverships) 67 (CVAs) and 170 (administrations).[95] The official figures contained in the Insolvency Service General Annual Report for the year 1999 show that there were 443 administrations and 475 CVAs embarked upon in Great Britain. This compares with the combined total of 16,537 for insolvent company liquidations and receiverships.[96] The improved performance of these rescue regimes owes much to a growing awareness of their potential, both amongst entrepreneurs and their advisers. Directors may also be reacting to countervailing pressures to act imposed by the more draconian climate in which they work. Although the wrongful trading sanction has not lived up to expectations, the expansion of the director disqualification jurisdiction, which by virtue of the Insolvency Act 2000 reforms can now operate through binding undertakings given outside the parameters of the court, must surely have concentrated minds. Powerful lobbies such as banks and, more latterly, the preferential creditors, have come under growing pressure to give business rescue proposals a fair wind. Indeed, it is clear that the sentiments underpinning *The Cork Report*[97] that the opportunity to access a rescue procedure should be subordinated to the vested interests of secured creditors has been officially abandoned. A perusal of the provisions of the Insolvency Act 2000, the conclusions of the Joint DTI/Treasury Review Group[98] and the proposals in the July 2001 White Paper[99] to push for abolition of the private remedy of administrative receivership would confirm that revolution.

One discernible trend in the evolution of corporate rescue law is the creeping introduction of the idea of 'debtor in possession'. This was permitted under the original consensual CVA model with minimal monitoring by the supervisor. The new CVA

---

92 One potential point of interface between corporate rescue procedures and the EU can be found in the rules on State aids. Although Article 92 of the EEC Treaty would not render unlawful a general regime for the rehabilitation of distressed companies, it might be used to question ad hoc attempts (albeit backed by legislation) to salvage particular undertakings in particular industries as this may potentially produce an anti-competitive effect. On this issue see: *Ecotrade (Case C-200/97)* [1999] 2 CMLR 804 and *Industrie Aeronautiche (C-295/97)* [2000] 3 CMLR 825.

93 [2000] OJ L 160/L (29 May 2000) – effective from 31 May 2002. See: Omar 'New Initiatives on Cross-Border Insolvency in Europe' [2000] *Insolvency Lawyer* 211 and Dawson 'The European Regulation on Insolvency Proceedings' [2001] 4 *Receivers, Administrators and Liquidators Quarterly* 345.

94 Source: *Companies in 1990–91* (London, HMSO, 1991) Table C2 at p 35.

95 Source: *Companies in 1993–94* (London, HMSO, 1995) Table C2 at p 39.

96 Source: *Insolvency – General Annual Report (1999)* (London, TSO, 2000) Table 3 at p 6.

97 Above n 15.

98 See above at n 75.

99 See above at n 84.

mechanism extends the idea by allowing the directors to operate with the benefit of a moratorium for several months before the CVA proposal is put to creditors. In practice administrators have not allowed directors to remain in managerial control, though it is open to administrators to allow them to participate. This rarely happens at present. The Review Group urges administrators to revisit the possibilities here by taking advantage of the latitude permitted by the law and thereby to reduce the management costs of administration.[100] This potential development must be watched carefully. Certainly, the evidence is that English law is moving away from the model of creditor control of corporate rehabilitation to a more US-based model in which the executives are left to dig the company out of the hole in which it finds itself. This would be a major cultural change for English law and needs to be fully assessed in the light of research suggesting that management failure is often the major cause of corporate collapse.[101]

A significant measure of the success[102] of the corporate rescue bandwagon is to be found in the recommendations in the White Paper *Insolvency – A Second Chance*.[103] If we move towards the notion that all distressed companies must go through a gateway in the form of the administration regime before their legal future is determined, that suggests a much more proactive approach on the part of the State with a presumption in favour of the possibility of rescue being evaluated.

Notwithstanding these advances, there are areas in the new law of corporate rescue that require further examination. At last the value of empirical research is being recognised as an essential tool by policymakers.[104] One issue requiring study concerns the long-term fate of companies that have undergone a rescue procedure. It would be disappointing if the evidence showed that recourse to these dedicated rehabilitation mechanisms only served to provide a new source of income for insolvency practitioners whilst merely postponing the inevitable collapse.[105] Sceptics of the corporate rescue bandwagon always contended that the game was not worth the candle and that it was in the long-term interests of a free market economy to allow businesses to fail. That hypothesis deserves proper scrutiny.

---

100 See n 75 above at para 77.

101 This significant factor behind corporate failure has been identified in successive surveys carried out by R3 (formerly the SPI); for the latest survey see Heis 'R3's Ninth Survey – Observations' [2001] (February) *Recovery* 24.

102 Success can be measured by other criteria. Certainly the corporate rescue phenomenon has attracted a voluminous body of academic discourse – leading contributions here would include A Belcher *Corporate Rescue* (London, Sweet & Maxwell, 1997), D Brown *Corporate Rescue – Insolvency Law in Practice* (Chichester, John Wiley & Sons, 1996). All leading texts on company law also offer discrete and generous treatment of this subject.

103 Above n 84. See now Enterprise Bill 2002, designed to implement these recommendations.

104 The Company Law Review has made constructive use of independent and empirical research as part of its process of iteration; see *The Final Report*, above n 1, at p 509. The Insolvency Service Review Group commissioned research by Professor Franks and Dr Sussman, academics at the London Business School, to study the role of banks operating intensive care facilities for distressed companies – see paras 53–59 of the Report of the Review Group, see n 75 above. The Insolvency Service Review Group referred to other such research in developing its arguments and has called for (at para 64) a continuing programme of research funded by the Government and private sector in order to inform future policy discussion.

105 The author is carrying out research on this issue with Gary Cook, Naresh Pandit and Andrew Griffiths as part of an ICAEW-funded study.

One unpalatable question that policymakers will be forced to address in the years to come is whether corporate rescue mechanisms can ever be a statistical success and match the performance of comparators in the personal insolvency sphere (such as the individual voluntary arrangement model). I doubt if they ever will. We must return to the fact that human motivation dictates that it is easier to cast aside a failing corporate vehicle than it is to decide to accept one's fate as a bankrupt, no matter how user-friendly bankruptcy as an institution might become in the years ahead. Whilst there are few limitations upon the right to incorporate with the benefit of limited liability that fact of life and human nature will not change.

That is not to say that we should reject the corporate rescue philosophy. It is worth reiterating that advances have been made and notable successes achieved. Rather, policymakers should accept that there is a law of diminishing returns operating in this arena and that after the next round of reforms have been progressed there is a good argument for letting this matter rest and investing more effort in studying and regulating the causes of corporate distress, rather than dealing with the consequences and symptoms. There are signs that this exercise in refocusing the scope of the investigation is already in motion in some quarters.[106] Certainly, the significance of a better understanding of these matters will be increased if (as seems likely) we in the UK move further towards debtor in possession rehabilitation regimes.

---

106 The insolvency profession has lead the way in investigating these matters – see the R3 Ninth Survey which is noted by Heis 'R3's Ninth Survey – Observations' [2001] (February) *Recovery* 24.

PART 5

FINANCIAL SERVICES AND MARKETS

DISCIPLINARY PROCEEDINGS AGAINST AUTHORISED FIRMS AND APPROVED PERSONS UNDER THE FSMA 2000

Jonathan Marsh

1 INTRODUCTION

On 26 July 2001, *The Final Report* of the Company Law Review was published. *The Final Report* made a number of recommendations aimed at supporting the creation, growth and international competitiveness of British companies and providing fair and proportionate regulation for companies. For financial services companies, *The Final Report* is not the only significant development from a governance and competitiveness aspect. Of greater immediate significance is the new Financial Services and Markets Act 2000, which came into force on 1 December 2001.

The Act has its origins in the perceived failure of its predecessor, the Financial Services Act 1986, to prevent failures in the financial system. In particular, the Government appeared to believe that the old system of regulation by numerous self-regulating organisations was confusing, ineffective and inefficient in that large financial institutions offering a range of services had to deal with more than one regulator. The new Act seeks to overcome these failings by the creation of a one-stop, statutory regulator, the Financial Services Authority ('FSA') with a range of new powers to meet four regulatory objectives, namely the maintenance of confidence in the financial system, the promotion of public understanding of the financial system, the protection of consumers and the reduction of financial crime.[1] In discharging its functions, the FSA is under a statutory obligation to have regard to a number of key factors such as the desirability of maintaining the competitive position of the UK's financial services industry and the principle that burdens imposed by the FSA should be proportionate to the benefits which the imposition of that burden seeks to achieve.[2]

The FSA is, therefore, required to maintain a balancing act between its regulatory objectives and the need not to reduce the competitive position of the UK as a centre for financial services by overburdening those it regulates. Nowhere is the tension more manifest than in the area of the FSA's enforcement powers. The purpose of this essay is to analyse this tension by examining whether the Act strikes an appropriate balance between the need to maintain market confidence and protect consumers on the one hand and the rights of financial services companies and their individual employees against arbitrary or unfair enforcement action on the other. For the purposes of this essay, my main focus will be on the FSA's right to take disciplinary action against those firms and individuals who are subject to its handbook of rules as opposed to its powers of criminal prosecution and its power to fine for market abuse. This is because the procedural

---

1 See The Financial Services and Markets Act 2000, s 2; hereafter FSMA 2000.
2 See FSMA 2000, s 2(3).

safeguards applicable to criminal proceedings apply in the latter two cases but not in the former.

2 OVERVIEW OF THE FSA'S ENFORCEMENT POWERS

The Financial Services and Markets Act 2000 provides the FSA with a range of criminal, civil and regulatory powers. As far as criminal prosecution is concerned, the FSA has the power to prosecute offences contained in the Act or in subordinate legislation[3] made under the Act, such as the offence of carrying on or purporting to carry on a regulated activity without authorisation or exemption.[4] In addition, the FSA can prosecute the offences of insider dealing (contained in Part V of the Criminal Justice Act 1993) and breaches of prescribed money laundering regulations.

In addition to the institution of criminal proceedings, the Act empowers the FSA to impose penalties on any person whose conduct falls within the statutory definition of market abuse.[5] Although outside the criminal system for domestic classification purposes, during the Parliamentary passage of the Act, the Government accepted that the market abuse regime was criminal in nature in terms of assessing compliance with the European Convention on Human Rights (ECHR) and, as a result, introduced a series of measures designed to reduce the possibility of a challenge under the ECHR. These included imposing restrictions on the FSA's use of compelled evidence[6] and ensuring the provision of subsidised legal assistance in appropriate cases.[7]

The FSA may institute criminal proceedings against and impose penalties in respect of behaviour constituting market abuse on anybody. In other words, the application of the FSA's enforcement powers in these two areas is not limited to the restricted class of entities specifically authorised under the Act[8] to carry on regulated activities ('authorised persons'). In contrast, Part XIV of the Act equips the FSA with disciplinary tools that are reserved for authorised persons. The FSA also has the power to discipline individuals required to be registered with the FSA as 'approved persons' for breaches of the FSA's principles and code of practice for approved persons. Before examining the nature of the FSA's enforcement powers over authorised persons, it falls first to identify the limit of this jurisdiction by giving a brief overview of the scope of activity requiring authorisation under the Act.

---

3   See FSMA 2000, s 401.
4   See FSMA 2000, s 23.
5   See FSMA 2000, s 118.
6   See FSMA 2000, s 174(2).
7   See FSMA 2000, s 134.
8   See FSMA 2000, s 31.

3 REGULATED ACTIVITIES UNDER THE FINANCIAL SERVICES AND MARKETS ACT 2000

The Financial Services and Markets Act 2000 prohibits the carrying on of regulated activity in the United Kingdom other than by an authorised person or an exempt person.[9] Section 22 of the Act gives the Treasury the power to specify 'regulated activities' by order and this power has been used to make the Regulated Activities Order.[10] The Regulated Activities Order has replaced the authorisation requirements under the Financial Services Act 1986, the Banking Act 1987 and the Insurance Companies Act 1982. In replacing the authorisation requirements of these three statutes, the Regulated Activities Order effectively bestows upon the FSA the power to regulate business that was previously regulated by a diverse collection of regulators such as the Bank of England, the Securities and Investments Board (SIB), the self-regulating organisations (SROs)[11] overseen by SIB, and the Department of Trade and Industry. As a consequence, the FSA will have direct regulatory jurisdiction over a huge number of businesses ranging from sole practitioner financial advisers through to major investment banks.

4 DISCIPLINARY MEASURES

The Financial Services and Markets Act 2000 gives the FSA two methods of dealing with the misconduct of authorised persons in addition to the power to institute certain criminal proceedings and the power to fine for market abuse. These are the power of censure[12] and the power to impose an unlimited financial penalty.[13] The inclusion of the power to fine marks a significant increase in the regulatory armoury as none of the statutory financial services regulators had previously had the power to impose a financial penalty. Whereas for companies which were subject to direct regulation by SROs, this power is little more than the continuation in statutory form of a power to which they were already subject; for those industry participants not falling within this category, this will be a new departure.

Introducing consistency by making all financial services industry participants subject to a power to fine is difficult to disagree with in principle. The more significant issue concerns the FSA's exercise of that power. Companies engaged in financial services will be keen to ensure that the FSA does not significantly increase the regulatory burden by overzealous use of these powers and that there is a fair process available to challenge an FSA decision to fine. These issues will be examined in detail during the course of this essay, but first, what type of misconduct is subject to a power to fine?

'Misconduct' in this context refers to a contravention of a requirement imposed by or under the Financial Services and Markets Act. In most cases this is likely to be a breach of

---

9   See FSMA 2000, s 19(1).

10 See Financial Services and Markets Act 2000 (Regulated Activities) Order 2001, SI 2001/544.

11 The Investment Management Regulatory Organisation (IMRO), the Personal Investment Authority (PIA) and the Securities and Futures Authority (SFA).

12 See FSMA 2000, s 205.

13 See FSMA 2000, s 206.

the FSA's rules made under Part X of the Act but will also include many other requirements imposed by or under the Act such as the requirement for an authorised person not to act otherwise than in accordance with the scope of a permission to carry on regulated activity.[14]

It is worth noting at this point that only those firms specifically authorised under the Act are subject to rules made by the FSA and promulgated in its handbook. Consequently only authorised persons can commit 'misconduct' giving rise to the FSA's disciplinary powers in Part XIV of the Act. The FSA's handbook of rules is voluminous and covers, among others, areas relating to conduct of business, market conduct and financial resources. Breaches of any one of the FSA's detailed rules could, in theory, give rise to disciplinary action against the transgressor.

It is important to note that because an authorised firm or an approved person is also subject to the general criminal law and to the market abuse regime which applies to the world at large, they could be subject to a number of overlapping disciplinary jurisdictions in respect of the same activity. For example, as far as conduct involving dealing on the basis of inside information is concerned, the FSA could choose to prosecute an individual for a criminal offence under Part V of the Criminal Justice Act 1993 or institute proceedings against an individual or a firm for market abuse or seek to impose a public censure or a fine for a breach of one of the rules applying to authorised persons such as the requirement to observe proper standards of market conduct.[15] In addition, the same conduct may be prohibited by the rules of a recognised investment exchange of which the authorised person is a member. This is significant because different processes with varying degrees of protection for the accused will apply depending on which of these routes the FSA chooses to take. As a result, in the aforementioned example, the FSA could decide to institute rule-based regulatory proceedings on the ground that, in the light of the prohibition on using compelled evidence in criminal or market abuse proceedings,[16] it is much more likely to succeed in securing a finding of guilt. It is submitted that whilst the technical nature of certain market-related offences makes criminal conduct difficult to prove and there is a clear public interest in bringing offenders to book, such reasoning is dangerous in that it could have the practical effect of denying an authorised person a proper opportunity to defend an allegation which is, as far as seriousness and reputational risk is concerned, criminal in nature.

Another, but related, area of concern for authorised persons is that the overlapping jurisdictions referred to in the previous paragraph not only give the FSA the ability to choose the option with the least safeguards for the defendant, but also subject authorised persons to the risk of double (or even multiple) jeopardy. An alleged insider dealer who is a member of an exchange could face disciplinary action by the FSA and by the exchange to whose disciplinary rules he is subject.[17] Although the FSA has been careful in its policy

---

14 See FSMA 2000, s 20.

15 See Principle 5, FSA's Principles for Business, *FSA Handbook of Rules and Guidance*; available at www.fsa.gov.uk/handbook/.

16 See, generally, *Saunders v United Kingdom* (1996) 23 EHRR 313.

17 See, for example, the cases of: *SFA v Rudolf Wolff* (SFA Board Notice 540 of 1 March 2000) and *LME v Rudolf Wolff* (LME notice 00/209: A203 of 10 May 2000) where the defendant was prosecuted and fined by both the SFA and the LME for what were, in effect, the same offences.

statements to give assurance that this type of overlap will be avoided,[18] there is no inbuilt protection in the legislation which prevents overlapping actions against the same defendant.

Having looked in overview at the regulatory enforcement powers available under the new Act, it falls now to consider the exact nature of the FSA's investigative and prosecutorial powers in so far as they relate to disciplinary proceedings against authorised firms and approved persons. In examining these powers I will also consider the statutory protections which apply in relation to investigation and prosecution.

5 INFORMATION GATHERING AND INVESTIGATIONS

Part XI of the Financial Services and Markets Act gives the FSA wide-ranging powers to investigate and gather information. As far as the latter is concerned, the FSA can compel authorised persons[19] and persons who used to be authorised persons[20] to provide information and documents. Although compulsory information and documentation provision is not a new concept – for example, the Serious Fraud Office has powers of this nature under the Criminal Justice Act 1987 – the number of circumstances in which these powers can be used by the FSA is wider. The only criterion necessary to trigger this power is that the information and documents must be reasonably required by the FSA in connection with its statutory functions. This general information-gathering power may be used in a wide variety of situations and is not confined to problems within the firm served with a notice of investigation. It is also worth noting that the FSA may exercise this power not just in relation to authorised persons but also in relation to persons connected with authorised persons, an operator, trustee or depositary of certain overseas collective investment schemes and recognised investment exchanges and clearing houses.[21]

A power related to the information-gathering powers concerns the FSA's right to require all authorised persons to provide a report on any matter which could have been the subject of the information-gathering powers in s 165 of the Act.[22] The person required to make a report under this section has to be nominated or approved by the FSA and must appear to the FSA to have the skills necessary to make a report on the matter concerned.[23] In practice, a skilled person so appointed is likely to be a lawyer, accountant or person with particular commercial experience. Significantly the cost of producing such a report falls on the firm. This means that, in theory at least, a firm could be required to pay significant amounts to a law or accountancy firm only for the report to give a clean bill of health. In such circumstances, the firm would not be entitled to any compensation.

Clearly, the technical and complex nature of many aspects of the financial services industry means that it would be difficult for the FSA to meet its regulatory objectives

---

18 Eg, response to CP17 paras 67 onwards.
19 See FSMA 2000, s 165(1).
20 See FSMA 2000, s 165(8).
21 See FSMA 2000, s 165(7).
22 See FSMA 2000, s 166(1).
23 See FSMA 2000, s 166(4).

without wide-ranging information-gathering powers and without the ability to call upon appropriate expertise. Given the significant resources available to many financial services industry participants, it is not surprising that the Government has sought to level the playing field in terms of access to technical expertise. However, even large corporations have legal rights and it would be invidious if the FSA were to invoke these powers to pursue mere fishing expeditions. Such an approach would create a significant regulatory burden which would call into question the FSA's statutory duty to have regard to the UK's competitive position as a financial services industry centre.

Another significant power given to the FSA is the power to carry out general investigations into the nature, conduct or state of the business of an authorised person, a particular aspect of that business or the ownership or control of an authorised person.[24] Again the barrier to use of this power is not particularly high in that the FSA can invoke it if it believes that there is good reason for doing so. Given the subjective and general nature of this test, it is difficult to envisage a successful challenge to the use of the investigative power on the ground that there was not a good reason for doing so. Once again the rationale appears to be that the FSA should not be unduly hampered in its investigative role by procedural burdens which might give rise to legal challenge. The public interest demands this approach and its acceptability will depend to a large degree on the FSA's approach to its use in practice.

The Act contains provisions relating to the conduct of investigations which are worth looking at as part of the analysis of the balance between protecting the FSA's rights as regulator and the regulated community. Where the FSA has appointed investigators, it must serve a written notice on the person under investigation confirming that investigators have been appointed, specifying the provisions under which the investigator was appointed and stating the reason for the appointment.[25] In addition, if there is a change in the scope of the investigation and the FSA believes that the person under investigation might be prejudiced by not being made aware of this, written notice of the change of scope must be served. Although written notice of investigation serves to delineate possible enforcement action and thus provides those subject to investigation with some means to take steps to protect their legal rights, there is no statutory basis to challenge the service of a notice. It is also worth noting that the provisions relating to a notice of change of scope are unlikely to offer much comfort given that it is for the FSA to decide whether lack of awareness of the change poses a risk of significant prejudice to a person under investigation.

Another key area, in terms of the balance of power between the FSA and those subject to its disciplinary jurisdiction, concerns the powers available to investigators. Investigators appointed to investigate suspected instances of misconduct may require those subject to investigation or those associated with them to attend for interview and to provide such information as the investigator may require.[26] In addition, any person can be required to produce documents.[27] In order to exercise these powers, the investigator must reasonably consider the question, information or document to be relevant for the

---

24 See FSMA 2000, s 167(1).
25 See FSMA 2000, s 170(4).
26 See FSMA 2000, s 171(1).
27 See FSMA 2000, s 171(2).

purposes of the investigation.[28] Failure to comply with a requirement imposed under Part XI of the Act can, provided that the court is satisfied that the defaulter had no reasonable excuse, lead to the defaulter being treated as though there were a contempt of court. Where the defaulter is a company, the court may deal with any director or officer as though they were in contempt.

In summary, the FSA has a wide range of powers which can be used in a wide range of circumstances with serious consequences befalling those who fail to comply with an investigative requirement. Of course investigative powers are only part of the process. An analysis of the protections available to those under investigation must also look at the law as it relates to the evidential fruits of the investigation. A firm suspected of misconduct will obviously care less about the powers available to an investigator if there are limitations on the use of evidence obtained by the investigator. With this in mind, let us turn next to evidential provisions of the new Act.

6 ADMISSIBILITY OF EVIDENCE

In the light of case law on the use of compelled evidence,[29] it is unsurprising that Part XI of the Financial Services and Markets Act deals not only with the investigative powers available to the FSA but also with the admissibility of statements made to investigators. A statement compelled as part of an investigation is admissible in evidence so long as it complies with any requirements governing the admissibility of evidence in the circumstances in question.[30] This somewhat strange drafting arises from the fact that the FSA's investigative powers relate not only to acts of misconduct by authorised firms but also to the criminal offences which the FSA may prosecute and to market abuse. The Act therefore has to take account of the fact that admissibility of certain types of evidence depends on the context in which that evidence is to be used: some types of evidence will be admissible in civil proceedings but not in criminal proceedings.

In the majority of criminal proceedings[31] or in proceedings relating to market abuse,[32] the statement cannot be adduced in evidence against the maker of the statement unless he or those acting on his behalf have themselves put the statement in issue in the proceedings.[33] The inclusion of these provisions is designed to ensure that the FSA is not in breach of the safeguards required in criminal proceedings by Art 6 of the ECHR. The fact that the restriction on admissibility extends to market abuse proceedings, which is not strictly a criminal offence, is a reflection of the fact that for ECHR purposes, there is a strong likelihood that the market abuse regime would, notwithstanding its classification under domestic law as a civil regime, be regarded as criminal in nature and therefore

---

28 See FSMA 2000, s 171(3).
29 See *Saunders v United Kingdom* (1996) 23 EHRR 313. See also the Lidbetter essay at p 319 above.
30 See FSMA 2000, s 174(1).
31 By virtue of FSMA 2000, s 174(3), compelled evidence will be admissible in certain types of criminal proceedings, such as proceedings under s 177(4) relating to the provision of false or misleading information pursuant to an obligation under Part XI; proceedings under s 398 for misleading the FSA; and certain offences under statutes dealing with perjury.
32 See FSMA 2000, s 123.
33 See FSMA 2000, s 174(2).

subject to the additional procedural safeguards required by Art 6 in criminal cases.[34] The applicability of the ECHR to the FSA's enforcement powers is considered in more detail below.

Part XI of the Act therefore gives the FSA significant investigative powers which, in the case of proceedings instigated against authorised persons under the Part XIV disciplinary measures regime, can result in compelled statements being adduced in evidence to the detriment of the maker of that statement. Part XI itself provides little basis for a person to challenge a decision to investigate. A challenge to the FSA's right to initiate a general investigation on the basis that the grounds for exercising the power had not been made out would require an aggrieved party to demonstrate that there was no basis for the FSA to believe that there was good reason to commence a general investigation: an extremely difficult evidential burden to overcome. As far as compelled evidence is concerned a party wishing to challenge the FSA's right to adduce such evidence in disciplinary proceedings under Part XI could argue that there are a number of factors which should result in the characterisation of such proceedings as criminal for the purposes of determining compliance with the ECHR and that, as a consequence, compelled statements should not be admissible in evidence. The merits of such an argument will be explored in more detail below.

7 THE DISCIPLINARY PROCESS

Having looked at the investigative powers available to the FSA and the extent to which the Act itself provides protection against improper exercise of those powers, it falls now to consider the procedures and safeguards which apply where the FSA wishes to fine or censure an authorised entity.

Before the FSA can take action, it must serve a warning notice setting out the proposed statement of censure or the amount of the penalty as the case may be.[35] As well as specifying the action which it intends to take, the notice must also specify a reasonable period of at least 28 days within which the recipient may make representations to the FSA.[36] Having served a notice, the FSA must then allow the recipient access to material on which it relied in deciding to commence disciplinary proceedings. It must also disclose any secondary material which it believes might undermine that decision.[37] Secondary material is defined as material which was not relied upon but which was either considered by the FSA in reaching the decision or which was obtained by it in connection with the matter to which the notice relates.[38]

The disclosure obligation does not apply in all circumstances. Material which has been intercepted under warrant or which indicates that such a warrant has been issued or

---

34 See the Joint Opinion of Lord Lester QC and Javan Herberg dated 27 October 1998, submitted to the Joint Committee on Financial Services and Markets and the Report of the Joint Committee on the Draft Financial Services of Markets Bill (London, TSO, April 1999).

35 See FSMA 2000, s 297.

36 See FSMA 2000, s 387.

37 See FSMA 2000, s 394.

38 See FSMA 2000, s 394(6).

executed is excluded from the disclosure obligation. In addition, protected items, that is, material covered by legal professional privilege,[39] are also excluded. The FSA may also refuse to disclose evidence if it believes that the granting of access would not be in the public interest or would be unfair, when balancing the likely significance of the material to the case in question and the potential prejudice to the commercial interests of a third party if the material were to be disclosed.[40] In such cases, the FSA must give written notice of its refusal and the reasons for it. Significantly, there is no statutory right of challenge to such a decision and an aggrieved party wishing to challenge an FSA decision to refuse access to material would be required to seek judicial review on the basis, for example, that such a decision was irrational. The effect of this is to reverse the burden of justifying the decision in that it will be for the person affected by this refusal to assert irrationality on the part of the FSA and the FSA will simply be required to demonstrate that its decision was not wholly irrational. Given the significant prejudice that a refusal to disclose evidence might engender, it might have been fairer to build in a statutory right of challenge under which the FSA would be required to justify its decision.

Having received the notice and been given an opportunity to consider disclosed material, the recipient may make representations.[41] If, notwithstanding these representations, the FSA decides to proceed with disciplinary action, it must serve a decision notice setting out the statement or penalty.[42] As in the case of a warning notice, a decision notice must be in writing and must give reasons for the FSA's actions.[43] In addition, a decision notice must state whether the statutory provisions relating to the recipient's right to access evidential material are applicable[44] and, if so, what that means and whether secondary material exists to which the recipient must be given access.[45] The decision notice must also indicate whether there is a right to refer the decision to the Financial Services and Markets Tribunal and the procedure on such a reference.[46]

The FSA cannot issue a decision notice under one part of the Act where a preceding warning notice was issued under another.[47] It would not, therefore, be possible to issue a decision notice relating to market abuse under Part VIII when the warning notice concerned a proposed penalty for a breach of the rules applying to authorised persons. The reason for this is that different procedural provisions and rights apply under different parts of the Act. This Part of the Act provides a safeguard for defendants by preventing the FSA from depriving a defendant of legitimate rights by taking initial procedural steps under one part of the process only to proceed under a different part.

Where a recipient of a decision notice does not refer the matter to the Tribunal or when the FSA moves to implement the Tribunal decision, the FSA must serve a final notice.[48] The statutory provisions relating to the final notice require the FSA to give

---

39 See FSMA 2000, s 413.
40 See FSMA 2000, s 394(3).
41 See FSMA 2000, s 387(2).
42 See FSMA 2000, s 208.
43 See FSMA 2000, s 388(1)(a) and (b).
44 See FSMA 2000, s 388(1)(c).
45 See FSMA 2000, s 388(1)(d).
46 See FSMA 2000, s 388(1)(e).
47 See FSMA 2000, s 388(2).
48 See FSMA 2000, s 390.

details of what will happen and when. For example, a final notice about a penalty must state the amount payable, the manner in which, and period within which it is to be paid, and details of the way in which the penalty will be recovered if it is not paid by the date given in the notice.[49]

Rather than containing detailed procedural provisions relating to the circumstances in which the FSA might use warning and decision notices, the Act obliges the FSA to publish a statement about its procedures for their use. This requirement acts as a safeguard in that the procedure adopted by the FSA must be designed to secure, among other things, that the decision which gives rise to the obligation to serve a notice is not taken by a person directly involved in establishing the evidence on which that decision was based.[50] The rationale here appears to be that such an approach is more flexible than incorporating guidance into the statute: another example of a desire on the part of the Government not to hamstring the FSA. No doubt those who fall within the FSA's disciplinary jurisdiction would prefer to have seen the procedures incorporated into statute on the ground that this would be a more effective form of safeguard. However, in reality it is difficult to believe that the FSA would not feel bound to follow its own published procedures even though they do not have statutory force.

The mechanism that the FSA has adopted in order to ensure compliance with this obligation involves the use of a Regulatory Decision Committee (RDC).[51] According to the FSA's proposed policy, the FSA staff will consider whether to recommend that enforcement action be initiated and, if they are minded to initiate action, they will recommend to the RDC that a warning notice be given.[52] After considering the staff recommendation, the RDC will decide whether to send a warning notice or to take no further action. If a warning notice is served, the RDC will consider both written and oral representations made by the recipient of the warning notice and will then state its decision in a decision notice or a notice of discontinuance.[53]

In order to ensure that the RDC is independent of the FSA staff involved in uncovering the evidence, it will be a body which will be directly accountable to the FSA Board but which is outside the FSA's management structure. Other than the chairman, none of the members of the RDC will be an employee of the FSA. This procedure achieves, ostensibly at least, the separation of powers required by the Act. Although it is difficult to envisage the FSA ever failing to follow its published procedures, it is worth noting that failure to do so will not, of itself, affect the validity of any notice,[54] but may be taken into account by the Financial Services and Markets Tribunal in considering any matter referred to it.[55]

As well as imposing an obligation on the FSA to publish details of its procedure in relation to the service of notices, the Act also requires the FSA to publish a statement

---

49   See FSMA 2000, s 390(5).
50   See FSMA 2000, s 395(2).
51   See the Enforcement Manual, *FSA Handbook of Rules and Guidance*; available at www.fsa.gov.uk/handbook/.
52   See FSA Consultation Paper 65a, at para 3.6.5 (London, FSA, August 2000).
53   See FSA Consultation Paper 65a, above n 52, at para 3.6.34.
54   See FSMA 2000, s 395(11).
55   See FSMA 2000, s 395(12).

setting out its approach to financial penalties under Part XIV.[56] The Act requires that the FSA's policy in relation to penalties must include having regard to the seriousness of the breach, the extent to which it was deliberate or reckless, and whether or not the person on whom the penalty to be imposed is an individual.[57] The FSA has, in fact, gone beyond its statutory requirement by publishing a statement of its general approach to the discipline of firms and approved persons which, among other things, describes the FSA's policy in relation to private warnings and explains the criteria which the FSA will use in determining whether to take disciplinary action.[58] In general terms, the factors which the FSA proposes to take into account in deciding whether to institute disciplinary proceedings include: the nature and seriousness of the breach, the conduct of the firm after the breach, the firm's previous disciplinary record, relevant guidance issued by the FSA, action taken by it in previous similar cases, and action taken by other regulatory authorities. The FSA has indicated in its *Enforcement Manual* that formal enforcement action will be reserved for a minority of breaches and that many cases will be resolved by discussion between the firm and the FSA or by the giving of an informal warning. In publishing details of its general approach to enforcement, the FSA introduces a form of safeguard in that it will be open to defendants to raise arguments relating to the FSA's failure to follow its stated procedures where appropriate. This fact together with the statutory safeguards referred to above goes a significant way toward reducing the prospects of the FSA exercising its disciplinary jurisdiction in an arbitrary fashion.

8 THE FINANCIAL SERVICES AND MARKETS TRIBUNAL

Having looked at statutory provisions which define the extent of the FSA's enforcement powers, this section deals with the primary statutory safeguard for persons wishing to challenge the issue of decision notices: the Financial Services and Markets Tribunal. Established under Part IX of the Financial Services and Markets Act, the Tribunal is administered by the Lord Chancellor's Department. As such, it is a first instance tribunal fully independent of the FSA. In accordance with Schedule 13 to the Act, the Lord Chancellor is required to appoint a panel of persons comprising lawyers with at least a seven-year qualification to serve as chairmen of the Tribunal and must also appoint members of a lay panel comprising individuals who are qualified by experience or otherwise to deal with matters of the kind that may be referred to the Tribunal.[59]

The Act deals with some of the elements of the procedure relating to the conduct of Tribunal proceedings, although the power to make certain procedural rules is delegated to the Lord Chancellor. These include the circumstances in which hearings may be heard in private and it is in this area that the Procedure Rules issued by the Lord Chancellor's Department have caused most controversy. Ironically, the controversy stems from the Lord Chancellor's Department's desire to respect the provision of Art 6 of the ECHR in relation to the right to a public hearing. Rule 19 of the Procedure Rules provides that all

---

56 See FSMA 2000, s 210.
57 See FSMA 2000, s 210(2).
58 See FSA Consultation Paper 65a, above n 52, at Chapter 12.
59 See FSMA 2000, Schedule 13, para 3(4).

hearings in front of the Tribunal are public unless upon application of one of the parties, the Tribunal is satisfied that a private hearing is necessary having regard to (a) the interests of morals, public order, national security or the protection of the private lives of the parties; and (b) any unfairness to the applicant or prejudice to the interests of consumers that might result from a hearing in public, if, in either case, the Tribunal is satisfied that a hearing in private would not prejudice the interest of justice.

Normally, transparency in relation to the disciplinary process is an important safeguard for the rights of defendants. However, in relation to regulatory enforcement involving commercial organisations, damage to reputation can arise simply from the fact that disciplinary proceedings have been taken. Given the commercial cost of reputational damage, firms authorised under the Act would prefer to maintain the spirit of the old regulatory authorities who were happy to conduct disciplinary proceedings in private. In order to ensure privacy under the new regime, firms will need to overcome the stiff hurdles presented by para 19 by persuading the Tribunal that a public hearing would have implications beyond damage to reputation. On some analyses, therefore, the provisions relating to public hearings will undermine the protections which an independent first instance tribunal should provide in that they may well deter firms from referring matters to the Tribunal.

If a defendant decides to refer a matter to the Tribunal, the reference must be made within 28 days of the decision notice or such other period as may be specified in the rules of procedure.[60] The FSA is prohibited from taking any action specified in a decision notice during the period within which the matter could be referred to the Tribunal.[61] If the matter is referred, the FSA must refrain from taking action until determination of the matter by the Tribunal and, if appropriate, the conclusion of any appeal from the Tribunal's decision.

In its original inception, the Tribunal was to be an appeal tribunal with limited jurisdiction to entertain factual evidence. Such an approach would have led to the RDC being treated as a first instance tribunal. Given that this body is administered by the FSA, it was deemed to be insufficiently independent to fulfill this role and lobbying on this point led to the Tribunal being given the powers to consider any evidence relating to the subject matter of the reference, whether or not it was available to the FSA at the material time.[62]

Giving the Tribunal full jurisdiction to entertain all matters of fact was but one of a number of significant changes which occurred during the Financial Services and Markets Act's Parliamentary progress as a result of concerns about its compatibility with the ECHR. Another significant change relates to the granting of the right, in certain circumstances, to legal assistance for defendants in Tribunal proceedings relating to market abuse. The reason for this decision is that the Government appeared to accept that the market abuse regime was, for the purposes of determining compliance with the ECHR, criminal in nature[63] and that the additional protections provided by Art 6(2) and (3) of the ECHR (see below) in relation to criminal cases, such as the right to financial

---

60   See FSMA 2000, s 133.
61   See FSMA 2000, s 133(9)(a).
62   See FSMA 2000, s 133(3).
63   See the Joint Opinion of Lord Lester QC and Javan Herberg, above n 34.

assistance to obtain legal advice and representation, should apply. However, because the Government does not believe that misconduct in the sense of breaches of the FSA's rules or principles by authorised firms or approved persons is criminal in nature, legal assistance will not be available to individual, approved persons who face disciplinary proceedings for misconduct no matter how serious the consequences of such proceedings might be. Whether the failure to extend the scope of the financial assistance provisions in this direction amounts to a breach of the ECHR is examined below.

Although the provisions relating to financial assistance are outside the scope of this essay in that such assistance is not available for breaches of the FSA's rules, it is worth noting that, to a certain extent, the financial assistance scheme places an unfair burden on companies authorised to conduct financial services. Unlike normal legal aid, legal assistance before the Tribunal will not be funded by the taxpayer, but by the financial services industry itself. This is achieved by giving the Lord Chancellor the power to issue demands to the FSA from time to time to cover the actual or anticipated costs of the scheme.[64] In order to enable it to meet such demands, the FSA is required to make rules requiring the payment to it by authorised persons, or any class of authorised persons, of specified amounts.[65] This means that as market abuse proceedings can be taken against authorised and unauthorised persons alike, the authorised community could be required to fund assistance provided to unauthorised persons.

Unlike a court of law, the Tribunal may not impose penalties itself. Rather, the Tribunal's role is to determine what, if any, is the appropriate action for the FSA to take in relation to a referred matter[66] and, on determining a reference, to remit the matter to the FSA with such directions, if any, as the Tribunal considers appropriate for giving effect to its determination.[67] In determining a reference, the Tribunal cannot go further than the FSA could in that it may not direct the FSA to take action which the FSA would have been precluded from taking itself. This prohibits the FSA from issuing a decision notice under a part of the Act different from that under which the preceding warning notice was issued.[68] A final point worthy of note in relation to the Tribunal's role is that it may, on determining a reference, make recommendations as to the FSA's regulating provisions or its procedures.[69] Although there is no obligation for the FSA to implement recommendations of this nature, they would be bound to be influential and, at the very least, this provision provides a useful, independent oversight mechanism.

Appeals from decisions of the Tribunal are to the Court of Appeal (or the Court of Session in Scotland). The only ground of appeal is on a point of law arising from a decision of the Tribunal disposing of the reference.[70] Such appeals may only be brought with the permission of the Tribunal or the relevant appellate court.[71] Where the appellate

---

64 See FSMA 2000, s 136(1).
65 See FSMA 2000, s 136(2).
66 See FSMA 2000, s 133(4).
67 See FSMA 2000, s 133(5).
68 See FSMA 2000, s 133(5).
69 See FSMA 2000, s 133(8).
70 See FSMA 2000, s 137(1).
71 See FSMA 2000, s 137(2).

court decides that the Tribunal's decision was wrong in law, it may remit the matter to the Tribunal or itself make a determination.[72]

9 IMPACT OF THE ECHR

The above sections on investigation, enforcement and the tribunal process demonstrate that the procedural safeguards available to those subject to disciplinary proceedings as opposed to criminal or market abuse proceedings are less robust. As already noted, this arises from the fact that in framing the Financial Services and Markets Act 2000, the Government viewed disciplinary proceedings as 'civil' in nature and that, as a result, the full range of ECHR safeguards did not need to be applied. As we have seen throughout this analysis, a central preoccupation of those responsible for framing the legislation has been to ensure that the FSA is flexible enough to deal with complex issues in a fast-changing marketplace and to avoid swinging the balance of power in favour of those subject to the FSA's oversight by including unnecessary procedural safeguards. Consequently, there is a strong incentive for the Government to be bullish in its approach to the classification of disciplinary proceedings as civil. This section looks at the impact of the Human Rights Act 1998 on the application of the FSA's disciplinary regime and, in particular, whether the decision to treat disciplinary proceedings as civil is open to challenge.

The Human Rights Act incorporates most of the rights contained in the ECHR into English law and allows parties to raise Convention rights either as a 'shield' in defence of actions brought by public authorities or as a 'sword' to sue for damages for breach of their rights.[73] Although apparently anomalous, given its emphasis on protecting the rights of the individual against the State, the protections bestowed by the ECHR extend to corporate entities and commercial organisations as well as individuals.

An entity will be regarded as a public authority for the purposes of the Human Rights Act if it is a court or a tribunal or if it is a body whose functions are public in nature.[74] Despite being a private body limited by guarantee, there can be no doubt that the FSA exercises public functions and that it will, therefore, be regarded as a public authority within the meaning of the Act.

The article of the ECHR most relevant to the FSA's disciplinary jurisdiction is Art 6 which guarantees the right to a fair trial. Article 6 distinguishes between cases involving the determination of civil rights and obligations where certain basic rights are guaranteed and a criminal charge where additional safeguards are imposed. Article 6(1) is applicable to both civil and criminal cases. It provides an entitlement to a hearing which is fair, public, within a reasonable time and before an independent and impartial tribunal. Case law of the European Court of Human Rights has interpreted the concept of a fair trial to include a requirement for adversarial proceedings[75] at which a party must have the right

---

72 See FSMA 2000, s 137(3).

73 See Human Rights Act, 1998, s 7(1).

74 See Human Rights Act, 1998, s 6(3).

75 See: *Mantovanelli v France* (1997) 24 EHRR 370; *McMichael v United Kingdom* (1995) 20 EHRR 205.

to be present,[76] the right to be heard on all important issues[77] and the right to have access to all necessary information to conduct the case effectively.[78] In addition, there is a requirement for equality of arms which, in particularly complex or serious cases, may require financial assistance to be provided to pay for legal representation.[79]

Article 6(2) and (3) provide extra protection in criminal cases. This protection includes a presumption of innocence until proof of guilt, prompt and adequate information about the charges, adequate time and facilities to prepare the defence, financial assistance (if needed) to obtain legal advice and representation, the right to call and cross-examine witnesses and the right to an interpreter.

10 DISCIPLINARY PROCEEDINGS: CIVIL OR CRIMINAL?

As additional protections apply to defendants in proceedings classified as criminal for ECHR purposes, it is important to ascertain whether disciplinary proceedings instituted by the FSA will be classified as civil or criminal. Clearly, criminal offences in respect of which the FSA has prosecutional powers will be dealt with by the criminal courts and the safeguards applicable to all defendants in criminal proceedings will apply. In addition, as we have already seen, the Government has accepted that, despite its classification as a civil offence for domestic purposes, market abuse is likely to be regarded as criminal in nature as far as compliance with the procedural requirements of the ECHR is concerned. As noted above, it was for this reason that the Government included a right to financial assistance for defendants in Tribunal proceedings relating to market abuse. It was also for this reason that statements taken under compulsion from a person accused of market abuse may not be used in subsequent proceedings against this person.[80]

As far as the Government is concerned disciplinary proceedings, as opposed to market abuse or criminal proceedings, are civil in nature and the additional safeguards provided by Art 6(2) and (3) of the ECHR are not applicable. Both individual approved persons as well as authorised firms could face proceedings which may result in unlimited fines and, in the case of individuals, effective loss of livelihood without having the right to resist the use of compelled evidence or the right to financial assistance for legal advice. The lack of these rights could be of particular significance in the case of individuals employed by financial services firms. In order to evaluate the Government's reasoning in relation to the characterisation of disciplinary proceedings, it falls first to analyse the law relating to the classification of an offence as criminal within the meaning of Art 6.

The European Court of Human Rights has emphasised that a restrictive approach to the characterisation of offences for the purposes of Art 6 would frustrate the aim and purpose of the provision, given that the right to a fair trial is a fundamental ingredient of a democratic society.[81] Correct characterisation of proceedings depends on an assessment

---

76 See *Monnell and Morris v United Kingdom* (1988) 10 EHRR 205.
77 See *Lobo Machado v Portugal* (1996) 23 EHRR 79.
78 See *McGinley and Egan v United Kingdom* (1999) 27 EHRR 1.
79 See *Airey v Ireland* (1979) 2 EHRR 302.
80 See FSMA 2000, s 174(2).
81 See *De Cubber v Belgium*, Series A No 86 (1985) 7 EHRR 236.

by reference to three criteria.[82] The first involves a consideration of whether or not the text defining the offence belongs, in the domestic legal system, to the criminal law. Secondly, consideration must be given to the nature of the offence, and thirdly the nature and degree of severity of the penalty that can be imposed must be examined.

In order to prevent States from being able to circumvent the requirements of Art 6(2) and (3), the classification of proceedings as civil under domestic law is deemed to be of relative value and no more than a starting point[83] and for this reason the second and third criteria have to be assessed. Under the second criterion, the first consideration is whether the offence applies only to a specific group or is of general application. The fact that regulatory proceedings only apply to persons engaged in a particular market or profession may help to sway the balance in favour of a civil classification but will not be conclusive in determining the issue. In *Campbell and Fell v United Kingdom*,[84] for instance, prison offences belonging to a disciplinary law rather than the criminal law under domestic classification were held to be criminal in nature by virtue of the seriousness of the penalty (deprivation of liberty through loss of remission and cellular confinement) even though the proceedings applied only to a limited population, namely prisoners.

The third criterion concerns the nature and severity of the penalty that may be imposed. This criterion is often decisive and, even if the second criterion is not met because the disciplinary jurisdiction is not of general application, the nature and severity of the penalty may still make Art 6(2) and (3) applicable.[85] The fact that fiscal penalties may be imposed, if they are punitive in nature, such as fines and disqualification, gives proceedings a criminal character for the purposes of characterisation under Art 6.[86]

In the light of the above, it is not surprising that the Government sought to provide additional safeguards for defendants in market abuse proceedings. There can be little doubt that the statutory nature of the market abuse offence, the fact that it may be committed by authorised and unauthorised persons alike and the severity of the unlimited fining power combine to make a compelling case for 'criminal' characterisation. The more difficult question is whether the general disciplinary offences, such as a breach of the FSA rules or principles, applicable only to authorised persons, would be deemed to be criminal in nature.

The Government's decision not to extend the additional safeguards required by Art 6(2) and (3) appears to be based largely on the fact that the regime applies only to authorised persons rather than the population as a whole and that the proceedings are, as a result, akin to the disciplinary proceedings of a professional body. On the face of it such an approach is open to challenge. Fines in respect of misconduct are without limitation and authorisation or approval may be withdrawn, resulting in loss of livelihood for individuals. These fiscal penalties are severe and are certainly punitive in nature. In addition, the restriction of the regime to authorised persons does not bear strict comparison to the disciplinary regimes of certain professions, such as those overseen by

---

82 See *Engel v Netherlands* (1976) EHRR 647.
83 See *Özturk v Germany* (1984) 6 EHRR 409.
84 See *Campbell and Fell v United Kingdom* (1985) 7 EHRR 165. Note also *R v Home Secretary* [2001] 1 WLR 1731.
85 See *Demicoli v Malta* (1992) 14 EHRR 47.
86 See *Lutz v Germany* (1988) 10 EHRR 182.

the General Medical Council in relation to the medical profession or the Law Society in relation to the solicitors' profession. Although in a strict sense, only a 'limited population' is subject to the FSA's disciplinary proceedings jurisdiction, the fact remains that the FSA is a large, powerful public body which regulates one of the UK's foremost industries. As a consequence, it is perhaps stretching things a little to view the large number of financial services players as a 'limited population'.

If a challenge to the Government's view of the FSA's disciplinary jurisdiction as 'civil' were successful a number of significant consequences would flow. Two of the most significant relate to the use of compelled evidence and the provision of financial assistance to obtain legal advice. As far as the first of these issues is concerned, the Financial Services and Markets Act 2000 provides that a statement made to an investigator is admissible in evidence in any proceedings except those relating to criminal offences or market abuse.[87] In criminal or market abuse cases, statements made by the accused under compulsion may not be used in subsequent proceedings against him. This exception is based upon the ruling of the European Court of Human Rights in *Saunders v United Kingdom*[88] where it was held that, whilst statutory powers of compulsion did not in themselves offend the ECHR, use of compelled statements made by the accused in evidence in a subsequent criminal trial against the accused would be a breach of Art 6, in particular the Art 6(2) presumption of innocence, and would render the trial unfair. It follows that if FSA disciplinary proceedings for misconduct were to be classified as criminal rather than civil, the right to use compelled evidence in such proceedings would be open to challenge.

Turning next to financial assistance to obtain legal advice, Art 6(3)(c) of the ECHR provides specifically for legal assistance to be provided free where the interests of justice so require. Whilst not relevant to authorised firms as they would not, in any event, be eligible for legal aid, the lack of availability of financial assistance in disciplinary proceedings involving approved persons charged in their personal capacity is highly pertinent. The FSA has the resources to support its enforcement actions with teams of investigators and lawyers including leading external law firms and barristers. An individual against whom disciplinary proceedings are taken is unlikely to have the resources necessary to bear equal arms and this may well result in a lack of due process.

The issue of criminal or civil classification in the context or regulatory proceedings was considered in the recent case of *Ex p Fleurose*.[89] This action arose from the Securities and Futures Authority (SFA) Disciplinary Tribunal's finding of guilt against Mr Fleurose in respect of a breach of the FSA's general principles and the subsequent dismissal of Mr Fleurose's appeal by the SFA's Disciplinary Appeal Tribunal. Mr Fleurose applied for judicial review of those decisions on the basis that the SFA's proceedings should have been classified as criminal for the purposes of the ECHR and that he should, therefore, have been given additional procedural safeguards. In particular, Mr Fleurose claimed the he had been deprived of the right not to have compelled evidence used against him in

---

87 See FSMA 2000, s 174(1).
88 See *Saunders v United Kingdom* (1996) 23 EHRR 313.
89 See *R v The Securities and Futures Authority Limited Disciplinary Appeal Tribunal of the Securities and Futures Authority Limited ex p Bertrand Fleurose* [2001] IRLR 784, upheld at [2001] EWCA Civ 2015.

that statements he made to the London Stock Exchange, in the course of its investigation of his dealings, were admitted in evidence before the SFA tribunal. He also claimed that he had been deprived of the right to legal assistance and that prosecution for breach of a vague general FSA principle breached Art 7 of the ECHR, which provides that there should be no retrospectivity in respect of offences and that acts which give rise to liability must be clearly foreseeable.

The court held that SFA disciplinary proceedings were not 'criminal' for ECHR purposes.[90] In arriving at this decision the court recognised the fact that the SFA process is not classified as 'criminal' under UK law was not decisive. However, the court took account of the fact that SFA disciplinary proceedings could only be brought against SFA-registered persons and not against the general public. In addition, any SFA fine (whilst potentially unlimited in amount) could only be enforced as a civil debt, without the sanction of imprisonment or contempt of court for failure to pay. Interestingly, the court also held that, despite its failure to classify the proceedings as 'criminal', the ECHR safeguards could still be relevant as part of the general right to due process available in all proceedings. In addition, it was held that it was a basic right in all disciplinary proceedings, civil or criminal, that the defendant should only be found guilty of misconduct if, at the time he committed the alleged offence, he knew or ought reasonably to have known that his actions constituted an offence. On the facts, however, Mr Fleurose was held not to have established that he had not known that what he had done was wrong at the time.

This case has some interesting implications as far as FSA disciplinary proceedings are concerned. The decision provides support for the Government's stance that the disciplinary process is not 'criminal' for ECHR purposes and, in particular, for the right of the FSA to use compelled evidence in disciplinary proceedings. Indeed, as far as this last point is concerned, the court in the *Fleurose* case held that restricting the use of compelled evidence in SFA disciplinary proceedings would hamper the regulator in its function of protecting the public and effectively force it to continue to accept as an authorised or approved person someone who, it knew, was unfit to be so.

On the other hand, the court did indicate that the ECHR might sometimes compel States to provide for legal assistance in some 'civil' cases where representation was considered to be indispensable for effective access to the court either because it was mandatory or because of the complexity of the case. The court also made some other general observations about the standards of fairness that would apply in any disciplinary proceedings, civil or criminal, which will be of particular relevance to disciplinary proceedings against authorised firms and approved persons. First, the court indicated that some of the rights specified in the ECHR as relevant to criminal proceedings have more general relevance to 'civil' cases. These rights include, in particular, the right to be informed promptly of the nature and cause of the charges, the right to adequate time and facilities to prepare a defence and the right to examine witnesses. Secondly, the court also indicated that a person against whom disciplinary action is being taken should not have to establish his innocence and that a 'sliding scale' would apply to the standard of proof

---

90 Cf Company Director Disqualification Act cases where it has been accepted that these types of cases are 'civil', see *Official Receiver v Stern* [2000] 1 WLR 2230.

such that the standard will vary according to the circumstances, and little, if any, practical difference is likely to be detectable in practice between 'civil' and 'criminal' discipline.

11 CONCLUSIONS

For companies engaged in financial services, the introduction of the Financial Services and Markets Act is a significant reform in that it creates a single regulator with a range of powerful enforcement tools at its disposal. For some, such as those engaged in mortgage lending, where, prior to the introduction of the Act, there was no formal regulation, the degree of regulatory oversight to which they will be subject will be an entirely new experience. For those previously subject to SRO regulatory oversight, the Act does not represent such a cataclysmic break with the past although there is inevitably a certain nervousness that, having been given an array of regulatory tools, the FSA will be seeking to use them on a regular basis.

Inevitably such nervousness is most manifest in the area of enforcement where the consequences of overexuberance on the part of the FSA would have the most damaging consequences on those subject to its regulatory oversight. The application of criminal procedural safeguards to the market abuse regime has gone some way to alleviating these concerns but, as we have seen, the safeguards have not been applied to disciplinary proceedings involving allegations of rule breach misconduct by authorised persons. Notwithstanding the court's findings in the *Fleurose* case, the Government's view that disciplinary proceedings are 'civil' in nature is open to challenge as it appears that, even in a 'civil' case, the basic right to a fair trial under Art 6 of the ECHR may require the application of additional safeguards on a case-by-case basis depending on the seriousness and complexity of the case in question.

On a practical basis, companies are not overly concerned with technical legal analysis and ECHR jurisprudence. They simply want to ensure that the FSA will not be oppressive in its use of disciplinary action. So, how likely is the FSA to be overburdensome in the discharge of its disciplinary function? The FSA's powers have been four years in the making during which period there has been intense Parliamentary scrutiny and widespread industry consultation. The FSA is a very visible, public body and, notwithstanding the theoretical scope of its powers, is most unlikely, for political reasons, to act in an arbitrary and unfair manner. To do so would undermine its credibility in the eyes of the financial services industry and the public at large. Such credibility is essential to the proper discharge of its regulatory function and its desire to maintain this is likely to prove a most effective procedural safeguard.

In addition, participants in the financial services industry have much to gain from a properly regulated industry. The competitive position of the UK as a place to conduct financial services business depends not only on avoiding overburdensome regulation but also on preserving the reputation of the UK as an international financial services centre. Orderly and well-regulated markets promote public confidence which, in turn, encourages use of those markets and more business for those providing financial services. Undoubtedly the FSA has to negotiate a difficult path between the interests of the public at large and the interests of the financial services industry but, given that these interests often overlap and that there is a significant political disincentive to the FSA abusing its powers, there are many reasons to be hopeful that the FSA will strike an appropriate balance between protecting the integrity of the marketplace and the rights of those engaged in the provision of financial services.

CHAPTER 19

THE MARKET ABUSE REGIME – RESHAPING INSIDER DEALING PROHIBITIONS

Lisa Linklater

1 INTRODUCTION

Insider trading has proved a particularly difficult nettle to grasp, not only in this jurisdiction, but elsewhere. How does one determine when the line has been crossed between opportunism and illegitimate behaviour? How does one define the type of information which may be used in or in relation to the financial markets? To what extent should the State, alternatively market users, be involved in setting these parameters? How does one ensure sufficient certainty in the law to preserve the liquidity of the markets, at the same time as maintaining enough flexibility in the law to react to new sharp practices? What sanctions are appropriate to this type of behaviour? What level of censure does insider trading deserve? How does one actually change market behaviour? These are some of the issues that have underpinned and continue to shape prohibitions against insider trading. They make formulating an appropriate response and articulating the policy supporting such response a complex task.[1] In this country, insider trading has primarily been addressed by the criminal law, most recently in the shape of Part V of the Criminal Justice Act 1993 (CJA). The Government has now taken the opportunity in the Financial Services and Markets Act 2000 (the Act) to create a new statutory offence of market abuse. The market abuse offence addresses two types of behaviour: misuse of information and market manipulation. The misuse of information offence will introduce a new and modern approach to insider trading,[2] which will supplement rather than supersede the criminal offence of insider dealing contained in Part V of the Criminal Justice Act 1993. The creation of the market abuse offence has been one of the most significant and controversial aspects of the new Act. This essay will put the misuse of information offence in context before considering how the new offence reshapes existing insider trading prohibitions.

Given that insider dealing has been prevalent for many years,[3] it may seem surprising that insider dealing was only first made a specific criminal offence under Part V of the Companies Act 1980. In fact, such legislation followed a decade of debate and unsuccessful attempts in Parliament to legislate on insider dealing in the 1973–74 and

---

1   As one writer has noted, 'despite widespread popular support for sanctions against insider trading, the reasons for such sanctions are hard to identify,' see Boyle 'A Theory of Law and Information: Copyright, Spleens, Blackmail and Insider Trading' (1992) 80 *California Law Review* 1413 at p 1429.

2   The offence of market abuse came into effect on 1 December 2001, along with many other provisions of the Financial Services and Markets Act 2000, by virtue of the Financial Services and Markets Act 2000 (Commencement No 7) Order 2001, SI 2001/3538; hereafter FSMA 2000.

3   See, eg, Robb *White Collar Crime in Modern England* (Cambridge, Cambridge University Press, 1992) and Banner *Anglo-American Securities Regulation* (Cambridge, Cambridge University Press, 1998). Commissioners appointed by Parliament in 1696 reported that the 'pernicious art of stockjobbing hath of late wholly perverted the End and Design of Companies' and illustrated this by reference to insider dealing: see *Journal of the House of Commons* 25 November 1696.

1978–79 parliamentary sessions, both of which were curtailed by general elections.[4] The criminal offence of insider dealing was re-enacted with minor amendments in the Company Securities (Insider Dealing) Act 1985. The European Union then played its role in shaping the criminal offence of insider dealing.[5] Insider dealing prohibitions were included within the 1992 single-market programme, culminating in the Council Directive Co-ordinating Regulations on Insider Dealing.[6] Member States were obliged to bring their legislation into line with this directive. Although one may think that the United Kingdom had been slow in introducing legislation to combat insider dealing, many of its European counterparts only introduced legislation prohibiting insider dealing following this directive.[7] Various amendments were made to ensure compliance with the directive, the result being Part V of the Criminal Justice Act 1993. The latter provisions remain and will continue to be the source of the criminal provisions against insider dealing.

While the criminal offence of insider dealing has hitherto been the primary direct response to insider trading, there are a number of other provisions that have indirectly addressed insider trading. First, directors and their associates are subject to obligations to disclose certain share dealings to both the company of which they are directors and the financial markets. These obligations are primarily contained in statute,[8] and supported by provisions such as the Listing Rules.[9] Statutory intervention was necessary to create such disclosure obligations because the common law has been constrained by the decision of *Percival v Wright*,[10] where the court held that directors of a company do not owe fiduciary duties to individual shareholders. Consequently, directors were not obliged to disclose material facts relating to the value of the company when negotiating with shareholders for the purchase of their shares.[11] The Model Code, which prohibits directors from dealing in securities in the company of which they are director for certain periods in a number of proscribed situations, provides another valuable source of indirect assistance to the criminal law.[12] Finally, mention should be made of the Panel on Takeovers and Mergers. This body was set up in 1968 on the proposal of the Governor of the Bank of England and the Chairman of the London Stock Exchange to address concerns of practices unfair to shareholders in a number of controversial takeovers. The City Code on Takeovers and Mergers (the City Code) contains provisions designed to ensure that select

---

4 See House of Commons Committee on Trade and Industry, Third Report, *Company Investigations* (1989–90) HC 36 at para 142 (London, HMSO, 1990).

5 The United Kingdom's membership of the European Union will continue to play an important role in shaping responses to insider trading. The European Commission issued a draft directive on market abuse on 30 May 2001; available at http://europa.eu.int/comm/internal_market. See also 'EU ministers agree curbs on insider dealing' *Financial Times* 14 December 2001.

6 Council Directive 89/592 EEC.

7 See, eg, McCormack 'Insider Dealing – New Departures in Ireland' (1991) 12 *Business Law Review* 146.

8 The Companies Act 1967, ss 27–30 required directors to disclose to the company details of interests which they or members of their families had in their company's securities and of any change therein. Similar provisions are contained in the Companies Act 1985, ss 324–29.

9 See, for instance, para 16.13 of the Listing Rules.

10 [1902] 2 Ch 421.

11 Recently, the strict application of this principle has been questioned in the context of unlisted companies, particularly small, family companies: see *Peskin v Anderson* [2000] 2 BCLC 1 at p 14 *per* Neuberger J and *Peskin v Anderson* [2001] 1 BCLC 372 at p 379 *per* Mummery LJ.

12 The Model Code for transactions in securities by directors, certain employees and persons connected with them, which forms an appendix to the Listing Rules. Consistent with the Financial Services Authority (FSA) taking over the role of UK Listing Authority from the London Stock Exchange on 1 May 2000, the FSA will prepare the Model Code.

groups of shareholders (for instance directors) cannot take unfair advantage of other shareholders in takeover bids. The common thread between these different provisions is that they seek to achieve fairness between market users by ensuring that those at the heart of the company are obliged to share price-sensitive information with others. By contrast with the criminal law, which is remedial in nature, these various provisions are directory.

However, the totality of provisions providing either prevention or cure fell short of providing an effective response to insider trading, albeit that they all have an important role to play. One drawback of the criminal law is that the cost of investigating and prosecuting white-collar crime is likely to be disproportionate to the public opprobrium it attracts. Further, as will be illustrated below, the prosecution are faced with real difficulties in crossing the various high hurdles of the narrowly drafted statutory offence, which is difficult to adapt to new circumstances. These difficulties are exacerbated by the fact that the prosecution must satisfy the court of the guilt of an accused beyond reasonable doubt. Further, the sanctions of the criminal law rather miss the point that this type of behaviour is all about money. Although an offender may face a penalty, the reality is that the sanctions of the criminal law fail to deprive an offender of his ill-gotten gains and do little to truly recompense 'victims' of the crime. Someone considering committing the offence of insider dealing may weigh all these heavy odds against a successful prosecution into the balance and consider that the risk of being caught is outweighed by the potential gain that may be made. If this is correct, the net effect is to undermine the force of the law. Further, the indirect responses to insider trading are just that – they are not and were not designed to be a complete response to such activity – the City Code is primarily concerned with takeovers and mergers and the Model Code is directed at a limited class of market users. As the financial markets became more accessible to a greater number of people in a wider number of jurisdictions, the need for a further direct response to insider trading became more compelling. Such response is the misuse of information offence introduced by the Financial Services and Markets Act 2000 as one aspect of the offence of market abuse. The market abuse regime borrows many of the assets of a self-regulatory regime, in particular by offering flexibility, informality and a set of rules which are significantly influenced by market users. However, the market abuse regime goes beyond self-regulation by offering effective investigatory and enforcement powers. At the same time, this is an essentially civil regime, which escapes many of the shortcomings of the criminal law in addressing insider trading.

However, it is important to note that the various existing provisions outlined above will not be superseded by the offence of misuse of information, but will retain an important role in the overall regulation of insider trading. It is particularly important to retain the criminal offence of insider dealing for a number of reasons. First, the criminal offence signals that the State perceives insider trading as serious conduct, in some cases meriting a term of imprisonment, and that such conduct is deserving of moral condemnation. Indeed, the criminal law underlines the various other provisions – for instance reference is made to the criminal offence of insider dealing in the introduction to the Model Code. The criminal law is also important from the perspective of the international regulation of financial crime.[13] The relevance of the criminal law is

---

13   For instance, insider dealing became an extraditable offence under the Criminal Justice Act 1988: see Rider and Ashe *Insider Crime* (Bristol, Jordans, 1993) at p 87.

underlined by the fact that the Financial Services Authority (FSA) (which has the overall responsibility for investigating and prosecuting the market abuse offence of misuse of information) has acquired power under s 402 of the Act to prosecute the criminal offence of insider dealing in England and Wales.[14] Some may nevertheless argue that the criminal law is of diminished significance, but it is suggested that such a view would overstate the use of the criminal offence of insider dealing in practice. A better view is that the role of the criminal law is now clearer, namely as a reserve power for the most heinous cases of insider trading. In addition, bodies such as the Panel on Takeovers and Mergers continue to have a particular role to play in ensuring fairness within the financial markets. Consequently, the misuse of information offence will run in tandem with the criminal offence of insider dealing, the City and Model Codes and the rules of Recognised Investment Exchanges such as the London Stock Exchange. Accordingly, a person must not only consider whether their behaviour amounts to market abuse, but also whether they have committed the criminal offence of insider dealing or fallen foul of regulatory provisions.

2 AN INTRODUCTION TO THE OFFENCE OF MISUSE OF INFORMATION

The offence of misuse of information introduced by the Act fills an important and substantial middle ground between the criminal law of insider dealing and the indirect responses to insider trading. The market abuse regime borrows from both the criminal law and self-regulation but offers an innovative approach in many areas. The most striking features of the offence of market abuse in the context of insider trading are its flexibility, scope and the new range of civil sanctions it introduces. At the same time, the market abuse offence has tailored and modernised the provisions of the criminal offence of insider dealing to fit the new misuse of information offence. The manner in which prohibited information is defined and the defences available are particular areas which deserve mention in this context. In addition, the powers of investigation applicable to both misuse of information and insider dealing have been revised.

Section 118 of the Financial Services and Markets Act 2000 creates the offence of market abuse, which includes the offence of misuse of information. The preliminary triggers for market abuse are that:

(a) the 'behaviour occurs in relation to qualifying investments';[15]

(b) 'traded on a market to which [s 118] applies';[16]

(c) 'which satisfies any one or more of the conditions set out in sub-s (b)';[17]

(d) 'which is likely to be regarded by a regular user of the market who is aware of the behaviour as a failure on the part of the person or persons concerned to observe the

---

14 This power is not however exclusive to the FSA; see further below at p 473 onwards.
15 See FSMA 2000, s 118 (1)(a).
16 See FSMA 2000, s 118(1)(a).
17 See FSMA 2000, s 118(1)(a).

standard of behaviour reasonably expected of a person in his or their position in relation to the market';[18]

(e) within the territorial scope of the Act.[19]

The relevant condition provided by s 118(2) of the Act in respect of the misuse of information offence is that:

> ... the behaviour is based on information which is not generally available to those using the market but which, if available to a regular user of the market, would or would be likely to be regarded by him as relevant when deciding the terms on which transactions in investments of the kind in question should be effected.[20]

3 THE MISUSE OF INFORMATION OFFENCE: A NEW APPROACH

3.1   Flexibility

One of the restrictions of the criminal offence of insider dealing are the rigid and narrow definitions used by Part V of the Criminal Justice Act 1993, some of which are considered in greater detail below. In addition, it is extremely difficult to adapt the law quickly to meet new situations. The Financial Services and Markets Act 2000 counters the criminal law by introducing a regime that is very flexible in a number of ways including the phrases it uses to define the offence, particularly the central concept of 'the regular user' and the use of the Code of Market Conduct. However, a flexible law must not become an arbitrary law if it is to maintain credibility. Further, the law must be sufficiently clearly defined so that a person may foresee the consequences of his actions. The Joint Committee of the House of Lords and House of Commons on Financial Services and Markets (hereafter the Joint Committee) acknowledged 'the Government's dilemma' on this point.[21] Some flexibility is necessary in order to make legislation effective, but too much flexibility may provide a potential 'means of escape' to wrongdoers[22] and lead to excessive caution on the part of business.[23]

The key components of the offence of market abuse used in the Act are vague and fluid, such as 'behaviour'; 'the regular user' and 'information that is not generally available'. Although these phrases are open-ended, they are barely defined in the Act. For instance, the only expansion upon 'behaviour' is that it includes both 'action' and 'inaction'.[24] Similarly, the Act sheds little light on when information will be regarded as 'generally available'.[25] The majority of guidance on the expressions used in the Act is set

---

18 See FSMA 2000, s 118(1)(c).
19 Defined by FSMA 2000, s 118(5).
20 See FSMA 2000, s 118(2)(a).
21 Joint Committee of the House of Commons and House of Lords on Financial Services and Markets (the Joint Committee), *Second Report*, 27 May 1999 (Session 1998–99) at para 29 (London, TSO, 1999).
22 See above, n 21 at para 7 of Appendix 9.
23 See above, n 21 at para 29.
24 See FSMA 2000, s 118(10).
25 The Act clarifies that information which can be obtained by research or analysis conducted by, or on behalf of, users of a market is to be regarded for the purposes of [s 118] as 'generally available', see FSMA 2000, s 118(7).

out in a document entitled the Code of Market Conduct ('the Code'), which forms part of the FSA's Business Standards in the FSA's handbook (known as 'the Handbook').[26] The Code will be supplemented by guidance given by the FSA to market users.[27] The FSA has been obliged by the Act to issue the Code of Market Conduct.[28] The Code is, therefore, not directly subject to the rigours of the parliamentary process, an issue which provoked considerable debate in the course of progress of the Financial Services and Markets Bill.[29] The Act provides that the Code of Market Conduct is only persuasive and not conclusive as to what amounts to market abuse.[30] By contrast, behaviour described in the Code of Market Conduct as not amounting to market abuse is conclusive according to the Act.[31] Behaviour within these descriptions (which are called 'safe harbours' in the Code) will be afforded a defence. This final scheme has been driven by two main factors. First, the desire for flexibility in this area of regulation – a too tightly drafted scheme allows the devious and clever room for sharp practice in behaviour that technically complies with the Code but is nevertheless market abuse.[32] Secondly, concerns as to unlawful delegation of power to the FSA if the Code were definitive as to what amounts to market abuse.[33]

The safeguard that has been built into the statutory scheme to answer concerns as to the extent of the powers vested in the FSA is the requirement that the Code be subject to public consultation before it is issued.[34] The consultation that has taken place has not been merely lip service. Consultation with market users has truly shaped the Code's development. This will undoubtedly help to give the Code credibility from the outset, which is clearly an important step towards creating an effective regime likely to have an impact upon the behaviour of market users. However, the FSA may circumvent consultation where it considers that there is 'an urgent need to publish the Code'.[35] While this may seem at first an apparent erosion of the protection afforded by consultation, two points alleviate such concerns. First, if the FSA wishes to maintain the authority of the regime, it must exercise this power sensitively and responsibly. Furthermore, any exercise of such power by the FSA would have to be accompanied by sufficient publicity to market users to ensure that offenders were aware of the consequences of their actions. This latter argument is supported both by principles of natural justice[36] and the European Convention on Human Rights ('ECHR'), [37] considered in greater detail below.

The central concept of the 'regular user' is one particular and important example of the flexible terms used by the Act. The 'regular user' sets two important standards in the context of the offence of misuse of information. First, the standard reasonably expected of

---

26 Available at www.fsa.gov.uk/handbook/mar.pdf.
27 See particularly Consultation Paper 59 ('CP 59'), chapters 10 and 11. The Enforcement Manual also underlines the significance of seeking and following FSA guidance, see, eg, the Enforcement Manual ('ENF') at 14.5.1(1)(c).
28 See FSMA 2000, s 119.
29 The point was addressed in some detail by the Joint Committee, see n 32 and 33 below.
30 See FSMA 2000, s 122(1).
31 See FSMA 2000, s 122(2).
32 The Joint Committee, First Report, 27 April 1999 (Session 1998–99) at paras 268–69 (London, TSO, 1999).
33 See above n 32, at para 271.
34 See FSMA 2000, s 121.
35 See FSMA 2000, s 121.
36 See further below at n 46.
37 Article 7(1) of the ECHR includes the principle that an offence must be clearly defined in law so that the individual may foresee the legal consequences of his actions, see further pp 465–66 below.

a market user is determined by whether behaviour is likely to be regarded as a failure to observe the standard of behaviour reasonably expected of the alleged offender by the 'regular user'.[38] Secondly, in the context of misuse of information, one must consider whether a 'regular user' would regard the information as 'relevant' when deciding the terms on which transactions in investments of the kind in question should be effected.[39] The only guidance in the Act is that the 'regular user' 'in relation to a particular market' is 'a reasonable person who regularly deals on that market in investments of the kind in question'.[40] Therefore, on a natural reading of the Act, one would expect the 'regular user' to be an actual market user. However, the Code of Market Conduct makes clear that a 'regular user' is in fact a hypothetical user of the markets.[41] Accordingly, behaviour may fall below the standards expected by a 'regular user', notwithstanding that behaviour may be accepted or tolerated by some market users.[42] Market users and their advisors must also bear in mind the standard expected will vary depending upon the markets or investments in question and the experience, level of skill and standard of knowledge that a regular user will expect from a person.[43] Given the crucial role of the 'regular user', it would seem important to determine who sets this standard. The FSA has recently asserted that the Financial Services and Markets Tribunal (FSMT) and not the FSA will set the standards of the 'regular user'.[44] The role of the FSMT is outlined in greater detail below in the context of enforcement. Although the FSA's view is technically correct, in practice the rare use of the Tribunal's predecessor, the Financial Services Tribunal, coupled with the likelihood of a high settlement rate suggests that there may be few Tribunal judgments to provide guidance to practitioners on the 'regular user' test. This is an example of the difficulties that may be presented in practice by the flexible regime.

Overall, the ECHR had a significant impact upon the drafting of the Financial Services and Markets Act 2000, by reason of the argument that the market abuse offence may be seen as criminal in nature.[45] The arguments based on the ECHR prompted many amendments to the Financial Services and Markets Bill. It has been persuasively argued that the failure to define the offence of market abuse itself more fully in the Act contravenes the principle contained in Art 7(1) of the ECHR (enacted into domestic law by s 1 and Sched 1 to the Human Rights Act 1998) that an offender must be able to foresee the consequences of his action. In fact, as one judge has recently noted,[46] this principle is really a branch of 'a basic understanding of natural justice'. However, the Government maintained its position on the scheme of the Act and the role of the Code of Market Conduct to provide guidance on the primary definitions. It is suggested that the contrary

---

38 See FSMA 2000, s 118(1)(a).

39 See FSMA 2000, s 118(2)(a).

40 See FSMA 2000, s 118(10).

41 The Code of Market Conduct at para 1.2.2. Paragraphs in the Code of Market Conduct are referred to in such code as 'MAR' and will be referred to in this manner henceforth.

42 See MAR 1.2.4.

43 See MAR 1.2.3.

44 FSA's policy statement on the Code of Market Conduct, *Feedback on CP 59 and Consultation Paper 76* ('CP 76'), April 2001 at para 1.5, available from the FSA.

45 See particularly the joint opinion of Lord Lester of Herne Hill QC and Javan Herberg, annexed to the Joint Committee's *First Report*, above n 32, at Annex C at para 63.

46 See Morison J in *R v Securities and Futures Authority ex p Fleurose* [2001] IRLR 784, upheld at [2001] EWCA Civ 2015.

argument is unlikely to succeed as a general criticism of the scheme of the new Act – the Code of Market Conduct has been carefully drawn, and it is suggested provides clear guidance to market users, particularly by its use of recognised market standards. Further, market users in borderline situations should seek guidance from the FSA. Indeed, it would be unfortunate if the scheme of the new regime failed on this basis – the informal and flexible approach of the Financial Services and Markets Act 2000 really offers the opportunity to have an impact upon insider trading and to keep pace with modern developments. However, the argument is likely to act as a useful check on the FSA's exercise of its extensive powers and encourage the FSA to fulfil its obligation to offer guidance to market users.

3.2 Scope

Many instances of insider trading will fall within both the criminal offence of insider dealing and the market abuse regime. However, a significant amount of behaviour will be caught by the market abuse regime that is outside the criminal law by reason of the broad scope of the new Act. This is of particular importance when one remembers that the market abuse regime, like the criminal law, applies to everyone whether or not they are regulated. The following features of the market abuse regime will embrace behaviour currently outside the criminal law: the move away from a requirement of 'knowledge' on the part of the offender in the offence of misuse of information; the lack of a requirement for a connection to an insider in order to establish liability; the types of activity it embraces and the definition of accessory liability.

The criminal offence of insider dealing requires the prosecution to establish that a person has 'information as an insider'.[47] In order to satisfy this requirement, a person must know both that the information is 'inside information' and that the information was received from an inside source'.[48] As a rule in isolation to address insider trading, this definition raises two particular obstacles. First, it presents difficulties of proof particularly where the offender has received information a number of steps removed from the company's inner sanctum. This in turn decreases the number of likely prosecutions for insider trading that may be justified and consequently undermines the force of the law. Secondly, it places an inquiry into the moral culpability on the part of an offender ahead of the fact that such behaviour has potentially damaged the financial markets – concerns in relation to insider trading stretch beyond the moral culpability of individual offenders.[49] In reality, in many cases of insider trading, the moral culpability in question will be insufficient to attract public opprobrium – the public are more likely to condemn a vicious crime against the person than insider dealing. Consequently, by allying itself to behaviour deserving moral condemnation, the criminal offence of insider dealing will often find that it is a low-priority crime for political reasons. Again, the net effect is a law without real authority. At the same time, a degree of moral culpability is appropriate to cases of insider trading, particularly where dishonesty is involved or a case has received such widespread publicity that confidence in the markets and consequently the country's

---

47 See CJA 1993, s 52(1). Since 1993 only seven people have been successfully prosecuted for insider dealing; see 'The brighter lights of regulation' *Financial Times* 12 November 2001.

48 See CJA 1993, s 57(1).

49 See further Joint Committee *First Report*, above n 32, at para 265 and CP 59 at para 6.14.

prosperity has been or is likely to be damaged. Further, the retention of moral culpability for certain cases of insider trading sends out a message that the collective body of the State will not tolerate the behaviour in question. Consequently, it is important that the criminal offence of insider dealing has been kept as part of the weapon to combat insider trading. However, a truly effective system of regulating insider trading will be concerned to have an impact upon market users' behaviour, in which case it will have a deterrent effect with corresponding benefits to the cost of regulation and the achievement of the objectives of regulation. The offence of misuse of information drops the requirement of 'knowledge' and instead is concerned with the standards set by 'the regular user'. Although the mental state of the person in question is not relevant to liability, it will remain relevant to the exercise of powers by the FSA to impose sanctions upon individuals.[50] The move to a perceived strict liability offence provoked criticism from the Law Society Company Law Committee who were concerned that the offence of market abuse was unduly severe and gave rise to potential injustice.[51] However, it is suggested that the final drafting may be supported on a number of grounds. First, 'morality' is not disregarded in the new regime, but 'culpability' is. After all, the 'regular user' may only set standards after considering what is 'right' or 'wrong' for a person in a particular position. Therefore, the new regime preserves a moral inquiry but one more concerned with the broader issue of standards of conduct than the particular perception or understanding of an individual offender. Secondly, the conduct of particular individuals may still be singled out for condemnation in appropriate cases by resort to the criminal law.

A further restriction of the criminal offence of insider dealing is that a person must have a connection with the company in question in order to commit insider dealing: the offender must have 'inside information' 'from an inside source'.[52] The classes of inside sources are narrowly defined, namely being a director, employee or shareholder of an issuer of securities or having access to the information by virtue of his employment, office or profession himself or directly or indirectly from one of these insiders.[53] The market abuse regime breaks the need for a nexus with the inside source. Such a connection is now merely a factor to be taken into account as part of the consideration of whether information is 'relevant'.[54] Specifically, the Code of Market Conduct describes proximity to the source of information as material to the reliability of information[55] – after all, the closer the source of information to the heart of the company, the more likely it is that the information is correct. The new approach would, therefore, catch situations that are probably outside the criminal law of insider dealing. For instance, someone who had taken price-sensitive information from bins outside the offices of a company and then dealt on such information would probably be outside the criminal law. After all, the scavenger is unlikely to have the information through being a director or through his

---

50 In particular, if there are reasonable grounds for the FSA to be satisfied following representations made to it in response to a warning notice that (a) the person believed, on reasonable grounds, that his behaviour did not fall foul of Part VIII of FSMA 2000, alternatively (b) that he took all reasonable precautions and exercised all due diligence to avoid behaving in a way which contravened Part VIII of FSMA 2000, the FSA may not impose a fine: FSMA 2000, s 123(2).

51 See Joint Committee *First Report*, above n 32, at para 264.

52 See CJA 1993, ss 56 and 57.

53 See CJA 1993, s 57(2).

54 See MAR 1.4.9.

55 See MAR 1.4.9.

employment and the person who is the precise source of the information may be unclear. Similarly, regulatory provisions would be unlikely to protect the markets in this situation. However, the lack of a direct connection to an inside source within the company would not prevent such a person being caught by the market abuse regime, although there might be issues as to the standards expected of such a scavenger by 'the regular user'. The move away from a nexus with an inside source is important not only because it broadens the scope of the regime by protecting a wider range of information but also because it refocuses the inquiry in cases of insider trading. The requirement of a nexus with the company is closely allied to traditional notions of breach of fiduciary duty. By contrast, the market abuse regime is more concerned with setting appropriate standards to be observed within the financial markets than with questions embedded in the law of trusts.

The criminal offence of insider dealing may be committed by a person who has 'information as an insider' if he either deals or encourages another to deal in certain securities or discloses information to another otherwise than in the proper performance of his employment, office or profession, subject to certain statutory defences.[56] The 'securities' are defined in Sched 2 of the Criminal Justice Act 1993.[57] By contrast, the Financial Services and Markets Act 2000 refers to 'behaviour ... which occurs in relation to qualifying investments traded on a market to which [s 118] applies'.[58] The market abuse regime is broader than the criminal offence of insider dealing in relation to prohibited activities in three respects. First, it is not confined to particular types of activity. The Act defines 'behaviour' merely as 'action and inaction'.[59] The guidance given by the Code of Market Conduct as to what amounts to 'behaviour' gives particular examples, but makes clear that this is not an exhaustive list.[60] Interestingly, providing corporate finance advice and conducting corporate finance activities are both specifically included within the current guidance in the Code of Market Conduct.[61] Secondly, the Act makes clear that 'inaction' is included within 'behaviour'. In the context of misuse of information, this may not be as sweeping as may first appear – after all behaviour must be 'based' on information,[62] connoting some element of active and not merely passive conduct. Therefore, the FSA's view that permitting another person to engage in abusive behaviour is a primary offence of market abuse may be viewed with suspicion.[63] Accessory liability (which it is submitted does cover such a situation) is considered in greater detail below. Finally, the Act does not tie behaviour to defined 'securities' but instead includes 'behaviour which occurs in relation to qualifying investments' within its scope. This phrase is expanded upon at s 118(6) of the Act which provides that it includes behaviour which occurs in relation to anything which is the subject matter, or whose price or value is expressed by reference to the price or value of those qualifying investments or occurs in relation to investments (whether qualifying or not) whose subject matter is those qualifying investments. The Code of Market Conduct also considers this phrase and

---

56   See CJA 1993, s 52.
57   See CJA 1993, s 54.
58   See FSMA 2000, s 118(1)(a).
59   See FSMA 2000, s 118(10).
60   See MAR 1.3.1.
61   See MAR 1.3.1(6).
62   See FSMA 2000, s 118(2)(a).
63   As set out in CP 76 at para 2.6.

gives examples of behaviour that is caught by this phrase in some detail.[64] Most strikingly, products 'whose price or value is expressed by reference to the price or value of those qualifying investments' are included. This is a potentially far reaching expression with the ability to reach activities outside the prescribed markets, but which nevertheless are linked to the financial markets. For instance, recently there has been an increase in betting on the performance of financial products, particularly through the Internet. The FSA has indicated in the Code of Market Conduct that in its view, spread-betting on baskets of shares traded on say the London Stock Exchange are within the scope of the market abuse regime.[65] It would appear to follow that betting on individual shares is also within the scope of the Act. If this view is correct, then it is a significant extension of the current law. For instance, a director who made a bet on securities in his company on the basis of material inside information before such information had been made generally available would be unlikely to be caught by the criminal offence of insider dealing (see particularly the narrow definitions contained in the CJA 1993) or regulatory regimes such as the Model Code. However, if the FSA's view is correct, there is a good argument that this activity, which clearly affords the director the opportunity to take unfair advantage of his position, is caught by the market abuse regime. Clearly, this type of activity is potentially a real threat to the financial markets, being in effect a form of insider trading, albeit without the use of securities. It is suggested that these various innovations are important steps in enabling the FSA to respond to novel sharp practices.

The market abuse regime permits the FSA to impose a penalty upon anyone 'requiring or encouraging' market abuse.[66] A person may be guilty of 'requiring or encouraging' market abuse where 'by taking or refraining from taking any action has required or encouraged another person or persons to engage in behaviour which, if engaged in by [the accessory] would amount to market abuse'.[67] The phrase is considered in greater detail in the Code of Market Conduct at MAR 1.8, although no legally recognised status is conferred upon such guidance by the Act. The FSA's view of 'requiring or encouraging' appears to include passive and not merely active behaviour. For instance, in the FSA's view, an intermediary may be guilty of requiring or encouraging market abuse where he knows or ought reasonably to know that the originator was engaging in market abuse.[68] The argument would appear to be that by failing to take action a person 'encourages' behaviour. This reasoning may be questioned – after all, how can a person 'encourage' another when that other's mind is already settled to act in a particular manner. Nevertheless, in principle there would appear to be merit in the FSA's concerns. If the FSA is able to establish conclusively the scope of 'requiring or encouraging' for which it contends by this example, the scope of the market abuse regime will be extended yet further. This view promotes a pro-active role by the financial community in combating insider trading by extending the scope of responsibility, which can only serve to reduce the incidence of insider trading. However, the FSA appears to have backed away from directly addressing employers' responsibilities for their employees in the final version of the Code of Market Conduct. In particular, the FSA has omitted the following guidance 'where an employer becomes

---

64 See MAR 1.11.6–MAR 1.11.11.
65 See MAR 1.11.11(a).
66 See FSMA 2000, s 123.
67 See FSMA 2000, s 123.
68 See MAR 1.8.8.

aware that one of its employees or any other person under its power or control is engaged in market abuse, but permits that person to continue to engage in the relevant behaviour, such behaviour amounts to requiring or encouraging'.[69] Compliance procedures are indirectly underpinned in the Enforcement Manual[70] and by parallel regulatory principles such as Conduct of Business Rule 2.4. Nevertheless, it is perhaps lamentable that the FSA has not addressed this particular issue more firmly – after all, prevention through effective compliance procedures is better than cure.

3.3   Enforcement

'To let the punishment fit the crime' is an extract from a well known aria from Gilbert and Sullivan's operetta, 'The Mikado'. However, previously the sanctions for insider trading have not really tied into the crime in question, as noted above. Under the Criminal Justice Act 1993, an offender may be liable to a fine or imprisonment.[71] The Act introduces a wide range of civil sanctions that offer the FSA a number of responses to different types of market abuse. These are modelled on the powers available to the FSA's counterpart in the United States, the Securities and Exchange Commission. The enforcement powers fall into two types: sanctions that the FSA may impose administratively and remedies that the FSA may seek from the civil courts. By contrast with the text of the market abuse offence itself, the precise scope of these powers is set out in some detail in the Act. The FSA has expanded upon when and how it will exercise these powers in a guide known as the Enforcement Manual in the Regulatory Processes section of the Handbook.

The primary sanction for market abuse or requiring or encouraging market abuse is a penalty, which the FSA may impose administratively.[72] The imposition of a penalty (whether by the FSA or the court – see further below) does not make any transaction void or unenforceable.[73] There has been disquiet by the fact that the Act does not set an upper limit for such penalty. Similarly, the FSA has decided not to use a tariff system in relation to penalties, although it has indicated that it will maintain a consistent approach.[74] These two particular factors maintain flexibility for the FSA in developing appropriate sanctions in this area. However, given that it appears that the fine income may go the FSA, there may be real concerns that the FSA has a self-interest in maximising the fee income. During consultation, the Joint Committee was content that fine income should go to the FSA. However, the committee recommended that it should be returned to the regulated community as a discount on fees with no offset for enforcement costs in order to give the

---

69   CP 59 at MAR 1.9.3.

70   See for example ENF 14.5.1(a) and ENF 14.6.2(5).

71   A person guilty of insider dealing may be liable on summary conviction or on indictment. The penalty for the former is a fine not exceeding the statutory maximum or imprisonment for a term not exceeding six months or both. Conviction on indictment may attract a fine or imprisonment for a term not exceeding seven years or both; see CJA 1993, s 61.

72   See FSMA 2000, s 123.

73   See FSMA 2000, s 131.

74   See ENF 14.7.2. Practitioners and market users will be able to build a picture of the approach of the FSA from the information, which the FSA is likely to publish; see FSMA 2000, s 391(4). Such information must be published in 'such manner as the Authority considers appropriate'; see FSMA 2000, s 391(7). The FSA is not obliged to publish information if publication would in the opinion of the FSA be unfair to the person with respect to whom the action was taken or prejudicial to the interest of consumers; see FSMA 2000, s 391(6).

FSA the least possible interest in maximising fee income.[75] To this end, the FSA must prepare and operate a scheme for ensuring that the amounts paid to the FSA by way of penalties imposed under the Act are applied for the benefit of authorised persons.[76] Whilst in theory this offers protection, the Act is loosely worded. Clearly, the responsible exercise of the power to impose penalties where a potential self-interest lies behind is extremely important in ensuring that the FSA and consequently the market abuse regime is not viewed with cynicism.

However, it should not be thought that the FSA's powers to impose penalties are without any check on such powers. First, the FSA is obliged to prepare a statement of its policy with respect to the imposition and amount of such penalties, which must comply with the requirements set down by FSMA 2000.[77] The FSA has complied with this requirement in Chapter 14 of the Enforcement Manual. Further, a person dissatisfied with a decision notice by the FSA to impose a fine upon him may refer the matter to the newly formed Financial Services and Markets Tribunal (FSMT).[78] The Tribunal will be run under the auspices of the Lord Chancellor's Department, and will have its own set of rules.[79] There are rather high expectations of the Tribunal – the Government rather grandly described it as 'a single, fully independent tribunal which will safeguard the rights of individuals and firms'.[80] However, the likelihood is that the vast majority of cases will be settled without recourse to the FSMT, following experience from the USA and the FSA's emphasis upon mediation.[81] There are many benefits for both offenders and the FSA in mediation, including a reduction of cost and time. From the point of view of the regulator, this allows further resources to be dedicated to more cases, with a corresponding impact upon market behaviour. However, there are also dangers in a system in which the majority of cases are settled, and commentators in the USA have raised their concerns in relation to the settlement policies of the FSA's American counterpart, the Securities and Exchange Commission (SEC).[82] It will be recalled that the FSA has stated that the FSMT will set the standard of the 'regular user'. However, if very few cases reach the FSMT, in practice the FSA will set the standard of the 'regular user' through its administrative enforcement action. This resurrects the concerns as to unlawful delegation of power to the FSA, which the Government has sought to avoid.

The FSA also has power to issue a public statement that a person has engaged in market abuse[83] or seek a restitution order administratively[84] where market abuse has been committed. In both cases, an offender dissatisfied with a final decision of the FSA

---

75 See Joint Committee *First Report*, above n 32, at p 5.
76 See FSMA 2000, Schedule 1 paragraph 16(2).
77 See FSMA 2000, s 124.
78 See FSMA 2000, ss 127 and 132.
79 See the Financial Services and Markets Tribunal Rules 2001, SI 2001/2476, made pursuant to FSMA 2000, s 132.
80 *Per* Miss Melanie Johnson, the then Economic Secretary to the Treasury; see House of Commons Standing Committee A, *Financial Services and Markets Bill*, 4 November 1999, at column 710 (London, TSO, 1999).
81 See Consultation Paper 65 (CP 65) at para 3.6.29.
82 See, eg, Flannery 'Time for a Change: A Re-Examination of the Settlement Policies of the Securities and Exchange Commission' (1994) 51 *Washington Lee Review* 1015.
83 See FSMA 2000, s 123(3).
84 See FSMA 2000, s 384.

may appeal to the FSMT, subject to the procedure for making such appeals.[85] It may also be some comfort to learn that there is a very specific procedure which the FSA must follow when imposing administrative sanctions[86] and that certain protections for the individual are built into the process. Most importantly, the FSA is obliged by the Act to ensure that it maintains its own Chinese Wall between those involved in investigation and enforcement in a particular case.[87] The FSA has created a Regulatory Decisions Committee (RDC) to meet this concern. This body is accountable to the FSA,[88] but is outside the FSA's management structure.[89] In fact, there is only one member of the RDC who is an employee of the FSA.[90] Whilst a credible team comprising the RDC may alleviate disquiet regarding the imposition of administrative sanctions, by reason of the notional distance from the heart of the FSA, the fact remains that such body receives delegated power from the FSA and is accountable to the same. The answer to the tension between the benefits of a fast, administrative system for sanctions and a real separation of powers may lie in creating a separate body independent of the FSA to take enforcement action in relation to market abuse. However, in practice, this might be seen as a retrograde step and contrary to the rationalisation of financial services regulation effected by the Act.

The FSA also has power to seek a wide range of civil remedies from the courts, including freezing orders and other injunctions,[91] as well as restitution orders and penalties. The Civil Procedure Rules[92] (being the procedural rules applicable to the civil courts) will apply to such applications. These rules permit an application to be made without notice to the other party where required by urgency or secrecy.[93] This may be contrasted with the administrative powers, in which the procedure to be followed does not permit enforcement action without notice to the offender. Therefore, the powers to seek remedies from the civil courts provide the FSA with the ability to react quickly and seek protective relief. For instance, if the FSA was concerned that a person who had engaged in insider trading was about to dissipate his assets, the FSA could apply to the court for a freezing order without notice to the other party in appropriate circumstances. Freezing orders are often regarded as a nuclear weapon within civil litigation generally, and will certainly form a significant part of the armoury available to the FSA.[94] The

---

85 See FSMA 2000, ss 127(4) and 386(5).

86 See FSMA 2000, ss 126 and 387.

87 See FSMA 2000, s 395.

88 See DEC 4.2.1.

89 See DEC 4.2.3.

90 See DEC 4.2.3.

91 There is a range of injunctions at the disposal of the FSA. The court has a power to make injunctions on the application of the FSA (1) restraining market abuse if it is satisfied (a) that there is a reasonable likelihood that any person will engage in market abuse or (b) that any person is or has engaged in market abuse and that there is a reasonable likelihood that the market abuse will continue or be repeated; (2) requiring a person to take such steps as the court may direct to remedy the market abuse if it is satisfied (a) that any person is or has engaged in market abuse, and (b) that there are steps which could be taken for remedying the market abuse; and (3) restraining a person whom the court is satisfied may be engaged in market abuse or may have been engaged in market abuse from disposing of, or otherwise dealing with any assets of his which it is satisfied that he is reasonably likely to dispose of or otherwise deal with if it satisfied that any person (a) may be engaged in market abuse or (b) may have been engaged in market abuse; see FSMA 2000, s 381.

92 SI 1998/3132 (as amended).

93 See Practice Direction to Civil Procedure Rules Part 23 at para 3.

94 For instance, the FSA has indicated that where criminal proceedings have been or will be commenced, the FSA may in appropriate cases seek an injunction or apply for restitution (see, eg, ENF 15.7.5).

power to freeze a person's assets will ensure that many of the other sanctions (such as the imposition of a penalty) are effective.

In addition to the above, the FSA may now institute proceedings for the criminal offence of insider dealing (except in Scotland).[95] For many years, such proceedings were only instituted in England and Wales by or with the consent of the Secretary of State for Trade and Industry or the Director of Public Prosecutions. The Companies Act 1989 gave the DTI powers to allow the Stock Exchange to prosecute cases directly.[96] The FSA is only one of a number of bodies that may prosecute insider dealing and will not necessarily prosecute such offence. Instead, it has agreed guidelines with other authorities in England, Wales and Northern Ireland who have an interest in prosecuting criminal offences.[97] Nevertheless, giving the FSA power to prosecute insider dealing is a logical move, which answers the criticism made over a decade ago by the Select Committee on Trade and Industry that 'inadequacies in the law and inexperience among both prosecutors and courts in dealing with cases'[98] were undermining successful prosecutions. It should also be noted that instances of market abuse might also overlap with cases which may be dealt with by the Panel on Takeovers and Mergers or Recognised Investment Exchanges such as the London Stock Exchange. Consequently, the need for co-ordination with such bodies is repeatedly underlined in the Enforcement Manual.[99] Effective co-ordination will be one of the keys to success of the FSA in maintaining the credibility of the market abuse regime.

Therefore, it may be said that the 'gap in the protections' to those using the markets[100] has been filled by the introduction of the market abuse regime. The new sanctions are particularly appropriate to insider trading since, as noted above, this type of offence is principally motivated by money. The wide range of tools available to the FSA allows it to tailor sanctions to fit the range of different offences. This move is to be commended – prohibitions on insider dealing only become effective if there is a sufficient threat of successful action. It is suggested that the range of sanctions now available will not only have a greater deterrent effect in relation to insider trading than the threat of the criminal law or other regulatory action, but also provide a more effective means of addressing this issue.

4 THE MISUSE OF INFORMATION OFFENCE – MODERNISING INSIDER TRADING PROHIBITIONS

Although there are many ways in which the misuse of information offence adopts a new approach, equally, such offence has borrowed certain parts of the criminal law of insider

---

95 See FSMA 2000, s 402(1). Section 402 FSMA 2000 further provides that the FSA must comply with any conditions or restrictions imposed in writing by the Treasury. Such conditions or restrictions may be imposed in relation to (a) proceedings generally; or (b) such proceedings, or categories of proceedings, as the Treasury may direct.

96 See *Company Investigations*, above n 4, at para 155.

97 See ENF 15.8.

98 See *Company Investigations*, above n 4, at para 153.

99 See for instance, ENF 6.6, 9.6, 9.10 and 14.9.

100 *Per* Miss Melanie Johnson; see House of Commons Standing Committee A, *Financial Services and Markets Bill*, 2 November 1999, at column 652 (London, TSO, 1999).

dealing and modernised the same for the purposes of the misuse of information offence. Examples include determining and defining which information may legitimately be used and defences to the offence. In addition, as will be seen, the Act applies powers of investigation into insider dealing and the offence of misuse of information without distinction, whilst revising such powers.

4.1 Determining and defining which information may legitimately be used

There are difficulties in determining and defining which information may be legitimately used in the financial markets, and when. Clearly, a flow of information is central to the efficient functioning of the financial markets. Second guessing the performance of companies and correspondingly their share value is in many ways the secret of success of market users. Further, one must ensure that market users clearly understand what information they may use if one is to ensure that market users feel sufficiently confident to continue to use information within the financial markets, thereby maintaining their liquidity. The definition of 'inside information' contained in the Criminal Justice Act 1993 is restrictive, requiring each of four conditions to be satisfied. These conditions are that information must:

(1) relate to particular securities or to a particular issuer of securities or to particular issuers of securities and not to securities generally or to issuers of securities generally;[101]

(2) be specific and precise;[102]

(3) not have been made public[103] (which is expanded upon in s 58 of the Criminal Justice Act 1993); and

(4) if it were made public would be likely to have a significant effect on the price of any securities.[104]

By contrast, the Financial Services and Markets Act 2000 characterises information as illegitimate where it is not 'generally available' and is likely to be regarded by a regular user as 'relevant' when deciding the terms on which transactions in the investments of the kind in question should be effected.[105] Whilst these expressions may seem to differ at first, a consideration of the guidance given in the Code of Market Conduct as to when information will be regarded as 'generally available' and 'relevant' makes clear that they share many similar characteristics.[106] For instance, both regimes allow for inequality between market users – after all, an enforced redistribution of resources is not part of the policy of the regulation of the financial markets. Consequently, a limitation of resources

---

101 See CJA 1993, s 56(1)(a). Information is treated as relating to an issuer of securities which is a company not only where it is about the company but also where it may affect the company's business prospects, see CJA 1993, s 60(4).

102 See CJA 1993, s 56(1)(b).

103 See CJA 1993, s 56(1)(c).

104 See CJA 1993, s 56(1)(d).

105 See FSMA 2000, s 118.

106 See MAR 1.4.5–1.4.11. For instance, the specific and precise nature of information is only a factor and not a condition of liability. Many of the other factors relate to the value of the information, eg, how current it is, how reliable it is and the extent to which information is new or fresh information.

and a corresponding limitation on research facilities do not prevent information from being illegitimate for the purposes of either law.[107]

However, there is a significant and important innovation in the misuse of information offence on this issue, which is introduced by the Code of Market Conduct. MAR 1.4.4(4) provides that information must relate to matters which a regular user of the market would reasonably expect to be disclosed to other users of the market on an equal basis, whether at the time in question or in the future. 'Information which has to be disclosed to the market in accordance with any legal or regulatory requirement' and 'information which is routinely the subject of a public announcement although not subject to any formal disclosure requirement'[108] are both included within this definition.[109] This serves the dual purpose of clarifying the class of information which may not be used and also of underpinning disclosure obligations.[110] This is a very good example of the clarity afforded by the use of the Code of Market Conduct. However, this qualification is important in two further respects. First, it applies recognised standards to all, whether or not they are regulated. Secondly, the use of categories of information affords the law clarity and a much more accessible definition than that used in the criminal offence of insider dealing. The Code also takes the opportunity to clarify areas which may be unclear, particularly as to what amounts to 'announceable information'. For instance, the Code states that the latter category includes information which is to be the subject of official announcement by governments, central monetary or fiscal authorities or regulatory authorities (financial or otherwise, including exchanges), as well as changes to published credit ratings of companies whose securities are 'qualifying investments'.[111] There had been doubt as to the extent to which government announcements had to be specific to particular companies or sectors in order to fall within the offence of insider dealing.[112] However, there is no logical reason not to include those with access to knowledge of a price-sensitive nature of this type, particularly where such knowledge has been obtained through public service.

4.2 Defences

The defences to the offence of misuse of information also draw significantly from the defences to the criminal law of insider dealing contained in Part V of the Criminal Justice Act 1993. The Criminal Justice Act 1993 sets out certain general defences and special

---

107 See CJA 1993, s 58(3) and MAR 1.4.6.

108 These are described in the Code as 'disclosable' and 'announceable' information respectively.

109 See MAR 1.4.12–MAR 1.4.16.

110 This is in keeping with the emphasis upon fair disclosure in regulating insider trading elsewhere. For instance, the Securities and Exchange Commission recently introduced Regulation FD (Fair Dealing) with a view to minimising selective disclosure by companies. Article 6(2) of the draft European Commission Directive on market abuse introduces a similar provision to Regulation FD at Article 6(2).

111 See MAR 1.4.15.

112 The position under the criminal law in respect of such information was unclear, by reason of the requirement that information must 'relate to particular securities or to a particular issuer of securities or to particular issuers of securities and not to securities generally or to issuers of securities generally' (CJA 1993, s 56(1)(a)). Information was treated as relating to an issuer of securities which is a company not only where it is about the company but also where it may affect the company's business prospects (CJA 1993, s 60(4)). Some commentators pointed out that this definition appeared to exclude confidential information relating to a particular Government policy; see, eg, *Insider Crime*, above n 13, at p 32.

defences to the offence.[113] The Code of Market Conduct has four specific safe harbours in respect of misuse of information: (1) dealing or arranging required for other reasons; (2) dealing or arranging not based on information; (3) trading information; and (4) facilitation of takeover bids and other market operations.[114] However, it should be noted that these defences are not identical to those to the criminal offence of insider dealing. Indeed, it is suggested that anomalies would have been created if they were identical. One example of a defence borrowed from the Criminal Justice Act 1993 and elaborated upon by the Code of Market Conduct is the safe harbour where 'dealing or arranging is not based on information'.[115] This misuse of information defence resembles the defence to insider dealing that a person 'would have done what he did even if he had not had the information'.[116] However, the Code of Market Conduct goes further than the Criminal Justice Act 1993 by providing presumptions. Significantly, in keeping with the emphasis upon setting standards, MAR 1.4.24 provides that where a person (whether authorised or not) establishes Chinese Wall arrangements in compliance with the FSA's Conduct of Business Sourcebook, such person will meet the conditions necessary to raise the presumption that they were not influenced in a decision to deal. The reinforcement of Chinese Walls in this manner is laudable, given what has already been noted, namely that prevention is better than cure. The Code of Market Conduct also creates a safe harbour relating to the facilitation of takeover bids[117] that is more tightly drafted than its counterpart in the Criminal Justice Act 1993.[118] In the context of takeover bids, the safe harbour conferred upon those parts of the Listing Rules listed in Annex 1G to the Code of Market Conduct should also be noted. These are examples of the opportunity taken by the new regime to tighten up on existing standards.

However, some defences have not been carried into the misuse of information offence. For instance, the defence to the offence of 'dealing' under the insider dealing regime on the basis that the alleged offender 'did not expect the dealing to result in a profit attributable to the fact that the information in question was price-sensitive information in relation to securities'[119] is not granted a safe harbour in the Code of Market Conduct. However, it is suggested that such a defence would be inconsistent with the misuse of information offence. The 'regular user' is not concerned as to profits or losses made, but only as to the failure to observe a standard. The impact of the failure to meet such standard is a secondary question, relevant to the sanction imposed. The making of a profit or avoidance of a loss is relevant to the question of whether to impose a financial penalty and if so the extent of such penalty[120] and is also a factor that is relevant in seeking restitution.[121]

---

113 See CJA 1993, s 53 and Schedule 1.
114 See MAR 1.4.19–MAR 1.4.30.
115 See MAR 1.4.21–MAR 1.4.24.
116 See for instance CJA 1993, s 53(1)(c).
117 See MAR 1.4.2.8–MAR 1.4.30.
118 See CJA 1993, s 53(4) and para 3 of Schedule 1.
119 See CJA 1993, s 53(1)(a).
120 See ENF 14.7.4(4).
121 See FSMA 2000, ss 383(4) and 384 and ENF 9.8.6.

4.3 Investigation

History records and common sense dictates that unless market misconduct may be successfully investigated, the likelihood of effective prosecution becomes remote.[122] Consequently, Miss Melanie Johnson, the then Economic Secretary to the Treasury said of the powers of investigation introduced by the Act: 'We make no apologies for wanting to be sure that investigations can take place as and when the circumstances suggest that they are needed. Nothing is gained by having a regulator that cannot respond quickly. Nothing is gained by encouraging wrongdoers to seek to prevent the launch of inquiries through procedural challenges in the courts'.[123] The Financial Services and Markets Act 2000 has modernised and extended the powers of investigation into insider dealing.[124] Given the essentially civil nature of the market abuse regime, one might expect the powers of investigation into market abuse to be less extensive than those into the criminal offence of insider dealing.[125] In fact, the powers of investigation into insider dealing apply without distinction to investigations into the offence of misuse of information or other forms of market misconduct.[126] As will be seen, the powers of investigation in relation to insider dealing have been modernised.

Logically, the power to appoint investigators has now been conferred upon the FSA in addition to the Secretary of State for Trade and Industry.[127] The threshold to appoint an investigator is low – there need only be 'circumstances suggesting' that the criminal offences of insider dealing and market manipulation or market abuse may have taken place.[128] The FSA and Secretary of State have a number of other powers to appoint investigators particularly where a suspected offender is authorised, but the FSA has indicated that it will usually rely upon the powers under consideration in cases of suspected market misconduct.[129] The particular power under which an investigator has been appointed is important, as the powers of investigation vary depending upon which power of appointment has been used. For instance, an investigator need not inform the subject of the investigation that they are being investigated where the investigator has been appointed to investigate market misconduct by contrast with investigators appointed by the FSA or the Secretary of State in other circumstances.[130] The FSA has set out factors that it will take into account in determining whether to appoint an

---

122 Previous experience of the need for effective investigative powers is underlined by the introduction of such powers in s 177 of the Financial Services Act 1986, and the recommendations in *Company Investigations*, above n 4. The Government had earlier rejected calls for such powers when insider dealing was made a criminal offence under Part V of the Companies Act 1980; see *Insider Crime*, above n 13, at p 86. The lack of effective investigation powers on the part of self-regulatory bodies was one of the deficiencies of this system. Hull and Bridges 'End of the Line for Insider Traders?' (1981) 14 *Bracton Law Journal* 13 at p 16.

123 Addressing House of Commons Standing Committee A *Financial Services and Markets Bill*, 23 November 1999 at columns 872–73 (London, TSO, 1999).

124 See generally FSMA 2000, Part XI.

125 Such powers are set out in Part VII of the Financial Services Act 1986.

126 See FSMA 2000, s 168(2) and (3).

127 The Economic Secretary emphasised that it was useful for the Secretary of State for Trade and Industry to retain a power of investigation (compare FSA 1986, s 105). In particular, a company investigation might move into areas concerned with financial services or a conflict of interest might arise: see above n 123 at column 862.

128 See FSMA 2000, s 168(2) and (3).

129 See CP 65a at para 2.7.1.

130 See FSMA 2000, s 170(2)(3).

investigator,[131] but in practice, given the low threshold to be satisfied in order for an investigator to be appointed, there are likely to be real difficulties in challenging the appointment of an investigator.[132]

The various powers are extensive, both in relation to the person under investigation and third parties, including their professional advisors and bankers. The investigators have a range of powers to require a person to give information and assistance pursuant to s 173 of the Act. These powers may be triggered where the investigator considers that such person 'is or may be able to give information which is or may be relevant to the investigation'. A person may be required to attend a particular venue at a particular time and answer questions or produce specified documents or documents of a specified nature at a certain time and place, pursuant to this requirement.[133] The use of information obtained by the investigators in compelled interviews is significantly curtailed by s 174 of the Act. According to this section, no evidence relating to any statement may be adduced and no question relating to it may be asked, by or on behalf of the prosecution or as the case may be the FSA, unless evidence relating to it is adduced, or a question relating to it is asked, in the proceedings by or on behalf of that person in most criminal proceedings[134] or in proceedings relating to an action to be taken against a person under s 123 of the Act (the imposition of penalties by reason of market abuse).[135] This departs from the general rule whereby statements made to investigators by a person in compliance with an 'information requirement'[136] are admissible in evidence in any proceedings, so long as it also complies with any requirements governing the admissibility of evidence in the circumstances in question.[137] The exclusion of compelled evidence in proceedings under s 123 followed concerns that without such a provision: 'the most serious potential mismatch between the statutory scheme and Art 6 of the [European Convention on Human Rights] [arises], and it is essential that the mismatch should be removed in the legislation itself, rather than leaving it to the courts to attempt to imply appropriate Art 6 safeguards into the legislation'.[138] It is suggested that the resulting drafting is rather clumsy since s 174(2) refers to 'proceedings in relation to action to be taken against a person under s 123'. However, this phrase is not defined further. Does it refer to the decision to take proceedings, the procedure leading to the penalty or the imposition of a penalty itself? It must be remembered that the various civil procedure

---

131 See ENF 2.6.

132 Certain critics voiced their concern at the Standing Committee stage that the Government had adopted the lower threshold (the earlier draft required 'reasonable grounds for suspecting that') in order to immunise itself from judicial review, a point that it is submitted overlooks the similar test which is used by s 177 of the Financial Services Act 1986.

133 See FSMA 2000, s 173(2) and (3).

134 Section 174(3) excludes the following offences (a) under ss 177(4) or 398 FSMA 2000 (b) under s 5 of the Perjury Act 1911 (false statements made otherwise than on oath); (c) under s 44(2) of the Criminal Law (Consolidation) (Scotland) Act 1995 (false statements made otherwise than on oath); or (d) under Article 10 of the Perjury (Northern Ireland) Order 1979.

135 See FSMA 2000, s 174(4).

136 These are defined by sub-section (5) as a requirement imposed by an investigator under ss 171, 172, 173 or 175 FSMA 2000.

137 See FSMA 2000, s 174(1).

138 See above n 45, at para 61. These concerns principally surrounded the compatibility of the legislation with the European Convention on Human Rights and the decision in *Saunders v United Kingdom* (1996) 23 EHRR 313, especially in respect of the market abuse regime which many believe will be regarded as criminal in substance in ECHR terms.

rules do not apply to administrative actions – there is no procedure of disclosure or other rules applicable to civil proceedings. Therefore, if a broad construction is made of s 123 of the Act, on which material will the FSA base its decision and how will the RDC be able to understand how the decision has been reached? There is a further anomaly – the power to impose a restitution order is not referred to in s 174(2) and yet could have as far reaching consequences for an individual as a penalty. These points apart, in any event, it should be noted that the protection conferred by s 174(2) is unlikely to apply where a statement has been given voluntarily[139] and it is suggested would not exclude statements by persons other than the accused. Further, as the Joint Committee noted, the FSA 'will still be able to use compelled evidence to suggest new lines of inquiry, to justify an injunction or an order for restitution or disgorgement or to proceed against a person other than the one who gave evidence'.[140]

The powers of investigation in relation to third parties have also been modernised. While legal professional privilege is preserved,[141] a lawyer may be required to furnish the name and address of his client pursuant to s 175(4) of the FSMA 2000. Perhaps more strikingly, the duty of confidence owed by bankers to their customers is significantly eroded by s 175(5) of the Act. This section goes beyond s 177 of the Financial Services Act 1986 which obliged a banker to disclose or produce any document in respect of which he owed an obligation of confidence by virtue of carrying on the business of banking unless either the person to whom the duty of confidence was owed consented or the making of the requirement was required by the Secretary of State. These provisions remain, but disclosure may now be required where the person to whom the duty of confidence is owed is under investigation or the banker himself is under investigation. Although this section may seem draconian, the key evidence of market misconduct may lie in a person's bank account. Further, as one commentator has noted: 'one of the main stumbling blocks to the effective investigation of economic crime has been the impenetrability of banking secrecy and confidentiality laws'.[142]

Finally, it should be noted that these various powers of investigation are reinforced by a number of sanctions for non-compliance. Section 177 creates a number of sanctions that reinforce the powers of the investigators. These are:

- being dealt with by the High Court (or in Scotland the Court of Session) as if in contempt of court, if the court is satisfied that such person failed without reasonable excuse to comply with a requirement imposed upon him by Part XI of the FSMA;

- the criminal offence relating to falsification, concealment or destruction of documents considered above;

- criminal offences in respect of the provision or reckless provision of false or misleading information.

Further, the FSA, the Secretary of State or the investigator may apply to a magistrate for a warrant to search premises and seize documents or information pursuant to s 176. The FSA or Secretary of State must give information to the magistrate on oath in order to

---

139 See ENF 2.10.5.
140 See above n 21, at para 20.
141 See FSMA 2000, s 431(1).
142 See Rider 'The Control of Insider Trading – Smoke and Mirrors!' [1999] *International Company and Commercial Law Journal* 271 at p 289.

satisfy the magistrate that the proscribed conditions for a search and seizure order are satisfied. These conditions are wide ranging, and relate not only to information concerning documents that have been withheld but also in the case of an authorised person to documents or information which could be the object of an 'information requirement' in circumstances where such requirement would not be complied with, or the documents or information would be removed, tampered with or destroyed. A search warrant is reinforced by a criminal offence attracting a term of imprisonment not exceeding three months or a fine not exceeding level five on the standard scale for any person who intentionally obstructs the exercise of any rights conferred by a warrant.[143]

5 CONCLUSIONS

The market abuse regime endured a rough passage before finally reaching the statute books and still has its critics. However, by creating of the offence of misuse of information, the Financial Services and Markets Act 2000 provides a fresh and modern solution to an old, but ever-present problem, which will fill a significant gap in the regulation of insider trading in this jurisdiction. At the same time, the criminal law as supplemented by self-regulatory provisions will retain an important role in the overall regulation of insider trading and will run parallel to the new regime. The Financial Services and Markets Act 2000 has taken the opportunity to extend the scope of the law, afforded the law flexibility, added further sanctions that assist in tailoring the response to insider trading to particular circumstances and have revised the powers of investigation into market misconduct. In fact, one may go so far as to say that there is a possibility that this legislation may 'set the pace for regulatory change internationally',[144] at least in the context of reshaping insider trading prohibitions. However, the FSA has a number of onerous responsibilities in ensuring that the regime maintains credibility and survives legal challenge in a climate in which criticism may never be far away.[145] It is hoped that the FSA will rally and set market standards internationally.

---

143 See FSMA 2000, s 177(6).
144 *Per* the then Chief Secretary to the Treasury, House of Commons Standing Committee A, *Financial Services and Markets Bill*, 6 July 1999 at column 6 (London, TSO, 1999).
145 See generally *Financial Times* 23 November 2001 at p 6.

APPENDICES

COMPANY LAW REVIEW PUBLICATIONS 1998–2001

1   Modern Company Law for a Competitive Economy – Published March 1998.

2   Modern Company Law for a Competitive Economy: The Strategic Framework (URN 99/654) – Published February 1999.

3   Modern Company Law for a Competitive Economy: Company General Meetings and Shareholder Communication (URN 99/1144) – Published October 1999.

4   Modern Company Law for a Competitive Economy: Company Formation and Capital Maintenance (URN 99/1145) – Published October 1999.

5   Modern Company Law for a Competitive Economy: Reforming the Law Concerning Overseas Companies (URN 99/1146) – Published October 1999.

6   Modern Company Law for a Competitive Economy: Developing the Framework (URN 00/656) – Published March 2000.

7   Modern Company Law for a Competitive Economy: Capital Maintenance: Other Issues (URN 00/880) – Published June 2000.

8   Modern Company Law for a Competitive Economy: Registration of Company Charges (URN 00/1213) – Published October 2000.

9   Modern Company Law for a Competitive Economy: Completing the Structure (URN 00/1335) – Published November 2000.

10 Modern Company Law for a Competitive Economy: Trading Disclosures (URN 01/542) – Published January 2001.

11 Modern Company Law for a Competitive Economy: Final Report Volume 1 (URN 01/942) – Published July 2001.

12 Modern Company Law for a Competitive Economy: Final Report Volume 2 (URN 01/943) – Published July 2001.

Copies of the above publications are available via the DTI Publications unit by telephoning 0870 1502 500; or via the DTI internet site at www.dti.gov.uk/cld/reviews/condocs.htm.

UK COMPANY LAW REFORM REPORTS 1837–1962

The following are the major reports on modern UK company law predating the DTI-sponsored Company Law Review of 1998–2001 which readers may find of interest when seeking to trace the origins of our current law.

1   Bellenden Ker Report (1837): *Report on the Law of Partnership*, Parliamentary Papers (HC) No 530, 14 July 1837 (86 pp)

2   Gladstone Report (1844): *First Report of the Select Committee on Joint Stock Companies*, Parliamentary Papers (HC) No 119, London, HMSO, 15 March 1844 (457 pp)

3   Davey Report (1895) C 7779: *Report of the Departmental Committee to Inquire What Amendments are Necessary in the Acts Relating to Joint Stock Companies Incorporated With Limited Liability Under the Companies Acts 1862–90*, London, HMSO, 1895 (196 pp)

4   Loreburn Report (1906) Cd 3052: *Report of the Company Law Amendment Committee*, London, HMSO, 1906 (44 pp)

5   Loreburn Report Appendix (1906) Cd 3053: *Appendix to Report of the Company Law Amendment Committee*, London, HMSO, 1906 (104 pp)

6   Wrenbury Report (1918) Cd 9138: *Report of the Company Law Amendment Committee*, London, HMSO, 1918 (14 pp)

7   Greene Report (1926) Cmd 2657: *Company Law Amendment Committee Report*, London, HMSO, 1926 (115 pp)

8   Cohen Report (1945) Cmd 6659: *Report of the Committee on Company Law Amendment*, London, HMSO, 1945 (115 pp)

9   Jenkins Report (1962) Cmnd 1749: *Report of the Company Law Committee*, London, HMSO, 1962 (223 pp)

UK COMPANY LAW STATUTES 1844–1989

The following are the main sources of modern company law legislation and are offered to enable the reader to trace the legislative history of our current company law. The primary Companies Acts are in bold capital letters.

1   **Joint Stock Companies Act 1844; 7 & 8 Vict c 110**

'An Act For The Registration, Incorporation, And Regulation Of Joint Stock Companies' (5 September 1844)

1   No official short title to this Act.

2   Repealed by Companies Act 1862, s 205 & Sch 3.

2   **Joint Stock Companies Amendment Act 1847; 10 & 11 Vict c 78**

'An Act To Amend An Act For The Registration, Incorporation, And Regulation Of Joint Stock Companies' (22 July 1847)

1   No official short title to this Act.

2   Repealed by Companies Act 1862, s 205 & Sch 3.

3   **Limited Liability Act 1855; 18 & 19 Vict c 133**

'An Act For Limiting The Liability Of Members Of Certain Joint Stock Companies' (14 August 1855)

1   Short title s 19.

2   Repealed by Joint Stock Companies Act 1856, s 107(3).

4   **Joint Stock Companies Act 1856; 19 & 20 Vict c 47**

'An Act For The Incorporation And Regulation Of Joint Stock Companies, And Other Associations' (14 July 1856)

1   Short title s 1.

2   Repealed by Companies Act 1862, s 205 & Sch 3.

5   **Joint Stock Companies Act 1857; 20 & 21 Vict c 14**

'An Act To Amend The Joint Stock Companies Act 1856' (13 July 1857)

1   Short title s 1.

2   Repealed by Companies Act 1862, s 205 & Sch 3.

6   **Joint Stock Companies (Amendment) Act 1857; 20 & 21 Vict c 80**

'An Act To Amend The Joint Stock Companies Act 1856' (25 August 1857)

1   No official short title to this Act.

2   Repealed by Companies Act 1862, s 205 & Sch 3.

7 Joint Stock Companies Winding-Up Act 1844; 7 & 8 Vict c 111

'An Act For Facilitating The Winding-Up Of The Affairs Of Joint Stock Companies Unable To Meet Their Pecuniary Engagements' (5 September 1844)

1 No official short title to this Act.

2 Commencement 1 November 1844 (s 32).

3 Repealed by Companies Act 1862, s 205 & Sch 3.

8 Joint Stock Companies Winding-Up Act 1848; 11 & 12 Vict c 45

'An Act To Amend The Acts For Facilitating The Winding-Up Of The Affairs Of Joint Stock Companies Unable To Meet Their Pecunary Engagements; And Also To Facilitate The Dissolution And Winding-Up Of Joint Stock Companies And Other Partnerships' (14 August 1848)

1 Short title s 4.

2 Repealed by Companies Act 1862, s 205 & Sch 3.

9 Joint Stock Companies Winding-Up Amendment Act 1849; 12 & 13 Vict c 108

'An Act To Amend The Joint Stock Companies Winding-Up Act 1848' (1 August 1849)

1 Short title s 34.

2 Repealed by Companies Act 1862, s 205 & Sch 3.

10 Joint Stock Companies Winding-Up Amendment Act 1857; 20 & 21 Vict c 78

'An Act To Amend The [Joint Stock Companies Winding-Up Act 1844], And Also The Joint Stock Companies Winding-Up Acts, 1848 And 1849' (25 August 1857)

1 Short title s 16.

2 Repealed by Companies Act 1862, s 205 & Sch 3.

11 COMPANIES ACT 1862; 25 & 26 Vict c 89

'An Act For The Incorporation, Regulation And Winding-Up Of Trading Companies And Other Associations' (7 August 1862)

1 Short title s 1.

2 Commencement 2 November 1862 (s 2).

3 Repealed by Companies (Consolidation) Act 1908, s 286 & Sch 6.

12 Company Seals Act 1864; 27 & 28 Vict c 19

'An Act To Enable Joint Stock Companies Carrying On Business In Foreign Countries To Have Official Seals To Be Used In Such Countries' (13 May 1864)

1 Short title s 1.

2 Repealed by Companies (Consolidation) Act 1908, s 286 & Sch 6.

13 Companies Act 1867; 30 & 31 Vict c 131

'An Act To Amend The Companies Act 1862' (20 August 1867)

1   Short title s 1.

2   1 September 1867 (s 3).

3   Repealed by Companies (Consolidation) Act 1908, s 286 & Sch 6.

14 Joint Stock Companies Arrangement Act 1870; 33 & 34 Vict c 104

'An Act To Facilitate Compromises And Arrangements Between Creditors And Shareholders Of Joint Stock And Other Companies In Liquidation' (10 August 1870)

1   Short title s 1.

2   Repealed by Companies (Consolidation) Act 1908, s 286 & Sch 6.

15 Companies Act 1877; 40 & 41 Vict c 26

'An Act To Amend The Companies Acts Of 1862 And 1867' (23 July 1867)

1   Short title s 1.

2   Repealed by Companies (Consolidation) Act 1908, s 286 & Sch 6.

16 Companies Act 1879; 42 & 43 Vict c 76

'An Act To Amend The Law With Respect To The Liability Of Members Of Banking And Other Joint Stock Companies; And For Other Purposes' (15 August 1879)

1   Short title s 1.

2   Repealed by Companies (Consolidation) Act 1908, s 286 & Sch 6.

17 Companies Act 1880; 43 & 44 Vict c 19

'An Act To Amend The Companies Acts Of 1862, 1867, 1877, And 1879' (24 March 1880)

1   Short title s 1.

2   Repealed by Companies (Consolidation) Act 1908, s 286 & Sch 6.

18 Companies Act 1883; 46 & 47 Vict c 28

'An Act To Amend The Companies Acts, 1862 And 1867' (20 August 1883)

1   Short title s 1.

2   Commencement 1 September 1883.

3   Repealed by Preferential Payments in Bankruptcy Act 1888, s 6 & Sch.

19 Companies (Colonial Registers) Act 1883; 46 & 47 Vict c 30

'An Act To Authorise Companies Registered Under The Companies Act, 1862 To Keep Local Registers Of Their Members In British Colonies' (10 August 1883)

1   Short title s 1.

2   Repealed by Companies (Consolidation) Act 1908, s 286 & Sch 6.

20 Companies Act 1886; 49 & 50 Vict c 23

'An Act To Amend The Companies Acts Of 1862, 1867, 1870, 1877, 1879, 1880, And 1883' (4 June 1886)

1   Short title s 1.

2   Repealed by Companies (Consolidation) Act 1908, s 286 & Sch 6.

21 Preferential Payments In Bankruptcy Act 1888; 51 & 52 Vict c 62

'An Act To Amend The Law With Respect To Preferential Payments In Bankruptcy, And In The Winding-Up Of Companies' (24 December 1888)

1   Short title s 7.

2   Commencement 31 December 1888.

3   Repealed by Companies (Consolidation) Act 1908, s 286 & Sch 6.

22 Companies (Memorandum Of Association) Act 1890; 53 & 54 Vict c 62

'An Act To Give Further Powers To Companies With Respect To Certain Instruments Under Which They May Be Constituted Or Regulated' (18 August 1890)

1   Short title s 3(1).

2   Repealed by Companies (Consolidation) Act 1908, s 286 & Sch 6.

23 Companies (Winding-Up) Act 1890; 53 & 54 Vict c 63

'An Act To Amend The Law Relating To The Winding-Up Of Companies In England And Wales' (18 August 1890)

1   Short title s 35(1).

2   Commencement 1 January 1891 (s 34).

3   Repealed by Companies (Consolidation) Act 1908, s 286 & Sch 6.

24 Directors Liability Act 1890; 53 & 54 Vict c 64

'An Act To Amend The Law Relating To The Liability Of Directors And Others For Statements In Prospectuses And Other Documents Soliciting Applications For Shares Or Debentures' (18 August 1890)

1   Short title s 1.

2   Repealed by Companies (Consolidation) Act 1908, s 286 & Sch 6.

25 Companies (Winding-Up) Act 1893; 56 & 57 Vict c 58

'An Act To Amend Section 10 Of The Companies (Winding-Up) Act 1890' (22 September 1893)

1   Short title s 2.

2   Repealed by Companies (Consolidation) Act 1908, s 286 & Sch 6.

26 Preferential Payments In Bankruptcy Amendment Act 1897; 60 & 61 Vict c 19

'An Act To Amend The Law Regarding Preferential Payments In The Case Of Companies' (15 July 1897)

1   Short title s 1.
2   Repealed by Companies (Consolidation) Act 1908, s 286 & Sch 6.

27 Companies Act 1898; 61 & 62 Vict c 26

'An Act To Amend The Companies Act, 1867' (2 August 1898)

1   Short title s 3.
2   Repealed by Companies (Consolidation) Act 1908, s 286 & Sch 6.

28 Companies Act 1900; 63 & 64 Vict c 48

'An Act To Amend The Companies Acts' (8 August 1900)

1   Short title s 36.
2   General Commencement 1 January 1901.
3   Repealed by Companies (Consolidation) Act 1908, s 286 & Sch 6.

29 Companies Act 1907; 7 Edw 7 c 50

'An Act To Amend The Companies Acts, 1862 To 1900' (28 August 1907)

1   Short title s 52(1).
2   General Commencement 1 July 1908 (s 52(3)).
3   Repealed by Companies (Consolidation) Act 1908, s 286 & Sch 6.

30 Companies Act 1908; 8 Edw 7 c 12

'An Act To Amend The Law With Respect To The Holding Of Land By Companies Incorporated In British Possessions' (1 August 1908)

1   Short title s 2.
2   Repealed by Companies (Consolidation) Act 1908, s 286 & Sch 6.

31 COMPANIES (CONSOLIDATION) ACT 1908; 8 Edw 7 C 69

'An Act To Consolidate The Companies Act 1862, And The Acts Amending It'

1   Short title s 295.
2   Commencement 1 April 1909 (s 296).
3   Repealed by Companies Act 1929, s 381(1) & Sch 12.

32 Companies Act 1913; 3 & 4 Geo 5 c 25

'An Act To Amend The Provisions Of The Companies (Consolidation) Act 1908, With Respect To Private Companies' (15 August 1913)

1   Short title s 2.
2   Repealed by Companies Act 1929, s 381(1) & Sch 12.

33 Companies (Foreign Interests) Act 1917; 7 & 8 Geo 5 c 18

'An Act To Prohibit The Alteration, Except With The Consent Of The Board Of Trade, Of Articles Of Association Or Regulations Which Restrict Foreign Interests In Companies And For Other Purposes Connected Therewith' (24 May 1917)

1 Short title s 3.

2 Repealed by Companies Act 1928, s 118(3) & Sch 3.

34 Companies (Particulars As To Directors) Act 1917; 7 & 8 Geo 5 c 28

'An Act To Provide For The Disclosure Of Certain Particulars Respecting The Directors Of Companies' (2 August 1917)

1 Short title s 4.

2 Repealed by Companies Act 1929, s 381(1) & Sch 12.

35 Companies Act 1928; 18 & 19 Geo 5 c 45

'An Act To Amend The Companies Acts 1908 To 1917 And For Purposes Connected Therewith' (3 August 1928)

1 Short title s 118(1).

2 General commencement 1 November 1929; s 118(4) & SR & O No 546.

3 Repealed by Companies Act 1929, s 381(1) & Sch 12.

36 COMPANIES ACT 1929; 19 & 20 Geo 5 c 23

'An Act To Consolidate The Companies Acts 1908 To 1928, And Certain Other Enactments Connected With The Said Acts' (10 May 1929)

1 Short title s 385(1).

2 Commencement 1 November 1929; s 385(2).

3 Repealed by Companies Act 1948, s 459(1) & Sch 17.

37 Companies Act 1947; 10 & 11 Geo 6 c 47

'An Act To Amend The Law Relating To Companies And Unit Trusts And To Dealing In Securities And In Connection Therewith To Amend The Law Of Bankruptcy And The Law Relating To The Registration Of Business Names' (6 August 1947)

1 Short title s 123(1).

2 Commencement 1 December 1947 and 1 July 1948; s 123(2) & SR & O 1947 No 2503 & SI 1948, No 439.

3 Repealed in large part by Companies Act 1948, s 459(1) & Sch 17.

38 COMPANIES ACT 1948; 11 & 12 Geo 6 c 38

'An Act To Consolidate The Companies Act 1929, The Companies Act 1947 (Other Than The Provisions Thereof Relating To Business Names, Bankruptcy And The Prevention Of Fraud In Connection With Unit Trusts), And Certain Other Enactments Amending The First-Mentioned Act' (30 June 1948)

1   Short title s 462(1).

2   Commencement 1 July 1948 (s 462(2)).

3   Repealed by Companies Consolidation (Consequential Provisions) Act 1985, s 29 & Sch 1.

39 Companies Act 1967; c 81

'An Act To Amend The Law Relating To Companies, Insurance, Partnerships And Moneylenders' (27 July 1967)

1   Short title s 130(1).

2   Repealed by Companies Consolidation (Consequential Provisions) Act 1985, s 29 & Sch 1.

40 European Communities Act 1972; c 68

(17 October 1972)

Section 9 ONLY.

1   Short title s 1(1).

2   Commencement 1 January 1973 (s 9(9)).

3   Repealed by Companies Consolidation (Consequential Provisions) Act 1985, s 29 & Sch 1.

41 Companies Act 1976; c 69

'An Act To Amend The Law Relating To Companies And, In Connection Therewith, To Amend The Law Relating To The Registration Of Business Names' (15 November 1976)

1   Short title s 45(1).

2   Commencement Various Dates Between 24 January 1977 and 1 January 1985; See s 45(3) & SI's: 1976 No 2188; 1977 No 165; 1977 No 529; 1977 No 774; 1977 No 1348; 1979 No 1544; 1980 No 1748; 1982 No 671; 1984 No 683.

3   Repealed by Companies Consolidation (Consequential Provisions) Act 1985, s 29 & Sch 1.

42 Companies Act 1980; c 22

'An Act To Amend The Law Relating To Companies' (1 May 1980)

1   Short title s 90(1).

2   Commencement Various Dates Between 23 June 1980 and 1 October 1983; See s 90(3) & SIs: 1980 No 745; 1980 No 1785; 1981 No 1683; 1983 No 1022.

3   Repealed by Companies Consolidation (Consequential Provisions) Act 1985, s 29 & Sch 1.

43 Companies Act 1981; c 62

'An Act To Amend The Law Relating To Companies And Business Names' (30 October 1981)

1   Short title s 119(1).

2   Commencement Various Dates Between 3 December 1981 and 1 January 1985; See s 119(3) & SIs: 1981 No 1621; 1981 No 1684; 1982 No 103; 1982 No 672; 1983 No 1024; 1984 No 684.

3   Repealed by Companies Consolidation (Consequential Provisions) Act 1985, s 29 & Sch 1.

44 Companies (Beneficial Interests) Act 1983; c 50

'An Act To Provide For Disregarding Certain Interests And Rights In Determining For The Purposes Of Provisions Of The Companies Act 1948 And The Companies Act 1980 Whether A Company Is Beneficially Interested Under A Trust Or Has A Beneficial Interest In Shares' (26 July 1983)

1   Short title s 7(1).

2   Repealed by Companies Consolidation (Consequential Provisions) Act 1985, s 29 & Sch 1.

45 COMPANIES ACT 1985; c 6

'An Act To Consolidate The Greater Part Of The Companies Acts' (11 March 1985)

1   Short title s 747.

2   Commencement 1 July 1985 (s 746).

3   Act still in force but has been amended.

46 Companies Consolidation (Consequential Provisions) Act 1985; c 9

'An Act To Make, In Connection With The Consolidation Of The Companies Acts 1948 To 1983 And Other Enactments Relating To Companies, Provision For Transitional Matters And Savings, Repeals (Including The Repeal, In Accordance With Recommendations Of The Law Commission, Of Certain Provisions Of The Companies Act 1948 Which Are No Longer Of Practical Utility) And Consequential Amendments Of Other Acts' (11 March 1985)

1   Short title s 35.

2   Commencement 1 July 1985 (s 34).

3   Act still in force but has been subject to many amendments since 1985.

47 Companies Act 1989; c 40

'An Act To Amend The Law Relating To Company Accounts etc ...' (16 November 1989)

1   Short title s 216.

2   Commencement s 215. The Act is now largely in force (a significant exception being the provisions relating to company charges contained in Part 4 of the Act) but was brought into force by numerous statutory instruments which will not be listed here.

INDEX